OFF SPRING

American Spirit

A History of the American People

Spirit of St. Louis

From the author

In May 1927, Charles A. Lindbergh made the first non-stop
flight from New York to Paris in the *Spirit of St. Louis*,
pictured on the cover. A young man of 25 at the time,
Lindbergh was born in Minnesota and learned to fly in
Nebraska. Some of the best pilots in the world had tried to fly
non-stop from New York to Paris, but all had failed.
Lindbergh and the *Spirit of St. Louis* successfully met every
obstacle. Flying alone, Lindbergh kept the plane on course
over the uncharted North Atlantic. Time and time again,
Lindbergh fought off sleep during the 33½-hour flight to Paris.
Together, pilot and plane became heroes. The *Spirit of St.
Louis* hangs today in the Smithsonian Institution in
Washington, D.C.—an enduring symbol of courage and of the
AMERICAN SPIRIT.

Clarence L. Ver Steeg

American Spirit

A History of the American People

Clarence L. Ver Steeg
Professor of History
Northwestern University
Evanston, Illinois

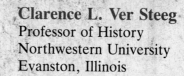

PRENTICE HALL

**Needham, Massachusetts
Englewood Cliffs, New Jersey**

American Spirit

About the author

Dr. Clarence L. Ver Steeg is Professor of History at Northwestern University in Evanston, Illinois. He received his master's and doctorate degrees at Columbia University and did post-graduate work at Northwestern University Law School.

His historical writings span a breadth of subjects—from home to high finance—and a scope of publications—from elementary textbooks to professional journals. Among his early historical books are *Robert Morris, Revolutionary Financier* which was awarded the Beveridge Prize by the American Historical Association, the widely acclaimed *The Formative Years 1607–1763*, the bestseller *The Story of Our Country*, and *Great Issues in American History: From Settlement to Revolution, 1584–1776*. His more recent books include *A People and a Nation*, *Origins of a Southern Mosaic: Studies in the Early Carolinas and Georgia*, and *World Cultures*. In addition to writing many history textbooks, he has contributed to others.

Often the recipient of fellowships and visiting lecturer status, Dr. Ver Steeg has served on many committees, including the Committee on the Commemoration of the American Revolution Bicentennial of the American Historical Association, a committee to plan the future of Northwestern University (the plan has been largely implemented), and a committee to advise in preparing the Master Plan for Higher Education for Public Institutions of the State of Illinois.

Credits

Executive Editor: Jeffrey M. Ikler
Project Editor: Mary Katherine O'Hare
Editor: Cormac Joseph Morrissey
Editorial Services: Joanna L. Gatanti, Mary Oates Johnson, Kenneth Kruse, Carole Wicklander
Production/Manufacturing Coordinator: Martha E. Ballentine
Copy/Production Editor: Sharon Buzzell
Product Marketing Director: Martha G. Smith
Product Marketing Manager: Darrell J. Kozlowski
Design Director: L. Christopher Valente
Design Coordinator: Stuart Wallace
Cover Design: L. Christopher Valente, Peter W. Brooks
Design Revision: Linda Dana Willis
Production, Design Services: Linda Dana Willis, Prentice Crosier
Photo Researcher: Laurel Anderson/Photosynthesis

Cover Art

"19th Hour," painting of Lindbergh's *Spirit of St. Louis* by Keith Ferris. Commissioned by Atlantic Aviation Corporation.

Teacher Consultants

Henry T. Conserva
Curriculum Specialist
San Francisco Unified School District
San Francisco, California

Kay Forrest-Zak
District Language Arts Coordinator
Teacher/Central School
Glencoe Public Schools
Glencoe, Illinois

Lovette Hood, Jr.
Instructional Coordinator
Atlanta Public School System
Atlanta, Georgia

A Simon & Schuster Company

Contents

Contents

Contents

Contents

Contents

Contents

Contents

The Reference Shelf

Focus On Skills

Focus On Lifestyles

List of Maps

Contents

Contents

List of Charts Graphs, and Tables (continued)

How To Use This Book

I N THIS SECTION you will take a walk through the pages of *American Spirit*. You will examine the parts that make up your text. You will discover what job each part is meant to do for you. You will see how each part relates to every other part. You will learn how to make each part work for you so that the story of the many people, places, and events of American history has meaning in your life.

Start your walk-through with the Table of Contents. It begins on page 5. The Table of Contents is a locator and an organizer. As a locator, it tells you where to find any important part of your text. As an organizer, it shows the parts into which your text is divided. Flip through the pages of the Table of Contents. See how the text is divided into large sections called units and into smaller sections called chapters. Notice that your text also includes a handy, good-size reference section called The Reference Shelf that contains an Atlas, Glossary, and Index, among other helps. Practice using the Table of Contents as a locator. Find the beginning and ending page numbers for Unit 1, for Chapter 13, and for the Index.

The Unit Opener

Take a minute to study pages 22-23, the opening pages of Unit 1. Look at other unit openers on pages 140-141, 250-251, and 364-365. Every unit's opening pages contain photographs. Some photographs are of people. Others show an event or an object. Each illustration calls to mind someone or something of importance in the unit.

Illustrations need to be read just as carefully as paragraphs of print. Use your powers of observation when you study an illustration. Use your imagination, too. Let each illustration "talk" to you from the past. If people are pictured, try to figure out who the people are and what part they might have played in the history of the times. Study their faces to see if you can tell something about their feelings. Study their styles of dress. Each illustration has some "nugget" of information that you can "mine."

Focus On The Unit

Each unit closes with a two-page review. Examine the Unit 1 review called *Focus On Unit 1* on pages 138-139. Each unit review has the same sections. "Lifestyles: Understanding Social History" allows you the opportunity to review the last chapter in each unit. "Making Connections" combines a time line with your knowledge of the unit in a series of skill questions. "Critical Thinking Skills" sharpens your critical thinking abilities. "Using Geography Skills" strengthens your

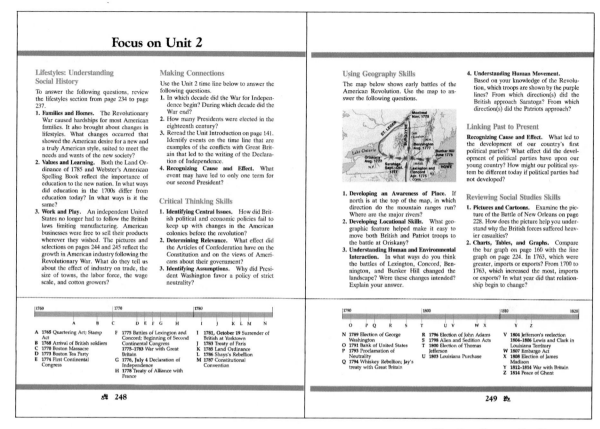

Focus on Unit 2

Lifestyles: Understanding Social History

To answer the following questions, review the lifestyles section from page 234 to page 237.

1. **Families and Homes.** The Revolutionary War caused hardships for most American families. It also brought about changes in lifestyles. What changes occurred that showed the American desire for a new and a truly American style, suited to meet the needs and wants of the new society?

2. **Values and Learning.** Both the Land Ordinance of 1785 and Webster's American Spelling Book reflect the importance of education to the new nation. In what ways did education in the 1700s differ from education today? In what ways is it the same?

3. **Work and Play.** An independent United States no longer had to follow the British laws limiting manufacturing. American businesses were free to sell their products wherever they wished. The pictures and selections on pages 244 and 245 reflect the growth in American industry following the Revolutionary War. What do they tell us about the effect of industry on trade, the size of towns, the labor force, the wage scale, and cotton growers?

Making Connections

Use the Unit 2 time line below to answer the following questions.

1. In which decade did the War for Independence begin? During which decade did the War end?

2. How many Presidents were elected in the eighteenth century?

3. Reread the Unit Introduction on page 141. Identify events on the time line that are examples of the conflicts with Great Britain that led to the writing of the Declaration of Independence.

4. **Recognizing Cause and Effect.** What event may have led to only one term for our second President?

Critical Thinking Skills

1. **Identifying Central Issues.** How did British political and economic policies fail to keep up with changes in the American colonies before the revolution?

2. **Determining Relevance.** What effect did the Articles of Confederation have on the Constitution and on the views of Americans about their government?

3. **Identifying Assumptions.** Why did President Washington favor a policy of strict neutrality?

Using Geography Skills

The map below shows early battles of the American Revolution. Use the map to answer the following questions.

1. **Developing an Awareness of Place.** If north is at the top of the map, in which direction do the mountain ranges run? Where are the major rivers?

2. **Developing Locational Skills.** What geographic feature helped make it easy to move both British and Patriot troops to the battle at Oriskany?

3. **Understanding Human and Environmental Interaction.** In what ways do you think the battles of Lexington, Concord, Bennington, and Bunker Hill changed the landscape? Were these changes intended? Explain your answer.

4. **Understanding Human Movement.** Based on your knowledge of the Revolution, which troops are shown by the purple lines? From which direction(s) did the British approach Saratoga? From which direction(s) did the Patriots approach?

Linking Past to Present

Recognizing Cause and Effect. What led to the development of our country's first political parties? What effect did the development of political parties have upon our young country? How might our political system be different today if political parties had not developed?

Reviewing Social Studies Skills

1. **Pictures and Cartoons.** Examine the picture of the Battle of New Orleans on page 228. How does the picture help you understand why the British forces suffered heavier casualties?

2. **Charts, Tables, and Graphs.** Compare the bar graph on page 160 with the line graph on page 224. In 1763, which were greater, imports or exports? From 1700 to 1763, which increased the most, imports or exports? In what year did that relationship begin to change?

1760		1770				1780		
	A	B	C	D E F G	H	I	J	K L M	N

A **1765** Quartering Act; Stamp Act
B **1768** Arrival of British soldiers
C **1770** Boston Massacre
D **1773** Boston Tea Party
E **1774** First Continental Congress

F **1775** Battles of Lexington and Concord; Beginning of Second Continental Congress
1775–1783 War with Great Britain
G **1776**, July 4 Declaration of Independence
H **1778** Treaty of Alliance with France

I **1781**, October 19 Surrender of British at Yorktown
J **1783** Treaty of Paris
K **1785** Land Ordinance
L **1786** Shays's Rebellion
M **1787** Constitutional Convention

1790		1800			1810		1820
O	P Q R S	T	U V	W X	Y Z		

N **1789** Election of George Washington
O **1791** Bank of United States
P **1793** Proclamation of Neutrality
Q **1794** Whiskey Rebellion; Jay's treaty with Great Britain

R **1796** Election of John Adams
S **1798** Alien and Sedition Acts
T **1800** Election of Thomas Jefferson
U **1803** Louisiana Purchase

V **1804** Jefferson's reelection
1804–1806 Lewis and Clark in Louisiana Territory
W **1807** Embargo Act
X **1808** Election of James Madison
Y **1812–1814** War with Britain
Z **1814** Peace of Ghent

248

249

The time line on the *Focus On* pages provides a good summary of the unit.

map-reading skills. "Linking Past to Present" challenges you to make the connection between events in our past and how these same events affect us today. The unit review concludes with "Reviewing Social Studies Skills," a review of the skills that you learned at the beginning of the unit.

Chapters Within a Unit

When you study a unit, you will see that the first chapter in the unit and the last chapter in a unit are different from the middle chapters in a unit. Take time to skim the chapters in Unit 1. Skim the first chapter, pages 24-41. The title tells you the chapter is about understanding time and place. Its job is to teach you the kinds of skills a historian uses to present the story of a place over time. A glance at the Table of Contents will tell you that the first chapter in each of the other units of *American Spirit* is also a chapter that teaches you how to use a historical skill.

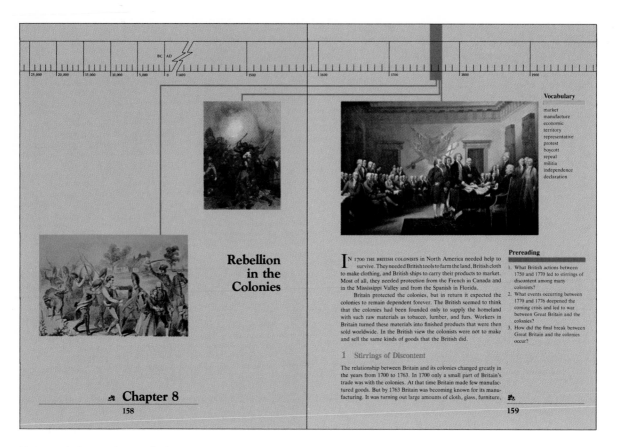

Within the illustrated textbook spread:

Vocabulary

market
manufacture
economic
territory
representative
protest
boycott
repeal
militia
independence
declaration

Rebellion in the Colonies

IN 1700 THE BRITISH COLONISTS in North America needed help to survive. They needed British tools to farm the land, British cloth to make clothing, and British ships to carry their products to market. Most of all, they needed protection from the French in Canada and in the Mississippi Valley and from the Spanish in Florida.

Britain protected the colonies, but in return it expected the colonies to remain dependent forever. The British seemed to think that the colonies had been founded only to supply the homeland with such raw materials as tobacco, lumber, and furs. Workers in Britain turned these materials into finished products that were then sold worldwide. In the British view the colonists were not to make and sell the same kinds of goods that the British did.

1 Stirrings of Discontent

The relationship between Britain and its colonies changed greatly in the years from 1700 to 1763. In 1700 only a small part of Britain's trade was with the colonies. At that time Britain made few manufactured goods. But by 1763 Britain was becoming known for its manufacturing. It was turning out large amounts of cloth, glass, furniture,

Prereading

1. What British actions between 1750 and 1770 led to stirrings of discontent among many colonists?

2. What events occurring between 1770 and 1776 deepened the coming crisis and led to war between Great Britain and the colonies?

3. How did the final break between Great Britain and the colonies occur?

⚓ **Chapter 8**
158

159

Make each illustration "talk" to you about the past. Study the vocabulary list. Use the questions listed in the margin as a guide in reading each main section in the chapter.

Now skim through the last chapter in Unit 1, pages 124-137. The title of this chapter tells you it is about the lifestyles of the times. The pages of a lifestyles chapter tell you about families and homes, about values and learning, and about work and play. Another glance at the Table of Contents reveals that a lifestyles chapter ends each of the other units of *American Spirit*.

The remaining four chapters in a unit—the middle chapters—tell the story of the unit. They are the narrative chapters. Examine pages 104-123 or one of the other narrative chapters in Unit 1. Each of these chapters discusses the actions of individuals and groups, describes places and events, and relates causes and effects.

Inside a Narrative Chapter

The opening pages of a narrative chapter present you with important study information. Use pages 84-85, for example. Notice the time line. You can tell what period of time the chapter covers by looking

🐛 **16**

at the section of the time line that is in color. You also see a number of photographs or other illustrations on these pages that can be "read" the same way you would read the illustrations on a unit's opening pages.

Another study aid on a chapter's opening pages is the list of important words used in the chapter under the heading "Vocabulary." The opening pages of every narrative chapter have such a list. Always check out the word list before beginning the study of a chapter. Look up each word in the Glossary so its meaning will be fresh in your mind. At the same time, check the pronunciation.

Still another study aid on these pages is a list of questions that guide your reading of a narrative chapter. Each numbered question or set of questions provides a guide for the reading of a main section in the chapter. For Chapter 4, the first main section has the title *Prelude to Settlement.* Read the question that guides the reading of this section. Find the next main section. It has the title *The Early Settlements.* Read its question. Do the same for the other two main sections of this chapter.

Now it is time to move beyond a narrative chapter's opening pages to the end of a main section. Again using Chapter 4, find the end of the first main section. In the margin you will find another list of questions. These are *Section Reviews.* Every main section ends with a list of review questions. These questions check your understanding of what you have read. It is a good study practice to make sure you know the answer to each question in a section-ending list before going on to the next main section.

Take a special look at the last question in this list. It is titled *Looking Ahead.* This question is a repeat of the second question from the list on the opening pages of the chapter. It is repeated to remind you what to look for as you read the next section of the chapter.

Each of the four narrative chapters in a unit includes a special two-page feature on people or on an important part of America's heritage. In Chapter 2, pages 58-59 highlight the heritage that people in the United States have received from Native Americans.

Finally, each narrative chapter has two closing pages called *Chapter Review.* Skim through pages 60-61, 82-83, 102-103, and 122-123. Each *Chapter Review* has a variety of exercises. "Chapter Summary" presents a recap of the chapter. "Reviewing Vocabulary" gives you a chance to show that you know your history vocabulary. "Understanding Main Ideas" and "Critical Thinking Skills" are good opportunities to review your understanding of the major concepts of the chapter and strengthen your critical thinking abilities. "Social Studies Skills" tests your ability to get information from

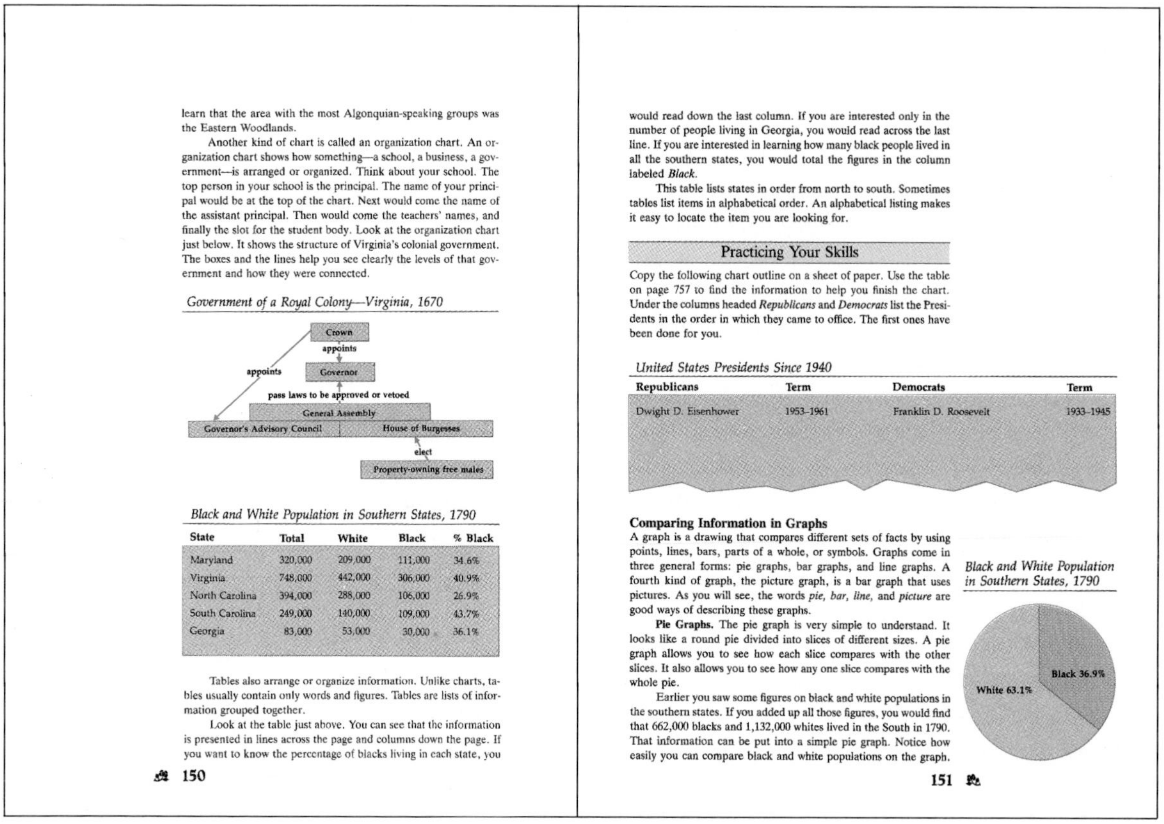

The following is a facsimile of pages 150–151 shown on this page.

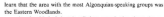

learn that the area with the most Algonquian-speaking groups was the Eastern Woodlands.

Another kind of chart is called an organization chart. An organization chart shows how something—a school, a business, a government—is arranged or organized. Think about your school. The top person in your school is the principal. The name of your principal would be at the top of the chart. Next would come the name of the assistant principal. Then would come the teachers' names, and finally the slot for the student body. Look at the organization chart just below. It shows the structure of Virginia's colonial government. The boxes and the lines help you see clearly the levels of that government and how they were connected.

Government of a Royal Colony—Virginia, 1670

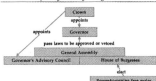

Black and White Population in Southern States, 1790

State	Total	White	Black	% Black
Maryland	320,000	209,000	111,000	34.6%
Virginia	748,000	442,000	306,000	40.9%
North Carolina	394,000	288,000	106,000	26.9%
South Carolina	249,000	140,000	109,000	43.7%
Georgia	83,000	53,000	30,000	36.1%

Tables also arrange or organize information. Unlike charts, tables usually contain only words and figures. Tables are lists of information grouped together.

Look at the table just above. You can see that the information is presented in lines across the page and columns down the page. If you want to know the percentage of blacks living in each state, you

150

would read down the last column. If you are interested only in the number of people living in Georgia, you would read across the last line. If you are interested in learning how many black people lived in all the southern states, you would total the figures in the column labeled *Black*.

This table lists states in order from north to south. Sometimes tables list items in alphabetical order. An alphabetical listing makes it easy to locate the item you are looking for.

Practicing Your Skills

Copy the following chart outline on a sheet of paper. Use the table on page 757 to find the information to help you finish the chart. Under the columns headed *Republicans* and *Democrats* list the Presidents in the order in which they came to office. The first ones have been done for you.

United States Presidents Since 1940

Republicans	Term	Democrats	Term
Dwight D. Eisenhower	1953–1961	Franklin D. Roosevelt	1933–1945

Comparing Information in Graphs

A graph is a drawing that compares different sets of facts by using points, lines, bars, parts of a whole, or symbols. Graphs come in three general forms: pie graphs, bar graphs, and line graphs. A fourth kind of graph, the picture graph, is a bar graph that uses pictures. As you will see, the words *pie, bar, line,* and *picture* are good ways of describing these graphs.

Pie Graphs. The pie graph is very simple to understand. It looks like a round pie divided into slices of different sizes. A pie graph allows you to see how each slice compares with the other slices. It also allows you to see how any one slice compares with the whole pie.

Earlier you saw some figures on black and white populations in the southern states. If you added up all those figures, you would find that 662,000 blacks and 1,132,000 whites lived in the South in 1790. That information can be put into a simple pie graph. Notice how easily you can compare black and white populations on the graph.

Black and White Population in Southern States, 1790

Black 36.9%
White 63.1%

151

Pages, such as these above, show you how to interpret and organize information in tables and charts. Other pages show you how to interpret maps, such as the one below.

such graphics as maps, charts, graphs, and political cartoons. "Writing About History" provides you with the chance to write about historical topics. "Your Region in History" presents an essay topic where you find out about the relationship between events in the nation and your community.

Inside a Skills Chapter

A skills chapter differs from a narrative chapter in several ways. Its opening pages have a list of important words used in the chapter. But these pages do not have a list of questions that guide your reading of a skills chapter. You know why you are reading. You are reading to learn a set of skills that will make your study of history easier and more meaningful.

A skills chapter has no *Chapter Review* pages to mark its close. In a skills chapter, a review exercise follows each main section. Called "Practicing Your Skills," these reviews let you master one skill before you move to another section and another skill. On what page in Chapter 1 do you find the first "Practicing Your Skills"

Area of Hohokam settlements

18

review? Check the Table of Contents once again. Look at the first chapter in each unit. What are some of the other skills you will learn as you use *American Spirit*?

Inside a Lifestyles Chapter

Turn to pages 124-137, the lifestyles chapter for Unit 1. A lifestyles chapter does not tell a story. It tells a *number* of stories, often in the words of people who lived in the past. The stories and the excerpts from letters, diaries, and other first-hand sources are grouped into three sections with four pages to a section. What are the titles of each of these three sections? Notice the section-ending list of questions on page 129. When these questions are discussed in class, listen carefully. The insights offered by classmates can broaden your understandings about the similarities and differences between life in the past and life today.

The Reference Shelf

The last 87 pages of your textbook contain a helpful reference section. Turn to pages 714-715, where the section begins. A reference section is one to which you refer as often as needed. You will use the various parts of this reference section time after time. It contains maps showing the growth and expansion of the United States. On what pages do you find these maps? It contains the Declaration of Independence and provides comments that help you understand its phrases. On what pages do you find the Declaration of Independence? This section also includes the Constitution and its amendments, again with comments to explain important points. On what pages do you find the Constitution? On what pages can you find information about the states of the Union? About Vice-Presidents of the United States?

On what pages do you find the Glossary? The Glossary contains every vocabulary word from the word lists on the opening pages of every skills chapter and every narrative chapter. The definitions given for each word are those that have a historical meaning. The Glossary also provides helps for the pronunciation of vocabulary words.

On what pages do you find the Index? You will find this alphabetical listing of topics a handy means of locating information in your text when writing reports.

Each of the many parts of your text is a study tool. This walkthrough has only introduced you to each tool. Now it is up to you to use each part, each tool, to help you study American history.

Introduction

History . . . is the memory of a nation. Just as memory enables the individual to learn, to choose goals and to stick to them, to avoid making the same mistake twice—in short, to grow—so history is the means by which a nation establishes its sense of identity and purpose. The future arises out of the past, and a country's history is a statement of the values and hopes which, having forged what has gone before, will now forecast what is to come.

President John Fitzgerald Kennedy

To the Student,

Think of all the things you do each day that are made easier because you have a memory. You know the route to school. You remember what classes you take each day. Names pop into your mind when you see familiar faces. You know the foods you like best. You know the words to a favorite song. You know what your room at home looks like. You can picture the face of a loved one. All of these everyday details are stored in your memory.

You have been collecting details in your memory since the day you were born. Memory plays such an important part in your everyday life that it is hard to imagine what life would be like without it. Without a memory you would not know what to expect from one moment to the next. Nothing would be "old," and everything would be new. Surprise would follow surprise. Without a memory you would live in a state of never-ending uncertainty, perhaps even fear. It would be like finding yourself in complete darkness in some unfamiliar place. Should you take a step forward? Should you reach out to touch something? Even if the unfamiliar space were suddenly to be flooded with light, the newness, the uncertainty, would not disappear. Without a memory you would not recognize a chair, a door, or even a parent walking into the room. Without a memory your bank of knowledge would always be empty.

Memory, however, helps you learn. Because you have taken many steps forward in the past, you know what to expect when you take another step forward. Memory gives you a sense of security because, in most cases, it tells you what to expect next. It tells you where you are, who you are, and who your friends and loved ones are. Memory gives you a sense of belonging—to your family, to your class, and to any other group of which you are a member.

Memory is as important to a nation as it is to a person. A nation's memory is its history. History gives the citizens of a nation a shared experience with every other person who ever took part in the events of the nation's past. This history gives each citizen a shared experience with every other person living in the present and who may live in the future. History is the link that unites the past with the present and the present with the future.

By studying the history of your country, you make yourself a link with its past, its present, and its future. The things you do and say become a part of your nation's history. The boys and girls who study the history of the United States in the next century will read about the events that took place in your lifetime. They will read about the cities, towns, or countryside in which you live. They will read about people you heard speak on the radio or television and the people you saw in person or on film. They will study your lifestyles. They may even read about something you did to influence the events of your lifetime.

21

LANDING AT JAMESTOWN.

Peopling the Nation

The Native Americans were the first humans to live in the Americas. They arrived from Asia more than 20,000 years ago. Over the centuries they settled large parts of both American continents. Different groups developed different ways of life.

Europeans did not become interested in the Americas until the first voyage of Christopher Columbus in 1492. Then people from Europe began to settle in different parts of the Americas. The Spanish conquered powerful Native American empires in Mexico and Peru after setting up colonies in the West Indies. French traders and trappers claimed a large part of North America for their nation. And after 1600 the English began to set up thirteen colonies along the Atlantic coast of North America. The thirteen English colonies thrived and later became the United States.

As you read about the peopling of the Americas, pay close attention to when and where each group of people lived. Understanding time and place is an important part of history.

Unit 1

Understanding Time and Place

🪶 Chapter 1

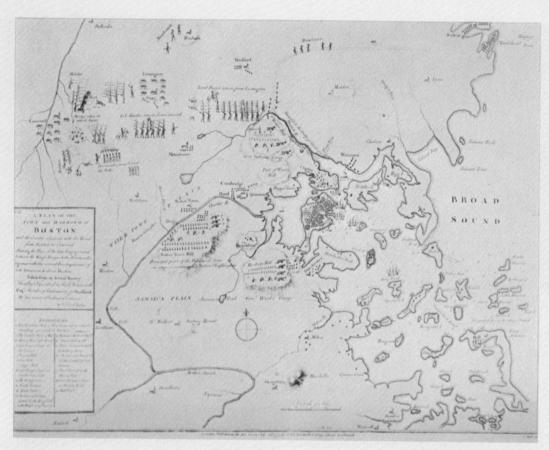

Vocabulary

lifetime	natural resource
century	mountain
decade	hill
generation	plateau
climate	plains
natural feature	elevation
landform	relief

Tﾍﾍﾍ IME IS IMPORTANT in your life. The passing of days and years affects you in many ways. Think back a year. Do you have the same teachers you had a year ago? Do you have new friends? Are you taller? What important things have happened to you over the past year?

Time is also important to your understanding of history. History is a record of change over a period of time. The things that happened in your life during the past year are a part of your history. The things that have happened in your country are a part of your country's history.

Place is also important in your life. If you lived in a different part of the country, you would attend a different school. If you lived in a different part of the world, you might speak a different language or eat different foods.

Understanding place is as important as understanding time when you study history. Earlier you read that history is a record of change over a period of time. To that definition you must now add a phrase. History is a record of change over a period of time that affects people living in a certain place.

The changing patterns of the sky mark the passing of time.

1 Learning About Time and History

Many scientists believe that human life on earth probably began about two million years ago. From the beginning, time has been a mystery to all who try to understand it. People see time passing, by the rising and setting of the sun. They see patterns of movement in the stars and planets that show time passing. People see time passing as they watch the seasons change from winter to spring. Everyone sees and experiences the passing of time, but few people can define it. Sixteen hundred years ago the philosopher St. Augustine puzzled over the meaning of time. "What then is time? If someone asks me, I know. If I wish to explain it to someone who asks, I know not."

Understanding Periods of Time

You know how long a minute lasts. You know how long a day, a month, and a year last. You have lived through the passing of each of these units of time. The average amount of time a person can live through—that is, the average human lifetime—is about seventy years.

Students of history must think about much longer spans of time than the average human lifetime. Longer spans of time are beyond human experience. People must use their imaginations to try to understand distant time.

You read that 1,600 years ago St. Augustine puzzled over the meaning of time. How long ago was 1,600 years? One way to understand such a long period of time is to use your imagination. For example, you know that an average person lives about seventy years.

Now imagine a world in which there is only one person living at a time. That person lives a whole lifetime, seventy years. The next person is born only when the first person dies. The next person also lives a full lifetime, and then a new person is born. The process continues. To span 1,600 years, about twenty-two people would have to live and die, one after the other. So 1,600 years equals about twenty-two lifetimes.

The last example used a unit larger than the year—the lifetime. Another way to imagine 1,600 years is to use a unit smaller than the the year, such as the day. In 1,600 years there are 584,000 days!

You also read that humans may have first appeared on earth about two million years ago. Two million years is even harder to imagine than 1,600 years. Two million years is equal to more than 28,000 lifetimes, or about 728 million days. Another way to imagine two million years is to try to show it on a chalkboard line. Let's say you wanted one inch (2.54 cm) to stand for one year. You would need a chalkboard that stretched nearly 32 miles (almost 52 km) to show two million years!

The history of your country does not span two million years. But the history of its people spans thousands and thousands of years—more than 20,000 years at least. Historians often divide such a great span of time into A.D. and B.C.

The letters A.D. stand for the Latin words *anno Domini.* In English, these two words mean "in the year of the Lord." The term A.D. refers to the years that follow the birth of Jesus of Nazareth, called "the Christ" or "the Lord." The year A.D. 1985 means 1,985 years after the birth of Jesus. A date that has neither A.D. nor B.C. by it is an A.D. date. Letters are needed only for B.C. dates.

The letters B.C. stand for the words "before Christ." They are written after the year rather than before it. The date 8000 B.C. means 8,000 years before the birth of Jesus. How many years ago was 8000 B.C.? To find the answer, you have to think through several steps. First, you know that 8000 B.C. means 8,000 years before the birth of Jesus. Second, you know that about 2,000 years have passed since the birth of Jesus. Finally, you can add the 8,000 years before Jesus to the 2,000 years after. You then know that 8000 B.C. was about 10,000 years ago.

Another way historians divide great spans of time is between history and prehistory. In its broadest meaning, *history* covers everything that has happened since human beings have lived on the earth. But it was not until about 3500 B.C. or 5,500 years ago, that people in some parts of the world began to develop written languages. Written records are the tools of historians. So history often means the years since the first written records. The many years before people kept written records are often called prehistory.

Prehistoric Native Americans are believed to have carved these pictures of arrows, people, and animals on Newspaper Rock in Petrified Forest National Park, Arizona.

Even though there are no written records of it, people can still study prehistory. Some groups of prehistoric people left tools, weapons, drawings, and other things they made. These things are useful clues about how those people lived. Remains of skeletons and clothing may even show what people looked like or how they dressed. When you study the first people to arrive in America, you will learn more about prehistory.

Another useful time unit in history is the century. *Century* can mean any period of 100 years. Historians often use the word to mean a certain century. You are living in the twentieth century. That means that you are living in the 100-year period between 1901 and the end of the year 2000. The first century A.D covers the years 1 through 100. The year 1776 was in the eighteenth century.

Decade is another useful word for a time unit. A decade is any period of ten years. Ten decades make one century. Writers of history often use the word to describe a special decade. For example, they may write about the 1770s, meaning all the years from 1770 through 1779. In what decade of the twentieth century were you born? In what decades have you lived?

Families play an important role in history. In stories about families, the word *generation* is sometimes used. *Generation* can measure time as well as show relationships among family members. A generation is the time span between the birth of parents and the births of their children. Think about your own class. You and your classmates are about the same age. You belong to the same generation. Your sisters and brothers also belong to your generation. Your parents and their brothers and sisters—your aunts and uncles—are older than you. They are another generation. Your grandparents are still another generation.

The average difference in age between one generation and the next is about thirty years. The actual age difference between parents and offspring may be more or less than thirty years.

Six Generations of Your Family

Your great-grandparents	their sisters and brothers	your great-grandaunts and great-granduncles	**Past Generation**
30 years average			
Your grandparents	their sisters and brothers	your grandaunts and granduncles	**Past Generation**
30 years average			
Your parents	their sisters and brothers	your aunts and uncles	**Past**
30 years average			
YOU		your sisters and brothers	**Present Generation**
30 years average			
Your daughters and sons	your sisters' and brothers' children	your nieces and nephews	**Future Generation**
30 years average			
Your granddaughters and grandsons	your sisters' and brothers' grandchildren	your grandnieces and grandnephews	**Future Generation**

Try to find out how many years difference there is between your age and the age of your parents.

Practicing Your Skills

1. The year 1976 was in the twentieth century. In what century was each of the following years?
565   1066   1492   1776

Critical Thinking

2. **Expressing Problems Clearly.** Young children often have special problems understanding periods of time. Write a paragraph explaining the word *century* in a way that a ten-year-old might understand.

Using Time Lines

Besides using words, historians draw time lines to show different spans of time. You read that you would need an eight-mile chalkboard (almost 13 km) to show 500,000 years if one inch (2.54 cm) stood for one year. But you can show the same span of time in only 5 inches (12.7 cm) if you let each inch stand for 100,000 years. Time lines are especially useful because they can show great spans of time in a small amount of space.

| 0 | 100,000 | 200,000 | 300,000 | 400,000 | 500,000 |

Every time line has a scale. The scale shows the period of time represented between the marks on that line. Look at the two time lines below. The first time line shows one decade. Each mark shows where a new year begins within that decade. The second time line shows a century. Each mark on it shows a decade within that century. Both time lines are the same length, but they have different scales.

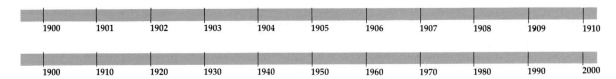

Look at the time line below. On this time line the spaces between the marks each stand for 500 years. The time line shows three events. It shows when written records begin, when Jesus was born, and when you are reading this chapter. It also shows the order in which these events occurred.

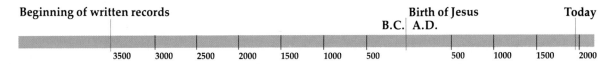

If you look closely, you can see something else on this time line. You can see that the time between the beginning of written records and the birth of Jesus is far longer than the time between the birth of Jesus and today. Time lines help you see events in the order they occurred. They also help you compare various spans of time.

There are two other times you have read about in this chapter that could be added to a time line. One is the time of St. Augustine, about 1,600 years ago. If you subtract 1,600 years from the present year you learn that St. Augustine lived in the late 300s. St. Augustine's lifetime can easily be added to the time line in the late 300s.

The other event you have read about is the beginning of human life on earth. That was about 500,000 years ago, according to many scientists. That date does not fit so easily on this time line. Since the marks on the line stand for 500-year periods, you would need a total of 1,000 marks to show so many years. But there is a way to show events in the far distant past on a time line. Historians use a jagged line to break the time line at the place where the scale changes. The time line below shows the additions of St. Augustine's lifetime and the probable beginning date of human life on earth.

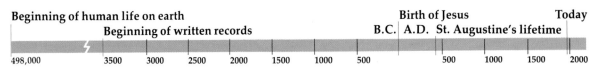

Massasoit and the Wampanoag lived in peace with English settlers for many years. The Pilgrims welcomed the visit of their friend Massasoit.

Practicing Your Skills

In the next chapter you will read about the Native Americans, the first people to live in America. In Chapter 4 you will read about the arrival of the English in North America. The following story is about the meeting in 1620 of one group of Native Americans, the Wampanoag (wäm′pə·nō′ag), and one early group of English settlers, the Pilgrims.

Critical Thinking

Expressing Problems Clearly. As you read this story, look for the words you have learned that refer to time. Note each date as you read.

A Wampanoag Century

The story of the Wampanoag century begins with the birth of the great Wampanoag leader, Massasoit (mas·ə·soit′). He was born sometime during the sixteenth century. The exact date is not known, but he was probably born about 1580. His place of birth was the area now known as Massachusetts.

The Wampanoag were farmers and hunters in the area of Massachusetts. They were governed by a chief of the tribe, called the sachem. Massasoit was the sachem when the Pilgrims came from England in 1620. The Pilgrims settled in the Wampanoag area.

The great chief Massasoit and the English made an agreement in 1621. They agreed to live in peace and help each other in case of war with other peoples. The Wampanoag agreed to leave their bows and arrows behind when they visited the English. The English agreed to leave their guns behind when they visited the Wampanoag.

Under Massasoit the English and the Wampanoag got along very well. The English spoke of Massasoit as a faithful friend. They were saddened when Massasoit died in 1661, some eight decades after his birth.

By that date a new generation of leaders had come to power among the Wampanoag and the English. These new leaders paid less attention to the original peace agreement.

Massasoit's eldest son, Wamsutta (wäm·sət′ə), became sachem when his father died. Trouble broke out between the Wampanoag and the English. Wamsutta was captured by the settlers. He died soon afterward.

In 1662 Massasoit's Second son, Metacomet (met′ə·käm′it), became the next sachem. Metacomet was able to keep peace with the English for almost a decade. But he saw more and more Wampanoag land being taken over by the English. The English wanted to treat the Wampanoag as subjects, not as equals. War finally broke out in 1675, almost a century after the birth of Massasoit. The English captured Metacomet's wife and son in August 1676. They were both sold into slavery. Metacomet was killed in a surprise attack later that same month. The English believed that Metacomet had betrayed them.

Only one century had passed from the birth of Massasoit to the death of Metacomet. But during that time the once proud and independent Wampanoag were defeated and made into slaves.

Use a separate sheet of paper. Copy the time line shown below. Skim over the Wampanoag story again. Show each event in its proper place on your time line. Two examples are done for you.

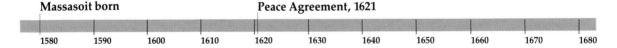

Massasoit born   Peace Agreement, 1621

1580   1590   1600   1610   1620   1630   1640   1650   1660   1670   1680

2 Learning About Place and History

In the story of the Wampanoag you read that the Native Americans lived in what is now Massachusetts. You also read that they were farmers and hunters. Where is Massachusetts? Why were the Wampanoag hunters and farmers? An understanding of place will help you answer these questions.

Understanding Natural Features

You have probably heard the expression "as old as the hills." It seems to say that the hills have been, and will be, around forever.

But hills, like everything, change over time. When the first people came to America tens of thousands of years ago, the continent was very different from the way it is today.

The earliest Americans lived during the last great Ice Age. During that time, temperatures all over the world were cooler than they are today. In the North, snow fell for thousands of years. It piled up into huge, moving mountains of snow and ice called glaciers. Glaciers spread out from the North Pole. They tore the land with the weight of millions of tons of ice. At the peak of the Ice Age, glaciers covered nearly all of what is now Canada and the northern part of the United States. The force of these moving mountains of ice was so powerful that it carved out great holes in the earth. Some of those great holes became the Great Lakes.

Then, by about 8000 B.C, or 10,000 years ago, the Ice Age ended. The climate warmed and the glaciers melted. Trees and other plants began to grow in places that were once cold and barren. Large grassland areas became deserts, with salty rather than freshwater lakes. Some woodlands turned to dry grasslands.

As the glaciers melted, land long buried under them began to appear. The Native Americans, who had come to America at the time of the Ice Age, continued to spread throughout the Americas. The generations of early Americans born after the Ice Age faced a new environment. This environment was more like the America you know today.

The Ice Age was the last great natural force to bring dramatic change to the land surface and climate of North America. But the millions of people who have lived on the land have made many changes in the environment.

Just over a century ago much of the Midwest was richly forested. Laura Ingalls Wilder, an American author, grew up in the Midwest in the 1870s. She recorded her memories in the book *Little House in the Big Woods*.

> The great, dark trees of the Big Woods stood all around the house, and beyond them were other trees and beyond them were more trees. As far as a man could go to the north in a day, or a week, or a whole month, there was nothing but woods. There were no houses. There were no roads. There were no people. There were only trees and the wild animals who had their homes among them.

But families such as Wilder's slowly cleared these wooded lands. The soil was rich and the climate good for farming. Forests were cleared in many other parts of the country. Irrigation turned dry lands into good farmlands. Small towns grew into large cities. Telephone and electric wires were strung across the land. Roads and rail lines crisscrossed the country. These and many other changes over time altered the face of your country's land.

Natural features are those that exist in an area naturally. They include landforms, bodies of water, climate, and natural resources. The natural features of the continent influenced peoples' lives and the course of your country's history. For example, gold and silver deposits discovered in the West in the mid-1800s led many people to migrate westward. This migration is part of America's history. It helped shape the West of today.

As historians study and record changes over time at a given place, they look for ways in which natural features have influenced those changes. As you read the following pages, think about which natural features are in the region in which you live and how they affect your life.

Landforms. There are four main landforms on the earth's surface: mountains, hills, plateaus, and plains. Geographers distinguish kinds of landforms by measuring the elevation. The elevation of a landform is its height above sea level. Geographers also measure a landform's relief. *Relief* refers to changes in elevation within a given stretch of land. If the land rises or drops sharply, it has a high relief. If the land rises or falls gently, it has a low relief.

Mountains are the landforms with the highest elevation and relief. Mountains rise 6,600 feet (1,980 m) or more. Within a given stretch of mountains, elevation may rise or drop as much as 1,000 feet (300 m) or more.

The land rises sharply along parts of the Oregon coast.

The Colorado River carved the Grand Canyon through a wide plateau in Arizona.

People who live in mountainous areas often live in valleys between mountain slopes. They live in valleys because the high slopes make travel and transportation very difficult. Most mountain areas have only a thin soil covering. But in some places the land can be used for farming or grazing. Mountains often are rich in mineral deposits or are heavily forested. Many people living in mountains work at mining or lumbering. Swift flowing mountain streams are also a good source of waterpower for electricity.

Hills are between 1,650 and 6,600 feet (495 to 1,980 m) high. They have a moderate relief. Hilly areas are usually more populated than mountainous areas. Transportation and farming are easier in the hills than in the mountains. In most other ways living in the hills is like living in the mountains.

Mountains and hills have influenced your country's history in a number of ways. Before there were airplanes, mountains and hills were often barriers to trade and travel. They often affected where people could settle and what kind of trade they could carry on. Mountains and hills sometimes formed a natural fort and served as protection from enemies.

Plateaus are flat landforms that are often higher than the land around them. Plateaus have an elevation of 1,650 feet (495 m) or

Farmers grow so much grain on the flat lands of the Midwest that the region is called the nation's breadbasket.

more, but they have very low relief. Rivers have carved deep canyons in some plateaus. The most famous of these is the Grand Canyon in Arizona. Plateau areas are often windswept, dry, and thinly populated. Herding is a common way to make a living on a plateau. In some places irrigation makes farming possible.

Plains are flat or gently rolling lands. They have a low elevation of 1,650 feet (495 m) or less. They also have a low relief. Most of the world's food is grown or raised on plains. And most of the world's largest cities are located on plains. Transportation is easy across the flat lands of the plains.

Plateaus and plains have also influenced the history of your country. The presence of plateaus in the United States helps explain why parts of the country have few people living in them. The wide stretches of plains help explain the large population in some areas of the country. They also explain the abundance of crops the country produces.

Bodies of water. Oceans, lakes, and rivers all affect the lives of the people who live near them. They are important transportation routes. Because bodies of water make trade possible, many large cities have grown up near them. Bodies of water are often important as sources for food. Rivers and freshwater lakes provide water for drinking and irrigating farmlands. Where dams are built, lakes and rivers also provide a source of waterpower.

Climate. Geographers study the climate of a natural region by measuring temperatures and precipitation. The temperature and the amount of moisture determine the kinds of plants that can grow in a region. Climate determines the growing season of a region. In some regions there is enough warm weather and enough rain to make farming possible year round. In other places the first frost comes early, and the growing season may be only six months long. The length of the growing season influences what crops people can grow or if they can farm at all. So climate has also helped shape the history of your country.

Natural resources. You have already read about some natural resources: soil, forests, minerals, and bodies of water. The resources in each region help determine how the people in that region will live. Long ago, people were limited by the natural resources in their region. If there were not enough animals to hunt in one place, people would have to move. Today people transport and trade resources from one place to another. Now they do not have to travel around to fill their everyday needs.

Landforms, bodies of water, climate, and natural resources all have influenced the way people have lived and worked throughout history.

Practicing Your Skills

Write out answers to the following questions about the region in which you live.

1. Which of the four landforms does your region have? How do these landforms affect the kind of life you have?
2. What are yearly temperatures like in your area? How much rain or snow does your region receive throughout the year? How does this climate affect the clothes you wear? The home you live in? The activities you enjoy?
3. Name at least three natural resources that your region has. How do people in your region use these resources?
4. How does your family earn its living? Would such a way be possible if you lived in any other region?
5. In what three ways have people changed your community in the last ten years?

Critical Thinking

6. **Predicting Consequences.** Imagine you were living 200 years ago. How might your answers to these same questions about your region be different?

REGIONS OF THE UNITED STATES

- Northeast
- Midwest
- South
- West

All the states but Alaska and Hawaii share a border with at least one state.

Using Maps

In the last section you learned about natural features. But you did not learn how these features are spread over the United States. How are landforms and bodies of water distributed in the United States? What are the climate zones of your country? Where are its natural resources located? Maps will help you answer these questions.

The United States is the fourth largest country in the world. It stretches from the Atlantic Ocean on the east to the Pacific Ocean on the west. Within it are all four kinds of landforms. It also has an abundance of water and natural resources. Because of its many kinds of natural features and its size, people often divide the country into four smaller regions. The map above shows how the fifty states of your country are divided into these four regions.

Maps, like time lines, have scales. Find the scales on this region map. This map shows the fifty states and their borders. It uses colors that are explained in the key. The colors show what states lie within each region. The map also shows you something about natural features. You can see the country's major rivers, lakes, and oceans on this map. But it does not show landforms, climates, or resources.

The following map shows many more of North America's natural features. This map also has a key that uses color and a scale. The color on this map shows various heights of land. By using the key on this graphic-relief map, you can tell if an area has mountains, hills, plateaus, or plains. For example, find the city of St. Louis, Missouri, on the map. Now find the color that is around St. Louis on

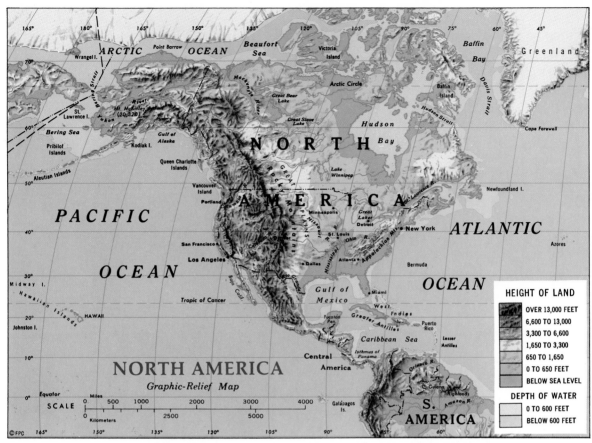

NORTH AMERICA

Graphic-Relief Map

HEIGHT OF LAND	
	OVER 13,000 FEET
	6,600 TO 13,000
	3,300 TO 6,600
	1,650 TO 3,300
	650 TO 1,650
	0 TO 650 FEET
	BELOW SEA LEVEL
DEPTH OF WATER	
	0 TO 600 FEET
	BELOW 600 FEET

Use the map key to find the elevation of your home region.

the key. You have learned that landforms with an elevation below 1,650 feet (495 m) are plains. Now you can tell that St.Louis lies in a plains area. Now find Denver, Colorado. If you use the same procedure, you can see that Denver lies in a mountainous area.

By comparing the region map with the graphic-relief map, you can learn how the four main regions of the country differ from one another. You can see that the West has more mountains than any other area and that the Northeast has more hills. You can also see that the main landforms of the Midwest and South are plains.

You read about the Wampanoag, hunters and farmers who lived in what is now Massachusetts. You can use maps to learn more about Massachusetts. The region map shows you that Massachusetts is in the Northeast region. The graphic-relief map shows you that the main landforms of Massachusetts are plains.

The climate map on the next page shows you even more about Massachusetts and other areas of the country. Look at the region map on page 38 to help locate Massachusetts on the climate map. If you study the key on the climate map, you will learn that the region receives abundant precipitation. Precipitation is necessary for farming. You can also learn that the summers are warm but the winters are cold. It is likely, then, that the Wampanoag farmed in the summer and had to hunt for food in the winter.

NORTH AMERICAN CLIMATE REGIONS

	Climate Type	Temperatures	Precipitation	Vegetation
	Tropical Wet	hot year-round	heavy year-round	rain forests
	Tropical Wet-and-Dry	hot year-round	heavy when sun is overhead	tall grasses, scattered trees
	Semiarid	variable	light	short grasses
	Desert	variable	very light	scrub, cactus, grasses
	Mediterranean	hot summers, cool winters	dry summers, wet winters	grasses, scrub, some trees
	Humid Subtropical	hot summers, cool winters	year-round, but heavier in summer	forests, grasses
	Marine	warm summers, cool winters	year-round, but heavier in winter	forests, grasses
	Continental	warm summers, cold winters	year-round, but heavier in summer	trees, grasses
	Subarctic	cool summers, cold winters	light	trees, some grasses, mosses
	Tundra	cool summers, cold winters	light	grasses, mosses, lichens
	Highlands	vary*	vary*	vary*

*depending on elevation and direction of prevailing winds

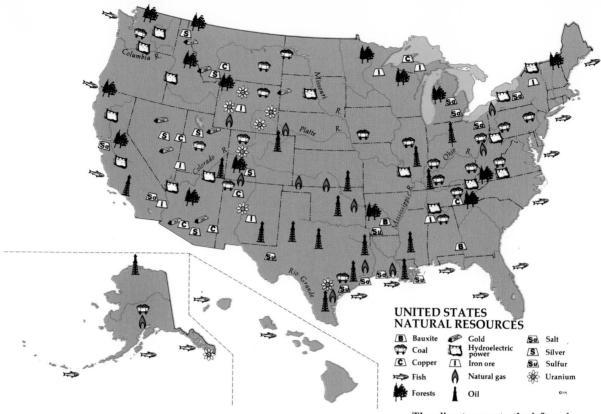

UNITED STATES NATURAL RESOURCES

B Bauxite		**Gold**		**Sa** Salt	
Coal		**Hydroelectric power**		**S** Silver	
C Copper		**I** Iron ore		**Su** Sulfur	
Fish		**Natural gas**		**Uranium**	
Forests		**Oil**			

The climate map to the left and the resources map above are both examples of a special purpose map.

Compare the climate map with the region map to understand more about how the regions are different. You can see that the South has warmer temperatures than the Midwest and Northeast. You can also learn that most of the West is drier than the other regions. The West also has the greatest variation in climate.

Throughout this book maps will help you understand how place is important in history. There are also special maps at the end of this book. Turn to page 716 and become familiar with the maps in the Atlas section. As you read about your country's history, these maps will help you understand the changes over time that have affected people in a certain place—the United States of America.

Practicing Your Skills

Compare the natural resources map on this page with the maps on pages 38, 39, and 40. Write out answers to these questions.
1. What region of the country has the most oil? What landform is common in regions where oil is found?
2. What regions have large amounts of coal? In what landforms is coal found?

Critical Thinking
3. **Drawing Conclusions.** In what ways might people living along the East Coast make their living?

The Native Americans

Chapter 2

Vocabulary

continent
descendant
ancestor
migrate
archaeologist
irrigation
drought
culture
delegate
council
environment
heritage

THE FIRST HUMANS to live in the Americas came from the continent of Asia thousands of years ago. Their daughters and sons became Native Americans, the first people born on the North and South American continents. Thousands of years later Christopher Columbus would name the descendants of these people Indians. He mistakenly believed that he had landed in the East Indies, which are islands off the coast of Asia. But the people Columbus met were not from India or the East Indies. Their ancestors had been Native Americans for more than 20,000 years.

1 The First Americans

There are no written records of when or how the first people came to America. But scientists in different fields have gathered bits and pieces of information. From these facts they have been able to piece together the story of the first arrivals.

Prereading

1. What two finds suggest that humans arrived in America more than 20,000 years ago?
2. How did farming change the Hohokam?
3. How did the Mound Builders use their mounds?
4. How were chiefs among the Iroquois chosen?
5. What two lasting effects did the abundant resources of the Pacific Northwest have on newcomers?
6. How did the Eskimo adapt to life in cold, Arctic lands?

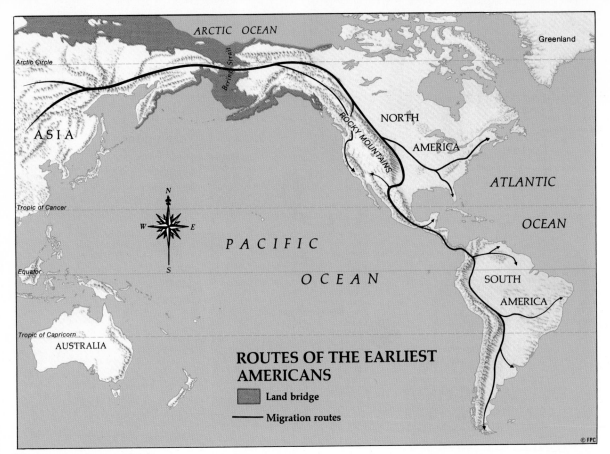

ROUTES OF THE EARLIEST AMERICANS

  Land bridge
— Migration routes

Many early migrants slowly traveled southward in search of food and comfortable climates

Early Migrations

The story of the first Americans begins more than 20,000 years ago, when the world was in its last Ice Age. During the Ice Age much of the Northern Hemisphere was frozen. Huge glaciers formed when parts of the Arctic Ocean turned to ice. As more and more water froze, the level of the sea fell. Land that was once underwater began to appear above the surface of what is now the Bering Strait. This new ground formed a wide land bridge between Asia and America.

Scientists believe that migrating Asians crossed this land bridge to North America on foot in search of food. They followed the animals that also crossed from Asia: shaggy bighorn sheep, giant bison, rugged bears, huge moose, caribou, and deer.

The early hunters, traveling in groups, crossed from Asia to North America carrying their hunting tools and a few goods for the home. They lived off their kill as they slowly made their way into the unpeopled continent.

The migrations lasted for thousands of years. Many generations of early Americans lived and died as the slow migrations continued. The early arrivals moved south into the land that is now the United States. They probably followed an ice-free path just east of the Rocky Mountains. Some of them may have used small boats to travel south along the Pacific coast. In time they moved into and settled almost every part of the Americas.

The Pieces of the Puzzle

Many scientists have worked on the puzzle of when and how these Asians came to the Americas. Some have studied rocks and landforms. Their findings helped show how the land bridge was formed. Discoveries by other scientists, called archaeologists, helped explain how the migrating people lived in the Americas. These scientists have uncovered deeply buried human remains as well as settlements. They also found the goods these early people used in their everyday lives.

One early find was made in 1908 near Folsom, New Mexico. A black ranch worker named George McJunkin was riding his horse beside a canyon that had been swept by floodwaters. He noticed some bones sticking out of a canyon wall, just below the rim. Curious, McJunkin climbed down and removed the bones.

The bones McJunkin found were larger than cattle bones. He could not guess from what animal they had come. Neither could other people who visited the site. Finally, in 1926, Jesse D. Figgins found that the bones were those of a huge bison that had lived there during the Ice Age.

Figgins and some helpers went to work digging at McJunkin's "bone pit." They found more bones from the Ice Age. Among the bones they found pieces of chipped flint. The flint points, made by humans for use as spearheads, told Figgins that Native Americans must have lived in New Mexico earlier than 8000 B.C., when the giant bison still roamed the land.

The findings at Folsom surprised many people who thought that Native Americans had come to North America thousands of years later. Other surprises were to come. In 1936 diggers in Los Angeles uncovered a human skull. Scientists who tested it for age have found that it dates from about 21,000 B.C. In 1966 there was another surprising find. Peter Lord, a Native American, discovered a carved caribou bone at Old Crow, Canada. It looked like a tool used to scrape flesh from animal skins. Scientists' tests showed that it dated from about 25,000 B.C. Because of these finds and others, most scientists believe that people have lived on the North American continent for more than 20,000 years.

By the time the Ice Age ended, about 8000 B.C., Native Americans had settled large parts of both American continents. It was not long before these groups were living in ways that were different from those of their big-game hunting ancestors. Groups living in eastern woodlands hunted deer instead of bison. Those living in western deserts gathered food where they could. Those who remained in the Arctic made warm clothing from animal skins and homes from ice. So different were their ways of living that the history of the early Americans is not a single story. It is many stories.

The spearheads found at Folsom, New Mexico, are more than 10,000 years old.

Section 1 Review

1. What chain of events during the Ice Age formed a land bridge between Asia and North America?
2. What two routes might early arrivals have followed in moving south into what is now the United States?
3. What did Figgins and his helpers find at McJunkin's "bone pit"?
4. How did Figgins's findings help him date the arrival of migrants in New Mexico?
5. What two other finds help date the arrival of newcomers to North America?

Critical Thinking

6. **Recognizing Cause and Effect.** Why did early Asians first cross the land bridge?

LOOKING AHEAD: How did the beginning of farming change the lives of early people in the Southwest?

45

2 Farmers of the Southwest

When the Ice Age ended, much of the southwestern part of North America became a desert. Only a few plants, such as cactus and mesquite (mə·skēt′), could grow there. Herds of large animals could no longer find enough food to eat. People living in the Southwest began to hunt smaller animals, such as rabbits. They also gathered wild berries, roots, and seeds. They learned to grind the wild seeds into meal with grinding stones. For thousands of years these people lived by gathering wild plants. Then they learned something that changed their whole way of life. They learned farming.

Scientists believe that Native Americans in Mexico were growing corn by about 5000 B.C. The skill of farming spread north from Mexico. By about 3500 B.C. people near Bat Cave, New Mexico, were growing corn, beans, and squash. The earliest farmers grew their corn in clumps of about a dozen plants. Because the soil was dry, these farmers left plenty of room for each plant. Otherwise the plants died in their search for enough water. After harvesting the corn, the early farmers used stones to grind it into a flourlike meal. They used the meal to make flat corn cakes, which they baked on hot stones. These cakes were like today's tortillas.

The Hohokam

Around 100 B.C. the Hohokam (hō′hō·käm′) farmers in what is now Arizona learned how to grow more food by using irrigation. The Hohokam dug canals from nearby rivers to channel water to their crops. Later they dug canals as long as 30 miles (48 km). They lined some canals with clay to keep the water from soaking into the ground too soon. In some canals the Hohokam controlled the flow of water with gates of woven grass.

As the Hohokam were able to grow more crops, they no longer needed to move about in search of food. They settled in one place and built pit houses. The Hohokam would dig a hole two or three feet deep and a dozen feet across. Over the pit they built a frame of branches. They wove reeds into a cover for the frame and coated it with mud. Pit houses protected the early desert farmers from the hot sun during the day and the sharp cold at night.

Besides canals and pit houses, workers have dug up beautiful painted pottery and clay figures at Hohokam sites. They have also found bowls carved from stone, jewelry made from shells, and mirrors of polished slate. Workers have discovered ball courts the size of modern basketball courts. On them the Hohokam played games, using rubbery balls made from the hardened juice of a desert plant. The object was to get the ball between stone markers at the end of the court. Players could kick or throw the ball to score a goal.

Area of Hohokam settlements

Through the invention of irrigation canals the Hohokam grew more food for more people. The canals, five to six feet deep, carried water to the fields from the Gila and Salt rivers.

The Anasazi

Another group of Native Americans, the Anasazi (än′ə·sä′zē), were even better farmers than the Hohokam. The Anasazi planted their crops near mountain streams in what is now Arizona, New Mexico, Utah, and Colorado. They chose places where there was plenty of rain. There they grew corn, beans, and squash.

Like the Hohokam, the early Anasazi lived in pit houses. Around A.D 900 they began to put up a new kind of building. The Spanish explorers later named these living places *pueblos* (pweb′lōz), the Spanish word for *towns*. The pueblos were four- or five-story

Area of Anasazi settlements

Section 2 Review

1. What two things did the Hohokam do to control the flow of irrigation water?
2. What four major steps did the Hohokam take in building pit houses?
3. What explanations do scientists offer for the sudden disappearance of the Anasazi around A.D 1300?

Critical Thinking

4. **Making Comparisons.** In what ways was life different for the people of the Southwest after they became farmers?

LOOKING AHEAD: How did the Mound Builders use their mounds?

Once the home of the Anasazi, Mesa Verde in Colorado has been preserved as a national park.

buildings made of clay or stone. One of the largest, Pueblo Bonito (bō·nē′tō) in New Mexico, had about 800 rooms. The pueblos were so well built that many of them are still standing.

The Anasazi built many of their pueblos against cliffs, high up on ledges of canyons. The most famous of these is Cliff Palace at Mesa Verde (mā′sə ver′dē) in Colorado. The people who lived in Cliff Palace got in and out by climbing on ladders through holes in the roof. Ladders also led up to the fields at the top of the cliff. The Anasazi could remove the ladders when enemies came.

The Anasazi made clay pots and jugs and beautiful turquoise jewelry. They wove cloth from cotton. The Anasazi lived in their cliff homes for a few hundred years. Then suddenly, sometime about 1300, they disappeared.

Scientists think that the Anasazi may have left because of a long dry spell. In such a drought the Anasazi would not have been able to grow enough food for all the people in the giant pueblos. The Anasazi are believed to have packed up and moved on to lands where the drought had not hit. New people from the north, the ancestors of the Navaho and the Apache, moved into the lands once farmed by the cliff-dwelling Anasazi.

3 The Mound Builders

Southwestern Native Americans were not the only people to learn farming. Diggers have found that at least one group in Kentucky raised squash and sunflowers in about 1000 B.C. Later these farmers also grew corn. As time passed, large farming settlements grew up in the Midwest and the Eastern Woodlands.

Many groups of Native Americans in the Midwest and East shared another practice besides farming. They built mounds out of earth. In the earliest mounds they buried their chiefs and other important people.

The oldest burial mounds in North America date from about 1000 B.C. The latest were built about 300 years ago. Some mounds still stand in many of the midwestern and eastern states. Some are only as high as your waist. Others are 100 feet (30 m) high, as high as a ten-story building.

The Native Americans built their mounds by filling baskets or clay pots with dirt in one place and dumping them in another. With each new load of soil the mound grew a little higher. Some of the biggest mounds must have taken many years to build.

The Mound Builders of the past left a treasure chest of facts about their everyday lives. In and near their many mounds—about 10,000 in the Ohio River Valley alone—are the remains of their cultures. These remains help tell the story of the Mound Builders.

This snake-shaped mound is in Ohio

Area of Adena settlements

The Adena

The oldest mounds were built about 3,000 years ago by people called the Adena (ə·dē′nə). These mounds are simple. When people died, their bodies were laid out on the ground along with a few simple everyday tools. Then they were covered over with dirt to form mounds a few feet high. Later the Adena built larger mounds. Some of these are 70 feet (21 m) high and hold many bodies.

Buried along with the bodies are copper jewelry and tools, pottery, and pipes carved from stone. Sometimes there are figures carved from sheets of mica (mī′cə), which is like soft, thin glass. Most Adena mounds also hold a stone tablet with a carving of a vulture on it. Archaeologists believe that this bird may have been sacred to the Adena.

Other objects found near the mounds tell us that the Adena lived mostly on food they hunted and gathered—deer, fish, and nuts. They probably also gathered sunflower seeds and other wild plants.

The Hopewell

Another group of Native Americans built mounds in the Ohio Valley. These Mound Builders, who lived between 700 B.C. and A.D 500, are called the Hopewell.

The mounds of the Hopewell are even bigger than those of the Adena. More goods, different from those of the Adena, are buried with the bodies. Diggers have found copper breastplates, freshwater pearls, carved shells, mica ornaments, pottery, and clay figures. The Hopewell did not make all these beautiful things themselves. They traded for them with people living hundreds of miles away in all directions.

Area of Hopewell settlements

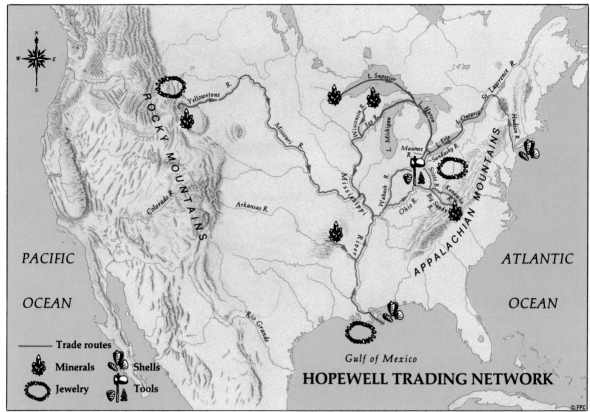

Minerals   Shells

Jewelry   Tools

—— Trade routes

PACIFIC OCEAN

ATLANTIC OCEAN

Gulf of Mexico

HOPEWELL TRADING NETWORK

Study this map to learn how the Hopewell used bodies of water to reach people and goods in other regions.

A Hopewell of long ago carved this figure from a piece of wood.

The Hopewell spread out into settlements along rivers, mostly in what is now southern Ohio and Illinois. They grew corn and other plants, fished, hunted, and kept up their lively trade. But during a war among people of the Eastern Woodlands, the Hopewell trade routes were no longer safe. By about A.D 500 their culture had died out, probably after a long drought.

The Mississippians

The latest group of Mound Builders were the Mississippians. They lived from about the early 700s until the mid-1700s. The Mississippians were good farmers. They lived mostly on corn, beans, squash, and the animals they hunted. Many lived along the Mississippi and Ohio rivers. Some of their towns were small, but others housed as many as 20,000 people.

One of the largest Mississippian settlements was the city of Cahokia (kə·hō′kē·ə) in what is now southern Illinois. Cahokia covered about 6 square miles (15.5 sq km). Around the center of the settlement was a wall of logs standing on end and coated with clay. This stockade enclosed about 300 acres (121 ha). Within the wall were houses, a marketplace, and many, many mounds.

Area of Mississippian settlements

NATIVE AMERICAN SITES AND SETTLEMENTS BEFORE A.D. 1500

- Hohokam
- Anasazi
- Adena
- Hopewell
- Mississippians
- • Archaeological sites

The cultures shown on this map are often called pre-Columbian because they existed before Christopher Columbus sailed to the Americas.

The marketplace was one of the most important places in the city. There people traded salt, furs, hunks of copper, and sharp-edged stones used for hoes. Artists traded their pottery and carved shells.

The many mounds in Cahokia were used in different ways. Corn and other crops grown along a nearby river were stored in some small mounds. Other mounds were platforms for the houses of important people. The largest mound was probably used for religious services. It stands 100 feet (30 m) high and covers 15 acres (6 ha). Its base is bigger than that of the Great Pyramid of Egypt. At one time a temple crowned its top. From there, one could see far beyond the city walls.

Outside the city walls there were more mounds, more houses, fields for farming, and a wide open square. People may have played games in this open space. Nearby was a huge sun calendar. To make

Section 3 Review

1. Of the Adena, the Hopewell, and the Mississippians, which group carried on trade over a wide area?
2. Which of the three groups developed a society divided into several classes?

Critical Thinking

3. **Making Comparisons.** In what two ways did the Hopewell mounds differ from the Adena mounds?

LOOKING AHEAD: How were chiefs among the Iroquois of the Eastern Woodlands chosen?

this calendar, the Mississippians arranged posts in a wide circle. On sunny days every post cast a shadow on the ground. By studying the changes in these shadows, the leaders in Cahokia decided when to plant their crops.

Sometime around 1600 the city of Cahokia lay empty. Its people had left, perhaps because the fields along the river could no longer grow enough crops to feed them.

Another settlement lasted longer than Cohokia. Near what is now Natchez, Mississippi, French fur traders found a large Mississippian settlement in 1704.

According to the French, the Natchez group was divided into several classes. Heading the group was a ruler called the Great Sun. He had the power of life and death over his people and was also their chief priest. Below him were lesser Suns, then Nobles, then a class called Honored People. Members of the lower class—farmers, soldiers, and slaves—could become Honored People by doing some dangerous deed or by fighting bravely in a war.

Some French traders were present when a Great Sun's brother died. At his death his two wives and several of his servants were killed to be buried with him. His body and the bodies of those who followed him to death were carried to the top of a mound. Weapons and ornaments were placed around his body. Then the grave was covered with dirt. Perhaps he still lies there, one of the thousands left buried by the Mound Builders.

4 The Iroquois of the Eastern Woodlands

Many groups living in the Eastern Woodlands were descendants of the Mound Builders. Among the most famous were the Iroquois (ir′ə·kwoi′). Most of them lived in the present-day states of New York and Pennsylvania.

The Iroquois lived in dwellings called longhouses that were grouped together in towns. Around the towns were stockade fences. Beyond the fences were the fields of corn and other vegetables.

The Iroquois Longhouse

The Iroquois built their longhouses on a frame of thin tree limbs. They stripped bark from elm trees and stitched the strips together to form the sides and roof. A typical longhouse was between 50 and 100 feet (15-30 m) long. Down the middle was a long hall with a door at each end. There were no windows or chimneys.

A longhouse held as many as twelve families. Each family lived in a part of the house on one side of the hall. The people slept on wooden shelves along the walls. They cooked in the hall on an open fire that they shared with the family living across from them.

Area of Iroquois settlements

In this model of an Iroquois longhouse a section has been cut away to show the inside.

Women in Iroquois Society

The longhouses, the fields, and everything the family owned belonged to the women of the group. Iroquois children took their mothers' names, not their fathers'. And families traced their roots through their mothers. When a man and a woman married, the husband went to live in his wife's longhouse.

Iroquois women held much of the governing power. They chose all the delegates to the council. The chief was named by the oldest women in the group and had to be accepted by a council of all the women. The chief could be removed from office by the women if they were not pleased with his leadership.

The Iroquois League

In the 1500s several Iroquois groups, or nations, were at war with one another. To put an end to the fighting among themselves, five nations banded together in 1570 to form the League of the Iroquois. They were the Mohawk, Oneida (ō·nī′də), Onondaga (on′ən·dô′gə), Cayuga (kē·ōō′gə), and Seneca (sen′i·kə). A sixth Iroquois group, the Tuscarora (təs′kə·rôr′ə), joined the league in 1722. The league tried to find peaceful ways to settle fights among Iroquois peoples and to form a stronger defense against their outside enemies.

The league was governed by a council of fifty men called peace chiefs. They were chosen as delegates for life by the women of the member nations. The league council met each summer to talk over disputes among members and sometimes to plan war with other groups. All members had to agree before the league could act. Sometimes all the people in a village would travel to the place where the league met. There they would listen to all sides of the questions.

The league lasted until 1784. European settlers admired its democratic ways of handling problems.

Section 4 Review

1. Describe an Iroquois town and its surroundings.
2. What steps did the Iroquois take in building a longhouse?
3. Which groups belong to the League of the Iroquois in 1722?
4. How was the league governed?

Critical Thinking

5. **Recognizing Cause and Effect.** Why did several Iroquois groups band together to form the League of the Iroquois?

LOOKING AHEAD: What two lasting effects did the abundant resources of the Pacific Northwest have on newcomers?

Native Americans of the Pacific Northwest carved cedar logs to make totem poles in honor of important people.

Area of Pacific Northwest settlements

5 Native Americans of the Pacific Northwest

Like the other earliest Americans, the first people to live on the Pacific coast of North America were most likely migrating hunters. But the environment these groups found was rich in resources. The rivers and streams flowing into the Pacific Ocean were full of fish. One person could catch amounts of salmon equal to his or her weight in just a few hours. Other food was also easy to find. In the forest there were berries and wild game. Many sheep and goats lived in the mountains. The ocean was alive with seals, otter, whales, porpoises, and fish. Soon after arriving on the coast, the Native Americans probably gave up their migrating ways and settled down near streams.

Forest Living

From nearby forests the early people of the Pacific Northwest took wood to build their houses. Cedar wood was most useful because it was soft and easy to split with stone axes and other tools. One group of Northwest Native Americans, the Haida (hī′də), built their houses by first pounding four thick corner posts into the ground. Then they made a frame out of cedar beams. Finally, they laid cedar boards across the frame to form the walls and roof.

The Haida found many uses for cedar bark. They wove baskets from it. They made mats to cover the floors and walls of their houses. They wove together threads of bark and of wool from mountain goats to make blankets.

Cedar was also used to make boats. The Haida built small boats for traveling on streams and long ships for ocean travel. They painted their boats in bright colors and carved figures on them.

The Haida also carved cedar logs to make totem poles. They set up these totem poles at the entrance to their houses. Sometimes the poles honored chiefs who had died. More often they honored the people living in the houses. The figures carved on the poles told of victories won and of other great deeds.

Potlatches

Because they had so many resources, the early people of the Pacific Northwest had more goods than they needed. Some people grew very wealthy. They enjoyed showing off their wealth at lavish parties called potlatches. The main event at a potlatch was the giving of gifts. Those who held the party, the hosts, gave away many valuable goods, perhaps to prove that they could always get more. They gave such gifts as dried salmon, fish oil, blankets woven of cedar fibers, fur robes, and carved wooden bowls and chests.

Both guests and hosts wore their finest clothing to these ceremonies. They wore robes made from the skins of otter, seal, and bear. Some wore headdresses carved with human faces that had shells for eyes.

There was always a great feast at the potlatch. The hosts served smoked salmon, roast duck or goose, deer or bear meat, and bowls of wild berries. After the feast, the gift-giving began. The feasting and gift-giving went on for two or three days. Then the guests gathered up their gifts and went home.

The guests did not keep their presents for long. They would soon be hosts at potlatches of their own. The guests were expected to pay back the host family by inviting them to a potlatch. In time, many blankets, robes, and carved dishes would find their way back to the people who first gave them away.

6   The Eskimo

The chill, raw land of the Far North often was the first stop in North America for each new wave of migrating Asians. The earliest migrants moved southward to better lands and warmer climates. The last wave of Asians to reach North America arrived between 3000 and 2000 B.C. By then the land bridge was once again underwater, so these later Asians must have crossed the Bering Strait by boat. These people, the ancestors of today's Eskimo and Aleuts (ə·loots′), did not migrate south. Instead, they settled in the cold northern lands, from the Aleutian (ə·loo′shən) Islands in the Pacific Ocean to Greenland in the Atlantic.

The Eskimo lacked abundant resources in their Arctic environment. Most Eskimo found the land frigid cold, with miles of trackless snow. There were no trees, few animals to hunt, and little or no land for farming. They had to spend most of their time building shelters, finding food, and keeping warm.

Eskimo Homes

The Eskimo built different homes in different seasons. In parts of the North, summer was a comfortable season. During the summer many

Section 5 Review

1. Name three things the Haida made from cedar wood.
2. Name three things the Haida made from cedar bark.
3. Name two purposes a totem pole served.

Critical Thinking

4. **Identifying Central Ideas.** Why did the early people of the Pacific Northwest hold potlatches?

LOOKING AHEAD: How did the Eskimo adapt to life in cold, Arctic lands?

Area of Eskimo settlements

Eskimo lived in tents made from animal skins. But during the winter their homes had to protect them from the Arctic cold. Some Eskimo were able to find stone or wood or whalebone. From these they built pit houses, which were designed to hold heat.

The Eskimo learned that warm air rises and cold air flows down. They entered their pit houses through an underground passageway that led to the living space above ground. This passageway trapped the cold air below and let the warm air rise into the house. Inside the living space sleeping platforms were built close to the ceiling, the warmest part of the dwelling. These platforms were spread with furs and animal skins for more warmth.

When they had no wood or stone, the Eskimo built igloos with blocks of ice and snow. An igloo took only a few hours to build. The ice blocks were laid like bricks. Snow was packed into the cracks between the blocks, where it froze into ice. Blocks of clear ice were used for windows. Sleeping platforms were also made of ice. As in the pit houses, these platforms were built near the ceiling in the warmest part of the igloo.

The Search for Food

Because food was hard to find, the Eskimo learned to be skillful hunters. Those living away from the sea hunted caribou. Sometimes they had to travel hours over ice and snow to find the animals. They carried their kill on sleds back to the village.

People living near the oceans caught fish and hunted seals, walruses, and whales. They built boats of wood and of animal skin. The small boats, called kayaks (kī′aks), had a closed top except for a hole in which the hunter sat. The larger boats, umiaks ($\overline{oo}$′mē·aks), had open tops. These carried about eight people and were used mostly for whale hunting.

The meat from two or three whales was often enough to feed a whole village over the long winter. The Eskimo found good uses for all parts of the whale. They used whalebone for making knives and tools. Eskimo artists carved beautiful figures of animals and people from whalebone. Whale fat, or blubber, was used to make oil for stoves and lamps. Whale skin was made into warm clothing.

Time for Rest

For the Eskimo, life was hard. They spent much of their time just staying alive. But, by using what they had in new ways, they were able to meet their needs and even have some time for fun. During the winter the men in a village would gather in a clubhouse to make and repair their hunting tools. Sometimes the women of the village joined them there. The men took time out from their work to see who could tell the best stories. Some men wrestled for fun.

The Eskimo wore goggles to protect their eyes from driving snow.

ARCTIC OCEAN

Greenland

Eskimo

Aleut

Eskimo

Eskimo

Tlingit

Eskimo

Haida

Hudson Bay

Chilcotin

Cree

NORTH

Nootka

Blackfeet

Chippewa

Algonquian

Chinook

Flathead

Mandan

Ottawa

Penobscot

Nez Percé

Menominee

Huron

Klamath

Shoshone

Crow

Dakota (Sioux)

Potawatomi

Iroquois

Wampanoag
Narraganset

Paiute

Cheyenne

Winnebago

Sauk
Fox

Mohegan
Pequot

Pomo

Ute

AMERICA

Omaha

Illinois

Miami

Erie

Delaware

Susquehannock

ATLANTIC

Chumash

Navaho
Hopi
Zuni

Pueblo

Pawnee

Kiowa

Shawnee

Powhatan

Tuscarora

OCEAN

Mojave

Osage

Cherokee

PACIFIC

Papago

Apache

Chickasaw

OCEAN

Pima

Comanche

Choctaw

Creek

Natchez

Apalachee

Calusa

Gulf of Mexico

Maya

Aztec

© FPC

NATIVE AMERICAN GROUPS IN THE 1500s

Mainly farming areas

Mainly fishing areas

Mainly hunting and gathering areas

Name the Native Americans who once lived where you live today.

Thousands of years before the first Europeans came to North America, lights from whale-oil lamps shone out of the clubhouses into the dark Arctic nights. Like other Native American peoples, the Eskimo had found ways to live on the American continent. Even after Europeans came to North America, the Eskimo lived much the same way they had for centuries. But, for most Native Americans, the coming of Europeans was to bring great changes.

Section 6 Review

1. When did the last wave of migrants reach North America?
2. How did the Eskimo find food?

Critical Thinking

3. **Testing Conclusions.** In what ways did the Eskimo depend upon the whale?

Heritage

Of Native Americans

The earliest Americans developed a variety of cultures that enrich the lives of today's Americans.

Time Line for Some Native American Groups

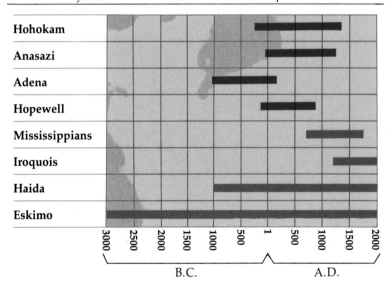

Hohokam
Anasazi
Adena
Hopewell
Mississippians
Iroquois
Haida
Eskimo

3000 2500 2000 1500 1000 500 1 500 1000 1500 2000

B.C. A.D.

■ Native American cultures that died out before the Europeans arrived

■ Native American cultures thriving when the Europeans arrived

These are only a few of the groups whose cultures enriched the nation.

Human culture in every group is passed along from the old to the young. How to speak, how to build, how to plant or to hunt, and how to worship are some gifts of older generations. These gifts become the heritage of the young. The United States has inherited its rich culture from many groups. From the beginning the Native Americans shared their lore with others.

Many Cultures

There is no single Native American heritage. Different groups developed different languages and cultures. When the Europeans arrived on this continent, Native Americans spoke more than 1,000 different languages. Each group had its own customs and beliefs. Even today the Seneca living in New York are different from the Sioux (sōō) in South Dakota or the Hopi (hō′pē) in Arizona.

Native American Foods

Native American ways affect you every day. Food crops first farmed by Native Americans are an important part of each person's diet. Corn was the main food for many early tribal groups in both North and South America. Today corn on the cob is still an American favorite. The popcorn that you eat at the movies was first made by Native Americans in Mexico. Native Americans in Peru were the first to grow the white potato, which you enjoy as French fries. Corn and potatoes, the gifts of Native American farmers, are among the world's most important food crops. Also on the long list of foods first farmed by Native Americans are beans, sweet potatoes, squash, tomatoes, pumpkins, tapioca, and cocoa.

Land Use

In their use of the land Native Americans showed how people can live without spoiling the world around them. They valued the land because they knew it filled their most important needs—food, shelter, and clothing. Those who want to save our environment today owe much to the Native American idea that people depend on nature.

Europeans could not live long in America without doing as the Native Americans had done. The English, the Dutch, the French, and the Spanish had to learn to plant corn and other American food crops. The Native Americans taught Europeans how to trap animals and how to net fish. Ponchos, parkas, and moccasins became part of American clothing.

Language Gifts

Words used every day in the United States were borrowed from Native Americans: *canoe, barbecue,*

Descendants of early Americans recreate a traditional corn dance.

toboggan, and *moccasin.* The word *buck,* meaning "dollar," goes back to the days when Native Americans traded buckskin for other goods.

Medicine

Native Americans discovered medicines still in use today. In Peru, Native Americans found a medicine in the leaves of the coca plant. Doctors today use the same medicine to fight pain. Native Americans used a poison on their arrows that doctors now use to relax muscles. Another medicine first used by Native Americans is used to treat malaria.

Family Ties

Family life was as important to Native Americans as it was to Europeans. In many groups, uncles, aunts, grandmothers, grandfathers, and cousins helped raise the children. Children without parents almost always found a home and a family. When Europeans forced the Tuscarora to move north in the 1700s, the Iroquois League took in all the Tuscarora people.

Religion and Nature

Religion, like the family, lay at the center of life for most Native Americans. Ceremonies often revolved around some part of nature. Most Plains groups held a sun dance each summer. The sun dance was a sign of the people's hope for enough buffalo and other game to hunt. More important, group members felt that the sun dance gave them new life.

In the snake dance the Hopi ask for good rainfall and healthy crops. During this dance group members hold snakes in their mouths and around their necks. Women spread cornmeal on the snakes. During the ceremony the snakes are not harmed in any way. At the end of the dance all the snakes are let go to return to the Hopi rain gods and tell of the ceremony.

In their respect for nature many Native American religions are alike. In most other ways, what the Native Americans believed about their gods and their world was as different as the many peoples who lived in the Americas.

Many places are known by their Native American names.

Native American Place-names

Connecticut	**Algonquian**	*at the long, tidal river*
Nebraska	**Oto**	*flat water*
Minnesota	**Sioux**	*cloudy water*
Kentucky	**Cherokee**	*land of tomorrow, or dark and bloody ground*
Ashtabula County, Ohio	**Algonquian**	*there are always enough fish moving*
Keya Paha County, Nebraska	**Sioux**	*turtle hills*
Kewanee, Illinois	**Potawatomi**	*prairie hen*
Opa Locka, Florida	**Seminole**	*big swamp*
Mississippi	**Algonquian**	*big river*
Schoharie Creek, New York	**Iroquois**	*driftwood*
Chehalis, Washington	**Chehalis**	*sand*

Chapter 2 Review

Chapter Summary

Most scientists believe the first humans arrived in North America more than 20,000 years ago. These ancestors of Native Americans were migrants from the continent of Asia. By 8000 B.C. their descendants had migrated to almost all parts of North and South America.

The early Americans developed a wide range of cultures and societies as they migrated south, west, and east. In the Southwest, the Hohokam and the Anasazi learned to farm and use irrigation. In the Midwest, the Adena began building mounds as burial places about 1000 B.C. These earliest Mound Builders were followed by the Hopewell and the Mississippians. In the Eastern Woodlands, the Iroquois developed a culture in which women held great power. In the Pacific Northwest, groups lived close to streams near the ocean and thrived in this plentiful environment. The final wave of Asian migrants, the Eskimos and the Aleuts, remained far north instead of moving south to warmer lands.

Reviewing Vocabulary

Use the following words to complete the sentences below. Write your answers on a separate sheet of paper.

continent   environment
descendants   migrate
ancestors   irrigation
archaeologist   cultures
drought   council
delegates   heritage

1. The farmers in the Southwest mastered their _____ by developing _____ systems to grow more food.
2. By looking at old bones and tools, a(n) _____ can tell a great deal about Native Americans' _____ and their _____.
3. The last two groups to _____ from the Asian _____ remained in the far north.
4. In periods of _____, early American groups often left their homes in search of more suitable conditions.
5. The Iroquois League was governed by a(n) _____ of men who, once elected, were considered _____ for life.
6. The _____ of the Mound Builders were groups living in the Eastern Woodlands.
7. The earliest Americans left behind a rich _____ that can be seen in aspects of our lives today.

Understanding Main Ideas

1. What evidence exists to support the claim that humans arrived in America more than 20,000 years ago?
2. How did farming affect the Hohokam?
3. Of what use were the mounds to the Mound Builders?
4. By what process were the Iroquois chiefs chosen?
5. The resources of the Pacific Northwest had what lasting effects on newcomers?
6. In what ways did the Eskimo adapt to the harsh environment of the Arctic?

Critical Thinking Skills

1. **Making Comparisons.** In what ways did the lifestyles of the Native Americans of the Pacific Northwest differ from those of the groups in the Southwest?
2. **Testing Conclusions.** Do you think that it is true that the Iroquois League was a democratic organization? Why?
3. **Identifying Assumptions.** Why do you think the Aleuts and the Eskimos chose to

Social Studies Skills: Using a Map Key

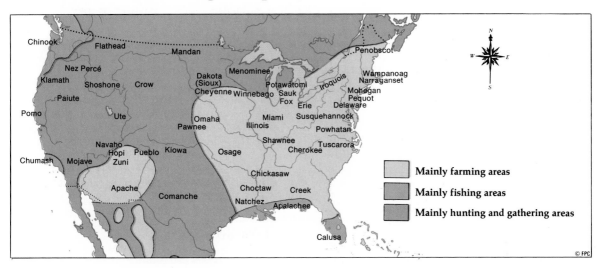

I. Farming Groups	II. Fishing Groups	III. Hunting & Gathering Groups

A map is one way to organize and present information. The map above details Native American groups in the continental United States. The map key on the far right of the map gives you information to understand the map. This same information can be organized another way—in a chart.

Skill Review: Copy the chart on the left onto a sheet of paper. Study the map and the information it contains. Then use the map and its key to place each group in the proper column on the chart.

---

remain in the far north rather than migrate to the south like their Asian predecessors?

Writing About History

Writing a Paragraph. Write a paragraph comparing the roles men and women played in Iroquois society and the roles they play in today's society. In what ways are they different? The same? Give at least two similarities and differences.

Your Region in History

Culture. Find out which groups of Native Americans had settled in or near your area. Think about the land, its water supply, and other natural resources that existed when the group lived there. Consider what food they ate, the duties that they performed, the leisure activities they enjoyed, and the culture that developed. Write a brief schedule describing a typical day in this Native American community.

BC AD

25,000 20,000 15,000 10,000 5,000 0 1400 1500

The Arrival of Europeans

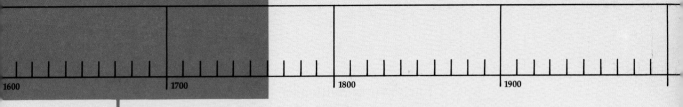
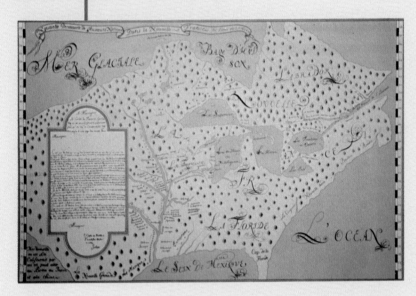

Vocabulary

seafarer
navigation
colony
empire
expedition
import
tributary
missionary

AT ONE TIME, students were taught that Christopher Columbus discovered America. But you have learned that this honor belongs to an unknown Asian who led the first settlers to the American continent. In this chapter you will learn how Europeans reached America. Although the Norse seafarers were the first Europeans to arrive, it was the Spanish voyage of Columbus that changed the course of American history.

1 A Widening World

Five centuries before Columbus's first voyage, a Norse seafarer landed on the eastern shore of what is now Canada. The Norse lived in the rocky and mountainous land of Norway in northeastern Europe. Norway is part of a peninsula that stretches south like a pointer into the North Sea. Sailing out from their many ports, the Norse seafarers explored the waters in and around northern Europe. They also sailed west into the stormy, open waters of the North Atlantic Ocean. The first European to land in the Americas was one of these seafarers.

Prereading

1. How was European interest in a widening world awakened in the 300 years following the Norse settlement in Vinland?
2. Where did the voyages of Christopher Columbus take him?
3. What was the extent of the Spanish claims in the New World by the middle of the sixteenth century?
4. How did the settlements of New France differ from those of Spanish America?

Early Norse Settlements

By about A.D. 870 the Norse had settled in Iceland, an island in the North Atlantic about 800 miles (1,280 km) west of Norway. Eric the Red, a venturesome fellow, brought his family there in the late 900s. By the year 985 Eric had discovered Greenland, a larger island to the west of Iceland. He founded a settlement there. Later a shipload of Norse settlers sailing west to Greenland got lost on the way. When the leader of this ship finally arrived in Greenland, he told of a land he had seen even farther to the west. Settlers in Greenland, where wood was hard to find, welcomed the news of a "land covered with trees." Eric's son Leif, a tall, good-looking man, decided to find out more about this unknown country.

Leif Ericsson set sail in the year 1001 with a crew of thirty-five. He soon landed on Labrador, then on the coast of Newfoundland—both now parts of Canada. Deciding to stay the winter, he and his crew built a small village of simple huts. Because the wild berries they found there looked like grapes, Leif and his crew named the place Vinland, or "wine land." The following spring they returned to Greenland with a load of wood and wild berries.

Norse trading ships once carried crews and cargoes to many places along the North Atlantic.

A few years later other Norse families settled in Vinland for about three years. During this time a son was born to a Norse couple. He was the first baby born in the Americas whose parents had come from Europe. This group of settlers came into contact with some Native Americans, whom they called Skrellings (skrā′lingz). The Skrellings may have been Eskimo. Fighting broke out between settlers and Skrellings, and the Norse finally packed up and returned to Greenland.

European Interest in Asia

At the time the Norse were finding their way to America, other Europeans thought of the Mediterranean Sea as the center of the known world. Europe lay to the north of the Mediterranean. Africa was to the south. The Middle East, leading to the Asian mainland, lay along the eastern rim of the Mediterranean. The people of southern and western Europe knew only the lands of North Africa and the Middle East. In the next 300 years Europeans became linked with peoples in almost every part of the world.

The Crusades

Europeans learned about the larger world during the Crusades. The Crusades were a series of religious wars fought from 1096 to 1291. In these wars Christians fought Muslims to gain back Jerusalem, then called the Holy Land. This territory is occupied today by the nation of Israel.

Most people in Europe were Christians. They followed the teachings of Jesus, who lived and died in the Holy Land. Christians had built many shrines there.

The Muslims, who ruled Jerusalem, practiced a faith called Islam. Their God was Allah. They believed that the prophet Mohammed heard Allah's words and wrote them in a holy book, the Koran.

After Mohammed's death in 632 the Islam faith spread throughout the Middle East and North Africa. Powerful Muslim rulers took over the land in which Jerusalem lay. They turned many Christian shrines into Muslim places of worship. In 1096, European Christians began the first of four Crusades to take back the Holy Land from the Muslims.

The first Crusaders did not win in their fight for the Holy Land. But those returning to Europe told of great cities, busy markets, and such riches as silks, jewels, and spices. In many parts of Europe people began to demand these goods.

Merchants in Venice and Genoa, seaport cities in northern Italy, made special trading arrangements with the powerful Muslim rulers. Only the Italians could deal in the much-valued goods carried along the trading routes between Europe and the Asian lands to the east. The Italians charged other Europeans high prices for the goods. To get around the Italian hold on eastern trade, other European nations began looking for a new sea route to Asia.

Marco Polo

A book written in the early part of the fourteenth century by an Italian named Marco Polo brought about even greater interest in the lands of Asia. As a young man, Marco had traveled to Asia. Once there, he had served in the court of the Great Khan, the ruler of China. In his book Marco Polo told of his adventures and travels. He told of seeing burning sand in the Middle East. It was oil. He wrote of rock that burned. It was coal. He described hundreds of elephants parading in jeweled harnesses edged with gold and silver. He told of the many carts hauling raw silk to the market. Marco Polo's story was read by many people in all parts of Europe. His story stirred adventurers, merchants, and rulers.

Portugal's Search for a New Route

Urged on by Prince Henry the Navigator, Portugal led the search for a new, less costly way to get Asian goods. Prince Henry believed that a route to Asia could be found by exploring the western coastline of Africa. Sometime after 1420 he began a school for sailors to teach the newest findings in navigation, shipbuilding, and mapmaking. Then he sent sailors on explorations along Africa's western coast.

Prince Henry did not live to see his ships reach Asia. But his work led to success later. In 1488 Captain Bartholomew Diaz reached the Cape of Good Hope at Africa's southern tip. Nine years later Vasco da Gama rounded the Cape. He sailed all the way to India, reaching it in 1498. Portugal opened the gates to the riches of Asia and began direct trade.

2 Christopher Columbus

There have been many brave explorers in the history of the world. But no explorer was more important to the history of the Americas than Christopher Columbus. He was born in Genoa, Italy, in 1451. Later he settled in Portugal and sailed on Portuguese ships to Iceland and down Africa's coast.

Columbus's Plan

His interest in the sea led Columbus to study many maps and books. He read and reread the books by Marco Polo. On his copy Columbus drew a finger pointing to Marco Polo's description of Japan as a country where houses had roofs of gold. He drew a star where Marco Polo said the China Sea was part of a large ocean, not a

Section 1 Review

1. What waters did the Norse seafarers explore?
2. Who was Eric the Red?
3. In what year did Leif Ericsson set sail for the "land covered with trees"?
4. What were the Crusades? Why were they fought?
5. Who was Marco Polo?
6. Why did Europeans seek a new, less costly way to get Asian goods?
7. What country was the first to search for another route to Asia?

Critical Thinking

8. **Predicting Consequences.** How might the history of the Americas have been different if the Norse had been in close contact with the rest of Europe around A.D. 1000?

LOOKING AHEAD: Where did the voyages of Christopher Columbus take him?

separate body of water. Columbus believed, though it was a mistake, that Japan was separated from Europe by an ocean only 2,500 miles (4,000 km) wide. As early as 1484 Columbus decided that he could reach China, Japan, and the Indies by sailing west from Europe. As a young sailor, Columbus had learned some navigation.

Columbus first proposed his plan to King John of Portugal. After listening to advisers, the king decided not to help Columbus. The advisers believed Japan was about 10,000 miles (16,000 km) away. No ship at that time could sail so far without running out of food and water. And Portugal's own search for an eastward route around Africa seemed more likely to bring success. Columbus then presented his plan to King Ferdinand and Queen Isabella of Spain. They weighed the small cost of a voyage that might fail against the great wealth Spain would gain if the voyage succeeded. They decided to back Columbus.

The First Voyage

On Friday, August 3, 1492, the *Pinta,* the *Niña,* and the *Santa Maria* slipped out of the harbor of Palos, Spain. The ships were very

In 1492 Columbus bid farewell to Queen Isabella and King Ferdinand of Spain. He sailed west in search of the Indies, but he found the Americas instead.

small—over a hundred times smaller than many of today's ocean vessels. Columbus's ship, the *Santa Maria,* was the largest of the three. It carried a crew of forty men and boys. Columbus could pace the ship from front to back with about forty good-sized steps. The *Niña,* the smallest ship, proved to be the sturdiest. It became Columbus's favorite.

After a stop in the Canary Islands off the western shore of Africa, Columbus set a course due west across the Atlantic. In the ship's log, a record kept by all captains at sea, Columbus noted how far the ships went each day. Columbus kept two logs, an open one for the crew and a secret one for himself. He feared that if the crew learned how far they had sailed they would refuse to go on. As the days passed with nothing but ocean water in sight, the crew became fearful and restless. They begged Columbus to turn back. But Columbus sailed on.

On October 7 the crew spotted a flight of birds. Columbus changed course to follow the birds, knowing they must be headed for land. Within a few days a sailor on the *Niña* picked up a green branch floating near the ship. Soon the sailors sighted more branches and even floating flowers. These signs of nearby land encouraged everyone. Then, on October 12, at two o'clock in the dark morning,

Dreams of new lands, gold, spices, and adventure lured European sailors on long voyages in small ships across dangerous seas.

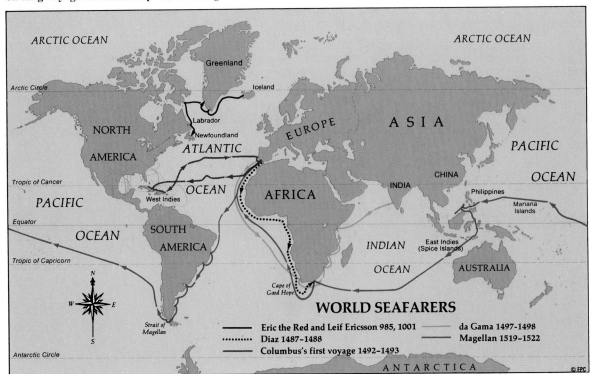

WORLD SEAFARERS

——— Eric the Red and Leif Ericsson 985, 1001	——— da Gama 1497–1498
········· Diaz 1487–1488	——— Magellan 1519–1522
——— Columbus's first voyage 1492–1493	

a sailor on the *Pinta* saw land off in the distance. Daybreak showed that the land was a gray cliff, a part of a small island. Columbus rowed ashore with his captains. He fell to his knees and thanked God for a safe voyage. He named the island San Salvador (Holy Savior) and claimed it for Spain. Today San Salvador is one of the many islands that make up the Bahamas.

Believing that he had reached the East Indies, Columbus called the people he met Indians. He was surprised that neither the people nor the land matched what Marco Polo had described. There were no great cities, no carts carrying raw silk to market, no baskets of spices, and only a little gold.

Other Explorations of Columbus

On his first voyage Columbus explored San Salvador, Cuba, and Hispaniola. In the next nine years Columbus made three more voyages to the lands across the ocean. On the second voyage he began a colony that gave Spain its foothold in the New World. He also explored the other Caribbean islands that came to be called the West Indies. Still he found no great riches. On the third and fourth voyages Columbus sailed along parts of the eastern coasts of South and Central America. Columbus died in 1506, never knowing that he had reached two continents unknown to Europeans of his time.

America—A Name on a Map

Other explorers quickly followed the lead of Columbus. One was Amerigo Vespucci (ăm′ə·rē′gō ve·spoo′chē), an Italian who sailed for Portugal. Vespucci wrote of his voyages and named the lands he had visited a "New World." A German mapmaker used Vespucci's writings in his own work. Because he thought that Vespucci had discovered the new lands, the mapmaker named them America after Amerigo Vespucci. The German's map was printed and used so often that America became the accepted name for the two continents first settled by Asians and later "discovered" by Leif Ericsson and Christopher Columbus.

3 Spanish Claims in the Americas

Following the voyages of Columbus, many Spaniards came to the Americas. Each person or group had to have the permission of the Spanish king, who ruled all the new colonies. Soldiers came looking for new lands to conquer. Fortune hunters came seeking gold. Priests came hoping to convert the Native Americans to Christianity. Servants came with their masters. Traders came to buy and sell goods. With this mix of Spaniards and with the Native Americans who already lived here, Spain founded its empire in the Americas.

Section 2 Review

1. What were the two passages Columbus marked in his copy of Marco Polo's book?
2. Why did the king of Portugal reject Columbus's plan?
3. Why did the king and queen of Spain support Columbus's plan?
4. How did the New World come to be called America?

Critical Thinking

5. **Determining Relevance.** What influence did Marco Polo's book have on Columbus's decision to sail west to reach Asia?

LOOKING AHEAD: What was the extent of the Spanish claims in the New World by the middle of the sixteenth century?

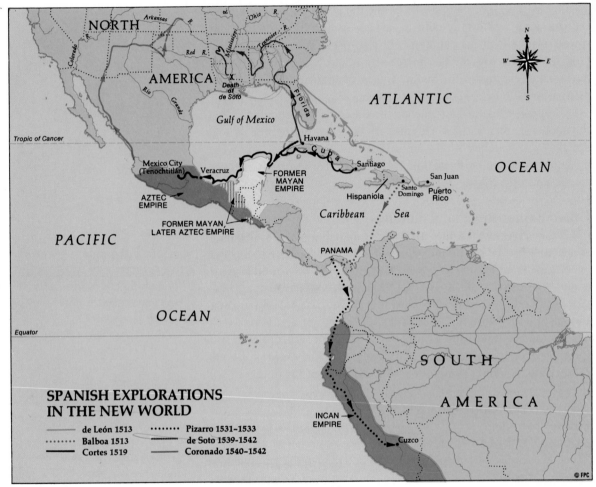

After Columbus, explorers pushed inland in their search for gold.

Explorers After Columbus

Juan Ponce de León (wän pän(t)s′ də lēón), while governor of the Spanish colony of Puerto Rico, heard tales of a fountain with waters that made an old person young. Deciding to find this "fountain of youth," he set off for lands to the north in 1513. Ponce de León never found this magic fountain, but he did reach a land so lovely that he gave it the Spanish name *Florida*, "the land of flowers." Later, in 1565, men and women came to settle in Florida. They established St. Augustine, now the oldest city in the United States.

Vasco Nuñez de Balboa (vas′kō nōō′nyəz də bal·bō′ə) came to the Americas as a farmer, settling on the island of Hispaniola. When he got into debt, he fled to Panama by hiding in a barrel aboard a ship. In Panama Balboa heard tales of a people who had so much gold they used it to make cups and dishes. In 1513, the same year Ponce de León explored Florida, Balboa set out westward across

Panama with almost 200 Spaniards and 100 Native Americans. Balboa never found the gold he was seeking, but he did find something else. After a difficult march across swamps and dark forests, Balboa reached the top of a high hill. He saw a wide, seemingly endless body of water. He named it the South Sea. Today we call it the Pacific Ocean, the name given to it by Ferdinand Magellan on his voyage around the world.

Magellan's Voyage

Magellan left Spain in 1519 with five ships described by an officer as "very old and patched . . . their sides as soft as butter." Magellan sailed west across the Atlantic, then south along the east coast of South America almost to its tip. There he found the passage, now called the Strait of Magellan, that would take him from the Atlantic to the Pacific. By the time Magellan entered this passage, he had only three ships remaining. High winds and stormy seas tossed his ships about. Huge rocks, appearing suddenly out of the water, made the passage dangerous. Magellan welcomed the peaceful waters at the western end of the strait. He named these peaceful waters the Pacific.

Months went by as the three ships sailed a westerly course. Food and water ran low. The crew ate biscuits that were little more than dust and worms, leather boiled to softness, and even rats. Eventually the ships reached the Mariana Islands, where they took on fresh supplies. They sailed on to the Philippines. There Magellan was killed in a fight with people living on the islands. The rest of the crew sailed quickly, leaving one sea-battered ship behind.

The two remaining ships reached the Spice Islands, now part of Indonesia. The crew traded beads and bells for spices. They loaded their valuable cargo on the *Victoria*, the last seaworthy ship. The *Victoria* continued sailing west, past India and around Africa, finally reaching Spain in 1522. Only eighteen persons lived through the nearly three-year voyage, the first in history to circle the world. But even with the loss of four vessels, the shipload of spices brought a handsome profit. The voyage of the *Victoria* proved that Asia could be reached by sailing west. It also proved that two continents, the Americas, blocked the westward passage from Europe to Asia.

The Conquest of Mexico

In 1519, the same year Magellan began his earth-circling voyage, Hernando Cortes (kôr·tez′) sailed from Cuba for Mexico. The Spanish had learned of a great empire in Mexico ruled by the Aztecs. Cortes meant to conquer these people.

Throughout much of their early history the Aztecs had wandered from place to place. But in the early 1300s they settled in the central part of Mexico. There they became farmers and developed many other skills needed to build a great empire. The Aztecs worshipped the sun and created a calendar based on the sun. They worked out ways of writing and numbering. And they built great temples and other buildings in honor of the sun.

The Aztecs built a grand capital city where Mexico City now stands. They also conquered other Native American groups. By the beginning of the 1500s the Aztecs' land stretched out in all directions from their capital. With the taxes paid by the peoples they defeated and with the gold and silver mined in the empire, the Aztecs became rich as well as powerful.

Cortes landed his army of about 500 men on Mexico's eastern coast near the present-day city of Veracruz. The soldiers then marched toward the Aztec capital. Along the way they were joined by thousands of other Native Americans who hoped to get revenge for their own defeat by the Aztecs. The Spanish had other advantages. Cortes had landed with horses. The people in Mexico had never seen horses and were frightened by them. Cortes's men were armed with cannons, crossbows, swords, spears, and axes. The Aztecs knew nothing about cannons and their firepower. The booming guns terrified them. The soldiers from Spain wore shining armor. That spears bounced off their armor made the Spanish soldiers seem like gods.

Montezuma (mänt′ə·zoo′mə), the Aztec leader, soon learned of the advancing army. He sent presents of gold, silver, jewels, and cloaks made of beautiful feathers. He hoped these presents would satisfy Cortes. But the sight of these treasures only spurred Cortes on. When he finally saw the Aztec capital, Cortes knew that he had found what so many others had sought—riches beyond belief.

An uneasy peace followed the first meeting between Montezuma and Cortes. That peace was soon broken. Cortes captured the Aztec leader. When fighting broke out, the Aztecs fought fiercely. They forced Cortes to retreat. But Cortes came back to fight another battle. In this one he defeated the Aztecs. For the next 300 years Spain would rule Mexico and its people.

The Conquest of Peru

The conquest of Peru also began with a search for wealth. Francisco Pizarro (frän·sis′kō pə·zär′ō) had explored Panama with Balboa. After Balboa's death Pizzaro continued to hunt for gold. He found it in Peru, where the Incas had risen to power.

The Incas formed a small empire in Peru about A.D. 1200. In the 1460s they began to take over new lands. Within thirty years the Incas controlled some 2,500 miles (4,000 km) along the western coast of South America. They ruled over what are today the countries of Peru and Ecuador and parts of Bolivia, Chile, and Argentina.

Tenochtitlan.

Cortes and Montezuma met in Tenochtitlán, the Aztec capital and site of present-day Mexico City. The peace following their first meeting did not last very long.

The Incas farmed, producing cotton and potatoes. They wore cloth from the wool of the alpaca and the llama. They shaped articles from gold, silver, tin, and copper. They made pottery, built good roads to bring together every part of their great empire, and kept careful records. These highly skilled people looked upon their ruler, whom they called the Inca, as a god. Like the Aztecs to the north, the Incas worshipped the sun. But, unlike the Aztecs, the Incas treated fairly the peoples they conquered.

In 1531 Pizarro landed in Peru with about 200 men. Although the Incas lived high in the Andes Mountains, Pizarro led his forces to their capital. He captured their leader, Atahualpa (ät′ə·wäl′pə). Pizarro bargained with Atahualpa. He would give the Inca ruler his freedom in exchange for a huge roomful of gold and other riches. Agreeing to the bargain, Atahualpa ordered his people to send in their gold and silver. Each day, runners arrived with all kinds of precious objects. When the room was filled, however, Pizarro broke his promise and killed Atahualpa. He appointed a new ruler. The

The Incas lived high in the South American Andes. But even their isolated mountain home could not protect them from takeover by Spain.

Spaniards then marched throughout the Incan empire and took control for Spain. This control lasted for nearly 300 years.

Explorations of Coronado and de Soto

After Magellan's voyage had proved that the Americas were a "New World," other explorers took up the search for gold begun by Balboa. For two years, beginning in 1540, Francisco Coronado searched the Southwest as far north as Kansas. He found pueblos and other villages, but he did not find gold or jeweled cities. Coronado returned empty-handed. But he had claimed for Spain all of the land through which he had traveled.

Another important Spanish expedition began in Florida in 1539. It was led by Hernando de Soto (hər·nän′dō də sōt′ō). For three years the group explored the Southeast from Florida to as far west as Texas. De Soto had planned to sail down the Mississippi River to its mouth and then return to Mexico. But he fell ill and died. His men buried him in the river, then followed his plan and returned to Mexico. De Soto's travels gave Spain its claim to all the lands he had explored.

The Spanish Colonies

By 1541, Spain claimed large parts of both Americas. Spain counted as its own nearly all of South America except Brazil, which Portugal had taken first. The Spanish held all of Mexico and Central America, which together they called New Spain. Included in New Spain were islands in the West Indies. Spanish rule also stretched from Florida to California across the southern part of what is today the United States.

The king and his appointed officials made all the laws for the Spanish colonies in America. They controlled all trade. The gold and silver mined in the colonies were shipped to Spain. Spain became the richest nation in Europe.

Wherever the Spanish settled, they took charge of all Native Americans and their lands. They also taught Native Americans the Christian religion. Spanish landholders made the Native Americans work for them in their fields, in their mines, and in their homes. Some Native Americans died because they were made to work long hours or were ill-treated. But many more died because they caught one of the many diseases the Spanish brought to America. In 1519, for example, there were about 25 million Native Americans living in New Spain. By 1605, less than a century later, so many had died that the Native Americans in New Spain numbered only about 1 million.

To have the workers they needed, the Spanish began to import Africans as slaves. Landholders in the West Indies bought most of the slaves shipped to the Spanish colonies. The first black slaves

75

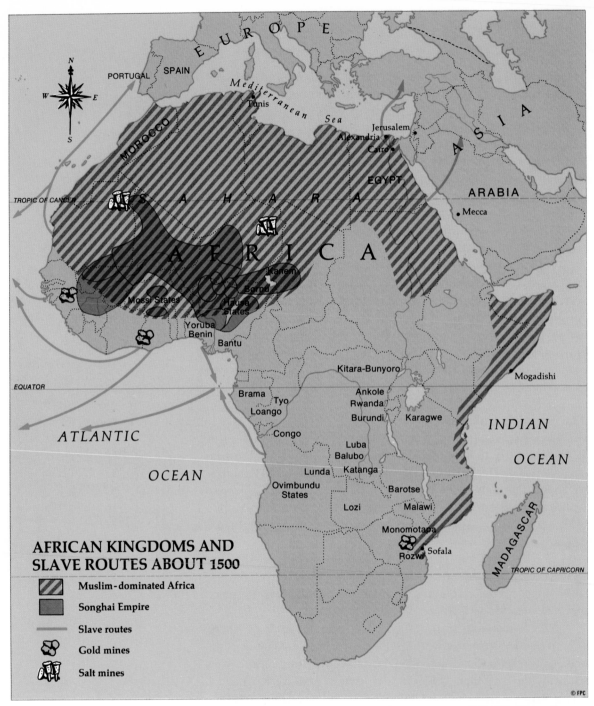

AFRICAN KINGDOMS AND SLAVE ROUTES ABOUT 1500

- Muslim-dominated Africa
- Songhai Empire
- Slave routes
- Gold mines
- Salt mines

Compare this map with the world map on pages 708–709. Name the present-day countries from which slaves were shipped in the 1500s. The voyage of slave ships across the Atlantic was called the Middle Passage.

were brought from West Africa on Spanish ships. Later, slaves were brought on ships sailing under the flags of other nations. As more nations founded colonies and made use of Africans, the black slave population of the Americas increased.

No one really knows how many Africans were captured and sold as slaves. Many blacks died from harsh treatment by slave traders in Africa before being shipped to the Americas. Those who were sent to the Americas usually were packed tightly onto ships. They were given little to eat or drink. The long journey across the Atlantic was called "the Middle Passage." The bodies of those who fell ill and died were tossed overboard. There is no accurate count of how many lived through the Middle Passage. But it is believed that at least ten million black men, women, and children were brought to the Americas before the end of the slave trade.

The Spanish Heritage

The Spanish left a heritage that has enriched the lands that later became the United States. Churches and other buildings put up by early Spanish settlers still stand in Florida and the Southwest. Today Americans have copied these buildings. The idea of the Spanish plaza—a large, open space surrounded by buildings—has been used in shopping centers and in large, city office areas.

A favorite pastime in the Southwest, the rodeo, came from the Spanish by way of Mexico. Many of the words heard at a rodeo— *bronco, lasso,* even *rodeo* itself—are Spanish. Some states, cities, rivers, and other land features have Spanish names. Other English words are the early Spaniards' way of saying Native American names. The Spanish language itself is part of our heritage. After English, Spanish is the most often used language in the United States. Every day, people come to the United States from Mexico, Puerto Rico, and Cuba, all once parts of the Spanish empire in the Americas.

Section 3 Review

1. What two Spanish explorations were carried out in 1513?
2. What two things were proved by the voyage of the *Victoria?*
3. Name three advantages that enabled Cortes to defeat the Aztecs easily.
4. How did Pizarro conquer the Incas?
5. Name three changes the Spanish made in the lands under their control.

Critical Thinking

6. **Recognizing Cause and Effect.** Why did Spain have a claim to much of the southern and southwestern parts of what is now the United States?

LOOKING AHEAD: How did the settlements of New France differ from those of Spanish America?

4 French Claims in North America

France, too, wished to find a westward passage to Asia. Like Spain, France had dreams of becoming rich and powerful.

Explorers for France

The first explorer to sail under a French flag was Giovanni da Verrazano (zhō·vän′ē də ver′ə·zän′ō). In the years 1523–1524 he sailed the coastline of North America as far south as the Carolinas and as far north as Canada's Newfoundland. The next explorer the French king sent to America was Jacques Cartier (zhäk kär·tyā′). Cartier explored the coastline of the Gulf of St. Lawrence in 1534. On a second voyage the following year he entered the St. Lawrence River and got as far as what is today Monteal. In 1541 Cartier made one more voyage to set up a French settlement. But the settlement did not last.

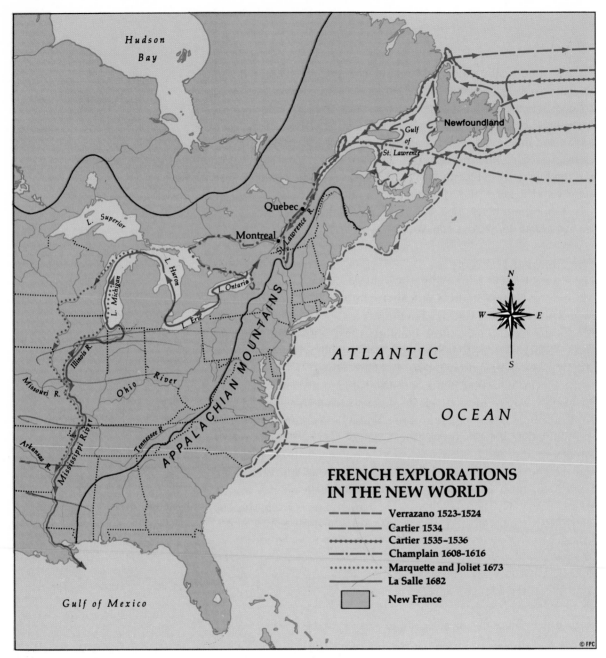

FRENCH EXPLORATIONS IN THE NEW WORLD

- - - - - - Verrazano 1523-1524
————— Cartier 1534
•-•-•-•- Cartier 1535–1536
-·-·-·-· Champlain 1608-1616
·········· Marquette and Joliet 1673
————— La Salle 1682
New France

With Spain holding much of Mexico and Central and South America, French explorers claimed territory in the more northerly reaches of the Americas.

More than half a century passed before Samuel de Champlain (sam′to͞o·əl də shäm′plān′) led another group to the land Cartier called Canada. In 1608 Champlain founded Quebec, the first lasting French settlement in America.

Two more expeditions gave France a claim to a great part of North America. The first began in 1673. Father Jacques Marquette (zhäk mär·ket′) and Louis Joliet explored the Mississippi River and claimed for France all the land they had covered. In 1682 Robert de La Salle followed the Mississippi to its mouth near present-day New Orleans. He claimed for France all the lands drained by the Mississippi and by its tributaries. La Salle called the land Louisiana in honor of King Louis XIV of France. The French founded New Orleans in 1718. By that time French claims stretched from the Gulf of St. Lawrence and the lands around the Great Lakes on the north to the Gulf of Mexico on the south.

Settlements of New France

Settlements in New France were different from settlements in Spanish America. The population of New France grew slowly. By 1663 Spain had more than 200,000 colonists in the Americas. New France had a much smaller number of settlers—only about 2,500. Much of New France was a broad, forested land over which a severe cold settled in the wintertime. Because the St. Lawrence and its tributaries froze in the winter, settlers could enter only in the spring or summer. Farming was difficult. In the beginning most settlers became fur traders or trappers. Many French settlements began as trading posts or as forts in the wilderness. By the 1700s the king had encouraged more people to move to New France. Most of these newcomers were willing to clear the wilderness for farmlands. New France began to flourish.

The French found their riches in furs, not gold. So, for the French, the Native Americans were more valuable as fur gatherers and as guides in the wilderness than as miners or farmhands. The settlers of New France and the Native Americans learned from each other. The French learned how to travel in the pathless woods and how to trap fur-bearing animals. And Native Americans learned about Christianity from French missionaries.

When the French began to farm, they had no need for extra workers. Settlers in New France were given only a few acres, not large landholdings like those in Spanish America. Most French farmers lived in nearby towns rather than on their small, narrow farm plots. The settlers of New France imported only a few blacks as slaves. It was too costly to buy, feed, and house slaves on their small farms, where winters were so long and cold.

The French lost New France to the English in 1763. But those parts of North America settled by the French still bear traces of them. Many French-speaking people today live around the Great Lakes, along the St. Lawrence River and its gulf, and in Louisiana. Town, lakes, and rivers with French names mark those places in the United States where the French first settled. Along with the Spanish, Portuguese, Africans, and Native Americans, the French left a lasting heritage that has enriched American life.

Section 4 Review

1. Who was the first seafarer to explore North America for France?
2. Was Champlain or Cartier the first to sail up the St. Lawrence as far as present-day Montreal?
3. Was Champlain or Cartier the founder of France's first permanent settlement?
4. When was this settlement made, and what was its name?
5. What three men explored the Mississippi, claiming for France the lands drained by the river?

Critical Thinking

6. **Testing Conclusions.** Explain why you agree or disagree with this statement: "Settlers in New France had great reason to stay on good terms with their Native American neighbors."

People As Explorers

Spanish and French explorers helped chart the lands of North America so that others could learn of the continent's riches.

In 1527 the Spanish sent an expedition of 600 persons, with supplies and livestock, to settle Florida. Cabeza de Vaca (kə·bā′zə də väk′ə) was appointed second in command. Esteban (es′tə·bän), an African black, was the slave of another member of the expedition.

Trouble at Every Stage

When the ships carrying the settlers arrived in the West Indies, some members of the party deserted. Later two ships were lost in a hurricane. The expedition finally landed on the west coast of Florida in April 1528. The ships then sailed on to Mexico, while the settlers marched inland.

Hard times became worse. Some people became ill and died. Others starved to death. Still others were killed when Native Americans, trying to protect their lands, attacked the Spanish.

Those who were left built several barges to carry them westward along the Gulf coast to Spanish settlements in Mexico. But so many were crowded into the barges that the boats rode low in the water. Some barges were lost at sea. De Vaca's barge was driven ashore on an island near present-day Texas.

The Native Americans

De Vaca and the others met some Native Americans who gave them food and taught them their language. In return the Spaniards hauled water, cut trees, and carried heavy loads of wood. Soon only de Vaca, Esteban, and two other Spaniards were left alive.

Explorers in North America helped open the land to settlers.

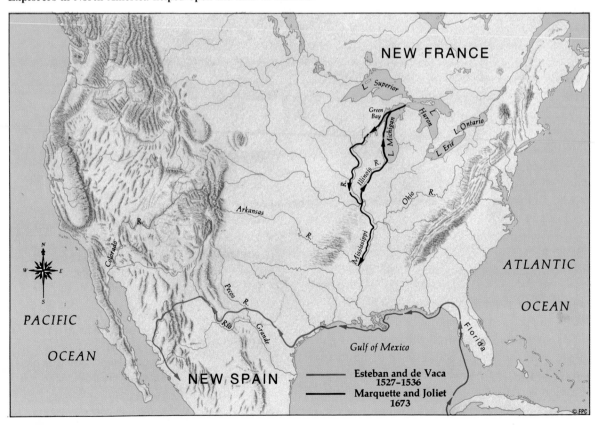

San Xavier del Bac was an early mission in what is now Tucson, Arizona.

The four men lived with Native Americans for five years. During this time they were asked to heal the sick. The strangers became famous among the Native Americans as medicine men.

In 1535 de Vaca and the others began walking westward, hoping to reach the Spanish settlements in Mexico. Naked and sunburned, they went from place to place, led by groups of Native Americans, who honored them as great healers. Finally, in 1536 the four men reached a Spanish outpost in northern Mexico.

No other Spaniard or black before them had crossed the land through which de Vaca and Esteban traveled. Their report told Spanish officials in Mexico much about the territory.

Later French Explorers

Another part of North America was explored by a French priest, Father Jacques Marquette. As late as 1672, Europeans still did not know where the "Great River of the West" flowed. Father Marquette proved that the "Great River" was the Mississippi and that it emptied into the Gulf of Mexico.

The Young Marquette

As a young boy in France, Jacques Marquette wanted to become a missionary-explorer. He knew that to do this he must train to be a Catholic priest. So he went to school for twenty long, hard years.

After completing school, Father Marquette was sent to the French colonies in North America, called New France. Father Marquette enjoyed the rugged life. He quickly learned several Native American languages and won the friendship of the peoples with whom he lived. But he dreamed of going to the land where the people called the Illinois lived. He wanted to teach them about Christianity.

In 1672 the governor of New France ordered the fur trader Louis Joliet to explore the Great River. Marquette was delighted when he was asked to join Joliet.

The Great River

On May 17 Marquette, Joliet, and five trappers set off from Green Bay in two birchback canoes. The Menominees warned them to turn back. Their Native American friends told of warring tribal groups, swift river currents, and unbearable heat. But Marquette said he would gladly give his life for his religion.

On June 17 the explorers entered the Great River. After days of paddling in the hot sun, the explorers reached the mouth of the Arkansas River. They were greeted by an Arkansas chief holding a pipe as a sign of peace. A large crowd gathered and Father Marquette preached a sermon.

Joliet and Marquette now knew that the Great River was the Mississippi and that it flowed to the Gulf of Mexico. They also knew that Spanish outposts were nearby. They feared capture by these enemies of France.

Marquette and Joliet decided to return to New France. They paddled up the Mississippi and Illinois rivers to Lake Michigan and reached New France in September.

Father Jacques Marquette's dream had come true. He had told the Native Americans about Christianity. And, like de Vaca and Esteban, he had helped others learn about North America.

Father Marquette greeted Native Americans with a peace pipe.

Chapter 3 Review

Chapter Summary

Seafarers from Norway, led by Leif Ericsson, were the first Europeans to arrive in the Americas. They came in A.D. 1001 and settled for a short time on Newfoundland, which they called Vinland. The next Europeans came in 1492 when Columbus made the first of his four voyages.

From its first colonies in the West Indies, Spain's empire expanded to the mainland. In 1519 Cortes sailed for Mexico and soon after conquered the Aztecs. A few years later Pizarro marched into Peru, adding the Inca lands to Spain's empire. Spain claimed lands explored by Coronado, Ponce de León, and de Soto in what is now the United States.

The French also claimed a share of the New World. They based their claims to land in North America on the voyage of Verrazano in 1524. Ten years later Cartier sailed into the Gulf of St. Lawrence. The next year he sailed up the St. Lawrence River. In 1608 Champlain founded Quebec, the first permanent French settlement in the Americas. Then in 1682 La Salle followed the Mississippi River to its mouth, claiming all the lands it drained for France. At its height, New France stretched from the city of New Orleans to beyond the Great Lakes.

Reviewing Vocabulary

Match each of the following words with its correct definition. Write your answers on a separate sheet of paper.

seafarer   expedition
navigation   import
colony   tributary
empire   missionary

1. a settlement of people from the same country living in a new country, but keeping ties with their old country

2. a river or stream that flows into a larger river or stream
3. a trip taken for a particular purpose
4. a person who goes to another country to teach a religion or to help others
5. to bring goods into one country from another country
6. one who helps run a ship; a sailor
7. the act of guiding a ship
8. a large territory or group of territories having a single government

Understanding Main Ideas

1. How was European interest in the world awakened in the 300 years following the Norse settlement in Vinland?
2. Where did Columbus explore in the Americas?
3. What territory had Spain claimed in the Americas by the mid-1500s?
4. Compare the settlements of New France to those of New Spain in terms of population, use of slaves, and source and amount of wealth.

Critical Thinking Skills

1. **Identifying Assumptions.** In what ways was Amerigo Vespucci correct in calling the Americas a "New World"? In what ways was he incorrect?
2. **Formulating Questions.** If you were a monarch deciding whether to fund a voyage of exploration in the 1500s, what questions would you ask the expedition's leader?
3. **Expressing Problems Clearly.** What negative effects did Spanish settlement in both North and South America have on Native Americans?

Social Studies Skills: Reading a Map

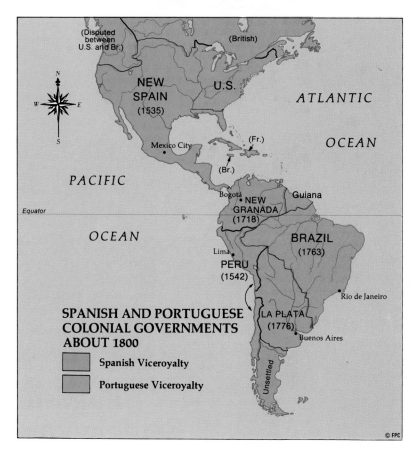

Study the map above. Use the map and the map key to answer the questions that follow. **Skill Review:** Approximately what time period is illustrated by the map? What do the brown areas represent? What nation settled the green area?

Writing About History

Writing a Letter.   Imagine that you were a member of a Spanish or French voyage of exploration. Write a letter to a friend in your homeland describing your leader, your role in the expedition, the lands you have explored, your feelings about your voyage, and your plans for the future.

Your Region in History

Economics.   Many of the early explorers of the Americas were disappointed because they did not find gold, silver, or other recognizable treasure. If any of the early explorers reached your area, what would they have found there? What is the most valuable product or resource in your area today?

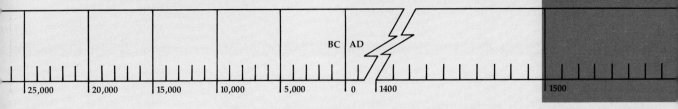

NOVA BRITANNIA.
OFFERING MOST
Excellent fruites by Planting in
VIRGINIA.

Exciting all such as be well affected
to further the same.

LONDON
Printed for SAMVEL MACHAM, and are to besold at
his Shop in Pauls Church-yard, at the
Signe of the Bul-head.
1609.

English Settlements in North America

🪶 Chapter 4

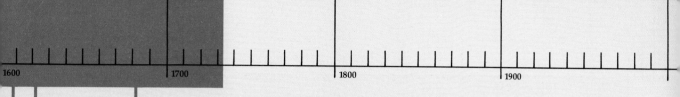

1600	1700	1800	1900

F IVE YEARS AFTER COLUMBUS landed in the New World, an English ship, the *Matthew,* sailed across the Atlantic. John Cabot, an Italian who had lived in England, was the captain of the tiny ship. Cabot was searching for a route to Asia shorter than the one that led south around Africa. But he never found this Northwest Passage. On his first voyage he sailed as far as Newfoundland before returning to England. The following summer, in 1498, Cabot made a second trip. He may have reached the Carolina coast. But the voyage ended in disaster. Cabot's ships were lost at sea, never to be heard from again.

1   Prelude to Settlement

More than a century passed between the voyages of Cabot and the first lasting English settlement in North America. For a long time Spain was powerful enough to keep other countries from challenging its claims in America. Also, England was undergoing great changes at home. The English had no time for exploration. They found themselves faced with problems of government, money, and religion. Besides delaying settlement in North America, these major changes made the English colonies different from those of Spain and France.

Vocabulary

legislature
profit
joint-stock company
charter
cash crop
proprietary colony
plantation
export
debtor

Prereading

1. What troubles within England and with Spain delayed English beginnings in North America?
2. What made the founding of Jamestown different from the founding of Plymouth Colony and Massachusetts Bay Colony?
3. How did each of the later Middle and Southern Colonies begin?
4. How did the English treatment of Native Americans differ from the treatment given to Native Americans by other European settlers?

85

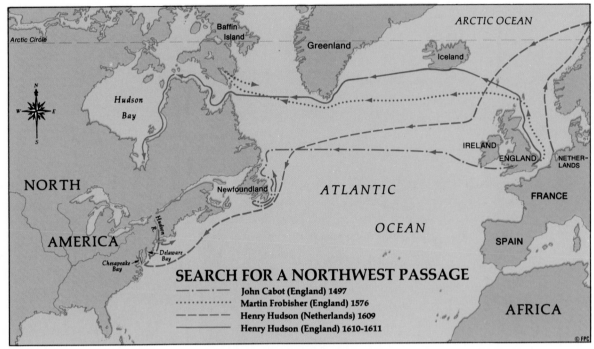

SEARCH FOR A NORTHWEST PASSAGE

— · — · — John Cabot (England) 1497
· · · · · · · · · · · Martin Frobisher (England) 1576
— — — — Henry Hudson (Netherlands) 1609
——————— Henry Hudson (England) 1610-1611

Cabot and others failed to find a river passage leading through North America to the Pacific or a sea route to Asia around the northern reaches of the continent.

Changes in England

Before 1500, England had been through several bloody civil wars. During the 1500s an English ruling family, the Tudors, tried to unite England and make it strong. The energy and money they might have used to explore new lands was used at home instead.

To bring the English people together, the Tudor rulers needed the help of Parliament, the English legislature. Parliament came to their aid. In return Parliament asked for and was given some powers of government. The Tudors also allowed local areas to rule themselves, as long as they followed the country's laws. By the time the English settled in America, they had become used to taking part in their own government. Spanish and French settlers had no such heritage of self-rule to bring to their colonies.

In 1500, merchants and ships from other countries handled much of England's trade. A century later English merchants shipped English goods throughout the world in English vessels. Often merchants formed large trading companies by pooling their money, ships, and crews. The public also put up money for these companies by buying shares of stock. In return the stockholders were given part of the companies' profits. These groups are also known as joint-stock companies. In 1500 almost no Engish trading companies existed. By 1600 these companies were trading everywhere in the world.

Money for the first English settlements in America was put up by trading companies. Stockholders hoped to gain huge personal profits. The Spanish and French colonies, in contrast, had been founded by persons acting for their rulers. In France and Spain, the Crown, not the public, stood to profit most from the colonies.

Old church ways in England also were undergoing change. In the 1400s most people in Western Europe were Roman Catholics. During the 1500s people began to protest the ways of the Roman Catholic Church. These protesters were called Protestants. In 1534 King Henry VIII of England made Protestantism the official religion of Engand. He set himself up as head of the country's new Protestant Church.

But many English people did not join the Church of England. Some remained Roman Catholic. Others believed that each religious group should make its own choices. These people felt that matters of faith were not rightly to be decided by the government. Differences in religious views became a mark of the English colonies in America. The Spanish and French in both Americas, in contrast, mainly belonged to the Roman Catholic Church.

Self-government, citizen-owned trading companies, and differences in religious belief made England and its settlements unique. But before the colonies could be setttled, England had to overcome the mighty power of Spain.

In 1497 John Cabot received a charter from King Henry VII to explore North America for England. He reached Newfoundland on his first voyage but was lost at sea on his second voyage.

The Challenge to Spanish Power

Sixteenth-century Spain was the most powerful country in Europe. Gold and silver from the Americas fed the Spanish treasury. Spain had built a great navy and a mighty army. Until the 1850s ships from other nations skirted Spanish sea-lanes for fear of being captured. English sea captains could not attack Spanish power directly. But they could stop lone vessels carrying treasure from the Spanish colonies to the homeland.

The most famous of these bold English sea captains was Francis Drake. In 1578 Drake sailed his ship, the *Golden Hind,* west from the Atlantic into the Pacific. There he surprised unarmed Spanish ships carrying treasure along the west coast of South America. His greatest catch was a vessel loaded with 52,000 pounds (23,500 kg) of silver.

Drake was afraid of being caught by the Spanish fleet if he returned to England by way of the Atlantic. So, after taking on fresh food and water near what is now San Francisco, he headed west across the Pacific and Indian oceans. The *Golden Hind* reached England in 1580, the second ship to sail around the world.

Partly to stop such raiders as Drake, Spain decided to conquer England. In 1588 Spain sent out a huge navy, called the Armada (är·mäd′ə). The Armada was made up of 130 ships and almost 28,000 soldiers and sailors. English sea captains, using small, swift sailing vessels, boldly attacked the Armada. Spain suffered a terrible defeat, losing about 80 ships and almost 15,000 soldiers and sailors. Although Spain remained strong in America for another 200 years, it could not keep other European countries from starting colonies.

2   The Early Settlements

About a decade before the defeat of the Spanish Armada, England began trying to plant colonies in North America. These early efforts failed. After defeating Spain, England turned to colonization with new fervor. This time it worked. Between 1607 and 1733 the English started thirteen colonies in North America. These colonies reached from what is now known as New England in the north to as far south as Georgia. The map on page 98 shows how the colonies can be divided into three main parts.

Some English colonies were set up to turn a profit. Others were founded as places of safety for people with different religious views. Still others were taken over by the English from other countries.

Failures of Gilbert and Raleigh

Sir Humphrey Gilbert, with a land grant from Queen Elizabeth I, twice tried to start a colony in North America. One attempt was

Section 1 Review

1. When did John Cabot give England its first claim to lands in North America?
2. Name two major changes that took place in England between 1500 and 1600.
3. Who was Francis Drake?
4. What was the Spanish Armada?

Critical Thinking

5. **Identifying Central Issues.** Why was England's defeat of the Spanish Armada important?

LOOKING AHEAD: What made the founding of Jamestown different from the founding of Plymouth Colony and Massachusetts Bay Colony?

Francis Drake was honored by Queen Elizabeth I for his bravery at sea. She titled him "Sir" in 1581.

When John White returned to Roanoke in 1590, all he found was the word *CROATOAN* carved on a tree. To this day the meaning of that message is unknown.

made in 1578 and the other in 1583. Both tries failed because of rough seas. Gilbert lost his life in a storm on the second voyage.

Sir Walter Raleigh made the next English attempts to found a settlement in America. First he sent out two groups to gather information. Members of the second group, sent out in 1585, returned with drawings and reports of the land and people they found.

On the basis of this information Raleigh sent out a third group in 1587. These people were to settle Roanoke (rō′ə·nōk′) Island, off the coast of what is now North Carolina. In the group were ninety-one men, seventeen women, two of whom were expecting babies, and nine children. Raleigh named John White governor of the colony. Among those at Roanoke Island were White's daughter and her husband. They became the parents of Virginia Dare, the first English child born in North America.

After four months White returned to England to get supplies. But England's war with Spain kept him from returning to the colony for three years. When he finally returned to Roanoke in 1590, he found no settlers. He searched for some sign of them. But he found no trace of his friends and family. The mystery of the Lost Colony has never been solved.

Jamestown

Jamestown, in Virginia, was the first lasting English settlement in America. Jamestown was founded in 1607. In that year, 104 men and boys landed on a swampy strip of land jutting into the James River. Money for the colony came from a group of London merchants. These men formed a trading company, the London Company. The

89

During a dispute with Chief Powhatan, Jamestown settlers captured the chief's daughter Pocahantas and held her captive on board a ship.

king gave the London Company a charter to found a North American colony. The settlers were directed to look for treasure, find a way to Asia, and bring back goods that could be sold for a profit in England.

At first the colonists at Jamestown were pleased with the "fair meadows and goodly tall trees, with fresh water running through the woods." They set up tents and built rough huts, as well as a fort. But soon sickness and hunger brought disaster. Before long, half of the arrivals had died.

Few settlers knew anything about farming. They were mostly interested in finding gold. Captain John Smith, one of the leaders, forced some of the men to cut down trees, even though they were not used to such hard work.

Times became worse when new members of the colony arrived without bringing enough fresh food. The winter of 1609-1610 became known as "the starving time." Only about 60 of the first 500 colonists who came to Jamestown survived.

Native Americans under their leader Powhatan (pou′ə·tan′) saved the settlement. The corn and meat they brought kept the settlers from starving.

Once the settlers learned to grow their own food and hunt wild ducks and geese, the colony took root. The first cargo the colonists sent back to England was not gold, but wood. Jamestown had nothing to sell at a profit until it started growing tobacco. Using methods they learned from the Native Americans, the colonists first raised this plant in 1612. Tobacco became the major cash crop that helped the colony grow.

Jamestown was first governed by a colonial council, chosen by the London Company. Later an all-powerful governor took the place of the council. In 1619 the London Company ordered the colonists to elect a lawmaking assembly. This first legislature, later known as the House of Burgesses, met at Jamestown in August 1619. The twenty-two members came from eleven towns and plantations. The meeting marked the beginning of self-government in the English colonies.

Even with a cash crop and a means of self-government, the colony lost money. So, in 1624, King James I took away the colony's charter. He made Virginia the first English royal colony, placing it under his direct control.

Plymouth and the Pilgrims

Plymouth became the second English colony in America and the first in New England. It was founded by a group of Separatists who believed in governing their own churches. They had broken away, or separated, from the Church of England. King James I, as head of the Church, found these beliefs dangerous. If the Separatists could defy the Church of England, they might defy the government next.

To avoid going to prison for their beliefs, a group of Separatists left England for Holland in 1600. They were allowed to worship as they pleased in Holland. Even so, they found that there were few jobs and life was hard. They also feared that their children were learning Dutch ways and losing their Separatist beliefs. So they looked to America as a place to improve life for their families.

To get to America, the Separatists made a deal with a group of London merchants. In return for ships and supplies, the Separatists would work to send profitable goods back to England.

Fewer than half of the Separatists in Holland chose to go to America. Those who went called themselves Pilgrims. The Pilgrims sailed for America on the *Mayflower* in 1620, leaving their friends behind. Of the 120 passengers, only about 30 were Pilgrims. The others were workers hired by the English merchants.

The Pilgrims landed on Cape Cod in New England in November 1620 and later moved to nearby Plymouth. New England was not governed by England at that time. So the settlers agreed to make fair laws and to obey them. Their agreement, called the Mayflower Compact, gave the colony a form of self-government.

Pilgrims and other English settlers used the region's abundant forest resources and their own hard work to build homes.

From the beginning Plymouth was different from Jamestown. Families settled Plymouth. Only men and boys began the Jamestown colony. Unlike Jamestown, Plymouth had no persons of high rank. Members of the Plymouth colony had always made a living working with their hands. They were prepared to do the same in America.

Even so, the Pilgrims had a rough beginning. They arrived in early winter when snow covered the ground. They struggled just to build huts and to stay alive. Of the eighteen married women in the group, only five survived. In all, about half of the colonists died during the first winter.

The following spring and summer the Pilgrims learned from the Native Americans how to plant corn and squash. They were helped especially by Squanto (skwän′tō), a member of the Wampanoag peoples. By 1625 the colony was well set. The Pilgrims traded with the Native Americans for beaver skins and even opened trading posts to the north and west. William Bradford, the governor of Plymouth, described the small band of Pilgrims as a candle whose light "shines to our whole nation."

Massachusetts Bay Colony and the Puritans

Another group in England wanted to simplify the ways of the Church of England. In their words, they wished to "purify" the church. These people became known as Puritans.

Puritan leaders in England organized the Massachusetts Bay Company. They obtained the right to some land in New England from King James I. Only Puritans who wanted to leave England could hold shares in the Massachusetts Bay Company. The shares gave them a vote in all elections held by the company. In this way the Massachusetts Bay Company became the government of the new colony.

Two large groups of Puritans arrived in New England in 1629 and 1630. The second group included more than 1,000 men, women, and children. Their seventeen ships were filled with farm animals, tools, food, and clothing. Among the colonists were landowners, as well as others schooled in law and business. From the beginning the colony did well. Boston became its leading town. The Puritans wished to build an ideal Christian community for others to follow. In 1691 the Pilgrims' Plymouth colony became part of Massachusetts.

Other New England Colonies

Other settlements in New England grew out of Massachusetts. Most were founded by people whose religious views were different from those of the Puritans.

Rhode Island was started by Roger Williams. Williams did not agree with many Puritan teachings. He believed that the Puritans should separate from the Church of England. He did not believe that the church should play a powerful role in government. And he believed that the land belonged to the Native Americans, not to the colony of Massachusetts Bay. The Puritan leaders found those ideas dangerous. They decided to send Williams back to England.

Warned about this decision by a friend, Williams fled. After buying some land from the Narraganset (nar′·ə·gan′sət) in 1636, he founded a settlement that he called Providence.

In 1638 Anne Hutchinson joined Williams in Rhode Island. She also had been driven from Massachusetts Bay because of her religious beliefs. She had told some Massachusetts Bay leaders that going to church was not necessary because many preachers were not true believers. For saying this, Hutchinson had been brought to trial. For her, the trial was a terrible ordeal. But she defended herself well. Finally, tired from endless questioning, she told her accusers that God would destroy them. When Hutchinson said this, the Puritan leaders pronounced her "unfit for our society." They ordered her to leave Massachusetts Bay.

In 1644 Williams was given the rights to his land by the English government. This land grant brought together several nearby settlements into the colony of Rhode Island. All persons in Rhode Island enjoyed the right to worship as they pleased. It was the first colony to stand for religious freedom.

Meanwhile, the Reverend Thomas Hooker was allowed by Massachusetts Bay to lead his followers westward in 1636 to the fertile Connecticut River valley. They traveled along trails made by Native Americans. They drove their cattle before them and carried the few things they owned in backpacks. These people started the town of Hartford. Others settled the towns of Windsor, Wethersfield, and New Haven. In 1639, leaders from some of these towns

The wintertime trial of Anne Hutchinson was held for long hours in an unheated room.

93

Some Early Colonial Laws

No garment could be made with short sleeves "whereby the nakedness of the arm may be discovered." *Massachusetts, 1639*
No one could sell cakes or buns except for special occasions such as weddings or funerals. *Massachusetts, 1639*
No one over seven years old was allowed to play, saunter, or sport on Sunday. *Massachusetts, 1653*
No plays, card games, billiards, dice, or any other games were permitted. *Pennsylvania, 1706*
Stealing someone else's slave was punished by death; killing a slave was punished by a fine. *South Carolina*
No one could sell or give any good hoe or any good dog to Native Americans. *Virginia, 1619*
No one could spend time idly or unprofitably. *Massachusetts, 1633*
No social gatherings were allowed on Sunday evenings, fast days, or Thursday lecture days. *Connecticut, 1709*
No worldly labor, games, hunting, shooting, horse racing, or social gatherings were permitted on Sunday. *New York, 1685*
No one was allowed to travel on Sunday except to go to church or to visit the sick. *Georgia, 1762*

Some Christian rules about Sundays were written into colonial law.

Section 2 Review

1. What happened to Gilbert's attempts to plant colonies in North America?
2. What directions did the London Company give to the settlers it sent to North America?

Critical Thinking

3. **Making Comparisons.** In what ways were the founding of Plymouth Colony and the founding of Massachusetts Bay Colony alike? In what ways were they different?

LOOKING AHEAD: How did each of the later Middle and Southern Colonies begin?

Lord Baltimore, founder of Maryland, believed that all Christians had the right to worship as they pleased.

drew up a plan for self-government called the Fundamental Orders of Connecticut. When the towns joined together in 1662 to form the colony of Connecticut, this plan became its written constitution.

Settlers also came to the northern part of New England. They moved into what are now the states of Maine, Vermont, and New Hampshire. New Hampshire was a part of Massachusetts for about fifty years. But in 1679 it became a separate colony. Maine was also a part of Massachusetts. It did not separate from Massachusetts until 1820, long after the Revolutionary War. The land of Vermont was claimed by both New Hampshire and New York. Like Maine, it was never formed into a separate colony.

3 Later Middle and Southern Colonies

Later colonies were not founded by trading companies. The colonies of Maryland, New York, New Jersey, Pennsylvania, and Carolina all began with one person or a group receiving a grant of property directly from the Crown. These were called proprietary colonies. The last colony to be formed, Georgia, was founded by a special group of persons called trustees. They promoted its settlement but did not own land in Georgia.

Maryland

Maryland was founded in 1634. The colony was a dream come true for the Calvert family. Sir George Calvert, who had the title of Lord Baltimore, became a Roman Catholic in 1625. Roman Catholics were not allowed to worship as they wished in England. So Lord Baltimore wanted to start a colony where Roman Catholics could worship. He was given some land in 1632 by King Charles I.

Two years later, two vessels—the *Ark* and the *Dove*—carried the first Catholic settlers to the shores of Chesapeake Bay. There they bought some land from the Native Americans and started the

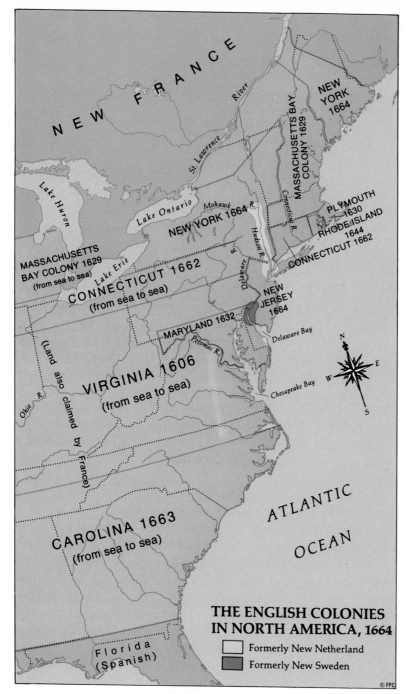

THE ENGLISH COLONIES
IN NORTH AMERICA, 1664

☐ Formerly New Netherland
■ Formerly New Sweden

By 1664 the English had taken over all Dutch settlements in North America.

settlement of St. Mary's. To protect religious freedom, the colony passed a Toleration Act in 1649. This important act allowed all Christian settlers to worship as they wished.

Dutch and Swedish Settlements

While the English were settling Jamestown and Plymouth, the Dutch were moving into North America. The Dutch based their claims on the voyage of Henry Hudson in 1609. By 1625 they had started a village on an island at the mouth of the Hudson River. The Dutch named the island Manhattan after the Native Americans who lived

On land bought from the Delaware peoples, Quakers began to build up Philadelphia.

there. The settlement itself was named New Amsterdam, after a large city in Holland. The Dutch also built a trading post near the present city of Albany, New York, and took as their own what is today New Jersey. These Dutch settlements became part of New Netherland.

Most people came to New Netherland for fur trading. A few came to farm. Wealthy people called *patroons* (pǝ·trōōnz′) received large grants of land along the Hudson River. A patroon had to pay the costs for bringing at least fifty persons to the new colony.

At about the same time, Swedish colonists settled New Sweden. This colony lay along the Delaware River near what is now Philadelphia. The Swedes founded Fort Christina in 1638, a settlement known today as Wilmington, Delaware. Swedish success with the fur trade upset the Dutch. A Dutch fleet from Manhattan Island captured the Swedish fort in 1655.

The Dutch held New Sweden until 1664. At that time the English captured all the Dutch settlements in North America. They changed the name of New Amsterdam to New York. The Dutch never won back their lands in North America. But Dutch influence in New York lasted for more than a century.

Pennsylvania

The Quakers had a loyal following in England. English leaders considered the Quakers dangerous because Quakers were against wars and fighting. The Quakers also would not swear an oath of allegiance to the Crown. Because the Quakers were not welcome in England, they looked to America as a safe home.

King Charles II owed Admiral William Penn a large amount of money. When the admiral died, the king owed this debt to the Admiral's son, William. William Penn was a Quaker who had spent time in jail for what he believed. In 1681 the king paid his debt to the son with a large tract of land north of Maryland.

Penn wanted to make Pennsylvania a "holy experiment" where people could worship as they pleased. Because he did not believe in fighting or in taking land or goods that did not belong to him, Penn bought the land from the Delaware peoples. The settlers and Native Americans lived in peace for seventy-five years. Penn called the chief city of the colony Philadelphia, meaning "brotherly love." From a population of 2,000 in 1682, Pennsylvania grew to a population of 12,000 by 1689.

In 1704 the settlers in the southeastern part of Pennsylvania decided to form their own colony. They felt that they were too far away from the government in Philadelphia. They named the new colony Delaware.

Later Southern Colonies

In 1663 King Charles II gave the land of the Carolinas to eight nobles. The first permanent settlement in the new colony was Charles Town, later called Charleston.

Many of those settling in Carolina were English colonists from the island of Barbados (bär·bād′əs) in the West Indies. When they came to Carolina, they brought their servants and slaves with them. Carolina was the first English colony in North America to have African slaves from its beginning. By 1710, Africans were the largest single group in the colony.

Some colonists raised cattle, using Africans as cowhands. Late in the 1600s the people of Carolina began to grow rice on plantations in the freshwater lowlands upriver from Charleston. Colonists also began to gather pitch and tar from pine trees. They sent these products, called naval stores, to England for use as waterproofing and glue in repairing and in building ships. But the most important Carolina export was deerskins, obtained from the Native Americans in trade for other goods.

By the 1720s the people of Carolina had become unhappy with the nobles' government. They asked King George II to take over. In 1729 Carolina became a royal colony and was divided into two parts—North Carolina and South Carolina.

Georgia was the last of the thirteen English colonies to be founded. No Europeans lived in the land between Spanish Florida and the English Carolinas. The English government thought it wise to settle in this territory to keep the Spanish from moving to the north. King George II gave the right to set up a colony to a group

In 1733 France held lands to the north of the English colonies and Spain held lands to the south. Powerful Native American groups lived to the west of the English colonies.

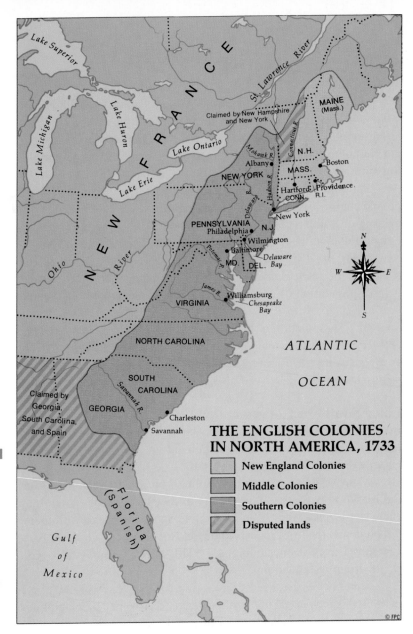

THE ENGLISH COLONIES
IN NORTH AMERICA, 1733

- New England Colonies
- Middle Colonies
- Southern Colonies
- Disputed lands

Section 3 Review

1. For what purpose did George Calvert found Maryland?
2. Which settlements were begun by colonists from the Netherlands? From Sweden?
3. What religious group settled the colony of Pennsylvania?
4. Who were the proprietors of the Carolinas?
5. For what two reasons was Georgia founded?

Critical Thinking

6. **Distinguishing False from Accurate Images.** James Oglethorpe, the first governor of Georgia, described the colony as "a calm retreat." How accurate do you think this description was? Explain your answer.

LOOKING AHEAD: How did the English treatment of Native Americans differ from the treatment given to Native Americans by other European settlers?

known as the Georgia Trustees. The Trustees made all the rules for the new colony. However, the Trustees did not own the colony's land, as founders of proprietary colonies had.

The first settlers arrived in 1733, founding Savannah. The colony was planned as a refuge for English debtors, people who were in prison because they owed money.

The colony did keep the Spanish from moving northward. But it did not become a refuge for debtors. Only a few debtors were freed from prison to settle in Georgia. The Trustees had also expected to export such new products as silk. But they could not grow the plants they needed for silk in that climate and soil. Quarrels broke out in the colony, and many settlers left. In 1752 King George II took over Georgia from the Trustees and made it a royal colony.

Native Americans held to their own ways of living even after the arrival of English settlers in the 1500s. This Virginia town, like many other Native American towns, was protected by a stockade.

4   The Role of Native Americans

The English, Spanish, and French colonists treated the Native Americans differently. The Spanish forced Native Americans to work in fields and mines. The French valued them as fur trappers and guides in the wilderness. The English viewed Native American groups as separate nations. They did not try to make Native Americans part of their colonies, as did the Spanish and French. While there was marriage between Native Americans and Spanish and French colonists, the English discouraged it. Also, Native Americans were not allowed to live in the English colonies. They were forced to leave their lands and move to the west.

The English made treaties with different Native American groups, just as they did with nations in Europe. Some of these treaties promised friendship. Others described each party's land or trade rights. But both sides sometimes broke these treaties.

Although they fought occasionally, the Native Americans and the English settlers were important to each other. Native Americans and colonists engaged in a vigorous trade. Deer and beaver skins were traded for blankets, iron kettles, guns, and other goods. More important, powerful Native American groups kept the English settlers near the coast. The Iroquois held western New York, and the Susquehannock (səs′kwə·han′ək) lived in western Pennsylvania. The Cherokee (cher′ə·kē) were strong in the land west of the Carolinas, and the Chickasaw (chik′ə·sô′) and the Creek surrounded Georgia. Not for a moment did either the English settlers or the Native Americans forget how closely their futures were tied together.

By 1733 the English colonies were spread all along the Atlantic coast. They were dramatically different from those of Spain and France in the way they were founded, in the way they grew, and in their dealings with the Native Americans. In the next chapter you will read about the different colonies and about the settlers from many lands who made the colonies grow.

Section 4 Review

1. How did the Spanish treat Native Americans?
2. How did the French treat Native Americans?
3. How did the English treat Native Americans?

Critical Thinking

4. **Making Comparisons.** In what ways did the English colonies differ from the French and Spanish colonies?

Heritage

Of the English Colonies

The government, economy, and society of the United States today have their roots in the early English settlements.

The heritage of the English colonies in North America is so much a part of you that you accept it without knowing. For example, English is the language most often spoken in the United States. And laws and customs followed in American courts today trace directly back through the colonists to old England.

The Gift of Freedom

The government of the United States rests on self-rule, a gift of the English settlers. The same is true of religious freedom. Among the people who settled in the English colonies were Puritans, Pilgrims, Catholics, Jews, Quakers, Presbyterians, Anglicans, and Baptists. So, today, the United States has no official religion. People are free to worship as they please.

The Free Market

The market system in the United States also began with the first English settlers. Today you use money to buy what you want—food, or records, or shoes. In some countries and at some times governments have told people what to buy and sell and where to work. But in Europe centuries ago people were allowed to earn and spend their own money as they chose. In England the market system grew particularly strong. The English settlers brought these ideas with them.

The settlers raised crops and made goods that they sold in exchange for products they wanted or needed. In this way the colonies grew larger and richer. The market system also helped the United States develop into one of the most powerful importing and exporting nations in the world.

Cultural Variety

The variety of cultural backgrounds in the United States today mirrors the variety that was part of the English colonies. Unlike Spanish and French colonies, the English settlements were made up of people who followed different ways of life.

Built in 1742, Faneuil Hall in Boston, Massachusetts, is once again a thriving marketplace.

Signs in a language other than English are common in the ethnic neighborhoods of many large cities in the United States.

began as early as 1642. In 1776 there were only two major universities in all of England, but there were nine colleges in the colonies. Today the United States has thousands of colleges and universities, far more than most countries in the world.

The most important and lasting gifts of the English colonists were their ideas of leadership and government. George Washington, Thomas Jefferson, and others who shaped the country were born and raised in the colonies. These leaders inherited a vision of what a democratic society should be. The achievements and influence of these leaders will never dim.

Over the years people from almost every country in the world have continued to make the United States their home. Every city or town is made up of neighborhoods. Many neighborhoods have a special identity, such as Polish, Jewish, Italian, African, Swedish, Chinese, Japanese, or Mexican. The list of people with different cultural backgrounds in the United States is almost endless.

People from different backgrounds brought different customs to the English colonies. The Puritans raised the church to a position of great importance by making it the very center of their lives. The Moravians in Pennsylvania, who came from what is today Czechoslovakia, brought with them their great love of music. The Germans in Pennsylvania introduced their own ways of farming and of building barns. Other Europeans learned from the Native Americans how to grow corn and tobacco. The French Protestants in Charleston, South Carolina, drew

on a history of play making when they started their theaters in the colonies.

Schooling and Leadership

Education was important in the English colonies. Schools were founded to teach reading, writing, and religion, especially in New England. There, public schools

Little-Known People

Many people, whose names are often overlooked, shared in the growth of this country. They farmed, made shoes, traded goods raised families, and took part in their own government. They made possible the founding of a nation of which you are a part. You share in their heritage.

So many town meetings were held inside Faneuil Hall that John Adams named it "the cradle of liberty."

Chapter 4 Review

Chapter Summary

Changes within England and England's rivalry with Spain delayed successful settlement in North America until the founding of Jamestown in 1607. By 1733 all thirteen of England's North American colonies had been founded.

Plymouth, founded by Separatists, was the first of the New England Colonies. It later became part of the Massachusetts Bay Colony. Other New England Colonies were Connecticut, New Hampshire, and Rhode Island.

The Middle Colonies began as proprietary colonies rather than trading colonies. When the English took over the Dutch colony of New Netherland in 1664, proprietors formed the colonies of New York and New Jersey. In 1682 William Penn began the "holy experiment" of Pennsylvania. Settlers in southeastern Pennsylvania formed their own colony of Delaware.

Maryland was the second Southern Colony to be settled. In 1729 King George II took over the Carolinas and divided them into North Carolina and South Carolina.

Reviewing Vocabulary

Choose the word that best completes each sentence. Write your answers on a separate sheet of paper.

1. The first (*legislature/plantation*) in the English colonies was the House of Burgesses.
2. The English Crown allowed more citizens to (*profit/separate*) from its colonies than did other rulers.
3. In a (*monopoly/joint-stock company*) stockholders share in a company's profits.
4. The King gave the London Company a (*tributary/charter*) to found a colony in North America.

5. A (*proprietary colony/royal colony*) was founded by a person or group receiving a grant of property directly from the Crown.
6. One might have seen rice growing on a Carolina (*plantation/patroonship*).
7. The Georgia Trustees expected their colony to (*import/export*) such new products as silk.
8. A (*debtor/lender*) owes money.
9. Jamestown prospered when a (*cash crop/trading company*) was developed.

Understanding Main Ideas

1. What delayed English settlement in North America?
2. Why were the early days of Plymouth and Massachusetts Bay colonies more successful than those of Jamestown?
3. Name each of the later Middle and Southern colonies and give the date of its founding, the name of its founder or founders, and the reason it was started.
4. Compare the way the English treated Native Americans to the way the French and the Spanish dealt with them.

Critical Thinking Skills

1. **Predicting Consequences.** What might have been the result if the Spanish Armada had conquered England?
2. **Making Comparisons.** Compare the English colonies to those of France and Spain in terms of government and the rights of settlers.
3. **Identifying Central Issues.** What was the lasting significance of Plymouth colony's Mayflower Compact signed in 1620?
4. **Expressing Problems Clearly.** Give at least three reasons why the English settlers and the Native Americans fought with each other.

Social Studies Skills: Reading a Chart

The Thirteen English Colonies

Colony	Date of English settlement	Type of colony at settlement	Type of colony in 1760/ Date of change
New Hampshire	1623	Proprietary	Royal/1679
Massachusetts Bay	1629	Joint-Stock	Royal/1691
Rhode Island	1636	Proprietary	Self-governing charter/1644
Connecticut	1636	Proprietary	Self-governing charter/1662
New York	1664	Proprietary	Royal/1685
New Jersey	1664	Proprietary	Royal/1702
Delaware	1664	Proprietary	Proprietary/1682 (Penn.)
Pennsylvania	1682	Proprietary	Proprietary/1694*
Virginia	1607	Joint-Stock	Royal/1624
Maryland	1634	Proprietary	Proprietary/1715**
North Carolina	1653	Proprietary	Royal/1729
South Carolina	1670	Proprietary	Royal/1729
Georgia	1733	Corporate	Royal/1753

*Was a royal colony in 1693
**Was a royal colony, 1691–1715

☐ New England ☐ Middle ☐ Southern

Charts are useful tools because they can present a great deal of information clearly. You can use the chart on this page in several ways. You might look for one specific piece of information, such as the date of the founding of South Carolina. You could examine the chart for a general idea of the types of English colonies. Another way to use the information presented in the chart is to compare the New England, Middle, and Southern colonies.

Skill Review: What four pieces of information does the chart present about each of the colonies? Into what groups does the chart divide the colonies? How is the division shown?

Writing About History

1. **Writing Persuasively.** Write a short pamphlet to attract settlers to one of the English colonies in North America. Describe at least three attractions of the colony. You may wish to illustrate your pamphlet.
2. **Writing an Eyewitness Account.** Imagine that you are a Native American in the 1700s who has witnessed the relationships between your fellow Native Americans and the French, Spanish, and English. Write a brief description of the pros and cons of each of these three relationships.

Your Region in History

Culture. When did the first settlers reach your area? Where did they come from? Are new groups of immigrants settling in your area today? Where do they come from? Do these two groups share any common goals?

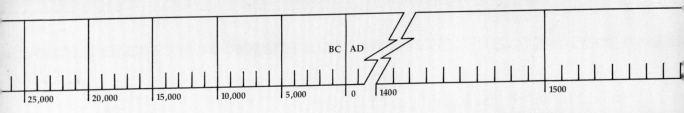

The Growth of the Thirteen Colonies

🐿 Chapter 5

Vocabulary

economy
immigrant
indentured servant
apprentice
militia
agriculture
ally
synagogue

F ROM THE BEGINNING each of the thirteen colonies had its own character. The people who came from other lands and the people born in America all left their mark on the colonies they helped form. They set up a system of self-government. And with their hard work they developed a strong economy, one suited to the geography of their region.

The British homeland also grew stronger over the years. In 1707, England and Scotland joined together to form Great Britain. Great Britain became the center of a worldwide empire based on trade. The colonies in North America became a more and more important part of this trading empire. Beginning in 1754, the importance of the colonies led Great Britain into a war with France. The outcome of this war made Great Britain stronger than ever.

1 Who Came and Why

Why did people in England want to found colonies in North America? Some founders stated their reasons outright. The London Company expected to find gold, trading goods, and a passage to Asia. The leaders of Massachusetts Bay Colony wished to build a model Bible community. Lord Baltimore wanted a refuge for Roman Catholics. And the eight founders of the Carolinas expected to make fortunes from their large grants of land.

Prereading

1. How did the arrival of non-English people, indentured servants, blacks, and women contribute to the growth of the thirteen colonies?
2. How did geography and the use of resources bring about differences between Great Britain and the colonies and among the colonies?
3. Why did Great Britain regulate colonial trading and manufacturing?
4. How did European rivalries lead to the end of French power in North America?

English settlers also came for different reasons. Thomas Shepard left for Massachusetts Bay to be with his friends. One reason John Winthrop decided to go to Massachusetts was to gain more land for his children. Caleb Heathcote came to New York to forget an unhappy love affair. And one mother sent her son to Virginia "to be tamed."

Changes in English Attitudes

In the 1600s English leaders wanted people to leave England for America. They believed that England was overcrowded. English leaders also believed that allowing such dissenting groups as Puritans, Separatists, Quakers, and Roman Catholics to go to America would improve conditions at home.

Most people who left England in the 1600s were farmers and other workers of the lower middle classes. Most of these people came to find what they could not find in England—work and the opportunity to better themselves.

By the 1700s the situation had changed. English leaders no longer wanted people to leave for America. England's economy had expanded. Workers were needed in factories. And workers were needed on the larger farms. After 1700, England encouraged only convicts to go to America.

The Arrival of Non-English People

While fewer English people came to the colonies in the 1700s, more people came from other countries. French Protestants who had been driven from their homeland were among the newcomers. The French settled in South Carolina, New York, and Massachusetts, hoping to build a new life. Jews from Europe also came to America. In much of Europe Jews were not allowed to practice certain trades or to own land. So they came to the colonies looking for equal rights and freedom to follow their faith.

Farmers from Germany flooded into Pennsylvania to escape European wars and to find good farmland. The Irish and Scots-Irish settled in Pennsylvania, western Virginia, the Carolinas, and Georgia. They were escaping hunger and hardship at home. All immigrants carried their heritage with them. Their languages, customs, dress, work skills, knowledge, and beliefs became a part of American life.

Indentured Servants

Many settlers in both the 1600s and 1700s came to America as indentured servants. Indentured servants were people who had their way to America paid by someone else. To repay these costs, they agreed to work four to seven years for their sponsors. When they

Estimated Colonial Population, 1630–1760

Year	Total population (white and black)	Percent black
1630	4,646	1%
1640	26,634	2%
1650	50,368	3%
1660	75,058	3%
1670	111,935	4%
1680	151,507	5%
1690	210,372	7%
1700	250,888	11%
1710	331,711	13%
1720	466,185	14%
1730	629,445	14%
1740	905,563	16%
1750	1,170,760	20%
1760	1,593,625	20%

After 1700, the number of immigrants from England dropped. But more people from Europe—Jews, French Protestants, and German, Irish, and Scots-Irish farmers—came to the colonies.

had worked the agreed number of years, indentured servants became free. In some colonies freed servants were given 50 acres (20 ha) of land and some livestock and seed to begin farming. Skilled carpenters, blacksmiths, and schoolteachers came to America as indentured servants. Before 1700, indentured servants came mostly to Virginia and Maryland. After 1700, most indentured servants settled in the Middle Colonies, especially Pennsylvania.

Many slaves did not survive the cramped and unhealthy quarters aboard ship. Those who did survive were sold into slavery when they reached the Americas.

The Arrival of Blacks

In 1619 Dutch sea captains brought the first African blacks to Virginia. Whether these Africans were sold as indentured servants or as slaves is not clear. But they certainly were brought against their will. Thirty years later there were both free blacks and slaves in the English colonies.

During the 1600s traders brought as many African slaves to Rhode Island and New York as they did to Virginia and Maryland. But after 1690, as more land in the Southern Colonies was planted in tobacco, rice, and indigo, the need for slaves grew. African slaves then became the chief work force in Virginia, Maryland, and the Carolinas.

The passage on slave ships from Africa to the colonies was frightful. Sometimes half the slaves on board died from sickness. One freed Virginia slave, Gustavus Vassa, wrote about his crossing. Vassa had been captured in Benin, Nigeria, and shipped to North America. He described the strong smell of men and women jammed below decks in stuffy holds. He wrote of Africans being chained together and being given little food or water. He told of slave traders punishing captured Africans who stood up for their human rights.

After the terrible trip, the slaves were sold and put to work in homes and in the fields. Black slaves came from many different regions of Africa. They brought with them their special skills as farmers, toolmakers, and traders. They also brought their customs, languages, and cultures. Their work helped the colonies, and their culture enriched American life.

Section 1 Review

1. Why did English leaders change their attitude after 1700?
2. Which non-English groups settled in Pennsylvania in the 1700s?
3. After what date did African slaves become the chief work force in the Southern Colonies?
4. What right did the colonial governments deny to all women?

Critical Thinking

5. **Identifying Central Issues.** Why were English leaders willing to allow colonists to leave for North America between 1600 and 1700?

LOOKING AHEAD: How did the geography and the use of resources bring about differences between Great Britain and the colonies and among the colonies?

As the number of Africans increased, most colonies passed strict laws to keep blacks as slaves. Slaves could not be taught to read and write. They could not leave their masters' plantations without written permission. But, most importantly, blacks were condemned to slavery as long as they lived. They were robbed of the chance to better themselves—the dream that brought white immigrants to the colonies. Many Africans resisted their slavery. In some cases they even revolted against their masters. But their efforts were put down by force.

Blacks made up the largest single group of immigrants to arrive in America between 1700 and 1775. By 1775 more than 400,000 Africans lived in the Southern Colonies alone. This number was about equal to the total population of New England. Slavery as a way of life continued until the 1860s.

Women in the Colonies

From the time of the earliest settlements women contributed to the growth of the colonies. Women were expected to take care of the house. But they often worked with men at other jobs. Many women were skilled workers. They sought jobs through the newspapers as shopkeepers, dressmakers, cobblers, gunsmiths, and teachers. Married women were not allowed to own land, and no women had the right to vote. But, even though women lacked many rights, they worked along with men in the development of the colonies.

2 Colonial Characteristics

As the thirteen colonies grew and changed, they became different from Britain and from one another. Each colony used its natural resources in different ways. And in each colony the heritage of the people who settled it colored its daily life.

Differing Ways: Britain and Its Colonies

Methods of farming in Britain differed from those in the colonies. In Britain land was scarce and costly. The British farmed their lands carefully to keep them fertile year after year. In the colonies land was plentiful and less costly. When the soil wore out in one field, farmers could clear a new field at little or no cost.

On the other hand, the colonies had fewer workers than Britain. Hiring workers was therefore more costly in the colonies than in Britain. Farmers in the colonies found ways of working that did not call for extra hands. For example, they seldom cut down trees to clear a field. Instead, they cut away some bark at the bottom of the tree, causing the tree to die. Then they burned the dead tree. Often they did not even clear out the remaining tree stumps.

The plains region of Syracuse, New York, was well suited to raising grain. Before they had machines, farmers had to harvest their grains by hand.

Sheep raising was another British activity that the colonists in North America could not keep up. The colonists did not have enough workers to give the sheep the extra care they needed. So they turned to raising pigs, which need little care. As a result, pork appeared regularly on the colonial table. Colonists ate other foods not often found in England. The Native Americans taught the colonists to grow corn and to use this grain in many ways. They also introduced them to such new foods as turkey, squash, beans, and pumpkins.

The Influence of Geography

You have seen that the colonies as a group differed from Britain in their use of resources. The colonies in one part of America also differed from the colonies in other parts. Because of geography, the New England Colonies depended for income on products that were different from those in the Southern or Middle Colonies. For example, the soil in Massachusetts was thin and rocky. And, because it was so far north, the colony had a short growing season. Massachusetts was better suited for grazing pigs and cattle than for raising grain crops. In time meat products became a major export of Massachusetts Bay.

Nearby fishing grounds also influenced the ways of life in the Massachusetts Bay Colony. A shelf of land, sometimes 200 miles wide, extends underwater from the coastline into the Atlantic. A cold ocean current flowing over the shelf creates ideal fishing grounds. Using these fishing grounds, Massachusetts Bay became known for its ships, sailors, and fishers. Port towns such as Boston and Salem grew up along the coast because the rivers of the Bay colony were too shallow for ocean ships. In time these port towns became the homes of merchants, skilled workers, and shopkeepers.

A lighthouse on Chesapeake Bay (above) once guided ocean vessels through the dark and fog. In New England, prayer meetings such as the one shown to the right were common among Puritans.

The geography of the Southern Colonies, on the other hand, led to different ways of life. For example, Chesapeake Bay forms Virginia's coastline. Many rivers, deep enough in colonial times for ocean vessels, emptied into the bay. Colonists settled along the rivers as far inland as ocean vessels could sail. They built docks to export tobacco and to import goods from England. No major port town grew up in Virginia in colonial times. There was also no important merchant class in Virginia until after the American Revolution. And skilled workers were as scattered as the plantations, not clustered in towns as they were in Massachusetts.

As in Massachusetts and Virginia, geography influenced the other colonies and helped give them regional character.

New England Ways

By the 1760s the people in Massachusetts Bay, Connecticut, Rhode Island, and New Hampshire had developed a strong sense of being New Englanders. Church life and town life each played a role in bringing about this sense of unity. Until the 1700s most New England towns were founded by church groups. In 1647, church leaders in Massachusetts Bay ordered every town with a population of fifty or more families to have a school. They wanted every child to be able to read the Bible and to study it. By 1671 every New England colony except Rhode Island, which had no official church, had passed such school laws.

Church leaders directed town life in other ways. They gave land to settlers. They also decided who could become members of the church. In the beginning it was important to be a church member, because only church members could vote for government officers. After the 1700s most New Englanders did not join the official church. Some joined other churches, such as the Baptist and Presbyterian churches. Others did not join any church.

This weakening of official church ties brought about changes in government and politics. Voting rights came to rest on ownership of property or payment of taxes rather than on church membership. And land was being given to individuals, not to church groups.

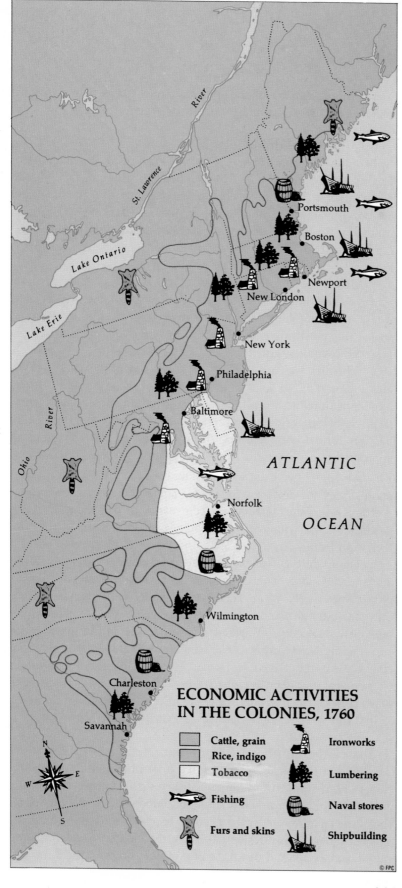

The geography of each colony influenced in part the kinds of economic activities the colony developed.

ECONOMIC ACTIVITIES IN THE COLONIES, 1760

- Cattle, grain
- Rice, indigo
- Tobacco
- Fishing
- Furs and skins
- Ironworks
- Lumbering
- Naval stores
- Shipbuilding

Portsmouth
Boston
Newport
New London
New York
Philadelphia
Baltimore
Norfolk
Wilmington
Charleston
Savannah

St. Lawrence River
Lake Ontario
Lake Erie
Ohio River
ATLANTIC OCEAN

N E S W

© FPC

Many people settled on farms away from towns. Yet the town remained the center of life in the New England Colonies.

People in the Middle Colonies

Unlike New England, where most colonists were descendants of English settlers, the Middle Colonies had a greater mix of people. In New York the Dutch influence on language, ways of building, and customs remained for more than a century. About 175,000 Germans came to settle in the Middle Colonies, mostly in Pennsylvania. And the flood of Irish became so great that one Quaker leader wrote: "It looks as if Ireland is to send all its inhabitants."

Most people in Pennsylvania lived on farms some distance apart. A few inland villages sprang up where major rivers met, where mills were built, or where Native Americans brought furs to trade. But most goods coming into or going out of Pennsylvania passed through the great port of Philadelphia.

Schooling was not required by law in any of the Middle Colonies. Some families sent their children to private schools. Others hired indentured servants to teach their children, either in a home or in a school supported by several families. Many youngsters never had any formal book learning. Instead, they learned a trade as an apprentice to a blacksmith, carpenter, printer, or other craftsworker.

An apprentice lived with the family of the craftsworker, obeying all rules the craftsworker made. Some youngsters became apprentices when they were only seven years old. The apprenticeships lasted until the youngsters were fully trained and ready to make their own livings.

The Middle Colonies harbored the followers of widely different churches and beliefs. Quaker Pennsylvania allowed religious groups such as the Moravians, Amish, and Dunkers to worship as they pleased. Maryland welcomed Roman Catholics as well as members of the Church of England. In New Jersey and in the counties surrounding New York City the Church of England was the official church. But the Dutch Reformed Church and the Presbyterian Church also had many members there. Because they came from so many different backgrounds, people in the Middle Colonies never shared the sense of unity that New Englanders did.

Traits of the Southern Colonies

The Southern Colonies are most often remembered for large plantations, stately homes, and the use of slaves. But most people in the Southern Colonies worked small farms and owned no slaves. Southern farmers grew such garden crops as corn, squash, and beans. They also raised livestock and made butter and cheese to sell. Some raised a small amount of tobacco or another crop for market.

The College of William and Mary in Virginia has the oldest academic hall in the nation.

The Church of England was the official church of every Southern Colony. But Baptists, Presbyterians, and people of other faiths could worship as they wished, as long as they paid taxes that went to the official church.

The Southern Colonies did not have any public schools. Some wealthy plantation owners hired teachers for their own children. Older boys who were later to run their families' plantations would be sent to England for higher learning. Children from less well-to-do families often went to schools far from home, run by ministers or educated gentlemen or gentlewomen.

Few white children in the Southern Colonies became apprentices. Most of the skilled workers were African slaves, and white parents did not want their children to learn from slaves.

Self-Government in the Colonies

Although geography and cultural background brought about regional differences, all colonies practiced self-government. By the mid-1700s each colony had three levels of government. These were the town or county government, the colonial government, and the government of the British empire.

Virginia's legislature was the first representative lawmaking body in America. From 1704 to 1780 the colony's government met in this building in Williamsburg.

113

Section 2 Review

1. Was land costlier in Great Britain or in the colonies? Were workers in greater supply in Great Britain or in the colonies?
2. What two English farming practices did settlers change when they reached North America?
3. In which group of colonies did life center around the towns?
4. In which group of colonies was there a greater mix of nationalities and church practices?
5. What three levels of government had developed in each colony by the 1750s?
6. What question expressed the real conflict that began to develop between the colonies and Great Britain?

Critical Thinking

7. **Demonstrating Reasoned Judgment.** In what way do you think the growing conflict between Great Britain and the colonies could have been resolved?

LOOKING AHEAD: Why did Great Britain regulate colonial trading and manufacturing?

The town or county government handled such matters as boundary disputes between local landowners. This local level of government cared for the poor. It made sure all local and colonial laws were obeyed. And it conducted all elections.

At the next level was the colonial government. Its powers were divided among a governor, a colonial council, and a lawmaking assembly. Most governors were appointed by the British Crown to speak for the Crown. The governors enforced Crown and colonial laws. They acted as the chief court officials. They also approved land grants and headed the militia. Members of the colonial councils were most often appointed by the Crown. They served as advisers to the governor.

Members of the lawmaking assemblies, on the other hand, were elected by the colonial voters. The assemblies made laws governing defense. They set taxes. They also decided who would have the right to vote. The members of the assemblies often did not agree on the issues of the day. But these differences gave rise to open and public debate before the voters for whom the lawmakers were supposed to speak.

The elected assemblies slowly gained power. As they did, the governors and the councils lost power. In most colonies the assembly decided how and when the governor should be paid. Sometimes an assembly would refuse to pay a governor until the governor approved all laws it had passed. The British Crown strongly protested such moves by the assemblies. And the assemblies protested when the Crown interfered with their actions.

The real conflict between the Crown and the colonies was far more serious than a difference of views on certain issues. The real question was, where did British rule and colonial self-government begin? A growing number of colonists believed that the British Crown and Parliament should not have the final say in all colonial matters. The Crown and Parliament saw no limit to their governing power. This difference of views surfaced again and again as the colonies became stronger. It grew so serious that it became a major cause of the American Revolution.

3 Britain and the Colonial Economy

Most colonists made their livings from agriculture. But other industries brought money into the colonies. Shipbuilding became important as more goods were traded. By the 1760s New England was building more than half the ships used in colonial trade.

There were ironworks in almost all of the colonies. Pennsylvania alone turned out more raw iron than Great Britain. In many colonies blacksmiths shaped the iron into tools and other useful

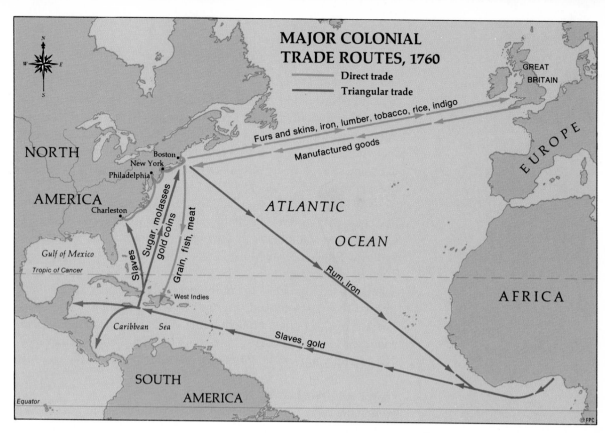

MAJOR COLONIAL TRADE ROUTES, 1760

— Direct trade
— Triangular trade

GREAT BRITAIN

NORTH AMERICA

Boston
New York
Philadelphia
Charleston

Furs and skins, iron, lumber, tobacco, rice, indigo

Manufactured goods

EUROPE

ATLANTIC

OCEAN

Sugar, molasses
gold coins

Grain, fish, meat

Slaves

Gulf of Mexico

Tropic of Cancer

West Indies

Caribbean Sea

Rum, iron

Slaves, gold

AFRICA

SOUTH AMERICA

Equator

© FPC

items. Where plenty of sand and limestone were found, people set up glassworks. The making of pitch, tar, and turpentine for building and repairing ships also brought good income. Everywhere in the colonies skilled workers turned out such goods as candles, barrels, and furniture. Others worked as cobblers, dressmakers, tailors, and printers. By 1770 the colonies exchanged so many goods with Britain that fully one third of all British trade was with North American colonies.

Trace the triangular trade routes connecting the Americas with Africa.

The Acts of Trade

From the beginning Britain believed that its colonies existed solely for its benefit. As early as 1624, Britain had restricted colonial trade to make sure it served British interests. As the colonial economies grew, Britain drew its trading ties even tighter.

Beginning in 1651, Britain passed several Navigation Acts. Almost everything the colonists traded was to go only to Great Britain or its colonies, and only in British or colonial ships. This was true for such goods as tobacco, indigo, and sugar. The Navigation Acts also stated that almost all colonial imports had to come from or through Britain. Only wine, salt, and servants could be imported directly from a country other than Britain.

The goal of the Navigation Acts was to increase Britain's trade and power. At the same time, Britain wanted to sap the strength of Holland, France, and Spain by stopping their trade with the British colonies.

The Navigation Acts hurt Britain's rivals. They also hurt the colonists, especially the tobacco farmers in Virginia and Maryland. All colonial tobacco had to go directly to Britain. Tobacco not sold there was stored. Then it was reshipped to other countries. The handling and storage costs were taken out of the profits that the tobacco farmers received.

In 1733 Britain passed the Molasses Act, another law that limited trade with its rivals. With this act Britain tried to end the molasses and sugar trade between the French colonies in the West Indies and New England. The Molasses Act was hard on New Englanders. They used sugar and molasses to make rum. New England merchants traded the rum for more sugar and molasses in the West Indies. They also shipped the rum to Africa, trading it for slaves. These slaves were then brought to the West Indies or to the colonies and traded for other goods. Many people did not obey the new law. They secretly moved the forbidden goods in and out of the country.

Other British Laws

As manufacturing grew in the colonies, Britain began to worry about a new rival—the colonies themselves. It feared that colonial goods would sell better than British goods and would hurt the British economy. So Britain began to block colonial manufacturing. The Hat Act, passed in 1732, stopped the export of beaver hats. This act hurt Pennsylvanians and New Yorkers most. They had been making hats at a small cost. They then sold them for less money than the British could sell their hats. Britain also passed the Iron Act in 1750. This act allowed the colonists to make pig iron and bar iron. But it stopped them from making finished iron products. Pennsylvania ironworkers were hurt the most by this law. The Pennsylvania Assembly refused to obey parts of the Iron Act to protect the jobs of many Pennsylvania workers.

Britain also took steps to keep the colonies out of banking and money-printing. In 1741 it forbade the colonies to form banks. A decade later it ordered New England to stop issuing paper money. By 1764 Britain had stopped all the other colonies from issuing money. Britain believed that it alone had the power to coin or control money.

British law offered some advantages for the colonies. Britain sometimes paid colonists extra money to produce the goods it needed, such as indigo. And Britain's warships protected colonial trading ships from warships of other nations. The colonists believed, however, that the disadvantages of the rules were greater than the advantages. They protested the laws governing trade, manufacturing, and banking. But Britain refused to change. So bad feelings between the colonies and Britain grew worse.

Section 3 Review

1. How much of Britain's trade in 1770 was with its North American colonies?
2. How did the Navigation Acts limit colonial export trade? Colonial import trade?
3. What was the main purpose of the Molasses Act?
4. What were two acts passed by Britain to block colonial manufacturing?
5. How did Britain limit the flow of money in the colonies?

Critical Thinking

6. **Recognizing Bias.** As an ironworker in England, how would you have felt about ironworking in the colonies?

LOOKING AHEAD: How did European rivalries lead to the end of French power in North America?

The Hat Act of 1752 barred colonial hatmakers from selling their goods outside of the colonies

4 European Rivalries

For a time the differences between Britain and its colonies were put aside. A more serious conflict arose between Britain and France. After 1700 these two European nations were locked in a contest for world power.

Britain had grown stronger and stronger with each step forward in its colonies and its economy. Britain's navy was the strongest in the world. Its trading ships sailed the globe. At the same time, France had become the most powerful country on the mainland of Europe. It had the largest and best outfitted army. It also had treaties of friendship with other powerful nations of Europe, such as Spain and Austria.

The Great War for Empire

Between 1689 and 1763 the great powers of Britain and France clashed in four wars. The last war, begun in 1754, was fought partly in North America. In America it became known as the French and Indian War. In Europe it was called the Seven Years' War. It is now known as the Great War for Empire, because it was fought to gain possessions in every part of the world.

The fighting in North America began with a dispute over the lands west of the Appalachian Mountains. Both Britain and France claimed these lands. Each country fought to make its claim good. Each also wanted Native Americans as allies in the fight. To gain Native American help, each country held out promises of trade and protection.

Some groups, such as the Hurons near the St. Lawrence River, mainly supported France. Other groups, such as the Iroquois in western New York and the Cherokee in the South, had ties with both groups. But neither the French nor the British made good on their promises to their Native American allies. When the fighting was over, Native Americans lost their lands to white settlers.

To hold its lands, France built forts along the Mississippi and Ohio rivers and around the Great Lakes. In 1753 the French started a fort near present-day Pittsburgh. At that time the British ordered the governor of Virginia to warn the French to leave. George Washington, then a young surveyor, delivered the governor's message. But

NORTH AMERICA IN 1763

⬚ The Thirteen Colonies	
■ British territory	▨ Ceded to Britain by France
■ French territory	▨ Ceded to Britain by Spain
■ Spanish territory	▨ Ceded to Spain by France

© FPC

After 1763, France was no longer a threat to English settlements in North America.

the French refused to leave. In 1754 the French defeated Washington and the band of soldiers sent to drive them out. The following year they defeated a larger force of 1,500 British regulars and 500 members of the colonial militia fighting under Edward Braddock, a British general. In this battle the British lost about 1,000 men, including General Braddock. Washington, who served with Braddock, had two horses shot out from under him. His clothing was ripped by small shot, but he escaped unhurt.

The war raged on, and it seemed certain that the French would win. In the next three years the French, led by General Louis Joseph Montcalm, defeated the British in several battles. In 1758 Britain finally rallied, guided by William Pitt, a powerful British political leader. Pitt sent more soldiers, as well as money to pay for supplies. He enlarged the British navy. He also sent two of Britain's very best generals to lead the fighting—General James Wolfe and General Jeffrey Amherst.

The Capture of Quebec

In 1758 Amherst's army defeated the French at Louisbourg, a fort on the coast of Canada. This victory opened the St. Lawrence River to the British navy. In the following year 250 British ships, carrying 8,500 soldiers and twice as many sailors and marines, sailed up the St. Lawrence. The leader of this mighty force was the young British general James Wolfe. His goal was to capture Quebec.

But Quebec was difficult to attack. It was built at the edge of steep cliffs. Below, the swift flow of the St. Lawrence made a landing dangerous for ships and men. For several months Wolfe tried to find a safe landing place. Finally, on a September morning, he found it. He saw some women washing clothes on the river bank below Quebec. He watched them take a hidden trail up to the city.

Wolfe led his men up this trail during the night. Early the next morning some 4,000 British troops were in place for a battle with the French. Both Wolfe and the French General Montcalm died in the battle, but the British finally won. Although the war lasted for four more years, it was the capture of Quebec that decided the fate of the French colonies in North America.

The Results of Peace

The peace treaty of 1763 put an end to French power in North America. France gave all its land in Canada and all its territory east of the Mississippi River to Britain. Because Spain had helped France fight the war, France gave Louisiana—its lands west of the Mississippi River—to Spain.

A new era began for Britain with the end of the Great War for Empire. Britain had won a vast territory from France, as well as Florida from Spain. Britain became the most powerful nation in the world. Its colonies, which spread around the world, now numbered more than thirty. But even Britain's power would not be able to keep it from losing its young colonies in North America.

A new era also began for the colonies and for the Native Americans living west of the Appalachians. With the French gone, the colonists felt they no longer needed British protection. Settlers began to enter the lands west of the Appalachians. These lands, once guarded by French strongholds, were now guarded by powerful Native American groups. The Native Americans, who had been caught in the struggle between Britain and France, were soon to be caught in a fight between Britain and its colonies. For the colonies in North America the new era would bring independence from Britain. For the Native Americans the new era would be a time of hardship.

Section 4 Review

1. By what other names is the Great War for Empire known?
2. What caused Britain's dispute with France in North America?
3. What did Britain and France promise Native Americans in return for their help in the dispute?
4. What battle decided the fate of the French colonies in North America?
5. At the war's end, what did France give to Great Britain? To Spain?
6. What did Spain give to Britain?

Critical Thinking

7. **Identifying Alternatives.** What might the United States be like today if France had won the Great War for Empire?

People of many different faiths came to America in search of the freedom to worship as they pleased.

Anne Dudley and her family lived well in England. Her father Thomas handled the affairs and lands of a well-to-do landowner. At home Thomas and Dorothy Dudley encouraged their daughter to read the works of important English writers. Anne began dreaming of being a writer herself someday.

A Puritan's Faith

As a young girl, Anne felt the strong tug of her parents' Puritan beliefs. She worried about her own feelings toward the god that her parents worshipped. Their god could be angry enough to destroy a person or far more generous than one could hope. Twice, as a child, Anne became very ill. Once she had smallpox, a disease that often killed its victims. Both times, Anne was sure she was being punished for her wrongdoings. She wrote that she was afraid she could no longer be close to God.

Marriage and Family

In 1628, at the age of sixteen, Anne Dudley married Simon Bradstreet, who worked for her father. Two years later Mrs. Bradstreet, her parents, and her husband left for Massachusetts Bay Colony. They wanted to build a Bible community with other Puritans.

The first years were hard. Food was scarce. Many friends died. But the Dudleys and the Bradstreets survived. In fact, Thomas Dudley and later Simon Bradstreet became governors of Massachusetts Bay Colony.

Many of Anne Bradstreet's poems were about her faith in God.

In 1633 the Bradstreets' first child was born. Anne had worried that God was not going to give them children. She should never have feared. The Bradstreets became the parents of eight children.

Verses from the Heart

Anne Bradstreet began to write poems about her feelings. Her verses reflected every part of her daily life: her faith, her family, her reading, her view of nature's beauty. Bradstreet's poems were taken to England by friends and printed there in 1650. English readers were surprised to learn that the poet was a woman who had raised eight children in a busy frontier settlement.

The Jews in America

The Levy family helped found the first Jewish community in the New World. At the time Europeans settled in America Jews had been driven out of many countries of Europe. Most Jews lived in Poland, Germany, and Holland, but they were seldom free to worship as they wished.

When Holland founded settlements in New Amsterdam, some Jews moved to America. They hoped to find the freedom they sought. But even in America Jews were not free at first.

In Dutch New Amsterdam, Jews could trade and buy land. But they were not allowed to be shopkeepers or skilled workers such as carpenters or cobblers. They could not hold services in a Jewish house of worship, called a synagogue. So they secretly held services in their homes.

Slowly all of this changed, mostly after the English captured New Amsterdam and made it New

Abigail Franks wanted future generations of her family to keep up Jewish ways.

Touro Synagogue in Newport, Rhode Island, is a lasting gift from early Jews in the United States.

York. By 1695 the Levys were one of twenty families who had established a synagogue in New York.

Abigail Levy's father led the Jewish communities in Baltimore and Philadelphia. And her husband, Jacob Franks, later guided the New York community. Under his leadership the New York Jews built their own house of worship in 1730.

Keeping the Tradition

The Jews in early America, like the Pilgrims and Puritans, feared that their children would marry someone who was not of their faith. When the Franks' daughter secretly married a non-Jew, Abigail became greatly upset. She thought their future grandchildren would not learn the Jewish way of life that she loved. Abigail wrote to her son: "My spirits was for some time soe depresst that it was a pain to me to speak or see any one . . . My house has bin my prison ever since."

To keep their faith strong, Jews in one colony sometimes asked for help from Jews in other colonies. In 1759 the Jews in Newport, Rhode Island, wrote to Jacob Franks. They asked for money to build a synagogue where they coud teach their children the Jewish ways and beliefs. The Newport group feared that the Jewish faith might be lost forever if the children remained "uninstructed in our most holy and divine law. . . ."

The Jewish people of New York gave generously. A synagogue was built in Newport. It stands today as one of the finest examples of early buildings of its kind in the United States. It is also the country's oldest synagogue.

Chapter 5 Review

Chapter Summary

As the thirteen colonies grew, they became different in many ways, both from their homelands and from each other. The New England Colonies, the Middle Colonies including New York, Pennsylvania, and Maryland, and the Southern Colonies all differed in their attitudes and their ways of life.

All colonies, however, practiced self-government on the local and colonial levels. Elected lawmaking assemblies slowly gained power. Many colonists began to question the Crown's right to make laws for the colonies in North America.

Beginning in 1651, Britain passed several Navigation Acts to increase its trade and its power over European rivals. These acts were not well received by the colonies. These bad feelings, however, were put aside when Great Britain went to war against France, its main rival both in Europe and in North America.

The French and Indian War began in 1754. It ended in 1763 with France giving away all of its land in North America. France gave all lands east of the Mississippi to Britain and all lands west of it to Spain.

Reviewing Vocabulary

Use the following words to complete the sentences below.

economy   militia
immigrant   agriculture
indentured servant   ally
apprentice   synagogue

1. Most colonists made their living from _____.

2. The defense of the colonies rested with armed civilians called the _____.

3. The _____ of the New England Colonies included fishing, trade, ironworks, and farming.
4. A(n) _____ is a person, nation, or group willing to help another person, nation, or group.
5. One way to learn a craft is as a(n) _____ to a skilled craftsperson.
6. A(n) _____ leaves his or her homeland to settle permanently in another country.
7. Jews worship in a _____.
8. After working for a period of years to repay the cost of his or her passage to the colonies, a(n) _____ was free.

Understanding Main Ideas

1. What contributions did each of the following groups make to the colonies: non-English people, indentured servants, blacks, women?
2. How did the colonies develop differences from Great Britain as a result of geography and the use of resources? How did these same factors contribute to differences among the colonies themselves?
3. What did Parliament and the King hope to gain by regulating colonial trade, banking, and manufacturing?
4. How did the French lose power in North America?

Critical Thinking Skills

1. **Determining Relevance.** What effect did geography have on New England schools? How did it discourage the development of schools in the Southern Colonies?
2. **Identifying Central Issues.** How were each of the following groups affected by the French and Indian War: British, French, colonists, Native Americans?

Social Studies Skills: Using a Pictograph

Estimated Slave Imports for Virginia, 1700–1709*

| = 100 slaves |

1700	🔻 🔻
1701	🔻 🔻 🔻 🔻 🔻 🔻 🔻 🔻
1702	🔻 🔻 🔻 🔻 🔻
1703	🔻 🔻
1704	🔻 🔻 🔻 🔻 🔻 🔻 🔻 🔻 🔻
1705	🔻 🔻 🔻 🔻 🔻 🔻 🔻 🔻 🔻 🔻 🔻 🔻 🔻 🔻
1706	🔻 🔻 🔻 🔻 🔻 🔻 🔻 🔻 🔻
1707	🔻 🔻 🔻 🔻 🔻 🔻
1708	🔻 🔻 🔻 🔻 🔻
1709	🔻 🔻 🔻

*Figures rounded to nearest hundred

Pictographs are useful tools for presenting statistics—numbers representing facts or data. The key is very important because it tells you what number of people or things each figure stands for.

Skill Review: Use the information in the pictograph to determine if each statement is true (write T), false (write F) or doubtful (write D). A conclusion is doubtful if the graph lacks the information needed to prove the statement either true or false.

1. Virginia received fewer slaves in 1700 than in 1709.
2. More slaves were imported in 1705 than at any other time.
3. Fewer than 900 slaves were imported into Virginia in 1704.
4. Slave imports increased each year between 1700 and 1709.
5. As many slaves were brought on English ships as on Dutch ships in 1703.

Writing About History

1. **Writing a Letter.** Imagine that you were a member of the British army during the Great War for Empire. You have been sent to the North American colonies. Write a letter to a loved one in England in which you describe the sights and sounds of a city or the countryside you have visited.

2. **Writing an Editorial.** Write an editorial for a Philadelphia newspaper supporting the Pennsylvania assembly's refusal to obey parts of the Iron Act.

Your Region in History

Citizenship. What was the first local assembly or legislature in your area? When and where did it meet? What is the official name for your state legislature today? Where does this assembly meet? How many people are elected to your state legislature?

Lifestyles:
Colonial Times

I N THIS UNIT you have read about the major events in the peopling of the American continents. You have read about Great Suns, kings and queens, brave explorers, and daring sea captains. You have also read about the not-so-famous people whose lives were touched by the history-making deeds of others.

The pages that follow offer glimpses into the daily lives of the settlers in North America. No matter where they settled, people took up the business of their daily lives and adjusted to their new homes. They built houses, fell in love, raised families, educated their children, worked, and relaxed. Reading the pages of their letters, diaries, and other written records can bring the people in history to life.

Families had to change many of their customs and habits when they moved to the New World. But they also kept some of the old ways from their homelands. Relationships between children and parents, and customs of dating and marriage remained much the same. The true stories that follow will give you an idea of what colonial family life was like.

Sons and daughters of well-to-do colonial families sometimes signed a marriage agreement before their wedding.

Permission to Date

These letters were written by two fathers whose son and daughter wished to go out with each other:

May 27, 1764
Dear Sir: My son, Mr. John Walker, [has] informed me of his intention to [date] your daughter Elizabeth, if he should be agreeable to yourself, lady, and daughter. [I find it proper] to inform you what I feel myself able to afford for their support [in the event that they decide to get married]. My [money] affairs are in an uncertain state, but I will promise one thousand pounds [next year], and one thousand pounds [the year after]. . . . The above sums are all to be in money or lands.

May 28, 1764
Dear Sir: Your son . . . applied to me for [permission to date] my daughter, Elizabeth. I gave him [permission], and told him . . . that my [money] affairs were in [a sad] state. . . . [I explained to him that it was] not in my power to pay him all the money this year that I intended to give my daughter, provided he succeeded [in winning her love]; but [I] would give him five hundred pounds more as soon as I . . . get the money.

A Colonial Midwife

An important person in colonial life was the midwife. Colonial mothers-to-be depended on the midwife to help bring new family members into the world. A Vermont history writer boasted about one very busy midwife.

[Mrs. Whitmore of Marlborough, Vermont] was very useful to the settlers, both as a nurse and as a midwife. She . . . frequently traveled through the woods on snowshoes . . . to relieve the distressed. She lived to the advanced age of 87 years, officiated at more than 2,000 births, and never lost a patient.

A Separated Family

Most black slaves lived in constant fear of being separated from their loved ones. Married couples usually were separated from some or all of their children. Often a wife was sold to one slave owner and her husband sold to another.

Josiah Henson was a slave whose family was broken up. Henson remembered the day at the slave auction when his brothers, sisters, and mother were all sold off:

My brothers and sisters were bid off first . . . while my mother, paralyzed by grief, held me by the hand. Her turn came, and she was bought by Isaac Riley of Montgomery county [Maryland]. Then I was [sold]. My mother . . . pushed through the crowd . . . to the spot where Riley was standing. She fell at his feet, and clung to his knees, [begging] him . . . to buy [Josiah] as well as herself, and spare to her one, at least, of her little ones. [Riley had no feelings for the mother, and removed himself from her.] . . . As she crawled away from the brutal man I heard her sob out, "Oh, . . . how long, how long shall I suffer this way!"

Slave traders sold the children of slave families to the highest bidder, just as they sold the parents. Families were broken up.

The first colonists lived mostly in simple huts built from sticks, mud, and clay. Some lived in caves. Later, as the colonists began to thrive in the new country, they developed different ways of living. Then they built more permanent and varied homes.

On the frontier, people lived in simple cabins. Most of these cabins had dirt floors. These frontier settlers made furniture from the wood of nearby trees. In larger settlements people lived in homes with one main room. This room served as a kitchen, dining room, and living room. People often slept in lofts built above this room. Some colonists added more rooms as their families grew.

Wealthier people spent more time and money building their houses. They built large homes, often with bricks brought from England. Wealthy planters and merchants used the finest goods money could buy in their homes.

The pictures on these pages show some of the different kinds of colonial homes and furniture. How are they different from homes and furniture of today?

This typical southern slave cabin is located on Boone Plantation near Mt. Pleasant, South Carolina.

Shelters dug from hills often served as early settlers' first homes.

The house at the right is the oldest in St. Augustine, Florida. Its builders used a Spanish design.

In many colonial homes a single room served as kitchen, dining room, living room, and playroom. In larger homes the kitchen was a separate room. The kitchen shown at the bottom of the page is in Alexandria, Virginia.

Notice the furnishings in this typical colonial bedroom in Dedham, Massachusetts.

Section 1 Review

1. In what ways did colonial parents help their daughters and sons get started in married life?
2. What colonial worker acted as nurse and doctor to women who were about to have babies?
3. What raw materials did colonists use most to build houses and to make furniture?

Critical Thinking

4. **Making Comparisons.** How are kitchens today like the kitchens of colonial times? How are they different?

Values and Learning

Every person has a set of values. Your values are made up of a group of beliefs, attitudes, and policies that show how you feel about life. You form values throughout your life. Each time you decide whether or not to do something, your set of values grows or changes. When you decide about something, you make a choice between two or more ways to act, believe, or feel. To make this choice you must judge the consequences of each action. What you decide will depend on what you most wish and value.

You learn values in a number of ways. You may learn them by watching or acting like other people. Friends, teachers, parents, and church leaders may teach them to you. Or you may learn them through experience and common sense.

Sets of values may be shared by groups of people. Often a society will make written rules and laws to make sure that all its members will live up to its values.

Values often change over the years. The following stories will give you an idea of some of the values held by society and individuals in colonial times.

Ben Franklin's Plan

Young Benjamin Franklin created a plan to help him live up to his values. He told about this plan in his *Autobiography:*

Ben Franklin's *Poor Richard's Almanac* included such famous sayings as "Early to bed and early to rise, makes a man healthy, wealthy, and wise."

Studying the values taught in the Bible was an important part of colonial life, even in a blacksmith's shop.

It was about this time (1721) that I conceived the bold . . . project of arriving at moral Perfection. . . . But I soon found I had undertaken a task of more difficulty than I had imagined. . . . I therefore tried the following method. . . . TEMPERANCE—Eat not to dulness; drink not to elevation. . . . SILENCE—Speak not but what may benefit others or yourself. Avoid trifling conversation. . . . ORDER— Let all your things have their places; let each part of your business have its time. . . . INDUSTRY—Lose no time; be always employ'd in something useful; cut off all unnecessary actions.

School of Good Manners

Colonial children formed many of their values from those held by their parents, teachers, and church leaders. Books also offered advice about values. One book, *The School of Good Manners,* listed rules on how children should treat their parents:

Never speak to thy parents without some title of respect, as, sir, madam. . . . Go not out of doors without thy parents' leave, and return within the time by them limited. . . . Quarrel not nor contend with thy [brothers] or sisters, but live in love, peace, and unity. . . . Bear with meekness and patience, and without murmuring or sullenness, thy parents' reproofs or corrections. . . .

Long Hair on Trial

Young people were often expected to accept their elders' values. Some officials did not want boys to wear long hair. A Massachusetts court had this to say about long hair in 1675:

. . . long haire, like weomens haire, is worne by some men . . . especially amongst the younger sort. This Court [declares] against this ill custome. . . . and the County Courts are hereby authorized to proceed against such delinquents either by [a warning], fine, or correction.

There were many distractions for young students studying at home as well as in one-room schoolhouses.

Young colonists were taught some of the same subjects you learn at school today. Colonial schools taught reading, writing, arithmetic, history, and geography. Many children also learned manners and religion at school. Some young people who did not go to school were taught these same subjects at home. Others learned job skills, instead of regular school subjects, at home or at places of business.

Rules for a Teacher

Teachers, like students, have rules to follow. In colonial times teachers had to follow strict rules about what, when, and how to teach. A New Amsterdam teacher received these instructions from colonial officials in 1661:

1. He shall take good care, that the children, coming to his school, do so at the usual hour, namely at eight in the morning and one in the afternoon.
2. He must keep good discipline among his pupils.
3. He shall teach the children and pupils the Christian prayers, commandments, baptism, Lord's Supper, and the questions with answers of the catechism. . . .
4. Before school closes he shall let the pupils sing some verses and a psalm. . . .

Busy Days at Religious School

Private religious schools provided education for some colonial children. Ursuline Sister Mary Magdeleine Hachard taught in New

According to the *New England Primer*, a good child was always to honor the king.

Section 2 Review

1. In what ways did colonial children learn values?
2. What did Benjamin Franklin mean by "temperance" and "industry"?
3. What is each person doing in the picture on page 132?
4. What two "Rules for a Teacher" would probably NOT apply to today's public classroom?

Critical Thinking

5. **Drawing Conclusions.** Based on the passage on page 131 from *The School of Good Manners,* how would you describe the rights of children in colonial families?

Orleans. She wrote to her father in 1728, telling him details of her busy days:

January 1, 1728
. . . We keep also a school to instruct the negro and Indian girls and women; they come every day from one o'clock in the afternoon to half-past two. You see, my dear father, that we are not useless in this country, I assure you that all our moments are counted and that we have not a single one to ourselves.

John Adams at School

Young John Adams learned to read at home under his father's guidance. John already was reading well by the time he started going to grade school. One of his first schoolbooks was the *New England Primer*. The *Primer* was used to teach "letters" and spelling. It was filled with religious and moral sayings. John and his classmates had to read such verses as:

> There is a heaven full of joy,
> Where godly ones must always stay;
> To [this] my soul must fly,
> As in a moment when I die.

Later John learned Latin, but this did not interest him. He often left class to go hunting in the woods. John told his father that he would rather be a farmer than go to college. His father disapproved.

Finally, John and his father came to an agreement. John promised that he would work harder on his studies if his father would arrange for a different teacher. The arrangements were made, and John kept his word. John's schooling helped prepare him to be a lawyer, a leader in the American Revolution, and the second President of the United States.

Schoolmaster at Charleston

Thomas Morritt, schoolmaster at the Charleston Free School during the 1720s, reported:

I have 10 boys sent me out of the Country beside one that came from [Philadelphia] & another that came from the Bahaman Islands which are Boarders & [I also have] 10 Charity Boys recommended by the [commissioners], two of [which] are Mulatos[.] In all [I have] 52 [boys]. . . . but . . . for those boys . . . such as are boarders I do intend . . . to make them read 3 times a week at least if not every night Classick History. . . . those books I will cause to be read an hour at nights between 8 & 9 & I shall not omit at that time to instruct them in Cronology & Geography & teach them the use of the Globes.

133

The early colonists were a hard-working lot. They spent much of their time meeting everyday needs—building homes, raising livestock, and growing crops. Even the richer colonists had much work to do. Later, after the colonists built their settlements, they had more time to do specialized work. They became blacksmiths, carpenters, storekeepers, ministers, silversmiths, cobblers, inventors—the list goes on and on. The following stories will give you an idea of some of the kinds of work the colonists did.

Neglected Merchants

The following letter appeared on January 21, 1733, in the *New York Weekly Journal*, edited by John Peter Zenger:

Mr. Zenger,
We, the widdows of this city, have had a Meeting. . . . We are House Keepers, Pay our Taxes, carry on trade, and most of us are she Merchants, and as we . . . contribute to the Support of Government, we ought to be Intituled to some of the Sweets of it; but we find ourselves entirely neglected. . . . we can . . . make as brave a Defence in Case of Invasion and perhaps not turn Taile as soon as some of them.

Black Farmers

Anthony Johnson and his wife Mary had been black indentured servants. They had earned their freedom after working a number of years on a Virginia plantation.

In 1651 the Johnsons bought 250 acres (100 ha) of land in Virginia and began planting corn and tobacco. To help them work, the Johnsons bought five servants, some of them whites.

The Johnsons and their plantation prospered. But one day a fire destroyed their home so they had to seek tax relief from the courts. On reviewing the Johnsons' hardship, the court ruled that they no longer had to pay taxes.

An Experienced Plowman

Robert Parke was an Irish Quaker who lived in Pennsylvania in 1725. He wrote his sister in Ireland about farming:

Dear Sister Mary Valentine:
. . . I am grown an Experienced Plowman & my brother Abell is Learning. . . . We have had a crop of oats, barley & very good flax & hemp, Indian Corn and buckwheat. . . . We also planted a bushel of white Potatoes . . . we had 10 or 12 bushels Increase. . . . All Sorts of Provisions are Extraordinary Plenty in Philadelphia market, where Country people bring in their comodities. . . . Dear Sister . . . tell my old friend Samuel Thornton . . . that in Plain terms he could not do better than to Come here.

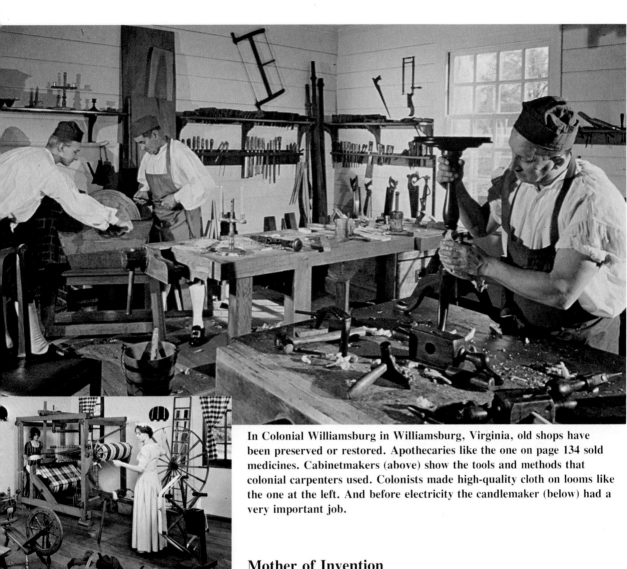

In Colonial Williamsburg in Williamsburg, Virginia, old shops have been preserved or restored. Apothecaries like the one on page 134 sold medicines. Cabinetmakers (above) show the tools and methods that colonial carpenters used. Colonists made high-quality cloth on looms like the one at the left. And before electricity the candlemaker (below) had a very important job.

Mother of Invention

Sybilla Masters, a Quaker, had four children. She was interested in mechanical invention. Masters invented a way to make cornmeal by stamping rather than grinding corn. On June 24, 1712, she told her friends that she planned to go to London to get a patent for her invention. A patent would give her the right of its ownership.

On November 25, 1715, the government gave a patent to Masters's husband, for "the sole use and benefit of 'a new invention . . . by Sybilla, his wife, for cleaning and curing the Indian Corn growing in the several colonies in America.'" Masters's husband was given the patent because law did not allow women to receive patents.

Masters later returned to Philadelphia and sold her cornmeal, which she called "Tuscarora Rice."

Colonists of all ages enjoyed the party game of musical chairs (top). Younger colonists enjoyed spinning tops (bottom left) and dolls. Wooden dolls were dressed in sometimes plain, sometimes elegant clothes.

The early colonists had little time for play. But as the people became settled in their new ways of life, they set aside more time for fun. People filled their leisure hours with games and activities they remembered from their homelands. They also learned other leisure-time activities from the Native Americans. And they made up a few new pastimes of their own.

Children's Toys

Colonial children's toys were made from everyday objects. Balls were made from old stockings, and dolls were fashioned from

On a pleasant afternoon many colonists enjoyed lawn bowling with friends. And children liked to see who could keep a hoop rolling the longest.

corncobs. Parents used knives to carve spinning tops, dolls, and other wooden playthings such as rocking horses.

Story Time

Another activity for young people was telling and listening to stories. Stories about Jack and the giant were among their favorites. Some people made up tall tales. One historian reports:

Sometimes boys and men would be content to sit around telling tales. . . . Out of such story-telling sessions came the "tall tale" . . . told for comic effect. A farmer might boast, for example, of the richness of his land. His watermelon vines grew so fast that they dragged the young melons along the ground at such a pace that they wore out before they had time to ripen.

Frontier Hunting Games

Frontier pastimes often imitated hunting and war. One man wrote:

Boys . . . [imitated] the noise of every bird and beast in the woods. . . . The imitations of the gobbling . . . wild turkeys often [attracted the turkeys to] within reach of the rifle. . . . Throwing the tomahawk, was another boyish sport. . . .

Colonial Dutch Customs

The Dutch introduced many amusements that became well-liked in the colonies. They played golf and a game similar to bowling called ninepins. Favorite winter activities were ice skating and going sleigh riding. In the summer they enjoyed fishing and picnics. The Dutch also introduced a custom that is known today:

The Saturday before Easter, every family boils a basket of eggs, colouring them in a curious manner. . . . each of the family takes several, goes among his [friends] challenging them. . . . The eggs are struck together, and the one that is broken given to the one who breaks it. There is much [amusement] in it. . . .

Section 3 Review

1. What "sweets" of the government might the widows of New York have wished to enjoy?
2. What crops were raised by the Johnsons in Virginia? By the Parke brothers in Pennsylvania?
3. What is a patent?
4. From what materials were many colonial toys made?
5. What amusements did the Dutch introduce?

Critical Thinking

6. **Drawing Conclusions.** In the letter on page 134, the "she Merchants" of New York City complain that they do not share the "sweets" of government. What do you think those "sweets" were?

Focus on Unit 1

Lifestyles: Understanding Social History

To answer the following questions, review the lifestyles section from page 124 to page 137.

1. **Families and Homes.** Families in the New World developed varied customs and habits while adapting to their new lives and surroundings. Reread the letters of the two fathers on page 126. What role did parents play in the courting process? What do these letters tell us about colonists' lifestyles and concerns?

2. **Values and Learning.** According to the passage on page 131, what four virtues did Benjamin Franklin feel were needed to arrive at "moral perfection"? Why do you think these virtues were valued in colonial times? Do you think they are valued today?

3. **Work and Play.** Colonial women are often described as staying at home to care for the children and run the household. Do the selections on pages 134 and 135 support this description?

Making Connections

Use the Unit 1 time line below to answer the following questions.

1. Based on the information in Chapter 1, how many generations passed during the period of time between A.D. 1400 and A.D. 1800?

2. In what century was the Iroquois League formed?

3. How many years passed between the arrival of the first people in the Americas and the landing of Leif Ericsson in North America?

4. Reread the Unit Introduction on page 23 and give examples from the time line that demonstrate active European interest in the Americas after Columbus.

5. **Recognizing Cause and Effect.** Which of the events in the 18th century led to the Great War for Empire?

Critical Thinking Skills

1. **Expressing Problems Clearly.** How did the organization of the Iroquois League prove helpful in solving problems?

2. **Making Comparisons.** What were some of the major similarities and differences between the Mound Builders and their immediate descendents?

3. **Recognizing Cause and Effect.** What were the underlying goals shared by the European powers in promoting exploration across the Atlantic?

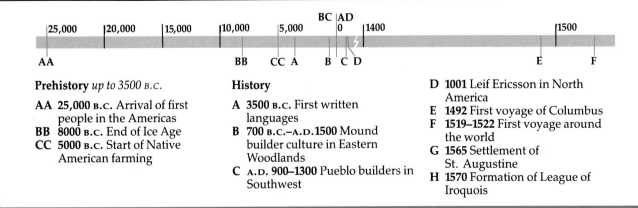

| 25,000 | 20,000 | 15,000 | 10,000 | 5,000 | BC | AD 0 | 1400 | | 1500 |

AA   BB   CC   A   B   C D   E   F

Prehistory *up to 3500 B.C.*

AA **25,000 B.C.** Arrival of first people in the Americas
BB **8000 B.C.** End of Ice Age
CC **5000 B.C.** Start of Native American farming

History

A **3500 B.C.** First written languages
B **700 B.C.–A.D. 1500** Mound builder culture in Eastern Woodlands
C **A.D. 900–1300** Pueblo builders in Southwest

D **1001** Leif Ericsson in North America
E **1492** First voyage of Columbus
F **1519–1522** First voyage around the world
G **1565** Settlement of St. Augustine
H **1570** Formation of League of Iroquois

Using Geography Skills

Use the map below to answer the following questions.

1. **Developing an Awareness of Place.** The Mayas lived on the part of Mesoamerica known as the Yucatan. The Yucatan juts out into the ocean and has water on three sides. What is land surrounded by water on three sides called?
2. **Understanding Human Movement.** Based on the information in this chapter, what do you think the thick black line and arrows represent?
3. **Understanding Human and Environmental Interaction.** Mesoamerica was the birthplace of several important civilizations. What kind of an environment do you think was needed to encourage the development of a civilization?
4. **Developing Locational Skills.** What present-day countries make up Mesoamerica? (See the map of North America on page 718 for present-day borders.)

Linking Past to Present

Predicting Consequences. If the French had been victorious in the French and Indian War, would the peace treaty of 1763 have been different? Who would have had control over New England? What changes might have taken place in Britain's colonies? How might the face of North America be different today?

Reviewing Social Studies Skills

1. **Time and History.** Review Chapter 3 "The Arrival of Europeans" and create a detailed time line showing the early exploration of the Americas. Be sure to include the voyage of Leif Ericsson as well as the voyages of later explorers.
2. **Place and History.** Examine the North American Climate Regions map on page 40 and the Growing Seasons map on page 724. How do these two maps help to explain the development of different economies of the northern colonies and the southern colonies?

I **1607** Founding of Jamestown
J **1619** Meeting of House of Burgesses
K **1624** Virginia: first royal colony
L **1629** Beginning of Massachusetts Bay Colony
M **1634** Founding of Maryland

N **1636** Founding of Rhode Island and Connecticut
O **1651** Navigation Acts
P **1664** English takeover of New York and New Jersey
Q **1679** Founding of New Hampshire
R **1682** Founding of Pennsylvania

S **1704** Creation of Delaware
T **1729** Split of Carolina into two parts, North and South
U **1733** Molasses Act
V **1750** Iron Act
W **1754–1763** Great War for Empire
X **1820** Separation of Maine from Massachusetts

Forming the Nation

The years between 1763 and 1815 brought great changes to North America and the world. As the years passed, the colonies grew and prospered. But conflicts with Great Britain also grew. In a bold move the colonists finally spoke up for their independence from Great Britain and fought a bitter war to achieve it.

General George Washington led the hard-fighting colonists to victory. The colonies became states, uniting under the Constitution in a new nation. Washington became the first President of the new nation and set the course for the future.

As other Presidents followed Washington, the young nation grew larger. But troubles continued. Within the country, conflicts between political parties often divided the people. And troubles outside the country finally led to another war with Britain—the War of 1812.

As you read about these exciting times, look carefully at the maps, charts, and pictures. They can often tell you as much as the printed word. And like the printed word, they take study to understand.

Unit 2

Regions of the World in millions of square kilometers

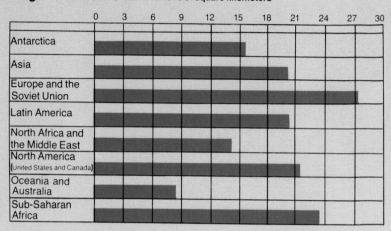

	0	3	6	9	12	15	18	21	24	27	30
Antarctica											
Asia											
Europe and the Soviet Union											
Latin America											
North Africa and the Middle East											
North America (United States and Canada)											
Oceania and Australia											
Sub-Saharan Africa											

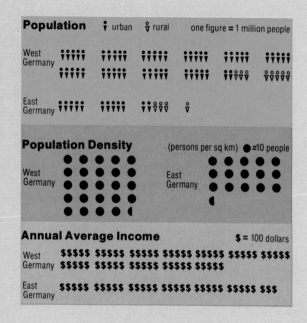

Population   ♀ urban   ♀ rural   one figure = 1 million people

West Germany

East Germany

Population Density   (persons per sq km) ● =10 people

West Germany

East Germany

Annual Average Income $ = 100 dollars

West Germany $$$$$ $$$$$ $$$$$ $$$$$ $$$$$ $$$$$ $$$$$ $$$$$ $$$$$ $$$$$ $$$$$ $$$$$

East Germany $$$$$ $$$$$ $$$$$ $$$$$ $$$$$ $$$$$ $$$

Understanding Graphics

Chapter 7

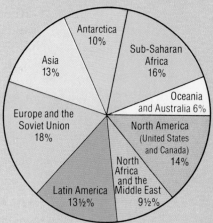

Land Area for Regions of the World

YOU SEND MESSAGES in many ways besides in writing. If you smile, you send a message. If you wave your hand in greeting, you send a message. If someone were to take a picture of you smiling or waving, your message would be recorded just as the written word is recorded. A hundred years from now people could look at the picture and read your message.

Pictures can send messages that are often hard to put into words. A map is one kind of picture. Imagine how hard it would be to put into words all the information that you can read from a map. Maps and other kinds of pictures that present facts and ideas—such as photographs, cartoons, charts, and graphs—are called graphics.

Some graphics—mainly tables, charts, and graphs—help to bring together different pieces of information. They can help you gather information and see how things are alike or different. They can also help you understand changes that take place over a length of time. The charts, graphs, and other kinds of graphics in this book contain as much information as the printed words. They must be read with as much care as the printed words. In Chapter 1 you learned how to read time lines and maps. This chapter will help you understand the messages that other graphics send.

Vocabulary

chart	caricature
graph	organization chart
graphic	pie graph
table	bar graph
caption	line graph
political cartoon	pictograph

1   Understanding Pictures and Cartoons

At the time Columbus sailed on his first voyage few Europeans knew how to read or write. For that reason paintings, drawings, and other kinds of pictures brought messages and information to people.

Beginning in the seventeenth century, more people learned to read and write. Printing helped spread the written word. People still used pictures, however, to add more facts or information to the printed word.

Gathering Information from Pictures

Pictures are full of interesting information. You can look at pictures from the past and see how people looked, dressed, ate, worked, and played.

To learn as much as you can from a picture, ask yourself questions about what you see. Compare what the picture shows with what you already know or with what you have learned from your reading.

Look at the picture on this page. It was painted in 1586 by John White, the governor of the lost settlement at Roanoke. You can see that the picture shows Native Americans fishing. But if you look carefully and ask yourself the right questions, you can see much more than that. You can learn that the Native Americans used spears, rakelike nets, and traps to catch the fish. You can learn that the Native Americans used canoes that were big enough to hold at least four people. You can also learn that some Native Americans did not use boats for fishing. They stood in the water and used spears to catch fish.

You might be puzzled about the fire in the boat. Why would the Native Americans build a fire in their boat? At first you might guess that they did it to keep warm. But if you look closely, you can see that this picture does not show a winter scene. If it were winter, there would be no plants along the shore. Read the words under the picture. They help explain the fire in the boat.

Pictures often have captions—words placed near the picture that tell something about the picture. You must read the caption as carefully as you read the picture. Often the caption will tell you something you need to know to understand a picture fully.

Now look at another picture. The drawing on page 145 was made in the late 1600s. This picture, like White's, shows people fishing. But it shows colonists rather than Native Americans. Look for other differences between the two pictures. Notice that the colonists are using fishing poles and lines rather than spears and traps. And they are fishing from the shore, not from boats. The clothing of the colonists is different from that of the Native Americans. The

Fish were an important part of the diet of eastern Native Americans. The fish were smoked over an open fire when they were caught so that they would keep longer.

Colonists brought not only their European ways of dress but also their fishing customs to North America. They fished as much for fun as for food.

caption may help explain the differences in clothing and ways of fishing.

You can learn much from every picture. Look at the people and try to understand what they are doing. Notice how they are dressed. Look for little things that will help you understand how people lived at the time of the picture. With practice you will learn many things from pictures.

Practicing Your Skills

Read the following picture and its caption. Then write out answers to these questions.

1. What city does the picture show?
2. What three ways of making a living does the picture show?

Critical Thinking

3. **Making Comparisons.** What is the population of this city today?

From a small village in 1752, Baltimore, Maryland, grew into a city of about 785,000 by 1980.

JOIN, or DIE.

Recognizing Opinions in Cartoons

Some pictures present opinions rather than information. One picture of this kind is the political cartoon. You can see political cartoons every day in newspapers. They are mostly about politics. But they always show an opinion of some kind.

Political cartoons began to appear in American newspapers in the mid-1700s. By that time many American colonists had become angry with the British government and the British king. Sometimes the colonists' anger took the form of cartoons that made fun of the king and his acts.

Some cartoons, such as the one on this page by Benjamin Franklin, called on the colonists to join together. This cartoon was first printed during the Great War for Empire. It was printed again at the time of the Stamp Act in 1765, and again in 1776. The letters near the pieces of the snake stand for the names of the colonies. The New England colonies are grouped together and form the head of the snake.

The words under the cartoon make Franklin's opinion very clear. He believed that the colonies had to join together to keep alive. By showing a living thing meant to be whole cut up into pieces, Franklin strongly expressed his opinion.

People who draw cartoons often use signs or symbols to help express their opinions. In many cartoons Uncle Sam stands for the United States (U.S.). A donkey is often the symbol for the Democratic party, and an elephant is the symbol for the Republican party. Animals are also used as symbols for some countries. The Soviet Union, a Communist country, is often shown as a bear. Great Britain is often shown as a lion and the United States as an eagle.

Look at the cartoon on page 147 by Bill Mauldin. The dove and the olive branch are both symbols of peace. The title of the cartoon will help you understand Mauldin's opinion. It might be explained in the following words. "The United States and the Soviet Union are very different from each other. But they have worked together to produce peace. They show off their peace proudly, just as a couple would show off their baby. But because the differences between the two countries are so great, the peace is, at best, an uneasy one." The cartoon makes the same point much more directly than the words. With symbols the point is made clearly and with humor.

The cartoon below is by Paul Revere. It is titled "A View of the Year 1765." The British government passed the Stamp Act in that year. This act forced the colonists to pay a stamp tax on all legal papers and newspapers. The colonists had no say in the matter. They soon rose up in anger against the Stamp Act.

In the cartoon the people to the left stand for the different colonies and their cities. *R-I* stands for Rhode Island. *B* stands for Boston. The people want to kill the winged monster—a symbol for the Stamp Act. The monster holds the Magna Charta, a famous British writing that promises certain freedoms for citizens. Underneath the monster lie two men crushed by the hated tax.

THE ODD COUPLE

The Liberty Tree stands to the right. *H-k* or *H*is majesty the king, George III, hangs from the tree. The men beside the tree comment: "There's that villain H-k. See he's got a high place." The king was the highest ruler in the land. So showing a king hanging from a tree was a powerful expression of the people's anger.

Revere's caption under the cartoon is hard to read. But you can perhaps make out some of the lines. The last lines of the middle column sum up Revere's point: "And each united Province faithful joins / Against this Monster and his curst Designs. . . ."

As you can see from the other political cartoons on pages 148-149, cartoonists often exaggerate a person's features. They may show a person with a large nose as a person with a *huge* nose. A

person with big teeth will have *very* big teeth. Eleanor Roosevelt and Jimmy Carter are easily recognized by their teeth in the pictures and the cartoons, called caricatures, to the left.

When you look at paintings or photographs, you look for information. But when you look at a political cartoon, you look for opinions. Cartoons can help you understand how some people viewed a person, a happening, or an issue in history.

Practicing Your Skills

The graphics below and on the next page show two views of President Theodore Roosevelt. One is a photograph. The other is a cartoon by John McCutcheon.

Theodore Roosevelt was President of the United States from 1901 to 1909. Many people voted for Roosevelt because they remembered him as the victorious leader of the Rough Riders in Cuba during the Spanish-American War.

Roosevelt was up for reelection in 1904 when the cartoon on page 149 appeared in the *Chicago Tribune*. Roosevelt ran as a candidate for the Republican party. The Republican party was nicknamed the Grand Old Party, or GOP. Roosevelt won by a huge vote.

With this information as a background, use your skills to complete the following practice exercises.

1. First look at the photograph and read its caption. Then write out answers to these questions.
   a. Where was this picture taken? Describe the area.
   b. What type of clothes and shoes is Roosevelt wearing?
   c. How does Roosevelt's outfit compare with outfits most Presidents wear?
   d. Who is the man with Roosevelt?
   e. Why might Roosevelt meet this man in this place?
   f. What can you learn about Roosevelt as a person from this picture? As a President?
2. Now look at the cartoon. Read the caption under the cartoon. Then write out answers to these questions.
   a. Why did the artist picture Roosevelt riding an elephant (pachyderm)?
   b. Does Roosevelt look like he can handle the elephant?
   c. Why did the artist show Roosevelt wearing riding boots and a western hat?
   d. What happening in history was the artist thinking of when he chose to show Roosevelt as a "rough and ready" rider?

Roosevelt poses with bearded nature expert John Muir in Yosemite Park.

Critical Thinking

3. Making Comparisons. Write a short paragraph about your ideas of Roosevelt based on the photograph and the cartoon. Try to answer the following questions.

a. In what ways is the idea you get of Roosevelt in the photograph the same as the idea in the cartoon?
b. In what ways are the ideas different?
c. What does the photograph tell you about Roosevelt that the cartoon does not?
d. What does the cartoon tell you that the photograph does not?

2 Understanding Charts, Tables, and Graphs

History is filled with facts and figures. Often such information is seen much more easily if it is organized. Charts, tables, and graphs are very useful for organizing facts. They also help you compare one fact or figure with others.

Organizing Information in Charts and Tables

Charts come in many different forms. But they are alike in one important way—they organize information. Facts are arranged on a chart to show how they are connected.

Like most of the Rough Riders who served under him in Cuba, Roosevelt was athletic and skilled as a horseman.

The Algonquian Language Family

Eastern Canada	Eastern Woodlands		Midwest	Plains
Cree	Abnaki	Nipmuc	Illinois	Arapaho
Montagnais	Chickahominy	Pamlico	Kickapoo	Gros Ventre
Nascapi	Delaware	Pamunkey	Menominee	Blackfoot
	Lumbee	Passamaquoddy	Miami	Cheyenne
	Malecite	Pennacook	Ojibwa	Cree
	Massachuset	Penobscot	Ottawa	
	Mattapony	Pequot	Peoria	
	Micmac	Powhatan	Potawatomi	
	Mohegan	Shawnee	Sauk	
	Nanticoke	Wampanoag	Fox	
	Narraganset	Wappinger		

The chart above organizes information about a major Native American language family—the Algonquians. How many different Native American groups spoke Algonquian languages? The chart can help you answer this question. If you add the number of names listed in all four columns, you learn that forty different groups spoke Algonquian languages. But the organization of this chart helps you learn more than that. You can learn that Algonquian speakers lived chiefly in four parts of North America. These were Eastern Canada, the Eastern Woodlands, the Midwest, and the Plains. You can also

149 🐌

learn that the area with the most Algonquian-speaking groups was the Eastern Woodlands.

Another kind of chart is called an organization chart. An organization chart shows how something—a school, a business, a government—is arranged or organized. Think about your school. The top person in your school is the principal. The name of your principal would be at the top of the chart. Next would come the name of the assistant principal. Then would come the teachers' names, and finally the slot for the student body. Look at the organization chart just below. It shows the structure of Virginia's colonial government. The boxes and the lines help you see clearly the levels of that government and how they were connected.

Government of a Royal Colony—Virginia, 1670

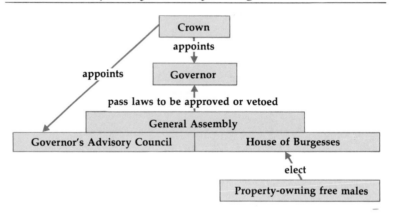

Black and White Population in Southern States, 1790

State	Total	White	Black	% Black
Maryland	320,000	209,000	111,000	34.6%
Virginia	748,000	442,000	306,000	40.9%
North Carolina	394,000	288,000	106,000	26.9%
South Carolina	249,000	140,000	109,000	43.7%
Georgia	83,000	53,000	30,000	36.1%

Tables also arrange or organize information. Unlike charts, tables usually contain only words and figures. Tables are lists of information grouped together.

Look at the table just above. You can see that the information is presented in lines across the page and columns down the page. If you want to know the percentage of blacks living in each state, you would read down the last column. If you are interested only in the number of people living in Georgia, you would read across the last line. If you are interested in learning how many black people lived in all the southern states, you would total the figures in the column labeled *Black*.

This table lists states in order from north to south. Sometimes tables list items in alphabetical order. An alphabetical listing makes it easy to locate the item you are looking for.

Practicing Your Skills

Copy the following chart outline on a sheet of paper. Use the table on page 757 to find the information to help you finish the chart. Under the columns headed *Republicans* and *Democrats* list the Presidents in the order in which they came to office. The first ones have been done for you.

United States Presidents Since 1940

Republicans	Term	Democrats	Term
Dwight D. Eisenhower	1953–1961	Franklin D. Roosevelt	1933–1945

Comparing Information in Graphs

A graph is a drawing that compares different sets of facts by using points, lines, bars, parts of a whole, or symbols. Graphs come in three general forms: pie graphs, bar graphs, and line graphs. A fourth kind of graph, the picture graph, is a bar graph that uses pictures. As you will see, the words *pie, bar, line,* and *picture* are good ways of describing these graphs.

Pie Graphs. The pie graph is very simple to understand. It looks like a round pie divided into slices of different sizes. A pie graph allows you to see how each slice compares with the other slices. It also allows you to see how any one slice compares with the whole pie.

Earlier you saw some figures on black and white populations in the southern states. If you added up all those figures, you would find that 662,000 blacks and 1,132,000 whites lived in the South in 1790. That information can be put into a simple pie graph. Notice how easily you can compare black and white populations on the graph.

Black and White Population in Southern States, 1790

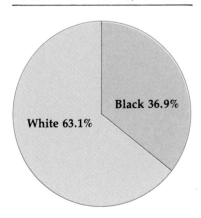
Black 36.9%
White 63.1%

Black and White Population in Southern States, 1790

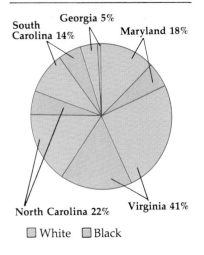

South Carolina 14%
Georgia 5%
Maryland 18%
North Carolina 22%
Virginia 41%

☐ White ☐ Black

The pie graph to the left has a little more information. It shows the total population, both black and white, for each of the five southern states. This graph helps you see that Virginia had the most people. You can easily see that South Carolina had about an equal number of blacks and whites.

Bar Graphs. Very likely you know how a thermometer works. The liquid in the glass rises or falls with the temperature. The liquid looks like a bar. To find out how hot or cold it is, you measure the height of the bar using the scale on the thermometer.

Suppose you check the temperature at noon each day for five straight days. Each day you draw a picture of the temperature reading as shown below. At the end of five days you can compare the five pictures to see how the noon temperature changed each day.

Noon Temperatures

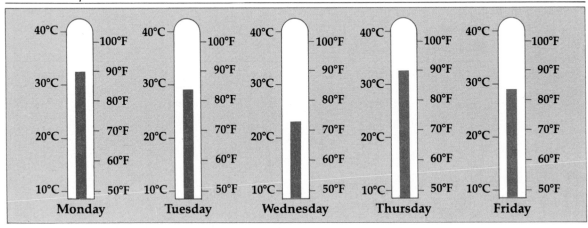

Monday   Tuesday   Wednesday   Thursday   Friday

But you really do not need five different pictures to compare these temperatures. You can turn your pictures into a bar graph as shown at the left on page 153. Now each day's bar can be checked against the Celsius or Fahrenheit scale along the left side of the bar graph. Read the scale on that bar graph from bottom to top. The higher the bar, the warmer the temperature. You can also turn this bar graph on its side and read the temperatures from left to right as shown in the graph at the right on page 153. In this graph the scale of temperatures runs along the bottom. You will come across both kinds of bar graphs in this book and other books.

Bar graphs always show amounts or numbers of something. The temperature graph showed number of degrees. Other bar graphs may show the number of people, dollars, tons of coal, or bushels of wheat.

Bar graphs, like pie graphs, allow you to compare figures or amounts. On the temperature bar graph you can compare Monday's

Noon Temperatures

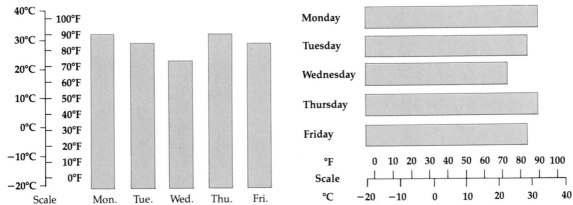

temperature with that of any of the other days. On the bar graph below you can compare the populations of the five biggest cities in the English colonies in 1760. The scale on this graph runs from left to right. The bar graph has two bars for each city. The first bar for Philadelphia shows the population of the city in 1760. The second bar shows Philadelphia's population in 1775. Using this graph, you can see how a city grew at different times. You can also compare the growth of one city with that of another. Philadelphia and New York grew rapidly, while Boston hardly grew at all from 1760 to 1775.

Populations of Five Cities in British North America, 1760 and 1775

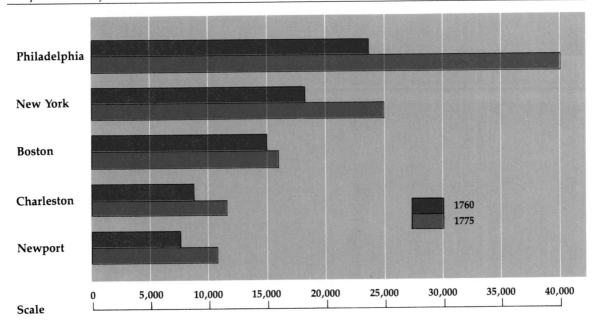

Line Graphs. Look again at the temperature graph on the opposite page. It measures one thing (temperature) over a period of time (five days). A better graph for showing this is a line graph. The graph at the top of page 154 shows how the temperature graph looks as a line graph. Here the temperature scale runs from bottom to top. The passing of time is shown from left to right.

Noon Temperatures

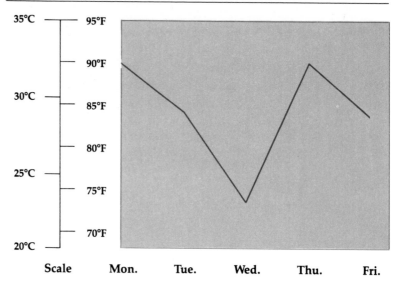

Time is a part of every line graph you will see in this book. The earliest time will always be at the left and the latest time at the right. Notice how a line graph allows you to see changes at different times. From Monday to Wednesday the temperature fell. The temperature rose from Wednesday to Thursday.

You can make a line graph that shows how the population of Newport, Rhode Island, changed between 1660 and 1775. Take a sheet of paper and make a set of crossed lines like the grid on the left below. The up-and-down part of the grid shows numbers of people. The left-to-right part shows the passing of time by decades. Transfer the scales to your grid.

Now take the information about Newport to the right below and put it on your grid. You can see that there are no figures for

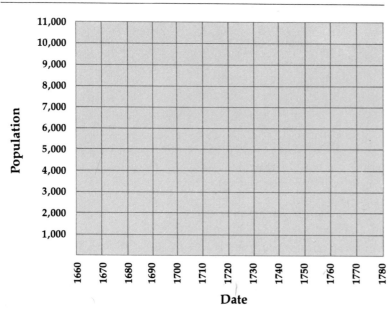

Population of Newport, 1660–1775

Year	Population
1660	700
1690	2,600
1720	3,800
1742	6,200
1760	7,500
1775	11,000

Population of Newport, 1660–1775

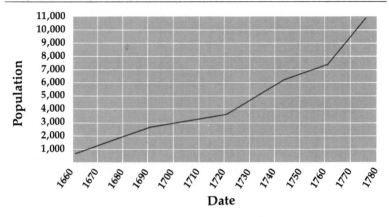

some of the decades between 1660 and 1775. That is because early population figures are often hard to find. You can also see that some of the dates do not fall onto an even decade. But you can still put information in the right place on your grid. For example, you can easily locate the year 1775 by finding the halfway point between 1770 and 1780.

For each year that there are population figures place a dot on your grid where the date meets the correct number of people. The first date is 1660. Find that year on your grid. The population that year was 700, so move up the grid line until you reach 700. The bottom line shows no population, or zero. The next line up is 1,000. A population of 500 would fall halfway between the zero line and the 1,000 line.

After you have placed all the dots correctly, connect them with straight lines. The line moving upward shows the rising population of Newport. The completed graph is shown above.

The next line graph is a little different. It shows the changing populations of two cities. It has two lines—one for each city. (New Amsterdam became New York in 1664 when the English took over the Dutch settlements.) The scale on this graph is different from the scale on the Newport graph. On this graph each mark on the population line stands for 2,000 people. The left-to-right time scale is the same as on the Newport graph.

Populations of Boston and New York, 1660–1775

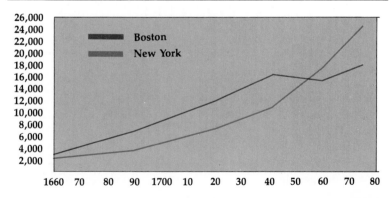

155

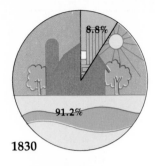

1830

1910

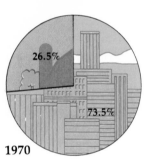

1970

Picture Graphs. Any graph may include pictures of some kind. The pie graph at the left uses pictures to illustrate its two parts. The farm picture stands for rural population. The city picture stands for urban population.

On a picture graph—sometimes called a pictograph—the pictures are not there just to look pretty. They are an important part of the graph. A picture graph is really a bar graph with pictures or symbols in place of the bars. Sometimes the symbols will be labeled to show what they stand for. More often the picture graph will have a key. The key to the pictograph below tells you that each symbol on the graph stands for 10,000 people.

You can see one important difference between a picture graph and a bar graph. On a bar graph a scale on the grid helps you see how many or how much of something is being shown. On a picture graph you need to check the key to see how many or how much each symbol stands for. Then you must count the symbols to get a total. On the picture graph below, count the symbols showing Maryland's population. There are thirty-two symbols, each one standing for 10,000 people. To learn Maryland's population you must multiply 10,000 by 32—for a total of 320,000.

Picture graphs show figures that are rounded off. If one symbol represents 10,000 people, it would take one-and-a-half symbols to show 15,000 people. And it would take one-and-a quarter symbols to show 12,500. But think of how hard it would be to show a population of 23,472 with symbols that represent 10,000 each.

Total Population of the Southern States, 1790

Maryland	⍓⍓⍓⍓⍓⍓⍓⍓⍓⍓⍓⍓⍓⍓⍓⍓⍓⍓⍓⍓⍓⍓⍓⍓⍓⍓⍓⍓⍓⍓⍓⍓
Virginia	(long row of symbols)
North Carolina	(rows of symbols)
South Carolina	(rows of symbols)
Georgia	(rows of symbols)

⍓ = **10,000 people**

156

You can see that picture graphs are not really exact. But they are useful. The pictures, or symbols, can help you get a general idea quickly. And they allow you to compare one part of a picture graph with another easily.

You have learned how to understand many kinds of graphics. The following exercises will help you practice what you have learned. When you finish them, skim through the rest of this unit. Stop to read the pictures, charts, tables, and graphs. By looking over the graphics in this way, you can begin to learn about the fiery events that led to the birth of your country.

Practicing Your Skills

On a separate sheet of paper, write out answers to these questions.
1. Look at the three pie graphs to the right.
   a. What change do you see between 1937 and 1978?
   b. When were the yes and no votes nearly equal?
2. Look at the bar graph. Which two states grew the most corn?

Critical Thinking
3. **Drawing Conclusions.** Based on the pictograph at the very bottom of the page, which regions of the country are good for raising cattle?

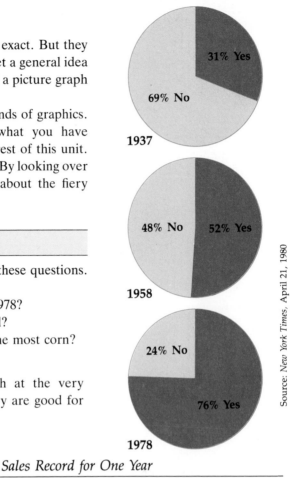

Source: *New York Times*, April 21, 1980

1937 — 31% Yes, 69% No

1958 — 52% Yes, 48% No

1978 — 76% Yes, 24% No

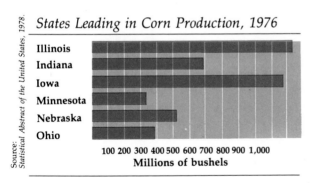

States Leading in Corn Production, 1976

Illinois, Indiana, Iowa, Minnesota, Nebraska, Ohio

100 200 300 400 500 600 700 800 900 1,000
Millions of bushels

Source: *Statistical Abstract of the United States, 1978.*

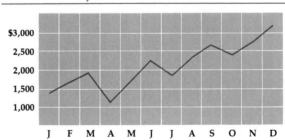

Sales Record for One Year

$3,000 / 2,500 / 2,000 / 1,500 / 1,000

J F M A M J J A S O N D

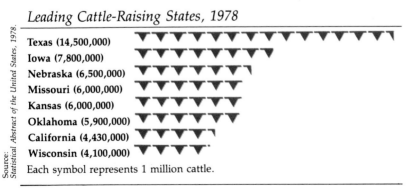

Leading Cattle-Raising States, 1978

Texas (14,500,000)
Iowa (7,800,000)
Nebraska (6,500,000)
Missouri (6,000,000)
Kansas (6,000,000)
Oklahoma (5,900,000)
California (4,430,000)
Wisconsin (4,100,000)

Each symbol represents 1 million cattle.

Source: *Statistical Abstract of the United States, 1978.*

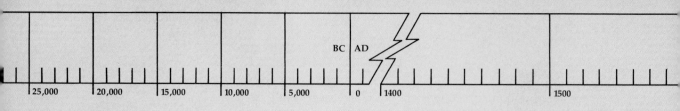

Rebellion in the Colonies

❧ Chapter 8

Vocabulary

market
manufacture
economic
territory
representative
protest
boycott
repeal
militia
independence
declaration

I N 1700 THE BRITISH COLONISTS in North America needed help to survive. They needed British tools to farm the land, British cloth to make clothing, and British ships to carry their products to market. Most of all, they needed protection from the French in Canada and in the Mississippi Valley and from the Spanish in Florida.

Britain protected the colonies, but in return it expected the colonies to remain dependent forever. The British seemed to think that the colonies had been founded only to supply the homeland with such raw materials as tobacco, lumber, and furs. Workers in Britain turned these materials into finished products that were then sold worldwide. In the British view the colonists were not to make and sell the same kinds of goods that the British did.

1   Stirrings of Discontent

The relationship between Britain and its colonies changed greatly in the years from 1700 to 1763. In 1700 only a small part of Britain's trade was with the colonies. At that time Britain made few manufactured goods. But by 1763 Britain was becoming known for its manufacturing. It was turning out large amounts of cloth, glass, furniture,

Prereading

1. What British actions between 1750 and 1770 led to stirrings of discontent among many colonists?

2. What events occurring between 1770 and 1776 deepened the coming crisis and led to war between Great Britain and the colonies?

3. How did the final break between Great Britain and the colonies occur?

Growth of Colonial Trade*

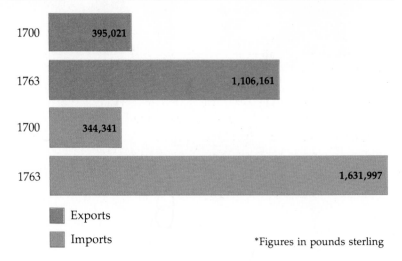

1700	395,021
1763	1,106,161
1700	344,341
1763	1,631,997

■ Exports
■ Imports

*Figures in pounds sterling

Colonists fought back when British laws and taxes threatened their growing trade with other countries.

and other household goods. Britain needed more raw materials. It also needed ever-larger markets for the goods it made. The colonies became more and more important to Britain as a marketplace for its manufactured goods.

Growth in the Colonies

As Britain came to depend more on the colonies for trade, the colonies came to depend less on Britain for survival. Their population grew from about 250,000 in 1700 to about 1,600,000 in 1763, almost half that of Britain. Philadelphia grew to about 24,000 people and became the second largest city in the British Empire. Only London was larger. With more people the colonies could grow more food and manufacture more goods. Growing economic strength and the defeat of the French in 1763 made the colonists less fearful of their powerful neighbors.

After more than a century of self-rule, the colonists knew how to govern themselves. They decided who could vote. They chose the members of the colonial assemblies and many local officials. They taxed themselves, and each colony had its own kind of local government. Many colonists, born and reared in America, became able political leaders. In population, in economic life, and in government the once-infant colonies had grown up.

Britain continued to rule the colonists as if they were powerless children. It followed old-fashioned ways of trading and governing. It questioned the colonists' right to self-government and tried to keep tight control. In 1759, for example, British leaders told the governor of Virginia that he could sign no colonial act until it had first been approved in Britain. And in 1761 the Crown gave British officials in America the right to search homes and stores for smuggled goods. In the same year, Britain declared its right to dismiss judges that the colonists in New York and New Jersey had chosen. These moves angered the colonists. But the colonists still needed Britain. So they avoided a showdown.

Disputed Claims on Western Lands

With the defeat of France in 1763 Britain won lands between the Appalachian Mountains and the Mississippi River. What should Britain do with the land? Some people wanted to start new colonies in this territory. Colonists in Pennsylvania and Virginia, which had land claims in the West, wanted to take part of the newly won lands as their own. But people in Rhode Island and Maryland, which had

King George III tried to solve the problem of disputed western lands by issuing the Proclamation of 1763.

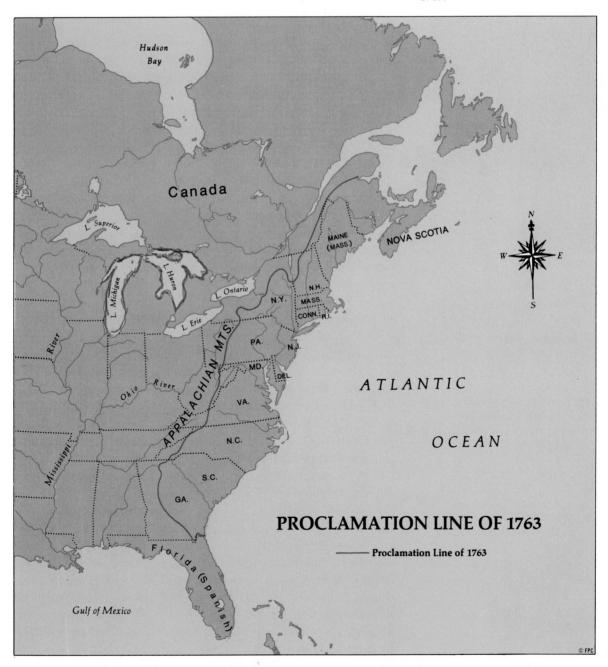

PROCLAMATION LINE OF 1763

———— Proclamation Line of 1763

no western claims, thought such a plan would be unfair. The colonists could not agree on how to divide the land. They took their dispute to King George III of Britain.

The king decided that no one would be allowed to settle in the lands west of the Appalachians. He issued this order in the Proclamation of 1763. Any answer Britain might have found would have angered some colonists. But this solution angered them all.

British Soldiers in the Colonies

The British faced another problem. How could they protect so much land from being retaken by France? The British decided to station 10,000 troops in important cities along the coast, including New York. To carry out its plans, the British Parliament passed the Quartering Act in 1765. This law forced colonists to house and feed British troops. Citizens in Britain and other parts of Europe had become used to opening their homes to soldiers. But such a practice was unknown in the colonies, and the people bitterly resented it. They also said that British soldiers were not needed along the coast. The soldiers would be too far away to defend the western lands.

When the British soldiers arrived, many New Yorkers would not have anything to do with them. The colonists made fun of the "redcoats" in their bright red uniforms who were overrunning the town. Sometimes the colonists rioted, sending the redcoats back to their forts for safety.

The New York assembly refused to obey the Quartering Act. As punishment, the British government said that the New York assembly could no longer make laws. This order took away New York's right of self-government and further angered the colonists.

The split between Britain and its colonies widened when Britain decided to tax the colonists. British leaders charged that the Great War for Empire had been fought mainly for the colonists. Britain, they said, had sent ships and soldiers at great cost to save the colonies from the French. So the British believed the colonists should help pay for the soldiers stationed in America.

The colonists took a different view. They said that the British soldiers were protecting Britain's own land and goods. They believed that Britain, not the colonies, had profited the most from the war. And they believed that Britain, not the colonies, should pay for it.

These different views raised a major question: Did Britain have the right to tax the colonies? The colonists had been taxing themselves since the earliest days of settlement. They firmly believed that Britain had no right to tax them, war or no war. There were no representatives to speak for the colonists in Parliament, where the British tax laws were made. The colonists said that "taxation without representation" was unfair.

The Sons of Liberty warned other colonists against using stamps issued by the British in 1765.

The Stamp Act

Despite colonial protest Parliament passed a tax law called the Stamp Act in 1765. Colonists had to buy stamps from the British government to use in their daily business. For example, colonists who wanted to put advertisements in the newspaper had to buy stamps from the British government to make the advertisements legal. They had to buy stamps for goods such as playing cards, for deeds to land, for school diplomas, and for court papers.

The colonists hated the Stamp Act more than any other British act. Many refused to obey it. Groups calling themselves the Sons of Liberty gathered in each colony to make certain that the Stamp Act was not obeyed. In Massachusetts the Sons of Liberty broke into the house of Lieutenant Governor Thomas Hutchinson. They caused much damage. "I had been [home] but a few minutes before the crew fell upon my house with the rage of devils," wrote Hutchinson. This hubbub even touched the daily lives of children in Boston and other towns. One person wrote that there was "no getting them kept to their set times of schooling, eating, going to bed, [and] rising in the morning." In South Carolina people ran through the streets at night with torches, looking for the hated stamps. In New York colonists laid hold of the stamps as soon as they arrived and locked them away. People in most colonies refused to use the stamps. The courts even stopped meeting so as not to use them. Ports were closed for the same reason. In Virginia, Patrick Henry publicly called anyone who obeyed the Stamp Act a traitor.

Some colonists publicly burned the British stamps in protest against the hated Stamp Act.

Colonial Protest

Colonists felt they had to join together to speak against the Stamp Act. Representatives from nine colonies attended a Stamp Act Congress in New York in October 1765. The representatives agreed that Parliament did not have the power to tax the colonists. They also agreed to refuse to buy British goods. They urged all the colonists to take part in this boycott and to dress in "decent, plain dresses made in their own country." The Congress believed that a boycott would force Britain to repeal the Stamp Act.

The Stamp Act was finally repealed in 1766. The boycott had worked. British merchants had lost much money and business. At the same time that Parliament repealed the Stamp Act, however, it said that Britain still had the right to tax its colonies.

The colonists welcomed the news of the Stamp Act repeal. Church bells rang, fireworks lighted the sky, people paraded in the streets. George Mason of Virginia told merchants in England that the colonists had grown tired of being treated like children. He no longer wished to hear the British say, "Pray be a good child . . . do what your Papa and Mama bid you . . . but if you are a naughty boy . . .

Colonial Exports, 1770

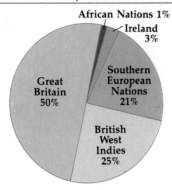

African Nations 1%
Ireland 3%
Great Britain 50%
Southern European Nations 21%
British West Indies 25%

By law the colonies were required to export most goods to Great Britain and its possessions.

Section 1 Review

1. How did the economic relationship between Britain and the colonies change between 1700 and 1763?
2. What did the Proclamation of 1763 forbid?
3. Why did the colonists feel that Britain had no right to tax them?

Critical Thinking

4. **Identifying Central Issues.** What was the major purpose of the Committees of Correspondence?

LOOKING AHEAD: What events occurring between 1770 and 1776 deepened the coming crisis and led to war between Great Britain and the colonies?

your Parents . . . will [need] to whip you severly." He warned his British friends that another tax similar to the Stamp Act "would produce a general revolt in America."

But the British did not listen to George Mason's words. In 1767, one year after repealing the Stamp Act, Parliament began taxing glass, paint, paper, and tea bought from Britain. Again colonists boycotted British goods, and again the boycott worked. In 1770 Parliament repealed all the taxes of 1767 except the one on tea. This law was kept on the books to show that Parliament still had the right to tax the colonies. But while Parliament in London was deciding to repeal most of the taxes, another conflict arose in Boston.

The Boston Massacre

In 1768 Britain had sent soldiers to Boston and New York to carry out the acts of Parliament. In both cities the soldiers drew trouble. On March 5, 1770, a big crowd of colonists gathered around several British soldiers on one of Boston's main streets. The colonists began by shouting and throwing snowballs at the redcoats. Then they attacked the soldiers, crying, "You lobster! You bloody back! You coward!" The town fire bell sounded. People streamed into the streets carrying axes, clubs, and muskets. One soldier was knocked off balance, and his gun fell to the ground. The other soldiers began to fire into the crowd. Three colonists were killed, two died later, and others were wounded. One of the dead was Crispus Attucks, an escaped black slave. A bystander claimed that Attucks had led the charge against the British.

Angry colonists called the brief but bloody fight the Boston Massacre. They tried the soldiers in court and found two of them guilty of manslaughter.

After the Boston Massacre, Samuel Adams, who was often called the "firebrand of the American Revolution," helped set up Committees of Correspondence in each colony. These groups shared news of happenings throughout the colonies. Each committee was prepared to act if the British again tried to limit colonial rights.

2 The Coming Crisis

After 1770 the only remaining British tax on the colonists was the tax on tea, the favorite drink of the time. The Committees of Correspondence tried to make certain that no one drank tea or paid the tax. Without warning, in 1773 the British passed a Tea Act. Under this act only the British could bring tea into the colonies, and only the British East India Company could sell it. The colonists realized that the British were testing to see how strongly the colonists believed in their right to tax themselves. A battle of wills had begun.

The Boston Tea Party

The colonists were quick to answer. Some British ships carrying tea were made to turn around and leave the colonies without unloading. Local leaders made other shippers store their tea in warehouses so it could not be sold. In Boston the protest was even stronger. One night in 1773 the Sons of Liberty made themselves up to look like Native Americans. Then they stole aboard a British ship and dumped its cargo of tea into the harbor. This event came to be called the Boston Tea Party. John Adams wrote: "Many Persons wish, that as many dead Carcasses were floating in the Harbour, as there are Chests of Tea. . . ."

King George and the leaders of Parliament were furious when they heard what had happened in Boston. Parliament passed four new acts in 1774. Three acts were meant to punish Massachusetts.

The first act closed the port of Boston, putting merchants, sailors, and shopkeepers out of work and keeping farmers from exporting their products. A second act took away the rights to hold town meetings, to choose certain representatives, to name judges, and to select juries, all key rights of self-government in Massachusetts. A third act allowed some officials charged with breaking the law in the colonies to be tried in Britain rather than in Massachusetts. This act went against the right of self-government in the courts. In the fourth act, the Quartering Act of 1774, the British ordered that their soldiers be given more food and supplies.

The British had expected people outside Massachusetts to take the British side. The Sons of Liberty had destroyed property. Both the British and the colonists believed that property must be protected. Most colonists, however, felt as did George Washington of Virginia. He wrote that if Britain could take away a right of self-rule in Massachusetts, it could also snuff out self-rule in Virginia.

Most Americans found Parliament's new orders too hard to bear and began to call them the Intolerable Acts. Instead of siding with Britain, the other colonies joined Massachusetts in opposing the hated acts.

The pace of the colonial revolt quickened. Parliament further angered the colonists in 1774 by passing the Quebec Act. This act gave the land west of the Appalachians and north of the Ohio River to Canada, home of the French settlers. Territory that the colonists had expected to settle was now going to their one-time enemies. To the colonists the Quebec Act seemed very unfair.

The First Continental Congress

Leaders from each colony met in Philadelphia in 1774 to decide what to do about the Intolerable Acts. They formed a group called the Continental Congress.

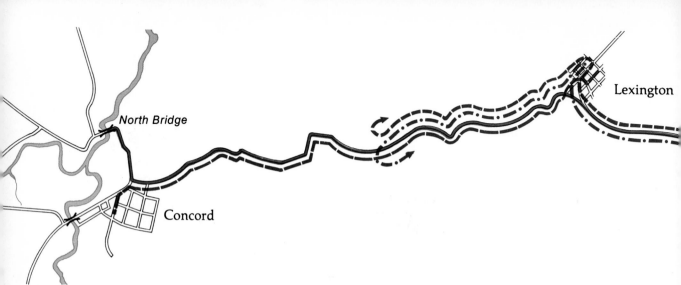

North Bridge

Concord

Lexington

The Congress agreed on several steps. First, it sent letters to King George to protest the Intolerable Acts. Second, it asked colonists again to boycott all British goods. Third, in case these peaceful means did not work, it decided that the colonies should gather supplies for war. Finally, it called for militia from all the colonies to defend colonial rights.

The leader of all British soldiers in North America was General Thomas Gage, who was stationed in Boston. Gage had lived in America for twenty years and was married to an American. He had warned the British that the colonists were gathering guns and supplies. He wrote: "If you think ten thousand men [British soldiers] enough, send twenty. If one million is thought enough, give two." A large British army, he wrote, might scare the colonists. But a "middling force" would only encourage them to fight and would "gain no friends."

Gage was ordered to attack and to capture key Massachusetts leaders, such as Samuel Adams and John Hancock. Gage called on his best soldiers. He planned a secret march to surprise the Massachusetts Sons of Liberty at Concord and take the military supplies stored there.

At ten o'clock on the night of April 18, 1775, the British troops quietly began to move out of Boston. The colonists had heard of Gage's plan and were watching. But they did not know what route the British would take. Paul Revere, a Boston silversmith, had arranged to have lanterns hung in the tower of the Old North Church in Boston. These lanterns would be seen by the colonists lying in wait outside the city. One lantern would signal that the British were traveling by land. Two lanterns would mean they were traveling by water. When Revere heard that the British were traveling on the river, he had a friend hang two lanterns in the tower. Then Revere met friends who were waiting to row him across the Charles River to Charlestown, where he would begin spreading the warning about the British attack.

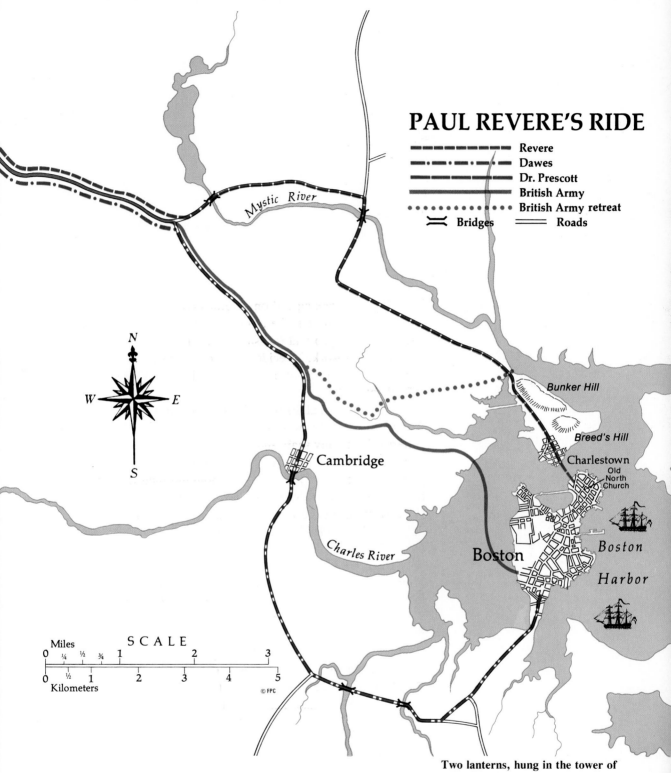

PAUL REVERE'S RIDE

— — — Revere
—·—·— Dawes
—— Dr. Prescott
—— British Army
·········· British Army retreat
)(Bridges   ═══ Roads

Mystic River

N
W *E*
S

Bunker Hill

Breed's Hill

Cambridge

Charlestown
Old
North
Church

Charles River

Boston

Boston

Harbor

SCALE

Miles
0 ¼ ½ ¾ 1   2   3
0   ½ 1   2   3   4   5
Kilometers
© FPC

Two lanterns, hung in the tower of Boston's Old North Church, told of the British approach by sea.

Revere suddenly discovered that he had forgotten to bring some cloth to muffle the creaking of the oars. So one of the men stopped at the home of a woman friend and borrowed a petticoat. The petticoat did the job. Revere was rowed across the river silently and in darkness under the guns of the British warships. More friends

Paul Revere alerted the colonists all along the 16-mile (26-km) route from Boston to Lexington.

waited on the other side with a swift horse. William Dawes joined Revere at Charlestown, and both set off for Lexington to warn colonial leaders of the British attack. The horsemen rode through the countryside crying, "The regulars are out!"

British soldiers caught Revere before he could reach Concord. Dawes escaped, but he was thrown from his horse. Another member of the Sons of Liberty, Dr. Samuel Prescott, rode on to Concord with the warning.

The British soldiers began to hear church bells rung and guns fired to warn of their attack. Lights began dancing in the dark countryside. The British knew then that the colonists had found out about their plans. They quickly sent for more soldiers.

Musket Fire at Lexington and Concord

Colonists near Lexington and Concord had gathered guns and ammunition. They had practiced marching together as soldiers. These members of the militia were called minutemen because they were ready to march at a minute's notice.

Now, warned by Revere and others, the minutemen dressed quickly and grabbed their guns. When the 700 British soldiers arrived at Lexington early on April 19, they found thirty-eight minutemen blocking their route to Concord. Someone fired a shot. In the shooting that followed the colonists got the worst of it—eight dead and ten wounded. Only one British soldier was hurt.

The British soldiers gave three cheers for their victory and marched on to Concord. But the colonists had already moved most of the weapons. The British came away empty-handed.

On the way back to Boston the British ran into a steady cross fire from hundreds of minutemen hidden behind stone fences and thick hedges. The British had more than 270 soldiers killed, wounded, or missing. Nearly 100 colonials were killed or wounded.

Most British leaders—but not General Gage—were surprised by the spirited defense of the colonists. These leaders never believed the colonists would fight. Earlier one British officer had written that at the sight of a British soldier, "the Boston voters will scamper

Patrick Henry, speaking in Williamsburg, Virginia, stirred up anti-British feelings among the colonists.

behind their counters." But he was wrong. Later General Gage wrote that, after the fighting at Lexington and Concord, "the flame blazed out in all parts at once. . . ."

The Second Continental Congress

Messengers sent by the Committees of Correspondence were soon in the saddle, carrying the news that fighting had broken out in Massachusetts. Patrick Henry made one of the most stirring speeches ever given in the English language. In March 1775 he addressed a meeting in Virginia. "If we wish to be free . . . we must fight! . . . There is no retreat but in submission and slavery! Our chains are forged. Their clanking may be heard on the plains of Boston!" His closing words have been repeated again and again. "Why stand we here idle? . . . Is life so dear, or peace so sweet, as to be purchased at the price of chains and slavery? . . . I know not what course others may take, but as for me, give me liberty, or give me death!"

Events moved swiftly. In May 1775 a Second Continental Congress met in Philadelphia. Feeling was divided. Some, echoing Patrick Henry, wanted to start an all-out fight. Others believed that colonial rights must be protected but that all fighting should end. No one as yet spoke up for independence from Britain.

3 The Final Break

The Continental Congress took steps to get more weapons. It set up a new Continental Army. It appointed George Washington of Virginia commander in chief. Washington's appointment showed how much the people valued him as a soldier. And the choice of a leader from Virginia to direct troops in Massachusetts showed that the colonies were united against Britain.

The Continental Congress feared that friends in Britain as well as future Americans might not know why they were taking such bold steps. So they wrote a long explanation of their reasons for taking up arms. They explained that they were fighting for the rights

Section 2 Review

1. In what three ways did the colonists inside and outside Boston protest the Tea Act?
2. What were the four British orders the colonists called the Intolerable Acts?
3. Why did the Quebec Act anger many colonists?
4. What four steps did the First Continental Congress take in response to the Intolerable Acts?
5. What was General Gage hoping to achieve by sending his soldiers to Concord?

Critical Thinking

6. **Identifying Assumptions.** Why were most British leaders surprised by the spirited defense of the colonists?

LOOKING AHEAD: How did the final break between Great Britain and the colonies occur?

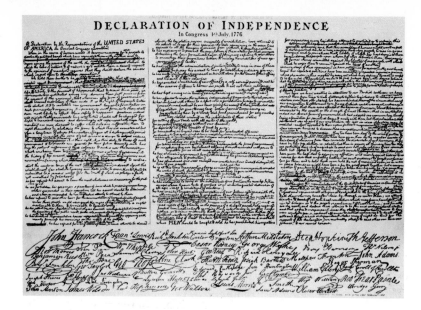

So large was John Hancock's signature on the Declaration of Independence that his name has come to mean any signature—as in "Write your John Hancock here."

of all British subjects, not just the rights of colonists. And for the first time the colonists spoke of separating from Britain. "Our cause is just. Our union is perfect." In these words the members of Congress were expressing a wish, not a fact. Their union was not perfect. Only after much debate did the colonists finally agree to fight the British and form a "more perfect union. . . ."

The Battle of Bunker Hill

Before Washington could take command of the soldiers in Massachusetts, the Battle of Bunker Hill broke out near Boston. On June 17, 1775, the British attacked colonial strongholds on Breed's Hill near the larger Bunker Hill. The first two British attacks failed. The third attack succeeded. But almost half of the British soldiers in the attacking force were killed or wounded on that hot, dry day. One British officer wrote: "A dear bought victory. Another such would have ruined us."

After the Battle of Bunker Hill, King George declared the colonies in rebellion. Then he began to hire soldiers from Hesse in Germany to fight in America. Hiring foreign soldiers was often done in Europe. The colonists, who still thought of themselves as subjects of the king, were troubled by the hiring of these outsiders. Many colonists believed King George could never again look after colonial rights.

The Declaration of Independence

In January 1776 Thomas Paine, who had been living in America for a little more than a year, printed a pamphlet called *Common Sense*. In it Paine declared that the king was a rascal who was trying to take away colonial rights. He called for separation from Britain. "The blood of the slain . . . cries, 'TIS TIME TO PART." Paine's pamphlet became a best-seller. Some colonists who were not sure what to do—even Washington—came to believe that Paine was right.

On June 7, 1776, Richard Henry Lee of Virginia brought two statements before the Continental Congress for a vote. The first called for the colonies to separate from Great Britain. The second called for Congress to form a new government, bringing the thirteen colonies into an independent union.

After almost a month of debate and by a very close vote, Congress decided that the thirteen colonies should separate from Britain. It asked five members to write a declaration of independence. Thomas Jefferson of Virginia wrote the first draft. But others helped him, especially John Adams of Massachusetts and Benjamin Franklin of Pennsylvania. Congress discussed the declaration and made many changes. It was finally accepted on July 4, 1776.

The Declaration of Independence is one of the most important papers in the history of the United States and the modern world. In only a few pages it lays out for all people the reasons why the colonies broke from Britain. The full text is on pages 730-733.

There are three parts to the declaration. The first part explains why it was written. It states that a government must be based on the consent of the governed. Only the people can decide how they are to be ruled and by whom. It also says that a government must ensure the people's right to "life, liberty, and the pursuit of happiness." The second part lists the colonists' complaints against the king and the British government. The third part says that the united colonies are free and independent of Great Britain. That statement changed the history of the world. It helped bring a new country into being, and it became a model for other countries in other parts of the world.

The colonial leaders could have declared their independence from Britain in a single sentence. Instead, they decided to tell exactly why they took such dramatic and drastic steps. They knew that revolution could lead to disunity in the colonies or even to no government at all. They had no new government to take the place of British rule. The Congress hoped that the stirring words of the declaration would unite all the colonists behind the cause of liberty.

The Declaration of Independence forced people to take a stand. Some people were for colonial rights but thought it unwise or impossible to separate from Great Britain. Others who had spoken out against the Stamp Act and other British laws finally decided to remain loyal to Britain. Families were sometimes divided in their feelings. For many, the decision to support independence or remain loyal to the Crown was heartbreaking. They knew their decision would change their lives forever.

Although the colonists had issued the Declaration of Independence, they were not yet independent. To win independence, they had to defeat the strongest nation in the world at that time—Great Britain.

Section 3 Review

1. What four steps did the Second Continental Congress take after it met in May 1775?
2. What two steps did King George III take after hearing about the Battle of Bunker Hill?
3. What pamphlet convinced many colonists that it was necessary to separate from Britain?
4. What were the two statements Richard Henry Lee brought before the Second Continental Congress for a vote?
5. What are the three parts of the Declaration of Independence?

Critical Thinking

6. **Checking Consistency.** Did the Declaration of Independence reflect the colonists' reactions to the Stamp Act and other British laws? Explain your answer.

People in the colonies, including Native Americans and blacks, had to make a difficult choice as they took sides in the conflict with Britain.

Deciding which side to take in the conflict between Britain and its colonies was hard for everyone. For Native Americans and blacks the choice was especially difficult.

Brant and the British

Joseph Brant, a Mohawk chief among the Iroquois, took the British side. Brant was born in a Mohawk outpost in Ohio in 1742. He spent his earliest years there learning to fish, hunt, trap, and swim. In time he became a strong, tall, well-built young man. Those who met him saw at once his dignity, strength, and self-confidence.

At the age of twelve Joseph met William Johnson, the British agent among the Six Nations of the Iroquois. Johnson had built a house in the Mohawk Valley of New York. He lived there with Molly Brant, Joseph's half-sister. Johnson took a special interest in Joseph's future.

A Young Soldier

When the Great War between Britain and France broke out in 1754, Brant fought for the British. Although only thirteen, he joined the Mohawk chief and William Johnson in the bloody Battle of Lake George in northern New York. The British defeated the French. Three years later Brant joined a combined British and Mohawk force to capture the French fort at Niagara in western New York.

After the war Joseph Brant went to a school for Native Americans in Lebanon, Connecticut. At school Joseph learned the English language and studied history, literature, and religion. He became a Christian, and he was taught to honor the king of England.

In May 1763 Brant received a letter from his sister ordering him home to help defend the Iroquois country from the flood of British and colonial settlers. But Brant had learned to honor the British Crown. So he decided not to fight against it.

In the showdown between the British and the colonists after 1773, Brant continued to favor the British. He was true to his schooling. But he also hoped the British would keep colonial settlers from overrunning Iroquois land.

An Honored Captain

Brant's support for the British grew stronger. In the fall of 1775 Brant sailed for England. He was received by royalty, admired by all, and showered with gifts. Artists painted his picture. Brant promised King George III he would lead 3,000 Iroquois in the fight for Britain.

As a captain in the British army, Brant fought many fierce battles in the Revolution. He was greatly admired. But the British could not defeat the colonists. Brant's dream of protecting Mohawk lands faded when the British lost the war.

When the war was over, Brant led the Mohawks to British Canada where they received a large land grant.

Brant died there in 1807. His tombstone honors "his fidelity and attachment to the British Crown."

Phillis Wheatley

In contrast to Joseph Brant, Phillis Wheatley—a black African—took

Brant stayed at the Johnson house.

People

Brant was known among the Mohawks as Thayendanegea.

Love of Freedom

The Wheatleys had treated Phillis well. But Phillis always remembered her early slave days. In one of her poems Phillis expressed her feelings about her slavery and her love of freedom.

> I, young in life, by seeming cruel fate
> Was snatched from *Afric's* fancied happy seat:
> What pangs excruciating must molest,
> What sorrows, labor in my parent's breast!
> . . . .
> Such, such my case. And can I then but pray
> Others may never feel tyrannic sway?

Late in 1775 Phillis wrote General George Washington, who had taken command of the militia at Boston. She wished him success "in the great cause you are so generously engaged in." She included a poem in which she praised him. Part of it read, "Thee, first in peace and honours . . . Fam'd for thy valour, for thy virtues more. . . ."

The later years of Phillis Wheatley's life were painful. Neither her own freedom nor the victory of the colonists could save her from hardships. Her friend and former owner John Wheatley died, her husband mistreated her, and she died in poverty in 1784.

the colonial side. As a child in 1761, she had arrived in Boston aboard a slave ship from Senegal. John Wheatley, a Boston tailor, bought her as a servant for his wife Susannah. The Wheatleys gave the eight-year-old youngster the name of Phillis.

Within a few months the family saw that Phillis learned quickly. Mrs. Wheatley and her daughter Mary taught Phillis the English language. Mary also taught Phillis geography, history, and Latin. The Wheatleys soon thought of Phillis as a daughter.

Phillis began to write poetry. Her first poem was printed in a Boston newspaper in 1770. Later the many poems she wrote were printed in a book that made her famous.

About 1773 Phillis's health began to fail. The Wheatleys sent her to England. Before she left, the Wheatleys gave Phillis her freedom. Phillis returned to Boston later that year when she learned that Mrs. Wheatley was ill. Mrs. Wheatley died in March 1774.

Wheatley was appreciated as much for her charming ways and witty conversation as for her poetry.

Chapter 8 Review

Chapter Summary

Beginning in 1763, a series of British actions —the Proclamation of 1763, the Quartering Act of 1765, and the Stamp Act of 1765— angered the American colonists. They protested in several ways including boycotting British goods. Both the Boston Massacre and the Boston Tea Party were the result of colonial protests.

When these protests were not successful, the colonists called the First Continental Congress to plan a course of action and prepare for war. The fighting began in 1775 with the battles of Lexington, Concord, and Bunker Hill. Finally on July 4, 1776, the Declaration of Independence was adopted and a new nation was born.

Reviewing Vocabulary

Match each of the following words with its correct definition. Write your answers on a separate sheet of paper.

market	boycott
manufacture	repeal
economic	militia
territory	independence
representative	declaration
protest	

1. having to do with producing, trading, and using goods and services
2. legislative action that nullifies a law
3. freedom to act on one's own
4. to make goods from raw materials
5. statement of one's position on an issue
5. citizens subject to military service
6. land which belongs to or is ruled by a government
8. refusal to do business with a company or a nation until certain conditions or practices are changed
9. a person who speaks for others
10. place where goods are bought and sold
11. a statement or a demonstration of disapproval

Understanding Main Ideas

1. What British moves between 1750 and 1770 began to cause feelings of dissatisfaction among many colonists?
2. What happened between 1770 and 1776 to increase the discontent and to cause the colonists to consider going to war against Great Britain?
3. What finally caused the colonies to break with Great Britain?
4. What did the appointment of Washington as commander in chief of the Continental Army show about the unity of the colonies against Britian?
5. What reaction did the members of Congress expect from the colonists after declaring independence?

Critical Thinking Skills

1. **Making Comparisons.** In what ways did the American colonies in 1763 differ from the way they were in 1700?
2. **Determining Relevance.** What was the relationship between the Battle of Bunker Hill and the writing of the Declaration of Independence?
3. **Formulating Questions.** If you had been King George III, what questions would you have wanted answered about conditions, attitudes, and feelings in the American colonies in 1775?
4. **Drawing Conclusions.** How did the slogan "no taxation without representation" reflect the colonists' view of the best type of government?

Social Studies Skills: Interpreting an Illustration

A historical picture can often be a valuable source of information. It can tell a great deal about when, where, and how an event took place. It may also show how the artist and the people felt at the time. Sometimes studying a picture carefully can also provide clues as to whether the picture is accurate or not.

Skill Review: Study the picture above, then answer the questions that follow.
1. What event is pictured in the drawing?
2. Do you think the artist was a colonist or British? Explain your answer.
3. Compare the picture with the information on page 165. Which details are accurate? Which are not?

Writing About History

Writing a Letter. Imagine you were a member of the Sons of Liberty who took part in the Boston Tea Party. Write a short letter to a friend in another colony describing the events of that night, the mood of the group, your thoughts, and what your actions were on board the ship.

Your Region in History

Government. Colonial Americans were angered by unfair taxation by the British. Taxation is still an issue to many American citizens. Through discussions with classmates, parents, and other members of your community, find out what local taxes affect you and your family.

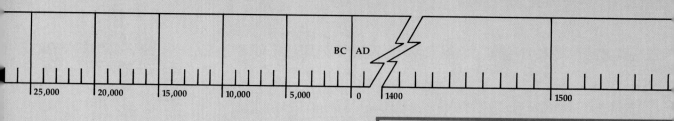

A
New
Nation

❦ **Chapter 9**

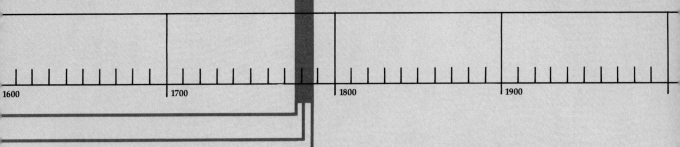

Vocabulary

constitution	executive
confederation	legislative
ratify	judicial
compromise	checks and balances
federal	amend

THE WAR BETWEEN GREAT BRITAIN and its North American colonies can be called by several different names. Each name highlights a different way of viewing the war. The name War for Independence shows the colonies fighting to separate from their parent country. The name American Revolution shows the colonists working toward a new form of government. Called a world war, the fighting in the colonies becomes part of a much larger conflict. In this conflict other European nations were trying to limit the world's most powerful nation—Great Britain.

The struggle can also be called a civil war, a war among citizens of the same country. British from the homeland fought against British in the colonies. Colonists fought against one another, sometimes against close neighbors or family members. By the end of the war, about 25,000 colonists—nearly 1 percent of all the people in the colonies—had died in battles, in camps, and as prisoners.

1 Upheaval in the Colonies

The British hoped that the colonies would be defeated by their lack of unity. As many as one third of the colonists were against independence. These Loyalists, as they called themselves, remained true to

Prereading

1. How did women, blacks and Native Americans contribute to the war efforts of both the Patriots and the British?
2. How did colonial leadership, military strategy, and French aid help the colonists defeat the British in the War for Independence?
3. What steps did the colonies take to become independent states, and what steps did the states take to form a national government?
4. How did the Constitution divide the powers of government to form a federal system?

Mary Ludwig Hays, better known as Molly Pitcher, filled in for her Patriot husband when he was hurt at the Battle of Monmouth.

the British government. Some of these people moved to Great Britain, Canada, and the West Indies. Others stayed behind. Most Loyalists who stayed behind favored the British in secret only. But some Loyalists fought openly for Great Britain.

Even families were divided by the war. Benjamin Franklin became famous as a Patriot leader. Patriots were those who supported independence. Franklin's son William, who was governor of New Jersey, became a Loyalist. Benjamin Franklin wrote: "Nothing has ever hurt me so much . . . as to find myself deserted in my old age by my only Son[.] [A]nd not only deserted, but to find him taking up Arms against me, in a Cause, wherein my good Fame, Fortune and Life were all at Stake."

Women at War

Patriot families found their home lives turned upside down by the war. Some women followed their soldier husbands to army camps. There they often cooked and mended clothes for the troops. Martha Washington left her home to be with her husband General George Washington. She was present at the siege of Boston in 1775-1776. And she lived with Washington at Valley Forge during the bitterly cold winter of 1777-1778. Later she said that she had heard both the first and the last shots of the Revolution.

When John Corbin from Virginia was killed during a battle at Fort Washington on Manhattan Island in 1776, his wife Margaret took his place in the battle line. The wounds she received left her crippled for life, and Congress gave her a pension for her bravery.

In 1776 Mrs. Mary Slocum of Pleasant Green, North Carolina, grew tired of waiting for her husband to return from battle. So one evening she rode on horseback toward the spot where she thought the battle might be. The next morning there was a burst of cannon fire. She rushed forward and came upon about twenty wounded men. She thought her husband was among them. Mrs. Slocum began to bandage the wounded with tree and bush leaves. Finally she found her husband, unhurt but "bloody as a butcher."

Both the Patriots and the British used women as spies because women were often allowed to move about freely in camp. Washington sent a young woman into Philadelphia to get news of the British. He then sent some soldiers to bring her back safely. Patriot and British soldiers spotted the woman at the same time. Swinging her onto his horse, the leader of the American group got away with the woman as pistol shots whistled past them.

Ann Bates, a one-time Philadelphia schoolteacher, spied for the British. With money they gave her she bought thread, needles, combs, and knives. As she sold these goods in Patriot army camps, she noted the number of soldiers, cannon, and horses. After the war the British rewarded her for the reports.

Women skilled in horseback riding were valued as war spies.

Black Soldiers

The first person to write about the part blacks played in the Revolution was William C. Nell, a black author. His book, printed in 1855, is called *The Colored Patriots of the American Revolution.*

Black soldiers such as Prince Estabrook and Peter Salem faced the British at Lexington. Estabrook was wounded. Salem, whose owners had freed him to fight the British, went on to fight at Concord and Bunker Hill. Among his many black fellow fighters at Bunker Hill was Salem Poor. Poor received a special award, praising him as a "brave and gallant soldier."

Some black slaves went to war with the Patriots. This painting shows a black working in the secret camp of Francis Marion, the Swamp Fox.

Despite their many brave deeds, black slaves were not allowed by law to join the Continental Army. Some officers were afraid to give slaves guns. Some believed that slave owners should be paid for their slaves. Would the Continental Army have to buy its soldiers from their owners? In October 1775 Congress passed a law keeping all blacks, slave or free, out of the army.

The British welcomed black soldiers. They even promised the slaves freedom. Some slaves took the offer and joined the British. In November 1775 the Earl of Dunmore, the Loyalist governor of Virginia, offered slaves in Virginia their freedom if they would join his army. Hundreds of slaves answered his call.

Dunmore's success caused the Patriots to change their minds about black soldiers. In January 1776 Congress passed a new law that allowed free blacks who had already been in the army to sign up again. No new black soldiers, however, were to be accepted. But the longer the fighting wore on, the more blacks the Patriot armies took in. In 1781 about one fourth of the soldiers in Washington's New York base camp were black. Blacks also served at sea.

Black soldiers were proud of their part in the Revolution. John Chavis, a free black teacher, said that when he died he wanted to be remembered by this line: "I am Black, I am a free born American and a revolutionary soldier. . . ."

Beginning in 1780 with Pennsylvania, many colonies began to free black slaves. Among these colonies were Connecticut, Rhode Island, New York, and New Jersey. However, freeing black slaves did not take hold in the colonies where most of the slaves lived—Maryland, Virginia, the Carolinas, and Georgia.

Native American Fighters

Native Americans, as well as blacks, had mixed feelings when the fighting broke out. The British and the colonists both wanted the Native Americans' lands and hunting grounds. Colonists had been streaming into the Ohio Valley to form villages and begin farming. Fear for the loss of their lands led the Delaware, Shawnee, Ottawa, Chippewa, Fox, and Miami living north of the Ohio to join the British. Most of the Iroquois nations in western New York and the Cherokee in western Carolina also became British allies. A few did not take sides or joined the colonists. The once powerful Iroquois League was split forever when its members chose different sides.

The British were never able to field a large Native American and British fighting force in the West. For this reason, the Patriots easily won the key battles in the West.

2 The War for Independence

When the fighting began, no one could foresee that the thirteen colonies would someday come together under a new government. During the war the Second Continental Congress, with representatives from each colony, served as the government.

Congress made winning the war its main goal. It raised money and war supplies. It sent people to France, Holland, Spain, and other European countries to seek aid. Some nations agreed to help the colonists. France, for example, gave aid in secret. France wanted its powerful enemy Great Britain defeated. But until France was certain the colonies had a chance to win, it did not become an open ally.

Congress also formed and guided the Continental Army. George Washington, named by Congress as commander in chief, had never led a large army. But he had shown himself to be a bold leader of militia. He often took big risks in battle, always trying to attack first. After several battles with the British, however, Washington learned to wait for the British to get tired or to make mistakes.

Section 1 Review

1. Did a Loyalist swear loyalty to the colonial cause or remain loyal to the British cause?
2. Why were women valuable to both sides as spies?
3. What prevented blacks from joining the Continental Army in great numbers?
4. Which colonies began to free black slaves starting in 1780? Which colonies did not?

Critical Thinking

5. **Recognizing Cause and Effect.** Why did the Delaware, Shawnee, Ottawa, and Miami side with the British?

LOOKING AHEAD: How did colonial leadership, military strategy, and French aid help the colonists defeat the British in the War for Independence?

Washington never forgot that he served the Continental Congress. As commander, Washington always told Congress in advance about his battle plans.

Early Battles

The army's first task under Washington was to drive the British out of Boston. In March 1776 the American troops encircled the city and began to shell the British without stopping. General William Howe, the new British leader, was forced to retreat by ship to Halifax, Canada. There Howe received more ships and soldiers. He and his troops then sailed for New York, where they expected Loyalists to join the British cause.

By April, Washington had moved his army to New York. Twice the British almost trapped Washington's army on Long Island. But the redcoats moved too slowly, and Washington's army slipped away. The British did force Washington to retreat from New York and across New Jersey to the Pennsylvania shore of the Delaware River. Many British thought the war was nearly over. General Howe settled down in New York City, leaving Hessian soldiers at Trenton, New Jersey, to watch Washington.

Washington launched a swift, unexpected attack. On Christmas night, 1776, his army crossed the ice-filled Delaware River in small boats and attacked the Hessians. The Hessians were caught by surprise. They had been celebrating Christmas and were not prepared to fight. At least 900 of them surrendered. A few escaped. Only four of Washington's soldiers were wounded, and none were killed. A week later Washington defeated a British army at Princeton, New Jersey.

These victories gave the Patriots new hope. They also gave Washington his winning plan: fall back before the larger British forces, then spring a surprise attack.

Britain's Grand Plan

In 1777, following defeats at Trenton and Princeton, the British leaders planned a way to cut off New England from the other colonies. General "Gentleman Johnny" Burgoyne (bər'goin') would march from Canada south along Lake Champlain to Albany. He would have 4,000 British, 3,000 Hessian, and 1,400 Native American troops. This army would meet British soldiers marching east from western New York and some of Howe's troops marching north from New York City.

But the grand plan failed! General Howe in New York did not follow the plan. He moved most of his troops south to attack Philadelphia. The British forces marching east from western New York took on the hard-fighting New York militia at Oriskany. Later the

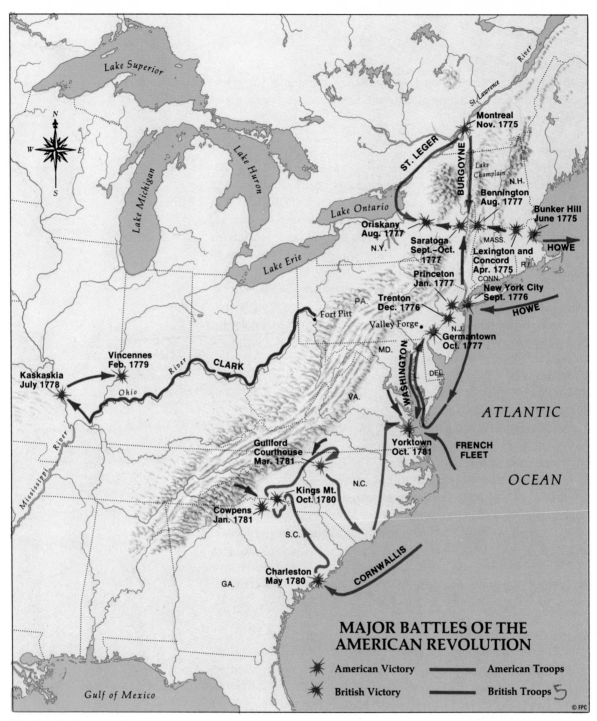

MAJOR BATTLES OF THE
AMERICAN REVOLUTION

American Victory · · · · · · · American Troops

British Victory · · · · · · · British Troops

The Revolution raged for six years—from the clashes over weapons thought to be hidden at Lexington and Concord to the surrender of Cornwallis at Yorktown.

British fled the area. Gentlemen Johnny was left to fight the Battle of Saratoga in northern New York alone. He finally surrendered his 7,000 British and Hessian troops to Patriot General Horatio Gates. The failure of the grand plan left a major Patriot army victorious in the field and ready to fight. The Battle of Saratoga was a turning point in the war.

While Gates was defeating Burgoyne, Washington was trying to keep General Howe out of Philadelphia. On September 11, 1777, the Continental Army lost the Battle of Brandywine, south of the city. Shortly after this the British took Philadelphia. Washington then ordered a surprise night attack on the British at Germantown, north of Philadelphia. The Continentals lost, but they fought well.

News of the victory at Saratoga and Washington's bold attack on Germantown made France believe the Patriots could win. In February 1778 France signed a treaty with the United States, promising soldiers, ships, and supplies to the Patriots. France had become an open ally.

The Winter at Valley Forge

After Germantown, Washington decided to make winter camp at Valley Forge about twenty miles from Philadelphia. Despite the cold, Washington used the time to mold his ragged, hungry soldiers into a skilled army. Washington never lost another battle.

In June 1778 Sir Henry Clinton, replacing General Howe, led the British troops from Philadelphia to New York City. Washington attacked them on the way, but neither side gained an advantage. The British finally holed up in New York City, never again to venture out to fight the watchful Washington.

Clashes in the West and South

Meanwhile, on July 4, 1778, Lieutenant Colonel George Rogers Clark and 200 other Americans took the British fort at Kaskaskia, a village in what is now southern Illinois. The British officer in charge gave up without firing a shot. Clark then marched on the British at Vincennes

In the winter of 1777-1778 Washington's army at Valley Forge numbered about 11,000 Washington said 2,873 of those soldiers were unfit for duty because they lacked shoes or enough clothes.

Nathanael Greene (top) led the Patriots in the Carolinas. Benedict Arnold (center) later turned traitor. German Baron Von Steuben (bottom) was with the Patriots at Monmouth and Yorktown.

French General Lafayette fought for the Patriots from Brandywine to Yorktown. Nathan Hale was hanged at twenty-one as a Patriot spy.

in what is now Indiana. He took the fort easily, but the British regained it later with help from Native Americans. In a surprise attack in February 1779, Clark again captured Vincennes—this time for good. These victories gave Americans the upper hand in the West.

While Washington kept one British army pinned down at New York City, the British sent another army under General George Cornwallis to South Carolina by sea. Cornwallis marched inland, winning several battles. But the Americans, led by General Nathanael Greene, would not give up. "We fight, get beat, rise, and fight again," said Greene. At the Battle of King's Mountain, Patriots surrounded a Loyalist army and captured or killed every person. At Cowpens, South Carolina, sharpshooter Daniel Morgan and his Patriots bested a British army of 1,000. Only a handful of British soldiers escaped.

Ethan Allen (above) captured Fort Ticonderoga. John Paul Jones (right) defeated the British ship *Serapis* at sea.

The Surrender of Cornwallis

Cornwallis still had enough troops to fight on. He marched north toward Virginia, only to be met by Patriots at Guilford Courthouse, North Carolina. There he suffered heavy losses. After securing more soldiers, he led them to Yorktown, Virginia. Before he could retreat, he was penned in from all sides.

Washington faked an attack on New York City and swiftly moved his army south to block Cornwallis's escape by land. In Virginia, Washington was joined by a French army of 5,000 led by General Jean Baptiste Rochambeau (zhän ba·tēst′ ro′sham′bō′). Admiral François de Grasse (frän′swä də gras′) had moved his French fleet from the West Indies into Chesapeake Bay. This move blocked Cornwallis's escape by sea. Cornwallis was trapped.

On October 19, 1781, at Yorktown, Cornwallis's army officially laid down their arms. Washington stood at the head of two lines, one of American soldiers and one of French soldiers. The British troops then passed in single file between the American and French soldiers to lay down their arms. As they did, the British band played "The World Turned Upside Down." The American band began to play "Yankee Doodle."

With the defeat at Yorktown the British lost the will to fight. Conflicts broke out from time to time for a year and a half more. But on September 3, 1783, Britain and the United States signed a peace treaty—the Treaty of Paris. Great Britain gave up everything in North America except Canada. The United States now stretched to the Mississippi River on the west, to Canada on the north, and to the border of Spanish Florida on the south.

Section 2 Review

1. What three things did the Continental Congress do to achieve its main goal of winning the war?
2. What was the winning strategy that Washington developed after the battles of Trenton and Princeton?
3. What effect did the Battle of Saratoga have for each of the following: the British, the Patriots, and the French?

Critical Thinking

4. **Testing Conclusions.** Is it true that without the help of the French the patriots would have lost the Battle of Yorktown?

LOOKING AHEAD: What steps did the colonies take to become independent states, and what steps did the states take to form a national government?

3 From Colonies to States: Problems of Government

After declaring independence in 1776, the colonists had to find a new form of government to replace British rule. For years the colonists had been self-governing at a local level. They knew their first step was to turn the colonies into states.

In May 1776 the Continental Congress advised each colony to form a government. Massachusetts's way of drawing up a state constitution became the one that would be followed throughout United States history. The voters of Massachusetts chose delegates to a special meeting called a constitutional convention. The convention's task was not to make laws. Its only goal was to write a constitution for the state. When the convention finished its work, the constitution was offered to the voters of Massachusetts. In 1780 the voters accepted it. By this time all thirteen colonies had become states. Each had a constitution of its own.

The Articles of Confederation

At the same time the states were writing their constitutions, the Second Continental Congress was working out a plan to unify the states. Such a union is called a confederation. A confederation allows many small governments to work toward goals shared by all. In November 1777 Congress approved the Articles of Confederation.

The Articles of Confederation divided the ruling power between the central government and the thirteen states. The Articles gave the central government power to deal with other countries, make war and peace, and issue and borrow money. The states kept the power to tax their citizens and to control their own trade. Each state had one vote in the Congress of Confederation, the lawmaking body of the new government.

The Problem of Western Lands

Before the Articles could go into effect, all thirteen states had to ratify the plan. By 1779 all states but Maryland had accepted the Articles. Maryland wanted the problem of land claims in the West settled first. Maryland had no claims in the area west of the Appalachians and east of the Mississippi. It did, however, have companies that wanted to share in the western land business.

By early 1781 some states claiming western land had agreed to turn the land over to the Confederation government. Maryland then ratified the Articles of Confederation, and the new union was official.

This step did not end the problem of the western lands. How were these lands to be divided and governed? The new national

---

Under the Articles of Confederation, Congress had the impossible task of governing and protecting the states without any way to collect taxes or raise an army.

Articles of Confederation

The Congress
of Confederation had

power to

pass laws with the consent of nine states
issue and borrow money
arbitrate differences between the states
establish weights and measures
establish a postal service
appoint military officers
declare war and make peace
establish an army and a navy
handle diplomatic affairs
handle affairs with Native Americans

no power to

enforce its own laws
collect taxes or duties
control trade between the states
raise troops
establish national courts to hear disputes between the states

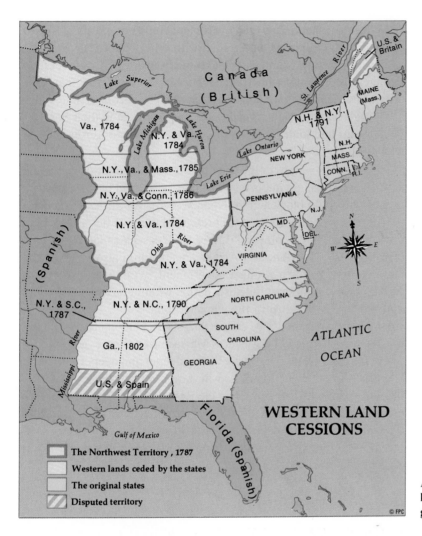

WESTERN LAND CESSIONS

The Northwest Territory , 1787
Western lands ceded by the states
The original states
Disputed territory

All states had turned over their
land claims to the United States
government by 1802.

government passed two acts. The first was the Land Ordinance of
1785. It set up a system to divide and sell lands north of the Ohio
River, east of the Mississippi, and west of the Appalachians. And the
Northwest Ordinance, passed in 1787, opened the way for new
states to be created out of the same territory. No fewer than three
and no more than five states were to be formed. Each state would
enter the Union free of slavery and with rights equal to those of the
other states.

Other Problems

Not all problems were resolved as well as those of the western lands.
For example, although the Confederation could make treaties for
foreign trade, it could not make the states obey them. Also, the
national government's only income was money it asked the states to
give. If a state refused, there was nothing the Confederation could

do. With these handicaps the government could not pay its bills. Nor could it protect citizens who traded with other countries.

Many people wanted to make the Articles of Confederation stronger. Merchants who traded between states feared that each separate state might tax the goods they shipped. Frontier states such as Georgia wanted the national government to defend their borders. People who had loaned money or goods to Congress during the war wanted to be paid back.

What was worse, every state had to vote in favor of important acts, such as a tax on imports, before the acts could become laws. A single state could block action. Noah Webster saw these weaknesses in the Articles and wrote, "Our pretended union is but a name and our confederation a cobweb." Other leaders such as George Washington, James Madison, and Alexander Hamilton also believed the new country needed a stronger government. Washington wrote to a friend: "We cannot exist long as a nation without having somewhere a power which will govern the whole union."

An uprising in 1786, called Shays's Rebellion, fed Washington's fears. Farmers in western Massachusetts were getting low prices for their crops. They were falling deeper and deeper into debt. County courts began to take away farms to pay these debts. So Daniel Shays, a former captain in the Revolutionary Army, formed a group to stop the court actions, by force if needed. The Massachusetts militia was called to arms, and Shays and his followers scattered. Washington feared that people in other states might do as Shays had done.

4 A New Constitution

In May 1787 fifty-five delegates from all the states except Rhode Island met at a convention in Philadelphia. They came together to discuss how to improve the Articles of Confederaton. The delegates soon decided improvement was not enough. A whole new constitution was needed.

The Need for Compromise

The convention met almost every day until their work ended in September 1787. So every person would feel free to speak out, the delegates decided to keep their talks secret. They planned to send the results of their work to the people of each state for approval.

The delegates disagreed on many points. Although all favored a Congress made up of representatives from all the states, delegates disagreed about how many representatives the states were to have. Delegates from such populous states such as Virginia, Massachusetts, and Pennsylvania believed that the number of representatives

Section 3 Review

1. What steps did Massachusetts take in drawing up its constitution?
2. What three powers did the central government have under the Articles of Confederation?
3. What two laws did the Confederation Congress pass to solve the problem of western lands?

Critical Thinking

4. **Identifying Central Issues.** What were two weaknesses of the central government under the Articles of Confederation?

LOOKING AHEAD: How did the Constitution divide the powers of government to form a federal system?

in Congress from each state should be based on the number of people in the state. The larger its population, the more representatives a state should have. Delegates from less populous states such as New Jersey and Delaware disagreed. They believed each state should have the same number of representatives. Otherwise the big states would outvote the small states every time.

After long debates the delegates agreed to the Great Compromise. Congress would be divided into two houses—the Senate and the House of Representatives. Each state, no matter what its population, would have two representatives in the Senate, thus pleasing the small states. In the House of Representatives states with large populations would have more representatives than would states with small populations. The large states were satisfied with this part of the compromise.

Delegates then began to debate whether slaves should be counted to determine the number of a state's representatives in the House. Delegates from the South, where most slaves lived, wanted slaves to be counted. Delegates from the North did not. Once again they compromised. Five slaves would be counted as three free people. This agreement has become known as the Three Fifths Compromise. The delegates also agreed that the importing of slaves from overseas could last until 1808.

Remembering the heavy-handed rule of George III, many delegates deeply feared giving great power to one person, the President. Some wanted the power to be shared by several people. After a long, heated debate the delegates finally agreed to give the power to one President but to give Congress and the courts the means to hold the President in check.

How to choose the President was another difficult question. Some people wanted Congress to select the President. Others thought the state legislatures should make the choice. And still others thought the voters themselves should choose. The delegates finally agreed that the people would vote for persons called electors, who would then vote for the President. If no person won a majority of electors' votes, the House of Representatives would decide.

The Federal System

After many large and small compromises, members of the convention finally agreed on the Constitution we have today. The new Constitution set up a federal system, made up of individual states and a union of states, the United States. The power given to each state and to the United States is based on the consent of the people. The people are the source of all governing power. Certain powers go to the United States—the federal government—such as issuing money and controlling trade among the states. Those powers not given to the federal government belong to the states. The people, as voters, elect others to speak for them. In this way the government is said to be representative.

The delegates to the convention decided to separate the powers of the federal government among the three branches—executive, legislative, judicial. In this way the convention hoped to make sure that no one branch of the government became too powerful.

The Legislative Branch

Congress is the national legislature under the Constitution. It makes laws. Only Congress can declare war. Only Congress can raise money to pay the costs of government. The legislature has other powers as well.

Congress is made up of the House of Representatives and the Senate. Representatives in both houses are chosen by the voters.

In addition to its own duties each branch of the government is charged with keeping the other branches from assuming too much power.

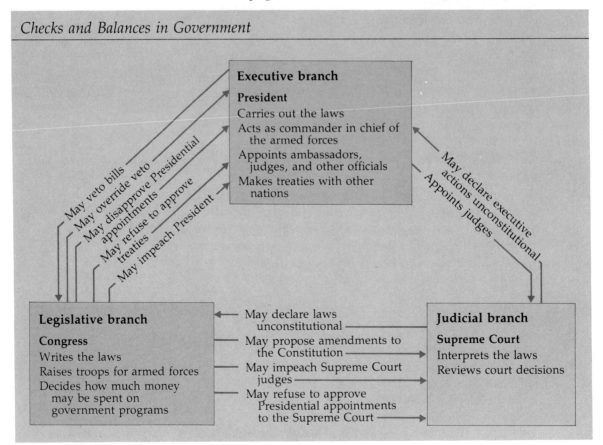

Checks and Balances in Government

Executive branch

President
Carries out the laws
Acts as commander in chief of the armed forces
Appoints ambassadors, judges, and other officials
Makes treaties with other nations

May veto bills
May override veto
May disapprove Presidential appointments
May refuse to approve treaties
May impeach President

May declare executive actions unconstitutional
Appoints judges

Legislative branch

Congress
Writes the laws
Raises troops for armed forces
Decides how much money may be spent on government programs

May declare laws unconstitutional
May propose amendments to the Constitution
May impeach Supreme Court judges
May refuse to approve Presidential appointments to the Supreme Court

Judicial branch

Supreme Court
Interprets the laws
Reviews court decisions

Representatives in the House serve two years at a time. Senators, on the other hand, serve six years.

The Executive and Judicial Branches

The President holds the executive power. The President carries out the laws that Congress makes and heads the armed forces. But the President also must obey the laws. The Senate can accept or reject the President's choices of people for different offices.

Under the Constitution there is a judicial system of national courts. The Supreme Court is the highest court in the land. Today it is composed of a chief justice and eight associate justices. The Supreme Court decides if a law is in keeping with the Constitution. The Supreme Court also rules on the meaning of a law if its wording is in question.

Checks and Balances

The separate powers of the three branches of government give each branch some check on the other two branches. For example, the President is commander in chief of the army. But this power is checked by Congress, since only Congress can fund an army. Congress can pass a bill, but the President must approve the bill before it can become a law. If the President does not approve it, Congress may still make it into law if enough lawmakers are in favor of it. In this way the legislative and executive branches check each other's power. If any one of the three branches reaches out for extra power, the other two branches can stop it. This separation and checking of powers is often called checks and balances.

The Supreme Law of the Land

The writers of the Constitution also worked out a way to carry out national laws and treaties peacefully. Under the Constitution all state courts must enforce the laws of the United States, as well as the laws of their own state. If the state and federal laws do not agree, the Constitution and the federal laws will win out. The Constitution is "the supreme law of the land."

The writers of the Constitution understood that as the country grew and changed, the Constitution might also need to be changed. They set up a way to amend the Constitution. When enough people want a change, an amendment can be added to make the Constitution meet new needs.

In six brief sections the new Constitution laid all the groundwork for the new government. The seventh section described how the new government would be approved. When nine states had ratified it, the new Constitution would go into effect. Many people were unsure that it would work.

Section 4 Review

1. What was the Great Compromise?
2. What two compromises were made to establish the office of President?
3. Into what three branches does the Constitution divide the national government?
4. How did the Convention make sure no one branch of government became too powerful?

Critical Thinking

5. **Determining Relevance.** What was the Three Fifths Compromise and how was it related to the Great Compromise?

Heritage   Of the Constitution

The Constitution is based on broad principles and is flexible enough to have lasted through two centuries.

Those who wrote the Constitution of 1787 believed that at best it would last a generation. Instead, it has become the oldest constitution in the world. The Constitution is based on ideas so broad that they apply as well today as they did in 1787.

Broad Principles

The most basic principle of the Constitution is that the people shall rule. That idea was new in 1787. Kings ruled; great families ruled; warlords ruled; generals ruled. But nowhere in the world except in the United States of America did the people rule.

A second principle is that the powers and limits of government must be described in writing. The people in the colonial age feared an *un*written constitution. Britain had such a constitution, made up of ideas and ways that had been followed for hundreds of years. But without a written constitution the British Crown could expand its powers whenever and however it saw fit.

The new United States citizens wanted what they believed and what they had learned about self-government to be set down in writing. This statement was to protect and guide future citizens of the United States.

The Principles at Work

The way the Constitution handles taxes shows both of these principles at work. Earlier the colonies and Britain had first argued and then fought over the right to tax. Without a written document there was no way to handle the problem. The two sides came to blows each time.

Americans wanted their individual rights spelled out in writing so that their new government could not take those rights away.

The Bill of Rights

1   Freedom of religion, speech, press, and peaceful assembly
    The right to ask government to correct wrongs
2   The right to keep and to carry firearms for self-protection
3   Freedom from housing and feeding soldiers in peacetime
4   Freedom from search of one's body, house, or papers by agents of the government without permission of the courts
5   The right to a grand jury hearing in cases of serious crime
    The right to be tried once, and only once, for the same crime
    The right to remain silent about the crime of which one is accused

    The right to due process of law
    The right to be paid for private property taken for public use by the government
6   The right to a fair and speedy trial
    The right to know the charges against one
    The right to face one's accusers
    The right to have witnesses and an attorney in one's defense
7   The right to a jury trial in cases involving property worth $20 or more
8   Freedom from very high bails or fines and from cruel and unusual punishments
9   All rights *not* mentioned in the Constitution retained by the people
10 All powers not given to the federal government nor forbidden to the states reserved to the states or to the people

The Pennſylvania Packet, *and Daily Advertiſer.*

[Price Four-Pence.]   W E D N E S D A Y, September 19, 1787.   [No. 2690.]

WE, the People of the United States, in order to form a more perfect Union, eſtabliſh Juſtice, inſure domeſtic Tranquility, provide for the common Defence, promote the General Welfare, and ſecure the Bleſſings of Liberty to Ourſelves and our Poſterity, do ordain and eſtabliſh this Conſtitution for the United States of America.

A R T I C L E I.

Sect. 1. ALL legiſlative powers herein granted ſhall be veſted in a Congreſs of the United States, which ſhall conſiſt of a Senate and Houſe of Repreſentatives.

Sect. 2. The Houſe of Repreſentatives ſhall be compoſed of members choſen every ſecond year by the people of the ſeveral ſtates, and the electors in each ſtate ſhall have the qualifications requiſite for electors of the moſt numerous branch of the ſtate legiſlature.

The people learned about the Constitution from their newspapers.

But under the written Constitution the right to raise taxes and decide how to use them was clearly given to the House of Representatives. If the people are unhappy with the decisions of their representatives, they can soon elect new ones. The written Constitution made taxes a matter for voters, not soldiers, to solve. With their votes the people rule.

Amendments

The amending process also shows both principles at work. Even after the Constitution was accepted in 1787, many people were concerned. They feared that the power of the federal government might be used to snuff out individual rights.

James Madison, the father of the Constitution, immediately saw the need to protect these rights in writing. So he brought before the first Congress a series of amendments. The ten amendments that were ratified became known as the Bill of Rights. They went into effect in 1791.

The amending process is one way the Constitution of 1787 has

been able to meet the changing needs of many generations of Americans. When enough people feel that the Constitution must be changed, they can add an amendment. Over the years the people of the United States have added twenty-six amendments to the Constitution.

Broad Language

Another reason the Constitution has kept pace with changing needs is that its broad language is open to changing meanings. Notice the word *people* in the first line. The Constitution begins with the words, "We the People of the United States . . ."

At the time the Constitution was written the word *people* had a narrow meaning. *People* were white males over twenty-one years of age who owned land. They were the only persons allowed by the states to vote. Women, blacks, Native Americans, and persons who did not own land were excluded. Later, in the 1820s and 1830s when most states changed their laws, white males who did not own land became *people* as well as voters.

In 1870 the Fifteenth Amendment to the Constitution gave black men the right to vote. But this right was often taken away from them by local laws and customs until the 1960s. Native Americans were not allowed to vote in all the states until 1948.

Not until 1920, when the Nineteenth Amendment to the Constitution was ratified, could women throughout the nation vote.

Since 1787, then, the definition of "We the People" has changed many times. The words of the Constitution are the same, but their meaning has changed to meet the changing beliefs of the people of the United States.

Those persons who most often redefine the Constitution are the judges in the federal courts and the Supreme Court. Each day these judges hear cases in which they must decide what is meant by certain phrases in the Constitution.

The broad ideas set forth in the Constitution and its openness to change have kept it meaningful. The wording of the Constitution allows people to work out useful solutions over changing times.

193

Chapter 9 Review

Chapter Summary

In 1781 the Continental Army, with the help of the French, forced the British to surrender at Yorktown. The War for Independence ended with the signing of the Treaty of Paris in 1783.

In the meantime, the former colonies had all become independent states. The Articles of Confederation formed a union of independent states, but lacked the power to solve national problems.

In 1787 delegates met and drew up the Constitution. This document established a federal system of government.

The Constitution was ratified in 1788. Ten amendments called the Bill of Rights were added later.

Reviewing Vocabulary

Choose the word that best completes each sentence. Write your answers on a separate sheet of paper.

1. By 1780 each of the former colonies had drawn up a (*charter/constitution*).
2. A (*confederation/constitution*) allows many small governments to work toward goals shared by all.
3. Before the Articles could go into effect, each state had to (*amend/ratify*) the plan.
4. Before the Constitution could be completed, delegates had to be willing to (*compromise/surrender*) their views on certain issues.
5. The Constitution established a (*federal/confederate*) system of government.
6. Under the Constitution, the President holds the (*legislative/executive*) power.
7. The Constitution established Congress as the (*executive/legislative*) branch of the national government.
8. The Supreme Court is part of the (*judicial/executive*) branch of the United States government.
9. The separation of powers of the three branches of government allows for a system of (*checks and balances/balanced power*).
10. The Constitution can be changed if enough people agree to (*veto/amend*) it.

Understanding Main Ideas

1. What important roles did women, blacks, and Native Americans play in the War for Independence?
2. How did colonial leaders, aid from France, and military strategy contribute to the victory of the colonists?
3. How did each of the thirteen colonies go about becoming an independent state and how did they take part in the formation of our first central government?
4. What is a federal system and how does the Constitution of the United States divide the powers of government?

Critical Thinking Skills

1. **Identifying Assumptions.** What two British beliefs influenced their military actions in 1776?
2. **Demonstrating Reasoned Judgment.** Why was it necessary for the delegates to the Constitutional Convention in May 1787 to reach a compromise on several difficult issues?
3. **Cause and Effect.** Consider the action of the Loyalist governor of Virginia, the Earl of Dunmore, in November 1775 and the length of the war. How did they influence colonial attitudes about blacks serving in the Continental Army?

Social Studies Skills: Interpreting a Map

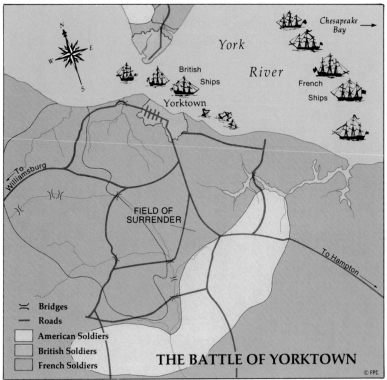

THE BATTLE OF YORKTOWN

Bridges
Roads
American Soldiers
British Soldiers
French Soldiers

A map key often is important in reading and interpreting a map.
Skill Review: Study the map and the map key. Then, answer the questions below.

1. Why were the British unable to march around the American soldiers and retreat to Hampton?
2. What country's soldiers stood in the way of a British retreat to Williamsburg?
3. Why did the British not try to cross the river and retreat northward?
4. Why was the presence and location of the French fleet so important? How did the fleet's position hurt the British?

Writing About History

1. **Rewriting History.** Write a paragraph describing the events that might have taken place in late 1781 and 1782 if the Patriots had not defeated the British at Yorktown.
2. **Writing a Report.** List the rights protected by the first eight amendments of the Bill of Rights. Write a report explaining which four rights are most important today.

Your Region in History

Government. As was agreed at the Constitutional Convention, the Constitution divides Congress into the Senate and the House of Representatives. Every state elects two senators. Who are the senators elected by your state? The number of representatives in the house depends upon the population of a state. How many representatives does your state have? Who is the member of Congress for your community?

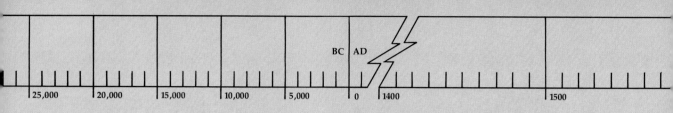

					BC	AD				
25,000	20,000	15,000	10,000	5,000	0	1400		1500		

The Constitution's First Test

❧ Chapter 10

1600   1700   1800   1900

Vocabulary

cabinet	proposal
justice	elector
tariff	candidate
excise tax	bribe
interest	platform
security	campaign

Prereading

1. What special problems did President Washington face during his first term?
2. What were the major points of Hamilton's economic program?
3. How did the views of the Federalists differ from the views of the Republicans?
4. What events made the Presidency of John Adams a stormy one?

AFTER ELEVEN STATES had approved the Constitution, the Congress called for national elections to be held in the fall of 1788. This first step in forming the government under the new Constitution was also the new government's first test.

Even in those states that had accepted the Constitution, many people were still against it. These people were called Anti-Federalists. George Washington feared that Anti-Federalists might be elected to Congress and undermine the Constitution. He wrote to a friend that people who favored the Constitution, called Federalists, must work hard to win the elections of 1788. Washington and his friends need not have worried. The supporters of the Constitution won a great victory.

1 Washington as President

As expected, George Washington was chosen President. John Adams of Massachusetts became Vice-President. At the time of his election Washington was the nation's hero. He had led his country through the dangers of the Revolution. He had presided over the Constitutional Convention. Now he was to head the government that was to make the Constitution work.

Washington as a Person

Most Americans know little about Washington as a person. They remember the painting by Gilbert Stuart that makes Washington look stern. As a young man, however, Washington was ambitious and fun-loving. He most wanted to be a large landowner. When he was sixteen, young George took a job as a surveyor of western lands rather than attend school. He wanted to learn about the lands that could be claimed and used for farming. When he was twenty, he joined the Virginia militia. He dreamed of becoming a British army officer like his brother Lawrence.

When Lawrence died, Washington became the owner of Mount Vernon, a plantation in Virginia. His landholdings grew when he married a widow, Martha Custis, who also owned a large plantation. But Washington spent little time at home. And instead of becoming a British officer, he became the only person in the eighteenth century to lead an army that soundly defeated the British.

Washington was a tall man who handled horses well. He was bold and daring, so daring that during the war he sometimes asked too much of his troops. His daring also led to some outbursts of temper, especially when others were not as brave as he was. But Washington also enjoyed parties and dancing. When he became better known, he liked the attention people gave him.

After the war Washington became the country's most honored citizen. In April 1789 he traveled from Mount Vernon to New York City to take charge of the new government. Cheering citizens went with him from town to town. At the Hudson River, which separates New Jersey from New York, he was met by a barge with thirteen oarsmen. The barge and its men stood for the Union with its thirteen states. With the barge came two boats filled with singers. As the boats approached the New York shore, thirteen cannons were fired. People on shore and on vessels in the harbor began to wave colorful flags and send out cheer after cheer. Church bells rang out. The crowd strained to see their hero. Washington was surprised and pleased. He was also fearful. He wrote, "I greatly apprehend [fear] that my countrymen will expect too much from me."

A New Course

On April 30, 1789, on the balcony of the Federal Hall in New York City, Washington swore to carry out his duties as President of the United States. He proudly wore a suit that was made in Connecticut rather than in Britain. As he read his speech, his feelings were strong. One observer wrote, "He trembled, and several times could scarce make out to read."

Washington set the course for the new government. He knew that those who were against the Constitution feared a powerful king.

On surveying trips into western Virginia young Washington bought some good land for himself.

With his hand on the Bible
Washington swore the Presidential
oath of office. Then thirteen guns
sounded a salute.

He did not want to awaken their fears. But he also knew that the country needed a strong leader. In a firm and quiet way Washington played some part in every policy made in the early years of the new government.

Washington's Cabinet

The new government began with a clean slate. There were no federal laws. No one had been given the right to speak for the United States in countries overseas. There were no government officials at home. James Madison, elected from Virginia as a member of the House of Representatives, said, "We are in a wilderness without a single footstep to guide us."

The members of the new government knew that every action they took set an example for future officeholders. Even such small matters as how to address the President had to be decided. Some people in Congress offered such titles as "His Excellency" and "His Highness, the President." Madison wisely suggested simply "Mr. President." This form of address was accepted and has been in use ever since.

A more important problem was how the President was to work with other government officials. Using the power given by the Constitution, Congress created four executive positions. The secretary of state was to handle relations with other countries. The secretary of war was to oversee military matters. The secretary of the treasury was to guide Congress in questions of money, and the attorney general was to handle matters of law.

With the approval of the Senate, Washington chose persons from different parts of the nation for these offices. He named Thomas Jefferson of Virginia, the author of the Declaration of Independence, as secretary of state. For secretary of the treasury he chose Alexander Hamilton of New York, a brilliant, colorful, ambitious man. Hamilton had served as Washington's aide during the war. The President selected General Henry Knox of Massachusetts as head of the war office. Knox's big, deep voice had guided Continental soldiers over the icy Delaware River to surprise the Hessian soldiers at Trenton. Finally Washington chose Edmund Randolph of Virginia as attorney general. Randolph had worked for approval of the Constitution in Virginia.

The Constitution did not say how these heads of departments should work with others. Some believed that the department heads should advise Congress. For example, Hamilton thought that he should appear in Congress to argue for his ideas about ways to raise money for the new nation.

The role of the heads of departments was finally decided by Washington. He needed facts and advice to make decisions. He asked his friend Madison to help him, and Madison did. The Constitution, however, states that Congress should make laws and the President should approve or reject them. As a member of the new Congress, Madison became more and more uneasy about advising the President. Washington asked advice from friends who were serving on the Supreme Court. They, too, believed it would be against the Constitution for them to advise him. Finally Washington turned to the heads of the departments. They were able and willing to advise him. Eventually they became known as his cabinet, and to this day cabinet members advise the President.

The President's Role in Treaty Making

Washington also set the course for all future treaty making. The Constitution gave the President the power to make treaties "with the advice and consent of the Senate." Washington believed these words meant that he should discuss the terms of treaties with the senators. But he soon found that this practice did not work.

In August 1789 Washington wanted to make a treaty with the Cherokee, Creek, Choctaw, and Chickasaw nations. He went to the Senate to talk about the terms. Members of the Senate greeted him warmly. But after the proposed terms of the treaty were read to them, there was a long silence. No one wanted to talk about the treaty in front of the President. Finally a senator proposed that the treaty be discussed first by a Senate committee. Angry and disappointed, the President left, saying "This defeats every purpose of my coming here."

After that, Washington decided that he or his representative would work out the terms of a treaty first. Once the terms were agreed to, he would seek the Senate's approval. All Presidents who came after him have followed Washington's example.

The Court System

The Constitution calls for a Supreme Court and a chief justice. It does not state how many justices should make up the Supreme Court. In 1789 Congress decided that the Supreme Court should have a chief justice and five other justices. The number of justices has changed over the years.

The Constitution also states that Congress may create "inferior" or lower courts. Many people believed that the existing state courts should serve as the lower courts. But many representatives in Congress had a different view. They believed the nation would be strengthened by a system of lower courts separate from the state courts. Congress, therefore, set up thirteen district courts and three circuit courts to enforce the Constitution, federal laws, and treaties. Although more district and circuit courts have been added since 1789, the federal court system has not changed. Today, as in 1789, a person breaking a federal law may be brought before a federal court to defend his or her rights. A case tried in the district court can be appealed to the circuit court. And if a federal law is in question, a case tried in the circuit court can then be appealed to the Supreme Court for a final decision.

2 Hamilton's Economic Program

The biggest problems facing the country were money problems. There were no federal taxes. The government had no money to pay its everyday expenses. To make matters worse, the new government was deeply in debt even before it started. It owed millions of dollars to its own citizens and to people in other countries. The individual states also owed money for war debts to their citizens.

Alexander Hamilton, Washington's secretary of the treasury, set about solving these problems. Hamilton believed in a strong central government. He believed that the new government needed the support of rich and powerful people. Therefore most of the financial laws Hamilton proposed to Congress favored this group.

New Tax Laws

Hamilton's first task was to find the money to pay the government's everyday costs. He supported Madison's proposal that Congress tax goods coming into the country. This kind of tax was called a tariff. Congress passed its first tariff in 1789. For more than a century tariffs were to be the main source of income for the federal government. To collect the tariff, Hamilton appointed 1,000 officials, making the treasury the largest department in the federal government.

In 1791 Hamilton proposed and Congress passed an excise tax on whiskey. Unlike a tariff, an excise tax is only for goods made in

Section 1 Review

1. What was Washington like as a person?
2. Who were Washington's first four cabinet members, and what departments did they head?

Critical Thinking

3. **Distinguishing Fact from Opinion.** James Madison said of the new government, "We are in a wilderness without a single footstep to guide us." Do you think this was a fact or simply an opinion? Explain your answer.

LOOKING AHEAD: What were the major points of Hamilton's economic program?

The Franklin penny—first coin minted by the United States—is also called the Fugio cent.

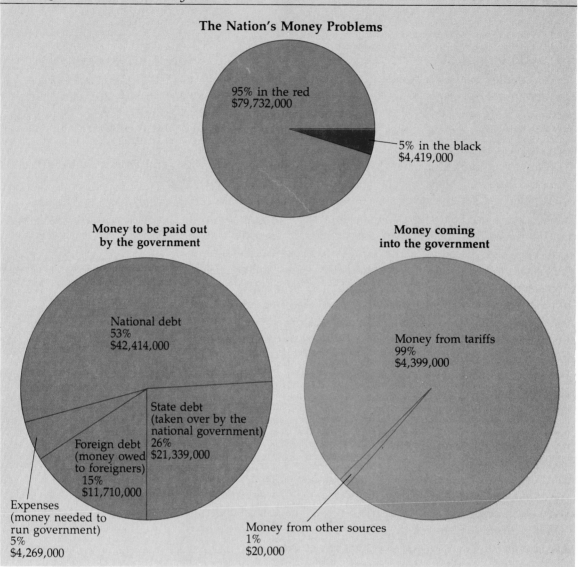

The Nation's Money Problems

95% in the red
$79,732,000

5% in the black
$4,419,000

Money to be paid out by the government

National debt
53%
$42,414,000

State debt
(taken over by the
national government)
26%
$21,339,000

Foreign debt
(money owed
to foreigners)
15%
$11,710,000

Expenses
(money needed to
run government)
5%
$4,269,000

Money coming into the government

Money from tariffs
99%
$4,399,000

Money from other sources
1%
$20,000

The young government needed great sums of money to pay its bills.

the home country. For farmers west of the Appalachians whiskey was a major source of income. They made whiskey from the corn they grew because whiskey was easier to ship than corn.

The whiskey tax raised money to pay the country's debts. Hamilton thought that the excise tax also showed westerners the power of the federal government. Hamilton wanted westerners to know that even though they lived far from the capital they could not get around federal laws.

Repayment of Debts

The new government started life with a huge debt. Most of it was left over from the Revolution. During the war, rich business leaders had loaned money to the government. In return they received notes

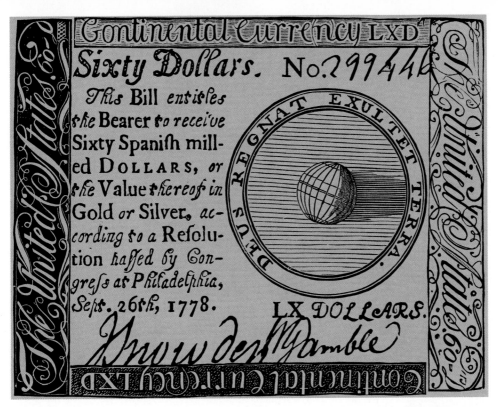

Though never worth as much as the amount shown on its face, a continental paper bill was considered worthless by war's end.

that promised repayment of the money with interest. Interest is the extra money paid as a fee for the use of loaned money. Farmers had given food, horses, and other supplies to soldiers. They, too, had received notes promising repayment by the Continental Congress. Soldiers also had been paid in notes rather than money.

As the war debts built up, many people began to doubt that the government would be able to pay back all that it had borrowed. Rather than risk getting no money, many people sold their notes to others for whatever prices they could get. Notes worth hundreds of dollars were selling for only a few dollars. People with enough money were willing to buy these notes at a low price. If the government failed to repay, the people who bought would lose only the low price of the note. But if the government did repay, they would get much more money than they had paid for the notes. By 1789, then, rich buyers owned most of the government notes.

Hamilton used the problem of repaying the money borrowed during the war as a way to win the support of wealthy trade and business groups. He proposed that the federal government pay back all the notes plus the interest with a new kind of note—a government security. Federal securities could be exchanged for gold or silver. These precious metals in turn, could be exchanged for federal securities. Hamilton also thought that money owed to people in other countries should be paid back on a regular schedule at the full value of the loan.

Many people, including many members of Congress, strongly disapproved of Hamilton's proposal. They said the money to repay the notes would have to come from taxes. Why should everyone be taxed to repay the wealthy at the full price of the notes? Why not pay back the notes at the low price?

While Congress debated this issue, Hamilton proposed another idea. He thought that the federal government should repay the money borrowed by the individual states during the Revolution. Hamilton believed this action would strengthen the ties between the national government and those people who had money to lend.

Some states, such as Virginia, had already repaid the borrowed money. Others, such as Massachusetts, had not. Madison of Virginia and some other members of Congress were strongly against Hamilton's plan. To get his proposals adopted, Hamilton made a bargain. If members of Congress from Virginia and other southern states would vote for his proposals, then he would favor a southern location for the capital of the United States. Congress adopted Hamilton's proposals. Washington, D.C., once a part of Maryland and Virginia, became the nation's capital.

A National Bank

Hamilton also proposed a national bank. The government would deposit its money and securities in this bank. The bank would also make money available for the use of business and merchant groups. It would print money, make loans, and pay dividends to those who bought stock in the bank. The government would put up $2 million of the $10 million needed to set up the bank. It would therefore own one fifth of the bank's stock and would share in its profits.

Many people feared that a national bank would put too much power in the hands of a few people. In Congress a representative from Georgia claimed that the bank would benefit northern merchants only, not small farmers or even large planters. A representative from Massachusetts replied that the bank was needed to strengthen trade and industry.

The main issue, however, was whether the bank was constitutional. Jefferson and Madison argued that the Constitution had not given the government the power to create a national bank. Hamilton replied that the government was allowed to issue money and to carry out money operations. As long as the Constitution did not forbid a national bank, said Hamilton, the government could create one.

President Washington was uncertain about forming a national bank. He finally sided with Hamilton and signed the bill in 1791. The Bank of the United States became an instant success with investors in the United States and with nations abroad. As a result, the value of federal securities was assured. People were willing to lend money to the government because they believed the government would pay them back.

Section 2 Review

1. What three major problems faced Hamilton when he took office?
2. What group did most of Hamilton's financial laws favor?
3. What two taxes did Hamilton propose to raise money for the government?
4. What is interest?
5. With what did Hamilton plan to repay government debts?

Critical Thinking

6. **Identifying Assumptions.** Why did some people fear a national bank?

LOOKING AHEAD: How did the views of the Federalists differ from the views of the Republicans?

3 The Rise of National Political Parties

The writers of the Constitution had not expected that national parties would develop. President Washington feared that political parties would weaken national unity. Instead, national political parties have helped keep the country together. Through political parties different views can be expressed and compromises can be worked out. For most of the nation's history there have been two major parties.

In Washington's day, the two parties were the Federalists and the Anti-Federalists. The Federalists were led by Washington, Hamilton, and Vice-President John Adams. The Anti-Federalists were led by Jefferson and Madison. The Anti-Federalists soon became known as Democratic-Republicans. By 1796 they were called Republicans.

Federalists and Republicans

The Federalists strongly supported the Constitution and President Washington. They feared disunity and weakness in the country. They believed that the national government should be stronger than the state governments. Most important, they were convinced that the leaders of the country should come from the better-educated, richer upper classes. Federalist laws tended to favor merchants, bankers, and other business owners.

The Anti-Federalists, or Republicans, also admired the Constitution. But they feared that the national government might become too powerful and state governments too weak. Most actions, they thought, should be taken by state governments rather than by the federal government. The Republicans won the support of those who were close to the soil—the southern planters and the small northern farmers. Jefferson wrote, "Those who labor in the earth are the chosen people of God."

The Whiskey Rebellion

The division between the two parties widened in 1794 with the Whiskey Rebellion. Farmers in western Pennsylvania could not sell the whiskey they made from their grain at a profit. It cost them more to make and ship the whiskey than people could afford to pay for it. Hamilton's whiskey tax of 1791 had added to the cost. Many farmers had refused to pay the tax.

To protest the whiskey tax, the small farmers in western Pennsylvania threatened to force local tax officials to give up their offices. They also made plans to march on Congress to force it to end the whiskey tax.

Washington, urged on by Hamilton, called up the militia in Pennsylvania and its surrounding states. An army of 13,000 men, larger than the armies in most Revolutionary War battles, gathered

Development of Two Political Parties

	Jefferson	Hamilton
1790		Federalists
1792	Anti-Federalists	
1796	Republicans	
1825	Democrats	National Republicans
1834		Whigs
1854		Republicans
Today	Democrats	Republicans

Almost from the start two political parties played major parts in the nation's government.

During the Whiskey Rebellion of 1794 government tax agents were sometimes smeared with tar, covered with feathers, and run out of town.

to put down the revolt. Washington and Hamilton themselves led the army. Before a showdown came, the farmers scattered. There was no shooting. But the nation was shaken. Because the farmers supported Republican candidates, Hamilton and Washington blamed the Republicans for stirring up trouble among the farmers. Jefferson blamed Hamilton's unfair tax.

Revolution and War in Europe

An even more serious conflict between the parties arose over foreign affairs—those issues that involved the relation of the United States to other countries. The Federalists believed in keeping close ties with the British. The Republicans held that the United States needed close ties with France.

In 1789 France was swept by its own revolution of the people against the king and the powerful nobles. France declared itself a republic in 1792 as a first step in providing equal rights for all classes of French citizens. Then war broke out in Europe. France battled against Holland, Austria, Spain, and Great Britain.

France asked the United States to honor the Treaty of Alliance it had made in 1778. The treaty stated that the United States would help France defend its territory in the West Indies. President Washington believed that the nation was not strong enough to go to war over troubles in Europe. In 1793 he issued a Proclamation of Neutrality. In it he stated that the United States would not take sides but would keep friendly ties with both France and Great Britain.

Even after the Proclamation of Neutrality, the war between France and Britain raised problems for Americans. The British, eager to stop trade between the United States and France, began seizing American merchant ships. They also removed some American sailors from the ships, claiming they were really British citizens. By December 1793, British ships of war had taken at least 250 unarmed United States trading ships, mostly in the West Indies.

Jay's Treaty of 1794

Washington believed it was time to answer these British actions. He sent John Jay, chief justice of the Supreme Court, to Britain to make a treaty. Jay was to get the British to stop taking American ships and sailors. He was also to try to open trade again with British colonies in the West Indies. His third goal was to settle the dispute over British forts in western territory.

Because Hamilton firmly believed in keeping close ties with Britain, he secretly told the British what Jay would offer. He also told them that Jay was easily swayed by praise. Perhaps because of Hamilton's warnings, Jay had a difficult time bargaining with the British. They finally agreed to give the United States just a few trade openings in the British West Indies.

Disappointed, President Washington first thought of giving up on the treaty. But finally he sent it to the Senate for approval. A bitter debate followed. Using a pen name in place of his own name, Hamilton wrote newspaper articles in favor of the treaty. Madison, also using a pen name, wrote against it. In a close vote the Senate finally accepted the Jay Treaty in 1795.

But the Jay question split the Federalists and Republicans even more. In South Carolina a dummy made to look like Jay was carried around in a cart of manure and ridiculed. Feeling ran so high that one person who was against the treaty scrawled angry words on the house of a neighbor who favored the treaty.

4   John Adams's Stormy Presidency

By 1796 Washington had served two terms as President. Some friends wanted him to run again. He refused. He believed he had already made the new government work. He also longed to return to Mount Vernon. Today, Washington is correctly rated as a wise leader and a strong President.

With Washington out of the running, Vice-President John Adams, a Federalist, was made President by a close vote. Thomas Jefferson, a Republican, was chosen Vice-President.

Before 1804 it was possible to have a President from one party and a Vice-President from another. Under the Constitution people in

Section 3 Review

1. Did the Federalists or the Republicans feel that government actions should favor farming interests over business interests?
2. Which political party favored close ties with France rather than close ties with Britain?
3. Why did Washington issue the Proclamation of Neutrality in 1793?
4. What issue in 1794 widened the split between the Federalists and the Republicans?

Critical Thinking

5. **Recognizing Ideologies.** Did the Federalists or the Republicans believe that the central government should have more power than the states?

LOOKING AHEAD: What events made the Presidency of John Adams a stormy one?

Election of 1796

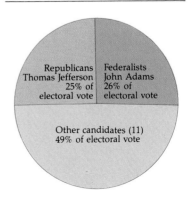

Republicans
Thomas Jefferson
25% of
electoral vote

Federalists
John Adams
26% of
electoral vote

Other candidates (11)
49% of electoral vote

each state were to vote for a certain number of persons called electors. These electors would cast a single ballot with two names on it.
Each name counted as one vote. The candidate getting the most
electoral votes became President. The candidate getting the second
highest number of electoral votes became Vice-President. In 1796
this method gave the country Adams and Jefferson, a President and
a Vice-President who had sharply differing views.

Trouble with France

President Adams faced a difficult four years in office. His biggest
problem was with France. The French became angry because the
United States was trading with Britain again. They said they would
seize American ships if they found even so much as a British-made
handkerchief on board.

Adams sent three representatives to France to settle the differences between the two nations. When the Americans arrived, three
French officials told them that talks could not begin until they paid a
bribe of $250,000. The Americans refused. President Adams told the
whole story to the newspapers. Instead of giving the real names of
the three French officials, Adams called them only *X, Y,* and *Z.*

The *XYZ* story shocked the country. Newspapers reported that
the United States delegates had said, "Millions for defense, and not
one cent for tribute [bribes]." The *XYZ* affair made Adams popular,
and Americans rallied behind their leader. The United States prepared for a possible war with France. Even children began to talk of
fighting the French.

Federalists used the troubles with France to pass a number of
laws in 1798. The Federalists hoped the laws would make their own
party stronger.

The Sedition Act was the harshest. It stated that anyone who
spoke against the President or members of Congress could be fined
or jailed. This act was passed to halt all criticism of the Federalists,
especially by Republicans. The law also went against the rights of
citizens to free speech and a free press, rights protected by the Constitution. At least three editors of Republican newspapers were sent
to prison.

Another law was called the Naturalization Act. It raised from
five to fourteen the number of years a person had to live in the
United States before becoming a citizen. Most immigrant citizens
joined the Republican party. Federalists hoped the law would keep
the Republican party from gaining new members. Under another
law, the Alien Act, the President could order noncitizens to leave the
country. This last law was not often used.

Republicans believed the Alien and Sedition Acts were unconstitutional. Vice-President Jefferson wrote a document to be voted on

by the Kentucky legislature, where there were more Republicans than Federalists. The paper stated that the Alien and Sedition Acts were unconstitutional and could not be enforced in Kentucky. Madison wrote a similar paper that was passed by the Virginia legislature. Both legislatures called on other states to find the Alien and Sedition Acts "void and of no force." Madison and Jefferson believed that states, acting together, had the right to overrule federal laws.

President Adams tried to stay out of the fight over the Alien and Sedition Acts. He believed that it was more important to keep peace with other nations. In 1800 he again sent representatives to France. This time the United States and France reached an agreement on trade.

The Election of 1800

Adams had kept the country out of war with France and decided to run for President a second time. But he and the Federalists had lost favor. The party itself was badly divided. Hamilton thought Adams was wrong to make peace with France. The weakened Federalists were torn between Hamilton and Adams.

The Republicans, on the other hand, had gained in public favor. Their candidate, Vice-President Jefferson, had led the Republicans in their fight against the Alien and Sedition Acts. The Republicans gained followers with their cry for freedom of speech. Jefferson's victory seemed certain.

On election day the electors followed the directions set down in the Constitution. Each elector wrote two names on a single piece of paper. Republicans wrote Jefferson's name first. They wrote Aaron Burr's name second. They expected Jefferson to be named President and Burr to be named Vice-President. But when the votes from all the states were counted, Aaron Burr had received as many votes as Jefferson. The election was a tie.

The Constitution requires the votes to be settled in the House of Representatives. Some Federalist representatives wanted to vote for Burr just to embarrass Jefferson. But Hamilton talked the Federalists into voting for Jefferson, whom he trusted far more than Burr. Jefferson finally became President, and Aaron Burr became Vice-President. Before the next election the Twelfth Amendment was added to the Constitution. This amendment states that electors must cast separate votes for the offices of President and Vice-President.

With the election of Jefferson a new party took charge of the government. It was the first change of parties in the country's history. No one could tell what might happen next. Would the Republicans build on what the Federalists had done? Or would they change everything? Some citizens of the new nation wondered if there was to be another revolution.

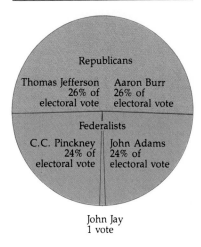

Election of 1800

Republicans

Thomas Jefferson
26% of
electoral vote

Aaron Burr
26% of
electoral vote

Federalists

C.C. Pinckney
24% of
electoral vote

John Adams
24% of
electoral vote

John Jay
1 vote

Section 4 Review

1. Who were X, Y, and Z?
2. What law stated that anyone who spoke against the President or members of Congress could be fined or jailed?
3. What did Jefferson and Madison ask the Kentucky and Virginia legislatures to do after Congress passed the Alien and Sedition Acts?
4. According to the Constitution, what group breaks a tie vote for President?
5. How did the Twelfth Amendment change electoral voting for President and Vice-President?

Critical Thinking

6. **Recognizing Cause and Effect.** Why did the French threaten to seize American ships?

Heritage   Of Political Parties

Political parties offer a means for expressing viewpoints, reaching compromises, and organizing election campaigns.

Political parties began in the 1790s when Hamilton and Jefferson, as members of Washington's cabinet, differed on major issues. President Washington—never a party member—feared the rise of parties. He believed they would destroy the Union. Washington's fears were needless.

Different Points of View

The right of citizens to hold different views on a matter lies at the heart of democracy. Political parties help people voice their differences. There have been at least two major parties through most of the country's history. So there have been at least two sets of views on major questions during that time.

Americans have proved over the years that party differences have made the Union stronger. At the same time, each party depends on a sharing of views. The more members sharing the same views, the stronger the party becomes. The shared opinions within a party have come to be called the party's platform.

Nominating Conventions

From the time of Jefferson's election in 1800 political parties have played a major part in naming candidates for major offices, especially for President of the United States. In the earliest Presidential elections party leaders held secret meetings to settle on a party choice for this high office. Only a few people took part in these meetings. Today the parties choose candidates at national conventions attended by hundreds of people. At these meetings almost everything is reported on television and radio and in the newspapers.

In some states, those who will vote at the national convention are chosen at a state convention. In other states, delegates are chosen at a meeting called a caucus. In still other states, delegates are selected at a separate election called a primary.

The Roll Call

Each party holds its national convention the summer before the Presidential election. Each gathering stirs up excitement and party feeling. Radio, television, and newspapers around the world send people to report on the doings of the delegates. Party members air their views and finally agree on what they want their party to stand for. So the delegates first spend some time drawing up the party platform. Then they open the meeting to nominations.

Often many people are named by the delegates, who make speech after speech. Then the nominations end, and the voting begins as the clerk calls the roll of the states. In some years everyone knows who the party's choice will be. In other years there is a great contest for the party's nomination. Then the people vote many times before settling on one person.

Finally the party members must select their nominee's running mate—a candidate for Vice-President. Most often the party's Presidential nominee chooses the

---

The Federalist vs. Republican Platform

Issue	Federalists	Republicans
1. Should the federal government repay the states' debts?	yes	no
2. Should a national bank be created and continued?	yes	no
3. Should there be a whiskey tax?	yes	no
4. Should there be support for Britain, France, or neither in European affairs?	Britain	France
5. Should the federal government be stronger than the state governments?	yes	no
6. Should the Alien and Sedition Acts be supported?	yes	no

These were the issues and answers in the election of 1800.

second person on the ticket, and party members agree with the choice. In a few cases the party nominee has allowed the delegates to make a choice of their own. When this has happened, nominating and voting take place just as they do in the naming of a Presidential candidate.

The Campaign Effort

After the conventions end, each party starts its biggest job—winning the election. Campaign workers in every state begin knocking on doors and meeting the people face to face. Some make phone calls to get out the vote. Others stuff envelopes and do anything else that will help the party get the people interested in voting for their candidate.

After election day—the first Tuesday after the first Monday in November every fourth year—the work of each party changes. The party whose candidate has lost does not drop out of sight for the next four years. Its leaders must speak for the party on major questions. Party members must make the people of the United States aware that there is more than one view on any issue. They must offer voters a choice.

In 1800 Thomas Jefferson stood for everything Republicans wanted in a leader and in their platform.

Television coverage of political campaigns and political cartoons about candidates and campaign issues often influence voters' choices.

Chapter 10 Review

Chapter Summary

President Washington appointed Thomas Jefferson as secretary of state, Alexander Hamilton as secretary of the treasury, General Henry Knox as secretary of war, and Edmund Randolph as attorney general. They became known as Washington's cabinet.

Hamilton and Jefferson later became leaders of the nation's first two political parties. Hamilton became a leader of the Federalists, a group that believed in a strong central government. Thomas Jefferson became a leader of the Anti-Federalists or Republican party. Republicans favored more power for the states and less power for the federal government.

In 1796, John Adams, a Federalist, was elected President. During his term in office, public demand for a war against France grew. President Adams's efforts to keep the peace and the passage of the Alien and Sedition Acts angered many Americans. In 1800, he was defeated in his bid for reelection by Republican Thomas Jefferson.

Reviewing Vocabulary

Use the following words to complete the sentences below. Write your answers on a separate sheet of paper.

cabinet
justice
tariff
excise tax
interest
security

proposal
elector
candidate
bribe
platform
campaign

1. Hamilton's _____ for both a(_____ to raise money called _____ and a(n) _____
2. President W_____ became known's advisers later _____

3. At a national convention, the _____ _____ is drawn up, a(n) _____ _____ is chosen, and the election _____, begins.
4. The XYZ affair arose when a _____ _____ was demanded from American representatives.
5. Money lent to the government was _____ repaid with extra money, called _____.
6. A(n) _____ is the person who actually casts a vote for the President.
7. Hamilton's _____ to pay back money with a government _____ met with opposition.
8. The Constitution calls for a Supreme Court and a chief _____.

Understanding Main Ideas

1. During his first term in office, what special problems had to be solved by President Washington?
2. Secretary Hamilton's economic program met with opposition from Congress over what three major points?
3. In what way did the Republicans and the Federalists differ regarding the nature of the government and those who should be favored by the government's policies?
4. President Adams's term was troubled by what events?
5. After the tie in the election of 1800, which house of Congress decided who would be President?

Critical Thinking Skills

1. **Predicting Consequences.** How might the nature of our national government have been different if George Washington had not been our first President?
2. **Recognizing Ideologies.** In what way did Secretary Hamilton's argument for the

Social Studies Skills: Interpreting a Flow Chart

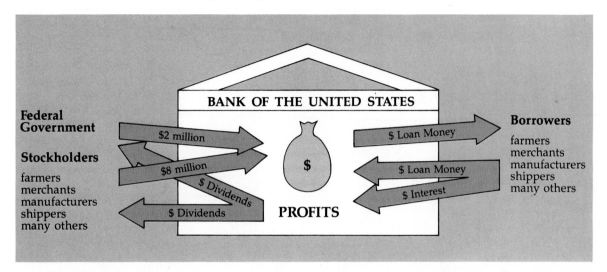

Study the flow chart above. The chart shows how the Bank of the United States, the national bank proposed by Alexander Hamilton, served the banking needs of individuals and the government.

Skill Review: After you have studied the chart, choose the correct ending to the statements below.

1. When the bank made a profit, stockholders received (a) interest (b) dividends.

2. The largest amount of money invested in the Bank of the United States came from (a) the United States government (b) individual stockholders.

3. Borrowers repaid their loans by paying (a) only the amount of money they borrowed (b) the amount of the loan plus interest.

4. When the bank made a profit it shared the profit with the United States government and (a) borrowers (b) other stockholders.

---

establishment of a national bank reflect his view of government?

3. **Testing Conclusions.** Is it true that the Twelfth Amendment has prevented disunity in our national government? Explain.

4. **Identifying Central Issues.** How did the Whiskey Rebellion reflect differences in American society?

Writing About History

Writing a Biography. Write a brief biographical sketch of George Washington. Include information about his youth, his life before the War for Independence, his military career, and his presidency. Conclude with your opinion of George Washington.

Your Region in History

Government. Today, as in 1789, the federal court system has district courts and circuit courts. Find out which federal court district your community is in. Who are the federal judges in your region?

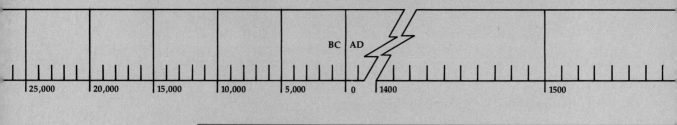

Republicans in Power

❧ Chapter 11

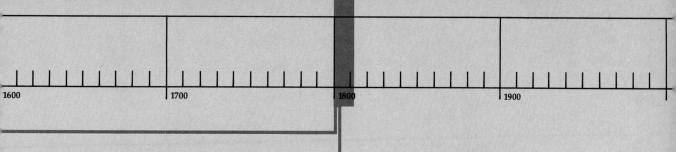

Vocabulary

disaster
inauguration
foreign affairs
stronghold
treason
neutral
foreign policy
blockade
impress
embargo
secession

THE FEDERALISTS believed the Republican victory in the election of 1800 was a disaster for the country. Republicans, said one Federalist newspaper, were "the worthless, the dishonest, . . . the vile, the merciless, and the ungodly." A Federalist clergyman of Connecticut said that the United States would now be "governed by blockheads." A New England woman wrote to a friend that she would rather see a cow in the White House than a member of the Republican party.

The Republicans, on the other hand, believed their victory had saved the nation from disaster. The Federalists, they felt, had stretched the Constitution beyond its limits. Thomas Jefferson spoke for the Republicans. He compared the government to a ship and said the Federalists had steered "with a view to sink her." Jefferson promised, "We shall put her on her republican tack, and she will show by the beauty of her motion the skill of her builders."

Prereading

1. Why was *Marbury* v. *Madison* such an important part of party changeover?
2. How did Europe's changing conditions lead to the sale of the Louisiana Territory?
3. How did the United States respond to the violations of its neutrality during Jefferson's administration?
4. Considering the results of the War of 1812, how do you think the War Hawks felt when the war ended?

215

1 Party Changeover

When it came time to swear in the new President, Jefferson offered a contrast to the formal fashions set by the Federalists. He refused to ride in a fancy carriage. Instead, he walked from his rooming house to the Capitol to take the oath of office.

Two political enemies joined Jefferson at his inauguration. Vice-President Aaron Burr sat on one side of Jefferson. His scheming would stir up trouble for Jefferson and the nation. Chief Justice John Marshall, a strong Federalist, sat on the other side. Under Marshall the Supreme Court would take a powerful part in interpreting the law of the land.

John Adams, the man whose place Jefferson was taking, was missing from the platform. Adams had left for his Massachusetts home because he was bitter about his defeat. His absence reminded Jefferson of his first task—to quiet Federalist fears about the change in parties.

Republican Guidelines

In his speech Jefferson asked everyone to forget the harsh words said during the campaign. He told the crowd: "We are all Republicans, we are all Federalists." He asked that states' rights be protected, calling state governments the best safeguard of people's liberties. He wanted a strong national economy, based on farming and aided by trade. In foreign affairs Jefferson asked for peace and friendship with all nations, but ties with none.

It was what Jefferson did, more than what he said, that helped calm Federalist fears. For example, Republicans under Jefferson kept the Bank of the United States. They followed through on Federalist plans to pay the debts of the American Revolution. Republicans under Jefferson quickly repealed the hated tax on whiskey. But they brought it back just as quickly when it was needed to meet the high costs of government. In foreign affairs the United States continued to struggle for its rights against a Europe torn by war.

Republican Appointments

The Republican victory in 1800 marked the first change in political parties in the national government. To make the party changeover, Jefferson named people to office who held Republican views. He chose James Madison as secretary of state; Albert Gallatin, secretary of the treasury; Robert Smith, secretary of the navy; Henry Dearborn, secretary of war, and Levi Lincoln, attorney general. Jefferson hoped that the choices of Dearborn and Lincoln from Massachusetts would win him favor in New England, a Federalist stronghold. Jefferson also replaced Federalists with Republicans in other offices.

Chief Justice John Marshall guided the Supreme Court as it defined, case by case, what the law of the new land meant.

Republicans, the Judiciary, and John Marshall

By July 1803 only 130 out of 416 offices in the national government were held by Federalists. Most of the Federalists still in office were judges in the federal courts. Jefferson could not fill these offices with Republicans because judges in the federal courts are chosen for life or for a set number of years. He complained that the Federalists, having lost the election of 1800, had "retired into the judiciary as a stronghold."

Jefferson's complaint was directed against the Judiciary Act of 1801. One part of this act, passed just before Adams left office, created forty-two federal judicial offices. President Adams had quickly appointed loyal Federalists to the new posts. The Republican newspapers, angry about what the Federalists had done, called the new judges "midnight judges." The newspapers claimed—incorrectly—that Adams had stayed up half the night on his last day as President to sign the new judges' papers.

William Marbury was one of these "midnight judges." In the confusion of the change in Presidents his papers had not been delivered before Jefferson took office. Without the papers Marbury could not sit as a judge. Marbury asked Madison, the new secretary of state, to hand them over. Madison refused. He knew that as long as the papers remained in his hands Jefferson would be able to fill the new post with a Republican judge.

Marbury then asked the Supreme Court to order Madison to deliver the papers. He based his case on a part of the Judiciary Act of

1789. The Supreme Court heard the case of *Marbury* v. *Madison*. The justices, led by Chief Justice Marshall, took two steps. They studied the Judiciary Act of 1789. They also studied Article III of the Constitution. This part of the Constitution sets forth the powers and duties of the federal courts, including the Supreme Court.

In 1803 Justice Marshall announced the Court's decision: the Court could not order Madison to hand over Marbury's papers. Marshall explained that Article III of the Constitution does not give the Court power to issue such an order to a President's official. Therefore, when Congress gave the Court this power in one part of the Judiciary Act of 1789, it went beyond the Constitution. So the Supreme Court called that part of the Judiciary Act null and void. That part of the act did not have to be obeyed. The Court found it unconstitutional.

The Court's decision in *Marbury* v. *Madison* had two immediate results. Marbury lost his judgeship, and Jefferson was able to choose a Republican judge. But the decision had a third, far more important result. For the first time in history the Supreme Court ruled on whether or not a law went against the Constitution. The justices had taken on the power of deciding how the words and sentences of the Constitution should be interpreted.

Marshall served as chief justice from 1801 to 1835. During his time in office the Supreme Court decided other important cases. Under Marshall the Court continued to uphold the Constitution as the chief law of the land. Marshall's work strengthened the federal government. It also strengthened the Supreme Court, making it equal in importance to Congress and the Presidency.

The rulings of Marshall and the other Federalist justices did not please Jefferson. Jefferson believed in a strict reading of the Constitution. He felt that each branch of the government could use only those powers clearly spelled out in the Constitution. And the Constitution did not state that the federal courts had the sole power to rule on the meaning of its words. Jefferson believed that the people through the President and Congress also had the power to say what was constitutional.

2 The Louisiana Purchase

Jefferson's belief in a word-for-word reading of the Constitution was soon tested when Louisiana was offered for sale. The story begins with Napoleon Bonaparte, who became the ruler of France in 1800.

Europe's Changing Conditions

Napoleon had a grand plan to expand French territory in both Europe and America. As part of this plan, he signed a secret agreement

Section 1 Review

1. What three guidelines did Jefferson give the people in his first inaugural speech?
2. What two actions did Jefferson take to calm Federalists' fears?
3. Whom did Jefferson appoint to his cabinet?
4. What was the only branch of government in 1803 that still had many Federalists?
5. What were the three results of the Supreme Court's decision in *Marbury* v. *Madison*?

Critical Thinking

6. **Expressing Problems Clearly.** Why did Jefferson criticize the federal courts?

LOOKING AHEAD: How did Europe's changing conditions lead to the sale of the Louisiana Territory?

with Spain on October 1, 1800. France agreed to give Spain some land in Europe. In return Spain deeded to France the territory of Louisiana, which stretched between the Mississippi River and the Rocky Mountains. The much-used port of New Orleans lay within this area.

Jefferson received hints of this secret agreement in 1801. The news troubled him. Since 1795, when the United States had signed a treaty with Spain, Americans had used New Orleans as a place to ship goods to and from the West. Jefferson feared that France might close the port to Americans.

A Golden Opportunity

Worried about what the French might do in Louisiana, Jefferson sent James Monroe to Paris to help Robert R. Livingston, the United States representative there. Jefferson told Livingston and Monroe to offer France cash for a small part of Louisiana along the coast that could be used in western trade.

In the meantime events in the French West Indies upset Napoleon's plan for a French empire in America. France had wanted Louisiana so it could be used to grow food for the French West Indies. But France lost Haiti, its largest colony in the West Indies. Haiti's 500,000 black slaves, led by Toussaint L'Ouverture (tōō′san lōō·vər·tyōōr′), had turned against their French rulers. When the revolt ended, L'Ouverture formed a new republic.

Napoleon sent thousands of soldiers to win back Haiti, but each attack failed. He knew then that his grand plan could not be carried out. So suddenly he offered to sell all of Louisiana—not just a part of it—to the United States. There was no time for Livingston and Monroe to check with the President. They leaped at the chance and drew up the treaty with France to buy Louisiana for $15 million.

The treaty was signed on April 30, 1803. Shortly before, the French representative spoke to Livingston and Monroe. He said, "You have made a noble bargain for yourselves." When they asked him what the boundaries of Louisiana were, he shrugged his shoulders and replied, "Make the most of it."

Importance of the Purchase

The chance to buy this land tested Jefferson's narrow reading of the Constitution. He searched its language. But the Constitution said nothing about the President's having the power to buy land. He knew that passing an amendment to grant the President that power might take years. So Jefferson sent the treaty to Congress anyway, and Congress approved it. He comforted himself by saying that if some President after him should go too far in using this power, the people could choose a new President in the next election.

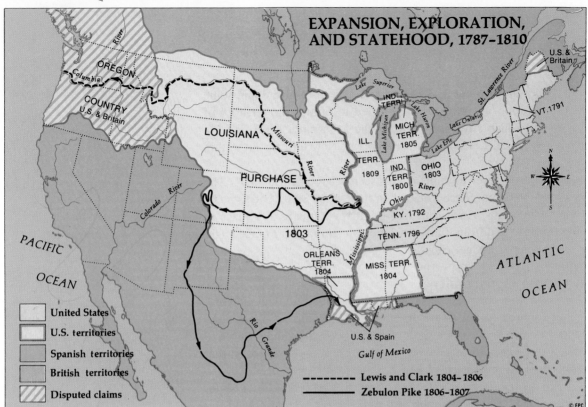

EXPANSION, EXPLORATION, AND STATEHOOD, 1787–1810

United States
U.S. territories
Spanish territories
British territories
Disputed claims

-------- Lewis and Clark 1804–1806
———— Zebulon Pike 1806–1807

After purchasing the Louisiana Territory in 1803, the United States rushed to map and claim the new land as its own.

The purchase of Louisiana had several important results. (1) It doubled the size of the country. (2) It ended all fears of a closing of the port of New Orleans. (3) It gave the United States minerals and other natural resources beyond anyone's hopes or dreams. (4) It allowed the people of the United States to settle beyond the Mississippi River.

Explorations of Lewis and Clark

Even before the Purchase, Jefferson had planned that Meriwether Lewis, his own secretary, and William Clark, the brother of George Rogers Clark of revolutionary war fame, would explore the Louisiana Territory. They were to seek a water route to the Pacific. They were also to report on the lands, people, and wildlife in the territory.

Lewis and Clark set out from St. Louis with nearly fifty men in May 1804. They traveled up the Missouri River to its source. They climbed the Rocky Mountains, crossed through dangerous passes, and reached the valley of the Clearwater River. Lewis and Clark's party then followed the Clearwater River to the Snake River. The Snake led them to the Columbia River, which in turn led them to the Pacific Ocean. Clark wrote in his diary: "Ocean in view! O! the joy!"

Clark also wrote about Sacajawea (sak′ə·jə·wē′ə) in his diary, calling her a woman of "fortitude and resulution." Sacajawea was a Shoshone (shə·shō′nē) and the wife of a French fur trapper. When the fur trapper joined the search party in April 1805, sixteen-year-old Sacajawea and her infant son went along. Sacajawea, acting as an interpreter and guide, proved to be an important and useful member of the group. She helped the explorers make friendly contacts with the Native American groups they met. Twice Sacajawea guided the explorers through tricky mountain passes.

Lewis and Clark spent four months learning about the lands near the mouth of the Columbia River. In March 1806 the explorers began their return journey. They reached St. Louis in September.

Lewis and Clark traced a route to the Pacific Northwest that settlers later followed. They made friends with a number of Native

By late fall 1804 Lewis (top) and Clark had reached the Mandan villages in present-day North Dakota. The following spring they crossed the Rockies.

The Mandan used dogs to pull sledges.

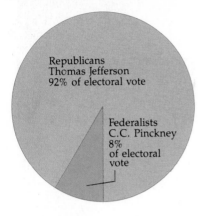

Republicans
Thomas Jefferson
92% of electoral vote

Federalists
C.C. Pinckney
8%
of electoral
vote

Section 2 Review

1. Why did the news that Spain had deeded Louisiana to France trouble Jefferson?
2. Why did Napoleon offer to sell Louisiana to the United States?
3. What four important results did the Louisiana Purchase have?
4. Why was Sacajawea a valuable member of the Lewis and Clark expedition?
5. Why was Aaron Burr charged with treason?

Critical Thinking

6. **Recognizing Cause and Effect.** Why was Burr found not guilty of treason?

LOOKING AHEAD: How did the United States respond to the violations of its neutrality during Jefferson's administration?

American groups. The diary Clark kept gave a good description of these peoples and of the region's wildlife.

Burr, the Federalists, and the West

In the election of 1804 the Republicans swept to victory as Jefferson won his second four years in office. The victory further weakened and divided the Federalists. Aaron Burr was especially angry with the Republicans. They had passed him over when they were choosing Jefferson's second-term running mate.

A small group of Federalists in New England wanted to take advantage of the break between Jefferson and Burr. They hated Jefferson so much that they plotted to break up the Union. They secretly planned to make up a new nation of the New England states and New York.

These Federalists persuaded the unhappy Burr to run for governor of New York in 1804. Burr agreed that, if chosen governor, he would back the plan to break up the Union. But Burr lost the race for governor, and the plan failed.

Burr then made trouble in the West. He planned to form a new empire in the Mississippi Valley with help from Britain or Spain. Between 1804 and 1806 Burr set up a base on the Ohio River. He tried to get the British to pay him for breaking up the United States. He asked for 100,000 pounds sterling, an amount equal to about $500,000. He also asked leading westerners for their help. When Jefferson heard what Burr was doing, he ordered Burr arrested on a charge of treason against the United States.

Burr was tried in 1807, but Chief Justice Marshall found him not guilty. Marshall said that treason could be proved only when the same act had been seen by two witnesses. No one could find two witnesses to testify to any *one* of Burr's acts. However, Burr's political life was at an end.

3   Foreign Policy Under Jefferson

During his first four years in office Jefferson had to turn his attention to trouble outside the United States. In his first inaugural address Jefferson had said he wanted friendship with all nations, but he wanted the United States to remain neutral. The United States would take no sides in conflicts between other countries. But nations overseas put Jefferson's ideas to the test just months after he first took office in 1801.

The Barbary Pirates

The first test of Jefferson's foreign policy came from the Barbary pirates. For many years pirates from the North African states of

Stephen Decatur, lifelong sailor and son of a sea captain, first won fame in 1804 for his daring attack on the Barbary pirates.

Morocco, Tripoli, Algiers, and Tunis had controlled the Mediterranean Sea. Nations that did not make a yearly payment to the rulers of these North African states had their ships and crews captured. Between 1783 and 1801 the United States had paid over $2 million in bribes. Like most of the leaders in Europe, Washington and Adams felt it was cheaper to pay the rulers than to fight their pirates.

In 1801, as Jefferson took office, the ruler of Tripoli demanded more money. President Jefferson decided to stop the payments. He also sent a fleet of United States ships to blockade and bombard the coast of Tripoli. For the next few years these ships attacked pirate vessels and blockaded their ports. In February 1804 Lieutenant Stephen Decatur, commanding a ship he had taken from the pirates, slipped into Tripoli harbor in a daring raid. His crew set fire to a captured United States ship so the pirates could not use it. Decatur and his crew then escaped. Finally the United States defeated the pirates at Tripoli in 1805. The other Barbary pirates, however, kept up their attacks until 1816, when their rulers signed treaties with the United States.

Troubles with Britain and France

Merchants and shippers of the United States had built up a booming trade with Britain, France, and the other nations of Europe. They expected to go on with this trade even when Britain and France began another war against each other in 1803. But Britain put up a blockade around western Europe to keep arms and food away from

United States Exports and Imports, 1790–1815

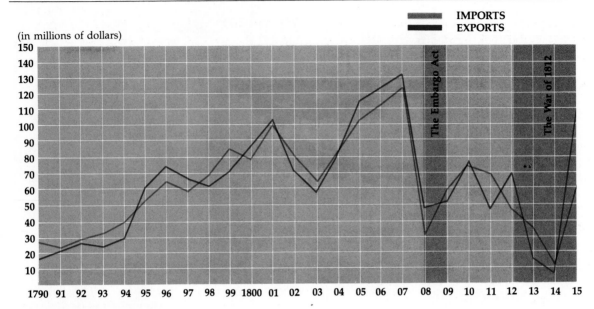

(in millions of dollars)

IMPORTS
EXPORTS

The Embargo Act

The War of 1812

Sales of United States goods abroad suffered greater setbacks than sales of foreign goods at home during troubled times in the early 1800s.

the French. In return France halted all shipping into and out of Great Britain. Both nations stopped United States vessels on their voyages to or from Europe. During the war the French seized about 200 United States ships. The British took about 500.

The British made far more trouble for Americans than the French. British ships often stopped United States vessels far from French ports. Then the British impressed, or took by force, sailors for their navy, saying that these sailors were British subjects. By 1811 the British had impressed at least 100,000 sailors from American trading ships.

Some of the impressed sailors *were* British subjects. These sailors had deserted British ships docked in United States ports. But many of the impressed sailors were citizens of the United States.

The Failure of Peaceful Measures

Jefferson grew tired of Britain's seizures of United States ships and sailors. But he believed in using peaceful means to stop them. He remembered the success of the boycotts on British goods in colonial days. He believed that example could be repeated. Congress approved Jefferson's idea of banning British imports and passed the Non-Importation Act in 1806.

This peaceful measure failed when a new crisis arose in 1807. On June 22 the British warship *Leopard* met the United States warship *Chesapeake* just off the coast of Virginia. The captain of the *Leopard* demanded that the *Chesapeake* stop and be searched for deserters. The *Chesapeake*'s captain refused, so the British opened fire and forced him to surrender. The British captain boarded the badly damaged United States vessel and took one British-born deserter. He also took three United States sailors: a black, a Native American, and a white man born in Maryland. Many people in the United States wanted to go to war at once. According to one, Britain's act struck "at the root of our independence."

Jefferson, refusing to give in to the cry for war, tried one more peaceful measure. This time he proposed that all United States trading ships presently in port be kept in port. Congress approved the idea and passed the Embargo Act on December 22, 1807. All the great eastern trading centers were suddenly shut down.

The Embargo Act hurt the United States far more than it hurt Britain. Farmers in the United States could not ship out their crops. The prices of farm goods slipped, land prices fell, and shipbuilding stopped. Exports dropped 80 percent in one year. Jefferson saw that his peaceful measures to end the British attacks against United States shipping had failed. Three days before his second term in office was up he signed a bill ending the embargo.

4   President Madison

In 1807 Jefferson stated that he would not seek office a third time. He supported Secretary of State James Madison for the Presidency. Madison had been a leading political figure since the early 1780s. Jefferson and Madison together had helped form the Republican party. Madison had served Jefferson as a friend, a true political ally, and a secretary of state. In the election of 1808 James Madison easily defeated the Federalist Charles Pinckney to become the fourth President of the United States.

A Call for War
Under Madison the United States made two more unsuccessful attempts to avoid war. In 1809 Congress passed the Non-Intercourse Act. This act opened trade with all countries except Britain and France. Trade with these two countries was to be closed until they lifted their blockades. But neither Britain nor France gave an inch.

In 1810 Congress replaced the Non-Intercourse Act with the Macon Act. The Macon Act allowed trade with all countries—Britain and France, too. But it also held a strange threat for both trouble-makers. If one of these two countries lifted its blockade before March 3, 1811, Congress would cut off trade with the other country within three months.

France quickly lifted its blockade to gain an edge over Britain. The United States kept its word. Madison ordered a halt to trade

Section 3 Review

1. What stand did Jefferson favor for the United States in conflicts between other nations?
2. Why did Jefferson decide to stop payments to the Barbary pirates?
3. Why did British seizures of American ships trouble the United States more than French seizures?
4. What was the purpose of the Non-Importation Act in 1806?

Critical Thinking
5. **Recognizing Cause and Effect.** Why did Jefferson end the embargo?

LOOKING AHEAD: Considering the results of the War of 1812, how do you think the War Hawks felt when the war ended?

Election of 1808

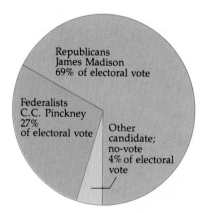

Republicans
James Madison
69% of electoral vote

Federalists
C.C. Pinckney
27%
of electoral vote

Other candidate;
no-vote
4% of electoral vote

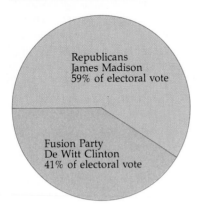

Republicans
James Madison
59% of electoral vote

Fusion Party
De Witt Clinton
41% of electoral vote

with Great Britain. But this step was not enough for some members of Congress. They called for war with Great Britain.

Among the members who wanted war was a group of westerners and southerners called the War Hawks. They wrongly believed that the British were stirring up trouble with Native Americans along the Canadian border. The War Hawks from the West wanted to attack Canada, that part of North America still under British rule. Some land-hungry farmers in Tennessee, Georgia, and Alabama joined the call for war. These southerners also wanted to take eastern Florida from Spain.

In 1812 President Madison asked Congress to declare war on Great Britain. Congress did so on June 18. But just two days before, Britain had finally decided to lift its blockade. Had the news of Britain's action reached the United States sooner, the call for war might have ended.

The War of 1812 at Sea

In the first few months of the war the United States navy won several surprising victories on the open sea. The *Constitution,* an American navy vessel, defeated the *Guerrière* and the *Java,* two British ships of war. Another naval vessel, the *United States,* defeated the British *Macedonian.* These victories shocked the British navy and gave the United States false hope. Within a year most United States warships were trapped in their home ports by a British blockade of the American coast.

The blockade crippled United States trade. A New Englander wrote: "Our harbors were blockaded; communications coastwise between our ports were cut off; ships were rotting in every creek and cove where they could find a place of security; our immense annual products were mouldering [rotting] in our warehouses; sources of profitable labor were dried up."

The War of 1812 at Home

Most people in the United States believed they could easily take Canada from the British. But the British won battle after battle. At last the United States scored two important victories. The first took place September 10, 1813, on inland waters. A United States naval fleet led by Captain Oliver Hazard Perry fought a British fleet on Lake Erie. After a fierce fight Perry reported, "We have met the enemy and they are ours." Perry's victory gave the United States control of the Great Lakes and stopped the British from entering the Ohio Valley.

A month later the second important battle took place on land. At the Battle of the Thames, General William Henry Harrison defeated a combined force of British and Native American soldiers.

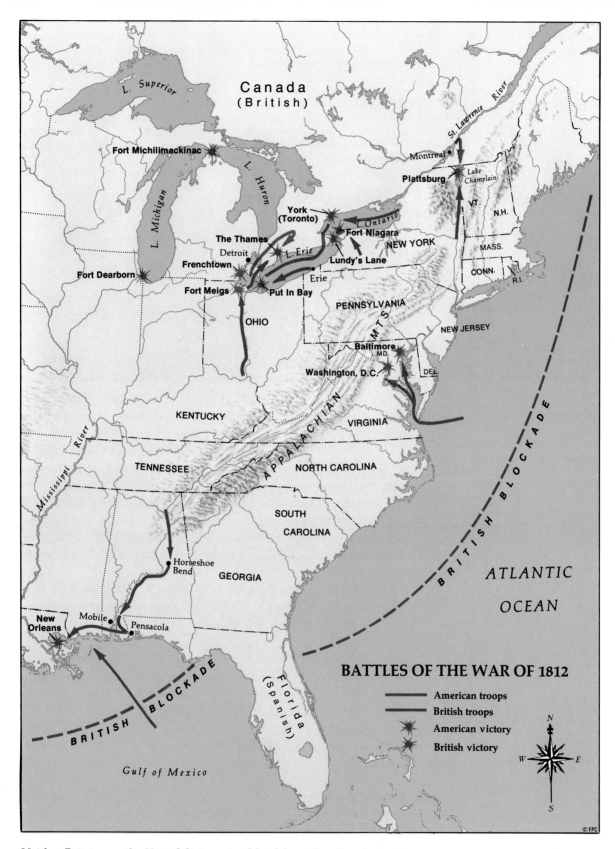

BATTLES OF THE WAR OF 1812

Map labels: Canada (British), L. Superior, L. Huron, L. Michigan, Fort Michilimackinac, Fort Dearborn, The Thames, Detroit, Frenchtown, Fort Meigs, Put In Bay, L. Erie, York (Toronto), Fort Niagara, Lundy's Lane, Erie, L. Ontario, St. Lawrence River, Montreal, Plattsburg, Lake Champlain, VT., N.H., MASS., CONN., R.I., NEW YORK, NEW JERSEY, DEL., OHIO, PENNSYLVANIA, Baltimore, MD., Washington, D.C., KENTUCKY, VIRGINIA, APPALACHIAN MTS., TENNESSEE, NORTH CAROLINA, SOUTH CAROLINA, GEORGIA, Horseshoe Bend, Mobile, Pensacola, New Orleans, Mississippi River, Florida (Spanish), Gulf of Mexico, ATLANTIC OCEAN, BRITISH BLOCKADE

Legend:
— American troops
— British troops
✶ American victory
✶ British victory

N W E S

© FPC

Neither Britain nor the United States gained land from the other during the War of 1812.

The worst defeat suffered by the British in the War of 1812 came at New Orleans, two weeks after the peace was signed.

Chief Tecumseh (tə·kəm′sə), a much-loved Shawnee leader, was killed during the fighting. His death ended all British hopes for more help from Native Americans and all British threats to the Northwest.

The British were most successful in attacking the eastern coast of the United States. They marched into Washington, D.C., on August 24, 1814. Government officials had to flee the city quickly. In fact President Madison and his wife Dolley had to leave their dinner on the table in their rush to escape. However, Dolley Madison did save some papers and paintings. The attacking British finished the Madisons' dinner and then burned the President's house and other public buildings.

The British next attacked a fort outside Baltimore. This time the United States forces held. The battle inspired Francis Scott Key to write the "Star-Spangled Banner."

The British attacked New Orleans on January 8, 1815. More than 7,000 British soldiers met General Andrew Jackson of Tennessee, whose troops included a unit of free black militia. Heavy musket and cannon fire killed about 300 British soldiers, wounded about 1250 and captured 500. The Americans had only 14 killed, 39 wounded, and 18 captured. The Battle of New Orleans made General Jackson a well-known hero. It later helped him become President.

Antiwar Views

From the beginning many Federalists were against the War of 1812. The war hurt the industries and trade of the New England states, where the Federalists were still strong. Young Federalist Congressman Daniel Webster asked, "Where is it written in the Constitution that you may take . . . parents from their children and compel them to fight the battles of any war in which the folly . . . of government may engage it?"

Federalists in New England did all that they could to undermine the war effort. Federalist governors refused to call out the militia when asked for soldiers. They also refused to gather supplies and to support measures to pay for the war.

Federalist anger at the war led to the Hartford Convention in 1814. Since Jefferson's election in 1800, the Federalist party had become weaker. New states had joined the Union. Most people in these states were Republicans. The delegates to the Hartford Convention discussed ways to keep their Federalist party alive and strong. Some spoke of secession—of leaving the Union to form a Federalist nation. When the meeting ended, the Federalists had prepared a final report to present to officials in Washington, D.C. This report did not call for secession. But it did ask for changes in national policies in exchange for New England's support.

By the time the Federalist delegates reached Washington, D.C., to give their report the war had ended. People in the capital were toasting the signing of a peace treaty with Britain and the news of Jackson's victory at New Orleans. The end of the war took away the Federalists' bargaining power. Talk of secession had hurt their cause. Within a few short years the Federalist party had disappeared from the national scene.

The Peace

Although neither Jackson nor the British general knew it, the treaty ending the war was signed two weeks before the Battle of New Orleans. It was signed on Christmas Eve, 1814, in the town of Ghent, Belgium. But news traveled so slowly that the Battle of New Orleans was fought after the official peace. The Peace of Ghent, as the treaty was called, stated that Britain and the United States would each keep the land it had held before the war. The pact said nothing about the impressment of sailors or the neutral rights of the United States.

The end of the war marked a change in the ways the United States and Great Britain treated each other. Both countries agreed to settle future differences peacefully. Never again did these two nations fight each other. The United States and Canada also agreed to settle all boundary questions peacefully.

The War of 1812 had other lasting effects. The United States proved its independence of Europe. Before the war, the political life of the nation mirrored events in Europe. After the war, events in Europe did not seriously affect the United States until the twentieth century. Future politics centered on issues at home rather than on foreign affairs.

Section 4 Review

1. After Madison became President, what two unsuccessful attempts did the United States make to avoid war?
2. What effects did the British blockade of the American coast have on American trade?
3. What American general became a national hero as a result of the Battle of New Orleans?
4. How did the peace ending the War of 1812 change the relationship between the United States and Great Britain? Between the United States and Canada?

Critical Thinking

5. **Recognizing Ideologies.** Why were many New England Federalists opposed to the War of 1812?

People

As Leaders

Although very different from each other, Alexander Hamilton and Thomas Jefferson were among the great leaders of the new nation.

The revolutionary war generation produced outstanding leaders. Among those who left a lasting heritage were Alexander Hamilton and Thomas Jefferson.

Hamilton the Federalist

Alexander Hamilton was born in the West Indies and spent much of his youth there. His mother was the daughter of a French family that had left its homeland because of religious persecution. His father, James Hamilton, came from Scotland.

James Hamilton, who failed in his business, left the family when Alexander was ten years old. Alexander soon went to work to help feed the family. At sixteen he was put in charge of a small business.

Alexander was eager to leave the West Indies to seek his fortune. Two friends agreed to back him. In October 1772 at the age of seventeen Alexander Hamilton set sail for New York.

Hamilton expected to become a doctor. Instead, he became a leader in the American Revolution and one of the nation's founders. His ideas were building blocks for a national political party.

Hamilton's Views

In 1774 at the age of nineteen Hamilton wrote a pamphlet against the British claim to unlimited power over the colonies. He wrote: "Perhaps, before long, your tables and chairs, and platters, and dishes, and knives, and forks, and every thing else, would be taxed. Nay, I don't know but they [the British] would find means to tax you for every child you got, and for every kiss your daughters received from sweethearts; and . . . that would soon ruin you."

Hamilton also favored colonial union. The colonists, he said, should stop arguing over small things. If Massachusetts or any other colony was in trouble, the others should come to its aid. The idea of strong union became *the* guiding principle of Hamilton's thoughts on government.

Power over States

At the constitutional convention in 1787 Hamilton pleaded for a strong central government. He wanted to do away with states and make the federal government the sole government. Later he changed his position somewhat and wrote papers in favor of the Constitution.

Alexander Hamilton lived from 1755 to 1804.

People

They were printed in a New York newspaper under the title *The Federalist.*

Hamilton's every thought was to make the federal government more powerful. He wanted the federal government under the Constitution to act energetically and show its power over the states.

Hamilton did not trust the judgment of people in choosing their own leaders. He believed leaders should be selected by and from persons with talent and money. Yet he played a big part in building a strong and prosperous nation whose government was based on the votes of the people.

Jefferson the Republican

Hamilton's rival, Thomas Jefferson, was born, reared, and educated in Virginia. Jefferson often needed to leave his home in Virginia to carry out his many duties. But he always returned home as soon as possible. He gloried in the land and disliked cities. He enjoyed art and spent time inventing useful tools for the house and farm.

Jefferson's Views

Unlike Hamilton, Jefferson believed in strong state government rather than strong central government. If such a central government became too strong, he feared it would cripple the states and endanger personal liberty. Jefferson also believed in "the good sense of the people." "They may be led astray for a moment," he wrote, "but will soon correct themselves."

Jefferson, like Hamilton, became a gifted political leader. He held almost every government office available during his lifetime. He was a member of the House of Burgesses. He was selected to speak

Thomas Jefferson lived from 1743 to 1826.

for Virginia in the Continental Congress. He was chosen governor of the state of Virginia, and later named by the Continental Congress as its envoy to France. Washington made him secretary of state. He was also elected third President of the United States. And he founded one of the two major national parties, the Democratic-Republican, the forerunner of today's Democratic party.

Love of Freedom

Yet Jefferson wanted to be remembered for three actions that had little to do with holding political office. First he wanted to be remembered as the author of the Declaration of Independence. To Jefferson, the Declaration was a lasting statement on political liberty.

Second he wished to be remembered for his role in ending government support of an official church in Virginia. Jefferson believed that church and state should be kept separate if the United States was to stay free.

Third he wished to be remembered for his role in starting the University of Virginia. In this act he stood for freedom of the mind and of ideas.

Under Hamilton the young United States showed strength, energy, and prosperity. Under Jefferson the nation developed its love of freedom—political, religious, and intellectual. Both leaders helped shape the future.

Chapter 11 Review

Chapter Summary

President Jefferson's two terms saw some landmark events in American history. For example, in the case of *Marbury* v. *Madison,* the Supreme Court, led by Chief Justice John Marshall, declared a law unconstitutional for the first time. Another landmark event was the Louisiana Purchase of 1803, which doubled the size of our nation.

During President Jefferson's term the United States became involved in the conflict between Great Britain and France. Both countries seized American ships. Congress responded by passing the Embargo Act.

Republican James Madison won the election of 1808. In his first years in office, Madison faced demands from many Republicans in Congress for a war against Britain. In June 1812, war was declared against Great Britain. The Republicans favored the war. Federalists in New England, however, refused to support the war effort and even spoke of seceding. The war ended with the Peace of Ghent in which both sides agreed to settle future disputes peacefully.

Reviewing Vocabulary

Choose the word that best completes each sentence. Write your answers on a separate sheet of paper.

1. Although both Britain and France seized American ships, only the British would (*impress/imprison*) American sailors.
2. President Thomas Jefferson wanted the United States to be a (*stronghold/neutral*) nation.
3. The election of 1800 was viewed by the Federalists as a (*victory/disaster*).
4. At his first (*inauguration/reception*), President Jefferson was joined by his Vice-President Aaron Burr.
5. At the Hartford Convention, some Federalists spoke of (*embargoes/secession*).
6. The (*Embargo/Non-Importation Act*) of 1807 was an attempt to maintain peace.
7. In (*foreign affairs/domestic affairs*) the President sought peace and friendship.
8. In 1803 Britain set up an (*embargo/blockade*) to keep supplies away from France.
9. Jefferson referred to the judiciary as a Federalist (*disaster/stronghold*).
10. The first test of Jefferson's (*domestic policy/foreign policy*) came from the Barbary pirates.
11. Although Aaron Burr was charged with (*secession/treason*), he was not found guilty.

Understanding Main Ideas

1. How did the party changeover in 1800 result in the case of *Marbury* v. *Madison,* and why was the case important?
2. The Louisiana Purchase was the result of what change in conditions in Europe?
3. What were the two steps taken by President Jefferson when Britain and France violated the neutrality of the United States?
4. Why might the War Hawks have been disappointed by the Peace of Ghent?
5. What were the three goals of the War Hawks?
6. How did France and Great Britain react to the Macon Act?

Critical Thinking Skills

1. **Recognizing Ideologies.** Why do you think the Supreme Court decision in *Marbury* v. *Madison* may have reflected the justices' Federalist beliefs?

Social Studies Skills: Interpreting a Diagram

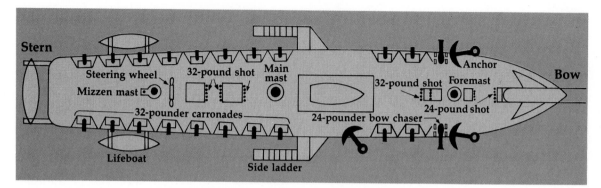

A diagram can be an important source of information, but it is helpful only if it is interpreted correctly. Study the diagram of the top deck of a fighting ship such as the U.S. Constitution.

Skill Review: After you have studied the diagram, look at the statements below. Decide whether each statement is true (T), false (F), or doubtful (D). A statement is doubtful if the diagram lacks the information to prove it true or false. Write your answers on a separate sheet of paper.

1. The *Constitution* was the first ironclad ship of its day.
2. The *Constitution* has three masts.
3. The mizzenmast was closest to the bow.
4. All but two of the cannons on the top deck used 24-pound shot.
5. The ship carried fifteen carronades on each side of the top deck.
6. The steering wheel was located between the main mast and the mizzenmast.
7. The lower deck immediately below the top deck held sleeping quarters.

---

2. **Checking Consistency.** Was the Louisiana Purchase in keeping with Thomas Jefferson's view of the Constitution? Explain your answer.
3. **Making Comparisons.** Compare the Macon Act of 1810 and the Non-Intercourse Act of 1809. How were the two acts similar and how were they different? Which act was more effective? Explain your answer.
4. **Distinguishing False Images from Accurate Images.** Although Aaron Burr was the third Vice-President of the United States, he is usually remembered as a traitor to his country. Is this a fair label? Explain your answer.

Writing About History

Writing a Journal. During the Lewis and Clark expedition, William Clark kept a diary, or journal. Imagine that you were a member of the expedition as it left St. Louis to explore the Louisiana Territory. Write a journal entry describing some of the events you might have experienced.

Your Region in History

Economics. Do you think your region was affected by Jefferson's embargo? Why or why not?

Lifestyles:
The
Revolutionary Era

✿ Chapter 12

THE REVOLUTIONARY WAR brought the United States of America into being. But the war took its toll in the daily lives of the people. Families were broken up, homes were destroyed or left behind, schools were closed, and many lives were lost.

Through the hardships, however, the people of the new nation held onto as much of their lives as they could. By the time the war ended the citizens of the new country were ready to take on the daily challenges of building their nation.

Lifestyles   Families and Homes

In *The Spirit of '76* T. H. Matteson shows a whole family helping a Patriot minuteman get ready for battle.

During the Revolution many families were separated and suffered hardship. Families who remained loyal to the Crown were often forced to leave America. Family members left behind felt sad and even hopeless. Husbands who fought in the colonial militia usually left their families behind. Marching soldiers and cannon fire made those who remained at home uneasy.

The war hurt most families. Some lost family members. Some lost property. Others had to move. All were faced with shortages. Schools for children closed. Towns and cities were taken over by rival armies. Even after the war political differences separated families and friends.

But life went on. People married. Parents raised children. People carried on their everyday lives as best they could.

After the Revolution some things changed. Most parents no longer made money arrangements for their children's marriages. But parents still had many children. Some had twelve, fifteen, or more. In a young country with much land and few workers large families made good sense.

A Romantic Problem

Like some of today's magazines, colonial magazines often ran advice columns. One woman wrote to the *Royal American Magazine* in 1774 about her love problem:

. . . [I] am courted by a young gentleman who has no accomplishment or qualification in my eyes . . . [except that he is rich]. My parents insist on my marrying him; and I really think he loves me; but . . . I never can like him; and besides there is a person of whom I am very fond . . . but has . . . [less money]. . . . Now, as I could wish to marry the first for his money, and the last for the love I have [for] him, as well as [his good sense] . . . :In these cases, what shall I do?

The answer was printed in a later edition of the magazine:

The road before you here is very plain. . . . marry the man you love.

Loyalist Family Woes

Joseph Galloway headed the colonial assembly of Pennsylvania. He once offered a plan of union for the colonies. But he was shocked when he heard of the Declaration of Independence. "Independency means ruin. If England refuses it, she will ruin us; if she grants it, we will ruin ourselves." He sadly took the British side and became a Loyalist.

In 1778 Galloway and his daughter left for England after the British took Philadelphia. His wife Grace stayed behind. She wrote in her journal:

. . . the Thought of My dearest Child & her father & [the] Uncertainty of our [fu]ture fate . . . are never from my thoughts. . . . that we may enjoy each others company once More is the great Desire of my soul.

A few weeks later she wrote,

"oh that I may live to get to england. . . ."

A Revolutionary Author

Mercy Warren wrote plays largely for political reasons. She had probably never seen a play herself.

Mercy Otis Warren of Massachusetts was a wife and mother of five. She was also a Patriot. Her brother James Otis was one of the most enthusiastic Sons of Liberty. In 1769 he started a fight in a Loyalist coffeehouse. He was so badly beaten that he never got well. Mercy decided to carry on her brother's fight with her pen. She wrote several plays that made fun of the British and the colonists who supported them. The plays were read and enjoyed throughout the colonies. The American troops loved *The Blockheads,* which made fun of British officers and troops.

In 1775 Warren began writing a history of the American Revolution. She kept on with this work for the next thirty years. The last part of her history was published in 1805 when she was seventy-seven years old. She died at eighty-six, outliving her husband and four of her children.

At the time of the Revolution most people lived on farms. They used the trees cleared from their fields to build their homes. Most houses were not painted. Usually the first floor had two rooms, one a kitchen with a large fireplace and the other a kind of living room. Sleeping rooms were on a second floor. Chairs, tables, shelves, and beds were often homemade.

In towns more and more people built houses of brick. Brick reduced the danger of fire and lasted longer than wood. Some of the houses were so well built that they are still used today.

The use of architects who drew up plans for buildings was new, too. Charles Bulfinch built in Boston a series of houses attached by shared walls. These houses made him famous. His way of building became known as the federal style. Bulfinch later was the architect for the Capitol building in Washington.

The kitchen pictured here stands at Stratford Hall in Virginia, birthplace of Robert E. Lee. The house was built in 1730. Row houses (bottom left), like those first designed by Bulfinch, were built in cities. The *Quilting Frolic* (bottom right) shows a popular pastime practiced throughout the colonies.

William Chappel's *House Raising in Grand Street,* 1810 shows another way colonists helped each other. Some furniture, such as the Shaker-made clothes cabinet above, was built in the colonies.

Section 1 Review

1. Name four ways the revolutionary war hurt most families.
2. What is a row house?
3. How did neighbors help one another build houses?

Critical Thinking

4. **Recognizing Bias.** Why would reading the play *The Blockheads* by Mercy Otis Warren tell you about her politics?

The new nation needed many public buildings. Benjamin Latrobe, a friend of Jefferson, designed and built many of them. Jefferson himself was an avid builder. He rebuilt his home in Monticello, Virginia, many times. He also laid out the plan for the buildings of the University of Virginia.

More and more the homes and public buildings of the new nation began to have their own special style. It was a style suited to the needs and tastes of the American people.

Wedding Gifts

"Bees" were fun for everyone. The *Quilting Frolic* shows a newly married couple being given a traditional gift. The gift was a quilt made by neighbors at a quilting bee. Neighbors enjoyed talk, food, and music as they worked on the quilt from start to finish. In the picture the completed quilt is being taken from its frame.

In some towns, neighbors held another kind of bee to raise a house in a single day. Neighbors from miles around would bring tools and food. When the house was finished, there would still be time for a party. Then the neighbors would travel the five or ten miles back to their own homes.

Shaker Simplicity

The Shakers of Pennsylvania, a religious group, did not believe in fancy houses or fancy furniture. Everything was built for use. Compare the Shaker cupboard with its built-in drawers with the kitchen cupboard on page 238. The Shaker cupboard is simple, while the other is decorated on top with carving.

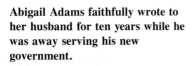

Abigail Adams faithfully wrote to her husband for ten years while he was away serving his new government.

The values stated in the Declaration of Independence are those of life, liberty, and the pursuit of happiness.

During and after revolutionary times many Americans believed that it was right to fight when they were treated unfairly. Sometimes, they believed, people had to act against the government to protect their rights.

Some of the leaders of the new country feared that these democratic ideas might be carried too far. They were afraid that crowd violence would destroy the country. They said that what was most important was to obey the law and respect people's property.

The Declaration of Independence also states that "all men are created equal." Many people understood that slavery went against this idea of equality. Even slaveholders voted for the Northwest Ordinance of 1787, which said that there could be no slavery in the new states.

Many values from this dramatic era are still held fast today.

Consumer Protest

Abigail Adams wrote her husband John in 1777 of how women took action against a stingy merchant in Boston. Respect for property was held as a value by many people. But the women in this story valued what they believed to be fairness even more.

. . . .*You know there is a great scarcity of sugar and coffee [which the women think is caused by merchants taking these goods off the market]. A number of [women], some say a hundred, some say more, assembled with a cart and truck [and] marched down to the warehouse . . . [When the merchant (a wealthy, stingy bachelor) refused to give the keys to the women,] . . . one of them seized him by his neck, and tossed him into the cart. . . . then [they] opened the warehouse, . . . [put the coffee on] the trucks, and drove off. . . . A large [crowd] of men stood amazed. . . .*

Ten-year-old Catharine Congdon's sampler (top) reads:

At home abroad in peace in war
Thy God will thee defend
Conduct thee through lifes
    pilgrimage
Safe to thy journeys end.

Patty Goodeshall also chose a religious thought for her sampler.

A black sailor was among those taken off the *Chesapeake* by the British.

Black Bravery

Sometimes people do brave things to protect something they value. During the War of 1812 many Americans bravely fought the British to protect their freedom. Black Americans, many of whom were slaves, also fought hard. Some people were surprised that black slaves, who had no freedom to protect, fought as bravely as free people.

On Wednesday, August 24, 1814, Commodore Joshua Barney of the United States Navy stopped the British advance up Chesapeake Bay. Barney had 400 seamen, a large number of whom were black. Before the battle President Madison was mistakenly worried that the blacks would not be brave. He asked Commodore Barney if the "[blacks] would not run on the approach of the British?" "No Sir," replied Barney. "They will die at their guns first."

Values in Needle and Thread

Girls were expected to learn needlework. The test of their skill was a piece of needlework called a sampler. On the sampler the girls sewed alphabets, numbers, and moral sayings. These sayings showed the values that people held at that time.

The Land Ordinance of 1785 and the Northwest Ordinance of 1787 provided for public schools. The schools were paid for by taxes. The reasons are stated in the Northwest Ordinance. "Religion, morality, and knowledge being necessary to good government, schools and the means of education shall be forever encouraged."

But public education was a new idea. It took many years to get started. In fact there were fewer schools after the Revolution than there had been before. Children whose parents could pay went to school. Other children were taught at home by their parents or by hired teachers. Most boys learned the skills they would need in life through work.

An American Best-Seller

Schoolmaster Noah Webster said that America was too dependent on British ideas and British books. So in 1783 he wrote the *American Spelling Book,* one of the most important best-sellers of all time.

Colonel Timothy Pickering bought a copy of Webster's book. He was so impressed that he wrote his wife the next morning:

The author [Webster] is ingenious, and writes from his own experience as a schoolmaster . . . and the time will come when no authority, as an English grammarian, will be superior to his own. It is the very thing I have wished for [to help my son with his education].

Webster's book contained pronunciation and spelling guides, and stories with a moral. Many American children used only one schoolbook—Webster's *American Spelling Book.*

These two pages of Webster's spelling book give the ending of one story, the beginning of another, and a table of words in which the letters *ch* sound like *k.*

In 1770 only a few children went to school. Most youngsters, like this blacksmith's apprentice, learned on the job.

Section 2 Review

1. Suggest two or three reasons why young girls were expected to learn needlework.
2. Why did Noah Webster write the *American Spelling Book?*
3. At what age did Thurlow Weed get his first job? How much did he earn at that job?

Critical Thinking

4. **Determining Relevance.** What did the Northwest Ordinance of 1787 say about slavery? About public education?

A Southern Student

Southern planters often hired teachers to teach their children at home. Philip Fithian taught the children of Robert Carter III in Virginia. In his journal Fithian described his student Ben who was sick in bed.

Thursday 15. [September 1774]
Ben is much better, he has return'd to his Bed in my Room. . . . I put him to begin & read . . . Horace [a Roman poet]. . . . He [hates] Greek, & therefore makes little or no progress in [it]. He has a [great] Love for Horses; he often tells me that he should . . . be more fond & careful of a favourite Horse than of a Wife . . . or than anything whatever! I never saw a Person . . . so full of Pleasure & enjoyment as he is when on Horse back, or even in the company of a Horse!

A Complete Education

For most people, learning took the form of practical, on-the-job training. Thurlow Weed, who became a printer's apprentice at age twelve, wrote of his early learning experiences:

My first [job,] when about eight years old, was in blowing a blacksmith's bellows for a Mr. Reeves, who gave me six cents per day. . . . I stood upon a box to reach the handle of the bellows. My next [job was working in a] tavern kept by a Captain Baker. . . . After the sheriff took possession of [the tavern, I became a] cabin boy on board the sloop Ranger. . . . I was then (1806) in my ninth year

The end of the rules limiting British trade meant that there were many more products made in the United States. More and more people worked at making products. Women and children were hired for many of the new jobs. Working hours were long, and the work was hard.

But after the Revolution, as before, most people worked on farms. Working hours on the farms were also long and hard. But many people took pride in their land and in the crops they raised.

Women and children found work in thread-spinning factories in New England. Some young boys dreamed of working at sea. Faraway places such as St. Eustatius in the West Indies lured them on.

Leaving Home

Like many young boys, Andrew Sherburne had long dreamed of living and working on a seagoing ship. In 1779 he finally got the chance to live out his dreams.

My father [at last] consented that I should go to sea. . . . I was not yet fourteen years of age. I had received some little moral and religious instruction, and was [amazed at] the habits of the town boys, [and the speech] of sailors. The town boys thought themselves [very] superior to country lads. . . . I was waiter to Mr. Charles Roberts, the boatswain. . . . Being ready for sea, we sailed to Boston . . . [and] proceeded to sea some time in June, 1779. [Since most of the crew were] raw hands and the sea rough, . . . many were [very] sick, and myself among the rest. We were [made fun of] by the old sailors.

A Growing City

Jabez Rogers was a proud resident of Middlebury Falls, Vermont. In 1793 he took note of the size of his city.

In April . . . I counted every building at Middlebury Falls and found the number to be 62.

About thirty years later another count numbered 604 buildings. Thirty-three of these were businesses—woolen mills, cotton mills, an iron foundry, a printing plant, a potter's works, two grist mills, two sawmills, and a marble mill with sixty-five very loud saws.

Encouraging Wages

As America grew, so did its need for factory workers. This help-wanted ad was printed in a Baltimore paper in 1808.

This manufactory will go into operation in all this month, where a number of boys and girls, from eight to twelve years of age, are wanted . . . and encouraging wages will be given; also, work will be given out to women at their homes, and widows will have the preference. . . . Applications will be received by Thomas White. . . .

The Cotton Gin: Just What Greene Ordered

Catherine Greene deserves some of the credit for the invention of the cotton gin. After the death of her husband General Nathanael Greene, she ran their Georgia plantation.

Eli Whitney, just out of school in 1793, was a guest at the Greene place. Greene wanted to meet Whitney. She thought some of his household inventions were good ones. During one of their talks she explained to him the South's great need for a machine that could separate cotton seeds from fiber. Whitney was interested. Within ten days Whitney had made a model cotton gin.

Before the invention of the cotton gin, workers could not meet the great demand for fibers brought on by the use of fast, water-powered spinning machines.

All generations of a family enjoyed the food and fun at a quilting party. Americans moving in high society entertained each other at fancy dress balls.

As before the Revolution, most citizens of the new country had little time for play.

But people from neighboring farms got together whenever there was an excuse for a gathering—a wedding, a house-raising, a quilting or cornhusking bee. There was always music, dancing, and plenty of food. Owners of large plantations gave even larger parties. Guests arrived with clothes and servants and stayed for several days of card playing and dancing.

Hunting, fishing, and riding were favorite ways to pass the time. New games such as football and golf were also well liked.

Dancing Fever

People from all parts of the nation loved to dance. In 1789 Reverend Jedidiah Morse wrote in his *The American Geography:*

Dancing is the principal and favorite amusement in New England; and of this the young people of both sexes are extremely fond.

Dancing was perhaps liked even better in the southern states. People sometimes had more than seventy guests at balls that lasted several days. Philip Fithian wrote about a ball given by the neighbors of the Carter family of Virginia:

. . . to-day I must dress and go . . . to the Ball. . . . I was introduced into a small Room where a number of Gentlemen were playing Cards. . . . With them I conversed till Dinner, which came in at half after four. The Ladies dined first. . . . About Seven the Ladies & Gentlemen begun to dance in the Ball-Room. first Minutes [minuets] one Round; Second Giggs; third Reels; And last of All Country-Dances [square dances]. . . . The Music was a French Horn and two Violins. . . .

Clothes in 1800 still looked European.

People often learned how to do all the latest dance steps at an early age. Ads such as this one encouraged young people to sign up for dance lessons.

James Robardet, respectfully informs the Ladies and Gentlemen of Philadelphia, that his Dancing School is opened. . . . A practising Ball will be given every fortnight [two weeks] . . . for the improvements of his pupils, when their parents will be gratefully admitted. . . . December 4th, 1792.

Section 3 Review

1. What were some businesses in Middlebury Falls, Vermont, in 1823?
2. Name one way factory owners let people know about job openings.
3. How did Eli Whitney get the idea for his cotton gin?

Critical Thinking

4. **Making Comparisons.** Name two ways that today's football differs from the game by the same name played in the nation's early years.

College Football

In our nation's early years the game of football was quite different from the game we know today. Football then was more like soccer or kick-the-can. People played the game in several different ways. William Bentley wrote in 1791:

Before winter comes on the Foot Ball . . . is differently pursued in different places. . . . even heads of families engage in it. . . . The bruising of shins [makes] it rather disgraceful to those of better education.

Disgraceful or not, people of "better education" soon fell in love with the game. In the early 1800s students at Yale University played football dressed in the most unusual way. Instead of wearing helmets and shoulder pads, the students played football in their tall top hats and tailcoats!

Focus on Unit 2

Lifestyles: Understanding Social History

To answer the following questions, review the lifestyles section from page 234 to page 237.

1. **Families and Homes.** The Revolutionary War caused hardships for most American families. It also brought about changes in lifestyles. What changes occurred that showed the American desire for a new and a truly American style, suited to meet the needs and wants of the new society?

2. **Values and Learning.** Both the Land Ordinance of 1785 and Webster's American Spelling Book reflect the importance of education to the new nation. In what ways did education in the 1700s differ from education today? In what ways is it the same?

3. **Work and Play.** An independent United States no longer had to follow the British laws limiting manufacturing. American businesses were free to sell their products wherever they wished. The pictures and selections on pages 244 and 245 reflect the growth in American industry following the Revolutionary War. What do they tell us about the effect of industry on trade, the size of towns, the labor force, the wage scale, and cotton growers?

Making Connections

Use the Unit 2 time line below to answer the following questions.

1. In which decade did the War for Independence begin? During which decade did the War end?

2. How many Presidents were elected in the eighteenth century?

3. Reread the Unit Introduction on page 141. Identify events on the time line that are examples of the conflicts with Great Britain that led to the writing of the Declaration of Independence.

4. **Recognizing Cause and Effect.** What event may have led to only one term for our second President?

Critical Thinking Skills

1. **Identifying Central Issues.** How did British political and economic policies fail to keep up with changes in the American colonies before the revolution?

2. **Determining Relevance.** What effect did the Articles of Confederation have on the Constitution and on the views of Americans about their government?

3. **Identifying Assumptions.** Why did President Washington favor a policy of strict neutrality?

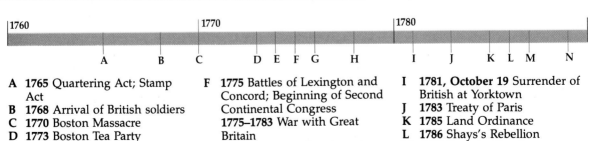

A **1765** Quartering Act; Stamp Act
B **1768** Arrival of British soldiers
C **1770** Boston Massacre
D **1773** Boston Tea Party
E **1774** First Continental Congress

F **1775** Battles of Lexington and Concord; Beginning of Second Continental Congress
   1775–1783 War with Great Britain
G **1776, July 4** Declaration of Independence
H **1778** Treaty of Alliance with France

I **1781, October 19** Surrender of British at Yorktown
J **1783** Treaty of Paris
K **1785** Land Ordinance
L **1786** Shays's Rebellion
M **1787** Constitutional Convention

Using Geography Skills

The map below shows early battles of the American Revolution. Use the map to answer the following questions.

1. **Developing an Awareness of Place.** If north is at the top of the map, in which direction do the mountain ranges run? Where are the major rivers?
2. **Developing Locational Skills.** What geographic feature helped make it easy to move both British and Patriot troops to the battle at Oriskany?
3. **Understanding Human and Environmental Interaction.** In what ways do you think the battles of Lexington, Concord, Bennington, and Bunker Hill changed the landscape? Were these changes intended? Explain your answer.

4. **Understanding Human Movement.** Based on your knowledge of the Revolution, which troops are shown by the purple lines? From which direction(s) did the British approach Saratoga? From which direction(s) did the Patriots approach?

Linking Past to Present

Recognizing Cause and Effect. What led to the development of our country's first political parties? What effect did the development of political parties have upon our young country? How might our political system be different today if political parties had not developed?

Reviewing Social Studies Skills

1. **Pictures and Cartoons.** Examine the picture of the Battle of New Orleans on page 228. How does the picture help you understand why the British forces suffered heavier casualties?
2. **Charts, Tables, and Graphs.** Compare the bar graph on page 160 with the line graph on page 224. In 1763, which were greater, imports or exports? From 1700 to 1763, which increased the most, imports or exports? In what year did that relationship begin to change?

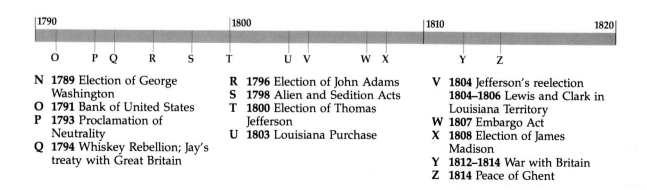

N 1789 Election of George Washington
O 1791 Bank of United States
P 1793 Proclamation of Neutrality
Q 1794 Whiskey Rebellion; Jay's treaty with Great Britain

R 1796 Election of John Adams
S 1798 Alien and Sedition Acts
T 1800 Election of Thomas Jefferson
U 1803 Louisiana Purchase

V 1804 Jefferson's reelection
   1804–1806 Lewis and Clark in Louisiana Territory
W 1807 Embargo Act
X 1808 Election of James Madison
Y 1812–1814 War with Britain
Z 1814 Peace of Ghent

BUILDING
THE
NATION

Between 1815 and 1850 the United States pushed its borders westward—first to the Mississippi and then to the Pacific. People from Europe and people born in the United States settled the West. As they migrated westward, settlers moved into lands once held by Native Americans.

Lifestyles changed dramatically as people discovered new ways of going from place to place and of making a living. New political ideas flourished. More people gained the right to vote, and the candidates they chose spoke more and more for the ordinary person. Differences in people's points of view gave rise to new political parties.

Slave labor and the cotton gin helped cotton production soar in many parts of the South. Many people opposed slavery and wanted to end its practice. But its defenders were afraid that giving up slavery would destroy the southern economy and way of life.

As you read about how the United States grew, think about the different historical sources you can use to learn more about history. Primary and secondary sources will help deepen your understanding of history.

Unit 3

Understanding Historical Sources

🪱 Chapter 13

HISTORIANS WRITE about what has happened in the past. The past has left many traces in many sources. Stories people tell, pictures, archaeological remains, letters, and diaries are all sources of historical information. To write a single page of a history book, historians may have to use dozens of different sources.

Historians must judge the worth or value of each source they use. They need to know whether a source is from the time under study or from a later time. They need to check the accuracy of written facts, choose the important facts, distinguish facts from opinions, and differentiate between real happenings and made-up stories. Knowing some of the skills used to write history will help you become better readers of history.

Vocabulary

accuracy	periodical
opinion	artifact
primary source	bibliography
autobiography	nonfiction
secondary source	evaluate
document	fiction

1 Finding Information

Historians generally like to use records of events made by people who lived through those events. These original records are called primary sources. Letters, journals, and autobiographies—true stories people have written about their own lives—are all primary sources.

Historians use pictures drawn in the period under study as sources of information. This sketch shows a tollgate on the Harrodsburg Pike.

So are drawings, photographs, movies, and sound tapes or videotapes made at the time a happening took place. Copies of such accounts—as long as the copies have not been changed from the original—are also primary sources. Sometimes the accounts are passed along as oral or spoken history rather than as written history. Buildings, tools, and other objects from the past are also primary sources of history.

Secondary sources are accounts written by people who gather the facts from primary sources. History books, biographies, and reference books are all secondary sources.

Identifying Primary and Secondary Sources

Many primary sources that historians use may be hard for you to find or to understand. But most libraries have some collections of original accounts. And some secondary sources contain copies from the originals, often with explanations that help the reader understand the originals.

Documents and **legal records** are useful primary sources. These include such important papers as the Constitution, as well as records of births, marriages, and deaths. Banks and businesses keep detailed records. Court records tell what is said in trials and other legal hearings. The United States *Congressional Record* is another legal record. Under different names it has been printed daily since 1789 and is an account of everything done in Congress.

Letters that have been written by famous people and printed or kept in collections are primary sources. You can go to the library and find volumes of letters written by John and Abigail Adams, Thomas Jefferson, and Daniel Webster, among others. Here is what Abigail Adams wrote to her sister about life in the White House.

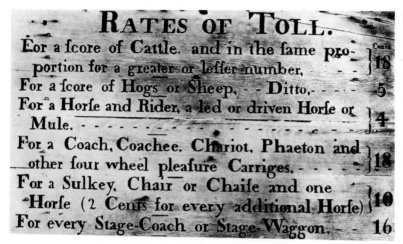

RATES OF TOLL.

For a ſcore of Cattle. and in the ſame pro- | 18
portion for a greater or leſſer number,

For a ſcore of Hogs or Sheep, - - Ditto, - - - | 5

For a Horſe and Rider, a led or driven Horſe or | 4
Mule. - - - - - - - - - -

For a Coach, Coachee. Chariot, Phaeton and | 18
other four wheel pleaſure Carriges. - - - - |

For a Sulkey, Chair or Chaiſe and one | 10
Horſe (2 Cents for every additional Horſe) |

For every Stage-Coach or Stage-Waggon. - - 16

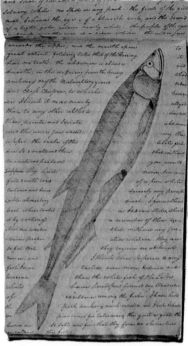

Objects used in the past, as well as drawings and diary entries, are primary sources. Historians have found such items as the toll rates board on the left above and the page from William Clark's journal useful in their research.

I had much rather live in the house at Philadelphia. Not one room . . . of the White House is finished. . . . It is habitable [only] by fires in every part, thirteen of which we are obliged to keep daily, or sleep in wet and damp places.

Letters help bring history to life. They remind readers that famous people from the past were real people, not just names in history books. Often, letters written by not-so-famous people about the events of their times are more interesting and important than the writings of famous people. Letters you write are primary sources and are a part of history.

Diaries and **journals** are day-by-day accounts. These accounts are also of interest to history students. Samuel Sewall, a Puritan who lived in Massachusetts, kept a diary from 1674 to 1729. His diary is often used as a source by people writing about daily life in early America.

The journals that Lewis and Clark kept as they explored the Louisiana Purchase tell of their everyday problems. Two entries show what camping was like before flashlights and bug spray.

January 13th 1806
. . . this evening we exhausted the last of our candles, but fortunately had taken the precaution to bring with us moulds and wick, by means of which and some Elk's tallow [animal fat] in our possession we do not yet consider ourselves [completely without] this necessary article. . . .

July 15th 1806
. . . the musquetoes continue to infest us in such manner that we can scarcely exist; . . . my dog even howls with the torture he experiences from them. . . .

Periodicals are such publications as newspapers and magazines that come out once a day, once a week, or once a month. By 1775

In the opinion of this cartoonist, Andrew Jackson acted more like a king than a president.

there were thirty-seven newspapers in the British colonies. These newspapers reported events leading up to the Revolution. After the Revolution, members of political parties used newspapers to express their views in articles and political cartoons.

Since colonial times periodicals have strongly influenced thought in the United States. People who were against slavery, for example, published their views in such newspapers as William Lloyd Garrison's *Liberator* or Frederick Douglass's *The North Star.* Their powerful words stirred many readers to take action against slavery.

Most libraries do not have periodicals dating back to 1775. But magazines and newspapers from later periods of history can probably be found at your library.

Some **books** are primary sources. Such famous people as Benjamin Franklin and Frederick Douglass wrote autobiographies. Autobiographies give firsthand accounts of the events in which the authors took part.

Pictures—drawings and paintings, editorial cartoons, old maps, still photographs, and moving-picture film—are also study aids. Only those made at the time of an event, however, are primary sources. Editorial cartoons are interesting because they show opinions about the issues of the day. Many libraries have collections of old drawings, photographs, and political cartoons. Such pictures are often used in history books.

Collections of oral history are also primary sources. Many Native American and African tribal groups had a special person whose job it was to remember the history of the group and to tell it to others. The storyteller might spend thirty or forty years learning the history and legends of the group. Then the history would be passed down almost word for word to another storyteller. In more recent times speeches and interviews have been recorded in writing, on sound film, or on sound tape. These speeches and interviews are also oral history.

Artifacts are items that remain from the past. These primary sources are usually found in museums rather than in libraries. Archaeologists who study artifacts write articles about them that you can study as secondary sources. In Chapter 2 there are pictures of artifacts used in studying Native Americans.

You probably already know many kinds of secondary sources. This book is one. Reference books such as encyclopedias, atlases, and almanacs are also secondary sources. Most reference books are found in the reference section of the library.

Articles in **encyclopedias** are arranged alphabetically. The articles may be on many topics or on only one subject. Your library might have encyclopedias on sports, music, medicine, photography, or technology.

An **atlas** is a book of maps and geographical facts. It often has in it a geographical dictionary called a gazetteer. This is a list of place-names that tells you on which map you will find each place.

Almanacs are usually published once a year. They give up-to-date information and statistics on a wide range of subjects. Almanacs include the major news stories of the year, lists of major accidents and natural disasters, lists of awards and prizes, charts about cities, and facts about people in the news. Some almanacs also give short accounts about events and people in world history. A **biographical dictionary** is most useful for historical research. The *Dictionary of American Biography,* for example, contains short articles on the lives of famous Americans.

Practicing Your Skills

On a separate sheet of paper, write out answers to these questions.
1. You have already studied many primary sources in this book. Identify the type of primary source presented on each of the following pages in this book: (a) page 45; (b) page 126; (c) page 131 (bottom); (d) page 146.
2. Look at the illustrations on pages 54, 135, and 149 (top). Which of these are primary sources? Which is a secondary source? Explain why in one or two sentences.

Critical Thinking
3. **Identifying Central Issues.** Which reference books (encyclopedia, atlas, almanac, or biographical dictionary) would you use to find the answer to each of these questions?
   a. How did the Federalist party begin?
   b. How far is Salt Lake City, Utah, from Nauvoo, Illinois?
   c. How many nuclear power plants were operating in your state last year?

Gathering Information from Sources

Historians follow several steps in preparing the record we call history. First they select a happening or a person from the past that interests them. Then they track down as many primary and secondary sources as possible about the subject they have chosen.

As a student of history you can follow the same steps to learn about an event or a person from the past. First choose a subject. Suppose you decide to study the forced march of the Cherokee to Oklahoma, known as the Trail of Tears (see pages 275-276).

The chart on page 258 lists the kinds of sources you may use to learn more about the Trail of Tears. One way to begin is to look in a general source, such as an encyclopedia. An encyclopedia often

Sources of Information About the Trail of Tears

Type of source	Type of information	Sources
Encyclopedia	Short summary articles, often with references to other articles in the encyclopedia and with bibliographies	*Compton's Encyclopedia* *Encyclopaedia Britannica* *World Book Encyclopedia*
General history of the United States	Description of Trail of Tears as one part of country's whole history	*American Spirit.* Clarence Ver Steeg, Chicago: Follett, 1982. *The American Heritage History of the Making of the Nation.* Ralph Andrist, ed. New York: American Heritage, 1968. *The Oxford History of the American People.* Samuel E. Morison. New York: Oxford University Press, 1965.
General history of the Native Americans in the United States	Description of Cherokee forced march as one part of whole history of all Native Americans in the United States	*The Broken Hoop: The History of Native Americans from 1600 to 1890, From the Atlantic Coast to the Plains.* Dan Georgakas. Garden City, N.Y.: Doubleday, 1973. *American Indian Tribes.* Marion E. Gridley. New York: Dodd, Mead, 1974. *The Indian Heritage of America.* Alvin Josephy, Jr. New York: Bantam, 1968.
General history of the Cherokee	Background information, including political, social, and economic life of the Cherokee	*Cherokee Sunset: A Nation Betrayed.* Samuel Carter III. Garden City, New York: Doubleday, 1976. *Indians of the Southeast: Then and Now.* Jesse Burt and Robert B. Ferguson. Nashville: Abingdon Press, 1973. *When Shall They Rest? The Cherokees' Long Struggle with America.* Peter Collier. New York: Holt, 1973.
History of the Trail of Tears	Report on the march itself with details of events leading up to and following the march	*The Cherokee Removal, 1838.* Glen Fleischmann. New York: Franklin Watts, 1971. *Only the Names Remain: The Cherokees and the Trail of Tears.* Boston: Little, Brown, 1972. *Cherokee Tragedy: The Story of the Ridge Family and the Decimation of a People.* Thurman Wilkins. New York: Macmillan, 1970.
Biography	Study of persons involved with the Trail of Tears	*Cherokee Chief: The Life of John Ross.* Electa Clark. New York: Crowell-Collier, 1970. *The Revolutionary Age of Andrew Jackson.* Robert V. Remini. New York: Harper & Row, 1976. *Sequoyah: Leader of the Cherokees.* Alice Marriott. New York: Random, 1956.
Journals, letters, diaries	Firsthand accounts of what happened	*Chronicles of American Indian Protest.* Council on Interracial Books for Children, eds. New York: Fawcett, 1971. *Native American Testimony: An Anthology of Indian and White Relations.* Peter Nabokov, ed. New York: Crowell, 1978. *Speeches on the Passage of the Bill for the Removal of Indians.* U.S. 21st Congress, First Session. Reprint. Millwood, N.Y.: Kraus Reprint Co., 1973.

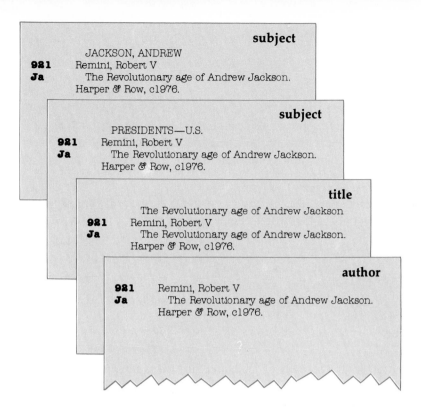

subject

JACKSON, ANDREW
921   Remini, Robert V
Ja   The Revolutionary age of Andrew Jackson.
          Harper & Row, c1976.

subject

PRESIDENTS—U.S.
921   Remini, Robert V
Ja   The Revolutionary age of Andrew Jackson.
          Harper & Row, c1976.

title

          The Revolutionary age of Andrew Jackson
921   Remini, Robert V
Ja   The Revolutionary age of Andrew Jackson.
          Harper & Row, c1976.

author

921   Remini, Robert V
Ja   The Revolutionary age of Andrew Jackson.
          Harper & Row, c1976.

contains a list of books—a bibliography—on the subject. It may also name people or other subjects that will help you.

To find nonfiction books in the library, look for three kinds of cards in the library catalog—an author card, a title card, and a subject card. These cards may be arranged in two ways. All author, title, and subject cards may be filed together alphabetically, or cards may be separated by author, title, and subject. Within these separate groups cards are also filed alphabetically.

As you gather information from different sources, you will be learning many facts about the Cherokee and the Trail of Tears. You will also be learning about attitudes—of the Cherokee who had to leave their land, of the white settlers who wanted to move into the land, and of the government officials who carried out the removal of the Cherokee. Understanding the attitudes of people in history brings new meaning to the bare facts of history.

Practicing Your Skills

On a separate sheet of paper write out answers to these questions.
1. To which source or sources listed on page 258 would you go for the following information?
   a. Names of Native American groups that had to leave their lands
   b. Events that led to the white settlers' need for more land
   c. The nature of Cherokee government
   d. The hardships the Cherokee suffered on the march
   e. The life story of John Ross, chief of the Cherokee
   f. The titles of other books that give facts about the Cherokee

2. Look over the first part of this chapter (pages 253-257). Try to name three sources besides those listed on the chart on page 258 that might tell about the Cherokee. Describe in one or two sentences what kind of information each might contain.

Critical Thinking
3. **Recognizing Bias.** How do you think the people who sang the song quoted below felt about the land rights of the Cherokees?

> All I want in this creation
> is a pretty little wife and big plantation
> way down yonder in the Cherokee Nation. . . .

2 Evaluating Sources

After finding sources of all kinds, historians must evaluate them. They must figure out when and how the accounts were written and who wrote them. They must decide whether or not the statements in the sources are fact, opinion, or even fiction. Some authors may have stated opinions as facts or even added details to tell a better story. To make these judgments, historians and students of history must be careful readers of both primary and secondary sources.

Distinguishing Fact from Opinion

If historical accounts were nothing but straight facts, they would be dull reading. Unless the reader already knows a subject well, facts by themselves do not always make much sense. The facts need to be explained. But no two historians see the facts in the same way. For example, here are parts of two historical accounts. Both describe the settlement of Texas by Anglo-Americans (white people from the United States). The first is from a biography of Stephen F. Austin.

> Of all the men who have figured in American History . . . there are no other two who have attracted so little attention from their contemporaries [those living at the same time] and have yet done things of such vast . . . importance as Moses Austin and his son Stephen. Their great work consisted in the making of Anglo-American Texas.

Two other historians have quite a different view of the Austins and of the other Anglo-Americans in Texas. The authors use the Native American word Téjas (tā′häs), meaning "friend," from which the name Texas comes.

> These first people fought their way in—killing and ruining the area around San Antonio. Most of them came from the slave states, and they brought a racist attitude with them. They

Artists often try to recreate historical events and figures. Frederic Remington painted this picture of the 10th Cavalry.

treated the Mexicans living in Téjas the same way they treated black people, and they showed no respect for the laws of Mexico. When Mexico abolished slavery in 1826, they just ignored the new law and kept on bringing in slaves.

Sometimes it is hard to separate fact from opinion. The first author has taken time out from his story to offer the view that Moses and Stephen Austin did "great work" of "vast importance" in Texas. In the second account, expressions such as "ruining the area" and "racist attitude" show that the authors believed the Anglo-American settlers were in the wrong. Even authors who try very hard to be fair to both sides in telling a story cannot always keep their opinions out of their histories.

In many cases the writers of primary sources were more concerned with expressing opinions or with pleasing their readers than with presenting facts. A careful historian learns to tell the difference.

Practicing Your Skills

The following exercises will give you practice in telling fact from opinion. On a separate sheet of paper write out answers to these questions.

1. Read the accounts on pages 280-282 and page 284 of this book about the settling of Texas by people from the United States. Compare these to the quotes about Stephen F. Austin on page 260. Which of the two quotes fits better with the account given in this book? Give three reasons for your answer.

Though they had a keen interest in the peoples of the Caribbean, Columbus and his crews were never able to live peacefully among them.

Critical Thinking

2. **Distinguishing Fact from Opinion.** Read the following account from the journal of Christopher Columbus about the people he found on San Salvador. As you read, look for facts and opinions. Then complete the activities following the reading selection.

I, in order that they might develop a very friendly disposition towards us, (because I knew that they were a people who could better be freed and converted to our Holy Faith by love than by force), gave to some of them red caps and to others glass beads, which they hung on their necks, and many other things of slight value, in which they took much pleasure. They remained so much our [friends] that it was a marvel, later they came swimming to the ships' boats in which we were, and brought us parrots and cotton thread in skeins and darts and many other things, and we swapped them for other things that we gave them, such as little glass beads and hawks' bells. Finally they traded and gave everything they had, with good will; but it appeared to me that these people were very poor in everything. . . . they bear no arms, nor know thereof; for I showed them swords and they grasped them by the blade and cut themselves through ignorance. They have no iron. Their darts are a kind of rod without iron, and some have at the end a fish's tooth and others, other things. [The people] are generally fairly tall and good looking, well built. I saw some who had marks of wounds on their bodies, and made signs to them to ask what it was, and they showed me that people of other islands which are near came there and wished to capture them, and they defended themselves. And I believed and now believe that people do come here from the mainland to take them as slaves. They ought to be good servants and of good skill, for I see that they repeat very quickly whatever was said to them. I believe that they would easily be made Christians, because it seemed to me that they belonged to no religion. I, please Our Lord, will carry off six of them at my departure to Your Highnesses, that they may learn to speak. I saw no animal of any kind in this island, except parrots.

Write out six facts that Columbus includes about these people. Write out three of his opinions. Then write three sentences explaining how the opinions Columbus expressed show either respect or disrespect for the Native Americans.

Judging Accuracy

One way to learn about history is through such novels as Harriet Beecher Stowe's *Uncle Tom's Cabin* or such television shows as "Roots" by Alex Haley. These can teach you much about life in the South between 1815 and 1850. But you must remember as you enjoy them that they are fiction, not fact. Stowe was inspired by real people, but the characters in *Uncle Tom's Cabin* are made-up people. Haley used real people and happenings for the story of "Roots," but he made up the dialogue between the characters and many of the details of the story.

You would not use made-up television shows or stories for information in a research report. They might not be accurate sources. Even some primary and secondary sources of history can be inaccurate. The best way to judge accuracy is to read as many

In staging such historical fiction as *Gone with the Wind*, moviemakers try to reproduce the life of the times. But movies are not reliable historical sources.

sources as possible. If you compare the facts presented in several sources and think about who prepared them and why, you can usually decide which is closest to the truth.

Here are two accounts of an event that took place in Boston on March 5, 1770. The British called it a riot, blaming the Americans. The Americans called it a massacre, blaming the British. As you read the two accounts, see if you can decide what really happened.

The first view of the Boston incident is from a letter written on April 10, 1770, by General Thomas Gage, the top commander of the British troops in North America.

> This Party [of British troops] was immediately attacked. Some [colonists threw] Bricks, Stones, Pieces of Ice and Snow-Balls at them, whilst others advanced up to their Bayonets, . . . calling out to them to fire if they dared, and provoking them to it, by the most [vulgar] language.
>
> Captain Preston stood, between the Soldiers and the Mob parlying [talking] with the latter . . . to perswade them to retire peaceably. Some amongst them asked him if he intended to order the Men to fire, he replyed by no means, and [remained standing] between the Troops and them. All he could say had no Effect, and one of the Soldiers receiving a violent Blow, instantly fired. Captain Preston turned around to see who fired, and received a Blow upon his Arm, which was aimed at his Head; and the Mob at first seeing no Execution done, and imagining the Soldiers had only fired Powder to frighten, grew more bold and attacked with greater Violence: continualy Striking at the Soldiers and pelting them, and calling out to them to fire. The Soldiers at length perceiving their Lives in Danger, and hearing the Word Fire all round them, three or four of them fired one after another, and again three more in the same hurry and Confusion. Four or five Persons were unfortunately killed, and More wounded. . . .

Here is another view of the Boston incident. It was written by a colonist and printed in a Boston newspaper on March 12, 1770.

> Thirty or forty persons, mostly lads . . . gathered in King street[.] Capt. Preston with a party of men with charged bayonets, came . . . to the commissioner's house, the soldiers pushing their bayonets, crying, make way! They took [their] place by the custom house and, continuing to push to drive the people off, pricked some in several places, on which they . . . it is said, threw snow balls. On this, the Captain commanded them to fire, and more snow balls coming, he again said . . . fire, be the consequence what it will! One soldier then fired, and a townsman with a [stick] struck him over the hands [so] that he dropped his gun; and rushing forward, aimed a blow at the

Captain's head which grazed his hat and fell pretty heavy upon his arm. However, the soldiers continued the fire . . . till seven or eight or, as some say, eleven guns were [fired].

By this fatal [firing] three men were laid dead on the spot and two more struggling for life. . . . the dead are Mr. Samuel Gray, . . . a [black] man named Crispus Attucks, . . . [and] Mr. James Caldwell, mate of Capt. Morton's vessel. . . .

How can you decide which account is more in line with what really happened? Whenever you need to evaluate a source, you should ask yourself the following questions.

1. Who is the author (or artist, or speaker)?
2. Is the source primary or secondary?
3. When was the source written (or made)?
4. Are the facts in this source the same as the facts in other sources?
5. What was the author's purpose?
6. For whom did the author write the account?
7. Does the author write about the event as a participant or as a reporter of things seen or heard?
8. What possible bias might the author have?

If you answer all these questions about the two accounts of the fight in Boston, you will better be able to judge them.

1. The author of the first account was General Thomas Gage, the British commander in North America. The author of the second account was a colonist.
2. Both accounts are primary sources. Both were written within a short time of the fight. Neither source, however, was written by an eyewitness to the fight.
3. Gage's letter was written over a month after the incident. The newspaper account was published a week after the clash.
4. Most of the facts in these two accounts do not agree. The British account has the colonists egging on the British with bricks, snowballs, and language. The colonial account has the British stirring up the colonists by pushing their way through the crowd with bayonets. Only then, the writer says, did the colonists throw snowballs. The British account also says that the captain never gave an order to fire. The colonial account says he gave such an order twice. Both accounts agree that the British captain received a blow on his arm. The British account says that six or seven soldiers fired, all in self-defense. The colonial account says seven or eight or eleven soldiers fired, with no mention of self-defense. The number of persons killed is also different in the two accounts—four or five in one and three in the other.
5. Gage's purpose was to let his superior in England know of the event. The colonist's purpose was to spread the news through the colony.

6. Gage wrote his letter for one person—a superior in England. The colonist wrote his account for a great number of colonists.

7. We do not learn from this account whether Gage himself was present at the event. Even so, his point of view is that of a reporter rather than of someone who took part. The newspaper writer probably was not at the scene. Words such as "it is said" suggest that he used the reports of others.

8. Gage might be eager to show his superior that the British were not at fault. As commander of the British in North America, he probably favored the British. The newspaper writer, whose readers were probably angry colonists tired of British laws and control, clearly favored the colonists.

It seems, then, that more research is needed before we can decide which account is more accurate. Many writers of secondary sources have checked different primary sources as you have just done. Like you, they have found that a primary source may have biases and mistakes. Remember that secondary sources may also have biases and mistakes.

Practicing Your Skills

1. The following is yet another account of the Boston incident. This one was written by the British Captain Thomas Preston on March 13, 1770. It is part of a letter sent to Britain.

> The mob still increased and were more outrageous, striking their clubs . . . against another, and calling out, come on you rascals, you bloody backs, you lobster scoundrels, fire if you dare . . . we know you dare not. . . . At this time I was between the soldiers and the mob, [doing] all in my power to persuade them to retire peaceably, but to no purpose. They advanced to the points of the bayonets, struck some of them and even the muzzles of the pieces, and seemed to be [trying to start a fight] with the soldiers. . . . While I was thus speaking, one of the soldiers having received a severe blow with a stick, stepped a little on one side and instantly fired, on which . . . asking him why he fired without orders, I was struck with a club on my arm. . . . On this a general attack was made on the men by a great number of heavy clubs and snowballs being thrown at them . . . some persons at the same time from behind calling out . . . why don't you fire. Instantly three or four of the soldiers fired, one after another. . . . On my asking the soldiers why they fired without orders, they said they heard the word fire and supposed it came from me. This might be the case as many of the mob called out fire, fire, but I assured the men that I gave no such order; that my words were, don't fire, stop your firing.

On a separate sheet of paper write out answers to all eight questions from page 265 about this account.

2. Now look at a picture made by Paul Revere. This picture was sold widely after the event in Boston took place. Write a paragraph answering the following question: If this were your only source, would you call the incident at Boston a massacre or a riot? Give at least three reasons for your answer.

Critical Thinking

3. **Identifying Central Issues.** Using the three written accounts, the information on page 164 of this book, and Paul Revere's drawing, write your own account of what happened in Boston. Try to use as many details as possible to give your account interest and life. Answer these questions as best you can in your account.

a. When and where did the event take place?
b. What did the setting look like?
c. How did the British dress? How did the colonists dress?
d. Who started the fight and why?
e. What happened after the fighting started?
f. Was the incident a riot or a massacre?

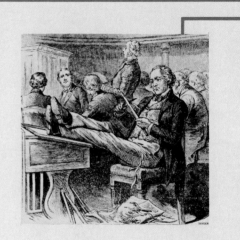

National Expansion

❧ Chapter 14

268

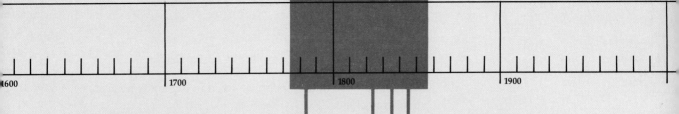

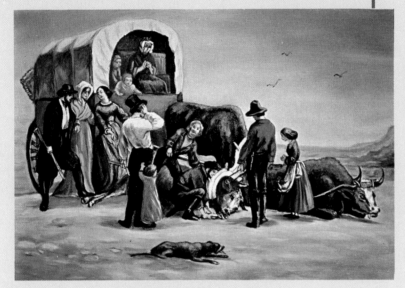

Vocabulary

prairie	migration
removal	mountain man
outpost	pueblo
pioneer	mission station
reservation	rancho
displace	expansion

THE DIRECTION OF United States history began to change about 1815. People in the United States looked west beyond the Mississippi River, rather than east across the Atlantic. The colonists had needed Great Britain before they claimed independence. And they had needed France, their ally, to make good their claim to independence. But after the Peace of Ghent was signed in 1814, the new country began growing beyond anyone's dreams. No foreign country seriously threatened its borders or the rights of its people. People in the United States felt that the future held promise—not only of land, but also of a new life. And the way to this land and new life for some lay west.

1   Westward Bound

Before 1815 few Americans had settled more than 300 miles (480 km) from the Atlantic coast. But from 1815 to 1850 the people of the United States swept across the continent to the Pacific coast some 3,000 miles (4,800 km) away. At the time the Constitution went into effect there were only 4 million people in the United States, most of them east of the Appalachian Mountains. By 1850 more than twice

Prereading

1. What routes did westward-bound settlers take into the new lands between the Appalachian Mountains and the Mississippi River?

2. How did the settlers and the United States government take over the lands of the Native Americans?

3. By what means did United States settlers cross the continent and reach the Pacific Ocean?

4. Why did United States citizens in Texas decide to declare their independence from Mexico?

5. Why did Mormons want to move to unsettled territory?

that number—10 million people—lived in the lands west of the Appalachians alone.

Trails to the West

William Calk wrote in 1775 of fighting with Native Americans for the western lands. He also tells how the land was divided.

Satrd April 8—we all pact up & Started Crost Cumberland gap, about one oclock this Day we Met a great maney peopel turnd Back for fear of the indians but our Company goes on Still with good courage. . . . tuesday 18th fair & cool . . . we come to where the indians fired on Boons Companey & kild 2 men. . . . thursday 20 . . . we Start Early & git Down to Caintuck [Kentucky] to Boons foart [fort] about 12 oclock wheare we stop. . . . fryday 21st Warm this Day, they Begin laying off lots

The trails west led settlers by land and water into the rich farmlands of the Lake and Gulf plains.

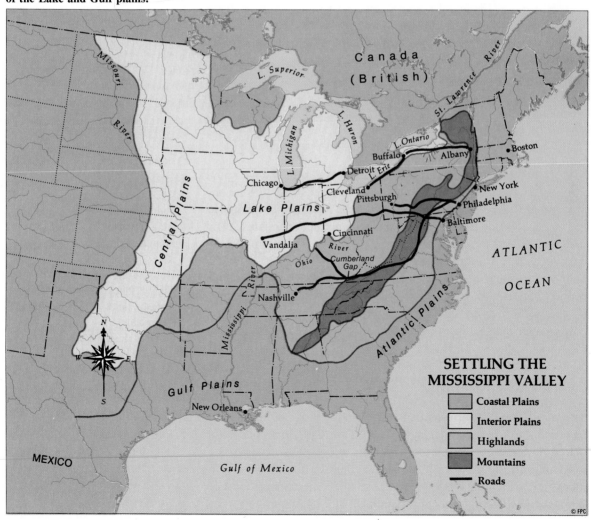

SETTLING THE MISSISSIPPI VALLEY

Coastal Plains
Interior Plains
Highlands
Mountains
Roads

© FPC

in the town. . . . Sunday April 23rd this morning the peopel meets & Draws for Chois of lots. . . . Monday 24th We all view our lots & Some Dont like them. . . . Wednesday 26th We Begin Building us a house & a plaise of Defence to keep the indians off. . . . Satterday 29th—We git our house kivered [covered] with Bark & move our things into it at Night and Begin houskeeping.

The first trail to the West started in several southern states. Its branches met at the Cumberland Gap, a pass through the Appalachians where Virginia, Kentucky, and Tennessee come together. There the trail divided. The Robertson Trail led south and then west to Nashville, Tennessee. The other—a rough, narrow, single-lane wagon trail—went directly west through the gap. This branch, the Wilderness Road, as it was called, led to Boonesborough and Harrodsburg, Kentucky.

Boonesborough was named for Daniel Boone, who blazed the trail through the Cumberland Gap. Boone—tall, blue-eyed, and blond—went to Kentucky in May 1769 with two partners to hunt for deerskins. He stayed there for two years and fell in love with the region. He decided to bring his own family and others to start a settlement.

A second trail to the West began in Philadelphia. It led to present-day Pittsburgh and then followed the Ohio River. At Pittsburgh people built or bought rafts on which they loaded everything they owned and set off downriver. The currents were swift and tricky. Sandbars often blocked the way. Many families lost everything they had when their rafts overturned.

A third trail led from Albany, New York, through the Mohawk Valley to western New York and to Lake Erie. The earliest settlers stopped and began farming the unclaimed land in western New York. Later settlers pushed farther west, moving by land and water to the Lake Plains.

New Lands East of the Mississippi

The northern trail and the trail down the Ohio River became gateways to the Lake Plains for the pioneers. The Lake Plains lie north of the Ohio River and reach west from the Appalachians to the source of the Mississippi. During the Ice Age huge glaciers leveled much of the land. When the glaciers melted, they left the Lake Plains covered with a layer of rich soil.

The southern part of the Lake Plains—now southern Illinois and Indiana—was covered by hardwood forests. Farther north—in western Indiana and central Illinois—there were endless miles of tall prairie grasses and only scattered clumps of trees. In Wisconsin and Michigan the northern Lake Plains were gently rolling, and the soil

Two river travelers struggle to bring their raft through the rapids near the village of Cedars. This village is probably the modern town of Cedar Rapids, Iowa.

was rich but sandy. Early settlers believed that crops would not grow where trees did not grow. So the settlers flocked to the southern hardwood forests and for a time kept away from the treeless prairies.

The Gulf Plains stretch from the Gulf of Mexico north to the Tennessee River valley and slightly west of the Mississippi River. Near the gulf, rainfall is heavy. At one time a belt of longleaf pine trees grew along the gulf.

The land and climate in the Gulf Plains between southern Tennessee and the longleaf pine region are ideal for growing cotton. North of Tennessee's southern border, frost comes too early for cotton growing. In time, people moved into all areas of the Gulf Plains. But the cotton-growing region attracted the most settlers, many of whom grew rich on their large plantations.

New States in the Lake and Gulf Plains

The Lake Plains in the North and the Gulf Plains in the South had been the home of Native Americans for hundreds of years. When the first white settlers arrived in the Lake Plains, they chose the hardwood forests to the south as their new home. Most were farmers who hoped to clear the land and begin growing crops. They came—thousands of them—mainly from the states south of the Ohio River. Many had been small-farm owners who could not compete with the large plantation system developing in the Southeast.

After 1830 more settlers came from New England and the Middle States, following the northern trail to the Lake Plains rather than the route along the Ohio Valley. Many settled first in Michigan. By 1837, Detroit, Michigan, had a population of 10,000—one fifth the size of Boston and the same size as Charleston, South Carolina. In 1831 a Detroit newspaper reported, "Almost every building that can be made to answer for a shelter is occupied and filled." Detroit soon had a theater, schools, churches, and libraries, as well as a water and waste system.

From Detroit settlers moved west along the Chicago Road to Illinois, turning Chicago from a lakefront village into a busy town by 1835. By then people had learned that crops could indeed grow in the treeless prairies. So they settled throughout northern Illinois as well as southern Wisconsin.

By 1850 more than 4 million of the nation's 23 million people lived in the Lake Plains. Under the terms of the Northwest Ordinance of 1787 five new states had entered the Union: Ohio, 1803; Indiana, 1816; Illinois, 1818; Michigan, 1837; and Wisconsin, 1848.

People in the South headed for the Gulf Plains. Some, mainly poor white farmers, settled near the longleaf pine region where they raised a few garden crops and cattle. Many more people settled in the cotton-growing region farther north. The hope of raising cotton drew so many people to the Gulf Plains that the trails west were jammed with would-be settlers. One Carolina planter compared the urge to move to a fever that "carried off vast numbers of our citizens." Between 1815 and 1840 about 40 percent of the people in South Carolina alone moved west. Slave owners brought their slaves with them when they moved. Almost half the 4 million people in the Gulf Plains were blacks, most of them slaves.

As the population increased, so did the number of states. Kentucky (1792) and Tennessee (1796) had joined the Union before 1800. Mississippi became a state in 1817, Alabama in 1819, and Florida in 1845.

New States West of the Mississippi

Soon after the Louisiana Purchase in 1803, thousands of new settlers poured west across the Mississippi River, especially in the South. With New Orleans as its center, Louisiana became a busy region of trade and of plantation farming. Louisiana became a state in 1812. By 1820 its population had grown to about 153,000.

Between 1815 and 1819 land-hungry settlers rushed into Missouri. They settled along the Missouri River and all the other rivers flowing into the Mississippi where the waters made the land rich for farming. Missouri quickly became a state in 1821. Farmers also began settling in Arkansas, again along the rivers. Between 1812 and 1835 the population of Arkansas grew from about 1,500 to about 70,000. Arkansas became a state in 1836.

The northern reaches of the Mississippi valley in Iowa and Minnesota were settled later. Until the 1830s the Native Americans—the Sauk, Fox, Iowa, Missouri, Omaha, Sioux, and Chippewa—held these lands. When federal treaties called for the removal of the Native Americans to areas farther west, white loggers and farmers moved in. Iowa became a state in 1846, and Minnesota in 1858.

Section 1 Review

1. Which two trails did settlers follow into Kentucky and Tennessee?
2. Which two trails became gateways to the Lake Plains?
3. What five states in the Lake Plains entered the Union between 1803 and 1848?
4. What five states in the Gulf Plains entered the Union between 1792 and 1845?
5. What five states just west of the Mississippi River joined the Union between 1812 and 1858?

Critical Thinking

6. **Recognizing Cause and Effect.** Why was cotton ideally suited to grow in the Gulf Plains between southern Tennessee and the longleaf pine region?

LOOKING AHEAD: How did the settlers and the United States government take over the lands of the Native Americans?

2 Displaced Native Americans

White settlers rushing westward settled on lands that had been the homes of Native Americans. Settlers cleared the land, started farms, and built homes. Native American groups tried to defend their lands, sometimes by fighting. The white settlers looked to the federal government for help in resolving the disputes.

Removal from the Lake Plains

On July 15, 1815, agents sent by President James Madison met with tribal groups in Wisconsin and Illinois. Land agreements were reached with some tribal groups, but the Fox and Sauk angrily left the meeting grounds. The Kickapoo and the Winnebago also were displeased with the government's offers.

Fearing more conflicts, the government strengthened old western outposts and built a chain of new forts along or near the Mississippi River. But some pioneers wanted the government to remove the Native Americans altogether. Between 1817 and 1830 the government gave the Shawnee, Wyandot, Miami, Potawatomi, and some others two choices. They were to move out of the Midwest or be confined to reservation lands set aside for them.

Some Native Americans thought they had a third choice. They fought back. In 1827 a warrior named Red Bird led some Winnebago in an attack on farmers near Prairie du Chien (prār′i′ də′ shēn′), Wisconsin. But other tribal groups did not come to their aid, and Red Bird was forced to give up. By 1837 the Winnebago had traded all of their land in Wisconsin for hunting grounds along the west bank of the Mississippi River.

The peaceful Sauk and Fox—farmers who lived in villages in western Illinois and Wisconsin—were also told to move west of the Mississippi River. The head chief, Keokuk (kē′ō·kôk′), advised his people to obey. But a lesser chief named Black Hawk refused to leave. He and his followers stayed in Illinois for two more years until the army forced them out. Later he returned with whole families in an attempt to settle peacefully among the whites. But Black Hawk and his people were once again driven away by soldiers. This conflict was called the Black Hawk War.

Two leaders of the Sauk and Fox were Little Stabbing Chief (top) and Keokuk.

Removal from the Southeast

Native Americans in the Gulf Plains also lost their lands. Between 1817 and 1825 the federal government made several separate treaties with the Chickasaw, Choctaw, Creek, and Cherokee. Members of these nations could move either to reservations in the Southeast or to lands west of the Mississippi River. To those who moved, the government offered money for supplies. But few chose to move.

The government then tried to make deals with some of the chiefs. The leaders of the Creek agreed that any chief making a deal to sell land to the federal government would be killed. In 1825 one chief, William McIntosh, sold some Creek lands in Georgia. The other chiefs condemned McIntosh to death.

The remaining Creek leaders could not hold their lands. Beginning in 1827 the federal government removed the Creek, first to Arkansas Territory, and then later to Indian Territory. The Choctaw and Chickasaw were also removed.

The Trail of Tears

The Cherokee story best shows the trials of the displaced Native Americans. The Cherokee, some 15,000 strong, were powerful and well organized. To keep their lands, they decided to set up their own government. They gathered at New Echota, Georgia, on July 4, 1827,

After 1830 most Native Americans living east of the Mississippi were forced to leave their homes for reservations in Indian Territory.

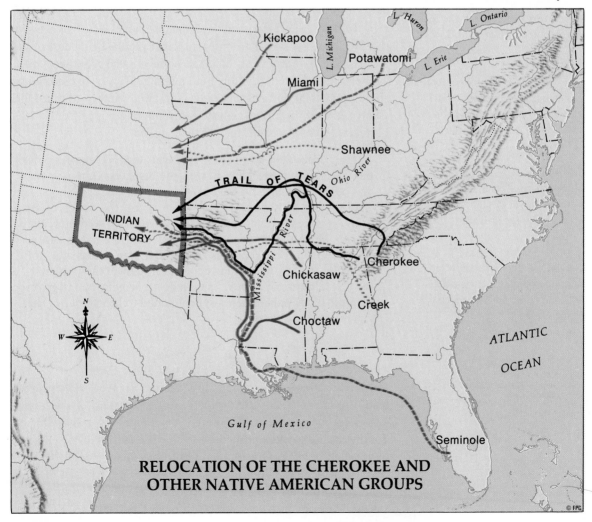

RELOCATION OF THE CHEROKEE AND OTHER NATIVE AMERICAN GROUPS

Section 2 Review

1. What four Native American groups were displeased with President Madison's settlement offers?
2. What happened to the Shawnee, Wyandot, Miami, and Potawatomi between 1817 and 1830?
3. What did Black Hawk do when the government ordered him to move west of the Mississippi River?
4. What two choices did the federal government offer the Choctaw, Creek, and Cherokee between 1817 and 1825?
5. What did the Cherokee do in an attempt to keep their lands?
6. What power did the Indian Removal Act give to the President?

Critical Thinking

7. **Determining Relevance.** Why is the removal of the Cherokee from Georgia called the Trail of Tears?

LOOKING AHEAD: By what means did United States settlers cross the continent and reach the Pacific Ocean?

Death and suffering marked the Cherokee's winter march.

and drew up a constitution for a Cherokee republic. In 1828 they elected Chief John Ross president. Officials from Georgia, however, reminded Congress that no group in the United States could set itself up as a separate nation.

In 1830 Congress passed the Indian Removal Act. This act gave the President the power to order all tribal groups living east of the Mississippi to move west. In 1838 some 13,000 Cherokee men, women, and children were forced to migrate. They were escorted by soldiers on their journey during a cold, wet winter. About 4,000 Cherokee died. In Cherokee history this migration is called the Trail of Tears. A vivid account tells of their march.

> They proceeded down along the river, the sick, the old people, and the smaller children, with the blankets, cooking pots, and other belongings in wagons, the rest on foot or on horses. The number of wagons was 645. It was like the march of an army, regiment after regiment, the wagons in the center, the officers along the line and the horsemen on the flanks and at the rear. . . . Somewhere also along that march of death—for the exiles died by tens and twenties every day of the journey—the devoted wife of John Ross sank down, leaving him to go on with the bitter pain of bereavement added to heartbreak at the ruin of his nation.

3 To the Pacific

Between 1825 and 1845, people surged to the Far West, following the lead of the trappers and the traders. Just to the west of the Mississippi were the newly resettled Native Americans. Beyond lay the dry Southwest. So settlers pushed on to the Pacific. By 1845, pioneers had settled in Utah, Oregon, and California. Many people believed that it was the fate, or destiny, of the United States to cover the land from coast to coast. This idea, later called Manifest Destiny, had a strong influence on Americans all through the 1800s.

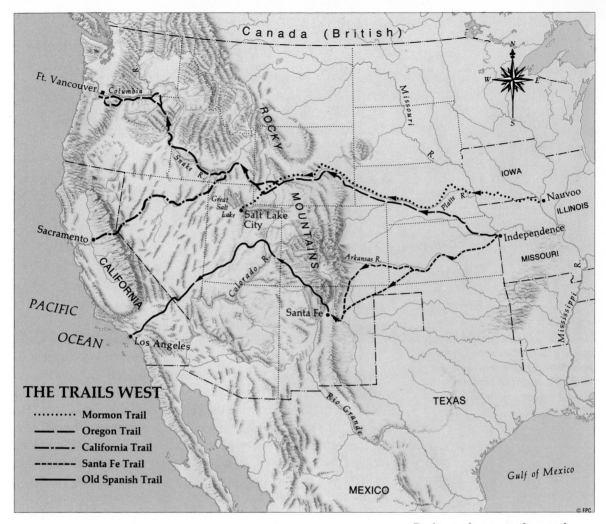

·········· Mormon Trail
———— Oregon Trail
—·—·— California Trail
----- Santa Fe Trail
———— Old Spanish Trail

Daring explorers, traders, and mountain men were soon followed west by equally adventurous settlers.

Trappers and Traders

The first white trappers and traders reached the central Rocky Mountains in the 1820s. These adventurers, called mountain men, were rough and tough. Each fall the mountain men scattered through the Rockies to trap beaver. Each summer they met at central trading points to exchange their furs for goods and money.

Although many mountain men made huge profits, they also suffered great hardships. One recalled hunger so great that he had "taken the soles of [his] mocassins, crisped them in the fire, and eaten them." In 1823 mountain man Hugh Glass was badly mangled by a bear. He managed to live and crawled more than a hundred miles to Fort Kiowa (kī′ə·wô′) in what is now South Dakota.

Glass also took part in developing exchanges between United States and Mexican traders at Santa Fe (sant′ə fā′). Each spring a train of wagons left Independence, Missouri, for Santa Fe. The wagons were filled with guns, pans, knives, forks, spoons, and dress goods. At Santa Fe these goods were traded for beaver skins and Spanish dollars. This yearly trade continued until 1844, when Mexico closed the Santa Fe post to Americans.

Troops stationed at Fort Laramie protected wagon trains along the Oregon Trail, while traders at the fort did business with Native Americans.

Although Santa Fe had a thriving trade, people did not want to settle in the Southwest. Some feared the attack of Native Americans. But most thought the land was useless. Zebulon Pike, for whom Pike's Peak in Colorado is named, had explored the area in 1806. He reported, "I saw in my route in various places tracts of land . . . where the wind had thrown up the sand . . . on which not a speck of vegetable matter existed." Even today many areas of the dry Southwest have few people.

By the mid-1840s the mountain men had trapped most of the beaver in the West. When they returned East, their stories of rich lands to the west made others eager to seek out these places. And their trails became the routes that later settlers followed.

Settlement of Oregon

As early as the 1820s, Congress and others had tried to settle the Pacific Northwest with little success. In 1833–1834 Nathaniel J. Wyeth, a Boston ice merchant, started a company for fur trading and salmon fishing in Oregon. The company failed, but Wyeth's travelers became the first white Americans to follow the route later known as the Oregon Trail. Three ministers—Jason Lee, Samuel Parker, and Marcus Whitman—learned the way from Wyeth and set out for Oregon. There they founded missions. A few others followed them. But blizzards, flash floods, and other dangers along the trail delayed settlement.

A party of 1,000 men, women, and children led by Peter H. Burnett proved in 1843 that Oregon could be settled. With Marcus Whitman as guide, the pioneers left Independence, Missouri, with more than 5,000 cattle and oxen and at least 120 wagons, divided into two columns. Burnett's party reached Oregon, and others soon followed. Oregon became a state in 1859.

The Spanish Background in California

In colonial times the Spanish had built pueblos, mission stations, and military outposts called presidios (pri·sēd′ē·ōz′) along the Pacific coast. By 1820 about 300 Spanish soldiers were scattered among the military outposts of San Diego, Santa Barbara, Monterey, and San Francisco. They lived in small forts made of wood and adobe—a mixture of mud, straw, and water. Small villages grew up around each post, bringing the total Spanish population to about 4,000. An additional 5,000 Spanish had settled in pueblos or villages such as Los Angeles, Santa Barbara, and San Jose (san′ə·zā′).

The most important Spanish settlements were the twenty-one mission stations stretching in a chain from San Diego to San Francisco. Priests ran these stations, which lay about one day's travel apart. About 30,000 Native Americans lived and worked on mission land. They raised livestock in the rich pastures. They dug irrigation canals to grow grain and other crops, especially grapes.

In 1821, after 300 years of Spanish rule, Mexico fought for and won its independence. Spanish priests continued to hold the missions in California for about ten more years. Then Mexican settlers began to call for free land. In 1833 the Mexican government opened the California mission lands to Mexican pioneers. As the settlers moved in, fighting broke out between them and the Native American mission workers. Buildings, crops, horses, and cattle were destroyed. In a short time the fighting stopped, and the newcomers were granted ranch lands called ranchos, ranging from 4,000 to well over 100,000 acres (16,000 to 400,000 ha).

United States Settlements in California

Mountain men—Jedediah Smith and thirteen companions—were the first persons from the United States to reach Mexican California.

The Santa Fe Trail became a popular southern route for settlers moving west.

They surprised the Mexicans in November 1826 when they camped outside San Gabriel mission. These long-haired, bearded men, clothed in skins from animals they trapped, were only the first of a number who came there each year.

John A. Sutter, a native of Switzerland, arrived in California by ship in 1839. The Mexican governor granted him 49,000 acres (196,000 ha) of land on the Sacramento River. He farmed, traded, and became a powerful landowner. In 1842 he built Sutter's Fort. It had thick walls on which he mounted cannon. Soon the fort blossomed into a village, with carpenters, bakers, toolmakers, and other skilled workers.

James W. Marshall was building a sawmill at Sutter's Fort in January 1848 when he noticed yellow flecks in a nearby riverbed. These yellow flecks turned out to be gold. By March the cry of "Gold! Gold!" reached everywhere. In 1849, people flooded into California in a great migration known as the gold rush.

Most gold seekers failed. Few knew how to find and hold their claims or how to work the streams. But still they came. The gold fever reached such a pitch that some people grew rich just housing the gold seekers. In San Francisco a canvas tent set up as a hotel brought in $40,000 a year. Some ships, abandoned in the bay by sailors gone gold-hunting, were used as sleeping quarters.

Mining camps with colorful names—Humbug Creek, Lazy Man's Canyon, Red Dog—grew up throughout the gold country. Camp members made their own rules, and lawbreakers were often swiftly punished.

California became a state in 1850. By this time Mexico had lost most of its land in present-day North America, including California, to the United States. The roots of the war that gave the United States most of the Southwest go back to the days when Americans first settled Texas.

4 Settlements and Conflicts in Texas

Before Mexico became independent in 1821, Spain ruled the area known as Texas. Few Mexicans wanted to settle in Texas, and the Spanish government had welcomed settlers from the United States.

The Austins in Texas

Moses Austin, an American, presented a settlement plan to Spanish officials in San Antonio in 1820. The officials approved his plan. But Moses Austin died before he could carry it out. Stephen F. Austin went ahead with his father's idea. He quickly enlisted 300 settlers and hired a vessel to take them along the Gulf of Mexico to the mouth of the Colorado River in Texas.

Section 3 Review

1. What was Manifest Destiny?
2. How did the mountain men help settle the West?
3. What two resources in Oregon attracted the group led by Nathaniel J. Wyeth?
4. What were the most important Spanish settlements in California in 1820?
5. When did California change from a Spanish to a Mexican possession?

Critical Thinking

6. **Demonstrating Reasoned Judgment.** What happened between Mexico and the United States that made it possible for California to enter the Union in 1850?

LOOKING AHEAD: Why did United States citizens in Texas decide to declare their independence from Mexico?

By the time the settlers reached Texas, Mexico had won independence. Austin had his plan approved by the new government. Meanwhile the Karankawa (kə·rangkə′wô′) and Tonkawa (täng′kəwə) groups attacked the Austin settlement, and a dry spell ruined the crops. Despite these setbacks Austin's colony gained a foothold. Its center was the village of San Felipe (san′ fä·lē′pä′) de Austin on the banks of the Brazos River. In four years the settlement gradually grew to 500 families and over 2,000 settlers.

In 1824 the Mexican government passed an act to encourage more settlement in Texas and other Mexican states. Those who came were to pay no taxes for ten years. In return they had to swear allegiance to the Mexican government. Many United States citizens moved to Mexico.

Trouble in Mexican Texas

Migrants from the United States soon outnumbered Mexicans in Texas ten to one. Problems developed. First, Mexicans were mostly Catholics, while most settlers from the United States were not. Second, Texas, as part of a larger territory called Texas-Coahuila (kō′ə·wē′lə), had only two representatives in the territorial government. With such a small voice United States settlers believed they were being ruled by outsiders. Third, disputes taken into the Mexican courts were not settled by local juries. People from the United States, who were used to trial by jury, felt deprived of rights. Fourth, the Mexican government wanted settlers to free any slaves they held, but the slave owners refused. Because of these disputes, the government of Mexico finally halted all settlement by United States citizens. And it stationed soldiers in Texas in case of uprisings.

By telegraph and newspaper the story of trouble in Mexico spread quickly around the country.

In their fight for independence from Mexico, Texans won their freedom at the Battle of San Jacinto.

In response each Texas settlement sent five delegates to San Felipe de Austin in 1832. The delegates swore loyalty to the government of Mexico. But they also wanted promises that their land would not be taken away, that migration to Texas from the United States would be reopened, and that the Mexican soldiers would be withdrawn. They also asked for their own separate assembly within the Mexican government, free from Texas-Coahuila.

At first it seemed as if the settlers and Mexico would reach an agreement. But a powerful Mexican leader, General Santa Anna, had just taken over the government. He set aside all compromise, sent more soldiers to Texas, and jailed Stephen Austin.

The Republic of Texas

Angry delegates from the Texas settlements met again in October 1835. They restated their wish to become a separate state within Mexico. They also agreed to take up arms if necessary. Soon Santa Anna sent an army against the defenders of Texas rights. Delegates to a meeting in March 1836 drafted a declaration of independence and wrote a constitution. The Republic of Texas was born.

A week later Santa Anna attacked the Texans at Fort Alamo in San Antonio. The defenders, among them such frontier heroes as Davy Crockett, William B. Travis, and Jim Bowie, were badly outnumbered. Every Texas soldier was killed. The victory was also costly to the Mexican army—1,544 soldiers killed.

The final showdown came at the Battle of San Jacinto (san′ jə·sint′ə) in April 1836. General Sam Houston, later president of the Republic of Texas, led the Texan troops. On April 21, just at noon when Santa Anna and his army were least expecting it, Houston attacked. "Victory is certain," Houston told his soldiers. "Trust in God and fear not!" Within hours Santa Anna was defeated.

Many Texans wanted their republic to become a state in the United States. But many members of Congress did not want Texas in the Union. They knew that Mexico might fight for it once again. Adding Texas to the Union raised another problem. In 1836 half the country's twenty-four states allowed slavery; the other half did not. Admitting Texas as a slave state would upset that balance and lead to conflict. Statehood would have to wait.

Section 4 Review

1. What part did Moses Austin play in the settlement of Texas?
2. How did Mexico encourage more settlement in Texas?
3. What three actions did General Santa Anna take after he took over the Mexican government?
4. When did Texans declare their independence as a republic?
5. What was the result of the Battle of San Jacinto?
6. For what two reasons were many members of Congress opposed to statehood for Texas?

Critical Thinking

7. **Expressing Problems Clearly.** What four problems led to trouble between Texans who had come from the United States and the Mexican government?

LOOKING AHEAD: Why did Mormons want to move to unsettled territory?

5 The Mormon Settlement in Utah

Present-day Utah was settled by members of the Church of Jesus Christ of Latter-Day Saints, better known as the Mormons. The church was founded in western New York in 1830 by Joseph Smith. Smith led his followers to Ohio, to Missouri, and finally to Illinois. By 1844 the Mormons had the largest and richest settlement in the state. Others envied them. The Mormons sometimes disagreed among themselves about religious questions. But they banded together when Smith was killed by a mob of non-Mormons.

Pioneer families needed the help of frontier guides who were wise in the ways of wilderness living.

Brigham Young's Migration

Under a new leader, Brigham Young, the Mormons decided to move where no one would bother them. In February 1846 the Mormons began the best-planned migration ever to travel beyond the Rocky Mountains. The first group to leave set up way stations to grow vegetables, raise livestock, and repair wagons. Smaller groups of 50 to 100 wagons followed the same route. In this way 15,000 Mormons traveled 1,500 miles (2,400 km) to Utah. Once there, the Mormons laid out a town beside the Great Salt Lake.

Federal Control of Utah

Because of past troubles, the Mormons did not want to join the United States or to have people with other religious views settling near them. But their lands in Utah—along with California and other western territories—were given up by Mexico to the United States in 1848. The Mormons immediately asked for statehood so they could continue to rule themselves.

The Mormons' appeal, however, was denied. Congress thought that the area they asked for was too large. Also there were too few people living there. So in 1850 Utah became a territory. After a brief clash in 1857, the United States government and the Mormon settlers reached an uneasy peace. About forty years later Utah became a state.

With citizens of the United States moving into Texas and California and with the government restoring order in Utah, the first thrust of westward expansion ended. It had affected almost every phase of life in the United States. New places were settled. More states came into the Union. Opportunities of all kinds arose. The young, growing nation was finding itself. Faster means of travel developed. Inventions speeded up work and increased production. New products appeared, and markets expanded. Even political ideas changed. You will study the consequences of the opening of the West in the following chapter.

Section 5 Review

1. Who founded the Church of Jesus Christ of Latter-Day Saints?
2. What made the Mormon migration beyond the Rocky Mountains so successful?
3. What was Utah called from 1850 until it became a state?

Critical Thinking

4. **Recognizing Cause and Effect.** Why did Congress deny the Mormon appeal for statehood?

The westward movement opened new doors for some people and shut others out.

In the nation's push westward, some leaders, such as Stephen F. Austin, had a chance to develop peaceful, strong, new communities. Others, such as Black Hawk, had to leave the communities they knew and loved.

A Community Builder

Stephen F. Austin came to Missouri with his parents in 1798 when it was still Spanish territory. At an early age he learned about the different peoples on the frontier and the need to live together for protection.

In 1822 Austin planted the first community of settlers from the United States in Texas. He became not merely the leader of the colony but its sole authority—the lawmaker, judge, and granter of land. He had the power to accept or reject persons who wished to join his colony. He mapped the area, encouraged trade with the United States, and built schools as well as sawmills. By 1825 Austin had settled 300 families; nine years later 750 new families had joined them. No other settlement in Texas was so successful.

Relations with Mexico

For a time Austin was able to keep good relations between the new settlers and the Mexicans. At the time he moved to Texas, he had given full allegiance to Mexico. He wrote: "I bid an everlasting farewell to my native country. . . ."

Later, when Texans were in conflict with Mexico, they sent Austin to Mexico City to speak for them. But Austin angered the Mexican leaders. They imprisoned him for a year, finally releasing him in 1835.

After Texas became an independent republic, Austin was a candidate to be its first president in 1836. Sam Houston defeated him in the election. Later that year Austin

Spanish and English traditions mingled in Texas. Stephen Austin (inset) started the first colony.

A German artist drew this version of the Battle of Bad Axe.

Black Hawk's statue overlooks the Rock River in Illinois.

died at the age of forty-three. But he had reached a goal that he had once written of in a letter. "My object is to build up, for the present as well as for future generations."

Black Hawk's Move

Black Hawk was a chief of the Sauk and Fox. Their villages lay near the mouth of the Rock River where it empties into the Mississippi River. The Sauk and Fox planted corn in the fertile soil and hunted for wild game.

White settlers moving west sought the rich soil worked by the Sauk and Fox. In Black Hawk's book of his life's story he recorded a meeting with a party of settlers: "I was out one day hunting . . . and met three white men. They accused me of killing their hogs; I denied it; but they would not listen to me. One of them took the gun out of my hand and fired it off—then . . . commenced [began] beating me with sticks. . . ."

Because of such acts, many Sauk and Fox moved to land west of the Mississippi River. At first Black Hawk and some others refused to go. But in 1831 federal soldiers threatened to attack them if they did not leave.

Black Hawk then led his people across the river into Iowa country. The season was too far along to plant corn and to build good shelters. Black Hawk and his followers were cold and hungry that winter.

Black Hawk dreamed of returning in peace to the rich Sauk and Fox lands. He gathered about 1,000 men, women, and children. On April 6, 1832, he crossed the Mississippi from Iowa into Illinois. Black Hawk reasoned that because 600 of his party of 1,000 were women and children, the white settlers would know that he was coming in peace, to settle rather than to make war.

The Bad Axe Massacre

The return of Chief Black Hawk and his group shocked the white settlers. False stories about his warlike plans swept through the territory.

A call went out for white volunteers. General Henry Atkinson, leading a party of 1,300 armed men, began to pursue Black Hawk and his band.

Black Hawk now knew that war was certain. He moved his followers into southern Wisconsin so he could hide the women and children. Flashes of fighting broke out in the summer of 1832. About 200 people on each side lost their lives.

Black Hawk decided to flee across the Mississippi. He and his people almost escaped, but when they reached the Mississippi, they were caught between the oncoming army of General Atkinson and a gunboat on the river.

Although Black Hawk tried to surrender, the gunboat and soldiers went on firing. At nightfall most of the surviving Sauk and Fox were captured. Black Hawk escaped, but he was caught later. After the Bad Axe Massacre—as this battle was called—Native Americans never again resisted white settlements north of the Ohio River.

Chapter 14 Review

Chapter Summary

After the United States had gained independence from Great Britain, settlers swiftly moved west of the Appalachian Mountains. This displaced many Native Americans from their lands. The federal government then forced the displaced Native Americans to live on reservations.

Pioneers moved across the Mississippi River to the Mexican territories of Texas and California and to the Pacific Northwest Territory of Oregon. Mormons migrated from Illinois to present-day Utah. Americans began to believe they were meant to control all the lands between the Atlantic coast and the Pacific coast. This idea was called Manifest Destiny.

Reviewing Vocabulary

Use the following words to complete the sentences below. Write your answers on a separate sheet of paper.

pueblos	mission stations
expansion	reservation
displaced	prairie
mountain men	outposts
ranchos	removal
pioneers	migration

1. Farmers settled the treeless _____ lands after federal treaties called for the _____ of Native Americans.
2. The journey of the _____ Cherokee to a _____ is called the Trail of Tears.
3. Adventurous _____ blazed the trails that _____ later followed west.
4. Spanish _____ and military _____ became the first settlements in California.

5. The most important Spanish settlements were twenty-one _____.
6. After 1833, Mexican settlers gained huge _____ in California.
7. Brigham Young led the Mormons in a well-planned _____ to Utah.
8. Westward _____ affected almost every phase of life in the United States.

Understanding Main Ideas

1. What trails were developed as pioneers moved to the land west of the Appalachian Mountains?
2. What methods were used by settlers and the United States government to take over the lands of the Native Americans?
3. What ways did pioneers find to travel across the continent to California and the Oregon Territory?
4. What reason did United States citizens give for their decision to secede from Mexico?
5. Why did the Mormons settle in Utah?

Critical Thinking Skills

1. **Expressing Problems Clearly.** What values, attitudes, and characteristics led pioneers to settle west of the Appalachian Mountains?
2. **Recognizing Ideologies.** How did Native American ideas about the land differ from those of white settlers? Considering these differences, could the two groups of people have lived peacefully on the same lands?
3. **Recognizing Cause and Effect.** In 1824 the Mexican government offered incentives to encourage United States citizens to settle in Texas. Less than a decade later,

Social Studies Skills: Interpreting a Bar Graph

U.S. Population by Old and New States, 1820–1850

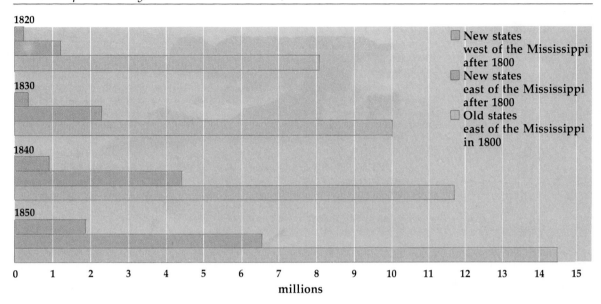

Skill Review: Use the bar graph to answer the questions below.

1. The population of new states east of the Mississippi almost doubled from **(a)** 1820 to 1830 **(b)** 1830 to 1840 **(c)** 1840 to 1850.

2. The population of new states west of the Mississippi did not pass the 1 million mark until **(a)** 1830 **(b)** 1840 **(c)** 1850.

Mexico halted all such settlement. What caused this change in policy?

Writing About History

1. **Writing Journal Entries.** Imagine that you took part in the westward movement sometime between 1815 and 1850. Write a series of dated journal entries describing your travels.

2. **Writing an Inscription.** Ponca City, Oklahoma, has a Pioneer Woman Monument honoring the role of American women in the westward movement. What inscriptions would you write for this monument?

Your Region in History

Culture. During what period in history was your locality a part of the American or Spanish frontier? How was frontier life in your locality similar to and different from life on one of the frontiers described in this chapter?

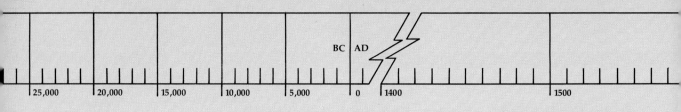

New
National
Forces

❧ Chapter 15

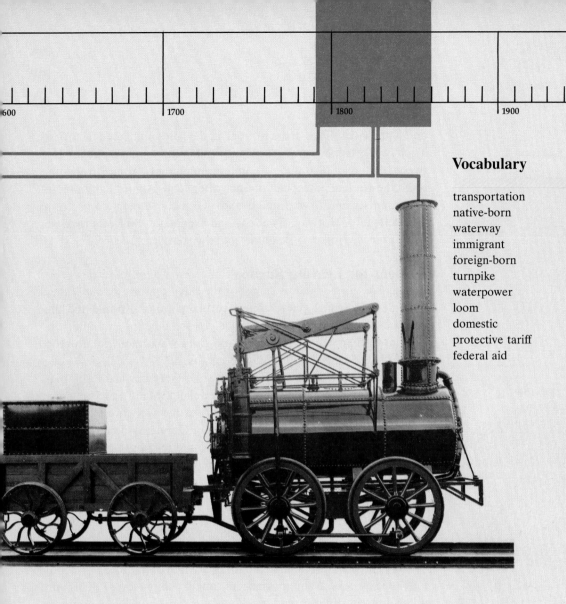

Vocabulary

transportation
native-born
waterway
immigrant
foreign-born
turnpike
waterpower
loom
domestic
protective tariff
federal aid

Prereading

1. Why did more immigrants settle in the East and the Lake Plains than in the Gulf Plains?
2. How did the transportation revolution change the movement of people and goods?
3. What changes in making a living resulted from the improvement of transportation?
4. What changes in political attitudes developed as sections of the country developed different economic interests?

N EW FORCES—of population, transportation, and economy—greatly influenced the growth of every part of the United States. Hundreds of thousands of people from Europe came seeking a better life in the United States. They wanted land of their own and freedom from hunger and despair. Some of these newcomers, as well as the native-born, traveled on newly made roads, waterways, and railroads that linked the different parts of an expanding nation. Ways of making a living changed as new goods were produced for growing markets.

1 Newcomers from Europe

Hundreds of thousands of Europeans came to the United States in the first half of the nineteenth century. They wished to become citizens of the new nation. They came to raise families in the farmlands

289

Origin of Immigrants to the United States, 1821–1850

1821–1830

Ireland
50,724
35%

England,
Scotland,
Wales
25,079
18%

All others
67,636
47%

1831–1840

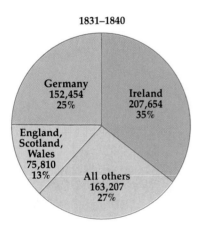

Germany
152,454
25%

Ireland
207,654
35%

England,
Scotland,
Wales
75,810
13%

All others
163,207
27%

1841–1850

Germany
434,626
25%

Ireland
780,719
46%

England,
Scotland,
Wales
267,044
16%

All others
230,862
13%

Growing numbers of immigrants came to the United States in search of jobs and freedom.

and in the cities. They came to work in the fields and in the factories. Their work helped strengthen and build the young republic. Between 1820 and 1860 about 4 million immigrants from Europe entered the United States, half of them after 1850. Almost half of these immigrants came from Ireland and Germany. Others came from Great Britain, Norway, Sweden, and Denmark. Still others came from France, Holland, Belgium, and Switzerland.

Reasons for Leaving Europe

People from these nations came for the same reasons that led other immigrants to come years earlier: bad conditions at home and the promise of a better life in America. In Ireland, for example, the peasant farmers could not find work. And when their potato crop failed in 1846, they had nothing to eat.

Unlike the Irish in the late 1840s the Germans had more reasons than survival for leaving their homeland. Many were unhappy with their governments. Others found that they were not allowed to worship as they pleased. Governments in Germany sometimes paid the cost of sending such persons to the United States. German peasant families packed all that they owned in knapsacks and headed for the nearest seaport. There they hoped to get passage on a boat to the United States.

During the voyage a family of six to ten people often had to stay in a boxlike compartment below deck. This space was about three steps wide, two steps long, and about as high as it was wide. The compartment became home for the length of the voyage—about four to six weeks. Many passengers caught "ship's fever." This and other diseases often spread quickly under such crowded conditions. Fifteen out of every hundred immigrants died during voyages to the United States.

Where Immigrants Settled

Most of the immigrants settled in the East, the Northeast, and the Lake Plains. Many Irish had only enough money to reach the United States. So they settled where they landed—in the ports of New York City, Boston, Philadelphia, Baltimore, and New Orleans. They looked for work in the shops, on the docks, and any other place where workers were needed.

Many Germans coming off the boats left the seaports and headed west. Some became farmers in Michigan, Illinois, Wisconsin, and Minnesota. Others settled in such cities as Cincinnati, Louisville, Chicago, and Milwaukee. In 1840 one third of the voters in Cincinnati were German. Three German immigrants—Adolph Sutro, Claus Spreckels, and Henry Miller—helped to develop California.

Only a few immigrants settled in the Gulf Plains. Most of them were unskilled workers and peasant farmers. They were not needed in the Gulf Plains, where slaves did the work. Also, the rich prairie soil in the North could be farmed at less cost than it would take to start a southern plantation.

Some newcomers did migrate to southern cities. In 1860 immigrants made up one out of every five persons in Savannah, Georgia, and almost one out of every three persons in Memphis, Tennessee. But many more settled in northern cities. In New York City, fully one half the people were foreign-born. And more than one half the people in Chicago, Milwaukee, and St. Louis were foreign-born. As the numbers of immigrants swelled, the American writer Herman Melville wrote: "We are not a narrow tribe. . . . No. Our blood is as the flood of the Amazon [largest river in the world], made up of a thousand noble currents all pouring into one. We are not a nation, so much as a world."

Opposition to Immigrants

Newcomers often had trouble finding jobs and housing. Many were treated harshly. People born in the United States were angered by those coming into the country from Europe. Many newcomers were willing to work for lower pay than were people born in the United States. Newcomers often had religious views and customs that seemed strange to native-born Americans. Some storekeepers and factory owners so disliked the foreign-born that they put up such signs as "No Irish Need Apply" (for work).

Some people formed secret groups to fight immigration. One such group founded in 1849, the Order of the Star-Spangled Banner, had members all over the country. They were called Know-Nothings because when asked about their sometimes violent acts against immigrants, they answered, "I know nothing."

The Know-Nothings formed a political party—called the American party—to oppose immigrants, especially Catholics. After 1850 the American party became powerful enough to win political offices at all three levels of government. Fighting sometimes broke out. The Know-Nothings tried to get people to burn Catholic convents and to break up Irish or German groups. Immigrants fought back. It was dangerous at times for outsiders to enter Irish or German parts of a city.

Other organizations were formed to help the newcomers. Some leaders spoke out firmly against the Know-Nothings, calling them un-American and undemocratic. Immigrants—both on their own and with the help of support groups—worked hard to become Americans. They made many contributions to the growing nation.

Section 1 Review

1. How many immigrants entered the United States between 1820 and 1860?
2. Name five European countries from which many immigrants came.
3. What were two reasons immigrants had for migrating to the United States?
4. What made the voyage to the United States a hard one for many immigrants?
5. What two reasons did many people born in the United States have for resenting foreign-born newcomers?
6. What was the purpose of the American or Know-Nothing party?

Critical Thinking

7. **Making Comparisons.** How did the opinions of the Know-Nothings differ from Herman Melville's?

LOOKING AHEAD: How did the transportation revolution change the ways people moved goods and traveled from place to place?

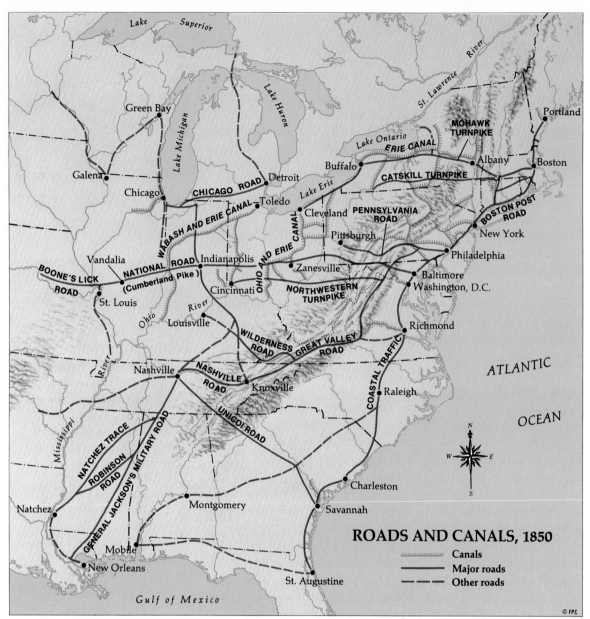

Private companies built many roads and canals in the early 1800's, taking their profits from the fees paid by travelers.

2 The Transportation Revolution

The movement of individuals and families, both native- and foreign-born, made improvements in transportation necessary. Wherever they settled, people grew crops and produced goods that had to be carried to market. To live, settlers needed tools, clothing, lumber, and other finished products. So older transportation systems such as roads and waterways were improved, and new systems—especially railroads—were developed.

Improved and Expanded Roads

A traveler going from Boston to Richmond after the American Revolution complained that the roads were nothing more than pathways. He also wrote of the torment inflicted by swarms of flies, mosquitoes, and gnats.

In the 1830s Fanny Kemble, an English actress visiting the United States, wrote of her experience in a horse-drawn coach over a wretched road: "Away galloped the four horses, trotting with their front and galloping with their hind legs: and away we went after them, bumping, thrumping, jumping, jolting, shaking, tossing and tumbling, over the wickedest road, I do think the cruellest, hard-heartedest road, that ever wheel rumbled upon."

Because they were the most heavily used in the nation, roads in the states along the Atlantic coast were improved first. Most roads in these states spread out like spokes of a wheel from the hub of a central city to neighboring towns and villages. Roads between major cities became part of a network of turnpikes or toll roads that the traveler paid a fee to use. By the 1820s, 146 turnpike roads were being built in Pennsylvania. At the same time New York built 4,000 miles (6,400 km) of turnpikes.

Robert Fulton (left), inventor, first began experimenting with steamships in France. His *Clermont* was the first such vessel in this country to make money for its owners by charging fares.

Inland Waterways

As more people and goods moved throughout the country, river travel improved. Inland waterways were used mostly for downstream trips until 1807 when Robert Fulton successfully piloted the steamboat *Clermont* both up and down the Hudson River. By the 1850s more than 700 steamboats were carrying people and goods on the Hudson, Ohio, Mississippi, and Missouri rivers.

Mississippi River travel had its dangers. Sandbars and floating logs often damaged boats. A typical Mississippi vessel usually lasted only about four to five years. English author Charles Dickens once wrote that being aboard a Mississippi steamboat was like sleeping on a powder keg about to explode.

Many states began building canals to connect their major rivers with other bodies of water. The first, the Erie Canal, was started in New York in 1817 and finished in 1825. It stretched 350 miles (560 km) from Albany to Buffalo. Called the Big Ditch, the Erie was some forty feet (12 m) wide and only four feet (1.2 m) deep. Thousands of men worked with picks and shovels to dig the canal. Horses and mules hitched to wagons hauled the dirt away.

The Erie Canal was so successful that canals were soon built in many parts of the country. Canals connected coastal cities or towns in the East with nearby rivers. Canals also linked rivers with the Great Lakes.

Not all the canals proved as successful as the Erie. But the canals made it easy for goods and people to spread into the Lake Plains. Farmers in western New York sent their wheat by water to New York City. And tools and clothing from New England were sent by water to the settlements in the Lake Plains. The cost of bringing goods to market dropped by at least 50 percent. Travel costs on inland water routes also dropped.

The Railroad Boom

The canal boom lasted for about twenty years. In the late 1840s the railroad boom took its place. Railroad track could be laid almost anywhere. A farmer living many miles from the nearest waterway could raise a crop and send it to market by rail. Trains ran when rivers and canals were covered with ice. Trains usually ran on time. And trains traveled faster than barges on rivers or canals.

The first useful steam locomotives appeared in the late 1820s. Train safety and service improved with each new invention. One special device helped locomotives hold the tracks on sharp curves. Another—the cowcatcher mounted on the front of the locomotive—pushed or held large animals away from the wheels. Hoses to drop sand on slippery tracks and closed-in cabs for the engineers also added to safety and comfort.

Charles Harvey (left, astride the horse), opened up the rich iron and copper country in the North by building the Soo Canals that linked Lakes Superior and Huron. Such early locomotives as the Atlantic (middle left) and the Tom Thumb (middle right) were gradually improved. The later Pioneer engine had an enclosed cab and a cowcatcher.

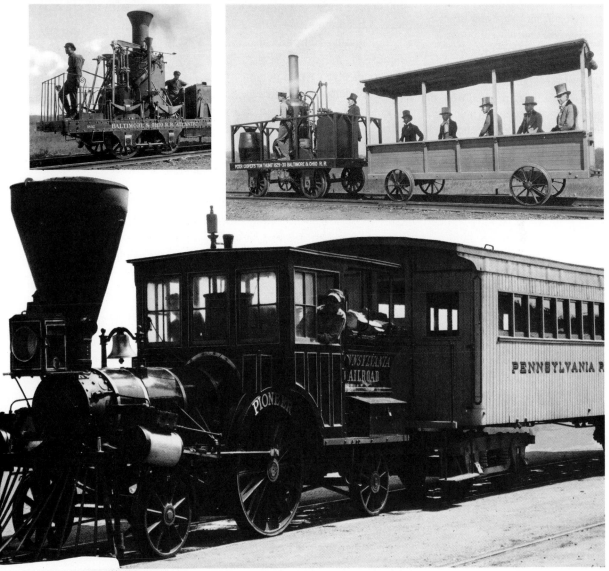

Section 2 Review

1. How did the steamboat make river travel easier and cheaper?
2. Name three ways that canals improved trade.
3. What four advantages did railroads have over waterways?

Critical Thinking

4. **Recognizing Cause and Effect.** How did the railroad boom result in additional jobs?

LOOKING AHEAD: What changes in making a living resulted from the improvement of transportation and the movement of people and goods?

The big boom in railroad building came about 1850. Four routes were laid to the West, and by 1860 a person could take a train from New York City all the way to Chicago. The cities of Atlanta, Richmond, and Chattanooga became rail centers in the South. Some cities, such as Cleveland and Detroit, enjoyed both cheap water travel and good rail service. Most railroads ran east and west rather than north and south, and there were more railroads in the North than in the South.

Railroads thrived, carrying more and more of the nation's goods and people. "Night before last *thirteen* carloads of first-class passengers went west in one train," reported Toledo's newspaper, the *Blade.* "The number [of passengers] can scarcely be less than 700. Three trains pass through each way daily. . . . The freight business is becoming large and will be immense."

Building railroads also created jobs for thousands of people. Thousands more people were needed to manage and maintain them. Railroads also carried persons from such eastern cities as New York and Philadelphia to Chicago, Cincinnati, or St. Louis in just a few days. Before the coming of railroads such travel took weeks by slow horse-drawn coach.

3 Changes in Making a Living

Major changes in the movement of people and of products from place to place affected the lives of all Americans in some ways. Each

Sam Slater started the cloth-making industry at his mill in New England. The new nation was soon matching the output of Britain.

part of the country developed its own special factory-made or farm products. Faster shipping led to giant increases in the exchange of goods within the United States and overseas. And cities and towns that were quickly becoming centers of trade and manufacturing drew in workers by the thousands.

The Manufacturing Revolution

In the early 1820s the older as well as the newer sections of the country became known for their special products. Shoes and cloth had been manufactured in New England ever since colonial times. But in the 1800s more tools, more workers, and waterpower for the mills gave new life to manufacturing in New England.

When Samuel Slater arrived from England in 1789, he brought with him valuable manufacturing know-how. England was the world's leading cloth maker. To protect its cloth-making secrets, it did not allow either the machines or the workers who ran them to leave the country. Slater, who was in charge of machinery in a cotton mill in England, left there in disguise. He did not bring drawings of the machines with him, but he was able to remember how the machines worked. Slater set up a cotton mill in Pawtucket, Rhode Island, using the new machinery. This cloth-making factory thrived.

Another improvement in New England cloth making was the development of looms for weaving yarn into cloth. In 1813 Francis Cabot Lowell of Massachusetts, with the help of Paul Moody, perfected a power loom like those used in England. With this loom New England factories could produce as much cloth each day as factories in England.

The cloth mills hired young unmarried women as workers. The women lived in large rooms called dormitories where they were carefully supervised. They had strict work rules, and they were required to be neat and to attend church.

Later, immigrants replaced the New England women workers. Entire immigrant families, including children, worked in the mills. The pay was poor, the hours long, and the conditions bad.

New York, New Jersey, and Pennsylvania shared in the rise of manufacturing. Large flour mills were built in western New York near the wheat belt. Factory towns grew up in New Jersey. And great deposits of coal were discovered in Pennsylvania between 1800 and 1850. Coal became a cheap fuel for iron making, increasing Pennsylvania's iron output.

Higher Yields for Farmers

Farm families in the Ohio and Mississippi valleys began to do well. So did the small towns nearby where farmers bought their tools and

Water and, later, steam were used to power weaving looms in the cloth mills. Other discoveries also helped speed up cloth production.

equipment. Better transportation opened up new lands for growing wheat and corn. With better plows and reapers each farmer could grow more grain.

In the South farming changed greatly after the Revolution. Tobacco lost its overseas market. Other nations began to compete successfully with the United States in the sale of pitch and tar. And rice could only be grown in a few lowland areas in South Carolina. The South needed a new product to make up for lost sales in tobacco and naval stores. The search for such a product led farmers and traders to cotton.

Before the 1800s separating the cotton seed from one pound (0.45 kg) of cotton fiber took one person about a day. But in 1793 Eli Whitney invented the cotton gin. With the gin one person could clean as many as fifty pounds (22.5 kg) of cotton per day. The machine came into use just as England and New England were seeking more cotton for their larger cloth-making factories.

In 1792 the United States raised only 138 thousand pounds (62,100 kg) of cotton. By 1800 about 17 million pounds (7,650,000 kg) of cotton were already being exported. By 1860 overseas shipments had reached 1,768 million pounds (795,600,000 kg). As each year's cotton output increased, the South became more dependent on a single crop—cotton—and on the slaves who produced it.

Southerners had always hoped to build cloth factories near the cotton fields. But the South had too little waterpower to run the factory machines. Also, money in the South was tied up in land and slaves. There was little left over for machines. The small output of some iron-making plants in Virginia and South Carolina could not begin to equal that of New England or even that of the upper Mississippi Valley.

Change in the Flow of Trade

As each area of the country came to depend more on other areas for goods and services, the flow of trade changed. In 1820 goods exchanged within the country flowed in a great circle. Wheat, flour, butter, and pork from the farms of the Ohio Valley, along with hemp and tobacco from Kentucky, were sent down the Mississippi River to New Orleans. There they were shipped on oceangoing vessels through the gulf to the eastern ports of New York, Boston, and Philadelphia. Finished goods, such as cloth, hats, shoes, and hardware, were shipped west along inland routes from the East coast to the Ohio valley.

As transportation improved, trade within the country grew, but its direction changed. Finished goods still flowed from New England and the Middle States to the Ohio Valley and the Lake Plains. But the food and grain from the Ohio and Mississippi valleys were sent directly east by rail or waterways, not through the port at New Orleans. The South had some trade ties with New York City, but its largest market for cotton—the nation's chief export—lay outside the United States.

By 1860 most exchange of goods was between the East and West. This change in trade flow worried the South, which began to believe its interests were being overshadowed by those of New England, the Middle States, and the Midwest.

Growth of Cities

In the early 1800s about 6 percent of the people in the United States lived in cities. By 1860, 30 percent lived in cities. New York, Boston, Philadelphia, Baltimore, and New Orleans grew because they were trade centers on the coasts. Newark, New Jersey, and Lowell, Massachusetts, grew because factories developed there.

Chicago was one city that had growing pains in the 1800s. In only one year—1833 to 1834—Chicago's population went from about 350 to 1,800. People bought and sold land in Chicago as if it were a precious metal. A local newspaper bragged that a plot of ground had doubled in value in a single day.

Chicago attracted persons of many types and interests. "Long John" Wentworth walked into town barefoot, a penniless immigrant

Section 3 Review

1. What three factors aided the growth of New England's manufacturing industry?
2. What discovery made it possible for Pennsylvanians to increase production in the iron-making industry?
3. Why did the South need a new product after the Revolution?
4. What two factors prevented the South from developing cloth factories in the 1800s?
5. Describe the changes that took place in the flow of trade as transportation improved.
6. What cities became centers of trade? What cities grew because of manufacturing?

Critical Thinking

7. **Drawing Conclusions.** What attracted people to Chicago in the early 1800s?

LOOKING AHEAD: What changes in political attitudes developed as sections of the country developed different economic interests?

carrying his shoes in his hands. He became Chicago's leading landholder and was later elected mayor. William B. Ogden came to Chicago to oversee his family's interests in land. As Chicago's first mayor, he helped make the city the nation's leading railroad center. Cyrus McCormick came to Chicago because he felt the market for his newly invented reaper was in the Middle West, where the prairies were fast becoming fields of grain. The hustle and excitement in the growing city led one Englishman to tell another before a trip to the United States: "See two things in America, if nothing else—Niagara and Chicago."

But Chicago, like all growing cities, had its problems. The land on which Chicago was built was only two feet above the level of Lake Michigan. To prevent flooding, engineers decided to raise the level of the whole city by twelve feet. They dug up mud from the Chicago River and used it to raise the level of the land. Steps led up or down from one part of town to another as the land rose slowly and unevenly. After 1855, Chicagoans for the first time could build houses with basements.

But the finest hotel, a brick building called the Tremont House, remained in the swamp as the land level rose. A New Yorker, George Pullman, said he could jack up the building without bothering the hotel guests by using new tools and 1,200 men. He made good his boast.

Living conditions usually grew worse as cities grew larger. People often needed more water than public wells could provide. There were few sewage systems to carry away wastes. Ankle-deep garbage often covered the streets. Rain turned streets into mudholes.

4 Changes in Political Attitudes

Great changes in travel, work, and home life raised new political issues. The three most often debated were the tariff, the role of the federal government in such tasks as road and canal building, and slavery. As each section of the nation grew and changed, its attitude toward these issues also changed.

The Tariff Issue

Since 1789, most federal income had come from tariffs. At that time the first Congress to meet under the new Constitution placed a tax on ships, steel, tobacco, salt, cloth, and other goods coming into the United States from other countries.

Between 1815 and 1830 the function of the tariff slowly began to change. It was still a source of income for the government. But it also became a means to keep out goods made in other countries that were also made in the United States. To pay the tax, producers in

The Briggs House, like the Tremont House, was raised out of Chicago's swampy streets by many workers using new tools and techniques.

other countries had to charge more for their goods than did domestic producers who had no tariff to pay. In this way the tariff protected home markets for goods made in the United States. Thus, it was called a protective tariff.

A protective tariff worked in the following way. If Pennsylvania nail makers wished to keep British nail makers from underselling them, they would ask Congress to place a high tariff on nails. Then the British had to pay not only the usual costs of making and shipping nails to the United States, but also a high tariff. Since their costs were higher, the price of their nails also had to be higher. British nails found few buyers in the United States. The protective tariff, then, stopped the British shipment of nails to the United States.

Those sections of the country that made money in the buying and selling of goods—mainly the East and Midwest—favored low tariffs. The more goods exchanged, the more money for the traders. Any government measure that reduced the amount of goods exchanged caused hardship for the traders.

The manufacturing sections of the country, or those sections that wanted to build up manufacturing, favored high tariffs. So did the Western farmers who wanted to protect the prices they received for their food crops.

In 1815 many southerners, expecting the South to turn to manufacturing for income, had leaned toward a high protective tariff. But southerners soon discovered that they lacked waterpower and ready cash for building up factories. And if a high tariff were placed on the imported goods that southerners depended on—clothes, furniture, cloth, and other finished products—these goods would cost them more money. By the 1820s southern leaders were strongly against high tariffs.

New Englanders also changed their minds about the tariff. In 1815 New England profited mainly from trade. So New Englanders favored a low tariff. But by the 1830s, New England had proved itself in manufacturing, and most of its leaders strongly favored the high protective tariff.

The Issue of Federal Aid for Improvements

The attitudes of southerners and New Englanders toward federal aid for roads, canals, and other internal improvements also changed as the regions developed. In 1815, southerners believed that their ties with the West would bring them prosperity. They favored the spending of federal tax money for government-built roads and canals. Senator John C. Calhoun of South Carolina said to Congress: "Let us then bind the republic together with . . . roads and canals. Let us conquer space."

In contrast, New England seemed cut off from the West in 1815. It did not yet have roads or canals leading west. The South and Middle States seemed better placed than New England for trade with the West. New Englanders, therefore, were against the use of their part of the nation's tax money for road and canal building.

As its manufactures grew, New England saw that its great market for clothing and other goods did indeed lie in the West. By 1830, New England was speaking out for federal aid in developing roads and canals.

By this time, however, southerners had changed their stand. They had seen a slow drop in the South's share of domestic trade. They were also learning that their chief source of wealth was in the cotton that they sold overseas. They began to resent the use of federal tax dollars to improve transportation in other sections. Calhoun, now Vice-President under Andrew Jackson, reversed his earlier stand: "The General Government [is] wholly unfit to carry on the works of internal improvements. . . ."

Westerners had favored federal aid for internal improvements from the beginning. They knew that the coming of roads, canals, and later, railroads would allow them to send their goods to market faster and at less cost. And as transportation costs for everyone went down, the cost of finished goods that westerners bought from the East—such as clothing, tools, and wagons—would also drop.

The Issue of Slavery in the New States

National expansion also raised new questions about the spread of slavery. When the Missouri Territory asked to enter the Union in 1819, a long debate started in Congress and the nation. Should slavery be permitted in a territory west of the Mississippi River?

A member of Congress, James Tallmadge of New York, led the argument against the spread of slavery. He wanted slave owners in Missouri to free their slaves over a number of years. He also wanted no more slaves to enter Missouri. Northerners believed that no slavery should be allowed in any territory west of the Mississippi River. They also believed that Congress had the power to keep slavery from spreading. They reminded southerners that the Northwest Ordinance of 1787 had outlawed slavery in the territory that later became the five free states of Ohio, Indiana, Illinois, Michigan, and Wisconsin.

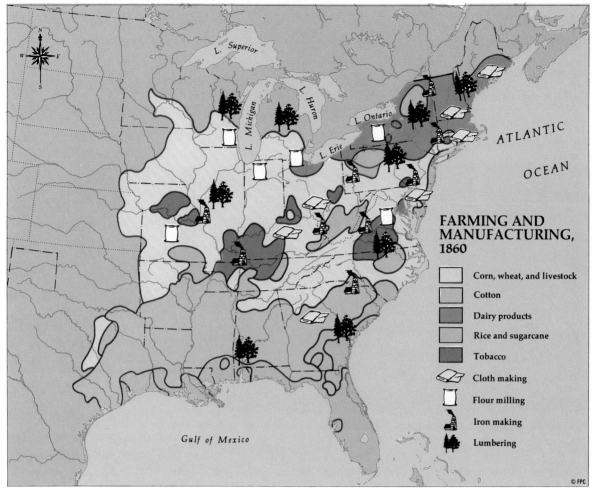

FARMING AND MANUFACTURING, 1860

	Corn, wheat, and livestock
	Cotton
	Dairy products
	Rice and sugarcane
	Tobacco
	Cloth making
	Flour milling
	Iron making
	Lumbering

Each part of the nation became known for its particular products.

Most southerners in Congress agreed that slavery was a great evil. But, they added, slaves are property, and property is protected by the Constitution. If Congress did not allow slavery in the West, then Congress would be making laws contrary to the Constitution. The southerners also pointed out that limiting slavery would limit the plantation system and destroy the economic life of the South.

Congress quieted for a time the long and heated debate when the lawmakers passed the Missouri Compromise of 1820. It was agreed that Missouri would be admitted as a slave state. Congress set the parallel of 36° 30′ N as the boundary. North of this line, slavery would be prohibited—except in Missouri. South of the line, slavery would be permitted. At the same time Missouri was admitted as a slave state, Maine was admitted as a free state. These two new states kept the number of free and slave states equal. As long as there was an equal number of slave and free states, political leaders felt sure that one section of the country would not rule over the other.

Some people thought the Missouri Compromise solved the issue of slavery in the territories once and for all. Others, including Thomas Jefferson, thought otherwise. Jefferson wrote that the issue filled him with terror. John Quincy Adams thought that the compromise was only the "title page to a great, tragic volume."

Section 4 Review

1. How did a tariff protect manufacturers of certain goods?
2. What sections of the nation favored high tariffs in 1815?
3. What sections of the nation favored high tariffs by the 1830s?
4. How did the South's position on federal aid for improvements change between 1815 and 1830?

Critical Thinking

5. **Determining Relevance.** How did the Missouri Compromise of 1820 quiet the debate about the spread of slavery west of the Mississippi River?

The United States has long been a nation of inventors.

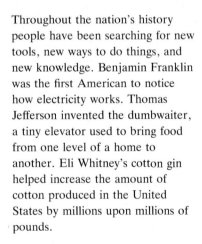

McCormick's reaper was first tested in Virginia in 1831.

Goodyear lived from 1800–1860.

Throughout the nation's history people have been searching for new tools, new ways to do things, and new knowledge. Benjamin Franklin was the first American to notice how electricity works. Thomas Jefferson invented the dumbwaiter, a tiny elevator used to bring food from one level of a home to another. Eli Whitney's cotton gin helped increase the amount of cotton produced in the United States by millions upon millions of pounds.

Interchangeable Parts

But Whitney's most important contribution was the idea of interchangeable parts. The use of interchangeable parts has been the cornerstone of modern industry. The example of the automobile shows how important interchangeable parts are. If a headlight or any part wears out, it can be replaced with a similar part. It is not necessary to get rid of the whole car or to make a special part for each car.

Whitney first used interchangeable parts in making muskets, a kind of gun. Instead of making the muskets one by one from start to finish, Whitney had workers make each part of the musket in great numbers and then put the parts together.

Whitney's gun factory became the forerunner of all factories in United States history. Television sets, cameras, and many other products you enjoy have been made on an assembly line that traces its beginnings to Eli Whitney.

Colt's Revolver

Samuel Colt followed Whitney's example when he invented the revolver. Colt's gun had a revolving cylinder that held the bullets. As one bullet was fired, the revolving cylinder would line up the next bullet with the barrel of the gun.

The first demand for Colt's revolver came during the Mexican War. The army placed an order for 1,000 guns, and Colt opened a factory that used an assembly line and interchangeable parts.

The Reaper

Cyrus McCormick and his father were farmers and managers in Virginia. For fifteen years Cyrus's father had tried to make a reaper and failed. But Cyrus was able to make a reaper in his log workshop in time for the harvest of 1831. His machine cut grain for others to tie in bundles. It changed farming for all time.

Vulcanized Rubber

In 1834 Charles Goodyear became interested in rubber, a newly discovered raw material. Goodyear tried many ways to turn rubber into

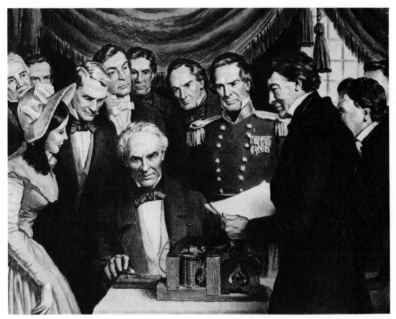

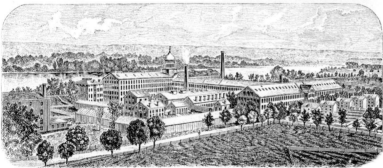

Morse's telegraph (top) and the use of assembly lines, as in Colt's gun factory, speeded up communications and manufacturing.

and no other boat could hold its way with us . . . and although the world and my country does not thank me for it, yet it gives me heartfelt satisfaction.''

After Robert Fulton's successful steamboat voyage on the Hudson in 1807, the steamboat began to be used on all inland waterways.

The steamboat soon gave way to the steam-powered railroad train as the new way of moving people and goods. Many people worked on perfecting railroads, an idea that started in Europe. They found ways to make lasting tracks, special brakes, and devices that coupled railroad cars together. After 1860, railroads became the main means of transportation in the United States until the coming of the automobile and airplane.

Other Inventions

Powerful looms made cloth swiftly and at small costs. The sewing machine made it possible to produce ready-to-wear clothes in large amounts.

Samuel F. B. Morse invented the first telegraph. Before the telegraph, sending messages took a long time. But a telegraph could send a message in seconds.

The heritage of invention still affects every person in the United States today.

Walter Hunt, inventor of the safety pin, sold all rights to it for $400.

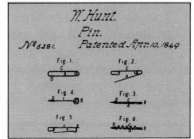

a material lasting enough to use in other products. All his early efforts failed. Then in 1839 he accidentally dropped a mixture of rubber and sulphur on a hot stove. Through this accident, Goodyear discovered vulcanizing—the process that made rubber lasting and flexible. This process has made possible the use of tires on cars, tractors, and trucks; rubberized clothing; and countless other items coated with or made of rubber. Today, however, synthetic materials have replaced the use of rubber in many items.

Energy from Steam

Between 1815 and 1850 steam power completely changed factories and transportation. Steam was turned into energy to run machines in factories. Its first use in transportation was in the steamboat.

Many people were trying to develop a steamboat, but perhaps John Fitch, a metalworker who lived in Philadelphia, was the first. His steamboat carried passengers on the Delaware River for several years. He wrote: ''We reigned as Lord High Admirals of the Delaware;

Chapter 15 Review

Chapter Summary

Between 1820 and 1860 about 4 million immigrants came to the United States, mainly from countries in northern Europe. Most of these newcomers settled in the North rather than in the South. Some people resented the immigrants because they were willing to work for low pay.

Other changes during this time included improvements in the nation's transportation system. A network of turnpikes or toll roads connected major cities. Steamboats and canals improved transportation by water, while a railroad boom made transportation cheaper and faster than ever.

As the nation grew, economic interests and political interests began to divide the nation. People in New England and the Middle States turned increasingly to manufacturing. In the West, most people were farmers. Cotton became the foundation of the economy in the South. Protective tariffs, federal aid for improvements, and slavery became major issues of conflict between North and South.

Reviewing Vocabulary

Choose the word that best completes each sentence. Write your answers on a separate sheet of paper.

1. In 1860 more than one half the people in Chicago, Milwaukee, and St. Louis were (*native-born/foreign-born*).
2. Some people born in the United States resented (*immigrant/domestic*) workers.
3. The movement of families and individuals created a need for improvements in (*transportation/manufacturing*).
4. Roads connecting major cities became part of a network of (*waterways/turnpikes*).

5. The development of (*water power/looms*) for weaving yarn into cloth improved the New England cloth-making industry.
6. (*Protective tariffs/Federal aid*) increased the price of goods that southerners needed to build factories of their own.

Understanding Main Ideas

1. Why did fewer immigrants settle in the South than in the East, the Northeast, or the Lake Plains?
2. What changes in the movement of people and goods resulted from the transportation revolution?
3. How did improvements in transportation bring about changes in making a living?
4. How did the development of different economic interests in sections of the country affect political attitudes?
5. Why did New England become the country's manufacturing center in the 1800s?
6. Why did cotton become the South's most important product?
7. What contributed to the growth of cities between 1800 and 1860?
8. What was the general purpose of a protective tariff?
9. Why did political leaders favor a balance of slave states and free states?

Critical Thinking Skills

1. **Making Comparisons.** Why did the railroad boom of the 1840s take the place of the canal boom?
2. **Drawing Conclusions.** What problems occurred as a result of the rapid growth of cities in the mid-1800s?
3. **Identifying Central Issues.** How did economic differences among sections of the nation affect attitudes toward slavery?

Social Studies Skills: Understanding Pictures

The picture on the left shows workers cutting grain with a scythe (blade) and cradle (wooden frame that catches the stalks). Workers who cut the grain then emptied the stalks from the cradle onto the ground.

The picture on the right shows a horse-drawn reaper with blades to cut the grain and a platform to catch the stalks. Workers had to rake the grain from the platform onto the ground.

Skill Review: Study both pictures. Then answer the questions below.
1. Which method used more human power?
2. Which method required workers to gather and stack grain?
3. In what ways was the reaper an improvement over the scythe and cradle?
4. How might you use additional workers to harvest grain more quickly with a single reaper?

Writing About History

1. **Writing a Letter.**   Imagine that you were an immigrant to the United States in the 1840s. Write a letter to your relatives back home. Describe your voyage to America. Tell where you settled and describe your living conditions. Express your feelings about your new homeland.
2. **Writing an Editorial.**   Choose either a northerner's or a southerner's point of view regarding the need for federal aid to improve transportation systems after 1830. Write a newspaper editorial defending that point of view.

Your Region in History

Science and Technology.   Make a list of inventions developed between 1800 and 1860. Which of these inventions do you think had the greatest impact on your community at that time? Explain your answer.

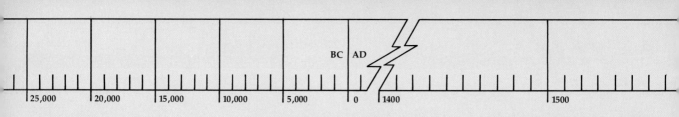

Democratic Politics and Reform

❧ Chapter 16

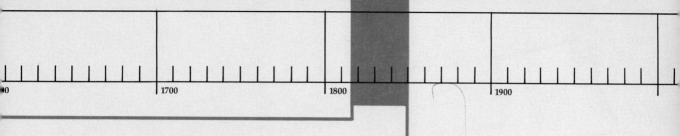

Vocabulary

border	veto
doctrine	reform
candidate	temperance
campaign	union
antislavery	strike
nullification	

I N THE EARLY NINETEENTH CENTURY the United States was new and its future was somewhat uncertain. Within a few years, however, great changes began taking place. The United States had a population that was growing swiftly. Its farm and factory products were reaching everywhere. Opportunities seemed unlimited. People living in the United States began to take special pride in their country. They began to develop a national democratic spirit.

Visitors to the United States noticed this growing national spirit. "It blazes out everywhere," an Englishman noted, "and on all occasions—in their conversations, newspapers, pamphlets, speeches, and books." People in the United States were proud to be part of a strong, new nation. Ralph Waldo Emerson, a New England author, wrote: "We will walk on our own feet; we will work with our own hands; we will speak with our own minds."

Prereading

1. What problems with other nations were solved?

2. How did democracy in politics bring about changes in voting, in candidate selection, and in political parties?

3. How did Jackson as President become a symbol of the new democratic spirit?

4. During the early 1800s, in what areas were efforts made to improve people's lives?

309

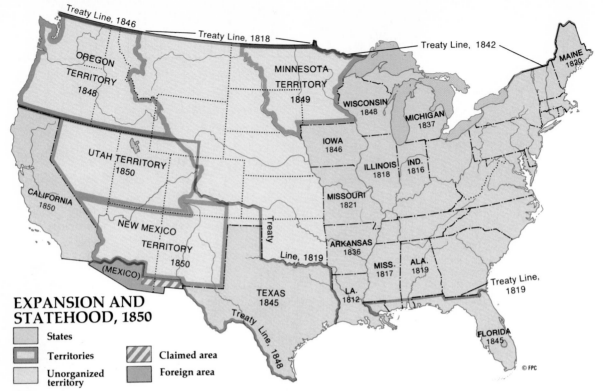

EXPANSION AND STATEHOOD, 1850

- States
- Territories
- Unorganized territory
- Claimed area
- Foreign area

Through purchase, war, and agreement the nation slowly took shape.

Treaty Line, 1846
Treaty Line, 1818
Treaty Line, 1842
MAINE 1820

OREGON TERRITORY 1848
MINNESOTA TERRITORY 1849
WISCONSIN 1848
MICHIGAN 1837

UTAH TERRITORY 1850
IOWA 1846
ILLINOIS 1818
IND. 1816

CALIFORNIA 1850
MISSOURI 1821

NEW MEXICO TERRITORY 1850
Treaty Line, 1819
ARKANSAS 1836
MISS. 1817
ALA. 1819

(MEXICO)
TEXAS 1845
LA. 1812
Treaty Line, 1819

Treaty Line, 1848
FLORIDA 1845

© FPC

1 Relations with Other Nations

Nowhere did the national spirit appear more strongly than in the relations of the United States with other countries, especially those in Europe. After 1815 the United States looked more to its own West and less to what was taking place in Europe. Yet the United States did not completely cut its ties with Europe.

Border Problems with Britain and Spain

The treaty that ended the War of 1812 was only a first step toward solving the problems between the United States and Great Britain. In the years that followed, the two nations peacefully settled a number of questions. In 1817 the United States and Great Britain agreed to limit the number of warships each of them would keep in the Great Lakes. In 1818 they set the border dividing the United States from British Canada between central Minnesota and the Rockies.

There remained some dispute about the Oregon Territory in the Northwest. After the Oregon Territory had been opened to trade, people from both the United States and Great Britain had settled there. In 1846 the two countries finally divided the Oregon Territory and agreed on another border—one that reached from the Rockies to the Pacific.

Problems with Spain were settled less peacefully. Spanish Florida had long been a sore spot to southerners. Native Americans, many of whom had been forced off their land, often crossed from Florida into Georgia and Alabama to attack white settlements. In the early 1800s Seminole groups often raided southern settlements and then returned to safety behind the Spanish border. The Spanish seemed unwilling or unable to stop the raids.

Southerners in the United States were also angry because escaped slaves often crossed into Spanish Florida. Once there, the slaves were safe from their owners. After the War of 1812 the United States government took action against Spain to stop the Seminole raids and the escape of slaves.

West Florida had already been taken by the United States between 1810 and 1813. In 1818, after the Seminole attacks, General Andrew Jackson led about 2,000 United States soldiers into Spanish Florida. Jackson believed the Spanish were more dangerous than the Seminoles. So he took and held Spanish forts in Florida.

Spain, weakened by wars in Europe and revolutions in its American colonies, knew it could not defeat the United States. In 1819 it sold all of Florida to the United States for $5 million. The two countries also agreed on a border between the United States and Spanish lands west of the Mississippi River.

Osceola led the Seminoles in their attempts to resist removal from Florida in 1835.

The Monroe Doctrine

Spain, once the strongest nation in Europe, began to lose its great empire in America. One by one, parts of Spanish America became independent countries in the early 1800s.

Some nations in Europe sent out a call to arms to help Spain win back its American colonies. These countries looked on Spain's loss as Europe's loss. They feared they might also lose their colonies in other parts of the world.

Russia was also becoming interested in northwest North America. It already claimed Alaska. In 1811 Russia set up a fort on the Pacific coast north of San Francisco. It wanted lands in the Oregon Territory that had already been claimed by the United States and Great Britain.

The leaders of the United States wanted to keep European nations out of North and South America. James Monroe had followed Madison as President in 1817. He was guided in his dealings with other countries by Secretary of State John Quincy Adams, the son of John Adams.

Adams advised President Monroe to take a stand against both Spain and Russia. In 1823 Monroe acted. In a speech to Congress he made four points that came to be known as the Monroe Doctrine.
1. No European nation could start a colony in the Western Hemisphere (North and South America).
2. Any such attempt would be seen as a threat to the United States.

As Spain lost its colonial holdings in Central and South America, the United States sought to strengthen its position in the Western Hemisphere.

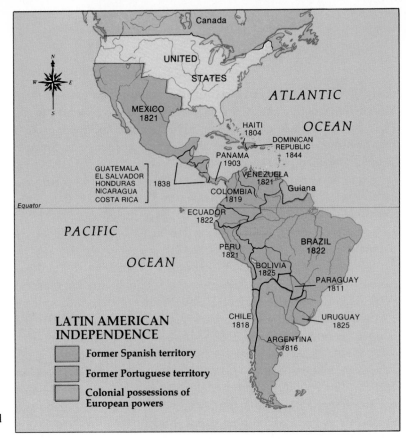

LATIN AMERICAN INDEPENDENCE

- Former Spanish territory
- Former Portuguese territory
- Colonial possessions of European powers

Section 1 Review

1. What three problems did Britain and the United States settle between 1817 and 1846?
2. For what two reasons were southerners in the United States angry at the Spanish government in Florida?
3. What settlement did the United States and Spain reach in 1819?
4. What two threats caused President Monroe to take a stand against European actions in the Americas?
5. What are the four main points of the Monroe Doctrine?
6. Why did Britain support the Monroe Doctrine?

Critical Thinking

7. **Predicting Consequences.** Would the Monroe Doctrine have been a success without Britain's support? Why or why not?

LOOKING AHEAD: How did democracy in politics bring about changes in voting, in candidate selection, and in political parties?

3. Any European nation that interfered with the new nations of Latin America would be treated as unfriendly to the United States.
4. The United States, in turn, would stay out of the affairs of Europe.

 The Monroe Doctrine was a bold step. The United States did not have a strong navy or army. Its brave stand depended on the aid of a powerful ally and former enemy—Great Britain.

 The British supported the Monroe Doctrine. With Spain and other European nations out of Latin America the British could trade with the new countries there. And the British, with their interests in Canada and Oregon, also wanted to keep Russia out of the lands south of Alaska. Britain used its powerful navy to back up the Monroe Doctrine and keep other nations out of the Americas.

 The Monroe Doctrine was a United States declaration of independence in foreign affairs. It is still in use today.

2 Democracy in Politics

The democratic spirit showed itself in local, state, and national politics between 1815 and 1850. More people gained the right to vote. By 1828 most states no longer made owning property a voting qualification. But only white men—no white women, Native Americans, or blacks—could vote, even after 1828. The democratic spirit also led to new ways of choosing candidates for office. And election campaigns were planned to win the support of all citizens who could vote.

Changes in Candidate Selection

Earlier in the nation's history Presidential candidates were chosen by small groups of congressmen who met privately. The voters had no part in choosing a candidate for their party.

In the 1830s this process changed. Citizens began to vote for delegates to a national convention. The delegates then chose the candidates. In this way the voters had a voice. At the national convention delegates' views on issues formed the party's platform.

Election Campaigns

Before the 1820s, a Presidential candidate made few if any speeches. There were no party platforms. After the 1820s, candidates and their followers worked hard to win voters, many of whom were voting for the first time. A newspaper printing the views of one candidate often became the voice of that candidate or his party. Parades, banners, and buttons brought the candidate to the voters' attention.

Candidates often went out of their way to interest the average person. Adolphus Hubbard, running for the office of governor of Illinois in 1826, made such speeches as: "I do not pretend to be a man of extraordinary talents. . . . Nevertheless, I think I can govern pretty well . . . for to tell the truth, fellow citizens, I do not think you will be hard to govern no how." In the Presidential election of 1840 William Henry Harrison, who was the rich son of a governor, ran as the "log-cabin" candidate.

Voters took a great interest in elections and were proud of being voters. In New England John Greenleaf Whittier wrote about the voter on election day:

> Today, of all the weary year,
>   A King of men am I.
> Today, alike are great and small,
>   The nameless and the known;
> My palace is the people's hall,
>   The ballot-box my throne!

Changes in Political Parties

James Monroe became President in 1817. In the election of 1816 he had run as a Republican, the party of Jefferson and Madison. The Federalist party was so weak by then that its candidate, Rufus King of New York, received the votes of only three states. By 1820, when Monroe ran for a second term, the Federalist party had died out. Monroe was reelected by all but one electoral vote. It seemed for a time that there were no more party differences. A Boston newspaper named the period the Era of Good Feelings.

But the good feelings were only on the surface. The Republican party was divided. In the election of 1824, Republicans fell into four

Election of 1816

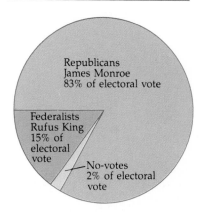

Election of 1820

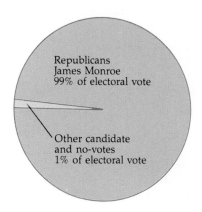

Election of 1824

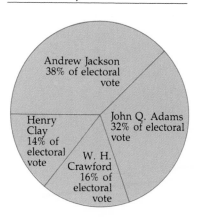

When Clay (addressing the Senate) threw his support to Adams (inset) in
the election of 1824, both were accused of wrongdoing.

main camps, each with its own candidate for President. Republicans
in Congress chose William H. Crawford as their candidate. People in
different parts of the country, however, were against this method of
choosing a candidate. So the New England state legislatures nominated John Quincy Adams. And some western states chose Henry
Clay of Kentucky. The fourth candidate, Andrew Jackson of Tennessee, had the support of both the West and the South.

Jackson received more popular and electoral votes than the
other three men. But he did not win a majority—more than 50 percent of the votes. The election therefore had to be decided by the

House of Representatives, as called for by the Constitution. Henry Clay, a key leader, threw his support to Adams. Adams then received enough votes in the House to win the election.

Jackson and his followers felt that Jackson had been robbed of victory. And when President Adams named Clay his secretary of state, Jackson said that Adams and Clay must have made a deal. He believed Clay had favored Adams in return for the office of secretary of state. Jackson wrote to a friend: "Was there ever witnessed such bare-faced corruption?"

Now there were two political parties again. Jackson's group became known as Democratic-Republicans and finally as Democrats—the same Democratic party you know today. Those who followed Adams and Clay began to call themselves National Republicans. Opponents of the Democrats, among them the National Republicans, later formed the Whig party, named after a party in Great Britain.

Between the 1830s and the 1850s the Democrats and the Whigs were the major parties in the United States. As the number of voters grew, the number of political views also grew. Party members could not always agree. Often some members would split off and form new third parties. These third parties usually held strong views about a single important issue. For example, the Liberty party was formed in 1839 as an antislavery party. Neither of the two main parties was willing to take such a stand for fear of losing some of its supporters.

3 Jackson As President

In the election of 1828 Democrat Andrew Jackson soundly defeated the National Republican candidate John Quincy Adams. Jackson was reelected in 1832. He came to stand for the democratic spirit in national politics. His terms of office were marked by great changes in social and political life and by sharp differences over such matters as tariffs and a national bank.

Jackson the Man

Jackson's father, a poor weaver, died before his son was born. Young Andrew Jackson lived with his mother in South Carolina before he moved to Tennessee. Unlike earlier Presidents who had come from eastern states, Jackson was a westerner, a man of the frontier. He had not spent much time at school. But he taught himself and became a lawyer, congressman, senator, judge, and army general. He became known as the hero of the Battle of New Orleans, the only important land battle won by the United States in the War of 1812. As a general, he was stern and tough. "Tough as hickory," someone

Section 2 Review

1. What important change in voting requirements had most states made by 1828?
2. How did the way of selecting Presidential candidates change during the early part of the 1800s?
3. How did election campaigns change during the 1820s?
4. Why did a newspaper label the period of Monroe's Presidency the Era of Good Feelings?
5. Why did Jackson feel he had been robbed in the election of 1824?
6. What were the two major political parties between 1830 and 1850?

Critical Thinking

7. **Expressing Problems Clearly.** Why did both the Whigs and the Democrats refuse to take a stand on slavery?

LOOKING AHEAD: How did Jackson as President become a symbol of the new democratic spirit?

Election of 1828

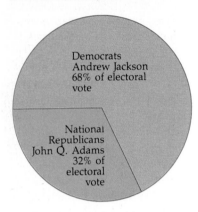

Democrats
Andrew Jackson
68% of electoral
vote

National
Republicans
John Q. Adams
32% of
electoral
vote

Election of 1832

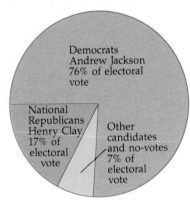

Democrats
Andrew Jackson
76% of electoral
vote

National
Republicans
Henry Clay
17% of
electoral
vote

Other
candidates
and no-votes
7% of
electoral
vote

said, giving first voice to the name that would be used for Jackson all his life: Old Hickory.

Jackson understood people. He believed he knew what was best for the United States. His enemies made his lack of learning seem worse than it was. One wrote that "his letters, with their crudities in spelling and grammar, would make the better educated angels weep." But the common people saw Jackson as one of them—a man born in a log cabin who rose to power because he was strong-willed and able.

Thousands of admirers came to Washington on the day Jackson took office in 1829. A huge crowd followed him to the White House after he took the oath of office and made a speech. They entered without being invited and took part in the celebration. Every room was packed with people. One congressman and his wife had to leave through a window because they could not reach a door. President Jackson himself escaped the crush by leaving through a back door. Finally, great tubs of punch were set up on the White House lawn to attract the crowd.

A member of the Supreme Court stated that on that day "the reign of King Mob seemed triumphant." But Jackson's followers replied, "It was a proud day for the people. General Jackson is *their own president.*"

The Tariff Problem

Tariffs had caused differences when New England developed manufacturing and the South did not. So southerners who had to pay a higher price on finished goods wanted lower tariffs. The tariff issue became a symbol for a political power struggle between industrial New England and the agricultural South.

The issue reached a crisis in 1828. In May of that year Congress passed and President Adams approved a high tariff on such raw materials as wool, iron, and molasses, as well as on finished goods. Those who were against the act called it the Tariff of Abominations. People in South Carolina led the opposition. John C. Calhoun, Vice-President under Adams and later under Jackson, became the state's spokesman.

Calhoun wrote a report for the South Carolina legislators that summer. He urged them to reject the new tariff and declare it null and void. Calhoun's stand became known as nullification—a state's right to refuse to obey an act of Congress and declare it null and void.

Nothing came of Calhoun's report until Congress passed another high tariff in 1832 when Jackson was President. South Carolina legislators were against this new tariff and called a convention in November. There they nullified the tariffs of 1828 and 1832. The legislators said no tariff duties would be collected in their state, because the tariff was unconstitutional. Also, they said, South Carolina might leave the Union.

In December President Jackson answered them. He said that as President he had sworn to uphold the laws of the land. Under these laws no state has the right to refuse to obey a law or to leave the Union. If South Carolina should try to do so, he would send soldiers into the state to crush the opposition. "Tell . . . the nullifiers from me," he said, "that they can talk and write resolutions and print threats to their hearts' content." But he warned that troops would be sent in if the laws of the United States were not obeyed.

The South Carolina governor asked for volunteers to defend the state. In the meantime Calhoun gave up the Vice-Presidency. He became a United States senator and together with Senator Henry Clay worked out a compromise tariff agreement.

The new tariff of 1833 passed Congress and was approved by Jackson in March. South Carolina accepted the lower tariff and changed its nullification stand. For the time being the hot issue of high tariffs died down.

A military man from 1802 to 1821, Andrew Jackson began his political career at age fifty-four.

The Bank Issue

The Bank of the United States was started by Hamilton and the Federalist Congress in 1791. It lasted for twenty years. A second national bank was begun in 1816, also with a twenty-year charter. In 1832, four years before the charter was to end, supporters of the bank passed an act to renew it. President Jackson, however, vetoed the act.

Jackson was against the bank for two reasons. First, he said, the national bank was unconstitutional. There was nothing in the Constitution that gave the national government the right to charter banks. Jefferson and Madison had also said this in 1791.

Second, the national bank was undemocratic. Jackson believed it favored big business, merchants, and bankers over the average person. The government, he stated, should not be used to make the rich richer and the powerful even more powerful.

Supporters of the bank came to the White House from all parts of the country. They tried to make Jackson change his mind. Newspapers, merchants, and members of Congress attacked Jackson's stand, but the President refused to change. "The Bank . . . ," he said, "is trying to kill me, *but I will kill it.*" When Congress failed to override the President's veto, the bank lost its charter.

Some historians feel that Jackson's stand was wrong. They say that the growing country needed a national bank to avoid slowdowns in the economy. Others believe Jackson was wise to resist favoring the wealthy.

Jackson's Policy on Native Americans

Along with many others, Jackson strongly favored the Indian Removal Act of 1830. Under the act the Cherokee, Choctaw, Creek, and other Native Americans living east of the Mississippi had to move to lands west of the Mississippi River.

As early as 1802, the federal government had promised Georgians that it would remove Native Americans from their state as soon as peacefully possible. For many years the Cherokee remained in Georgia. But when more land was needed and when gold was discovered on Cherokee lands in the 1820s, Georgians tried to take over the lands on their own.

The Cherokee asked for help from the Supreme Court, headed by Chief Justice John Marshall. They wanted the Supreme Court to keep the Georgia government from taking their lands. The Cherokee argued that they were a foreign nation and that the Constitution allows such nations to be heard before the Supreme Court. But Marshall, in the 1831 ruling on the *Cherokee Nation* v. *Georgia,* declared that the Cherokee were not a foreign nation. Rather they were a dependent nation, protected by the United States. As such, they had no right to bring a case before the Supreme Court.

A year later, however, another case before the Supreme Court brought in a ruling that favored the Cherokee. Georgia had passed a law that white missionaries were not to settle among the Cherokee unless they first swore loyalty to the state of Georgia. One missionary, Samuel Austin Worcester, refused to take the oath. He was sent to jail, and his case reached the Supreme Court. Chief Justice Marshall said that the Georgia law was unconstitutional. Only the federal government, he said, and not Georgia's state government, had authority over the Cherokee.

At first there was rejoicing among the Cherokee and those who wanted to help them. But it soon became clear that President Jackson and the Georgia officials were going to ignore the ruling. They would go ahead with the removals.

Jackson believed that his policy of removal was best for the Native Americans. In his farewell address of 1837, he stated: "This unhappy race—the original dwellers in our land—are now placed in a situation where we may well hope that they will share in the blessings of civilization."

4 Improvement in People's Lives

A democratic spirit also began to surface in social welfare reform. Many people acted to improve the lives of all groups in the nation—the young, the poor, the sick, the workers, the women, the handicapped, and many more.

Section 3 Review

1. How was Jackson's background different from that of earlier Presidents?
2. Why did many people, especially in the South, call the tariff of 1828 the Tariff of Abominations?
3. How did the South Carolina legislature react to the continuation of a high tariff in 1832?
4. How did Jackson respond to the nullifiers?
5. On what two grounds did Jackson oppose the Bank of the United States?
6. According to Chief Justice John Marshall, who had authority over the Cherokee?

Critical Thinking

7. **Recognizing Bias.** What opinion about Native Americans was reflected in Jackson's farewell address?

LOOKING AHEAD: During the early 1800s, in what areas were efforts made to improve people's lives?

The spirit of reform brought education to the physically handicapped. Pictured is a class of deaf and mute students in New York in 1859.

Public Schools for All

Most schools in the young nation were run by church groups or private citizens. But after 1820 the cause of free elementary schooling for everyone, paid for by taxes, gained supporters. These people believed that all children should have the chance to learn how to read, write, and think. The drive to provide schools for every youngster became known as the movement for common schools.

The Constitution says nothing about setting up schools. So most public schools founded after 1820 were run by state or local governments. The Land Ordinance of 1785, however, set aside a part of all federal lands to be used for raising money for schools. Many state universities were funded in this way.

High schools came into being in the 1820s. The first was a school for boys only, built in Boston in 1821. Boston also opened the first high school for girls in 1826. Massachusetts soon made the high school a part of its school system. Other states followed its lead.

Massachusetts was the home of Horace Mann—one of the most important reformers of public schooling. Mann was in charge of his state's schools from 1837 to 1848. He tried to convince people that schooling was important. He started the first teacher-training schools in the country. He helped set up fifty new high schools in Massachusetts, and he helped bring ways of teaching up to date.

Blind, deaf, and mute, this student communicates with his hands.

Samuel Howe was director of the Perkins School for the Blind, Boston, from the time it opened in 1832 until he died in 1876.

Social Reforms

The early 1800s were marked by many different reform movements. Some reformers even tried to build a perfect society. They set up small communities in which every person was equal and in which wealth was not important. If they could reach their goal, they felt, such groups would spring up everywhere in the United States. But their plans usually failed. The writer Nathaniel Hawthorne lived for a time at Brook Farm, one of these "perfect societies." Disappointed in it, he wrote, "A man's soul may be buried and perish under a dungheap, or in a furrow of the field, just as well as under a pile of money."

Other reformers had greater success. Thomas Hopkins Gallaudet (gal′ə·det′) worked with the deaf. Gallaudet went to Europe in 1815 to learn a language using hand signals. Two years later he founded the first free school for the deaf in the United States. The ways of teaching used at this school in Hartford, Connecticut, spread all through the country.

Dr. Samuel Gridley Howe worked with the blind. He started a school in his father's home where he taught blind people the alphabet. He pasted string on cardboard to form raised letters that the blind could read by touch.

Dorothea Dix became a reformer after she was asked to teach a Sunday School class for women in a Massachusetts prison. There she found that persons with mental illness were thrown into dirty cells with criminals. This practice angered Dix. She spent the rest of her life working for better conditions in hospitals for the mentally ill.

Dix visited hundreds of such places in the 1840s, and she reported to lawmakers about the terrible conditions she found. She was told that nothing could be done. But Dix answered that she knew no such word as *nothing*. Kind treatment and clean rooms, she said, would help cure the mentally ill. Over forty years she helped build hospitals for the mentally ill in fifteen states and in Canada.

A drive to limit the drinking of liquor, called the temperance movement, had the largest following of all reform movements between 1820 and 1850. Temperance societies were formed in every state and in almost every town. Members of these groups believed that the government should do something about drunkenness. They tried to get laws passed to limit drinking. They refused to buy from stores that sold liquor. Some states outlawed liquor for a few years because of the work of the temperance groups.

The many social reform movements were part of the growing national spirit in the first half of the nineteenth century. For some, this spirit meant that they were proud of their history. To them, honoring flags and marching in Fourth of July parades were ways of showing their pride. But to many others the national spirit meant

Dorothea Dix began a lifelong crusade in 1841 to help mentally ill patients after she found that they were housed with criminals in Massachusetts.

working for a better life for all people. The true genius of the United States, said poet Walt Whitman, was "always most in the common people, south, north, west, east, in all its states."

The Labor Movement

Life was hard for workers in the early nineteenth century. Men, women, and children often worked fourteen to sixteen hours a day. Factories had little light and hardly any fresh air. Workers had to use noisy and often dangerous machinery. Anyone hurt on the job usually lost that job. The average skilled factory worker was paid about two dollars a day in the early 1850s. Unskilled workers received half that amount, hardly enough to keep a family alive. Workers who tried to band together to form unions often lost their jobs or were put in jail.

Still, workers' groups spoke out for shorter hours, higher pay, and better working conditions. Workers went on forming unions. In 1827 fifteen trade unions in Philadelphia banded together to gain strength. By 1836 thirteen other cities had such associations of unions. Union leaders worked hard to teach union members about

Those attending the First International Convention of Women in Washington, D.C., in 1888 paused for this group picture.

politics. They wanted members to vote for lawmakers who were willing to make conditions better. Workers also used the power of the strike. In a strike, workers walk off their jobs and refuse to return until their demands are met. In 1824 women weavers in a Rhode Island mill went on strike with the men workers for more pay. It was the first strike in which women workers were known to take part.

Many people—most of all business owners—thought that unions and strikes should be outlawed. But in 1842 a Massachusetts court ruled that it was legal for workers to form unions and to go on strike. This ruling made the labor movement stronger. In the years 1830–1860 more and more skilled workers won ten-hour workdays, but unskilled workers failed to win better conditions.

Women's Rights

Women also had to fight for their rights in the 1800s. Politics and business were still thought to be only for men. Not one single state before 1890 allowed women to vote. In many states married women could not even own property. They had no power over legal decisions affecting their children.

After the 1820s a few states gave all women the right to own property. Slowly women began to enter such fields as teaching, writing, and medicine. Oberlin College, founded in Ohio in 1833, was the first college to offer women the same kind of schooling it offered men. Mount Holyoke in Massachusetts became the first women's college in 1837. Catherine Beecher and Emma Willard were pioneers in training women to be teachers. Susan B. Anthony, one of the greatest of the early leaders who fought for women's rights, also

Owners of cotton plantations, such as this one in Mississippi, contented themselves with a slave-supported system. Sojourner Truth (inset) and other activists in the North spoke out against slavery.

worked to get more women hired as teachers. It had long been thought that only men should teach. Some said that women were not as gifted as men. Anthony called this idea "absurd."

To gain strength, supporters of women's rights formed a group. Led by Elizabeth Cady Stanton, they held a national meeting in 1848 at Seneca Falls, New York. There they drew up a declaration of independence that stated, "All men and women are created equal." They insisted that all women should immediately be given all their rights as citizens of the United States.

By 1850 this goal had still not been reached. Wyoming Territory was the first to grant women the right to vote in 1869. Other western states followed Wyoming's lead. But women had to wait until 1920 for a constitutional amendment—the nineteenth—that gave them the right to vote in national elections.

Some men advised women to wait patiently. At a meeting in Akron, Ohio, Sojourner Truth, born a slave in New York, listened to the argument that women were weaker than men. She replied: "That man over there says that women need to be helped into carriages and lifted over ditches and have the best place everywhere. Nobody ever helped me into carriages or over mud puddles, and aren't I a woman? Look at me! I have plowed and planted and gathered into barns, and aren't I a woman? I have borne thirteen children and seen them sold, and that little man says women can't have as many rights as men."

In the 1840s and 1850s the antislavery movement began to take away energy and effort from all the other movements. It seemed that this great issue had to be settled before all others.

Section 4 Review

1. What governments ran most of the public schools after 1820?
2. In what four ways did Horace Mann reform public schooling in the United States?
3. For what groups of persons did Dorothea Dix work to improve conditions?
4. What was the goal of temperance societies?
5. What two methods did union members in the early 1800s use to improve their working conditions?

Critical Thinking

6. **Identifying Central Issues.** What was the goal of the Seneca Falls convention in 1848?

Heritage   # Of Reform

Throughout the nation's history people have been working to improve their own lives and the lives of others.

The heritage of working for a better life for people in the United States goes back to colonial times. People came from almost every country of western Europe to settle in the colonies. They came mainly to improve their own lives. They wanted greater opportunities for themselves, their children, and their children's children. This dream has never died.

Helping Others

There is a second part to this dream. Not only should a person improve himself or herself, but every person should work to help others. As the lives of others improve, the whole society improves, making life better for everyone.

This reasoning helps explain why reform has been so important in the United States. For example, those who worked to improve the schools believed that public education would lead to well-informed citizens. Well-informed citizens, would make better choices of leaders, and the whole country would be better off. Those who worked for the rights of women and minorities believed that the nation would be helped by the contributions of *all* its citizens. Those who worked to free slaves believed that equal rights and freedom for blacks would bring equal rights and freedom for all.

Reform Cycles

Reform movements have a rhythm in United States history. The first one began in the 1820s and lasted until the war between the North and South in the 1860s. This is the reform movement you have been studying. A second reform movement began slowly in the 1880s and 1890s and reached its peak early in the twentieth century. It ended when the United States entered the First World War in 1917. You will study this reform movement later.

Another reform movement began in the 1930s when the nation was suffering through hard times. It ended when the United States entered World War II in 1941.

This rhythm suggests that throughout the country's history, the people have put their energy into making a better life for themselves and others. When war or some other happening redirects those energies, the reform movement dies down—at least for a time.

Today's supporters of equal rights for women (left) continue the work started by Elizabeth C. Stanton and Susan B. Anthony (above).

Children were employed in this glassblowing factory in the 1800s.

Minority Rights

Each movement focused on a different aspect of reform. For example, the first movement brought greater social equality for women. The second gave them greater political equality. A third movement—presently underway—is seeking equal economic rights for women. Today's women struggle for equal opportunity in getting jobs and in getting equal pay for equal work.

Reform movements for blacks and other minorities followed the women's movement step by step during the same years. The antislavery movement in the 1800s ended with the freeing of black slaves. The second and third movements sought but failed to win political and economic equality for blacks. Political equality has come slowly in the 1960s and 1970s. But economic equality for blacks and other minorities—and for women— is a goal still to be won.

The Role of Labor

Working people—among them women and minorities—are a part of each reform movement. In the first movement the working people most wanted better schooling, paid for by taxes. In the second reform movement they struggled for the right to form unions to achieve economic equality. In the third reform movement workers fought for shorter hours, better pay, and a way to handle grievances. They won the right to bargain as a group with employers over working conditions and pay.

The idea of giving each group an equal voice in government and a fair share of the nation's riches is still with us. Listen to the promises in any election campaign. You will learn that those in office want to meet the needs and wishes of those who elect them. Reform movements push officeholders into action. People interested in bringing about change get together and direct the attention of the voters to important issues. The process is slow, but Americans will not give up their goal of improving people's lives.

On an assembly line, employers may use fewer and less skilled workers.

Chapter 16 Review

Chapter Summary

A national spirit developed as the United States successfully dealt with its foreign affairs. Treaties in 1818 and in 1846 settled border problems with Canada. The purchase of Florida from Spain in 1819 increased United States territory while the Monroe Doctrine, issued in 1823, increased United States influence in world affairs.

Meanwhile, the political scene at home was changing. By 1820 the Federalist party died out and the Republican party split into two groups. The followers of Andrew Jackson, mainly from the South and the West, became known as Democrats. The National Republicans, who opposed the Democrats, were mainly from New England. The parties clashed over many issues, including the tariff and the national bank.

Reviewing Vocabulary

Use the following words to complete the sentences below. Write your answers on a separate sheet of paper.

antislavery	candidates
reform	temperance
border	veto
campaigns	doctrine
nullification	union
strike	

1. Two treaties with Britain established the _____ between the United States and Canada from central Minnesota to the Pacific.
2. President Monroe set forth a _____ that closed the Western Hemisphere to European colonization.
3. After the 1820s, political _____ planned election _____ to win voter support.
4. Neither the Democrats nor the Whigs were willing to support the _____ movement for fear of losing votes.
5. President Jackson took a strong stand against _____ and used his _____ power to defeat the national bank.
6. Of all the _____ movements, _____ societies had the largest following.
7. _____ workers used the power of the _____ to win better working conditions.

Understanding Main Ideas

1. How did the United States solve its problems with Great Britain and Spain?
2. What changes in voting rights, in the method of selecting candidates, and in political parties resulted from the growth of democracy?
3. In what ways did President Jackson symbolize the new democratic spirit?
4. What reform movements in the early 1800s attempted to improve people's lives?
5. What was the role of third parties in the two-party political system of the mid-1800s?

Critical Thinking Skills

1. **Recognizing Ideologies.** How did the Monroe Doctrine reflect the national spirit of the United States?
2. **Distinguishing False Images from Accurate Images.** Andrew Jackson became the symbol of the democratic spirit in the early 1800s. Would you have chosen him to represent the spirit of democracy? Explain your answer.

Social Studies Skills: Interpreting a Picture

Study the picture showing Andrew Jackson on the way to his inauguration.

Skill Review: Decide whether each of the items below states a fact or an opinion that you can gather from the picture.

1. The stage stopped outside the United States Post Office.

2. Most of the men listening to Jackson wore hats.

3. Most of the people in the crowd agreed with Jackson's views.

4. Jackson made many stops along the route to greet his admirers.

5. The weather was cold on inauguration day.

Writing About History

1. **Writing a Report.** Write one paragraph describing the inauguration of Andrew Jackson for an anti-Jackson newspaper. Write another paragraph describing the same event for a pro-Jackson newspaper.

2. **Writing a Testimonial.** In your opinion, who was the greatest social reformer of the mid-1800s? Write a testimonial for that person. Describe the reformer's accomplishments and tell why you admire the person.

Your Region in History

Citizenship. Look at the map on page 310. What was the status of the area where you live in 1850? Was the part of the United States where you now live a state or a territory in 1850? In what year was your state admitted to the Union?

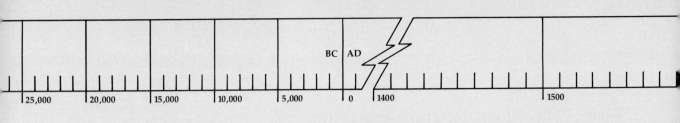

					BC	AD			
25,000	20,000	15,000	10,000	5,000	0	1400		1500	

The South
and Slavery

🐚 **Chapter 17**

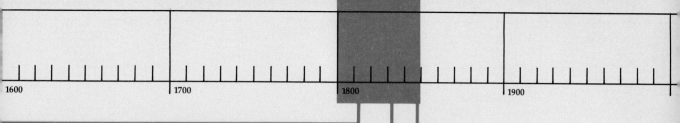

1600	1700	1800	1900

Vocabulary

plantation
cash crop
abolition
overseer
slaveholder
census
discrimination

Prereading

1. What ties were there among southern whites?
2. How did the slave system work, both for the slave owners and for the slaves?
3. What were the lives of free blacks like?
4. How did slaves, free blacks, and other groups aid the antislavery movement?

MANY REFORMERS who wanted a better life for everyone came to see that the greatest evil of all was slavery. Reformers believed that as long as men, women, and children were held as slaves, the nation itself was not fully free. At an antislavery meeting in New England a farmer stated: "It is as bad to enslave black people as white; and if you enslave any, it enslaves everybody else; and if you allow slavery in the country, you can't keep liberty."

The Constitution allowed the slave trade to go on until 1808. Many people hoped that after that date slavery would die out. Slave labor did not fit in with the economy of the North. So slavery in the North died out. But in the southern states, with the opening up of new land and the development of new crops, the need for slaves grew.

1 The Southern Economy

In the early 1800s the South thrived, but its growth did not match that of the North. Population in the South grew at a slower rate. And southern goods were neither as varied nor as profitable as those of the North.

Southern Crops

Most of the South remained agricultural. But ways of life and products differed among southern farmers. On large plantations planters used hundreds of slaves to raise cash crops. On smaller farms the owners worked from 150 to 500 acres (60 to 200 ha) of land, often with only a few slaves.

Farmers living in states close to the North—Kentucky and Missouri, for example—often had more in common with their northern neighbors than with the owners of the plantations farther south. There were more small farms and fewer large plantations in states close to the North. Southerners who lived up-country and in the mountains owned little land and had no slaves. Most of these people earned hardly enough to survive.

The owners of large plantations used their valuable land and slaves to grow rice, sugar, tobacco, and cotton. Land and climate allowed farmers to grow rice only along the rivers in the lower Gulf Plains, no more than 20 miles (32 km) inland. Between 500 and 600 plantations in this part of the South grew rice. Sugar plantations did well in Louisiana because of its warm, wet climate and its rich soil. Tobacco remained an important crop in Virginia, Maryland, Tennessee, North Carolina, and parts of Kentucky and Missouri. The best part of the South for growing cotton stretched from southern Tennessee to the longleaf pine region along the Gulf coast.

Southerners had always tried to grow cotton. But cotton growers had not been able to make much money on the crop. The chief drawback was separating the cotton fibers from the seeds. Until the cotton gin came into use the separating had to be done slowly by hand. The new speed possible with the cotton gin helped to make "King Cotton." Many southerners then moved west of the Appalachians, planting cotton in the rich, untilled soil. They tapped the growing market for cotton in English cloth-making factories. With the great boom in cotton the South needed slaves more than ever.

The Southern Planter

The richest landowners in the South were the planters. They owned plantations covering thousands of acres on which they grew cotton, rice, sugar, or tobacco. A plantation was both a home and a factory.

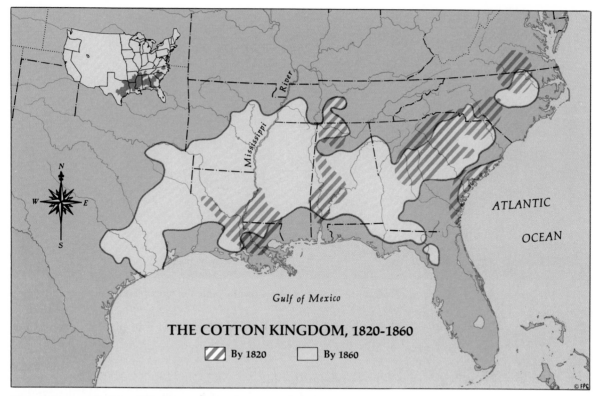

THE COTTON KINGDOM, 1820-1860

By 1820   By 1860

Slaves alone made it possible for southern planters to farm large plantations profitably in the 1800s.

As a home, it had a big house with fancy furniture, curtains, and rugs—goods often imported from Europe. There the owner held dinners and parties with neighbors and friends.

As an agricultural factory, a plantation had a large number of slaves. Each slave had his or her own job. House slaves became cooks, maids, butlers, children's nurses, and general servants. House slaves made life more comfortable for a planter and his family. But most slaves were field hands, who lived in small cabins near the planter's home. The field hands planted, hoed, and harvested the crops. Other slaves learned skills such as separating cotton with a cotton gin or curing tobacco. Still others worked as shoemakers and weavers, blacksmiths and brickmakers, barrelmakers and mechanics. Each part of a working plantation helped produce something its owner could exchange for money or goods. The slaves did all of the many different jobs that all the workers in a town might do. A large plantation was like a town in itself.

When planter families gathered at parties or dinners, talk would turn to the latest fashions, the best horses, the price of crops,

Life on the plantation was comfortable for most planter-owners.

politics, and the values of southern life. The planters praised the southern way of life as the ideal life.

The Farmer-Planter

Although the owners of large plantations held most of the South's land, owners of small farms—the farmer-planters—made up the largest group of whites in the South. They lived mostly in the up-country regions between the plantations on the Atlantic coast and the Appalachian Mountains. Farmer-planters owned about 300 acres (120 ha) or less. They raised garden crops—mainly corn—for home use and small amounts of a cash crop such as cotton or tobacco. Most of them also owned pigs, cattle, horses, and mules. Unlike the southern planters with large homes, the farmer-planters lived in small log cabins or frame houses with only one or two rooms. The furniture and rugs were simple, often homemade.

Some farmer-planters worked their farms alone. Others owned a few slaves—no more than ten. The slave owner and slaves generally worked side by side in the fields. One or two slaves might help with the housework. They lived in cabins near the farmer's house. Though the small-farm owner in the North and South shared much the same way of life, the southerner dreamed of becoming a rich planter and the owner of many slaves.

The poorest white southerners lived in run-down log cabins in the pine region on land with sandy soil. They scratched out a living by farming a few acres of garden crops and raising a few pigs and chickens. Some lived in the mountains where farming was hard. People in the mountains generally hunted and fished to get enough to eat. These poor whites—about one tenth of the South's people—were often sick, since they did not have enough good food. Few of them ever learned to read and write. The poor whites owned no slaves. And, though they sometimes lived less well than the black slaves, they looked down on the blacks.

Ties Among Southerners

Money and land in the South were not divided equally among the whites. In the 1850s the large planters held most of the fertile land and were able to add to their holdings over the years. In Alabama the large planters held more than two thirds of the land. Small-farm owners had trouble earning enough money to buy more land. In the 1850s the income of about 1,000 planter families put together was $50 million a year. All the rest of the southerners—about 660,000 families put together—earned only about $60 million.

There were many differences among southern whites, but certain ties linked them together. For one, most southerners were farmers. Of every hundred southerners, black and white, ninety-two lived on farms or plantations. Only eight of the hundred lived in cities. New Orleans as a port and Richmond and Atlanta as railroad centers did grow, but they grew more slowly than most northern cities. There was some industry, such as iron making, in the South. Yet the South's industry was far behind that of the North, so large industrial cities did not spring up.

Southerners were also linked by the need to find markets outside the United States for their goods. Some cotton, tobacco, rice, and sugar were shipped to markets in the United States. But most of the South's cash crops were shipped to other countries. Great Britain was the chief market for southern cotton.

Southerners also shared views on most political issues. The planters with the largest and richest holdings had the most influence in local, state, and national politics. Yet nearly all southerners, from planters with many slaves to poor whites with no slaves, favored low tariffs. Most of them opposed federal aid for building roads and canals. They were against a national bank. And most whites believed that abolition—doing away with slavery—would destroy the South.

2 The Slave System

Slavery more than anything else set the South apart from the North. By 1850 only two out of every hundred northerners were black. In the South one out of every three persons was black, and most blacks were slaves. A few southerners freed their slaves. In his will George Washington gave his slaves freedom after his death. Most southerners, however, even those without slaves, defended the slave system.

Section 1 Review

1. What were the four major southern crops?
2. What three factors combined to make cotton "king" in the South?
3. How were southern plantations similar to factories?
4. What group made up the largest population of whites in the South?
5. What group was the richest and had the most influence in politics in the South?

Critical Thinking

6. **Identifying Assumptions.** Why were most southern whites against doing away with slavery?

LOOKING AHEAD: How did the slave system work, both for the slave owners and for the slaves?

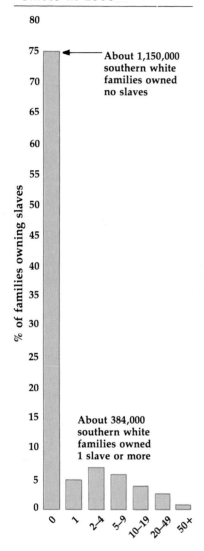

Percentage of Southern White Families Owning Slaves in 1860

% of families owning slaves

About 1,150,000 southern white families owned no slaves

About 384,000 southern white families owned 1 slave or more

0, 1, 2-4, 5-9, 10-19, 20-49, 50+

A few white families owned most of the slaves in the South by 1860.

Patterns of Slaveholding

The number of slaves was different from one southern state to another. On the South Carolina coast, where rice was grown, eight out of ten persons were black slaves. In western Virginia, North Carolina, and large parts of Kentucky and Tennessee only two persons out of ten were slaves. In some cotton-growing parts of Mississippi as many as nine out of ten persons were slaves. In general, the slave population compared to the white was largest where there were plantations earning huge profits.

By far the greatest number of slaves—2,500,000 by 1830—worked on farms and plantations. But a large number—about 500,000—did other kinds of work. Many were servants to people who lived in towns and cities. Others worked in the building of roads, canals, and bridges. The building of southern railroads depended greatly on slaves. Black slaves could be found doing all kinds of work in towns and cities.

Black slaves also worked in factories. Some factory owners found they could save costs by replacing free white workers with slaves. Some slaves belonged to the factory owner. Others were hired out by planters who had more slaves than they could use, especially in winter when there was less work on the plantations.

Work Rules for Slaves

The work lives of slaves were not all the same, but nearly all slaves had a long, hard day. One Arkansas slave owner described the workday on a plantation: "We . . . have everybody at work before day dawns . . . and we continue in the cotton fields . . . till it is so dark we can't see to work."

Most small-farm owners worked along with their slaves. But owners of large plantations did not. These planters often hired one or more white overseers to assign tasks to the slaves and to see that these tasks were carried out.

Some planters gave orders to the overseers, in person or in writing, on how to plant the crops and manage the slaves. The overseer reported directly to the master if a slave became sick or failed to do his or her task. Many overseers treated slaves roughly to get the work done.

The slaves working under an overseer were sometimes divided into smaller work groups or crews. A "driver" chosen from among the slaves was put in charge of each work crew. The driver's job was to see that the crew finished the work it was to do. Sometimes a driver set the pace for the group. A few drivers reported directly to the slave owner instead of to the overseer.

Another way of managing the work of slaves was the task system. A driver or overseer gave each slave a specific task, such as planting a certain number of rows of cotton or cultivating a certain number of rice plants. A slave who finished his or her task could return to the slave quarters, even if the day was not over. The task system was used most often on rice plantations. It was also used on cotton plantations on the Carolina coast and in factory work.

Treatment of Slaves

Slaves whose work was not satisfactory to an owner or overseer were often whipped. Overseers often gave a slave twenty lashes for

The cotton gin made part of the slave's work easier.

even a small offense and many more for a greater one. Most planters, however, used the whip sparingly. They knew that a slave who was wounded by the whip might not be able to work. Moreover, a slave with lash marks would be less valuable if sold to another owner. Other ways to punish a slave were taking away privileges, giving the slave extra work, or locking the slave up for a time.

Between 1820 and 1850, when the North's movement to free slaves became stronger, southern legislatures passed laws that made the lives of slaves even harder. Slaves were not allowed to leave their plantations without a written pass. After a certain hour only house slaves were allowed outside the slave quarters. When captured, runaway slaves were severely punished. No one was to teach a slave to read or write. And, in some states, slaves could not join a church. In most places slaves were not allowed to carry guns for fear they would revolt.

On some plantations the slave cabins were out of repair, dirty, and full of fleas. On others, like those of Jefferson Davis or Henry Clay, the slave quarters were made of brick, and the inside walls were whitewashed and clean. Most slave cabins were single rooms, with a fireplace on one side and a place for sleeping. Five or six persons lived in each cabin, even on the best-kept plantations.

Sometimes slaves were given a small patch of ground and were allowed to raise vegetables for themselves. On some plantations, if slaves raised more garden crops than they needed, they could sell the produce and keep the money. Some slaves who knew a trade could hire themselves for work outside their plantation. A few slaves managed to save enough money in this way to buy their freedom. But many slaveholders did not allow slaves the freedom to work elsewhere.

Slave Families

Black slaves found it hard to have a family life. A few owners encouraged their slaves to marry. Many others did not because they feared trouble if the husband and wife lived on different plantations or if one member of the couple was sold.

Slave families were sometimes broken up when an owner died and the plantation was divided among the owner's children. Slave sales also broke up families. And sometimes owners would hire out one member of a slave family to a factory or another plantation. Many slaves ran away, not to escape to freedom, but to join their families.

It was at slave auctions, however, that families were most often broken up. "Who buys me must buy my son too," one slave is reported to have shouted from the auction block. Often husbands, wives, and children were bought by different owners.

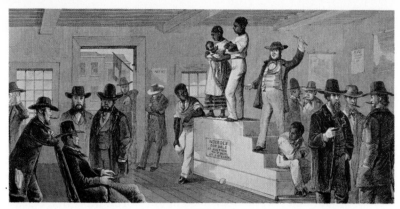
Family ties among blacks were of little interest to many slave dealers.

Trade in Slaves

Trading in slaves was big business. Under the Constitution the overseas slave trade could last until 1808. But slave traders continued to smuggle in slaves even after that date. In 1828 the government declared such slave trade to be an act of piracy. Yet slave trade lasted until as late as 1860.

As more land was settled in the West, and as cotton and sugar growing made more money, the demand for slaves became greater. Slave prices went up 500 percent between 1820 and 1850. By 1860 a strong field hand sold for about $1,500 in New Orleans. Those who had learned a trade, such as blacksmiths, sold for even higher prices. Slave smugglers grew rich in these years, while blacks remained in slavery year after year after year.

Supporters of Slavery

Fourteen percent of the people in the United States in 1850 were black slaves. Along with the Native Americans, these people were shut out of the American dream that hard work, skill, and talent could bring about a better life. Every person born of a black slave mother entered—and usually left—the world as a slave. Meanwhile, slave owners became rich. Slaves were property, worth much money to their owners, and the owners did not want to free their slaves.

The South seemed caught in a system based on slavery that southerners believed was impossible to change. Many, in fact, did not want to change it. By the 1850s slavery was an important part of what many southerners thought to be a perfect society.

The North was growing rapidly. Its industries, cities, and railroads were booming. Southerners watched northern power grow. They feared that the North would gain more political power than the South and that the southern way of life would be destroyed.

Southerners still had enough votes in Congress to block laws that they did not like. There were more southerners than northerners on the Supreme Court. And no one could hope to win the Presidency without southern votes. Yet the South feared what might happen as the North grew and developed. So southerners defended slavery and their way of life all the more strongly.

Section 2 Review

1. Where did the greatest number of southern slaves work?
2. What other kinds of work besides farming did slaves do?
3. What two methods were sometimes used to get work done on a large plantation?
4. In what three ways did southern legislatures limit the activity of slaves between 1820 and 1850?
5. What practice made it difficult for slaves to have a family life?

Critical Thinking

6. **Recognizing Ideologies.** Why did many southerners argue strongly in favor of slavery?

LOOKING AHEAD: What were the lives of free blacks like?

3   Free Blacks

As you have learned, all black people in the United States were not slaves. Some slaves worked to buy their freedom. Others escaped to freedom. Many had always been free. The census of 1850 showed 434,000 free black men, women, and children living in the United States. About half that number lived in the North. Most free blacks in the South lived in Maryland, Virginia, and North Carolina. Far fewer were found in the lower South and in the western states. A large number of free blacks lived in New Orleans.

Free blacks in the South often moved to the towns and cities, where they found more jobs and had less fear of threats from the authorities. Frederick Douglass wrote that life in Baltimore at its worst was like heaven compared to plantation life. Free blacks did not have to live apart from whites in the towns and cities. Blacks lived in whatever houses they could afford, side by side with whites.

A Hard Life

In spite of some freedom in the towns and cities, most free blacks had a hard life in both the North and the South. Local and state laws restricted the lives of free blacks in the South almost as much as the lives of slaves. A free black person in the South could be arrested on the charge of not having a way to make a living and could be sold to be a slave for a period of time. Blacks arrested for minor reasons could be sold as slaves in some southern states. Free blacks were not allowed to go where they pleased or even to hold meetings. In some

Of the total population in 1850, 16 percent were blacks; 14 percent were black slaves.

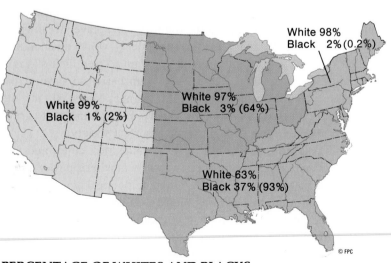

White 98%
Black   2% (0.2%)

White 99%
Black   1% (2%)

White 97%
Black   3% (64%)

White 63%
Black 37% (93%)

© FPC

PERCENTAGE OF WHITES AND BLACKS IN FOUR REGIONS, 1850
(figures in parentheses show percentage of blacks who were slaves)

states laws kept free blacks from getting jobs that whites wanted. In most of the South all black people were thought to be slaves unless they could prove otherwise. Free blacks had to carry papers proving they were free. In Florida and Georgia there was a law that all free blacks must have a white "guardian."

The treatment of free blacks in the North was not much better. Many northern states, as well as every southern state, had passed laws keeping free blacks from voting, from giving evidence in court, or from serving in the state militia. In 1842 John C. Calhoun and other senators tried to keep blacks from serving in the United States army and navy. The bill failed to pass in the House of Representatives, so black men continued to serve, usually in all-black units or as cooks or servants to officers.

Several blacks are shown in this winter scene painted in Brooklyn, New York, in 1816. Though some blacks lived comfortably in the North, whites there still did not treat them as social equals.

Work and Education

Free blacks held many kinds of jobs. Census records in North Carolina before 1860 show that free blacks were doing seventy different kinds of work. All through the country free black men and women could be found doing nearly every kind of job. Most did unskilled work. Some were in professions—teachers, dentists, and lawyers. A few were successful southern farmers. Some even owned slaves.

A few blacks managed to build small fortunes in business. Jehu Jones owned a hotel in Charleston, and James Forten manufactured sails in Philadelphia. Forten gave much of his money to the antislavery cause.

There were many black ministers in both the North and the South. Two of them, Samuel Ward and Henry Garnet, served white churches in New York. The African Methodist Episcopal Church and the Baptist Church gained many black members. Free blacks could attend services in some white churches, but they usually had to sit separately from the whites.

Free blacks had a better chance for public schooling in the North than in the South. Southern blacks had to be taught secretly because teaching them was against the law. In 1820 Boston started separate schools for blacks, and many northern towns followed. New York, New Jersey, Pennsylvania, and Ohio had separate schools for blacks. Only Boston and New Bedford, Connecticut, finally let both blacks and whites attend the same schools in 1855.

Discrimination in the North

Some white northerners did not believe blacks should be allowed the same schooling or job opportunities as whites. In 1831, citizens of New Haven, Connecticut, refused to allow for a black college. In 1834, whites in Philadelphia destroyed the African Presbyterian Church and burned the homes of some of its members. Many white northerners showed as much discrimination against blacks as did most southern whites.

Some free blacks began to write books and publish newspapers protesting slavery in the South and discrimination against blacks in the North. John Brown Russwurm, along with Samuel E. Cornish, started the first black newspaper, *Freedom's Journal,* in 1827. Frederick Douglass, who had escaped from slavery, wrote the story of his life, *My Bondage and My Freedom.* He later started another antislavery newspaper, *The North Star,* and gave speeches all over the North. William C. Nell was the author of a book called *Services of Colored Americans in the Wars of 1776 and 1812.*

In 1853 the National Council of Colored People was formed. That group stated that, except for Jews, no one had suffered more discrimination than "free colored people of the United States."

Section 3 Review

1. Why did many free blacks in the South move to towns and cities?
2. What were three restrictions that often made life difficult for free blacks in the South? In the North?
3. Identify each of the following: Jehu Jones, James Forten, John Brown Russwurm, Frederick Douglass.

Critical Thinking

4. **Making Comparisons.** Was life better for free blacks in the north than in the South? Explain.

LOOKING AHEAD: How did slaves, free blacks, and other groups aid the antislavery movement?

OUR COUNTRY IS THE WORLD—OUR COUNTRYMEN ARE ALL MANKIND.

BOSTON, MASS., FRIDAY, JUNE 14, 1850.

4 The Antislavery Movement

Voices had been raised against slavery since it first began. Throughout the first half of the nineteenth century the protests grew stronger. Whites, slaves and free blacks, northerners, and some southerners—all played a part in the movement to free the slaves.

Slave Revolts

Slaves had their own ways of protesting slavery. Many slowed down their work, a strategy also used by factory workers in the North. They tested almost every new overseer to see how slowly they could work without being punished. Slaves also protested by pretending to be sick to get out of work. They broke farm tools. Other slaves protested by running away in the hope of finding freedom.

But the form of protest southerners feared most was the slave revolt. By the 1830s hundreds of slave revolts had already shaken the South. In August 1800 more than a thousand slaves met outside Richmond, Virginia. They expected to march into the city. But a bad storm delayed their march and gave the Virginia militia time to put down the revolt. More than twenty years later, in 1822, a free black named Denmark Vesey nearly succeeded in organizing a revolt in Charleston. But the secret leaked out. Vesey and other leaders were hanged.

In 1831 a slave revolt in Virginia upset many in the South. It was led by Nat Turner, a preacher and slave leader from Southampton County. About sixty whites and nearly a hundred slaves were killed. Turner was caught, tried, and hanged. So were a number of his followers.

On the left side of the masthead of Garrison's paper, blacks are shown at auction. On the right a black family looks with excitement on the army of people pouring through a distant gate called Emancipation.

341 🜚

News of the Turner revolt frightened many white southerners. One woman felt that life in the South was like life near a volcano. "We know not when, or where, the flame will burst forth, but we know that death in the most horrid form threatens us." Nat Turner's revolt led to the passing of stronger laws against slaves. White southerners tried to keep slaves from learning about freedom movements in other places. Maryland and other southern states made it a crime to stir up trouble among slaves.

The American Colonization Society

Some antislavery people wanted to return all blacks to Africa—the home of their forebears. In 1817 the American Colonization Society was formed to raise money for such a plan. The society hoped to form a colony in Africa for free blacks. Slaves were also welcome if their masters decided they could go.

The society had greater support in the South than in the North. One slave owner in Virginia offered freedom to any of his slaves who would agree to go to Africa. Another in Mississippi wrote in his will that all of his 123 slaves would be freed on his death if they would move to Africa. Many blacks left the United States to settle in Liberia in western Africa. By 1830 about 1,500 blacks from America had settled there. In 1847 Liberia became the first independent republic in all of Africa. But many who settled there had trouble adjusting. The United States had become their home, and they were not used to the lands and people in Africa.

Most free blacks and slaves refused to leave the United States. In 1817 James Forten of Philadelphia headed a group of 3,000 blacks who spoke against leaving. Blacks in other northern cities did the same. "This is our home," one group stated, "and this is our country. Beneath its soil lie the bones of our fathers. For it, some of them fought, bled, and died. Here we were born and here we will die."

The Abolition Movement

Around 1830 the antislavery movement began to grow stronger. Northern white leaders spoke out openly against slavery. People who wanted to abolish, or end for all time, the keeping of slaves came to be called abolitionists. One of the best-known abolitionists was William Lloyd Garrison. Garrison started a newspaper called *The Liberator* on January 1, 1831. In it he asked that slavery be ended everywhere in the United States at once. "I am in earnest," he wrote. "I will not excuse—I will not retreat a single inch—AND I WILL BE HEARD."

Garrison's words caused a split between those who wanted the gradual end of slavery and those who wanted its immediate end. Many who believed it should end gradually also believed that the

federal government should pay the southern planters for their slaves. This movement had its greatest number of followers in Ohio, Indiana, Illinois, and Michigan. It also included white southerners such as Sarah and Angelina Grimké (grim′kē) who left their family and their South Carolina plantation to fight against slavery. Angelina Grimké's pamphlet "Appeal to the Christian Women of the South" was publicly burned in her old home state.

Most free blacks wanted immediate freedom for slaves. As early as 1800 the Free African Society of Philadelphia took this stand. By 1830 there were at least fifty black antislavery groups. Frederick Douglass became president of the New England Anti-Slavery Society in 1847. He spoke against slavery all over the North.

Black women also played an important part. Sojourner Truth, who had been a slave in New York until 1827, could neither read nor write. But she was a strong speaker against slavery. Harriet Tubman acted rather than spoke. After escaping from slavery in Maryland, she returned to the South many times to help hundreds of slaves escape. Southerners offered rewards totaling $40,000 for her capture.

Many other people—white and black, northerners and southerners—helped run what came to be called the Underground Railroad. Escaped slaves would be given aid, food, and shelter as they followed this route to freedom in the North or in Canada.

Some abolitionists died for the cause. The Reverend Charles T. Torrey helped about 400 slaves escape to freedom. He was put in jail in Maryland in 1844 and died there. In Alton, Illinois, Elijah P. Lovejoy, a minister and newspaper editor, spoke out for the gradual end of slavery. Several times people attacked him and destroyed his printing presses. Lovejoy refused to leave Alton or to change his stand. "Why should I flee from Alton?" he asked. "Is this not a free state?" But an angry crowd turned on him and killed him in 1837.

Such acts made the antislavery movement part of a larger movement for free speech and the rights of all people. Men and women who cared about freedom for all and for the bettering of all people's lives were sure that slavery was the greatest evil. With antislavery movements growing in the North and proslavery attitudes stiffening in the South, the stage was set for the war that would divide the United States.

Section 4 Review

1. Name four ways slaves protested their condition.
2. Which form of protest did southerners fear the most?
3. What were three effects of Nat Turner's revolt on southern whites?
4. What was the goal of the American Colonization Society?
5. Why did many blacks refuse to return to Africa?
6. What was the goal of William Lloyd Garrison and his followers?
7. How did Frederick Douglass, Harriet Tubman, and Sojourner Truth fight slavery?

Critical Thinking

8. **Determining Relevance.** Was the antislavery movement a part of a larger movement for the rights of all people? Explain your answer.

Douglass and Tubman—among many others—worked tirelessly for freedom for black slaves.

Frederick Douglass (far left) wrote and spoke for black freedom. Harriet Tubman (below at the left) helped slaves escape.

Frederick Douglas and Harriet Tubman were both slaves who escaped from their owners and later played an important part in freeing others.

Hardship for Douglass

Douglass was born in about 1817. When he was about eight years old, he was sent to Baltimore where he worked as a house servant for seven years. He learned to read and write. He also worked in a shipyard. When his owner died, he was sent back to a plantation 40 miles (64 km) from Baltimore where he worked as a field hand. About 1836 Douglass tried to escape, but he was thrown into jail.

Later, Douglass was sent back to Baltimore. There he suffered great hardship. He was severely beaten— at one time every day for six months. But he also learned a trade—to caulk or glue seams between boards in shipbuilding. In 1838 he managed to escape, disguised as a free black seaman.

He went to New York City where he married Ann Murray, a free black he had first met in Baltimore.

Life in the North

Douglass and his wife went to live in New Bedford, a port in Massachusetts. For a time he worked at odd jobs. He was not able to practice his shipbuilding trade because whites working on vessels refused to work with him or with any other blacks.

Douglass soon began to read William Lloyd Garrison's abolitionist newspaper, *The Liberator*. In 1841 he attended a meeting of the Massachusetts Anti-Slavery Society on Nantucket Island. Douglass spoke with such

feeling about his life as a slave that the society hired him to represent it at meetings elsewhere. Before long Douglass had become a key figure in the New England Anti-Slavery Society.

Douglass was a religious man. When the church he attended made him and other blacks sit apart from the whites, Douglass joined an all-black church. He became a leader in the black church, as a powerful and persuasive speaker and writer.

In 1845 Douglass left for Great Britain and Ireland where he met many antislavery leaders.

Douglass returned to the United States in 1847. He finally bought his freedom—up to this point he had been a runaway slave—and started a newspaper. It was called *The North Star.* That was the star that slaves escaping to the North followed in search of freedom. The paper was printed for seventeen years.

Douglass also supported women's rights, temperance, and other reform movements. He later became an ambassador to Haiti and a leader of Howard University.

When Douglass died in 1895, he was known throughout the world.

Tubman's Slave Life

The life of Harriet Tubman took a different course. She was the daughter of Benjamin Ross and Harriet Greene, both slaves. Her owner ordered her to marry John Tubman when she was about twenty-three years old.

Although Harriet was not strong, she was able to work long, hard hours. As a slave she worked in the field. She was once badly hurt when a heavy weight was thrown at her head by an angry owner. She

suffered from beatings. But she overcame her hardships and became very strong.

Tubman had deep religious beliefs. She firmly believed that God would care for her, no matter what the dangers.

As Tubman watched older sisters being taken away in a chain gang to be sold, she became desperate to escape. In 1849 she left with her brothers. After traveling a short distance, Tubman's brothers became frightened and returned to their owner.

Liberty or Death

But Tubman pressed on. As she said later, she followed the North Star to freedom. She said, "There was one of two things I had a right to, liberty, or death; if I could not have one, I would have the other; for no man should take me alive."

In the years that followed, Tubman made over fifteen trips back to Maryland to help about 300 slaves escape.

She would let other slaves know her escape plans for them by walking nearby and singing a hymn. As a sign that the coast was clear, she sang:

O go down, Moses,
Way down into Egypt's land,
Tell old Pharoah,
Let my people go.

Tubman became the best-known freedom driver on the Underground Railroad. She worked endlessly in the cause of equal rights for blacks until she died in 1913.

The first runaway listed on this fugitive slave poster was worth $25 in reward money to his finder.

The Levi Coffin house in Fountain City, Indiana, was once referred to as "the Grand Central Station" of the Underground Railroad.

Chapter 17 Review

Chapter Summary

The slave trade became illegal in 1808, but slavery lasted many more years. The demand for slave labor increased with the South's growing dependence on cotton. Most southern whites believed that the abolition of slavery would destroy the South's economy.

One out of every three persons in the South was black, and most blacks were slaves. Most slaves worked on farms and plantations. Many became runaways, either to escape to freedom or to rejoin their families. Slave owners made every effort to recapture runaways.

An active antislavery movement began. Frederick Douglass, a free black who urged the end of slavery, became the editor of *The North Star*. The American Colonization Society was formed to resettle blacks in Liberia. A few white southerners, such as the Grimké sisters, became abolitionists, but most abolitionists were from the North. William Lloyd Garrison used his newspaper *The Liberator* to call for an immediate end to slavery.

Reviewing Vocabulary

Match each of the following words with its correct definition. Write your answers on a separate sheet of paper.

abolition	census
slaveholder	cash crop
discrimination	overseer
plantation	

1. a large farm, usually planted with a single crop and usually requiring a large local workforce
2. a farm product raised to be sold for a profit
3. the work of ending slavery
4. a supervisor of slaves on a plantation
5. the owner of a person bought as property
6. an official count of the number of people living in a given area
7. an act that judges people on the basis of something other than individual merit or value

Understanding Main Ideas

1. In what ways were southern whites alike in their way of life, their economic needs, and their political views?
2. What was life like for slave owners and for slaves under the slave system?
3. How did the lives of free blacks differ from the lives of slaves?
4. What role did slaves, free blacks, and other groups play in the antislavery movement in the North and South?
5. How did farmer-planters differ from plantation owners?
6. Why did southern legislatures pass laws to limit the activity of slaves between 1820 and 1850?
7. In what ways did slavery affect family life for southern blacks?
8. Why did southerners defend slavery?
9. How did northern states limit the rights of free blacks?
10. What were William Lloyd Garrison's views on the abolition of slavery? How did his position cause a split between antislavery groups?

Critical Thinking Skills

1. **Distinguishing Fact from Opinion.** Most southern whites believed that abolition would destroy the South. Do the facts found in your text support this opinion? Explain your answer.
2. **Checking Consistency.** Why did northerners favor abolition yet discriminate against free blacks?

Social Studies Skills: Interpreting a Chart

Year	Total of Blacks in U.S. Population	Total of Free Blacks in Population	Percent of Free Blacks in Total Black Population	Percent of Slaves in the Total Black Population
1790	757,208	59,527	7.9%	
1800	1,002,037	108,435	10.8	
1810	1,377,808	186,446	13.5	
1820	1,771,656	233,634	13.2	
1830	2,328,642	319,599	13.7	
1840	2,873,648	386,293	13.4	
1850	3,638,808	434,495	11.9	
1860	4,441,830	488,070	11.0	

Copy the chart above and complete the fourth column by subtracting the percent of free blacks from 100.0.

Skill Review: Use your completed chart to decide whether each of the following statements is true or false.

1. At each census between 1790 and 1860, the total number of blacks in the United States population increased.

2. At each census between 1790 and 1860, the total number of free blacks in the United States population decreased.

3. After 1830, the percent of black slaves in the total black population increased.

4. In 1860 the percent of free blacks in the total black population was less than it had been in 1830.

5. The highest percent of slaves in the total black population was in 1860.

3. **Demonstrating Reasoned Judgment.** Which of the abolitionist speakers do you think was most convincing to audiences of the time? Why?

Writing About History

1. **Writing a Speech.** Imagine that you were an abolitionist in the 1850s. Write a persuasive speech to gain support for the antislavery movement. Indicate whether your speech is written from the viewpoint of a northerner, a southerner, a white, a slave, or a free black. Also indicate the audience for which your abolitionist message is intended.

2. **Writing Historical Fiction.** Choose one of the following topics: life on a plantation, escape to freedom, free blacks. Then write a fictional account about the topic you chose based on the facts presented in the chapter.

Your Region in History

Culture. Look at the map on page 338. What was the percent of whites and blacks in the region where you live in 1850? What attitudes toward slavery do you think most people in your region had at that time? Be prepared to explain your answer.

Lifestyles:
The
Growing
Nation

☙ Chapter 18

Between 1815 and 1850 Americans were building a new nation. The size of the country doubled, and the population tripled. Newly arrived immigrants settled in and around eastern industrial cities. Other Americans pushed west where land was cheap, though life was often hard. In the South, where cotton growing became more profitable, much new land was planted with cotton.

In the growing nation some people became rich while others remained poor. Some attended school. Others learned by doing. Some spoke against slavery. Others favored it. More and more, the part of the country in which people lived shaped their family lives, jobs, opportunities, and ideas.

As in earlier years, couples in the 1800s usually had many children. When the children grew up, they often moved west to buy land of their own. Families of slaves were often broken up by their owners. A few women decided that, since wives had so few legal rights, they were better off single than married. Some women–married and single–went to work outside the home.

Family on the Move

Eliza Donner was one of the survivors of the Donner party, which met with disaster on the trail to California in 1846. Her family had started out from Springfield, Illinois, in high spirits.

. . . The members of our household were at work before the rosy dawn. We children were dressed early in our new . . . travelling suits; and as the final packing progressed, we often peeped out of the window at the three big white covered wagons that stood in our yard. . . .

I sat beside my mother with my hand clasped in hers, as we slowly moved away from that quaint old house on its grassy knoll, from the orchard, the corn land, and the meadow. . . . her clasp tightened, and I, glancing up, saw tears in her eyes and sorrow in her face. . . .

In Independence, Missouri, the Donners joined others.

Elderly matrons spent most of their time in their wagons, knitting or patching designs for quilts. The younger ones and the girls passed their [time] in the saddle. They would scatter in groups over the plains to investigate distant objects, then race back, and with song and banter join husband and brother, driving the loose cattle in the rear. The wild, free spirit of the plain often prompted them to invite us little ones to seats behind them, and away we would canter with the breeze playing through our hair and giving a ruddy glow to our cheeks. . . .

Lifestyles

Among blacks and whites alike, marriage was often an occasion for community celebration.

A Slave Marriage

When he was eighteen and a slave in Kentucky, Henry Bibb met a slave woman named Malinda, who lived on a neighboring farm. Later in his life he wrote about their marriage.

. . . before I was aware of it, I was deeply in love. . . . After having [asked her to marry,] I informed her . . . that I was decided on becoming a free man before I died; and that I expected to get free by running away, and going to Canada. . . . [Two weeks later,] clasping each other by the hand, pledging our sacred honor that we would be true, we called on high heaven to witness [our marriage]. There was nothing that could be more binding upon us as slaves than this; for marriage among American slaves, is disregarded by the laws of this country. . . . I was permitted to visit [Malinda] only on Saturday nights, after my work was done, and I had to be home before sunrise on Monday mornings. . . .

Marriage Under Protest

Lucy Stone had decided that she would never marry. In her day a woman who married gave up all her legal rights. Twenty-six-year-old Henry Blackwell met Stone when she cashed a check at his hardware store in Cincinnati. Stone was then thirty-three and was traveling around the country lecturing for the American Anti-Slavery Society. Two years later Henry came to Lucy's home with a letter of introduction from William L. Garrison. When Henry proposed marriage, Lucy refused. But Henry assured her, "Equality with me is a passion." After two years Lucy agreed to marry him.

At their wedding in 1855, Henry read the protest they had written against the existing marriage laws.

. . . We protest . . . against those laws which give to the husband:

1. *The custody of the wife's person.*
2. *The exclusive control and guardianship of their children.*
3. *The sole ownership of her personal [property], and use of her real estate. . . .*

351

The well-to-do, such as this family in Hartford, Connecticut, could carpet their living rooms and surround themselves with paintings and musical instruments.

Those few people who became rich from manufacturing or from cotton planting often built costly new homes. They furnished these homes with the finest furniture, carpets, and decorations that could be brought from Europe.

Those who moved west built one-room log cabins or sod houses on their new farms. As the farmers made more money, they built larger, more comfortable houses. Whale-oil lamps gave better light than candles. Carpets replaced rag rugs. Stoves replaced fireplaces. A few homes had indoor plumbing.

Cities grew and became more like those of today. Fire and police protection, water, and street lighting were supplied by the city to those who lived there. But more and more immigrants crowded into the poorer neighborhoods of cities with new industries. The lives of the workers often became less, rather than more, comfortable as the 1800s went on.

A Heavenly Place

Later in his life Samuel Clemens [Mark Twain] remembered how he loved to visit his uncle's farm in Missouri during the 1830s. His uncle had eight children and about twenty slaves.

It was a heavenly place for a boy, that farm. . . . The house was a double log one with a spacious floor (roofed in) connecting it with the

The Winnebago of 1852 lived in wigwams made with hides.

kitchen. In the summer the table was set in the middle of that shady and breezy floor. . . .

I can see that farm yet . . . the family room . . . with a "trundle" bed in one corner and a spinning wheel in another . . . the vast fireplace, piled high on winter nights . . . the lazy cat spread out on the rough hearthstones; the drowsy dogs braced against the jambs . . .; the slick and carpetless oak floor . . .; half a dozen children romping in the background. . . .

A "Den" for the Newly Arrived

One member of a reform group—the New York Children's Aid Society—described the homes of some immigrant families.

I visited lately one of their lodging houses for the newly-arrived—a den such as I had no idea existed in New-York. . . . A number of ragged children were playing at the door; within, the hall was dark and reeking with the worst filth. I climbed the dirty stairway, knocked at the door, and entered a little room where some women were cooking; in . . . a little closet of a place, half-a-dozen . . . girls were sitting, making coarse straw bags, "for a cent a-piece". . . .

The upper part of the house was . . . all very filthy. The people seemed very poor, honest . . . , not long here, and without work, usually. Women and men, evidently not of the same family, were herded into the same rooms. . . .

On the land where they had cut down trees to build houses the settlers often began to plant their crops.

Section 1 Review

1. How did the Donner children feel about the move west? How did their mother feel?
2. Why might Henry Bibb have felt he had to tell Malinda about his intention to run away?
3. What household items, comparable to whale-oil lamps and stoves of the past, are signs of prosperity today?

Critical Thinking

4. **Identifying Central Issues.** When Lucy Stone and Henry Blackwell married, what of hers legally belonged to him? Did their protest change that?

A person's values determine the choices he or she will make in life. Different people make different choices. Some value wealth and security. Some give up money and comfort to help others. In the 1800s most people believed that children needed to be taught proper values.

Contrasting Values in California

Doña María de la Concepción (kōn·sep′sē·ōn′) was one of the nine children of Don José Argüello (dōn hō′zā′ ar·gwē′yō′). Don José owned a large ranch of 35,000 acres (12,343 ha) near San Francisco in Spanish California. When Doña María was fifteen, she fell in love with a young Russian nobleman who had come to her father's ranch as the representative of the Russian colony in California. Soon afterward he left for St. Petersburg, Russia, to obtain the czar's permission to marry Doña María. But he never returned.

Doña María devoted her life to teaching Native Americans the ways of Christianity. As Sister Domenica, she became the head of the convent of Santa Catalina at Monterey. She worked for better lives for the poor. When she died in 1857, she was called La Beata (lä bā′ä′tä), the Saintly One.

Many other Californians were more interested in getting rich than in helping the poor. Reverend Walter Colton, the mayor of Monterey, described the 1849 "gold fever":

In their search for gold, prospectors often used a tilted trough called a sluice box. They washed stream water over the ridges in the box and collected any gold particles trapped there.

Catherine and Levi Coffin helped more than 5,000 slaves escape.

The family who had kept house for me caught the moving infection. Husband and wife were both packing up; the blacksmith dropped his hammer, the carpenter his plane, the mason his trowel, the farmer his sickle, the baker his loaf. . . . All were off for the mines. . . .

An Underground Railroad

Levi Coffin and his family could have lived in peace and comfort in Indiana. But they chose to serve as "conductors" on the Underground Railroad. This decision endangered their property and their lives. Coffin described one group of escaping slaves.

The largest party of slaves ever seated at our table, at one time, numbered seventeen. . . . [They] arrived at our house about dawn one morning, having been brought in two covered wagons from Salem, a settlement of Friends in Union County. The distance was about thirty miles, and the journey occupied the most of the night. . . . when I went out, I found the fugitives all seated in the room, my wife having welcomed them and invited them to take chairs and sit down. . . . Several of our near neighbors came in to see this valuable property seated around our table, and estimated that, according to the owners' valuation, they were worth $17,000. . . . many of them were in need of garments and shoes. These were furnished to them, and when all were made comfortable, I arranged for teams and suitable conductors to take them on to the next station. . . .

Schoolbook Values

"A Kind Brother" was a lesson in the Second Reader of a famous series published by William Holmes McGuffey in 1836. For many years *McGuffey's Readers* were used in nearly all the elementary classrooms in the country. Over 120 million copies were sold. In addition to reading, children learned about honesty, thrift, and patriotism. Good won over evil in every story.

At the end of a story about a little boy who was hurt when he did not obey his parents, McGuffey adds this moral:

Lit-tle chil-dren may learn from this, that they should al-ways o-bey their par-ents. . . . I once knew of a lit-tle girl who was told not to cross the street be-fore a car-riage. But she would not stop; and when the car-riage came up, it ran di-rect-ly o-ver her.

Even history books taught moral lessons. A text written in the 1850s explained why America had become a great nation.

The founders of this nation were honest, true men. They were sincere in all they said, upright in all their acts. They . . . strove to live at peace with their neighbors. When they were attacked, they fought like men, and, defeated or victorious, would not have peace till their point was gained. Above all, they insisted, from the very first, on being free themselves, and securing freedom for you, their children.

At Watertown, Wisconsin, in 1856 Mrs. Carl Schurz taught the nation's first kindergarten—a class of German-speaking children.

Many people in the 1800s learned the skills they needed in life on their own or from an experienced person. The public school movement, however, meant that more and more children attended the early grades of school. Teachers were often not well trained. And many subjects studied in school today were not taught then.

Mark Twain

Samuel Clemens's education did not end when he left the schoolhouse. Like many boys who lived along the Mississippi, he had dreamed of being a steamboat pilot. When he was twenty-two years old, he had a chance to become an apprentice to Horace Bixby, pilot of the *Paul Jones*. Later, Clemens took the steamboat term for a water depth of 12 feet (1.8m), "mark twain," as his pen name.

"My boy," Bixby said, "there's only one way to be a pilot, and that is to get [to know] this entire river by heart. You have to know it just like A B C."

That was a big job. But Clemens boasted,

. . . before we reached St Louis . . . I had a notebook that fairly bristled with the names of towns, points, bars, islands, bends, reaches etc. . . . When I had learned the names and position of every visible feature of the river . . . I judged that my education was complete. . . .

A New England School

In 1831 a teacher described a school in rural New England.

The new building erected about five years since . . . is of brick; the room is larger and higher; it is better lighted, and has an improved fire place. The writing desks for the pupils are attached to the walls, and the seats for the smaller pupils have backs. . . .

Males have been uniformly employed [as teachers] in winter [term], and females in summer [term]. . . . Many of them, both males and females, were from sixteen to eighteen years of age, and a few, over twenty-one. . . .

The school books have been about the same for thirty years. Webster's Spelling Book, the American Preceptor [a reading book], and the New Testament, have been the principal books used. . . .

Until within a few years, no studies have been permitted in the day school, but spelling, reading, and writing. Arithmetic was taught by a few instructors, one of two evenings in a week. But in spite of a most determined opposition, arithmetic is now permitted in the day school, and a few pupils study geography.

With the aid of a device held between the teeth this class of hearing-impaired students "listens" to a musical concert.

Section 2 Review

1. Of religious, moral, and economic values, which played the greatest role in the actions of Doña María de la Concepción? Of the gold seekers? Of the Coffin family?
2. What was a "station" and who was a "conductor" on the Underground Railroad?

Critical Thinking

3. **Making Comparisons.** Name some subjects today that were not studied in New England in the 1830s.

Talking Leaves

Sequoya, a citizen of the Cherokee nation, spoke no English. But he admired the way that some English-speaking people could make marks on sheets of paper ("leaves," Sequoya called them) and make the marks "talk" back to them. In 1809 he began making a set of symbols for the sounds in the Cherokee language. When he was finished, he had an alphabet of eighty-five characters. Within a few months several thousand Cherokee had learned to read and write their language and were teaching others.

The Cherokee council passed laws to set up better schools and an academy. In 1827 the council established a printing press and a newspaper for the Cherokee nation. The *Cherokee Phoenix* printed news, public documents, and commentary in both English and Cherokee.

Sawyers in sawmills (above) and blacksmiths were valued workers in most communities in the 1800s.

Most people in the 1800s still worked on farms. Better tools such as steel plows and threshing machines made farm work easier, and the farmers could make more money. Working conditions and pay in the factories, however, became worse rather than better in the 1800s. And slaves' work did not change because slaves had no way of bettering their positions.

Factory Girls

Harriet Robinson was younger than ten when she started work in the Lowell cloth factory. Hours were long and wages were a little less than two dollars a week. But in 1836, when Harriet was eleven years old, wages were cut, and the Lowell "factory girls" called a strike. Harriet later wrote of her part in the strike:

. . . when the girls in my room stood irresolute, uncertain what to do, . . . I . . . started on ahead, saying . . . "I don't care what you do, I am going to turn out." . . . As I looked back at the long line that followed me, I was more proud than I have ever been since. . . . About 1,500 girls took part in the strike. As they marched through the streets, they sang:

> *"Oh! isn't it a pity, such a pretty girl as I—*
> *Should be sent to the factory to pine away and die?"*

From Slave to Inventor

Benjamin Bradley, a slave from Maryland, found people to help him buy his freedom. He also put up money himself, and later he paid back everyone who had helped. This letter was sent to one of Bradley's helpers.

Dear Sir:—I am very happy to inform you that the freedom of the slave Benjamin Bradley has been accomplished by the payment of $1,000, to which you contributed the final $122 necessary to make it up. . . .

Bradley was owned by a master in Annapolis, Maryland. Eight years ago he was employed in a printing office there. He was then about sixteen, and showed great mechanical skill and ingenuity. With a piece of gun-barrel, some pewter, a couple of pieces of round steel and some materials, he constructed a working model of a steam engine.

His master soon afterwards got him the place of a helper in the department of Natural and Experimental Philosophy in the Naval Academy at Annapolis. He sold his first steam engine to a Midshipman. With the proceeds, and what money he could lay up (his master allowing him five dollars a month out of his wages), he built an engine large enough to drive the first cutter of a sloop-of-war at the rate of sixteen knots an hour. . . .

As people settled down, traders built more lasting quarters.

Gimbel's Palace of Trade

Adam Gimbel came to New Orleans from Bavaria, Germany, with five dollars in his pocket. He traveled up and down the Mississippi valley with a pack, selling shoelaces, yarn, and other notions.

In 1842 Adam set up a trading post called the Gimbel Palace of Trade in Vincennes, Indiana. He was the first to give refunds, even on unfair complaints. He promised "fairness and equality to all patrons whether they be residents of the city, plainsmen, traders, or Indians." People liked this stand, and Gimbel's Palace did a lot of business.

Gimbel and his wife had seven boys, all of whom worked in the Gimbel store. Later, Gimbel opened new stores. When Adam died, his son Isaac became president of the chain of Gimbel Department Stores.

Maria Mitchell, Astronomer

Maria Mitchell had an interesting career in the day when most women could find work only at home, in a factory, or in a schoolroom. Maria had been interested in astronomy since she was a little girl. She had helped her father, William Mitchell, record an eclipse of the sun. She was so good at arithmetic that some people wanted her to open a navigation school for whalers. Instead, she became a librarian.

Mitchell spent most evenings searching the sky with a telescope. On October 1, 1847, she discovered a comet, which was later named for her. The next year she became the first woman elected to the American Academy of Arts and Sciences in Boston. She continued to study astronomy when she later taught at Vassar.

In the 1800s people enjoyed swimming, attending museums, and playing parlor games. Ball playing remained popular among Native Americans. And on the Fourth of July people across the United States honored the birthday of their country.

Nothing to Do

Mrs. Frances Trollope, an Englishwoman visiting America, found Cincinnati very dull.

I never saw people who appeared to live so much without amusement as the Cincinnatians. Billiards are forbidden by law, so are cards. . . . They have no public balls, excepting . . . during the Christmas holidays. They have no concerts . . . no dinner parties.

Proper Amusements

In the 1800s books and magazines began to suggest ways for people to have fun. In 1834 *Family Magazine* printed some calisthenics for men who wanted to keep in shape. As a warm-up, the magazine told readers to "hop and strike the lower part of the back with the feet."

Barnum's Museum

On January 1, 1842, P.T. Barnum opened the American Museum in New York. He advertised its "Great Model of Niagara Falls, With Real Water" and "Free Music for the Millions!" In a year, thanks to interesting but sometimes misleading advertising, Barnum's museum became most popular with New Yorkers.

Philadelphians in 1853 danced in the elegant ballroom of the Assembly Building.

The Barnum & Bailey Greatest Show on Earth promised "remarkable dives" and "double and triple somersaults" from the La Moyne Brothers.

The mystery of Barnum & Bailey's wandering globe was how it traveled up and down a spiral inclined plane.

Five-year-old Charles S. Stratton of Connecticut joined Barnum's museum as an attraction. His mother was surprised to see him described as "General Tom Thumb, a dwarf eleven years of age, just arrived from England."

Creek Team Sports

Hundreds of Native Americans came to ball-playing tournaments. Each player on a team had a stick with a hoop of woven net at one end. The ball was made of deerskin and stuffed with hair. The players were to catch the ball in their nets and fling it over the opposing team's goal. Basil Hall, an English traveler and sea captain, described a game he watched the Creek play in 1828.

One of the chiefs . . . cast the ball high in the air . . . [about] thirty players rushed forward . . . a fine scramble took place. . . . At length an Indian, more expert than the others . . . ran off with [the ball] like a deer. . . . [the others tried] by any means to prevent his throwing [the ball] through the opening between the [branches of the trees] at the end of the [playing field]. Whenever this grand purpose of the game was accomplished, the successful party announced their right to count one by a fierce yell of triumph. . . .

Jingle Bells

When snow came, sleighs came, too. The sport was enjoyed because young ladies could ride with men. In 1821 Adam Hodgson described sleighing in New York.

Painted sleighs with scarlet cloth and buffalo skins are dashing along in all directions at a [great] speed. . . . Everybody seems to make the most of the snow while it lasts, and night does not put an end to its festivity. The horses have a string of bells around their necks, and in the fine moonlight nights I hear them dashing away long after midnight.

Fourth of July

The Fourth of July has been celebrated in many ways. On July 4, 1843, James W. Nesmith was on his way to Oregon from Maine as part of Burnett's group, guided by Whitman. Nesmith wrote in his diary:

The glorious Fourth has once more rolled around. Myself, with most of our company, celebrated it by swimming. . . . there seems to be some of our company [thinking] about luxuries [consumed] in different parts of the Great Republic on this day. Occasionally you hear something said about . . . soda, ice cream . . . [etc.], but the Oregon emigrant must forget these luxuries and . . . submit to hard fare, and put up with . . . cold-water celebrations . . . namely, drinking cold water and wading and swimming in it all day.

Section 3 Review

1. How much money did Benjamin Bradley have to raise to buy his freedom?
2. List five items sold in today's department stores that Gimbel would not have had for sale.
3. How do Americans today celebrate the Fourth of July?

Critical Thinking

4. **Recognizing Ideologies.** Would Harriet Robinson have been in favor of laws limiting child labor? Why or why not?

Focus On Unit 3

Lifestyles: Understanding Social History

To answer the following questions, review the lifestyles section from page 348 to page 361.

1. **Families and Homes.** Reread the accounts of the marriage of Henry Bibb and Malinda, and of Lucy Stone and Henry Blackwell on page 351. In what ways did the marriage ceremonies of these two couples reflect the social, political, and economic conditions of the time?
2. **Values and Learning.** Many people today believe that values *should* be taught in school. What values did children learn from such textbooks as McGuffey's Readers and the history book quoted on page 355? What do these schoolbook values indicate about the purpose of education in the 1800s? Do you think these values should be taught in today's schools? Explain your viewpoint.
3. **Work and Play.** The United States is often viewed as a land of opportunity. How do the stories of Harriet Robinson, Benjamin Bradley, Adam Gimbel, and Maria Mitchell on pages 358 and 359 support this view of the United States? In what ways do they contradict it?

Making Connections

Use the Unit 3 time line below to answer the following questions.

1. Who was President when each of the following events took place: The Missouri Compromise? Completion of the Erie Canal? Passing of the Indian Removal Act?
2. How was the formation of the Republic of Texas in 1836 related to Mexican Independence in 1821?
3. Reread the Unit Introduction on page 251 and give examples from the time line that demonstrate the effects of westward migration on Native Americans.
4. **Determining Relevance.** Which events on the time line reflect the democratic spirit of the nineteenth century?

Critical Thinking Skills

1. **Recognizing Cause and Effect.** What events led settlers west of the Appalachian Mountains, then west of the Mississippi River?
2. **Predicting Consequences.** How might southern attitudes toward the tariff, federal aid for improvements, and slavery have been different if the South had succeeded in building clothing factories?

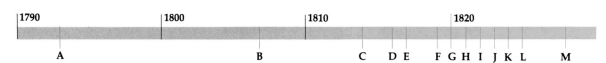

1790	1800	1810	1820
A	B	C D E	F G H I J K L M

A **1793** Whitney's cotton gin
B **1807** Fulton's steamboat
C **1814** Peace of Ghent
D **1816** Election of James Monroe
E **1817** American Colonization Society
F **1819** Purchase of Florida

G **1820** Monroe's reelection; Missouri Compromise
H **1821** Mexican Independence
I **1822** Establishment of Liberia, first African republic

J **1823** Monroe Doctrine
K **1824** Election of John Quincy Adams
L **1825** Completion of Erie Canal
M **1828** Election of Andrew Jackson; Tariff of Abominations

3. **Recognizing Bias.** What attitude did Ralph Waldo Emerson express about foreign relations in the following quote: "We will walk on our own feet . . . we will speak with our own minds"?

4. **Identifying Alternatives.** What different methods did abolitionists in both the North and the South propose to end the practice of slavery?

Using Geography Skills

Use the map below to answer the following questions.

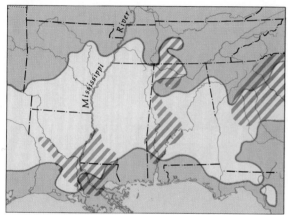

1. **Understanding World Regions.** What region does the area shown on the map represent?

2. **Developing Locational Skills.** What states on the map were once part of the Cotton Kingdom (areas marked in red and yellow)?

3. **Developing an Awareness of Place.** Why do you think the Mississippi River was important to southern planters?

4. **Understanding Human Movement.** Why do you think American settlers took their slaves with them to Texas?

Linking Past to Present

Determining Relevance. How did the spirit of reform improve life for most Americans in the mid-1800s? Is this same spirit evident in the United States today? What reform movements exist today? How are current reform movements similar to those of the mid-1800s? How are they different?

Reviewing Social Studies Skills

1. **Finding Information.** Make a list of possible sources of information about slavery. Identify each one as a primary or a secondary source.

2. **Evaluating Sources.** Write a list of questions you would use to evaluate each of the sources you identified above.

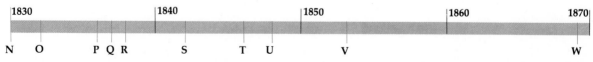

| 1830 | | | | | 1840 | | | | 1850 | | | | 1860 | | | | 1870 |
| N | O | | | P Q R | | | S | | T U | | V | | | | | | W |

N **1830** Indian Removal Act
1830–1832 Black Hawk War

O **1832** Jackson's reelection; Jackson's veto of the national bank

P **1836** Formation of Republic of Texas; Battles of the Alamo and San Jacinto

Q **1837** Opening of Mount Holyoke (Mass.), first women's college

R **1838** Trail of Tears

S **1842** Unions and strikes legal in Massachusetts

T **1846** Irish potato crop failure; settlement of border problems with Canada
1846–1847 Mormon migration

U **1848** Seneca Falls convention

V **1853** National Council of Colored People

W **1869** Granting of vote to women in Wyoming

SAVING THE NATION

The vast political, economic, and social changes in the United States between 1815 and 1850 sharpened differences between the North and South. Despite many efforts to settle these differences by compromise, the results of the election of 1860 split the nation.

The North and South fought a bitter war between 1861 and 1865. The South tried to set up a new nation, while the North struggled to preserve the Union. Both sides fought fiercely and bravely. But the North finally won out.

The Civil War ended slavery and forced both blacks and whites in the South to find new ways of living after 1865. Conflicting views about how the southern states should be treated led to clashes between the President of the United States and Congress.

After the mid-1800s thousands of people moved west. Once again Native Americans lost their homelands.

As you read about the Civil War era, think about people's decisions and their reasons for making them. Understanding decision-making will help you see how people affect their country's history.

Unit 4

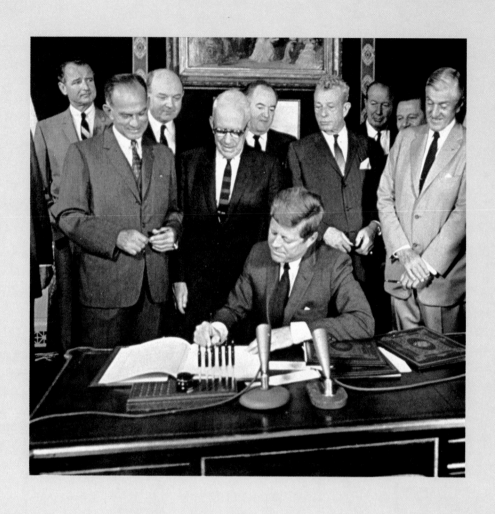

Understanding
Historical
Decisions

Vocabulary

decision	impeach
define	evidence
identify	appeal
option	opinion
evaluate	dissent
consequence	

T HE COUNTRY YOU LIVE IN TODAY has been shaped by the decisions of its people and their leaders. The Patriots made decisions that led to a revolution. The framers of the Constitution made decisions about the government of the new country. Since then, members of federal, state, and local governments have made decisions about laws and how to carry them out. People make important and not-so-important decisions every day. These decisions affect their lives and the lives of those around them. Some of these decisions may also affect the history of the United States.

In this chapter you will study the decision-making process—the steps that must be taken in making a decision. You will also study some decisions that have changed history. The skills exercises will help you understand how decisions are made and how decisions may be analyzed.

1   Understanding the Decision-Making Process

Anytime you make a studied, thoughtful choice, you are using the decision-making process. You are taking a series of steps. Your first step is to define the problem. What is it that you need to decide? Your next step is to identify the options—courses of action—that are open to you. In a third step you make a choice. And your final step is to evaluate the results of your choice. You can remember the steps in this process by thinking of the letters in the word *dice*—D for *define*, I for *identify*, C for *choose*, and E for *evaluate*.

When you think about some of your past decisions or the decisions made in history, it is easy to see the steps that led to a decision. But in everyday decision making these steps are not so clear-cut. One step may seem to flow into another. All steps may seem to take place at the same time. Or they may take place in a different order. Sometimes steps may seem to be repeated.

The word *dice* is handy for helping you remember the steps in the decision-making process. But the decision-making process is not a game of chance. Thoughtful decision makers try to leave as little as possible to chance.

Defining Problems and Identifying Options

In most cases the first step in decision making is to define the problem that requires a decision. For example, you may be faced with many decisions as you prepare for high school. Maybe you will need to decide which school to attend. Or, if that is already decided, you may need to decide which program of study to take or which after-school activities you wish to join. Decision makers often zero in on one decision at a time. In zeroing in they are defining the problem that calls for a decision. Suppose you zero in on the problem of what to study. You have defined the problem and are ready for the next step—identifying the options.

The high school you will attend will tell you about all the programs of study. Your school may offer programs that stress math and science or art and music. It may offer a program for students planning to go to college. It may also offer a program for those planning to get a job right after high school. Once you know all the programs the school offers, you have completed the second step of the decision-making process. You have identified your options.

For Frederick Douglass, the process of defining his problem and identifying his options took several years. Douglass was born a slave in Maryland, probably in 1817. When he was sixteen years old, he realized that he did not want to be a slave any longer. In his

When you find that your decisions have not turned out as you expected, you may need to apply the DICE method to your new problem.

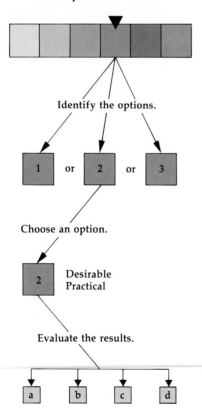

The Decision-Making Process (DICE)

Define the problem.

Identify the options.

1   or   2   or   3

Choose an option.

2   Desirable
    Practical

Evaluate the results.

a   b   c   d

autobiography he described how he came to this realization. One day he became angry when the man he was working for, Edward Covey, knocked him down. Douglass fought back. "This battle with Mr. Covey was the turning point in my career as a slave," he wrote. "I now resolved that, however long I might remain a slave in form, the day had passed forever when I could be a slave in fact." Douglass had not yet decided how he would change his situation. But he had defined his problem: he could not be a slave.

From this point he began to identify and consider his options. He could continue to fight. He could dismiss his feelings and accept being a slave. Or he could find a way to escape. In considering these options, Douglass had to decide which was more important to him: safety or freedom. If he remained a slave and controlled his impulse to fight back, he would be safe. If he risked his life and tried to escape, he had the chance to gain freedom.

Douglass decided to try for freedom. After failing once to escape in 1836, he tried again in 1838, when he was about twenty-one years old. This time he succeeded. In later years he risked his life many times by traveling from state to state, speaking against slavery. Until he bought his freedom years later, Douglass could have been jailed as a runaway slave and returned to his owner.

Marie Zakrzewska (zak·shef′ska) also had a difficult decision to make. She had to decide whether to stay in Europe or to make a new life in a new country. Zakrzewska had been interested in medicine since she was a young girl. Her mother had attended the school for midwives at the Charité Hospital in Berlin. Midwives are people who help women give birth. Marie sometimes helped her mother, who served as a midwife at the hospital.

When Zakrzewska was eighteen, she applied for admission to the school her mother had attended. At first she was turned down because she was too young. But two years later, in 1849, she was accepted. She was such a good student that she was named chief midwife and professor at the hospital school when she was only twenty-two. But people were against her appointment because she was a woman. They forced her to resign.

Zakrzewska decided to go to the United States. She hoped that she would be able to practice medicine there. She and her two sisters arrived in New York in 1853. They earned their living by setting up a small knitting business. In 1854 Zakrzewska was introduced to Dr. Elizabeth Blackwell, who had been the first woman in the United States to earn the degree of Doctor of Medicine (M.D.). Dr. Blackwell helped Zakrzewska learn English and gain admission to the Cleveland Medical College. After Zakrzewska received her medical degree, she worked with Drs. Elizabeth and Emily Blackwell to start a hospital for women and children in New York. In 1862 she set up

In two years the immigrant Zakrzewska learned to speak English and earned a medical degree from Cleveland Medical College.

a similar hospital in Boston. She hired only women doctors at her hospital because almost no other hospital employed women as physicians. Although medicine remained her chief interest, Zakrzewska also spoke out against slavery and for women's rights.

Practicing Your Skills

Write out short answers to these questions.

1. After his escape, Frederick Douglass chose to remain in the United States and speak out against slavery. Name three other options he might have chosen instead.

Critical Thinking

2. **Recognizing Cause and Effect.** Imagine that Zakrzewska was your sister in Berlin. Although you understand her problem, you do not want her to move away. Write a letter trying to convince Zakrzewska to stay in Germany. Give reasons that might make her want to stay.

Choosing an Option and Evaluating the Decision

Once the options have been identified, the decision maker comes to the hardest part of the decision-making process. The decision maker must choose an option and act on the decision.

In similar cases different people choose different options because of differing goals. For example, you may choose the art and music program in high school because you plan to be a music major in college. Your brother or sister may choose a program that teaches skills needed to get a good job after high school.

Besides considering which option is most likely to achieve a desired goal, decision makers must also consider which options are most practical. Sometimes the option that seems most desirable is not practical because it is too dangerous. For example, Frederick Douglass did not attempt to run away until he had a practical plan to do so. Good decisions are both desirable in terms of the decision maker's goals and values and practical in terms of the situation.

Some decisions have consequences that reach beyond the life of one person. Some decisions, especially those made by government leaders, can affect a whole town, state, or nation. Leaders must always think about the effects of their decisions on those they lead.

Joseph, chief of the Nez Percé, was about thirty-seven when he first faced a decision that would affect those he led.

Chief Joseph, a leader of the Nez Percé (nez′ pərs′) of Oregon and Idaho, faced decisions in 1877 that affected the future of his people. The United States wanted all Nez Percé chiefs to sign a treaty that would take away three fourths of the Nez Percé land. The rest of the land would be made into a Nez Percé reservation. All Nez Percé chiefs except Chief Joseph's father signed the treaty.

When his father died in 1873, Chief Joseph carried on his father's work. But in 1877 the government sent soldiers to force Chief Joseph and his people onto the Nez Percé reservation in Idaho. Chief Joseph looked at his options. He could fight the government soldiers, or he could give in. The soldiers promised peace if Chief Joseph saw that his people moved within thirty days.

Chief Joseph's masterful planning brought the Nez Percé to within 40 miles (64 km) of escape across the Canadian border.

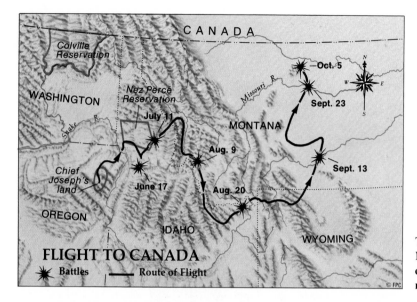

FLIGHT TO CANADA

⁕ Battles ——— Route of Flight

The four-month-long march of the Nez Percé—men, women, and children—covered more than 1,300 miles (2,080 km).

Chief Joseph decided to give up his land. "Better to live at peace than to begin a war and lie dead," he said. But several of his group slipped away in anger and killed eleven white people. The killings forced Chief Joseph to make a new decision. He decided the Nez Percé should try to escape to Canada. Armies pursued them, and they fought many battles. But always Chief Joseph's people kept moving closer to Canada. Finally, in a battle they fought just south of Canada's border, many Nez Percé were killed. The army leader promised that if Chief Joseph surrendered, his people could go in peace to the Nez Percé reservation. Chief Joseph surrendered.

Like Chief Joseph, many decision makers have few, if any, good options open to them. They try to make the least harmful choice. Chief Joseph's words when he gave himself up showed that he had no more good choices left:

> I am tired of fighting. Our chiefs are killed. The old men are all dead. . . . it is cold and we have no blankets. The little children are freezing to death. My people . . . have run away to the hills. . . . I want to have time to look for my children. . . . My heart is sick and sad. I am tired. From where the sun now stands, I will fight no more forever.

The Nez Percé were not allowed to go to the reservation in Idaho as they had been promised. They were sent first to Kansas and then to Oklahoma. Hundreds became sick and died. In 1885 the few Nez Percé who were left—but not Chief Joseph—were allowed to return to the reservation in Idaho. Chief Joseph died on a reservation in Colville, Washington, of what the attending doctor called a "broken heart."

Chief Joseph was about sixty-four when he died in 1904 in Colville, Washington.

Practicing Your Skills

Write out short answers to these questions.

1. After his people had been sent to Oklahoma, Chief Joseph looked back at his decision to surrender. He wrote that if he had known that his people would not be allowed to return to Idaho at once he would never have surrendered. What other choice was open to Chief Joseph? Which option would you have chosen in his place? Why would you have chosen that option?

2. As you have read, Chief Joseph is not the only person in this story who made decisions. The warriors who disobeyed Chief Joseph

also made a decision that cost the lives of eleven white people. How might the story of the Nez Percé have ended if these men had decided to obey their chief? Would the outcome be very different? If so, how? If not, why not?

3. As you read the story below, think about why Elizabeth Van Lew decided to become a Union spy during the war between the North and South. Then answer the questions following the story.

Elizabeth Van Lew was born in 1818 to a rich family in Richmond, Virginia. From her mother she learned strong anti-slavery views. These views were strengthened during the years she attended school in Philadelphia. A few years after her father's death in 1843 the Van Lew family freed the slaves who had been their house servants.

In 1861 the war broke out. The Van Lews' home state of Virginia joined the southern states that had left the Union. But Van Lew remained loyal to the northern states of the Union. She and her mother were allowed to take food, books, and clothing to Union army prisoners at the military prison in Richmond. At the prison Elizabeth was given southern army plans, which she sent secretly to the Union forces. Soon she had agents in many places. One agent even managed to be taken on as a servant in the home of Jefferson Davis, the president of the southern government. Van Lew was able to carry on as a spy because she dressed and acted as though she were out of her mind. Her neighbors called her Crazy Bet.

In 1864, when Union soldiers were stationed close to Richmond, Van Lew maintained five relay stations between Richmond and Union headquarters. Her messengers carried coded messages in the soles of their shoes. Van Lew hid a copy of the secret code in her watch.

In 1865 the southern army retreated from Richmond. Van Lew raised a huge American flag over her house to welcome the Union soldiers to her city. General Ulysses S. Grant, the leader of the Union army, assigned a special guard to protect her from angry neighbors. He thanked her in person for the help she had given his army.

After the war Van Lew worked for the post office department in Washington, D.C. When she was almost seventy, she retired to her home in Richmond. During her last years there, she fought on her own for women's rights by refusing to pay taxes on her land. She argued that women should not pay taxes until they were given the right to vote. It was a case of "taxation without representation," she said. Her neighbors would have nothing to do with this strong-minded woman. She lived as an outcast until her death at the age of eighty-two.

a. What were Van Lew's options when war broke out between the North and the South?

b. What values influenced her choice to support the Union?

Critical Thinking
c. **Drawing Conclusions.** Which values influenced Van Lew's choices later in life?

2 Understanding Decisions of National Importance

Some historians define history as a record of important decisions. The people who made these important decisions could not know all of the consequences that their decisions would have. And historians who look back cannot know all of the reasons that guided people to the decisions they made. But it is useful to think about how history might have been different if key people had made different choices. For example, if the British Parliament had decided in 1773 not to adopt the Tea Act, would there have been a Boston Tea Party? Would there have been an American Revolution? And if the United States ministers in France had decided in 1803 not to buy the Louisiana Territory, would the western border of the United States now be the Mississippi River?

You can see that some decisions made in the past had great influence on the future. Legal decisions, including those of the Supreme Court, are most important. Each Supreme Court decision explains some part of the Constitution. As such, the decision becomes part of the law of the land. As long as the decision stands, it is binding on everyone who lives in the United States. It can be overruled only by a constitutional amendment or by a future Supreme Court decision.

Judging the Importance of Decisions

You can judge the importance of a decision made in the past by thinking about the consequences of that decision. When war broke out between the North and South in 1861, Robert E. Lee had a difficult decision to make. It was a decision that changed his life. And it was a decision that affected the history of his country.

Lee was fifty-four years old and a colonel in the United States cavalry. Most of his life had been spent in the army. He had graduated second in his class from the U.S. Military Academy at West Point. He had worked as an army engineer in St. Louis, New York, San Antonio, and other places. He had served in the Mexican-American War and as officer in charge of West Point.

Lee's father had fought in the American Revolution under George Washington. Washington had always been a hero to Lee. Lee had grown up in Alexandria, Virginia, not far from Washington's hometown. He had married Mary Custis, who was Martha Washington's great-granddaughter.

Lee was stationed in Texas when he first heard that the southern states might leave the Union. He had no sympathy for that idea. He loved the Union. Lee no longer held slaves himself, and he showed no special interest in the southern economic system.

Early in 1861 Lee was recalled to Washington, D.C. In April President Abraham Lincoln offered him the full command of the United States Army. But he decided not to accept the offer. The next day he learned that Virginia, his home state, had voted to leave the Union. Lee felt that he could never fight against Virginia. So he made another decision. He resigned from the United States Army and went to Richmond. When Virginia asked him to command the state's armed forces, he accepted. In June 1862 Lee became commander of the Army of Northern Virginia.

In every battle that Lee fought against Union forces he had fewer soldiers than his enemy had. But his skill as a general was so great that he won many of these battles. In 1865, badly outnumbered and without supplies, he decided that it would be hopeless to fight on. On April 9 he surrendered to Union General Ulysses S. Grant. In

Robert E. Lee had many hard decisions to make, probably none harder than the one to surrender at Appomattox.

the years after the war Lee became a hero in the South and North. He accepted defeat and called on the people of the South to work for peace and national unity. He died in 1870, knowing that he had done his duty to his country and to Virginia.

To judge the importance of Lee's decision, try to think how history might have been different if Lee had chosen to go with the Union. The Union won the war even without Lee on its side, so the Union would probably have won the war in any case. But if Lee had served with the Union instead of against it, perhaps the Union would have won sooner. And perhaps Lee, not Union General Grant, would have later become President. If Lee had accepted Lincoln's offer, the history that you will read in this unit might have been dramatically different.

Practicing Your Skills

As you read the following story, think about why Edmund G. Ross made his decision. Then judge the importance of his decision and write out answers to the questions that follow the story.

After the war between the North and South, many Republicans in Congress believed that the South should be punished for its rebellion. They wanted soldiers to guard the South. And they wanted to treat southerners as though they had lost all rights to govern themselves. Andrew Johnson, who became President after Abraham Lincoln, believed that southerners should be allowed to reenter the Union with little trouble. The Republicans in Congress passed bill after bill meant to punish the South. Even though President Johnson vetoed each bill, most were passed again over his veto.

Congress also passed a law in 1867 that said the President could not remove certain government officers without the Senate's approval. When President Johnson fired his secretary of war, the Republicans in Congress claimed that he had broken this law. They thought they had at last found a way to get rid of this stubborn President. In 1868 the House of Representatives voted to impeach the President, which is the first step in removing a President from office. The final step would require a two-thirds majority vote of guilty in the Senate.

Edmund G. Ross had been a Republican senator from Kansas for only one year. He had worked to put an end to slavery and had been a major in the Union army. He did not like Johnson. The Republicans in Congress were sure they could count on his vote to find Johnson guilty.

As the trial in the Senate went on, Ross saw that it was not a fair trial. Most senators did not study the evidence. They were interested only in whether there would be enough votes

Senators listen as Edmund Ross votes "not guilty" in the Senate trial of President Johnson.

to convict President Johnson. When an early count of votes was taken, Ross refused to make a decision. He wanted to hear the evidence first.

When the trial was over, the senators voted. Ross voted not guilty. The Republicans failed by only one vote—Ross's vote—to get the two-thirds majority needed to convict the President. Johnson remained in office. Ross was called a skunk, a liar, and a traitor. He was not reelected to Congress. He and his family were hated in Kansas. To escape being treated badly, Ross's family moved to New Mexico Territory. Not until 1907, about forty years later, did anyone praise Ross for standing by his beliefs. A Kansas newspaper wrote, "He did his duty knowing that it meant his political death. . . . He acted for his conscience. . . . he acted right."

1. How would history have been different if Ross had voted against Johnson?

Critical Thinking

2. **Drawing Conclusions.** Study Article 2, Section 4, of the Constitution. On what grounds may a President be impeached?

Understanding Legal Decisions

The United States Supreme Court is the highest court in the country. Cases tried in state and federal courts can be appealed to the Supreme Court. Once a case is brought before it, the Supreme Court also has the power to decide whether state or federal laws and orders of the President follow the guidelines of the Constitution.

When Supreme Court justices make decisions, they refer to the Constitution and to earlier court decisions. As the country changes, and as the values of people in the United States change, Supreme Court decisions also change.

During the 1880s and 1890s many southern states passed laws requiring black and white people to use separate washrooms, restaurants, and other public facilities. In 1896 a man named Homer Plessy

379

Because of the *Plessy* v. *Ferguson* decision in 1896, this southern movie house of the 1930s could legally require its black patrons to enter by the rear door.

appealed to the Supreme Court to rule on such a law regarding separate railroad cars in Louisiana. Judge John H. Ferguson of Louisiana had upheld that law. Plessy hoped the Supreme Court would overturn Ferguson's ruling.

Before the Supreme Court, Plessy's lawyers argued that the Louisiana law violated the Thirteenth Amendment, which abolished slavery. They also argued that it violated the Fourteenth Amendment. This amendment says that the states may not "deprive any person of life, liberty, or property, without due process of law; nor deny to any person . . . the equal protection of the laws." Seven justices finally ruled that the Louisiana law allowing separate facilities did not violate the Constitution as long as those facilities were equal. In a written explanation, called an opinion, Justice Henry Brown explained the views of the majority. "That [the Louisiana law] does not conflict with the Thirteenth Amendment . . . is too clear for argument. . . ." He went on to say that the Fourteenth Amendment was not violated either. He explained that laws allowing separate but equal treatment do not stamp blacks "with a badge of inferiority."

One justice, John Marshall Harlan, disagreed with the others. Although the majority rules on the Supreme Court, Justice Harlan wrote out his own opinion, called a dissent. "If a white man and a black man choose to occupy the same public conveyance on a public highway, it is their right to do so, and no government proceeding on grounds of race, can prevent it without infringing the personal liberty of each. . . . Our Constitution is color-blind. . . . I am of the opinion that the statute of Louisiana is . . . hostile to both the spirit and the letter of the Constitution of the United States." Harlan's dissenting view finally won out—but not until 1954.

Practicing Your Skills

1. Read Amendments 13 and 14 on page 750. Then write a short paragraph agreeing or disagreeing with Justice Harlan's view that a separate but equal policy for blacks and whites is hostile to the Constitution. Explain your reasons for agreeing or disagreeing.
2. As you read the following about the 1954 Supreme Court decision in *Brown* v. *the Board of Education,* think about why the Court chose to find the separate but equal policy unconstitutional. Then write out answers to the questions that follow.

   Many states used the Supreme Court ruling on *Plessy* v. *Ferguson* to justify separate schools for blacks and whites. Experience over the years, however, showed that separate schools were hardly ever equal. White pupils often received a better education.

   In 1952 a group of four cases concerning separate schools came before the Supreme Court. This group of cases was named for the first case filed, *Brown* v. *the Board of Education of Topeka.* The Court did not rule on these cases until 1954. When it did, the decision of the Court was unanimous.

   Chief Justice Earl Warren wrote that it was "obvious" that separate schools kept black children from getting an equal education and caused "feelings of inferiority" in black children. Therefore separate schools denied the equal rights promised in the Constitution. "In the field of public education the doctrine of 'separate but equal' has no place. Separate educational facilities are inherently unequal."

   a. The justices who ruled on *Plessy* v. *Ferguson* in 1896 and the justices who ruled on *Brown* v. *the Board of Education* in 1954 relied on the Constitution for their decisions. In what ways are the two decisions different? What might have led the justices in 1954 to decide "separate but equal" was unconstitutional?

Critical Thinking

   b. **Predicting Consequences.** Find a story in a newspaper that reports in some detail on a legal decision. The story may be about either a court case or a new law. Write a paragraph explaining in your own words what questions the decision makers had to answer before they reached their decision. Also try to identify what consequences the decision in the story will have.

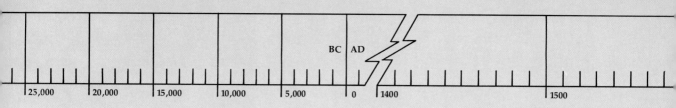

UNCLE TOM'S CABIN;

OR,

LIFE AMONG THE LOWLY.

BY

HARRIET BEECHER STOWE.

VOL. I.

The Gathering Storm

Chapter 20

Vocabulary

economy
controversial
boundary
parallel
cede
cession
acquisition
nullify
secession
preservation
popular sovereignty

THE STORMY EVENTS between the late 1840s and 1861 led to war between the North and the South.

Some historians believe that the war came mainly because of the different interests of the South and North. The economy of the South was based almost entirely on products from the soil, which were sold outside the country. The economy of the North was more broadly based on farms, factories, trade, and banking. Other historians argue that fighting broke out mainly because the nation lacked able leaders who could work out useful compromises. Such leaders, they say, would have softened the differences between the North and South. These leaders would have kept the country together by calling to mind the experiences that the two regions shared in creating and building a nation. Still other historians hold that slavery so sharply divided the North and South that the gulf between them could never be bridged.

Prereading

1. How did the extension of slavery become the central issue that led to the crisis of the Civil War?
2. What steps did leaders in the nation take to settle the extension of slavery question between 1850 and 1854?
3. Why did the Dred Scott decision and John Brown's raid turn the United States into a house divided?
4. How did the election of 1860 lead the southern states along the road to secession?

1 Background of the Crisis

President Andrew Jackson left office in 1837. In the following years the politics, economy, and borders of the United States were wide

383

Election of 1836

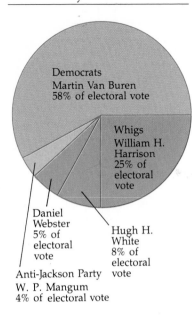

Democrats
Martin Van Buren
58% of electoral vote

Whigs
William H.
Harrison
25% of
electoral
vote

Daniel
Webster
5% of
electoral
vote

Anti-Jackson Party
W. P. Mangum
4% of electoral vote

Hugh H.
White
8% of
electoral
vote

Election of 1840

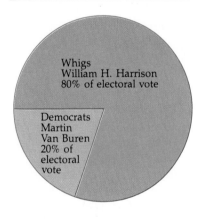

Whigs
William H. Harrison
80% of electoral vote

Democrats
Martin
Van Buren
20% of
electoral
vote

Election of 1844

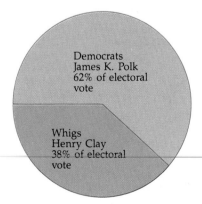

Democrats
James K. Polk
62% of electoral
vote

Whigs
Henry Clay
38% of electoral
vote

open to change. The United States was acquiring vast lands in the South and West. The central issue of the 1850s was whether or not slavery would be allowed in the new lands.

Political parties were unable to produce strong Presidential candidates around whom the whole nation could rally. Without able political leaders to help resolve differences of opinion, the conflicts over slavery became more and more bitter.

Politics After Jackson

Martin Van Buren, a Democrat from New York, became President after Jackson in 1837. Van Buren's term was marked by hard economic times. Businesses failed, people were out of work, and farmers who were in debt lost their lands. Voters in the election of 1840, therefore, were looking for new direction. Van Buren lost that race to William Henry Harrison, a member of the Whig party. Voters thought of Harrison as another Jackson—a man of the people. They saw him as a westerner born in a log cabin, the hero of the Battle of the Thames in the War of 1812, and the territorial governor of Indiana. Harrison's skills as President, however, were never tested. He died a few weeks after taking office.

Harrison was followed by Vice-President John Tyler, also a Whig. Tyler could do little as President because he could not win the backing of his party's most powerful congressional leaders—Daniel Webster of Massachusetts and Henry Clay of Kentucky.

Because neither the Whigs nor the Democrats could settle the country's differences, many voters turned to third parties. Most third parties were based on a single issue and lasted for only a few years. For example, the Liberty party in New York stood solely for freeing the slaves. The American party formed in the 1850s sought to stop immigration. Other third parties favored free land in the West or reform. Such parties, however, never attracted enough votes to win the Presidency. The issues they stood for were too controversial.

National Expansion Under President Polk

In the election of 1844 Whig leader Henry Clay ran against James Polk, a Democrat from Tennessee. Clay had been a major political leader for more than thirty years. Always well dressed, Clay was also a charming speaker. Polk had served in the House of Representatives for fourteen years—four of those as Speaker.

The Democratic platform in 1844 called for settling Oregon's border with British Canada at the 54°40′ line and bringing Texas into the Union. The Democrats promised the westward-looking American ". . . Oregon for his summer shade, and the region of Texas as his winter pasture. . . . he shall have the use of two oceans—the mighty Pacific and the [stormy] Atlantic shall be his. . . ." Polk ran on

Pyramid Lake in Oregon Territory was on part of the land granted to the United States by Britain in the 1846 boundary settlement.

that platform of national expansion. He won the election by a narrow margin.

Before Polk's election the United States had been willing to settle the Oregon boundary at the 49° parallel. But when the British representative refused this offer without even asking his government, President Polk pushed for nothing less than the 54°40′ parallel. If necessary, the United States would fight, he said.

The British, however, did not want to fight the United States. They offered to settle the boundary peacefully, but at the 49° parallel. A treaty setting that boundary was finally approved by the Senate on June 15, 1846. Never again did Britain and the United States have a major quarrel.

Bringing Texas into the Union was not as peaceful as settling Oregon's border. During Polk's campaign, debate had continued to rage over statehood for Texas. Northerners feared that admitting Texas would give the South the voting edge in Congress. Northern antislavery groups also were against statehood for Texas because many Texans were slave owners. Before Polk took office in 1845, however, Congress overrode northern opposition and paved the way for Texas to become the twenty-eighth state in the Union.

President Polk's diary brought to light his plan to obtain New Mexico and California as well as Texas during his term of office. Except for Texas, all of this land still belonged to Mexico. Within three years Polk had achieved his goal—and more. But the United States had to wage war with Mexico to win these lands.

The Mexican-American War

Mexico had never fully accepted the independence of Texas after 1836. Therefore it could not agree that Texas had the right to join the United States. And, aside from this issue, Mexico believed that the Nueces (nōō·ā′səs) River was the western boundary of Texas.

The United States, however, claimed that the western boundary of its new state was the Rio Grande, many miles southwest of the Nueces River. President Polk sent John Slidell to Mexico late in 1845. He told Slidell to settle the boundary of Texas at the Rio Grande and also to buy the land that is now New Mexico and California. The Mexican government refused to talk with Slidell.

Polk had already sent federal troops under General Zachary Taylor to guard the territory between the Nueces River and the Rio Grande as United States land. Mexico, in turn, had sent General Mariano Arista (mä′rē·ä′nō ə·rēs′tə) with soldiers to guard the same land for Mexico. When scouts from both armies fought with loss of life in May 1846, the United States declared war against Mexico immediately.

General Taylor moved one United States army into Mexico from the north. He crossed the Rio Grande and defeated the Mexican army at Monterrey in 1846. General Taylor followed up this victory with a series of winning battles that gave the United States control of northern Mexico.

Meanwhile Colonel Stephen Kearny captured Santa Fe, New Mexico, in 1846 without firing a shot. With about 100 soldiers

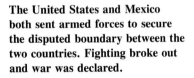

The United States and Mexico both sent armed forces to secure the disputed boundary between the two countries. Fighting broke out and war was declared.

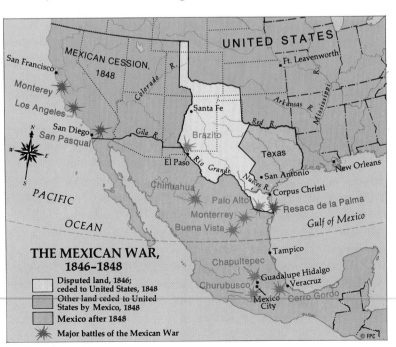

THE MEXICAN WAR, 1846–1848

☐ Disputed land, 1846; ceded to United States, 1848
☐ Other land ceded to United States by Mexico, 1848
☐ Mexico after 1848
✴ Major battles of the Mexican War

Kearny then marched overland to California. There he found that the United States Army and Navy had already begun to take over California.

In 1847 another force, led by General Winfield Scott, fought along the eastern coastline of Mexico. Scott first captured Veracruz on the coast. Then he marched inland and took Mexico City.

With their capital taken, Mexicans were willing to come to peace terms in 1848. Mexico ceded to the United States more than 500,000 square miles (1,300,000 sq km) of land. The Mexican Cession included land that is now the states of California, Nevada, and Utah. Mexico also gave up what is now most of New Mexico and Arizona and parts of Wyoming and Colorado. In return the United States paid Mexico $15 million, a tiny sum compared with the value of the territory. The Mexican Cession was the third largest land acquisition in United States history.

2 Efforts to Compromise

Gaining the lands of the Mexican Cession raised again the issue of slavery. Should the new western lands fall under the terms of the 1820 Missouri Compromise, which allowed slavery only south of the 36°30' line? Or should Congress find some new solution? Between 1846 and 1850 Congress considered several solutions but accepted none. Its leaders seemed powerless to keep the North and South from moving farther apart on the slavery issue.

Clay's Compromise of 1850
To break the deadlock, Senator Henry Clay of Kentucky, by then seventy-three years old, stepped in with a compromise. He suggested that the many bills then being debated in Congress be pulled together into a single package. Clay's compromise included the following points:
1. California would enter the Union as a free state.
2. New Mexico and Utah would be made territories. Any decision about slavery should be left to the people living there.
3. Trading of slaves in Washington, D.C., would end.
4. Slaveholding in Washington, D.C., could be brought to an end only with the approval of people living in Maryland. If Congress chose to end slavery, the government would have to pay slave owners in full for the loss of their slave property.
5. The return of runaway slaves would be enforced by federal law.
6. Congress would declare that it had no power to act against the trading of slaves among the states in the South.

Though Clay tried to please everyone, his plan was not to anyone's full liking. The debates in Congress were long and loud. The

Section 1 Review

1. Why did many voters turn to third parties in the 1840s?
2. Why did northerners oppose statehood for Texas?
3. Why did Mexico oppose Union statehood for Texas?
4. Over what issue did the Mexican-American War begin?
5. What peace terms ended the Mexican-American War?

Critical Thinking
6. **Recognizing Cause and Effect.** Was the withdrawal of Texas from Mexico a cause of the Mexican-American War? Explain your answer.

LOOKING AHEAD: What steps did leaders in the nation take to settle the extension of slavery question between 1850 and 1854?

Though they represented widely different views, Daniel Webster (left), Henry Clay (center), and John C. Calhoun together helped write the laws that guided the nation between 1815 and 1850.

South's long-time leader, Senator John C. Calhoun of South Carolina, now too weak to deliver his own speech, argued that antislavery groups were the major problem. The North, he said, was gaining too much power. He believed that the South should be given the right to nullify federal laws to protect itself from acts favoring the North. Calhoun was proposing a drastic change in the Constitution which forbids any state the right to nullify federal laws. Senator Jefferson Davis of Mississippi strongly favored another course only hinted at by Calhoun. Davis called for secession—for the South to cut its ties with the Union.

Senator Daniel Webster of Massachusetts spoke in favor of the compromise. He believed the Union was in danger. He began his speech with the words: "I wish to speak to-day, not as a Massachusetts man, nor as a northern man, but as an American. . . . I speak to-day for the preservation of the Union. . . ." He warned the southern states that they could not cut their ties with the Union through secession without bringing on a war.

Webster was strongly criticized in his own New England, especially by antislavery groups. They believed Clay's compromise favored the South. They thought it destroyed all hope of ending slavery. James Greenleaf Whittier, a New England poet who hated slavery, called Webster a "fallen angel."

A rising young senator from Illinois, Stephen A. Douglas, spoke out boldly for the compromise. He took over for Clay when the older man, worn out from speaking seventy times in defense of his ideas, left Congress for a rest. Douglas used his political skills to bring the lawmakers together.

One by one the points in Clay's plan were signed into law, and the tension eased. Webster, now treated as an outcast by Massachusetts voters, thought the crisis of secession had passed. Senator Douglas, urged people to "stop the debate, and drop the subject. If we do this, the Compromise will be recognized as a final settlement." Some Georgians and Mississippians thought the settlement was good. The Alabama *Journal* also supported the compromise. Secession, the *Journal* said, would not help the South, but instead would bring hardship. Even northern congressmen who favored the compromise were generally reelected to office.

The Compromise of 1850 marked the end of the careers of three giants who held the political stage between 1815 and 1850. They were Henry Clay, Daniel Webster, and John C. Calhoun. By 1853 all three had died. With their deaths an era came to an end.

The Public on Fire

Despite promising signs that the Compromise of 1850 would be accepted, differences over slavery did not end. In 1851 an escaped slave named Shadrach (sha'drak') was arrested in Boston. He was rescued by a group of fellow blacks. "The rescue of Shadrach," wrote antislavery supporter Wendell Phillips, "has set the whole public afire." A Maryland slave owner, reclaiming two of his runaway slaves in Pennsylvania, was killed by a mob. In New York, a well-known black named James Hamlet was captured. A Maryland woman claimed that he was a runaway. Hamlet was taken directly to Maryland without a court hearing and without being allowed to see his wife and children. These acts touched off public outcries.

In 1852 the public was also stirred by a book called *Uncle Tom's Cabin* by Harriet Beecher Stowe. It soon became the basis of a popular play. *Uncle Tom's Cabin* presented a vivid picture of cruel slave owners and despairing blacks. It also described kind southerners and heroic blacks. About 100,000 copies of the book were sold within a month and 300,000 within a year. The book was banned in the South, but some southerners read it. In the North and outside the United States *Uncle Tom's Cabin* fed the fires of antislavery.

The Kansas-Nebraska Act of 1854

A new political crisis arose when Senator Douglas introduced a bill in Congress to form the territory of Nebraska into a state. It once again raised the issue of slave state or free state.

Under the Compromise of 1820 Nebraska would enter the Union as a free state. Slavery was not to be permitted in states north of the 36°30′ line. But southerners feared that a new state, free of slavery, would tip the scales of power in Congress to the North.

Far more issues were at stake at that time than the question of slave state or free state. For example, Douglas favored building a railroad to link the Middle West to the lands along the Pacific Ocean. This idea raised several familiar questions. What route should the railroad follow? Would it be built on federal land with federal money? Who stood to gain from it, the North or the South?

Another issue had to do with Missouri. If Nebraska entered the Union as a free state, the slave state of Missouri would then have free states on three sides. This prospect worried Missouri slave owners. One newspaper warned. "There will always be men and means to assist in the escape of our slaves. . . ."

There was still another side to the Nebraska question. Senator Douglas wanted to become the Democratic Presidential candidate. He needed help from the South where the Democratic party was strong. To win southern favor, Douglas introduced the Kansas-Nebraska Bill. The bill set aside the Missouri Compromise of 1820. It called for popular sovereignty—the idea that settlers in a territory should be allowed to decide for themselves whether or not they wanted slavery. It also called for dividing the Nebraska Territory into two parts: Nebraska to the west of Iowa and Kansas to the west of Missouri.

Douglas knew the Kansas-Nebraska Bill would raise a storm. Antislavery people and other northerners would have nothing to do with it. Southerners generally favored Douglas's bill because they expected to make Kansas a slave state.

Congress left the question of slavery or no slavery to the voters in the new states of Kansas and Nebraska in 1854. By so doing, it hoped to avoid further conflict.

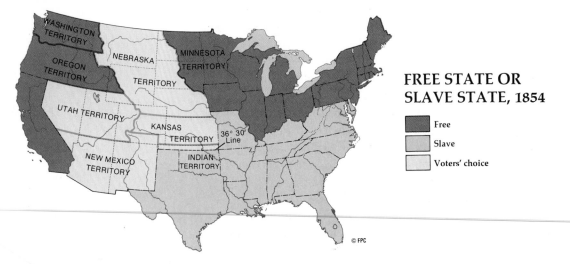

FREE STATE OR SLAVE STATE, 1854

- Free
- Slave
- Voters' choice

Missourians crossing the border into Kansas to vote for slavery came prepared to fight.

In 1854, the Kansas-Nebraska Act passed in Congress by a narrow margin. But the storm over slavery never again died down.

Bleeding Kansas

After the Kansas-Nebraska Act was passed, Kansas became a battleground between free state and slave state forces. Power struggles, fighting, and killing became commonplace as southerners and northerners both rushed to settle Kansas. Soon the territory was called "Bleeding Kansas."

In one of the first elections 1,700 Missourians crossed into Kansas on horseback and by wagon and river ferry just to vote for slavery. In May 1856 some 800 raiders, mostly from Missouri, destroyed the town of Lawrence, Kansas, where antislavery groups had settled. They smashed the newspaper presses, burned houses, and destroyed the Free State Hotel. John Brown, an antislavery fanatic, decided to strike back. Together with his sons and a few friends he murdered five unarmed proslavery settlers at Pottawatomie Creek. Proslavery Kansans then attacked Brown, killed one of his sons, and burned the settlement of Ossawatomie.

Violence also crept into Senate debates. Senator Charles Sumner of Massachusetts spoke against the proslavery views of Andrew Pickens Butler of South Carolina. A few days later Butler's cousin, a representative from South Carolina, walked into the Senate chamber. He found Sumner seated at his desk writing. He then clubbed Sumner with a heavy cane until Sumner fell to the floor unconscious. The issue of Kansas and slavery was slowly turning into a national nightmare.

Some onlookers are smiling in this cartoon that denounces the attack on Sumner in the Senate.

Section 2 Review

1. What were the points that Congress enacted as the Compromise of 1850?
2. Who proposed organizing the territory of Nebraska as a state?
3. What were the three main points of the Kansas-Nebraska Act? What is popular sovereignty?
4. What were the three major ideas on which the Republican party was based?

Critical Thinking

5. **Determining Relevance.** How was *Uncle Tom's Cabin* related to the antislavery movement in the North?

LOOKING AHEAD: Why did the Dred Scott decision and John Brown's raid turn the United States into a house divided?

Formation of the Republican Party

Out of this controversy a new political party was born, the Republican party. The Whig party was slowly losing its strength. After Polk, Zachary Taylor—a Whig and hero of the Mexican War—had become President in 1849. His Vice-President, Millard Fillmore, became President when Taylor died in 1850. The real leaders of the Whig party, however, were Clay and Webster. The Whig party seemed to gain its strength from its leaders rather than from the stands that it took. When the leaders died, the party faded. The party's last Presidential candidate, Winfield Scott, was defeated by Democrat Franklin Pierce in the election of 1852. As Whigs lost power, members of the party looked for another political home.

Some Whigs found that home in the Republican party, which was first formed in 1854 and had roots in the American party. The Republican party was founded on three major ideas: free land in the West; laws favoring manufacturing, banking, and business; and no new slave states. The party ran local and state candidates in 1854. In 1856 it supported John C. Frémont for President.

Frémont had explored the West and had fought against Mexicans in California. He was narrowly defeated in 1856 by James Buchanan, a Pennsylvania Democrat. A frightened South had warned that it would leave the Union if Frémont won. "The election of Frémont would be the end of the Union, and ought to be," wrote one southerner. Frémont and the Republicans gained no backing in the South. In 1856, for the first time in United States history one of two main political parties lacked support from all parts of the country.

3   A House Divided

President Buchanan took office in 1857. That same year saw the end to an economic boom. Prices of most farm products fell. People stopped buying many manufactured goods, so factories lay idle. These economic problems made the slavery questions even harder to solve. A new compromise seemed out of reach.

Dred Scott Decision

A Supreme Court case in 1857 reopened all the old slavery questions. The case was brought by Dred Scott, the slave of an army officer who lived in the slave state of Missouri. In 1834 Scott moved with his owner to army posts in the free state of Illinois and later to the free Wisconsin Territory. Then he returned to Missouri with his owner. There antislavery supporters encouraged Scott to sue his owner for his freedom in 1846. Scott and his backers argued that he had become free when he had lived where slavery was not allowed. His case reached the Supreme Court.

In 1857 the Court held that Scott was not a citizen. As a slave and noncitizen, he had no right to bring a case in court. The Court also stated that the Constitution protected property. Because slaves were "property," they could be taken by their owners into any part of the nation and remain their property. The Dred Scott decision sent a shock wave throughout the North, even among people who were not active abolitionists.

A Divided Party

The slavery issue in Kansas surfaced again in 1857. This issue, which had already split the North and the South, now split the Democratic party. President Buchanan asked Congress to accept a state constitution from Kansas Territory that allowed slavery. But antislavery settlers had boycotted the convention that had formed the document.

Senator Douglas—Buchanan's major rival in the Democratic party—was against the Kansas constitution. Douglas said that it did not stand for the views of all of Kansas. The Democrats split into two groups on the question—one backing Buchanan, the other, Douglas. The Kansas constitution was voted down in Congress. Only in 1861, after fighting had broken out between the North and South, did Kansas become a state—a free state.

The Lincoln-Douglas Debates

In 1858 Douglas ran for reelection as a senator from Illinois. A rising new Republican, Abraham Lincoln, ran against him.

Lincoln was born in a Kentucky cabin. As a boy, he moved to Indiana and then to Illinois with his family. He had little formal

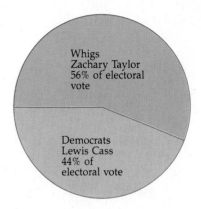

Election of 1848

Whigs
Zachary Taylor
56% of electoral
vote

Democrats
Lewis Cass
44% of
electoral vote

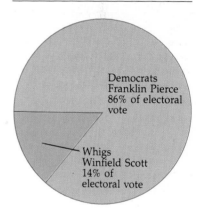

Election of 1852

Democrats
Franklin Pierce
86% of electoral
vote

Whigs
Winfield Scott
14% of
electoral vote

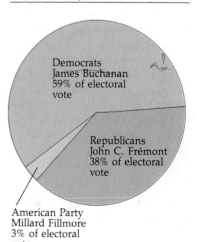

Election of 1856

Democrats
James Buchanan
59% of electoral
vote

Republicans
John C. Frémont
38% of electoral
vote

American Party
Millard Fillmore
3% of electoral
vote

Lincoln and Douglas appeared in Alton, Illinois, on the Mississippi River, in the last of their seven debates.

schooling, having taught himself. He worked on a farm, in a store, and at other general tasks. He learned law by reading on the subject with the help of a lawyer. He slowly but surely gathered around him a circle of political friends. He charmed them with his funny stories. But he often worried that his life was a failure.

Lincoln described himself as a Clay Whig. By that he meant he favored a high tariff and federal money to build roads, canals, and railroads. Lincoln believed that the spread of slavery must be stopped. Otherwise it could become lawful in all the states.

The highlight of the Senate campaign was seven debates between Lincoln and Douglas. Often as many as 15,000 eager listeners would stand long hours under a hot prairie sun to hear the two men debate. Each candidate was popular. Douglas was thick-set, short, spirited. Some said he had a fighting bulldog look. Lincoln, on the other hand, was tall—six feet four inches (193 cm). He usually wore a stovepipe hat, which also served as a place to store his important papers. Lincoln stayed in one place as he spoke. At times he stood on tiptoe, jabbing the air with his arm to make a point. Or he would step back and tell a funny story. Unlike Lincoln, Douglas was always moving, walking from one side of the platform to the other as he spoke.

They talked on every issue, including slavery. Lincoln did not speak for a complete end to slavery, but he called slavery morally wrong. He believed that it should not be allowed in the new territories. He warned the crowds that "a house divided against itself cannot stand." Douglas believed in popular sovereignty. He argued that people living in the new territories should decide for themselves whether or not they wanted slavery.

Douglas defeated Lincoln in the Senate race. But the debates made Lincoln a national figure whom the people did not forget.

John Brown's Raid

Some antislavery people grew tired of waiting for an answer to the slavery problem. One of these was John Brown, the same man who murdered the proslavery settlers in Kansas. In October 1859 he decided to act. Brown thought that he and his sons and a few friends could take over a government store of arms at Harpers Ferry, Virginia. They planned to hand over the weapons to slaves, who could then revolt. With this plan Brown hoped to end slavery in the South.

State militia, along with federal soldiers led by Colonel Robert E. Lee, broke through Brown's defenses and took him prisoner. Brown was tried in a Charlestown court for treason against the state of Virginia. He was convicted and hanged. After Brown's raid many outraged southerners felt certain that antislavery groups would stop at nothing to free southern slaves.

4 The Road to Secession

The idea of secession—that one state or several could leave the Union peacefully—was not new. Some New Englanders had favored secession during the War of 1812. South Carolina had taken a like stand over the tariff during the Presidency of Andrew Jackson. During the election of 1856, secession was widely discussed throughout the South. After the 1860 election, however, secession became a reality.

The Election of 1860

The Democrats were badly divided when they met in Charleston, South Carolina, in April 1860 to choose a candidate for President. A few of their number, often called "the fire-eaters," favored secession. They wanted slavery in every territory in the Union. Northern Democrats, and many southern ones as well, could not agree that slavery should be so widespread.

Senator Douglas received more votes than anyone else. But he needed two thirds of the votes to be named the candidate. He fell short of two thirds, and the convention was stalled.

The delegates then agreed to meet in Baltimore in June. The fire-eaters were kept out of this second gathering. Without them Senator Douglas was chosen to run for the Democrats. The fire-eaters then chose their own candidate, John C. Breckinridge of Kentucky. Breckinridge favored secession.

Section 3 Review

1. Why did Dred Scott sue his owner for his freedom?
2. What did the Supreme Court rule in the Dred Scott case?
3. How did a disagreement over the Kansas constitution split the Democratic party?
4. How did Lincoln's stand and Douglas's stand on slavery in the territories differ?
5. What was John Brown's plan to bring an end to slavery in the South?

Critical Thinking

6. **Identifying Assumptions.** What led Abraham Lincoln to oppose the spread of slavery into new territories?

LOOKING AHEAD: How did the election of 1860 lead southern states along the road to secession?

— 1812 — NE favored secession during war

— 1860 — Democrats were badly divided

— Douglas recieved more votes — but convention was stalled

— Breckinridge

(Handwritten annotations in margins:)

Lincoln elected

*— Confederate States of America
Feb 4
made own
Constitution*

— Davis elected

*— March 1861
Lincoln
took office*

Election of 1860

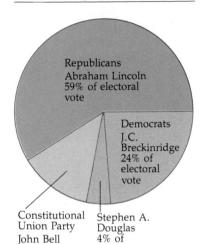

Republicans
Abraham Lincoln
59% of electoral
vote

Democrats
J.C.
Breckinridge
24% of
electoral
vote

Constitutional
Union Party
John Bell
13% of
electoral vote

Stephen A.
Douglas
4% of
electoral vote

Southerners who were unhappy with both Douglas and Breckinridge formed the Constitutional Union party. They chose John Bell of Tennessee as their candidate. Like Douglas, Bell stood for the Union.

The Republicans met in Chicago to name their candidate. Many names were suggested, but Abraham Lincoln was chosen.

With the Democrats so divided, Lincoln won the election. When his victory became known, many people in the lower southern states took steps to secede. Alexander Stephens of Georgia begged other southerners to wait and see what Lincoln would do. But more than two months before Lincoln was to take office, on December 20, 1860, South Carolina voted for secession. By February 1, 1861 Mississippi, Florida, Alabama, Georgia, Louisiana, and Texas had followed South Carolina's lead. Eight slave states in the upper South, however, remained uncommitted.

A Southern Government

On February 4, 1861, the states that seceded sent delegates to Montgomery, Alabama. There the delegates formed a government called the Confederate States of America. The Confederate states believed they were strong enough to win in a showdown with the federal government.

The Confederate States of America adopted a constitution like that of the Union, but with a few important changes. For example, the Confederate constitution named slaves as property to be protected. It barred the high tariffs so harmful to the South. It forbade the Confederate government to pay for building roads, canals, and railroads. It also gave greater power to the separate states than to the central government of the Confederacy.

Jefferson Davis of Mississippi was elected President and Alexander Stephens of Georgia was elected Vice-President of the Confederacy. Davis had attended the military school at West Point and served with courage and honor in the Mexican War. Davis felt his duty as Confederate president was to serve the South, but he hoped to avoid war. He told the United States Senate, "I hope . . . for peaceful relations with you, though we must part."

President Buchanan failed to settle the differences between the Confederate states and the federal government. When Lincoln took office in March 1861, he faced a divided nation. In his inaugural speech Lincoln, like President Jackson before him, rejected the right of any state to leave the Union. In his view the Constitution of the United States and the laws of its Congress remained the law of the whole nation—North and South. At the end of his speech he directly addressed the seven states that had seceded. "In *your* hands, my dissatisfied fellow-countrymen, and not in *mine*, is the momentous

OUR NATIONAL BIRD AS IT APPEARED WHEN
HANDED TO JAMES BUCHANAN . MARCH . 4 . 1857

THE IDENTICAL BIRD AS IT APPEARED . A . D . 1861 .

The 1861 bird stands on a peg leg labeled "Secession" and wears a shoe called "Anarchy."

issue of civil war. . . . We are not enemies, but friends. . . . Though passion may have strained, it must not break, our bonds of affection."

Outbreak of Fighting

Lincoln's call for peace would not halt military action in the South. Confederate troops had taken over most federal forts in the southern states. Their next target was Fort Sumter, a federal army base on an island in Charleston harbor. The soldiers defending Fort Sumter needed supplies. President Lincoln, eager to keep Fort Sumter, decided to send in food but not arms.

When the supply ships drew near Charleston, they were not allowed to enter the harbor. Confederate General Pierre Beauregard, under orders from Jefferson Davis, called for the surrender of Fort Sumter. The federal commander, Major Robert Anderson, refused. He said he could not surrender with honor until his supplies were gone. Unwilling to accept this answer, the Confederates opened fire on the fort shortly before dawn on April 12, 1861. Firing on the flag of the United States was an act of open rebellion.

The formation of the Confederacy and the firing on Fort Sumter turned the debate between the North and South into a civil war. The hardship and fighting lasted four years. A higher percentage of Americans lost their lives in the Civil War than in any other war in United States history. After the fighting began, one question overshadowed all others: Would the Union be saved?

Section 4 Review

1. Who became the candidate of the northern Democrats in the Presidential election of 1860?
2. Whom did the Democrats in the South—the fire-eaters—choose as their Presidential candidate?
3. Why did a third group form the Constitutional Union party? Who became its candidate?
4. What state was the first to vote for secession?
5. What was Lincoln's view of secession?
6. What Confederate action opened the Civil War?

Critical Thinking

7. **Making Comparisons.** In what three ways did the Confederate constitution differ from the constitution of the United States?

People   And Principles

The Grimké sisters spoke out for human rights in the midst of conflict in the nation.

The South Carolina family of John and Mary Grimké included fourteen children. The Grimké sisters, Sarah and Angelina, were born in Charleston—Sarah in 1792 and Angelina in 1805.

Southern Roots

In 1819 Sarah visited Philadelphia, where she was attracted to the Quaker faith. Angelina soon followed Sarah's lead. In time, however, both sisters found the Quaker faith too exacting.

The Grimké sisters decided to move to Philadelphia. In later years they lived in New Jersey. But they never forgot their beginnings in South Carolina, a slave state.

A Stand Against Slavery

Both sisters disliked slavery. Angelina wrote a letter praising the stand of abolitionist William Lloyd Garrison. To her surprise, her letter was printed in Garrison's *Liberator*. Angelina longed to do more for the antislavery movement. In 1836 she wrote her "Appeal to the Christian Women of the South." In this pamphlet she stated that slavery went against the Declaration of Independence. She called on southern women to speak out against slavery. "The women of the South can overthrow this horrible system of oppression and cruelty . . . and wrong."

Many southern women shared her views, but they did not speak about them openly. One wrote in her diary that she thought of moving to a free state. "There we

Sarah (left) and Angelina Grimké were both against slavery. So was Garrison (below), who suffered for his views in Boston in 1835.

hope to be relieved of many unpleasant things, but particularly of the evils of slavery, for slaves are a continual source of trouble." Another wrote, "I must say that my mother never did like slavery and did not hesitate to say so."

Angelina's pamphlet won support among antislavery groups in the North. But it was publicly burned in South Carolina.

Angelina was invited to speak out in public in the North. She drew huge crowds, especially in Massachusetts. But a local minister was alarmed, saying he "would as soon be caught robbing a hen roost as encouraging a woman to lecture." A Massachusetts ministers' group came out against women acting as church leaders and reformers.

Women's Rights

Sarah Grimké took the lead in speaking out for women's rights. She wrote *Letters on the Equality of the Sexes and the Condition of Woman.* In this book she stated that "the page of history teems with woman's wrongs."

Angelina joined her sister in speaking out for women's rights. She compared them with the rights of slaves. "I recognize no rights but human rights. I know nothing of men's rights and women's rights. . . . the rights of the slave and woman blend."

Crisis at the Doors

In 1838 Angelina married Theodore Weld, an abolitionist. For a time she made few public speeches. But when the great questions of the 1850s arose—the Kansas-Nebraska Act, the Dred Scott decision, and the election of Lincoln—Angelina began to speak publicly again against slavery.

In 1854 she wrote her friend Gerrit Smith, who was serving in Congress: "Go on, my brother, and a new era must dawn upon the history of Slavery in this country. . . . Slaveholders know now *where* you stand. . . ." When she feared that Smith might leave his government post, she begged him to stay: "I have long hoped that the South could be reached by moral power, and your presence in the Congress brightened my hopes—but I begin to despair. . . . If you do indeed resign—then I should believe that the great crisis is near[,] even at the doors."

A War of Principles

During the war Angelina and Sarah gathered petitions asking that Congress pass a law to end slavery. When black troops began to fight for the Union, Angelina wrote, "Instead of *our* fighting for the Negro, now he is fighting for us, and will yet save us and himself too."

When northern soldiers moved into South Carolina, Angelina thought of returning to her home state, which she had not seen for over thirty years. Instead she returned to the public platform, comparing freedom for blacks with freedom for all. "This war is not, as the South falsely pretends, a war of races, nor of sections, nor of political parties, but a war of PRINCIPLES; a war upon the working classes, whether white or black. . . . and now *all* who contend for the rights of labor, for free speech, free schools, free suffrage, and a free government . . . are driven to do battle in defense of these or fall with them. . . ."

Sarah Grimké died in 1873 at the age of eighty-one. Angelina died in 1879. Though the Grimkés kept ties with their family in the South they held fast to their ideals throughout their lives.

Angelina favored the election of Lincoln (above) in 1860. She also admired the blacks who fought for the Union.

Chapter 20 Review

Chapter Summary

James K. Polk won the presidential election of 1844. Under Polk, the country saw a period of rapid territorial growth.

As the United States gained more land, the question of slavery in the new territories arose. The Compromise of 1850 and the Kansas-Nebraska Act were only temporarily successful in reducing tensions over the slavery debate.

The slavery issue continued to divide the nation as fighting broke out in Kansas. The Supreme Court decision in the *Dred Scott* case angered people in the North, while John Brown's raid angered people in the South.

Abraham Lincoln, facing a divided Democratic party, won the 1860 presidential election. But before his inauguration, seven southern states seceded from the Union. Those states formed a new government called the Confederate States of America.

Reviewing Vocabulary

Match each of the following words with its correct definition.

economy   acquisition   parallel
controversial   nullify   cede
boundaries   secession   cession
preservation   popular sovereignty

1. The conflict over setting _____ in the northwest was the last major dispute between Great Britain and the United States.
2. Calhoun claimed the South should be given the right to _____ federal laws to protect itself from the North.
3. The South's _____ was based on goods grown on large plantations.
4. The Mexican-American War resulted in the largest land _____ in United States history.
5. A(n) _____ is an imaginary east-west line on a globe.
6. To _____ is to award or grant something to another party.
7. The Mexican _____ took place in 1848.
8. During the 1850s, the freeing of slaves and the restriction of immigration were _____ issues.
9. _____ allowed people in their own territory or state to determine policies for themselves.
10. Part of the _____ from Mexico to the United States included New Mexico.
11. A major concern for Abraham Lincoln was the _____ of the Union.

Understanding Main Ideas

1. What were the events that made the spread of slavery the central issue that led to the Civil War?
2. What steps were taken to reach a compromise and end the spread of slavery between 1850 and 1854?
3. How did John Brown's raid and the *Dred Scott* decision divide the United States?
4. How did the South react to the 1860 Republican victory?

Critical Thinking Skills

1. **Recognizing Bias.** Why was *Uncle Tom's Cabin* so popular in the North?
2. **Testing Conclusions.** Consider the following opinion: "If the decision in the *Dred Scott* case had been different and Dred Scott declared free, the Civil War would not have happened." Explain why you agree or disagree.
3. **Demonstrating Reasoned Judgment.** Which of the three opinions on the causes of the Civil War presented on page 383 do you support? Why?

Social Studies Skills: Reading a Map

ELECTION OF 1860

- Lincoln
- Breckinridge
- Douglas
- Bell

(12) number of electoral votes

© FPC

Study the map above. It shows the electoral votes cast for each presidential candidate in the election of 1860.

Skill Review: On a separate sheet of paper, answer the statements that follow as true (T) or false (F).

1. Electors in thirteen states and two territories voted for Breckinridge.
2. New Jersey was the only state to split its electoral votes.
3. Breckinridge received the majority of his electoral votes from the South.
4. Lincoln received electoral votes only from states in the northeast.
5. New York had more electoral votes than any other state.

Writing About History

Writing an Editorial. Write an editorial from the point of view of a southerner or a northerner on one of the following topics: The Compromise of 1850; popular sovereignty; the right to secede; or the election of Abraham Lincoln. Explain where you stand on the issue that you have chosen, as well as the reasons for your position.

Your Region in History

Geography. Take another look at the map above. How many electoral votes did your state have? What candidate did your state support? If your region was a territory, which candidate might your region have supported? Based on what you have read in the chapter, explain the voting behavior of your state or territory.

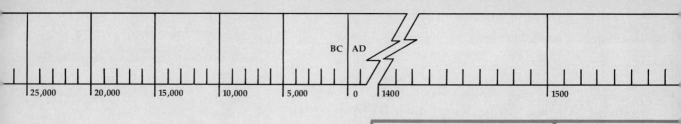

A Nation Divided

Chapter 21

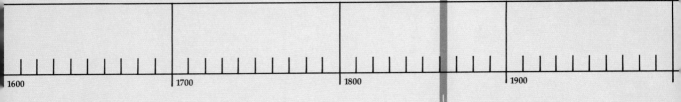

1700   1800   1900

Vocabulary

opposition
volunteer
draft
bonus
enlist
shortage
phase
proclamation
surrender
duty

THE WAR BETWEEN THE NORTH AND SOUTH turned into the most bitter fight in the nation's history. The suffering left a lasting mark, but the outcome freed the slaves and saved the Union.

The war is known by different names. In the South it is often called the War Between the States. Many southerners looked upon the conflict as a struggle between the states of the Confederacy and the states of the Union. Many northerners called the conflict the War of Rebellion. They believed the South was rebelling against the lawful government organized under the Constitution of 1787. Certainly it was a civil war, because it divided friends, neighbors, and families into warring groups.

Whatever name the war is given, no one at the beginning could foresee its lasting effects. Every mind and heart was filled with more immediate problems. The two rival governments reached into the lives of everyone for support. Men and boys stepped forward, offering to fight and even to die for what they believed. Women and children laid down their peacetime tasks to take up the burdens of war. Homes stood empty, and the soil lay untilled. President Abraham Lincoln rightly said, "This is essentially a people's contest."

Prereading

1. What problems did the two rival governments face as the Civil War began?

2. How did the North and the South organize for war behind the lines?

3. What advantages and disadvantages did each side face during the war's first two phases?

4. What events in the last two phases of the war led to Union victory?

403

1 Rival Governments

The Union and Confederate governments faced serious problems. Neither President Abraham Lincoln nor President Jefferson Davis had experience as managers of government. Yet both faced the key task of winning over those states that had not made a choice. And they needed to prepare for war while facing opposition at home.

The Two Presidents

When Lincoln entered office, he knew little about the Presidency. The federal treasury was empty. Seven states had left the Union. Lincoln drew no support in the South. Even many political leaders in the North were against him. Members of his own cabinet were divided on what should be done. And the officers in his government did not work together well.

But the untested, new President acted forcefully. Without asking Congress, President Lincoln called for 75,000 volunteers to put down the "rebellion." He also spent federal money without the approval of Congress, an unconstitutional act. He ordered some courts to stop trying cases. In place of the courts he ordered military rule, another unconstitutional act. Lincoln believed the danger of the times called for these drastic measures.

President Jefferson Davis of the Confederacy also acted on his own. He formed armies. He planned military moves. He took over army posts, post offices, and other federal services in the South. He tried to open talks with Britain, France, and other nations. But he seldom asked the Confederate Congress what they thought. One Senator in that Congress called him a "Confederate dictator."

The Border States

Both Lincoln and Davis worked at fever pitch to win promises of aid, especially from the border slave states. Without the help of some border states the Confederacy was sure to fail. It had only one sixth of the population of the United States. It did not have a single foundry to make steel plate or cannons. It had neither a gunpowder works nor a major factory.

Both sides won some border states. Five days after the firing on Fort Sumter, Virginia voted to secede from the Union. During the following month the Confederacy also won Arkansas, Tennessee, and North Carolina, in each case by a divided vote. The Choctaw, Creek, Chickasaw, and Seminoles in the West also came to the side of the South. The Cherokee were undecided.

With four border slave states now lined up with the South the population of the Confederacy doubled. These border states also

404

provided foundries, factories, and other resources needed for war. And their skilled leaders joined the Confederate cause.

Lincoln knew the importance of keeping the remaining border slave states in the Union. "I think to lose Kentucky is nearly the same as to lose the whole game," he wrote. "[With] Kentucky gone, we cannot hold Missouri, nor, as I think, Maryland. These all against us, and the job on our hands is too large for us."

Lincoln finally held on to the remaining states. Delaware, Maryland, Missouri, and Kentucky were all won over, but not without conflict. A few western counties in Virginia refused to secede with the rest of that state. These counties also came to the Union. In 1863, while the war was in progress, they formed the new state of West Virginia. Native Americans living on the northern Great Plains also cast their lot with the North.

The lines were now drawn, Union states against the Confederacy. Besides fighting each other, however, each side had to fight opposition from within.

Political Opposition at Home

Neither Lincoln in the North nor Davis in the South could win the full support of his region. Members of a peace movement in the North, called Copperheads, thought the southern states should be allowed to secede. Copperheads were so strong in some states that they blocked laws geared to further the Union's war plans.

Moreover, some northern cities or counties were pro-southern. For example, New York City had profitable trade links with southern planters and businesses. Many of its people favored the South rather than the Union. They were against the war and against Lincoln's conduct of the war.

One by one the states of the South seceded from the Union. The border states of Virginia, Arkansas, Tennessee, and North Carolina followed.

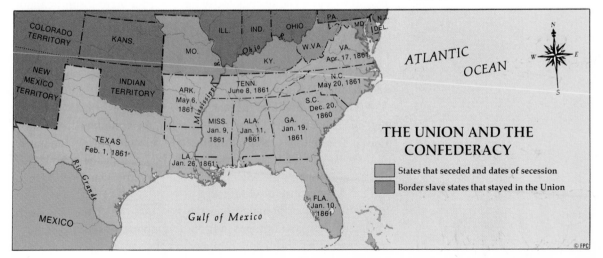

THE UNION AND THE CONFEDERACY

States that seceded and dates of secession

Border slave states that stayed in the Union

People made fun both presidents by drawing cartoons —

Section 1 Review

1. What seven problems did Lincoln face as he took office?
2. What kind of opposition did Jefferson Davis face from southern governors?

Critical Thinking

3. **Demonstrating Reasoned Judgment.** Why was it important to the Confederacy to win the support of some border states?

LOOKING AHEAD: How did the North and the South organize for war behind the lines?

White fighters brought own weapons

1861 — 16,402 men for Union

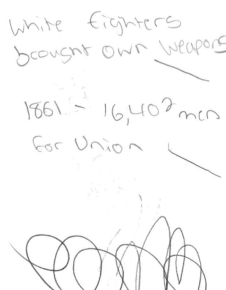

Lincoln's leadership was challenged again and again. Newspaper cartoons often poked fun at Lincoln. And several members of his cabinet lacked respect for his leadership.

Davis also faced opposition. A peace movement in the South favored an end to talk about secession. And because of the South's strong belief in states' rights, state governors in the Confederacy were not always cooperative. At one time the governor of Georgia refused to send troops for the Confederate army, arguing that his soldiers were to protect his state, not the whole Confederacy. Other governors sometimes held back supplies.

Some Confederate states went counter to the laws of the Confederacy. Some states kept Confederate tax collectors from carrying out their duties. Georgia even negotiated on its own with other countries. At times these problems delayed and weakened the actions of President Davis and the Confederate government.

2 Behind the Lines

To fight the war, the rival governments needed soldiers, sailors, and weapons on a scale unknown in United States history. Those serving needed to be paid. Supplies needed to be made and bought. Farmers, planters, and workers responded to the call for soldiers. When they joined up, others stepped in to pick up their tasks. In one way or another every home was affected by the war.

The Call for Troops

At first the Union and the Confederacy depended solely on white volunteer fighters. People on both sides were eager to join up. A college student in Ohio became so anxious to join the Union army that he wrote: "The lessons today have been a mere form. I cannot study. I cannot sleep."

In the South, community leaders formed volunteer companies. The persons who joined usually brought their own weapons. After an election of officers the company offered its services to either the state or the Confederacy.

At the outbreak of the war in 1861 the Union army had 16,402 men and officers. The Union usually asked for volunteers from state militia. The militia organized themselves, elected officers, and gave their services to the federal government. Before long the Union army had such groups as the Michigan Volunteers, the Ohio Volunteers, and the Massachusetts Volunteers.

The flood of volunteers in the first months of the war overwhelmed both governments. Often a company turned up without arms or supplies. Both governments lost the services of hundreds of thousands of volunteers for lack of supplies.

The Union soldiers on the left belonged to the New York state militia. The Confederates on the right rode with Jeb Stuart's cavalry.

As the fighting wore on, the need for soldiers was greater than the number of volunteers. So the Confederacy and the Union began to draft men into the army. The Confederacy adopted a draft law in April 1862. Every able-bodied white male between the ages of eighteen and thirty-five was declared eligible for service.

People believed to be more valuable on the home front did not have to serve. Among those excused from duty were teachers with more than twenty pupils, college professors, mail carriers, and overseers of twenty or more slaves. The draft law and its exceptions drew outspoken complaints. Drafted soldiers asked why they had to fight while planters with twenty or more black slaves were excused. In their view the poor were fighting for the rich. The exceptions to the draft were gradually reduced. Even so, only 20 to 30 percent of the soldiers in the Confederate army were drafted. The rest volunteered.

The Union passed a draft law in March 1863 when it sorely needed some 300,000 soldiers. The draft applied only in states that failed to produce their share of volunteers. The Union draft also allowed for exceptions. Opposition to the law led to riots in New York City and elsewhere. And for all the trouble it caused, it provided only 10 percent of the Union soldiers.

The Union also paid bonuses to those who enlisted or reenlisted. Soldiers sometimes tried to cheat on the offer. John O'Connor enlisted and then deserted thirty-two times, receiving a bonus each time he joined up again.

Blacks and the War Effort

Free blacks rushed to join the Union forces, but their enlistments were not accepted. When several Union generals began to enlist escaped slaves, Lincoln stopped them. He reasoned that black troops

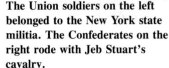

407

Northern farmers worked shorthanded but did well during the Civil War.

[handwritten margin note: formed military clubs until stopped by police]

would be unwelcome in the important border slave states that had stayed in the Union.

Free blacks formed military clubs in several cities. Until stopped by police, blacks in New York City met regularly to practice military drills. Free blacks meeting in Boston declared, "Our feelings urge us to say to our countrymen that we are ready to stand by and defend our government as the equals of its white defenders. . . ." Free blacks in Philadelphia wanted to go South to start slave revolts, a plan quickly stopped by the federal government.

Blacks were accepted slowly in the Union army. Before the war ended in 1865 at least 186,000 blacks had served as Union soldiers. About half of them came from the states that seceded from the Union. The others came from the border states and the North. Frederick Douglass and other black leaders helped sign them up. Blacks served in every division of the army. A few were troop leaders. Some were doctors, ministers, scouts, and spies. Every major battle in the Civil War after 1862 included black soldiers.

In the South slaves were forced into work gangs for the Confederate army as early as 1862. In March 1865, as the war neared its end, the Confederate Congress promised freedom for slaves who would join its forces. But this step came so late that few blacks served as Confederate soldiers.

Foreign Affairs

Both the Union and the Confederacy sought help from Britain. Britain and other nations, however, decided not to back either side. Their neutrality angered the Union, which saw itself as the legal government of the United States.

At first the Confederacy expected British cloth mills to be so in need of southern cotton that Britain would have to come to the aid of the South. When fighting broke out, however, these mills had much cotton on hand. As it turned out, because of a crop failure, Britain needed grain and corn from northern farms more than it needed southern cotton.

Moreover, the British people disliked slavery, so they favored the Union. But if the Confederacy could win its independence, Britain knew it would have to recognize the Confederate states as a nation. Then other countries would have to do the same.

Although the British did not take sides, they did sell war goods to the Confederacy. Even more important, the British built ships for the Confederate navy. One vessel alone, the *Alabama,* captured more than sixty Union ships.

The Home Front

Throughout the North and South the war affected production on farms and in factories. Cotton production in the South fell from 4 million bales in 1861 to 300,000 bales in 1864. One reason for the drop was that a Union blockade of southern ports cut off the British market. Another reason was the Confederate need for food, not cotton, for the troops and on the home front. And as plantation owners and overseers left to join the armies, fewer people remained to tend the fields. Slaves also escaped as the Union troops advanced.

In contrast Northern farmers fared well. The British market expanded, as did the market at home. Wheat rose from 65 cents a bushel in 1860 to $2.26 a bushel in 1864. There was a shortage of farmhands because so many joined the Union army. But women on the farms took the men's places. And more farm machines were being used. Cyrus H. McCormick sold 165,000 reapers during the war, compared to a few thousand each year before 1861.

Factories in the North and South produced clothing, guns, and other supplies for the fighting forces. During the war years the number of northern women employed in manufacturing rose from 270,000 to 370,000. Groups of women in the North and South rolled bandages, sewed uniforms, and served food at train stations to soldiers coming through. One southern woman reported, "Ladies who never worked before are hard at work making uniforms and tents."

In the South most of the schools closed. In the North schools and colleges generally stayed open. More and more women took over teaching and other jobs that were once filled by men.

On the whole, northerners did not suffer marked shortages, but many southerners did. Clothing, coffee, and even such everyday goods as buttons were in short supply. Salt also was hard to find. Without salt to preserve it, meat quickly spoiled.

The price of goods in the South soared, especially in cities. J. B. Jones, a clerk in the Confederate war office, kept a diary. In May 1864 he reported that flour in Richmond, Virginia, sold for $400 a barrel. A pair of shoes cost several hundred dollars.

Union civilians—men and women—turned out such war materials as shells and gunpowder.

Section 2 Review

1. How were officers in volunteer companies often chosen?
2. Why did the Confederate draft law draw many complaints?
3. How did the Union encourage men to enlist or reenlist in the army?
4. Why did Lincoln order Union generals to stop enlisting escaped slaves in the army?
5. Why did Britain not support the Confederacy?
6. For what four reasons was there a drop in southern cotton production?

Critical Thinking

7. **Drawing Conclusions.** How did the war affect northern farms and factories?

LOOKING AHEAD: What advantages and disadvantages did each side face during the war's first two phases?

3   The War's First Phases

In the early years of the war neither side gained an edge. The two sides were roughly equal in advantages and disadvantages. Confederate and Union soldiers also equaled each other in courage. The victories of the Confederate armies in the East weighed evenly with the victories of the Union in the West and on the sea.

Advantages and Disadvantages

The Union had some advantages over the Confederacy. The Union could draw its army from a population almost twice the size of the Confederacy. The North also had better roads, canals, and rail lines. Its numerous factories produced weapons and supplies. Its government had existed for seventy years. This government was able to raise money for the war effort through tariffs, income taxes, and excise taxes. The federal government could also borrow money from banks and citizens and print paper money. Users of the paper money could expect full repayment in gold or silver.

The Union also had some disadvantages. To win, the North needed to attack the South and force its defenders to surrender. A larger army and more powerful weapons are needed to attack than to defend. Lincoln had difficulty finding a Union general with the ability to strike decisively against the South until late in the war.

The South had many advantages. In contrast to the North, the South was defending its home ground. Most Confederates believed they were fighting for a way of life. Men and boys of the South were

These soldiers served together as an all-black unit in the Union artillery.

better trained in the use of weapons and horses than were men and boys of the North. The South had a strong military tradition. Many of its most important leaders, including President Jefferson Davis, had trained at West Point to become professional soldiers.

The South also had the advantage of a great military leader, General Robert E. Lee. President Lincoln had offered Lee, an officer in the army of the United States, leadership of all the Union forces. Lee refused, saying he could not take up the sword against family and friends in his home state of Virginia. He later became commander of the Army of Northern Virginia and the Confederacy's outstanding battle leader. Lee's quiet daring, his ability to outthink other generals, and the love he won from his troops made him a serious challenge to the Union.

The South suffered great disadvantages, mainly in raising money and supplies for the war. The Confederate government had outlawed tariffs. And the South had few banks and little paper money. Most of its capital was invested in land and slaves. For these reasons the South could not easily borrow money. It paid for the war by printing its own paper money. But by 1864 a Confederate dollar bill was worth only five cents. By the end of the war it was worthless.

The Soldier's Life

Union soldiers were supposed to wear blue uniforms. Confederate soldiers were to wear gray. But neither army was well clothed. And the southern soldiers always seemed short of footwear. One of the bloodiest battles of the war was triggered when Confederate troops entered the town of Gettysburg looking for shoes.

Soldiers in the Union army were called Billy Yank. Soldiers in the Confederate army were called Johnny Reb. For both, fighting was a hard life. A Confederate soldier wrote his parents that one hole in the seat of a trooper's pants meant that he was a captain. Two holes meant he was a lieutenant. "And the seat of his pants all out" showed he was an everyday soldier.

The loss of life on both sides was staggering. At the Battle of Antietam the Union lost 12,000 men killed or wounded in a single day. The Confederates lost 9,000. Altogether the two armies at Antietam lost 20 percent of their soldiers—all in one day.

Yet three times as many soldiers died of typhoid fever, smallpox, and other diseases as were killed in battle. In total the Union lost 360,000 soldiers. The Confederates lost about 329,000.

Though enemies, Billy Yank and Johnny Reb sometimes swapped Yankee coffee for Rebel tobacco in lulls between battles. Such acts helped soldiers live on in the midst of disease and death. Many were frightened. But both sides showed courage. A Union soldier wrote his father: "We got the worst of it but . . . I didn't run."

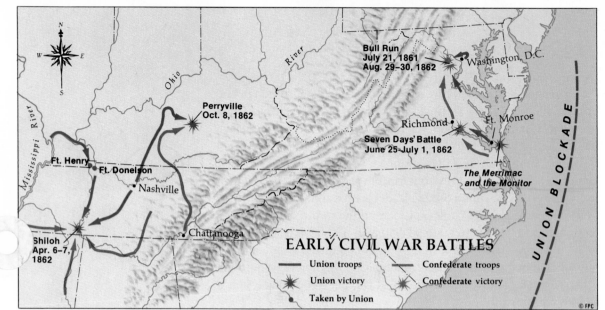

EARLY CIVIL WAR BATTLES

- —— Union troops   —— Confederate troops
- ✳ Union victory   ✳ Confederate victory
- • Taken by Union

Early in the war Union forces were most successful at sea, along the Mississippi, and in the West.

A private from Atlanta, Georgia, wrote his wife: "I want to come home as bad as any body can . . . but I shant run away."

Early Battles

Each side expected a quick victory, misjudging how long the war would last. The war took place in four phases. In the first phase the North attacked the Confederate border states. It also set up a naval blockade around the South. In the second phase General Lee's Confederate forces marched into Maryland. They fought their way close to the Union capital at Washington, D.C., and almost struck a final blow. In the third phase the Union armies captured key ports along the Mississippi River, dividing the Confederacy. In the fourth phase the Union armies swept through the weary Confederate states.

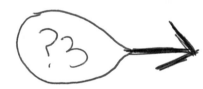

The first major battle of the war came when the Union army marched from Washington, D.C., through Virginia. Their goal was to take the Confederate capital at Richmond. General Irvin McDowell and his Union soldiers expected an easy victory. But the troops under Confederate General Pierre Beauregard stopped McDowell at Bull Run, thirty miles from Washington, D.C.

The Union forces turned, running pell-mell for their capital city. Union soldiers threw away their knapsacks, guns, canteens—anything to lighten their load. The Confederates were too disorganized to take advantage of their victory. But the Battle of Bull Run showed that the war would be long and hard fought.

President Lincoln chose General George B. McClellan to replace McDowell. McClellan planned to seize Richmond, using Fort Monroe on Chesapeake Bay as his base. But General Lee outwitted McClellan in a series of battles near Richmond in 1862.

The Union navy, however, was gaining an upper hand. Just after the firing on Fort Sumter Lincoln had ordered a blockade of southern ports. Each year the blockade cut off more goods going into

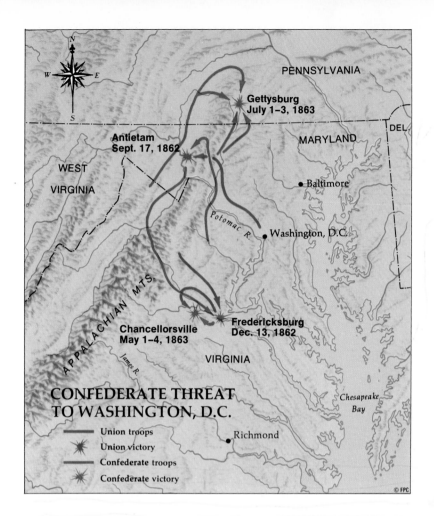

CONFEDERATE THREAT TO WASHINGTON, D.C.

Union troops
Union victory
Confederate troops
Confederate victory

© FPC

Though neither side won the bloody battle at Antietam, the North gained a decided advantage there.

and out of the Confederacy. In 1862 the Union navy also won control of the Mississippi River between the Gulf of Mexico and New Orleans in the south and between the Ohio River and Memphis further north. The South could not offset these Union gains. Jefferson Davis later said, "We were without a navy while they had a powerful fleet."

The Confederacy turned the *Merrimac*, a captured Union ship, into an ironclad vessel and renamed it the *Virginia*. And the Union built its own ironclad, the *Monitor*. The two ships battled near the mouth of Chesapeake Bay on March 9, 1862. The sea battle—the first in United States history between ironclads—ended in a draw.

A Union army in the West under General Ulysses S. Grant was more successful. In February 1862 it captured two key Confederate forts in Tennessee and in April won a bloody battle at Shiloh. The Confederate army lost one fourth of its troops at Shiloh and the Union one fifth. When others complained about Grant's battle losses, Lincoln answered, "I can't spare this man. He fights."

Meanwhile General Lee led the war into its second phase as he marched into Maryland in September 1862. His goal was to take over Washington, D.C., and force the Union to accept the southern Confederacy as an independent nation.

413 🐌

At first Lee did not know that his plan had been discovered by accident. A Union private had found a copy of Lee's orders wrapped around some cigars that had fallen from a Confederate general's pocket. From this lucky find General McClellan knew exactly where Lee's army would be. The Battle of Antietam that followed on September 17, 1862, brought on the bloodiest day of fighting in the whole war. Neither side won or lost. But one Union general said, "We hurt them a little more than they hurt us."

The Emancipation Proclamation

Many historians believe that the Battle of Antietam was the turning point in the war. That battle allowed Lincoln to issue the Emancipation Proclamation on September 22, 1862. This proclamation freed all slaves in the Confederate states.

Since the beginning of the war, the President had wrestled with the slavery problem. He feared he would lose the backing of slave-holding border states in the Union if he took a stand against slavery. Even in the North antislavery groups were in the minority. When Britain let it be known that it might recognize the Confederacy, however, Lincoln acted. He knew Britain's stand against slavery.

President Lincoln's first goal had always been to save the Union—with or without slavery. Against the advice of his cabinet and others, Lincoln now decided that the Union could best be saved by freeing the slaves. He stated, "The moment came when I felt that slavery must die that the nation might live."

Of course, the Confederate states did not honor this ruling from their rival government. No slaves were really freed. And the proclamation was silent about slaves in border states loyal to the Union. But Lincoln's stand and the slight Union edge at Antietam convinced Britain not to recognize the Confederacy.

4   Union Victory

As the war moved into its third phase, greater numbers of soldiers and supplies began to tip the scales in favor of the North. But the South refused to give up.

The Last Battles

The Union armies won two major battles in July 1863. One was fought for three days at Gettysburg, Pennsylvania. The second took place at Vicksburg, Mississippi. The Union victory over General Lee at Gettysburg ended Confederate threats to Washington, D.C., and the North. The victory at Vicksburg and at a nearby Confederate stronghold gave the Union control of the whole Mississippi River, cutting the lifeline of the western Confederate states to the East.

Section 3 Review

1. What three taxes did the North use to raise money for the war?
2. What United States military leader from Virginia chose to join the Confederate cause rather than fight for the Union?
3. What were the four phases of the Civil War?
4. What did the Battle of Bull Run show about the war?
5. What was the role of the Union navy in the first phases of the war?
6. What was the Emancipation Proclamation?

Critical Thinking

7. **Recognizing Cause and Effect.** What discovery gave General McClellan an advantage at the Battle of Antietam?

LOOKING AHEAD: What events in the last two phases of the war led to Union victory?

Four months after the battle at Gettysburg, President Lincoln visited the field to dedicate a national cemetery. At the ceremony he spoke briefly. "We here highly resolve that these dead shall not have died in vain—that this nation, under God, shall have a new birth of freedom—and that government of the people, by the people, for the people, shall not perish from the earth."

After the Battle of Gettysburg, the war entered its final stage. The Union army severed the key Confederate supply line at Chattanooga, Tennessee. This victory freed the Union forces under General W. T. Sherman from strong opposition. His army swept into the southeastern states, destroying everything in its path.

Meanwhile Grant had been appointed commander in chief of all Union armies. He personally led the Army of the Potomac against General Lee's Northern Army of Virginia near Richmond. Both sides suffered heavy losses. Finally, outnumbered, outgunned, and without food and other essentials, Lee surrendered April 9, 1865.

Both Grant and Lee had attended West Point. Each had served in the Mexican War. At the surrender at Appomattox Court House, Grant and Lee met in a farmhouse and talked briefly about happier days. Then Grant wrote in pencil the terms of surrender. The Confederate army would be allowed to return home. At Lee's request Grant let the soldiers keep their horses and mules so they could begin farming again when they returned home.

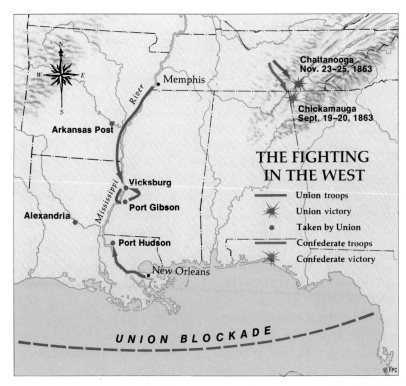

THE FIGHTING IN THE WEST

Victory at Gettysburg in the summer of 1863 effectively halted the South's drive on Washington, D.C., begun the year before.

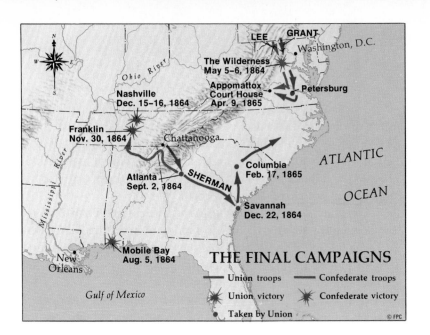

THE FINAL CAMPAIGNS

Following the capture of Atlanta, Union General Sherman began his famous "march to the sea."

After the agreement was signed Lee walked out on the porch of the farmhouse. Three times he slowly struck the gloved palm of his left hand with his right fist. Then he mounted his horse. Grant saluted him by raising his weather-beaten campaign hat. Lee raised his tailored hat in turn and rode off. The war was over.

Republican Politics

When the Confederacy was formed, representatives from the seceding states had left Congress to take part in their new government. As a result, Republicans held full sway in Congress. They were free to adopt new tariffs, set new policies on western lands and internal improvements, and pass other laws favoring the North.

Congress had passed a higher tariff after Lincoln's election but before he took office. Each year Congress raised duties on iron products, coffee, tea, sugar, clothing, and other everyday goods brought into the country. By 1865 many of the duties were equal to the cost of making and shipping the products.

The Republicans also chose a northern route for a railway to the Pacific. Congress passed a law in 1862 that set up the Union Pacific Railroad Company. Union Pacific was to build a line west from Omaha, Nebraska. The Central Pacific Railroad would build east from Sacramento, California. The plan was to "strengthen the bonds of Union between the Atlantic and Pacific coasts."

Congress also gave these railroads ownership of millions of acres of land along the route. All rights held by Native Americans to any of this land were set aside. The government also gave money to the railroads for each mile of track they laid.

The Republican Congress also adopted the Homestead Act in 1862. It granted 160 acres of public land for a small fee to anyone who lived on the land for five years. By 1865 the government had granted over 2.5 million acres of land under the act.

General Lee and one of his officers waited as General Grant drew up surrender terms at Appomattox.

During the war Congress also passed the Land-Grant College Act, which southerners had always opposed. The act gave to each state 30,000 acres of public land in the West for each of the state's senators and representatives in Congress. Sale of the land was to finance the founding of "agricultural and mechanical colleges." Cornell University in New York and Iowa State University are among those that were first organized as land-grant colleges.

Death of Lincoln

In the election of 1864 Lincoln ran for a second term against Democrat George McClellan, a former general in the Union army. Lincoln promised to end the war and to bring the South back into the Union. He won the election in November.

Suddenly, only two days after the official surrender of Lee's army in 1865, a tragic event shocked the country—North and South. On April 14 President Lincoln was shot by John Wilkes Booth. Booth, a fervent and unstable champion of the Confederate cause, had been hatching a plot to kidnap Lincoln. He planned to hold the President to win compromises for the Confederacy. Lee's surrender made Booth all the wilder.

Booth was an actor who often worked at Ford's Theatre in Washington, D.C. Lincoln and his wife attended a play there. Booth entered the President's theater box and shot the President. Lincoln died the following morning. Church bells throughout the city tolled in mourning. Telegraph wires carried the grim news to a stunned nation.

Lincoln's untimely death did not end his influence. He continues to live in history, in part because of the wisdom of his words. In his second inaugural address, delivered hardly a month before his death, he pointed up the importance of peace and forgiveness. "Let us strive on to finish the work we are in; to bind up the nation's wounds . . . to do all which may achieve . . . a just and lasting peace among ourselves, and with all nations." It remained to be seen whether his wise words would be followed.

Election of 1864

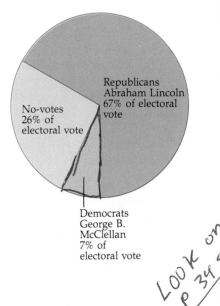

Republicans
Abraham Lincoln
67% of electoral vote

No-votes
26% of electoral vote

Democrats
George B. McClellan
7% of electoral vote

Look on p 348

Section 4 Review

1. What was the main importance of the Union victory at Gettysburg? At Vicksburg?
2. What were four major results of Republican politics during the Civil War years?

Critical Thinking

3. **Checking Consistency.** How did the actions of Congress during the war reflect a continuing attitude toward Native Americans?

Heritage   Of the Union

During and after the war a sense of unity among citizens still endured.

Though long and bloody, the Civil War had saved the Union. In the end the ties binding together the North and South were stronger than the forces pushing them apart.

Ties Among Soldiers

The ties of lasting union were strong, even when the fighting first broke out. For example, the federal government allowed members of the United States Army and Navy to leave peacefully to fight for the Confederacy. Soldiers and sailors who had trained and fought together took different sides. But they did not lose respect for one another. Confederate General Thomas "Stonewall" Jackson, admired by North and South alike for his skill and daring, had been a classmate of Union General George B. McClellan at West Point. They— as well as other officers—had shared the same training. They were taught by the same teachers. Some were close friends.

Generosity in Victory

The generous terms of the surrender at Appomattox also show the ties of once-united citizens. General Ulysses S. Grant did not call for the jailing of the defeated Americans from the South. He even allowed officers and soldiers to keep their weapons. Grant also suggested that General Robert E. Lee go to Washington to speak to President Lincoln about fair treatment for the losing side. Seldom if ever had a winning general offered so much.

Ties of Government

The Union and Confederacy also shared similar forms of government. The Confederacy adopted many laws of the United

Like the cadets of a later year shown at the left, Confederate General Stonewall Jackson (above) and Union General George McClellan (below) were classmates at West Point in 1846.

States. Even on their flag the Confederates used the stars, bars, and colors of the Union flag.

More important, both sides preserved representative government. Each allowed critics from within to speak out against policies and leaders. And despite the turmoil of a civil war both sides held open and free elections.

More Rights for Blacks

In addition both sides gave blacks more rights. President Lincoln's Emancipation Proclamation of 1862 called for freeing slaves in the Confederate states beginning in January 1863. Not until the Thirteenth Amendment was passed in 1865, however, was slavery outlawed by the United States Constitution.

Slaves had been used by the Confederate army for duties other than fighting from the outset of the war. In 1863 President Jefferson Davis issued orders that any slave needed for Confederate service would be taken and the owner would be paid a monthly fee.

Slowly the Confederacy began to look on slaves as fighters and to think of promising them their freedom if they served. In February 1865 General Lee called the use of slaves as fighters necessary. The following month the Confederate Congress called for 300,000 soldiers, black or white. Black troops began to join the army. In effect, emancipation of slaves in the South had begun. In time the base of representative government in the

This member of the Phalanx guard in Grant's camp was one of thousands of black soldiers fighting for the Union before war's end.

United States came to include more than 4 million freed slaves.

Regional Differences

Although saving the Union and freeing the slaves were the most important outcomes of the Civil War, an acceptance of regional differences also emerged. The balance between a central government and regional interests is a key feature of the United States today.

Some historians believe that the South as a region with common interests did not really exist before 1861. They point to differences between the border states and the cotton-producing states, the small farmers of the up-country and the plantation owners of the lowlands. They note the different interests of a railway center such as Richmond and a port city such as New Orleans. These historians argue that there were many, many Souths—

not one single South. These historians believe that the South as a single region rose out of the fight for independence as a confederacy. Fighting the war together made southerners more aware of their roots in the soil of the South.

Peace Among Regions

Regional differences are still apparent and accepted today. Each region has its own ways of speaking. Different regions also have different lifestyles and political leanings. The people earn their living in different ways.

The Civil War put the heritage of the Union to the test. The Union held, and its heritage became enriched. Today's United States is a mix of national interests and regional differences. After the Civil War, which had threatened to divide them forever, the separate states never again talked of secession.

Chapter 21 Review

Chapter Summary

The Union and Confederate governments faced the tasks of preparing for war and winning over those states that had not yet chosen sides.

The Union and Confederate governments each tried to gain the support of countries in Europe, particularly Great Britian. The European powers, however, decided to remain neutral.

The expectation of a short war was shattered at the Battle of Bull Run. A long and costly war became a reality. The North had a better transportation system, more factories, and the ability to raise money and supplies. The South had the advantage of defending its home ground. It also had better military leadership.

The Battle of Antietam is considered by many to be the turning point of the war. After the battle, President Lincoln issued the Emancipation Proclamation. The naval blockade, Union victories at Gettysburg and Vicksburg, and General Sherman's march through Georgia convinced General Lee that the war was lost. On April 9, 1865, Lee surrendered to Grant at Appomattox Court House. Five days later, President Lincoln was assassinated by John Wilkes Booth.

Reviewing Vocabulary

Use the words below to complete the following sentences.

opposition	shortage
volunteer	phase
draft	proclamation
bonus	surrender
enlist	duty

1. The North paid a(n) _____ to men who decided to _____.

2. To raise money, the Union government placed a(n) _____ on a number of imported goods.

3. Both President Lincoln and President Davis faced _____ to their policies during the war.

4. General Grant decided the terms of _____ at Appomattox Court House.

5. Although most of the soldiers in the Union and Confederate armies had chosen to _____, both sides later had to _____ men into service.

6. Women in the North entered the workforce at the homefront due to the _____ of male workers.

7. Following the Battle of Antietam during the second _____ of the war, President Lincoln issued a _____ that freed the slaves in the Confederate states.

Understanding Main Ideas

1. At the beginning of the war, what two problems had to be solved by both the North and the South?

2. How did the North and the South prepare for war behind the lines?

3. During the early phases of the war, what advantages and disadvantages did the North and the South have?

4. In the third and fourth phases of the war, what were the Union victories that brought the war to an end?

5. What railroad policies did the Republican Congress follow during the course of the Civil War?

6. What were the features of the Homestead Act of 1862?

7. What promises did Lincoln make in the 1864 presidential election?

Social Studies Skills: Interpreting Political Cartoons

Study the political cartoon at the right. The cartoonist chose to illustrate the meaning of the following statement made by Lincoln during the Lincoln-Douglas debates in 1858: "A house divided against itself cannot stand."

Skill Review: Answer the following questions according to the cartoon.

1. What has happened to the North and South?
2. What is President Lincoln attempting to do?
3. Choose the caption below that most accurately expresses the cartoonist's message:
   (a) President Lincoln can hold the Union together.
   (b) President Lincoln would let the South secede.
   (c) Only Stephen Douglas can maintain peace.
   (d) Loyalty to the Union will hold the North and the South together.

Critical Thinking Skills

1. **Making Comparisons.** How did the roles played by women in the North and South reflect differences in the two societies?
2. **Identifying Assumptions.** Why, at the beginning of the Civil War, did both the North and the South expect victory and a short war?

Writing About History

Writing an Advertisement. Assume that you are in charge of encouraging enlistments in either the Union or Confederate army. Write an advertisement that convinces would-be volunteers to join the war effort for the North or for the South.

Your Region in History

Economics. At the time of the Civil War, what was your region's primary economic activity? Did your region's economy have an impact on the outcome of the war? Has the economy in your region changed? Would the economic activities going on today in your community have changed the course ·of the Civil War?

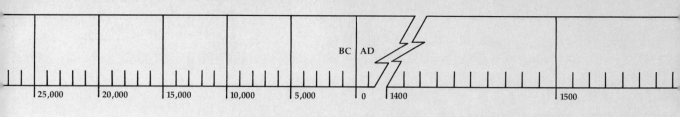

Reconstruction

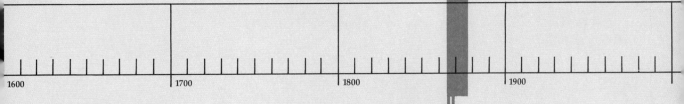

Vocabulary

tenant farmer
sharecropper
prejudice
black code
bribery
graft
corruption
commission
fraud

GENERAL LEE'S SURRENDER at Appomattox brought the Civil War to an end. Although the Union had been saved, there were angry differences to settle before the Union could be reconstructed, or put together again. Northern political leaders studied a number of questions. Should the South be punished for its so-called rebellion? How should the southern states be brought back into the Union? What was to become of the 4 million former slaves—now free men, women, and children?

The Reconstruction period lasted from 1865 to 1877. Decisions made in those years affected the South, relations between the North and South, and the lives of black people for nearly a century.

1 After Appomattox

At the war's end in 1865, soldiers from both armies began to return home. What they found back home depended on whether they went home to the North or the South. The North had suffered little damage to farms, homes, and businesses from the war. Most battles had been fought in the South. Loss of northern lives, however, had been high. And those who lived through the war often came home with

Prereading

1. What changes took place in the South after Appomattox?
2. How did the politics of Reconstruction lead to a clash between Congress and the Presidency?
3. How did Reconstruction change the South?

423

After the war, people turned again to settling the Great Plains.

wounds they would bear for the rest of their lives. Still the North was prospering. Industries that had sprung up during the war were growing. New railroads were being built. More new farmland was to be had in the ever-expanding West. When about a million Union soldiers returned to peacetime life in 1865, most had little trouble finding a way to earn a living.

Destruction in the South

In the South the picture was very different. Returning soldiers found parts of the South almost totally destroyed. Cities had been burned, roads and bridges wrecked, and farmlands ruined. Homes and livestock were gone. Trains and railroad tracks were too damaged to use. The South's cotton—the little that was left—had been seized by the North. Many wondered how new crops could be grown in the untilled soil. Union General Philip Sheridan is reported to have said of the once green-growing Shenandoah Valley, "A crow cannot fly down the valley without carrying its own provision."

A visitor to Charleston, South Carolina, described what had become of that major port. It was now, he said, a city of "vacant houses, of widowed women, of rotting wharves, of deserted warehouses, of weed-wild gardens, of miles of grass-grown streets, of acres of pitiful and voiceless barrenness."

The loss of human life in the South was also tragic. One out of every twenty white male southerners had been either killed or wounded. The South had lost most of its younger generation—those who might have been its leaders.

424

The South had also lost its slave labor force. After the war the South was forced to accept the laws of the federal government—including the Emancipation Proclamation. When they lost their slaves, many planters also lost their wealth. Before the war each slave was worth about $1,000. Even farmers who owned only a few slaves could find no one to help them with their crops after the war. These southerners had to learn how to run their farms without slave labor. For many slave owners the end of slavery meant the end of southern civilization as they knew it. Some were crushed by the change. Others left the South in despair.

The Union victory stirred strong feelings of bitterness between North and South. Many northerners thought of the southern whites as rebels who deserved all their troubles. Southern whites, in turn, did not look kindly on the Yankees who had defeated them in war and humbled them in peace. It would be decades before these hard feelings were laid aside.

The Joys and Problems of Freedom

For many former slaves freedom was the fulfillment of a dream. They sang about their joys:

Slavery chain done broke at last!
Broke at last! Broke at last!
Slavery chain done broke at last!
Gonna praise God till I die!

For most southern blacks, however, the joy of freedom was short-lived. Many, if not most, rejoiced in their new-found freedom by leaving their owners. They soon discovered, however, that they had no place to go. One black described the feeling of many former slaves. Freedom, he said, "came so sudden on them they weren't

By 1865, parts of Richmond, Virginia, were entirely burnt out.

425

prepared for it." They left the plantation, he continued, "with nothing in the world but what they had on their backs."

Freedom meant choosing a name, because many slaves had never been given last names. It meant the right to own property, form schools and churches, vote, and even seek political office. But above all it meant finding a way to earn a living. How could freed slaves own property if they had no money to buy it? Freed slaves with skills—carpenters, bricklayers, blacksmiths—outnumbered white skilled workers by five to one. But few blacks had or could borrow the money to buy property and begin a business.

Tenant Farmers and Sharecroppers

Freed slaves who had worked the land had even fewer chances than skilled workers to own property. Many hoped the government would give them "forty acres and a mule"—enough to get them started in farming. A few blacks, particularly in South Carolina, did manage to buy small farms. But most remained without land. They were forced to become tenant farmers or sharecroppers on land owned by whites.

Though they did not own land, tenant farmers usually had more freedom than sharecroppers. A tenant farmer rented a piece of land just as people today rent an apartment. Tenant farmers could decide for themselves what crops to plant, and they usually sold their own crops. At the end of the season they would pay the landlord in either money or a share of the crop.

Sharecropping became more common than tenant farming. Most black farm workers had to accept sharecropping even though it was only slightly better than slavery. Unlike tenant farmers, sharecroppers were told what to plant—usually cotton and tobacco. The owners often directed the workers in their planting and harvesting, just as owners or overseers had directed the slaves. Sharecroppers were seldom allowed to plant their own gardens.

At harvest time the crop was shared by the black sharecropper and the white owner. Sharecroppers who provided only labor—most of them—usually got one third of the selling price. The few who were also able to bring with them seed and farming equipment got two thirds of the selling price.

Most sharecroppers had to depend on the owners or on local storekeepers for their everyday needs—food, clothing, and housing. The high prices these people charged left most sharecroppers in a never-ending state of poverty. They were hardly able to get through a year and never able to save enough to break free.

Over the years sharecropping hurt almost everyone. The workers were forever in debt. The land wore out because of too much planting of a single crop. Landowners had little money to spend on the latest farming machines or methods. Only the storekeepers made money. Sharecropping weighed heavily on the South and held back southern farming for a century.

The Urban Black

Many freed slaves moved to southern towns and cities in search of freedom and jobs. In cities such as Richmond and Charleston there were more blacks than whites. Some blacks who came to the cities, especially those with needed skills, managed to earn a living. Others could not find work.

Crowded into shantytowns at the edge of a city, blacks were faced with increasing prejudice from whites in both North and South. Many southern cities passed laws called black codes that were like those in use before the war. Under these codes, blacks were kept off the streets at night. Jobless blacks could be told to leave town or face arrest. Or they could be pressed into street gangs that had to work for the city. Blacks could not serve on juries or be witnesses at trials.

Few blacks in the cities had time to go to school. Jennylin Dunn, whose parents settled in Raleigh, North Carolina, hoped to attend one of the new schools set up for young blacks. But she later reported, "Most of us were so busy scrambling around making a living that we had no time for school."

blacks crowed into one town but couldn't serve on juries

The Freedmen's Bureau

Some freed blacks succeeded in going to school, many with help from the Freedmen's Bureau. Set up by Congress just before the war

The Freedmen's Bureau helped blacks with daily needs and work agreements.

Schools for blacks

Section 1 Review

1. Why did Northerners and Southerners have bitter feelings toward each other after the war?
2. In what four ways did freedom change the lives of former slaves?
3. How is the life of a sharecropper different from the life of a tenant farmer?
4. How did black codes limit the freedom of blacks?
5. What were the two main purposes of the Freedmen's Bureau?

Critical Thinking

6. **Expressing Ideas Clearly.** How did Reconstruction help former slaves and how did it fail them?

LOOKING AHEAD: How did the politics of Reconstruction lead to a clash between Congress and the Presidency?

ended, the Freedmen's Bureau was to help former slaves and people displaced by the war. The bureau was to help them find homes, jobs, and education.

The Freedmen's Bureau had its greatest success in setting up thousands of schools for blacks. Before the war, teaching a slave to read and write had been against the law in much of the South. Now freed blacks who could attend flocked to the new schools. Many schools ran day and night to teach the thousands, young and old, who wanted an education. Teachers from the North and South, both black and white, taught in the new schools.

The Freedmen's Bureau also founded and put up the money for colleges and universities. Fisk University in Nashville; Howard University in Washington, D.C.; Hampton Institute in Hampton, Virginia; and Atlanta University are the best known.

The bureau also set up hospitals that cared for nearly half a million cases of illness. It offered food and homes to those without jobs or money. And it helped black workers get fairer pay and treatment from their employers.

Some Freedmen's Bureau activities succeeded while others failed. The bureau depended on Congress for money, and some of its programs failed for lack of funds. Some bureau officials were more interested in lining their own pockets than in helping newly freed blacks. They took money from employers in return for finding them cheap labor. Dishonest dealings led to the closing of the Freedmen's Bank in 1874. Those few blacks who had saved money in the bank lost it all. And though some bank officers tried hard to help them, few blacks became independent landowners.

2 The Politics of Reconstruction

As the South was pulling itself together, leaders in Washington were debating questions that had surfaced long before the end of the war. The most important question was, who should govern the South during Reconstruction? Two other questions stirred attention in the capital. Who had the right to decide when the southern states would be allowed to reenter the Union—Congress or the President? And what steps should be followed to bring the former Confederate states back into the Union?

Government at Odds

The writers of the Constitution had never expected the secession of several states from the Union. The Constitution, therefore, held no clear answers. President Lincoln and many others believed that acts of secession were the illegal acts of lone citizens rather than of whole states. Using this reasoning, Lincoln argued that the Confederate

no answer for secession

Tuskegee Institute in Alabama was founded by ex-slave Booker T. Washington. By about 1902 the college was offering students work in chemistry.

states had never really left the Union. He believed his task was to put down the rebellion of the individual citizens. Acting on this belief, he had used his powers as commander in chief to call out the armed forces. Lincoln also believed that the President had the power to decide how citizens of the former Confederate states were to be taken back into the Union.

Long before the Civil War ended, President Lincoln spelled out his plan for restoring the southern states. Except for some high government and military officers, he would pardon any southerner who would swear to obey the laws of the United States. A state could rejoin the Union when 10 percent of all its people who had voted in 1860 took the oath. Citizens of that state could then form a legal state government and vote for members of Congress.

The Republicans who were running Congress did not agree with Lincoln's plan. They believed the Confederate states *had* left the Union. Once defeated, they argued, these states no longer existed. They had become federal territory. And the Constitution gave Congress the power to make rules for territories and to admit new states. Congressional Republicans believed, therefore, that only they had the right to decide when and how the former Confederate territory would be readmitted to the Union. They also believed that only

Congress had the right to decide who from the South would be allowed to be a representative in Congress.

These differences set the stage for a political battle—this time not between two parties but between two branches of government. On one side stood Lincoln, a strong President and a masterful politician. On the other side stood Congress, a branch of government led by such strong-willed Republicans as Representative Thaddeus Stevens of Pennsylvania and Senator Charles Sumner of Massachusetts. The struggle over Reconstruction turned out to be as hard fought as any political battle in the country's history.

Congress vs. the President

Lincoln announced his 10 percent plan in December 1863, before the war ended. By that early date thousands of voters in Louisiana and Arkansas had already signed an oath of loyalty to the Union. State governments were formed, and representatives were elected to the United States Congress. Blacks could not vote in any state at that time, so they remained unrepresented.

Congress, however, refused to seat representatives from Louisiana and Arkansas. Congress had not even counted the electoral votes of those two states in the national election of 1864. In 1865 Tennessee organized its new government under the 10 percent plan. But again Congress refused to seat its representatives.

Leading Congress against Lincoln's plan were the Radical Republicans. The Radicals—a small but powerful group—had several goals. They wanted to make sure that former slaves were given their proper rights, including the vote. They wanted to see the leaders of the Confederacy punished. They wanted to keep the federal government in the firm hold of the Republican party. The Republican tariff and the Homestead Act were not to be overturned. If the southern states were seated in Congress again, the Republicans might be outvoted. As one Republican said, the South would cast a solid "rebel vote." For all these reasons the Radical Republicans wanted Congress, not the President, to be in charge of Reconstruction.

In July 1864 Congress passed its own Reconstruction plan, which was much more punishing than the President's. Lincoln refused to sign the bill. This veto angered Congress, and both branches of government prepared for another round.

When President Lincoln was killed five days after Lee's surrender at Appomattox, Vice-President Andrew Johnson of Tennessee became President. Johnson was a border-state Democrat who had been chosen as Lincoln's running mate to show unity during the war. Johnson strongly opposed secession, and his plans for Reconstruction were like Lincoln's. So the dispute between the President and Congress over Reconstruction continued with Johnson.

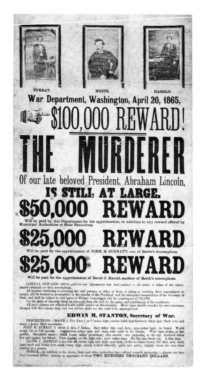

Of the three men shown on the poster, only John Wilkes Booth and David Herold were involved in the plot to kill Lincoln.

When a number of southern states adopted black codes, the Radicals won the votes they needed in Congress to pass exacting measures against the South. The black codes alarmed northerners. They saw little difference for blacks between conditions under the codes and under slavery. The codes convinced other members of Congress to vote for Radical Republican measures. Congress finally won the contest over control of Reconstruction in the South.

Congress in Control

In April 1866 Congress passed a civil rights act over President Johnson's veto. This act gave the freed blacks their rights as citizens. It also gave federal courts, rather than state and local courts, the right to try civil rights cases. The Congress knew that blacks had little chance of being heard in white southern courts. The civil rights acts passed in the 1960s were partly based on the act adopted in 1866.

Some members of Congress wanted to be sure that the Civil Rights Act was constitutional. So they had earlier begun a movement to amend the Constitution to leave no doubt about the rights of black people. The Thirteenth Amendment had already been passed by Congress and ratified by the states in 1865. That amendment made all slavery illegal.

The Reconstruction Congress added two other amendments to the Constitution. The first of these, the Fourteenth Amendment, was proposed in 1866 and ratified in 1868. Its first section defines citizenship and declared that no state may "deprive any person of life, liberty, or property, without due process of law." The section goes on to state that every person is entitled to "the equal protection of the laws." In other words all men—black or white—should have the same legal rights. The second section of the amendment says that any state denying any of its male citizens the right to vote could have its representation in Congress reduced. Thus, if half a state's voters were black and all blacks were denied the vote, that state could lose half of its representatives in Congress. With this amendment Congress warned the South not to deny the vote to blacks, though no state was ever punished under it.

With the Fifteenth Amendment, proposed in 1869 and ratified by the states in 1870, Congress took an added step. The Fifteenth Amendment declared that "The right of citizens of the United States to vote shall not be denied . . . on account of race, color, or previous condition of servitude [slavery]." This amendment assured blacks who were eligible—at that time, males over the age of twenty-one—of the right to vote. Despite the amendment many blacks were denied the vote for 100 years more.

To become a part of the Constitution, an amendment must be approved in three fourths of the states. Neither the Fourteenth nor

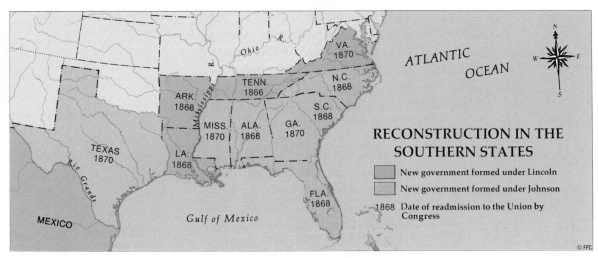

RECONSTRUCTION IN THE SOUTHERN STATES

VA. 1870

TENN. 1866

N.C. 1868

ARK. 1868

S.C. 1868

MISS. 1870

ALA. 1868

GA. 1870

TEXAS 1870

LA. 1868

FLA. 1868

MEXICO

Gulf of Mexico

ATLANTIC OCEAN

New government formed under Lincoln

New government formed under Johnson

1868 Date of readmission to the Union by Congress

© FPC

Ex-Confederates bitterly opposed Reconstruction. Readmission to the Union for four southern states was delayed until 1870.

the Fifteenth amendment adopted by Congress could have been ratified without the approval of some southern states. Congress knew the South would not vote for these amendments. So ratification became part of its Reconstruction plan. Any state seeking to be readmitted to the Union first had to ratify the Fourteenth Amendment.

Congress went on to pass a set of Reconstruction acts, all of them over the veto of President Johnson. The most important act divided the South into five military districts, each directed by a general of the Union army. The generals were given the power to see that new state governments were formed. They could hire or fire state officials and decide who had the right to vote. While blacks could vote, many leading Confederates could not.

The Impeachment Trial

Led by the Radical Republicans, Congress was now in full control. Some of the laws it passed may have been unconstitutional. But no case calling those laws into question was ever brought before the Supreme Court. President Johnson kept vetoing Congress's bills, and Congress kept overriding his veto. For a time it seemed as though the constitutional system of checks and balances no longer worked.

As a final display of power, Congress tried to remove President Johnson from office in 1868. According to the Constitution, Congress can remove a President for misconduct. This misconduct is defined as treason, bribery, or "other high crimes and misdemeanors."

In such cases the House of Representatives impeaches, or agrees to bring charges against, the President. The Senate serves as jury and the Chief Justice of the Supreme Court as judge.

The House voted to impeach Johnson before holding either a formal hearing or a debate. The House drew up eleven charges against the President. All were flimsy. None had anything to do with

President Andrew Johnson was handed a summons (left) to be tried by the Senate on eleven counts. Spectators needed tickets to attend the trial.

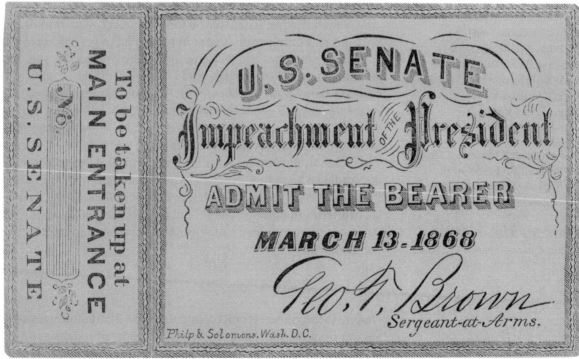

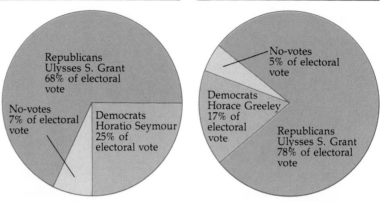

Election of 1868

Republicans
Ulysses S. Grant
68% of electoral
vote

No-votes
7% of electoral
vote

Democrats
Horatio Seymour
25% of
electoral vote

Election of 1872

No-votes
5% of electoral
vote

Democrats
Horace Greeley
17% of
electoral
vote

Republicans
Ulysses S. Grant
78% of electoral
vote

Section 2 Review

1. What was Lincoln's plan for restoring the southern states to the Union?

2. Why did the Republicans in Congress believe that only Congress had the right to decide how southern states would be readmitted to the Union?

3. For what four reasons did the Radical Republicans want Congress in charge of Reconstruction?

4. How did the Thirteenth Amendment complete the work of Lincoln's Emancipation Proclamation?

5. What did the Fourteenth Amendment declare?

6. What did the Fifteenth Amendment declare?

7. What issue did the Congress use as an excuse to impeach President Johnson?

Critical Thinking

8. **Recognizing Ideologies.** How did the political beliefs of the Radical Republicans affect their actions?

LOOKING AHEAD: How did Reconstruction change the South?

treason, bribery, or high crimes and misdemeanors. Eight charges were based on a single action by President Johnson—his firing of Secretary of War Edwin M. Stanton. This action, the Congress claimed, was illegal.

The Stanton issue arose over the Tenure of Office Act—a law passed by Congress over Johnson's veto. The law barred the President from firing certain federal officers without the Senate's permission. President Johnson believed this law was unconstitutional. In fact, many years later, in 1926, the Supreme Court declared the law unconstitutional. But when Johnson fired Stanton, who favored the Radical Republicans, the House of Representatives used the firing as an excuse to impeach the President.

The trial in the Senate ran on for more than two months. It was like a hit play or movie; everyone in town tried to get a ticket to see it. Though no crimes and misdemeanors were proved, the vote was breathtakingly close. A two-thirds majority of the Senate was needed to convict the President. The Radicals failed by just one vote to get the needed two-thirds majority. Seven Republicans, certain that the charges were not supported by fact, voted against their party. None of the seven was reelected.

Johnson finished his term of office in 1869. Ulysses S. Grant, the leading Union general in the Civil War, followed Johnson as President. Grant ran as a Republican in the election of 1868. During his two terms in office he backed the congressional plan for Reconstruction, putting an end to the conflict between the Congress and the President.

3   The South Under Reconstruction

Despite the harsh terms of Reconstruction the South slowly began to recover from the war. Most southern states reorganized their governments, even in the face of turmoil. More people—whites as well as blacks—received the right to vote. More people qualified for public office. Tax-supported schools were begun or improved. Roads, bridges, and railways were repaired and extended. States also opened hospitals and offered other needed services. Farmers slowly began to produce even more than they had before the war.

But Reconstruction also had its failures. Industry in the South grew very slowly. Some political officeholders cheated the citizens. And though black people made important gains, they were seldom treated as the equals of whites.

Blacks in Southern Governments

Blacks—some of them former slaves—held political offices in the Reconstruction governments of the South. Two blacks, both from Mississippi, served in the United States Senate. Hiram K. Revels, who served in the Senate for one year, filled the seat once held by Jefferson Davis, the former president of the Confederacy. The other, former slave Blanche K. Bruce, served a full six-year term. Fourteen blacks were also elected to the House of Representatives. Six of them came from South Carolina, where black voters outnumbered white voters for a short time.

Blacks served as lieutenant governors in several southern states. They also held such state offices as secretary of state, state treasurer, speaker of the house, and superintendent of education. Many served in state legislatures. Blacks also took part in the conventions that drew up new state constitutions. And many played important parts in their local communities.

Some southern whites criticized blacks who held state and local offices. They accused them of cheating and claimed that the blacks were tools of the northern Republicans. But the record shows that most blacks used their political power to make independent choices. Some blacks, going against the Republicans, favored restoring political rights to former Confederates. Once their own rights were made sure, a group of South Carolina blacks said, "We will ask no further protection from the Federal Government, for then united with our white friends in the South we will be able to secure for ourselves every desired or desirable means of prosperity."

Unlike southerners, northerners did not elect a single black person to Congress or to a major state office during Reconstruction.

Corruption: South and North

Throughout Reconstruction the Republican party controlled the South. Joining the blacks who held political office were so-called carpetbaggers and scalawags. Carpetbaggers were northerners who went south looking for new ways to earn a living. Some of them were elected to political office. Others worked for the Freedmen's

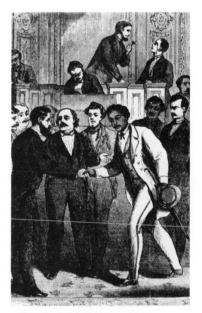

John W. Menard of Louisiana, first black representative, was welcomed to the House but never served there because his election was challenged.

435 ❧

Bureau, taught in the new schools, or set up businesses. Scalawags were southerners who worked together with freed slaves and favored congressional Reconstruction.

Though most carpetbaggers and scalawags were honest, hardworking people, the few who were corrupt gave a bad name to all. They took bribes from railroads that were in search of land on which to build rail lines. They also accepted money to vote for laws that favored certain businesses.

The North also had crooked officials. None of the southern governments matched the double-dealing that went on in New York City. A political leader called Boss Tweed controlled the politics of the city and the state. He laid away millions of dollars, using the taxpayers' money for his own gain or for that of his friends. He used his power to fake street repairs or to have the city buy overpriced goods from him. At the federal level, businesses and individuals were able to bribe northern officers to keep them from collecting taxes. Some firms that the government hired to sell goods to the Native Americans took the money and delivered either low-grade stock or nothing at all. Some members of Congress accepted favors for granting federal money to businesses and railroads.

Perhaps the most serious threat of lawlessness came with the appearance of the Ku Klux Klan and other secret groups in 1865. Through such bands southern whites hoped to regain control of their states. They used force or the threat of force against black voters. In 1871 alone 163 blacks were murdered in one Florida county. Some 300 blacks were murdered around New Orleans.

The Election of 1876

The question of who would govern the South surfaced in the national election of 1876. Graft and corruption in Grant's administration had hurt the Republican party. To save its reputation, the party named Rutherford B. Hayes—a man known for his honesty—for the Presidency. The Democrats nominated Samuel J. Tilden, who had taken steps to break up the Boss Tweed ring.

When the electoral ballots were counted, Tilden won 184 of the needed 185 votes. Hayes received 165 votes. Twenty other electoral votes, nineteen from three southern states, were in question.

An electoral commission was set up to settle the dispute. It was made up of five members from the House of Representatives, five from the Senate, and five from the Supreme Court. Seven commission members were Democrats and eight were Republicans. The commission, by a vote of eight to seven, gave Hayes all the disputed ballots. Republican Hayes was elected President.

For a time it seemed that the Democrats in Congress might not accept the ruling of the commission. In the end they agreed, but only

Election of 1876

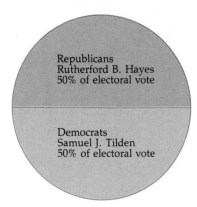

Republicans
Rutherford B. Hayes
50% of electoral vote

Democrats
Samuel J. Tilden
50% of electoral vote

This 1870 cartoon (left) illustrates the South's argument against Reconstruction. Some southerners resorted to criminal action and lynched blacks, carpetbaggers, and scalawags.

in return for certain favors. Hayes was to choose at least one southerner for his cabinet. Federal money was to be spent on improvements in the southern states. And Hayes was to pull all federal troops out of the South.

The Results of Reconstruction

Hayes kept his word and removed the federal troops from the South. This act marked the end of Reconstruction. The Democratic party once again controlled the vote of the "solid South." For decades to come a Republican could not hope to be elected there. State laws that by-passed the new constitutional amendments kept black people in most parts of the South from voting and holding office. Keeping whites and blacks separated became a way of life.

Historians still argue over Reconstruction. Some believe that Radical Reconstruction had been a mistake and a failure. They point to the continued ill will between North and South and between whites and blacks as the main fault in Reconstruction. Other historians hold that much of the work of Reconstruction was destroyed after 1877. Still others stress the advances—the efforts to help the freed slaves and to restore the economic life of the South. They point to the Fourteenth and Fifteenth amendments on which significant civil rights actions in the mid-1900s were based. These historians believe that Reconstruction introduced important social reforms. Though halted for a time after 1877, these social reforms were picked up again later and carried out.

Certainly Reconstruction left deep wounds. The entire South was condemned to poverty for almost a century. The blacks lost the rights they had so painfully acquired. At times Reconstruction promoted lawlessness.

Slowly these wounds healed. When southern-born Woodrow Wilson became President many years later, in 1914, he said: "I yield to no one . . . in love for the South. But *because* I love the South, I rejoice in the failure of the Confederacy. . . ."

Section 3 Review

1. What part did blacks play in southern governments during Reconstruction? In northern governments?
2. Who were carpetbaggers and scalawags?
3. What was the purpose of the Ku Klux Klan?
4. What three demands did Democrats in Congress make before they accepted the electoral commission's decision in 1876?
5. What were some of the failures and successes of Reconstruction?

Critical Thinking

6. **Testing Conclusions.** Do you agree with President Wilson's conclusion that: " . . . *because* I love the South, I rejoice in the failure of the Confederacy . . ." Why or why not?

Blanche K. Bruce and Thaddeus Stevens served the country as public officials committed to their ideals.

As a young lawyer, Stevens had defended many runaway slaves.

Uncompromising Views

After his election to the House in 1848, Stevens strongly fought Clay's Compromise of 1850 on the grounds that it favored the South. He spoke against members of Congress who were from the South. He called them slave drivers.

After Lincoln's election in 1860, Stevens warned the southern states not to leave the Union. He said, "Our next United States will contain no foot of ground on which a slave can tread, no breath of air which a slave can breathe." His speeches against the South became so critical that his friends in the House once had to form a circle around him to protect him from the southern members of Congress.

During the Civil War Stevens held a key position in the House of Representatives. He saw nothing wrong in the arrest of many

During Reconstruction the first black elected to the United States Senate for a full term was Blanche Kelso Bruce. He represented the state of Mississippi. Almost 100 years passed before a second black was elected to the Senate.

The election of blacks to public office was made possible in part by Thaddeus Stevens, Radical Republican leader in the House.

Outspoken Stevens

Stevens was born in Vermont in 1792. He and his four brothers came from a poor family. Thaddeus was a good student in school. With hard work Stevens became a lawyer and settled in Pennsylvania.

Stevens became a leading, but outspoken, public figure in Pennsylvania. His foes, and sometimes his friends, were frightened by his strong and critical language in debates. Stevens believed in high tariffs, federal money for railroads and highways, and a national bank. He disliked slavery and believed it should be brought to an end.

Senator Bruce favored restoring the vote to white ex-Confederates.

People

southerners and the taking of their property, including slaves. He favored stiff punishment for most southerners and death for some.

Stevens believed the South was a small, defeated part of the country that was properly under the control of the federal government. He also believed that the Republican party had to remain in power. Only in this way, he thought, could the country be sure of long life for such Republican measures as high tariffs, homesteads in the West, and federal aid to railroads.

Stevens championed voting rights for freed slaves. With those rights finally granted, the way was cleared for the election of Blanche Kelso Bruce to the United States Senate.

Senator Blanche K. Bruce

Bruce was born a slave in Virginia in 1841. He moved to Missouri as a youngster. He attended Oberlin College in Ohio for two years. In 1868 he became a planter in Floreyville, Mississippi. He also served in county offices in that state. Then he was elected to the United States Senate in 1874 where he served a full term from 1875 to 1881.

A Cold Welcome

On his first day in the Senate Bruce was not warmly welcomed. Usually new senators taking the oath of office are accompanied by the senior senator from their state. As Senator Bruce started up the aisle, the senior senator from Mississippi, James Alcorn, remained in his seat. So Bruce walked alone toward the front of the room.

When Bruce was halfway up the aisle, a tall man came up to him. "Excuse me, Mr. Bruce, I didn't see that you were without an escort. Permit me. My name is Conkling." Senator Roscoe Conkling of New York linked arms with Bruce, and the two marched up the aisle together so that Bruce could take the oath of office.

Senator Bruce favored increasing business between the states. He worked for the improvement of the Mississippi River for the transport

Conkling befriended Bruce.

of goods and people. He also tried to end election fraud.

Champion for Minorities

Senator Bruce was most effective in working for civil rights. He spoke out for the rights of blacks, Native Americans, and other minority peoples. When a law to stop Chinese immigration into the United States was discussed in the Senate, he spoke against it. He declared, "Mr. President, . . . representing as I do a people who but a few years ago were considered essentially disqualified from enjoying the privileges . . . of American citizenship . . . I shall vote against this bill."

When congressional Reconstruction ended in Mississippi, blacks were once again kept from voting. Bruce spent his remaining years in several minor government posts, filled by Presidential appointment rather than election.

The influence of both Stevens and Bruce was brief. Their goal of equal rights for blacks was hard to reach. Stevens had helped make it possible for Bruce to be elected. But prejudice would keep other black leaders out of Congress for many years to come.

Just after the war many blacks exercised their new right to vote.

Chapter 22 Review

Chapter Summary

Reconstruction lasted from 1865 to 1877. Presidents Lincoln and Johnson favored a "soft" plan regarding the readmittance of the Confederate states to the Union. Congress, led by Radical Republicans, favored a harsher policy to punish the South and its leaders. Overriding President Johnson's vetoes, Congress passed its plan, which included the Fourteenth and Fifteenth amendments.

Following the war, newly freed Southern slaves were unable to find jobs. They could not afford to buy land. They became tenant farmers or, more often, sharecroppers. Black codes limited their freedom. Reconstruction policies in the South were carried out by northern carpetbaggers and by southerners called scalawags.

In the presidential election of 1876, disputed electoral votes left both candidates without enough votes for election. In return for congressional support, Hayes agreed to remove federal troops from the South. When Hayes became President in 1877 he honored the agreement and Reconstruction came to an end.

Reviewing Vocabulary

Choose the word that best completes each sentence. Write your answers on a separate sheet of paper.

1. None of the impeachment charges against President Johnson mentioned treason, (*prejudice/bribery*), or high crimes and misdemeanors.
2. The dispute that arose from the election of 1876 was decided by an electoral (*vote/commission*).
3. The Republican party was hurt by the (*fraud/corruption*) in government during Grant's administration.

4. A (*sharecropper/tenant farmer*) rented land and paid the landlord at the end of the season.
5. Life for blacks in southern cities was harsh because of (*grafts/black codes*) that limited their freedom.
6. Senator Blanche K. Bruce worked to end (*fraud/prejudice*) in elections and to gain civil rights for blacks.
7. For most blacks in the South, life as a (*sharecropper/tenant farmer*) was little better than slavery.
8. Charges of (*graft/bribery*) were made against Grant's administration.
9. As blacks moved into cities, they faced increasing (*prejudice/fraud*) in the North and in the South.

Understanding Main Ideas

1. How did life for Southern blacks and whites change after Lee's surrender at Appomattox?
2. What were the issues during Reconstruction that led to conflicts between Congress and the President?
3. What changes occurred in the South during Reconstruction?

Critical Thinking Skills

1. **Recognizing Cause and Effect.** How did the attempt to remove Johnson from office strengthen our system of government?
2. **Demonstrating Reasoned Judgment.** Historians have different opinions about the results of Reconstruction. Which of the views do you find most convincing? Explain your reasons.
3. **Checking Consistency.** Did President Hayes's favors to congressional Democrats mirror Radical Republican goals?

Social Studies Skills: Interpreting a Map

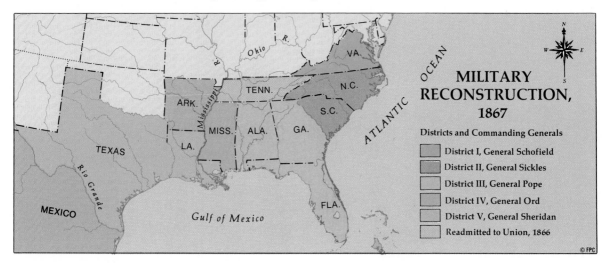

Study the map on this page. It shows the military districts into which the South was divided in 1867.

Skill Review: Based on the map, decide whether each statement below is true (T), false (F), or unknown (U). A statement is unknown if the information on the map fails to prove the statement is either true or false.

1. The South was divided into five military districts.
2. Each former Confederate state was part of a military district.
3. General Pope was a commander in the Civil War.
4. General Sheridan was in charge of military operations in District V.
5. Tennessee had been readmitted and was not part of a military district.
6. Alabama, Arkansas, and Mississippi were part of District IV.
7. The last of the federal troops were withdrawn from Georgia, North Carolina, Mississippi, and Arkansas in 1877.
8. District I only included Virginia.

Writing About History

Writing a Diary. Imagine that you are a senator the night before the vote on the charges against President Andrew Johnson. In your diary, write how you intend to vote and the reasons behind your decision. Do you support the congressional plan for Reconstruction? Do you feel the charges against Johnson are unfounded? How do you think your vote is going to affect the country?

Your Region in History

Geography. The Civil War divided the United States in half, setting neighbors and even family members against one another. What side did your region support? Was your region an active participant in the hostilities? Summarize the contributions and the sacrifices that your community made during the Civil War. Does any evidence of the role your region played exist today?

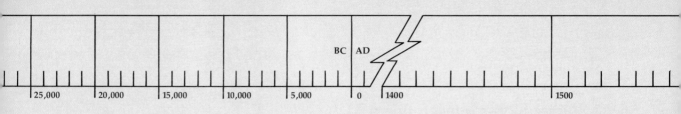

The Last Frontier

✤ Chapter 23

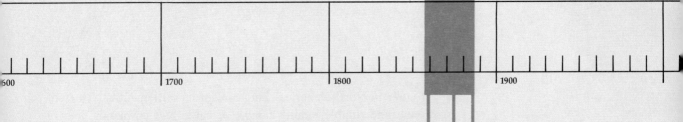

DON'T STOP THE GAME. PAGE FENCE WILL STOP THEM.

Vocabulary

frontier	massacre
deposit	reservation
claim	roundup
bison	longhorn
grassland	trail
warrior	range

Prereading

1. How did miners contribute to the settlement of the last frontier?
2. What changes did white settlement of the last frontier bring to Native Americans?
3. How did the cattle industry influence the settlement of the Great Plains?
4. How did farmers change the Great Plains into a settled territory?

EVEN AS THE WAR between the North and South raged, people continued to move west. Since the founding of the first English settlement, there had always been a frontier—largely unsettled land. The last frontier was the middle country that lay between the Missouri River to the east, California and Oregon to the west, Canada to the north, and the Gulf of Mexico to the south. This broad, open land was called the Great Plains–Rocky Mountain region.

People had crossed the Plains to settle in California, Oregon, and Utah. And they had put down roots in parts of Texas. But for the most part the Plains had been a place to pass through, not a place to stop. Unlike the Eastern Woodlands and the Far West, the Plains were dry. Some maps even called parts of the Plains "the great American desert." Trees were few. Tall buffalo grass spread as far as the eye could see. Beyond the Plains in several directions were the steep, treacherous Rocky Mountains.

Different Native American groups had lived in parts of the Great Plains for centuries. In the middle to late 1800s the Great Plains–Rocky Mountain area attracted other settlers—those seeking adventure, fortune, or land. Except for Alaska, it was the nation's last

443

frontier in North America. The story of its settlement is a story of rough and tumble mining camps, of cattle and cowhands, and of struggling farmers. It is also a story of the end of a way of life for the Native Americans of the Great Plains.

1 The Miners

Between 1858 and 1876 thousands of people migrated into the land that is now the states of Montana, Idaho, Wyoming, the Dakotas, Nevada, Colorado, and Arizona. Most were not looking for rich farmland or well-watered grazing land. They were searching for precious metals—gold and silver.

So-called gold fever brought a fortune to a few people and disappointment to many. But the rush to mine precious metals proved that there was great wealth under the land that many believed to be worthless. And the mining camps left behind some settlements that became thriving, present-day towns and cities.

Pike's Peak or Bust

The gold strike of 1848 lured thousands of settlers to California. By the late 1850s the best diggings there had been claimed. Gold seekers began to look elsewhere. Two of them—Captain John Beck, a Cherokee, and W. Green Russell of Georgia—led some miners to the Pike's Peak area of Colorado. In the summer of 1858, near what is now Denver, they found small amounts of gold. The word spread like fire on dry prairie grass. By the spring of 1859 the rush was on. The *St. Louis News* reported:

> It is astonishing how rapidly we learn geography. A short time since, we hardly knew, and didn't care, whether . . . Pike's was in Kansas or Kamchatka. . . . Now Americans hear of nothing, dream of nothing but Pike's Peak. . . . It seems that every man, woman, and child . . . is moving Pike's Peakward.

More than 100,000 people set off for Colorado, many with signs saying "Pike's Peak or Bust." Some travelers gave up before reaching Colorado. Half of those who finished the trip soon returned home. Merchants, eager to make money off of the settlers, had misled them with success stories. Most gold deposits were mined out.

Yet thousands of people remained. Some kept hunting for gold and silver in Colorado. Others took up work in Denver, a town that sprang up almost overnight to house the many newcomers.

More towns—Boulder, Canon City, Pueblo—were started in other parts of Colorado. Pike's Peak turned out to be a bust for most gold hunters. But its lure had helped settle the territory. In 1876 Colorado entered the Union as a state.

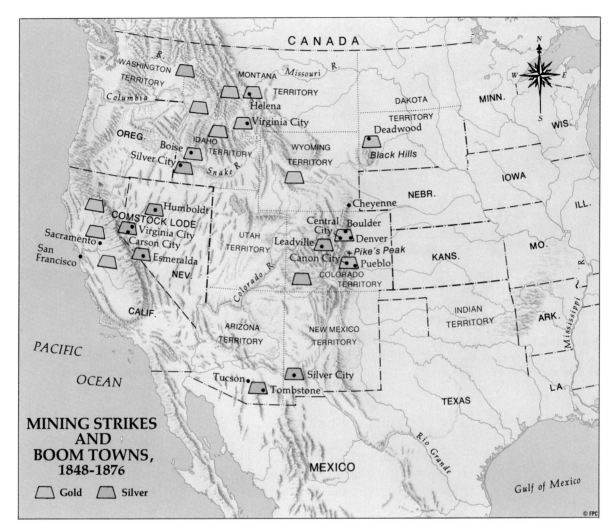

MINING STRIKES
AND
BOOM TOWNS,
1848-1876

☐ Gold ☐ Silver

Mining Towns

Denver and many later mining camps had similar beginnings. Thousands of people rushed into an area. A town sprang up, usually on land belonging to the government or to Native Americans. Miners and small business owners arrived first. Gamblers and outlaws often followed, looking for quick, sometimes dishonest, ways to make money. Saloons and gambling halls lined the streets, and lawlessness became a part of everyday life.

The people of the town usually made their own laws—and practiced frontier justice. Outlaws found guilty at trials were often hung immediately. Other lawbreakers got the message and left town as soon as possible.

When the gold and silver ran out, some towns remained and prospered. Denver and Boulder in Colorado, Tucson and Tombstone

The discovery of gold in California brought a flood of prospectors to the West. The gold seekers then began working their way back east.

Deadwood City was the last of the big boom towns brought into being by the discovery of gold.

in Arizona, Virginia City in Nevada, and Deadwood and Custer City in South Dakota are a few of the many living monuments to the mining days.

The Comstock Lode

One group of disappointed California gold miners decided to try their luck on the eastern side of the Sierra Nevada Mountains. In 1859 two partners found a rich deposit of gold and silver in present-day Nevada. They were soon joined by Henry T. P. Comstock. Other miners called Comstock the laziest man at the diggings, but he talked himself into a successful partnership. He spoke so often about "his" claim that the discovery became known as the Comstock Lode. A lode is a deposit of ores laid down in the cracks between rocks. The Comstock Lode was the richest deposit in the United States.

Once again news of the gold and silver strike spread like wildfire. Once again thousands of people rushed in, this time to Nevada. A settlement of caves, tents, and saloons grew into Virginia City. The writer Mark Twain described Virginia City as the liveliest town that the nation produced in so short a time. Sidewalks swarmed with people. The stream of wagons, carts, buggies, and other vehicles filling the streets seemed endless. Twain wrote that money-getting plans "were seething in every brain."

Individuals and partners laid thousands of claims throughout the Nevada territory, but less than a dozen turned a profit. These few profits, however, were beyond belief—more than $15 million within four years.

In 1873 a group of miners calling themselves the Consolidated Virginia Company brought in heavy digging machinery. As they dug deeper, they found that the rich lode widened. At a depth of more than 1,100 feet (330 m) they found the Big Bonanza, an area 54 feet (16.2 m) wide loaded with gold and silver ore. This rich find brought a profit of about $200 million.

Gold in the Black Hills

Nothing matched the Comstock Lode, but other discoveries kept gold seekers searching around the western half of the country looking for new finds. A mining boom in Arizona in 1862 gave life to the town of Tucson. And a series of gold and silver strikes led people into Idaho and Montana in the 1860s. The final big strike was made in the Black Hills of the Dakota Territory.

The Black Hills area was occupied by the Sioux. Federal troops were stationed there to keep white settlers out of the territory. As the gold fever grew, the army sent in an expedition of soldiers and scientists. Government leaders thought they could avoid conflict between the Sioux and white settlers by proving that there was no gold in the Black Hills. But the group, led by Lt. Col. George A. Custer in the summer of 1874, found just the opposite. The territory contained rich gold deposits.

And so the rush began. Again and again miners tried to enter the territory. Again and again federal troops chased them out. Finally the soldiers gave up. In October 1875 they allowed the miners to go in and risk conflict with the Sioux. By 1876, Deadwood, the last of the "wild west" towns, had a population of 7,000. It quickly became known as the "wickedest" mining settlement of all, the home of such colorful characters as Wild Bill Hickok, Poker Alice, Calamity Jane, California Jack, and Deadwood Dick—a former slave.

After the Black Hills rush, the days of the mining booms ended. There were still rich deposits of gold, silver, and other useful ores throughout the West. But mining began to enter a new phase. Large mining companies that could afford costly digging equipment took over. The day of the lone prospector who carried all he needed on the back of a mule had ended.

2 Native Americans of the West

Before the Civil War Native Americans of the Great Plains were generally left in peace by incoming settlers. These few white pioneers believed that the Plains lacked fertile soil and were similar to "the desert of Siberia."

The Native Americans knew better. Though the Plains were dry, they supported plentiful animal life: jackrabbits, prairie dogs,

Calamity Jane, as Martha Jane Canary was nicknamed, was expert in handling horses and guns.

Section 1 Review

1. When did the gold rush to Pike's Peak begin?
2. What was the name of the deposit of precious metals that turned out be the richest in the United States?
3. Why did federal troops try to keep miners out of the Black Hills?

Critical Thinking

4. **Drawing Conclusions.** How did mining change after the Black Hills boom?

LOOKING AHEAD: What changes did white settlement of the last frontier bring to Native Americans?

antelope, coyotes, and above all, bison. The American bison, often called buffalo, thrived on the Plains. Great herds of them, numbering in the millions, wandered about the grasslands.

Mounted Hunters

Many different Native American groups lived in the Great Plains–Rocky Mountain area. Among those to the north were the Sioux, Blackfeet, Crow, Cheyenne, and Arapaho (ə·rap′ə·hō′). To the south were the Comanche, Kiowa (ki′ə·wô′), Ute (yo͞ot), Southern Cheyenne, Apache, and Navaho.

The Spanish had brought the horse to the Americas hundreds of years earlier. By the mid-nineteenth century the tribal groups on the Plains had become skilled and daring riders. They hunted bison by surrounding a running herd and shooting the animals with lances and arrows. The young men of a tribe, mounted on swift horses, did the killing. Older men as well as women and children followed on foot. They would skin the animal and cut up the meat.

Many Plains groups wandered from place to place, following the herds of bison. Their way of life was built around this magnificent animal, which was their main source of food. They also made clothing and tents, or tepees, from bison hides. The tepees were easy to take down and to pack for moving.

Their way of life made the Native Americans of the Plains hard to fight. They had no crops to destroy and no permanent villages to burn. They could move quickly to avoid attack.

The Native Americans of the Plains were also skillful riders and warriors. A settler armed with a single-shot rifle was no match for a mounted hunter. Until the invention of the repeating rifle and the Colt revolver, a fast-moving Sioux, Cheyenne, or Comanche— armed with a bow and arrows or a lance—had the advantage.

Native Americans of the Plains followed the bison as the herds moved from place to place.

What Custer thought was a gathering of about 1,000 hostile Native Americans at Little Big Horn was actually a meeting of about 2,500 to 5,000 warriors. Custer and his whole troop were killed when they attacked the camp.

Wars of Desperation

The government had made treaties promising the Native Americans trouble-free use of the land "as long as the waters run." But the gold fever and growing interest in land for cattle grazing and farming led to broken promises and forgotten treaties. Miners paid little attention to the rights of Native Americans as they settled into an area. When ranchers and farmers arrived later, they often asked federal soldiers to protect them. With the soldiers' help settlers often took the land of the Native Americans.

The Native Americans fought back. Typical of the terrible warfare was the Sand Creek Massacre of 1864. A group of volunteer militia in eastern Colorado attacked a band of peaceful Cheyenne whom federal troops were supposed to protect. The militia killed more than 450 men, women, and children. News of the massacre reached other tribal groups, and soon the Plains became a battlefield. The Cheyenne, Sioux, and others went on the warpath.

There were massacres on both sides. Both attacked and brutally killed women and children as well as fighters. Federal troops stationed in western forts sometimes tried to keep peace. But more often they became the chief enemy of the Native Americans. In June 1876, Lt. Col. Custer and his entire command of 264 soldiers were wiped out by the Sioux at the Battle of Little Big Horn.

The Native Americans had many great leaders, among them Red Cloud of the Sioux, Sitting Bull and Crazy Horse of the Teton-Dakota, Geronimo of the Apache, and Chief Joseph of the Nez

449

Percé. But even such leaders could not protect them as one by one the tribal groups were forced to live on reservations.

Another blow was the killing of the bison. White hunters slaughtered the beasts by the thousands, skinning them for their hides. William F. Cody earned the nickname Buffalo Bill after killing more than 4,000 of the animals in about a year and a half. In the 1850s some 20 million bison roamed the Great Plains. By 1883 the herds had been largely destroyed.

With the bison gone, a way of life for the Native Americans of the Plains had ended. Slowly the tribal groups were moved to small reservations. There they settled down to live poorly on government supplies, never again to hunt the bison on the open plains.

The Five Tribes

Some Native Americans of the Plains were given reservations in western Oklahoma in what was called Indian Territory. Already living in this territory were the five tribal groups moved there from the Southeast in the 1830s—the Cherokee, Creek, Choctaw, Chickasaw, and Seminole. After their forced move these groups had adapted to their new home. Many became farmers, ranchers, and small business owners. They printed newspapers in their own languages. They also ran their own schools.

During the Civil War most of the Five Tribes had favored the South. After the war the federal government punished the Five Tribes by forcing them to sell part of their land. At first the territory was used as reservations for some Plains groups. It was later opened to white settlers and called Oklahoma Territory.

As whites continued to move west, settlers pressured the federal government into opening additional parts of Indian Territory. The Five Tribes had to sell all their land to the government. Finally Congress opened nearly 2 million acres of this land to new settlement. The land was divided into 160-acre (64 ha) homesteads. Settlers could claim these homesteads—and smaller town plots—on a first come, first served basis beginning April 22, 1889.

On that day 100,000 land-hungry settlers gathered along the edge of the territory. They waited for the gun to sound at noon as a sign of the official opening. When the shot was fired, they all rushed in—on horseback, in wagons and carriages, on foot, and even on bicycles. Trains carried hundreds more people.

Within a few hours the territory was completely settled. Oklahoma City came into being instantly with 10,000 people. Guthrie had nearly 15,000. More Oklahoma land was opened to settlement in the 1890s. By 1907 half a million people lived in what by then had become the state of Oklahoma. Members of the Five Tribes were confined to their own 160-acre (64 ha) plots of land.

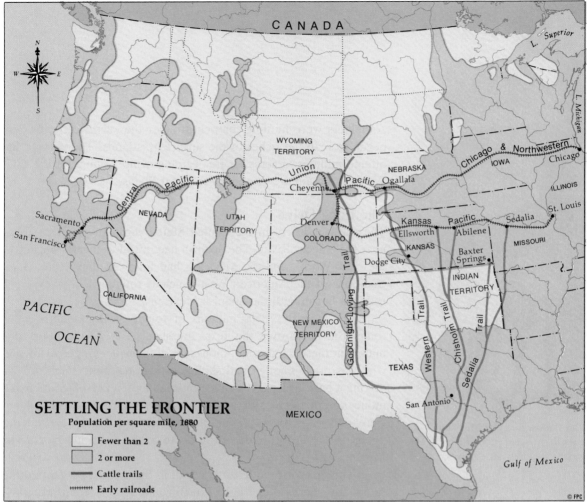

Once completed, the railroad became the focus of most western life.

The Dawes Act

The standing of Native Americans in the United States changed with the passing of the Dawes Act of 1887. Under this act the tribal leaders could no longer speak for the group in dealings with the government. The government would look on Native Americans only as individuals, not as groups. Tribal lands were divided into 160-acre (64 ha) plots for each adult head of a family. Unmarried persons and children got smaller plots. After a period of twenty-five years Native Americans were to become full citizens of the United States.

Those in favor of the Dawes Act believed it would help bring the Native Americans into United States society. But the act led to problems. Some Native Americans did begin to blend in with their white neighbors. But others resisted, trying to keep their tribal ways alive. Much of the land the Native Americans received was not fertile, and much of it was bought by white settlers.

In 1924 Congress finally gave full citizenship to all Native Americans in the United States. In the end these people had gained a country but lost a continent.

Section 2 Review

1. Name five Native American groups that lived in the Rocky Mountain–Great Plains area.
2. How did the horse change the life of groups on the Plains?
3. Why was the bison so important to the Native Americans?
4. What happened to the Five Tribes after 1889?

Critical Thinking

5. **Recognizing Cause and Effect.** What problems did the Dawes Act cause for Native Americans?

LOOKING AHEAD: How did the cattle industry influence the settlement of the Great Plains?

3   Cattle and Cowhands

As miners were hunting for riches under the earth, cattle owners began to reap the riches of the surface grasslands. The wide plains offered millions of acres for free cattle grazing. Soon after the Civil War a cattle empire arose on the Great Plains.

The Long Drive

The cattle industry in the United States began in southern Texas near the Nueces River. The Spanish had introduced cattle raising in the New World, and the Mexicans had followed their lead. Many traditions of the American West—such as roundups, cowboys, and rodeos—began with the Spanish-Mexicans.

In the early 1860s millions of tough, wild longhorn cattle roamed in herds over the Texas grasslands. They were fierce animals. But these longhorns—thousands of them—belonged to anyone who was brave enough and skillful enough to round them up. By driving a herd to a point along a railroad line, a person could make money shipping the cattle east to market. By 1865, railroad builders were moving across Missouri toward Kansas. Texans started the "long drives" to bring the cattle north to the new railway stops in Missouri and Kansas.

The first long cattle drive began in the spring of 1866. During the winter, herds of cattle had been rounded up. When the grasslands turned green, cowhands drove their herds north. About 250,000 cattle crossed the Red River in Texas on the way to northern markets that year. Some of the cattle reached Sedalia, Missouri, and were shipped by rail to Chicago. Most were sold to cattle breeders in Kansas, Missouri, and Iowa.

The cowhands faced many problems on the first long drive. Much of the trail led through wooded areas. The cattle, used to the open range, were frightened by the trees. Mad with fear, the animals were more dangerous than ever. Another problem arose when many farmers in Kansas and Missouri tried to keep the herds off their land. They did not want the longhorns trampling their crops. Farmers also were afraid that the cattle might be carrying Texas fever. Such a disease could spread to their own herds. These problems made the long cattle runs "a heap of trouble." But the money to be gained made the work and the worry worthwhile. Longhorns costing $4 to $5 a head in Texas could be sold for $30 to $40 in the North.

By 1867, railroads had reached well into Kansas, making drives farther west possible. A new route, called the Chisholm Trail, led from southern Texas to Abilene, Kansas. This route was set by Joseph G. McCoy, an Illinois meat dealer. He chose Abilene as the trading point and made special deals with the railroads to carry the

Cowhands, like this Mexican caballero, spent many hours in the saddle on long cattle drives.

cattle to Chicago and other cities. In a few years Abilene changed from a sleepy little town to a busy, somewhat lawless cattle stop.

Between 1868 and 1871 nearly a million and a half cattle were shipped through Abilene. As the railroads moved farther west, the cattle trails moved with them, first to Ellsworth, Kansas, then to Dodge City. Farther west still was the Goodnight-Loving Trail, named after trail drivers Charles Goodnight and Oliver Loving. This trail led to the Union Pacific Railroad at Cheyenne, Wyoming. Years later Goodnight declared: "All in all, my years on the Trail were the happiest I ever lived. There were many hardships and dangers but . . . most of the time we were solitary adventurers in a great land as fresh and new as a spring morning. . . ."

The Cowhand's Life

Thousands of books, movies, and television shows have made the American cowhand an exciting figure. For the most part, however, a cowhand's life was hard and filled with dull jobs. Riding the dusty range day after day tired even the hardiest of the hands. For weeks at a time cowhands had to catch quick naps, sleeping with their boots on and using a saddle as a pillow. Their Colt revolvers were never out of reach. And there was always the danger of a stampede. The wild longhorns, frightened by any strange noise, would scatter in all directions, crushing everything in their path.

Much of a cowhand's life was spent doing daily chores on a large Texas ranch. There were no fences between ranches, so the cattle roamed freely during most of the grazing season. To keep cattle on the owner's ranch, cowhands rode all day back and forth along the property lines. Cattle drifting over the rancher's border were driven back. This job was called line driving.

Despite line driving, cattle still drifted from ranch to ranch. The herds became mixed. To return cattle to their rightful owners, ranchers held roundups—usually two a year. In the spring newborn calves would be rounded up for branding. Each ranch had its own brand, a mark that identified the owner. In the fall came the beef roundup, when the ranchers chose the cattle to be driven to market.

All the ranchers in an area joined in the roundup. Each rancher sent a group of cowhands and a chuck wagon with a cook. The cowhands would gather a huge herd of cattle. Then they would separate the cattle by brands. When one herd was separated, the process was repeated with another herd. The roundup lasted for weeks.

Though the rich rancher—the so-called cattle baron—was the ruler of cattle country, the cowhand was its hero. Most hands were young men, often in their teens. About a third of them were blacks or Mexican-Americans. Cowhands worked for room and board and about $40 a month. They carried or wore everything they needed.

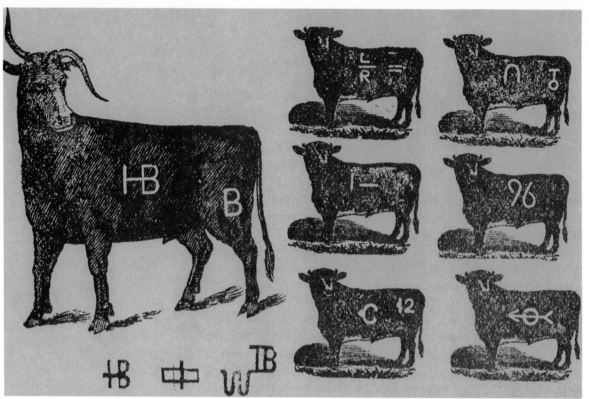

Cattle brands helped cowhands sort out the animals in a herd.

Section 3 Review

1. What was the purpose of a "long drive"?
2. What were two difficulties cowhands had to face while on the trail?
3. What three factors helped end the era of open-range cattle raising in the late 1880s?

Critical Thinking

4. **Making Comparisons.** How did a spring roundup differ from a fall roundup?

LOOKING AHEAD: How did farmers change the Great Plains into a settled territory?

Most precious of all a cowhand's belongings was the saddle. One person commented about a cowhand: "He might sell his gun or his coat or his boots, and he cares nothing how many times he changes his horse. . . .But he will never part with his saddle."

The Changing Cattle Industry

In the late 1860s cattle raising spread into Kansas, Nebraska, Colorado, Wyoming, Montana, and the Dakotas. It even crossed the border into Canada. Northern ranchers bred the Texas longhorns with eastern cattle to produce bigger, stronger animals.

Open-range cattle raising throughout the Plains reached its peak in the mid-1880s. Then, almost as quickly as it started, it came to an end. So many cattle were reaching the market that the prices dropped. Also, the winter of 1885-1886 was so cold that many herds starved or froze. The following summer was hot and dry. Grass withered, and streams dried up. The cattle died of hunger and thirst. The following winter brought savage blizzards and temperatures as low as $-68°$ F ($-56°$ C). Cattle died by the thousands. Some ranchers lost as many as 90 out of 100 animals.

4 The Farmers' Frontier

Open-range cattle raising also declined because more farmers moved into the Plains. Farmers built fences around water holes and fields of crops to keep the roaming herds away. Sometimes there were range wars between cattle owners and farmers.

Even the cattle barons began to fence in land and grow hay crops for winter feed. Many old-time cowhands were saddened by the change. One complained:

> I remember when we sat around the fire the winter through and didn't do a lick of work for five or six months of the year. . . .Now we go on the general roundup, the calf roundup, then comes haying—something that the old-time cowboy never dreamed of—then beef roundup . . .and, after all this, a winter of feeding hay. I tell you, times have changed.

The New Farming Settlers

Miners and cattle ranchers had proved that the Great Plains were not a desert wasteland. The settlers who followed turned the grasslands into farms and towns. They came for the same reasons people settled earlier frontiers—cheap land and a better life. The largest group came from states along the Mississippi River. During the 1870s so many people left this area that all but two states bordering the Mississippi declined in population.

A second large group of settlers were immigrants from Europe. The greatest numbers came from northern Europe. Germans by the thousands settled in Texas, Kansas, Minnesota, Nebraska, and the Dakotas. Farmers from Norway, Sweden, and Denmark usually settled in the northern Plains, especially in Minnesota and the Dakotas. Many thousands of Irish who helped build the western railroads stayed on in the Plains.

A third, somewhat smaller group of settlers came from the southern states. These were blacks—freed slaves who found life impossible in the South after Reconstruction. Many left to escape white cruelty. Others left to find jobs in the West because jobs in the South were so few.

People traveled to the Plains by train, by riverboat, and by stagecoach. Some even walked, pulling their few belongings in small carts. Many southern blacks walked up the Chisholm Trail from Texas to Kansas. Most settlers, however, liked the covered wagon. It served as home until they could build a shelter.

Federal Land Acts

The federal government aided in new settlement. Under the Homestead Act of 1862, for example, any adult could claim a homestead of 160 acres (64 ha) for a fee of only $10. The family could keep the land if they farmed it and lived on it for five years.

Problems developed with the Homestead Act and other land acts. Many acres ended up in the hands of land agents, who then resold them at a high profit. There was also some cheating. One land act stated that the farmer had to build a permanent dwelling on the land to claim the land. One clever fellow built a house on wheels and rented it to settlers for $15 a day. The renters could then honestly say there was a house on the land. The house would be wheeled away the next day and rented to someone else.

Another problem was the size of the homesteads. A farm of 160 acres (64 ha) was large enough for farming in the East. But in the Great Plains, where rainfall was light, farms had to be larger to be successful. Later acts of Congress slowly increased the amount of western land that people could claim.

Farming on the Plains

Plains farmers grew mainly wheat and corn, but they lacked two major resources—trees and water. The few trees in the Plains grew only along rivers and streams. So the farmer had no wood for building houses and fences. Fences were needed to keep farm animals from wandering off and to keep grazing cattle out of the crops. A farmer in DeKalb, Illinois—Joseph F. Glidden—solved the fence problem. Glidden, looking for a cheap way to build a good fence, hit on the idea of twisting wire into strands with sharp edges, or barbs, at regular points. He put his barbed wire on the market in 1874. Before long he was selling hundreds of miles of it every day.

Some farmers could afford to build frame houses with lumber brought in by railroad. Most had to settle for small dwellings made of sod. Sod houses tended to be dreary and uncomfortable inside. Rain often caused the walls or the ceiling to leak.

But farmers welcomed rain for the crops. Snowfall and rainfall in the Great Plains is low—between 10 and 20 inches a year. Before they could live on the Plains, farmers had to have water.

Those lucky enough to have a stream near their land hauled water to their homes in buckets or barrels. Others drilled deep wells and used windmills to pump the water out of the ground. Some people had no source of water other than what they could collect in rain barrels. A dry year—and there were many—could ruin a farmer.

Successful farmers managed in one way or another to get enough water for drinking, cooking, washing, and watering farm animals. But water for the crops was always a problem. A few people irrigated their lands, but most depended on the rains.

Farmers adapted their methods to the dry environment. They developed dry farming. Rain usually came in the summer, when the hot sun and the ever-present winds quickly dried the soil. Farmers learned to turn the soil over after a rain, burying the wet earth under a layer of dry earth. Then the plant roots could soak up the moisture before the soil dried out. Farmers also learned to set their plants far apart so the roots would not be competing for scarce water. Because

With enough rain, settlers can grow abundant crops on the Plains.

of the wide spacing between plants, farms in the Plains had to be larger than those in the East.

Wheat, a form of grass, was the most successful dry-farming crop. But because the farms were large and all the soil had to be turned after each rain, the farmers needed machines. Heavy farm equipment was being built in the East where an age of machines was dawning. New machinery for farming helped turn the Great Plains into a breadbasket for the nation.

Miners and cattle ranchers played their part in settling the Great Plains. But year after year the farmers faced the wild middle country—nearly half of what was then the United States—and tamed it. They struggled against the heat of the summers and the bitter cold of the winters. They lived through dry seasons when their crops died and great clouds of dust blew over the Plains for days and even weeks at a time. In some years they watched as swarms of grasshoppers—millions and millions of them—darkened the sky and ate everything in their path.

Some settlers gave up. They could not face the hardships and the loneliness of living month after month without seeing a single neighbor. Others stayed on in the Great Plains, closing the nation's last frontier.

Section 4 Review

1. From what three areas did the farmers who settled the Great Plains in the 1870s come?
2. Why did many southern blacks settle in the Plains?
3. How did the Homestead Act encourage settlement of the Great Plains?
4. What two needs made farming difficult for people on the Plains? How did the invention of barbed wire solve one of these problems?

Critical Thinking

5. **Drawing Conclusions.** Why was dry farming so important in the Plains?

Heritage   Of the Frontier

The frontier experience has helped shape the unique character of the United States.

Historian Frederick Jackson Turner believed that the frontier was the single most important influence in the nation's history. He defined the frontier as the leading edge of the westward advance of white settlement. On the frontier, said Turner, white society renewed itself by being born again and again.

The Frontier Life Cycle

The process of rebirth on the frontier had a cycle of its own. First came the white traders who lived among Native Americans. They exchanged clothing, tools, and beads for hides and furs. Their life was dangerous. Traders rarely put down roots to build a house or raise a family. They were the link between the Native Americans of the Plains and Rockies and the whites who were always moving westward.

Ranchers: Stage Two

The traders were followed by people who would live in the wilds of the new frontier. Sometimes these people were called ranchers. Ranchers built rough dwellings with dirt floors to house their families. Sometimes they cleared a few acres to plant garden crops. But more often they lived off a few pigs and the game they could kill with a hunting rifle. Ranchers moved often to the next frontier, always expecting to find more game animals, better soil, and a place apart from other white settlers.

Farmers: The Final Stages

After the ranchers came the farmers. These farmers were often too poor to buy land. By planting a few crops, they might raise enough money to buy a few tools. They tried to get ahead by improving the land and by building a cabin and sometimes sheds to house tools or grain. Some pioneer farmers moved more than six times in their lives, always hoping to better themselves.

As the pioneer farmers moved on, settled farmers—those with money to buy land and with animals and seed—moved in. These farm families built homes and turned any cabins already on the land into corn bins. Most of all, these farmers were certain to get proper title to the land. Together a number of farm families formed a community. They built sawmills and grain mills, set up schools and churches, and started businesses.

This last step completed the cycle of settlement. Society was

Ranchers (left, above) built cabins to satisfy their most immediate needs. Settled farmers (left below) bought land and built permanent homes.

born again in the process, said Turner.

The American Spirit

Turner believed that this cycle of white settlement on the frontier gave rise to what he called the "American spirit." People living in the wild country away from others were inventive and independent. Individualism—the belief that the well-being of each person was more important than the well-being of the group—flourished. All peoples on the frontier were equal. Their advantages were based solely on their ability. Turner believed the frontier taught self-rule and strengthened democracy. The frontier also furthered ideals— mainly a faith in better things to come. In Turner's view the frontier experience made the United States different from all other nations.

Other Views

Other students of history look at the frontier differently. Some see that each frontier has its own heritage. For example, the songs of the cowhands on the Great Plains are part of one tradition. So are the dances of the Hopi. Some historians today also point to the mixed heritage of the frontier—the exchange of folkways between the white settlers and the Native Americans they met in their move west. Each group—settler and Native American, cowhand and farmer—left its lasting mark.

Equally important, some historians say, are the other events and people that shaped the United States and its ways of life. People coming from Africa, Europe, Asia, and other continents flooded into the new country, bringing with them their different cultures and talents. The factory worker as well as the farmer, the city dweller as well as frontier folk, people of the East and people of the West—all these and many more have left their mark on society in the United States. The frontier was only one part of the nation's heritage that shaped its history.

But Turner's idea is basic in the study of history. He saw that different people coming to one place—the frontier—at a certain time made history. He understood the important links among time, place, and people in the frontier chapter of United States history.

The Hopi Snake Dance, held each year for nine days, is a prayer for rain and good crops.

M. Wright Gill

Chapter 23 Review

Chapter Summary

Our nation's last frontier stretched westward from the Missouri River to the borders of California and Oregon, and from Canada southward to the Gulf of Mexico. It was called the Great Plains-Rocky Mountain area. The Great Plains, a dry grassland, was the home of many Native Americans. They traveled the plains following the herds of bison or buffalo that were the basis for their way of life.

However, life for Native Americans on the Great Plains changed. Following the Civil War, white settlers entered the area to mine, to raise cattle, and to farm. The Native Americans fought for, but eventually lost, the lands and the rights guaranteed them by treaties.

The search for gold and silver first brought the miners to the area. As cattle ranching grew, herds were driven across the Plains to railroad towns for shipment to the East. The Homestead Act provided cheap land and made it possible for settlers to move into the Great Plains and set up farms and towns.

Reviewing Vocabulary

Match each of the following words with its correct definition. Write your answers on a separate sheet of paper.

frontier	massacre
deposit	reservation
claim	roundup
bison	longhorn
grassland	trail
warrior	range

1. the herding together of cattle
2. a buffalo; a wild ox of the American Great Plains
3. open country where cattle graze
4. a mass of matter, such as gold, formed by natural forces
5. a large area of flat or rolling land covered by grass
6. land staked out as one's own
7. a piece of public land set aside by the federal government for the use of Native Americans
8. one who is experienced in warfare
9. a path through unsettled country
10. a large-scale killing of defenseless people
11. a boundary between settled and largely unsettled land
12. a breed of cattle derived from Spanish stock that once roamed wild in the southwestern United States

Understanding Main Ideas

1. In what way did the discovery of gold and silver lead to the settlement of the Great Plains?
2. How were Native Americans affected by the settlement of the west?
3. What changes took place in the Great Plains area as a result of the growth of the cattle industry?
4. How did farmers transform the Great Plains into a settled region?

Critical Thinking Skills

1. **Recognizing Cause and Effect.** What impact did the discovery of gold and silver have upon the way of life of Native Americans such as the Cheyenne and the Sioux?
2. **Recognizing Bias.** Did the federal government's actions during the settlement of the Great Plains reflect an attitude toward Native Americans? Explain.
3. **Identifying Assumptions.** Why were the Great Plains the last area to be settled?

Social Studies: Comparing and Interpreting Pictures

The Big Horn Store

Compare the picture of the town of Deadwood in 1888 on this page with the picture of Deadwood in 1876 on page 446.

Skill Review: After comparing the pictures, answer the following questions.
1. How had the size of the town of Deadwood changed?

2. How do the streets and roads in 1888 compare with those in 1876?
3. What new information about the location of Deadwood can be learned from the 1888 picture?
4. What new building material had been used in Deadwood by 1888?
5. How had The Big Horn Store changed?

Writing About History

Writing a Report. Assume you are the federal agent in charge of a reservation in the late 1890's. Write a report that you will send to the President explaining why the groups of Native Americans from the Great Plains are having a hard time adjusting to a new way of life on the reservation. Explain how their previous way of life was different.

Your Region in History

Economics. The settlement of the Great Plains was largely begun by miners lured to the region by the promise of gold and silver. Was your region ever considered to hold such treasure? What were the natural resources that attracted your region's founders? Are any of these resources still a part of your region's economy today?

Lifestyles:
The
Civil War Era

❧ Chapter 24

THE CIVIL WAR brought deep suffering to the North and South. In comparison with the total population more soldiers were enlisted in the Union and Confederate armies than have served in any war before or since. And as a percentage of the total population, more soldiers died in that war than in any war before or since.

The end of the war brought great changes. Slaves were freed. Relations between farm workers and landowners in the South changed. In the North people flocked to the cities to work in the new factories. And in the West more and more miners, ranchers, and farmers moved into the Great Plains and the lands beyond the Rocky Mountains.

Everyone pitched in to help when it was time to wash and hang out the clothes on the ranch in frontier Texas.

In any war families suffer from separation. But the Civil War directly affected almost everyone in the United States. In many families one member favored one side while other members favored the other.

With fathers and brothers serving in the Union and Confederate armies, the women left at home had to feed, clothe, and care for the rest of the family. Some wives wrote to government leaders, asking that their husbands be allowed to come home and help. After the war many families moved westward as the last frontier was settled.

Brother Against Brother

John C. Pratt lived in Boston, Massachusetts. His brother Jabez D. Pratt lived in Baltimore, Maryland. Both were businessmen in their forties. A few days after the Civil War began, Massachusetts troops marched through Baltimore on their way to Washington, D.C. Fighting broke out between the Union soldiers and some Baltimore residents who sided with the Confederacy. When John heard about the fighting, he invited Jabez to bring his family to Boston. They could remain there, John wrote, until the war was over.

Jabez replied angrily that he and his wife had decided not to run, especially not "into the arms of . . . abolitionism." He wrote further that he and his son intended to fight the Union soldiers if there was any more trouble. "If he would not fight, I would disown him," Jabez said of his son.

Bitter feeling grew up between the brothers. But in one apologetic letter, Jabez expressed warm feelings toward his brother.

. . . I reciprocate [feel in return] your brotherly feeling toward me, and . . . I hope I may not be compelled to meet you in hostility. I would much prefer to meet you as a brother. I don't think you would shoot at the next man to me, and I assure you that such would be my feelings.

Letters Home

The soldiers fighting in the Civil War grew homesick and were troubled about their families. Robert Gill wanted to know if "little Callie speaks of her 'pa.' Does she remember me?" D. Hunter wrote to his wife, "I want to see the children very bad . . . their [are] sevril [several] men in the same fix that I am [with] young bab[e]s at home that they never saw." Jerome Yates worried about the crops. He wanted to know "how high the cotton and the corn [were.] . . . How the Cows look . . . How many Chickens you have."

Writing letters helped to ease the pain of separation. Most soldiers wrote home often and were eager to get letters from

Farm families were often photographed, along with some of their furniture and animals, in front of their sod houses on the Plains.

home. W. Norton said that letters from home were like "angels' visits." And William Whatley felt that "To now be denied the pleasure of writing to and hearing from those I love would be next to death."

Visitors

In her book *Little House in the Big Woods* Laura Ingalls Wilder wrote about her early childhood in the 1870s in Wisconsin. Families there were not able to visit with their neighbors or relatives often, so a visit was a big event for Laura and her family.

Now it was summertime, and people went visiting. Sometimes Uncle Henry, or Uncle George, or Grandpa, came riding out of the Big Woods to see Pa. Ma would come to the door and ask how all the folks were, and she would say: "Charles is in the clearing." Then she would cook more dinner than usual, and dinner time would be longer. Pa and Ma and the visitor would sit talking a little while before they went back to work.

Sometimes Ma let Laura and Mary go across the road and down the hill to see Mrs. Peterson. The Petersons had just moved in. Their house was new, and always very neat, because Mrs. Peterson had no little girls to muss it up. She was a Swede, and she let Laura and Mary look at the pretty things she had brought from Sweden— laces, and colored embroideries, and china.

During the Civil War hundreds of thousands of soldiers learned to live under the open skies. At best, they lived in tents or simple shelters. Where the battles were fought, many people lost their homes. Parts of many cities in the South were destroyed. After the war new buildings went up in both southern and northern cities. And in the West sod houses dotted the countryside.

Lincoln and his family—left to right, Mary, William (Willie), Robert, and Thomas (Tad)—lived in their Springfield home (below) until February 1861.

The Lincolns at Home

Mary Todd and Abraham Lincoln were married on November 4, 1842. At first they lived in a boardinghouse in Springfield, Illinois. Later they bought a house of their own.

Mary Lincoln loved to entertain friends and relatives. One visitor in 1860 wrote his impressions of the Lincoln home.

The house was neatly without being [lavishly] furnished. . . . There were flowers upon the table; . . . pictures on the walls. . . . The thought that [came to mind was] "What a pleasant home Abe Lincoln has."

A Temporary Home

Lawrence Van Alstyne served in the 128th New York Volunteers. His diary gives an account of daily life at training camp.

September 17, 1862
We are in a field of 100 acres, as near as I can judge, on the side of a hill, near the top. . . . A blanket spread on the ground is our bed while another spread over us is our covering. A narrow strip of muslin, drawn over a pole about three feet from the ground, open at both ends [is our tent], the wind and the rain . . . beating in upon us, and water running under and about us; this, with all manner of bugs and creeping things crawling over us, and . . . great hungry mosquitos biting every uncovered inch of us. . . .
. . . I will say something about our kitchen, dining room and cooking arrangements. Some get mad and cuss the cooks, and the whole war department, but that is usually when our stomachs are full. When we are hungry we swallow anything that comes and are thankful for it. The cook house is simply [part] of the field we are

Most private homes in the Civil War period had a parlor, or separate room, where the family entertained guests.

in. . . . We each get a piece of meat and a potato, a chunk of bread and a cup of coffee with a spoonful of brown sugar in it. . . . We settle down, generally in groups, and the meal is soon over. . . . We make quick work of washing dishes. We save a piece of bread for the last, with which we wipe up everything, and then eat the dish rag.

Becoming One of the Neighbors

Anna and Olof Wing left their home in Sweden in 1870 for a one-room log cabin in Polk County, Minnesota. The family prepared for their first winter, storing enough food and fuel to keep them full and warm. Anna and Olof wanted to make friends with their neighbors, but they did not speak English. In her diary Anna wrote:

It is like standing outside looking in, with the door locked on both the inside and the outside. You cannot go in and they cannot let you in, but I have decided that I shall be one of the neighbors. I am going to learn the American language.

How to Be the Perfect Housewife

Godey's Lady's Book was the first American magazine for women. Many of the articles concerned cooking, sewing, and keeping house. One article printed in 1859 was entitled "How to Economize [Save Money] and Conduct a Home." It advised women to strive for luxury and comfort in their homes.

. . . it must be your ambition to know how to make the best appearance . . . to appear . . . richer than you are, or at least quite as rich as you are. . . . a good dinner, deliciously white table linen, brightly-polished glass, and well-made knives and forks . . . create an appearance of a superior income. . . .

Section 1 Review

1. Which of the Pratt brothers was on the side of the Confederacy?
2. What is a boardinghouse?
3. Name three hardships facing Lawrence Van Alstyne and his fellow soldiers.
4. How did Anna Wing propose to become one of the neighbors in Minnesota?

Critical Thinking

5. **Recognizing Cause and Effect.** Why was summertime the season for visiting in Laura Wilders's region?

Lifestyles   Values and Learning

As in other times, decisions made by individuals during these war years were based on personal values. Many decided to fight for what they believed right. Many died and were honored by both North and South. In the West a shortage of police and courts meant that many people took the law into their own hands. And there were often differences in values between Native Americans and the white settlers.

A Quiet War

Henry David Thoreau, the author of *Walden,* believed that the Mexican War was wrong and would spread slavery. To protest this war, he refused to pay his taxes. He explained his actions in an essay called "Resistance to Civil Government."

I cannot for an instant recognize that political organization as my government which is the slave's *government also. . . . I do not care to follow the course of my dollar . . . till it buys a man [a slave] or a rifle to shoot one with. . . . In fact, I quietly declare war against the state in my own way.*

Thoreau went to jail for one night in his hometown of Concord, Massachusetts, for refusing to pay his taxes.

A Hard Decision

When the Civil War started, many young men dropped out of school and joined the army. One student from the South explained why in this 1862 letter to his father.

. . . I believe I know the value of an education . . . but the time has come when even this can be neglected. . . . I hope and pray you will not [let] it be said that there was even one, capable of bearing arms, not on the list of his country's defenders.

The First Memorial Day

The Hollywood Memorial Association of Richmond, Virginia, declared May 31, 1866, as its first Memorial Day. On May 30 the young men of the city, carrying picks and shovels, marched to the cemetery. As they passed down the road, men, women, and children joined them. At the cemetery everyone helped rake up rubbish and replace fallen boards and stones that marked the graves. The next day they decorated with flowers. Richmond had not forgotten its war dead.

Frontier Justice

In 1882 Roy Bean of Langtry, Texas, got himself appointed justice of the peace. He held court in his saloon and kept most of the money paid in fines by wrongdoers. Although he had no law degree and only one law book, he was known as the "Law West of the Pecos."

Judge Bean fell so in love with a picture of English actress Lillie Langtry that he named his saloon "the Jersey Lilly."

A prisoner was once brought before Judge Bean for stealing horses. The thief had been caught in the act and shot in the ear while trying to escape from the horses' owner. Judge Bean said:

Poor shot, Jack, but if you had got him he would not have been properly finished as becoming a horse thief. It's my ruling that the prisoner is guilty. The rest is your business, Jack. You'd better buy him a drink before you string him up. Court is adjourned.

Kiowa Values

Satanta was a Kiowa chief. He made this speech in 1867 when he and other Kiowa leaders signed a treaty agreeing to go to a reservation.

I don't want to settle. I love to roam over the prairies. There I feel free and happy, but when we settle down we grow pale and die. . . . A long time ago this land belonged to our fathers; but when I go up to the river I see camps of soldiers on its banks. These soldiers cut down my timber; they kill my buffalo; and when I see that, my heart feels like bursting. . . . Has the white man become a child that he should recklessly kill and not eat? When the red man slay game, they do so that they may live and not starve.

In the South many schools and colleges closed during the war for lack of teachers and pupils. After the war, freed slaves were eager to learn. Schools were established for them. Immigrants to America often taught themselves English. On the Great Plains a sign language developed among the many different peoples there.

A School for Freed Slaves

On November 20, 1866, members of the First Congregational Society of Washington, D.C., set up a seminary for freed slaves and others. General Oliver O. Howard, a religious man, a Civil War hero, and head of the Freedmen's Bureau, was present. One member suggested that the school be named Howard Theological Seminary.

Later the society decided to offer courses in more subject areas. The members worked to get a charter from Congress for Howard University. The school accepted its first students in 1867. Howard students honor their university in its song:

Reared against the eastern sky
Proudly there on hilltop high,
Far above the lake so blue
Stands old Howard firm and true. . . .

Passing the Exam

In 1872 former slave Booker T. Washington walked about 300 miles to get to Hampton Institute in Virginia. In his autobiography, *Up From Slavery,* he wrote about his first day there.

This Gros Ventre man "signs" his message with his hands.

. . . I presented myself before the head teacher for assignment to a class. Having been so long without proper food, a bath, and change of clothing, I did not, of course, make a very favorable impression upon her, and I could see at once that there were doubts in her mind about the wisdom of admitting me as a student. . . . After some hours had passed, the head teacher said to me: "The [next classroom] needs sweeping. Take the broom and sweep it."

It occurred to me at once that here was my chance. . . . I knew that I could sweep. . . .

I swept the [classroom] three times. Then . . . [a]ll the woodwork around the walls, every bench, table, and desk, I went over four times with my dusting-cloth. . . . I had the feeling that . . . my future depended upon the impression I made upon the teacher in the cleaning of that room. When I was through, I reported to the head teacher. . . . She went into the room and inspected the floor and closets; then she took out her handkerchief and rubbed it on the woodwork about the walls, and over the table and benches. When she was unable to find one bit of dirt on the floor, or a [piece] of dust on any of the furniture, she quietly remarked, "I guess you will do to enter this [school]."

Booker T. Washington (right), graduate of Hampton Institute and founder of Tuskegee, is shown here with his secretary Emmett Scott.

In 1881 Booker T. Washington was to found a school himself. That school became Tuskegee Institute in Tuskegee, Alabama.

Section 2 Review

1. In what ways did the nation honor those who died in the Civil War?
2. What subjects might be taught at a theological seminary?
3. Why did Booker T. Washington's teacher at first have doubts about admitting him?

Critical Thinking
4. **Recognizing Ideologies.** What does a person value who is against slavery?

Learning English

Carl Schurz, born in Germany, came to America in 1852. Later he described how he taught himself the English language.

I resolutely began to read—first my daily newspaper. . . . I worked through editorial articles, the news letters and [stories], and even as many of the advertisements as my time would allow. . . . Then I proceeded to read English novels. . . . I never [skipped] a word the meaning of which I did not clearly understand, and I never failed to consult the dictionary in every doubtful case.

A New Language

Native American groups on the Great Plains spoke many different languages. When they came into contact with each other and with white settlers, they needed a way to communicate. A system of gestures, or sign language, slowly developed that was understood by Native American groups all over the Plains.

During the Civil War, women in both North and South managed farms and plantations. Many others, especially in the North, worked in factories. After the war, slaves became free laborers, greatly swelling the free work force. Many blacks had skills as craftsworkers. But selling their labor was new to them. In the West whites and blacks worked as cowhands. In both East and West people with fresh ideas were inventing new products.

After the war most blacks continued to live and work in the South (inset). Titusville, Pennsylvania, was the site of the nation's first oil well, called Drake's Folly.

The Home Front

Union troops forced Mrs. Judith McGuire and her family to flee from Alexandria to Richmond, Virginia. In her diary Mrs. McGuire wrote about how she supported her family there.

March 5, 1863
. . . Several of us are making soap and selling it. [Another lady is] making pickles and catsups for the restaurants. . . . This kind of [activity] works two ways: it supplies our wants, and gives comfort to the public. . . . The blockade [of the South] has taught our people [to use] their own resources.

A Contract for Farmers

In 1868 a group of black farm workers signed a contract with John Mitchell in Yallabousha County, Mississippi. Each person agreed to work as a farmhand for one year. The workers would pay the daily expenses of the farm. Mitchell would provide the land, stock, housing, tools, and fuel. Farm income would be divided equally between Mitchell and the workers. If a farmhand became too sick to work, part of the money would be held back. Because most of the workers could neither read nor write, they signed their names on the contract with Xs.

Danger on the Long Drive

On long cattle drives cowhands were in the saddle all day. The dangers of the drive were many, as Andy Adams's account shows.

. . . before a mile had been covered, the leaders [the animals in front] again turned, . . . milling and lowing in their fever and thirst. . . . No sooner was the milling stopped than they would surge hither and yon, sometimes half a mile, as ungovernable as the waves of an ocean. After wasting several hours in this manner, they finally turned back over the trail, and the utmost efforts of every man in the outfit failed to check them. We threw our ropes in their faces, and when this failed, we resorted to shooting; but in defiance of the [shooting] and the smoke they walked sullenly through the line of horsemen across their front. . . . then for the first time a fact dawned on us that chilled the marrow in our bones—the herd was going blind.

The Real McCoy

The phrase "the real McCoy" can be traced back to the black engineer Elijah McCoy. Born in Canada in 1843, McCoy studied in Edinburgh, Scotland, before settling in the United States.

In 1872, while working for the Michigan Central Railroad, McCoy invented a device that continuously oiled the moving parts of a machine. Over the years he adapted his invention to many other machines. Soon no machinery was considered complete unless it could oil itself. Machine inspectors began to ask, "Is it the real McCoy?" "The real McCoy" came to mean "the real thing" and was applied to other things besides machinery.

Elijah McCoy's fame spread as he found new ways to apply his invention to different machines.

Pants for Miners

In 1850 Levi Strauss, a twenty-year-old Jewish immigrant from Bavaria, sailed from Boston for San Francisco. He carried silk and other cloth for making clothes. He also had canvas duck for making wagon covers and tents. By the time he reached San Francisco, only the canvas was left.

One day Strauss heard a miner complaining about how quickly his pants wore out in the mines. Strauss decided to make the canvas into pants. The miners bought all he could make.

When he ran out of canvas, Strauss began making the pants out of denim, a tough cotton fabric. Levi Strauss's blue denim pants have remained popular for over 100 years.

In both South and North, hunting, fishing, ice skating, and other outdoor sports continued to be popular after the Civil War. Baseball, boating, and croquet became the rage. Indoors, people played checkers, dominoes, cards, and other games.

Games for Soldiers

Milton Bradley introduced his first game, The Checkered Game of Life, in 1860. When the Civil War began, Bradley went to work for the Union army at the armory in Springfield, Massachusetts. There, groups of Union soldiers often sat in their off-duty hours with little to do. Bradley made a game kit just for them—one that fit into a soldier's pocket or knapsack. The kit included backgammon, checkers, chess, dominoes, and The Checkered Game of Life.

Both women and men enjoyed the sport of baseball in the 1800s. The teams shown in the bottom picture are the Red Stockings and the Atlantics.

Playing croquet with many others in the park could turn a humble family pastime into a social event.

Section 3 Review

1. What daily expenses might John Mitchell's farmhands have had to pay?
2. What was dangerous about the herd's going blind in Andy Adams's story?
3. Name three popular sports besides baseball played by professionals today.
4. What games, if any, have replaced croquet as a family pastime?

Critical Thinking

5. **Making Comparisons.** What games might be found in a soldier's game kit today?

Baseball Mania

In 1828 a reporter for the *New York Evening Post* complained about "large groups of men and boys playing ball and filling the air with their shouts and yells." But the noise over baseball was just beginning. The game gained more fans every year.

On June 19, 1846, the Knickerbocker Club and the New York Nine played the first game between two organized teams. The Knickerbockers wore straw hats, blue trousers, and white shirts. Pitchers had to throw the ball underhanded, and outfielders caught fly balls in their hats.

During the Civil War, soldiers often played baseball. After the war the magazine *Galaxy* reported: "It is a mania. Hundreds of clubs do nothing but play, all summer and autumn."

In 1869 the Cincinnati Red Stockings became the first professional baseball team. All of the players were paid for playing. In 1876 the National League was formed. Baseball was on its way to becoming the national sport.

Croquet by Day and by Night

In the late 1860s and the 1870s croquet was played in all parts of the country, even the West. The equipment—hoops, pegs, mallets, and balls—was inexpensive and could easily be set up in a yard. Almost all members of a family could play. When a family bought a set, the neighbors came over for croquet parties. People enjoyed the game so much they refused to stop playing when it got dark. They continued by the light of the moon or by lantern light. In 1875 the hoops in one croquet set came with candle sockets.

Soda Sensations

In the 1830s John Matthews of New York invented a machine to make carbonic acid gas. With the gas he made soda water, which was sold as a refreshing drink in the stores. About 1838 Eugene Roussel of Philadelphia added flavors to his soda drinks. People liked them. Soon almost all soda fountains offered several flavors of soda water. When soda-fountain owners started adding ice cream to their drinks in the 1870s, people liked them even more.

Soda fountains built by Matthews and others became quite elaborate. There were wall models that looked like marble altars. One fountain offered 300 flavors. And some models could be wheeled about the streets. Matthews wrote this flowery advertisement for his soda cart:

Youth, as it sips its first glass, experiences sensations which, like the first sensations of love, cannot be forgotten but are cherished to the last.

Focus On Unit 4

Lifestyles: Understanding Social History

To answer the following questions, review the lifestyles section from page 462 to page 475.

1. **Families and Homes.** The Civil War was a time of hardship for many American families. Reread the letter from Jabez Pratt to his brother on page 464. What effect did the Civil War have upon their relationship? What do the readings tell you about the soldiers' homes?
2. **Values and Learning.** Attitudes and values shape peoples' actions. How did the attitudes and values of Thoreau, the southern student, and Booker T. Washington presented on pages 468 and 470 affect their actions?
3. **Work and Play.** After the Civil War, the nation enjoyed rapid economic growth and new opportunities for workers. Reread the accounts of the farm workers and of Elijah McCoy on pages 472 and 473. What new opportunities were opened for blacks?

Making Connections

Use the Unit 4 time line below to answer the following questions.

1. What action occurred right after Lincoln's election to his first term as President of the United States?
2. What event in the 1870s increased the migration of people westward?
3. Reread the Unit Introduction on page 365. In which years were compromises between the North and the South reached?
4. **Demonstrating Reasoned Judgment.** In which decade shown on the time line do you think the greatest efforts were made to protect the rights of black Americans? Support your answer.

Critical Thinking Skills

1. **Determining Relevance.** What relationship exists between the election of 1844 and the disputes between the North and the South?
2. **Formulating Questions.** If you were the governor of a border state, what questions would you have wanted Abraham Lincoln to answer immediately after his election in 1860?
3. **Predicting Consequences.** How might Reconstruction have been different if Lincoln had not been assassinated?
4. **Drawing Conclusions.** How was the settlement of the Great Plains linked to new inventions?

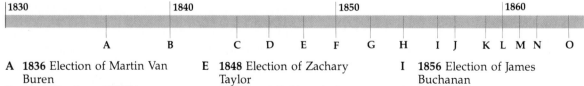

1830		1840			1850				1860		
	A	B	C D	E F	G	H	I J	K L M N	O		

A **1836** Election of Martin Van Buren
B **1840** Election of William Henry Harrison
C **1844** Election of James Polk
D **1846–1848** War with Mexico

E **1848** Election of Zachary Taylor
1848–1876 Gold rush days
F **1850** Clay's Compromise
G **1852** *Uncle Tom's Cabin*; election of Franklin Pierce
H **1854** Kansas-Nebraska Act; birth of Republican party

I **1856** Election of James Buchanan
J **1857** Dred Scott decision
K **1859** John Brown's raid; discovery of Comstock Lode
L **1860** Election of Abraham Lincoln

Using Geography Skills

Use the map below to answer the following questions.

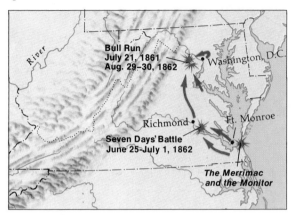

1. **Developing an Awareness of Place.** Where is Bull Run in relation to Washington, D.C.?
2. **Developing Locational Skills.** Was the battle between the *Merrimac* and the *Monitor* fought off the coast of the North or the South?
3. **Understanding Human and Environmental Interaction.** Why was Fort Monroe's location important to an army whose navy controlled the seas?
4. **Understanding World Regions.** What physical characteristics of the region probably influenced the movement toward Washington, D.C.?

5. **Understanding Human Movement.** Based on what you have learned in Unit 4, what do the arrows represent?

Linking Past to Present

Predicting Consequences. If gold and silver had not been discovered in California and in the Rocky Mountains, how might the history of the United States have been different? Would the West have been settled so quickly? How would the nation look different today?

Reviewing Social Studies Skills

1. **The Decision-Making Process.** Review the discussion of Clay's Compromise of 1850 in Chapter 20. Study Senator Daniel Webster's decision on whether or not to support the Compromise of 1850. Describe the problems he faced, identify his choices, and analyze his final decision using the decision-making process outlined on page 368.
2. **Understanding Decisions.** Considering the state of the nation in 1862, how might the outcome of the Civil War have been different if President Lincoln had not decided to issue the Emancipation Proclamation? Explain your answer.

M 1861 Formation of Confederate States of America
1861–1865 Civil War
N 1862 Emancipation Proclamation
O 1864 Lincoln's reelection
P 1865 Assassination of Lincoln; Johnson President; Thirteenth Amendment

Q 1866 Civil Rights Act
R 1868 Fourteenth Amendment; Johnson impeachment trial
1868–1876 Grant's Presidency
S 1870 Fifteenth Amendment
T 1873 Big Bonanza discovery

U 1875 Black Hills gold rush
V 1876 Battle of Little Big Horn; election of Rutherford Hayes; end of Reconstruction
W 1887 Dawes Act
X 1896 *Plessy* v. *Ferguson*

TRANS-FORMING THE NATION

Between 1876 and 1914 the nation became a leading industrial power. Factories turned out goods, and transportation networks linked all parts of the nation. Thousands of people moved to the cities in search of opportunities. Some businesses grew into giant corporations.

Farmers and workers protested the rise of big business and achieved some reforms through the Populist (People's) movement.

In world affairs the United States joined the race for empire. By the early 1900s the United States had holdings or ties in so many parts of the world that events in distant lands affected the United States directly. The United States had become a world power.

As you read about the transformation of the country, look for ways in which political, economic, and social matters influence one another and the flow of history. And look for causes and effects in the chain of events that have helped make the United States a world power.

Unit 5

Understanding
Historical
Focus

❧ Chapter 25

Vocabulary

strand
political
focus
analysis
economic
cultural
intellectual
synthesis
cause and effect
conclusion
value judgment
balance

A HISTORY BOOK such as *American Spirit* is made up of many different strands. Besides stories about famous persons, it offers details about the everyday lives of ordinary people. It tells about what has happened in trade, business, and industry. It tells of political parties, elections, changes in government, and the passing of laws. And it tells of peaceful relations as well as wars with other nations.

All of these separate strands come together to form the full story of your country. And events in one strand often affect events in another. A sharp change in the nation's business life, for example, will often bring about changes in the way people live and work and play. Or it may affect the kinds of laws that are passed.

In this chapter you will learn how to think critically about the different strands of history. You will also see how each strand can bring about change in the others. You will see that historians—in focusing on a single strand or in tying the strands together—often arrive at different conclusions and hold different points of view.

1   Understanding Historical Analysis

An analysis is a careful study to discover how something works. When you analyze something, you take it apart to study its pieces and to see how these pieces work together. In an English class, for example, you might analyze a sentence by separating it into parts. You can divide a sentence into two major parts—subject and predicate—or further divide it into nouns, verbs, adjectives, and so on. Breaking down a sentence will help you understand how all the parts, or words, work together to give the sentence meaning.

Analyzing Historical Statements

You can also analyze sentences in a history book. But you would use a different kind of analysis from that used in an English class. You might take a single sentence from a history book and think about all the different ideas that lie behind it. Consider this sentence:

The Declaration of Independence was signed on July 4, 1776.

Think of all the ideas that lie behind that simple sentence. Who declared independence from what? Why? What caused this to happen? What happened because of it? You could ask dozens of questions like these—all about a single sentence that says something happened at a certain time. These are the kinds of questions a historian must ask—and answer.

Few events in history happen without causing or affecting other events. For example, after signing the Declaration of Independence, the former colonists found themselves at war with Great Britain. They had to fight not only to hold their own in a war, but also to form a new kind of government and make that government work. The life of every citizen, even those who lived far from the battles of the Revolution, was changed by the Declaration of Independence.

The following paragraph describes some events you will read more about in this unit. What questions might you ask about each sentence in the paragraph?

Between the end of the Civil War and the early years of the twentieth century the United States became the world's leading manufacturing nation. With the rise of industry, cities grew rapidly, drawing immigrants from other countries and Americans from their farms. At the same time, a small number of business leaders became so powerful that many citizens wanted the government to pass laws controlling business. Reformers and labor leaders tried to improve conditions for working people at home and on the job. As American industrial might grew, the United States began to influence countries in other parts of the world.

Analysis of old photographs, such as this one taken in a machine shop, can reveal details of economic and social history.

Now let us look at the paragraph one sentence at a time. Each sentence will be followed by some questions you might ask about its topic. You need not try to answer any of these questions. But think about how they relate to the sentence. Many of the answers will come as you study the rest of this unit.

Sentence 1
Between the end of the Civil War and the early years of the twentieth century the United States became the world's leading manufacturing nation.

a. How did the United States become the world's leading manufacturing nation?
b. What kinds of manufacturing led the way in the United States?
c. In what cities and states did some industries spring up?
d. Did its lead in manufacturing change the way other countries of the world viewed the United States? If so, how?
e. What changes came about because of industrial growth?

Sentence 2
With the rise of industry, cities grew rapidly, drawing immigrants from other countries and Americans from their farms.

a. How is growth in industry connected with the growth of cities?
b. What cities grew rapidly?
c. What drew people to the cities?
d. What kinds of jobs did people find there?
e. How did farming change as more people moved to cities?
f. What was home life like in the cities?
g. Why did immigrants come to the United States?
h. Where did the immigrants come from?
i. What kinds of jobs did immigrants find here?
j. What was life like for the new immigrants?
k. In what ways did the growth of cities influence city politics? National politics?

483

Sentence 3

At the same time, a small number of business leaders became so powerful that many citizens wanted the government to pass laws controlling business.

a. Who were the business leaders who gained so much power?
b. What businesses were these people in?
c. How did they become so powerful?
d. Why were people worried about the power of business leaders?
e. Were all people troubled by the strength of big business?
f. What were the differences of opinion about big business among the political parties? Among political leaders?
g. How did government try to check the power of big business? Was it successful?

Sentence 4

Reformers and labor leaders tried to improve conditions for working people at home and on the job.

a. What was daily life like for most working people in the late nineteenth century?
b. What were working conditions like?
c. What conditions needed to be improved?
d. Who were the reformers? What did they try to do?
e. Who were the labor leaders?
f. What did labor leaders try to do for working people?
g. How did labor leaders work for change?
h. Were they able to improve conditions for workers?

Sentence 5

As American industrial might grew, the United States began to influence countries in other parts of the world.

a. Which did the United States want more, imports or exports?
b. With what countries was the United States seeking more trade?
c. What did the government of the United States do to protect and build up foreign trade?
d. Did the United States gain new territory abroad because of its trading ties? Where?
e. Did everyone in the United States favor holding territory abroad?
f. Was United States influence welcomed by people in other lands?
g. Were people from other lands welcomed in the United States?

As you can see, many questions lie behind each sentence. Some questions are about people's everyday lives. Some have to do with jobs and the working world. And some deal with government, lands, and politics at home and abroad. All phases of American life are part of the country's history.

Practicing Your Skills

Critical Thinking

Formulating Questions. Read the following paragraph carefully. The sentences are numbered for you.

(1) The Great Plains-Rocky Mountain area was the last frontier to be tamed. (2) Before the Civil War most of this land was settled only by Native Americans. (3) After the war more and more white people moved in. (4) Miners came looking for gold and silver. (5) Cattle raisers first used the open plains for grazing land, but later they fenced it in. (6) Settlers gradually solved the problems of raising crops in the grasslands.

What are some questions you might ask about each sentence in the paragraph? Write as many as you can, following the example on pages 483–484. Think of questions that have to do with such subjects as homes, ways of living, work, business, and transportation.

Identifying Historical Strands

A history can be written on almost any subject: a history of tools, of buildings, of schools, of your school. You can write a history of your family, of your town or city, or of your state. Almost every subject you can think of has a history.

The photograph below and the pictures on pages 486 and 487 tell part of the history of travel in the United States.

The title for this picture, made in 1886, calls the train "a ship of the plains."

There are many kinds of history books. Some, like this one, tell the general history of a nation. Others cover the history of several nations. A history of Europe, for example, would tell about events in all the countries on the European continent. A world history would give facts about all or most of the countries in the world.

Other history books cover only certain periods of time, such as the nineteenth century. A history book even narrower in time would be one on the United States during the 1920s. A whole book might even be written about a single event, such as the election of 1876 or the Spanish-American War.

There are also books that cover a single strand of history. One such history might focus on politics in the United States. Such a book would tell of political parties, elections, Presidents, and acts of Congress. It would also cover the country's foreign affairs—its relations with other governments. But it would tell little about the daily

George Pullman built lavish sitting room cars (left) and sleeping room cars for well-to-do travelers.

lives of people in cities, small towns, and farms. It would also probably not have much to say about business and industry or about jobs and labor unions. These subjects would be brought in only as part of the nation's political story.

Political history, such as the account just described, is one of three main strands in history. Economic history is the second. It concerns how people earn a living and how they make and use goods. Agriculture, industry, trade, business, and transportation are some main topics you would read about in an economic history.

Social history covers people and groups. The daily lives of people—rich, poor, or middle class—are important in social history. A social history will teach you about families and homes at different times in the past. You would read about people's customs and about their free-time activities. Many of the stories in the Lifestyles chapters of this book are part of social history.

Some books focus on a fourth strand: cultural and intellectual history. This strand follows the course of religion, education, art, and literature over time. Sometimes this strand is woven into social history, as it is in the Lifestyles chapters.

Unit 5 will show you the different historical strands untangled. Chapter 26, The Age of Machines, deals mainly with economic history. It covers the growth of business and industry in the late nineteenth century. It also tells about workers and their problems and about the growth of labor unions. The next chapter, City Lights, is mostly social history. It also records some facts about cultural and intellectual history. Chapters 28 and 29 are political history. The first one treats events within the nation. The second takes up political events abroad, or foreign affairs.

As you read these chapters, you will see that the strands of political, economic, and social history are often mixed together. Look at the paragraph above the heading "Big Business" on page 507, for example. The paragraph tells about the growth of the automobile industry—a part of economic history. But it also tells about some results of that growth. Suburbs grew up around big cities because people could now drive to and from work in their automobiles. People also used cars to travel for pleasure. This is part of social history.

Even a single sentence may touch on several strands. Here is an example. *Rapid industrial growth often came hand in hand with sprawling city slums and the bribing of lawmakers.* In this sentence the phrase *rapid industrial growth* refers to economic history. *Sprawling city slums* is a topic in social history. And *the bribing of lawmakers* has to do with political history.

Look again at the five sentences of the paragraph on page 482. Sentence 1 concerns economic history. Sentence 2 may seem difficult to place because several strands are present. Look at the questions based on Sentence 2. Some are related to politics, some to economic life, and some to social life. Sentence 3 is about political history, and Sentence 4 has elements of both economic and social history. The part of Sentence 5 that reads *the United States began to influence countries in other parts of the world* is related to the foreign affairs part of political history.

All three strands of history are intertwined in this photograph taken during the May Day parade of the Socialist party in 1903.

A child working in a sweatshop (inset) and a Jewish immigrant living in a coal cellar are part of the story of industrial growth in the United States.

Thus, only two of the five sentences are about a single strand only. And even those two sentences can raise questions about other strands. All of the sentences are general statements. The more detailed a sentence is, the easier it is to see a single strand of history in the sentence.

Practicing Your Skills

1. Look carefully at the questions following each of the five sentences (pages 483-484). Then write out answers to the questions below.
    a. Which question after Sentence 1 covers the foreign part of political history?
    b. What strand of history is the subject in Sentence 2, question e?
    c. Which questions about Sentence 3 are *not* concerned with economic history?

d. Which questions after Sentence 4 have to do with social history? Which with economic history?

Critical Thinking

2. **Expressing Problems Clearly.** In the Practicing Your Skills exercise on page 485 you wrote some questions of your own. Make a chart with these three column heads: Political History, Economic History, and Social History. List each of your questions under the proper heading. List a question more than once if it seems to fit in more than one column. Do any sentences not fit any of these headings? If so, make your own heading for a fourth column.

2   Understanding Historical Synthesis

You have been practicing historical analysis. You have been taking history apart and dividing it into political, economic, and social strands. In this way you have focused on the separate elements in history. Now you will put the parts together again to see how each may affect the other. This process is called synthesis.

Combining Historical Strands

The events in any one strand of history can have a bearing on other strands. When you analyze history, you separate the strands. To synthesize history you need in part to know how one strand can act on another. You need to see relationships.

Cause and effect is one kind of relationship between events. You can see cause and effect in the paragraph analyzed earlier in this chapter. One sentence tells you that "As American industrial might grew, the United States began to influence countries in other parts of the world." In this sentence greater industrial might is a cause. The growing influence of the United States on other countries is an effect.

The rise of business and industry in the United States caused cities to grow, caused more people to find work in cities, and caused business leaders to become rich and powerful. These are only a few of the many effects caused by the spread of business and industry. The cause—industrial growth—is part of economic history. So are some of the effects. Other effects are part of political and social history. All are interrelated.

You can build a long chain of events and see how they are linked by cause and effect. Look at the following chain. The first event is a cause. The second is its effect. Then number 2 becomes a cause leading to number 3, which in turn becomes the cause for effect number 4.

1. Industry expanded greatly. (economic)
2. There were more jobs to be had in industry. (economic)

Edison invented the first electric lamp in 1879. The picture on the next page shows one effect of his invention.

3. People left farms to seek jobs in industrial cities. (economic and social)

4. There was not enough good housing for all the people who flocked to the cities. (social)

5. Many had to live in crowded slums. (social)

6. Reformers tried to improve conditions for people in the city slums. (social and political)

7. Laws were passed to improve living conditions. (political)

Notice how an economic cause leads to both social and political effects.

This is a very simple chain of events. You could build dozens of different chains of events, all based on the growth of industry. Suppose, for example, event number 2 was "Business leaders became rich and powerful." Then an entirely new chain of events would follow. But again you would probably have events that ran through more than one strand of history.

For almost any important historical event you should be able to see the causes and effects and decide whether they are political, economic, or social. The Civil War, for example, was a political event, as is any war. But it had both economic and social causes. Slavery was an important part of the South's farm economy. It was also at the heart of the South's social order. The North's economy did not rest on slavery. And some northerners were strongly against slavery. Thus, social and economic differences led to a political

491

result—a war. That war in turn sent waves through the political, economic, and social life of the North and South.

The Civil War is a good example of how events may have many causes and effects. When you study cause and effect, you often think of a single cause and a single effect. But just as an event may have more than one effect, it may also have more than one cause. To say that slavery caused the Civil War is too simple. Slavery was one important economic and social cause of the Civil War. But there were other causes. Northerners and southerners held different views on tariffs, a political and an economic cause. Northerners and southerners did not agree about the right of states to secede from the union, a political cause. Many economic, social, and political factors led the North and South into an armed conflict.

You will understand history better if you study causes and effects. You must be careful, however, to avoid seeing a cause-and-effect relationship where there is none. Just because two things happen at the same time, or one event follows another in time, does not always mean that one caused the other.

During a political campaign you might hear people say, "The Democrats are the party of war. Every time we have a Democratic President we get into a war." Others might say, "The Republicans are the party of big business. They don't care about the working people." Such people are pointing out what they consider to be causes and effects. Elect a Democratic President (cause) and a war will follow (effect). Elect a Republican (cause) and business will prosper, but workers will suffer (effect).

People who make such statements are not good historians. Their causes and effects do not agree with the facts. And they are missing some facts. It is true that the United States got into wars under Democrats Woodrow Wilson, Franklin Roosevelt, and Harry Truman. It is also true that wars began during the terms of Republicans Abraham Lincoln and William McKinley. Moreover the record shows that in each of these cases there were far more causes for war than the election of a President.

In the same way, you can look at history and see that both Republicans and Democrats have favored business. Both parties have stood for the working people. And both parties have drawn blame from both business and labor. Good times and bad times for business or for workers are also the result of many causes and are not linked to a single political party.

Historians look for causes and effects, but they must study all the facts. They analyze a historical event by looking at all of its separate parts. Then they synthesize by putting the parts together in a way that shows how the parts are related. They state their findings based on their analysis and synthesis of the facts.

Readers of history also must study the facts. They too must judge why and how a historian has come to a certain conclusion.

Practicing Your Skills

1. Following are some sentences from Chapter 23. Make two sentences out of each one listed below. The first should state a cause; the second, an effect. The first example is done for you.
   a. The 1848 gold strike lured thousands of settlers to California.
      1. In 1848 there was a gold strike in California. (cause)
      2. Thousands of settlers were lured to California.
   b. One group of disappointed California gold miners decided to try their luck on the eastern side of the Sierra Nevada Mountains.
   c. With the bison gone, a way of life for the Native Americans of the Plains had ended.
   d. As the railroads moved farther west, the cattle trails moved with them.
   e. Farmers adapted their methods to the dry environment.

Critical Thinking

2. **Recognizing Cause and Effect.** Go back to the pairs of sentences you wrote in the first exercise. Next to each sentence write whether it shows an economic, social, or political cause or effect. Some may relate to more than one strand.

Drawing Historical Conclusions

Historians draw conclusions about the events of the past. In doing so they sometimes make value judgments. That is, they decide that one or more events or actions of the past have had a good or bad result. In Chapter 22 you read that some historians have called the Reconstruction period a "tragic era." This is a value judgment. Historians who say this think that much of what happened in the years following the Civil War had a bad effect.

You will also remember, however, that other historians did not agree with this conclusion. These historians see good results in the civil rights acts and the Fourteenth and Fifteenth amendments of that time. They have shown that, in spite of some corruption, organizations such as the Freedmen's Bureau gradually improved the lives of black people.

Although historians carefully evaluate the facts, they do have their own points of view. These points of view may color their conclusions. Two historians looking at the same set of facts often arrive at different conclusions.

Such a difference of opinion can be seen in the way historians have looked upon industrial expansion in the late nineteenth and early twentieth centuries. Some historians admire leaders such as Andrew Carnegie in the steel business or Henry Ford in the automobile industry. Such historians believe that Carnegie, Ford, and others like them made the United States a great industrial giant. Industry made more jobs, improved the standard of living, and helped the United States become a world leader.

Other historians have seen the period from a different point of view. They have labeled it the age of the "robber barons." They believe that many business leaders were selfish. They point to the bribes paid to lawmakers and the other unlawful means used by leaders of big business to pile up fortunes. These historians weigh the acts of men such as Carnegie and Ford against the long hours, low pay, and miserable factory conditions for many workers.

Most readers of history do not have to choose between two such extreme views. Historians usually present a more balanced account of the period. They describe the bribery and corruption. But they also show that more and better goods produced at cheaper prices made life for the average person more comfortable. Working

In the extreme view of this cartoonist big business took money from everyone—the farmer, the gardener, the mechanic, the laborer, and the merchant.

EVERY MAN TO HIS OWN GAME—

BUT IT'S ACTION THAT DRAWS THE AMERICAN GALLERY

In the eyes of this pro-business cartoonist the American way has everything the "fans" want— youth, strength, speed, and skill.

people did have serious problems, but they also spoke up for and won better working conditions. A balanced historical study will weigh the facts on both sides.

Balance is important in history. Few periods or movements or even single events in history can be called all good or all bad. Able historians present clear evidence to support their conclusions. Even so, the reader of history needs to study the facts. As a reader, you may want to challenge a historian's conclusion. You may want to form a conclusion of your own.

Practicing Your Skills

Critical Thinking

Distinguishing Fact from Opinion

a. Imagine you are a white settler. Write a paragraph about moving west during the late nineteenth century. Use information from Chapter 23. Present enough clear evidence to make a value judgment about whether the move west was good or bad for you.

b. Write another paragraph on the same topic. This time imagine you are a Native American living in the Great Plains as the white settler moves in. Again, include a value judgment.

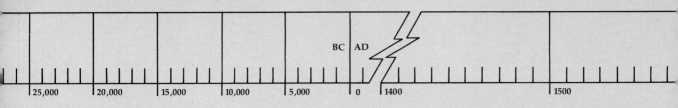

The Age of Machines

✿ Chapter 26

Vocabulary

energy
communication
charter
invention
corporation
competitor
assembly line
shareholder
stock
trust
holding company
monopoly
labor
union
strike
enterprise

Between the 1870s and 1914 the United States became the world's leading manufacturing nation. It built more railroads, produced more steel, and developed more new industries than any other country. A leader in the steel industry boasted, "The old Nations of the earth creep on at a snail's pace; The Republic [United States] thunders past with the rush of an express." The explosive growth in the use of new sources of energy and new machines affected every person living in the United States.

The roots of American industry go back to the 1630s when iron products were made at Saugus, Massachusetts. But industry's main growth came after 1815. Textile mills and shoe factories in New England, flour mills in New York and Pennsylvania, and iron and other manufactures in Pennsylvania and parts of Virginia were early signs of what was to come. During the Civil War the numbers of factories in the North and South multiplied. And after the war the nation seemed to turn all its energies from politics to industry.

Prereading

1. What changes in transportation and communication furthered the growth of industry between 1870 and 1914?

2. What developments in industry were brought about through the work of forward-looking individuals?

3. What new ways of managing and organizing businesses arose as industries grew larger?

4. What problems did labor leaders try to solve for workers in growing industries?

497

1 Changes in Transportation and Communication

The key to the growth of industry was bigger and better nationwide transportation and communication systems. At the start of the Civil War about 30,000 miles of railroad track had been laid across the United States. By 1910 slightly more than 210,000 miles of track crisscrossed the nation—a jump of 700 percent. More people, goods, and raw materials could move over great distances by train faster than ever before.

Communication changed and grew almost as much as transportation. Messages once carried by riders on horseback began to travel by telephone wire. The telephone changed people's daily lives and the way they conducted business.

The Revolution in Railroads

In 1869 the first railroad linking the Midwest to the Pacific was completed. Work had been started during the Civil War. At that time Congress chartered the Union Pacific to lay track west from Omaha, Nebraska. The Central Pacific Railroad Company was chartered to lay track east from Sacramento, California. For every mile of track laid, each company received generous amounts of government money and land. So the two companies raced toward each other to get the most track laid.

The two railroads finally met on May 10, 1869, at Promontory Summit, about fifty miles from Ogden, Utah. As the two engines from each line faced each other, the last track was set in place with a gold spike. A telegraph message from the scene was flashed across

Many Chinese workers who helped build the railroads stayed on in the United States. These young men were winners of a fire-fighting hose team race in Deadwood, Dakota, in 1888.

MAJOR TRANSCONTINENTAL RAILROADS, 1900

the nation. "One, two, three—done!" This railroad link to the Pacific was welcomed in the East with parades and merrymaking.

Even before the first coast-to-coast line was completed, other railroads were being built or planned. By 1900 five different lines connected railroad centers in the Midwest with cities on the West Coast. Still other lines brought North and South together. Short "feeder" railways linked with longer lines to form a large railway network. By 1900 nearly every settled part of the country was within easy distance of a railroad.

New inventions continued to improve train service. More and stronger steel for tracks brought greater safety, smoother rides, and longer-lasting rail beds. With the invention of the refrigerator car, meat and other foods could be shipped long distances without spoiling. Locomotives became more powerful and pulled larger loads. Trains could travel faster and more safely after George Westinghouse invented air brakes in 1869.

By selling much of the land the federal government gave them, railroad companies raised the money to lay new tracks.

Effects of Railroad Expansion

Railroads brought people and products together from all parts of the country. Local markets became national markets. Railroads carried needed raw materials from faraway places to factories built near the homes of the workers.

The railroads carried passengers as well as freight—more and more every year. By 1890 the railroads were collecting more than

500 million passenger fares per year. Yet travel was not always comfortable. At first, passengers had to sit or sleep on hard wooden benches. Many people carried their own food to avoid the high prices and the mad rush to eat when the train made a brief stop. Slowly rail travel improved. Cushioned seats were put on trains. George Pullman's Pullman car was fitted with beds, or berths, in which travelers could sleep. Pullman also introduced the dining car for long trips.

Trains soon replaced riverboats and stagecoaches for cross-country travel. Until the automobile came along in the early twentieth century, and the airplane still later, railroads were the main form of transportation for people and goods.

Communication

Since colonial times, people had sent messages from place to place by stagecoach or by riders on horseback. Individuals and trading firms often sent two or three copies of important letters, hoping that at least one would be delivered to the right place—sometimes months after being sent.

To speed mail delivery to the West Coast, the pony express was organized in April 1860. Young men and boys took turns riding fast horses from St. Joseph, Missouri, to San Francisco, California,

Air kept under pressure in a system of tubes moved message containers from place to place in the Western Union Telegraph Company in New York.

and back. Horse after horse, rider after rider, the mail moved day and night. The complete trip from Missouri to California took ten days—an unheard-of speed.

Yet, after only nineteen months of service, the pony express ended—killed off by the telegraph service. When the first coast-to-coast telegraph line was completed in late 1861, messages could be sent cross-country in a matter of minutes rather than days. Telegraph communication improved as quickly as rail transport. In 1878 the Western Union Telegraph Company had laid over 200,000 miles of wire and had sent about 24 million messages. By 1900 the miles of wire had increased fourfold and the number of messages threefold.

New means of communication were the center of attention at the 1876 Philadelphia World's Fair honoring the hundredth birthday of the Declaration of Independence. The star of the show was a small device—the telephone—invented that year by Alexander Graham Bell. By the end of the century well over a million telephones were in use in the United States. By 1920 more than 13 million had been installed.

Invention of Office Machines

Another invention—the typewriter—quickly became part of every business office. Christopher Sholes, a Milwaukee newspaper worker, built the first useful model in 1867. An improved model was sold to the Remington Arms Company in 1873. The device was further improved and widely used. Mark Twain, the famous writer, said about the machine, "I believe it will print faster than I can write. . . ." Other useful office devices followed, among them the fountain pen and the adding machine.

2   New Developments in Industry

Several developments taking place at about the same time explain the burst of industrial growth in the late nineteenth century. (1) New deposits of fuels and ores such as coal, oil, and iron were discovered. (2) Transportation and communication systems stretched to all parts of the country. (3) New inventions improved manufacturing processes. (4) Population grew rapidly, giving rise to more workers for factories and more buyers for manufactured goods. (5) Industry attracted imaginative people whose ideas made doing business more efficient and, above all, more profitable. The money to be gained drew still more people into business and industry.

The Steel Industry

The story of the steel industry shows how these developments worked together for growth. In the 1840s new deposits of iron ore, a

Section 1 Review

1. How did the Civil War encourage the growth of industry in the United States?
2. How did the invention of the refrigerator car, more powerful engines, and air brakes aid the growth of rail transportation?
3. Name at least three ways that changes in railroad transportation contributed to industrial growth.
4. Name two inventions that appeared in business offices in the last half of the nineteenth century.

Critical Thinking

5. **Recognizing Cause and Effect.** Why was the Pony Express in business such a short time?

LOOKING AHEAD: What developments in industry were brought about through the work of forward-looking individuals?

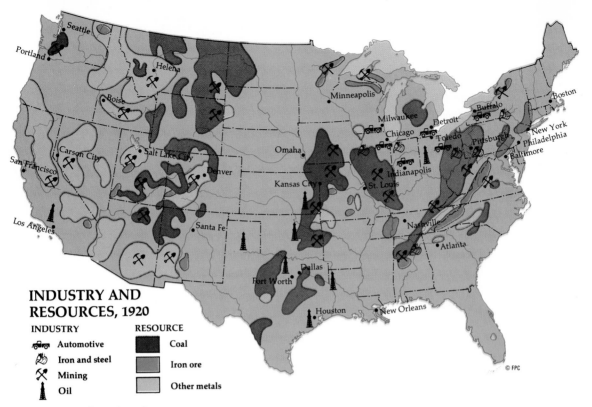

INDUSTRY AND RESOURCES, 1920

INDUSTRY
- 🚗 Automotive
- ⚒ Iron and steel
- ⚒ Mining
- 🛢 Oil

RESOURCE
- ▰ Coal
- ▰ Iron ore
- ▰ Other metals

© FPC

The discovery of ore deposits, coupled with the building of cross-country railroads, brought the products of mine and factory together.

raw material from which steel is made, were discovered in Upper Michigan and Minnesota. Nothing came of this find because the leading ironworks were located close to coalfields in Pennsylvania—more than a thousand miles away. But the railroads, moving across the country in the 1870s and 1880s, could carry the rich ore to the distant mills. Finished steel was then moved by rail to factories where it was shaped into farm machines, tools, and other goods.

The steel industry also grew with the help of new inventions. The Bessemer furnace, first used in the United States in the 1870s, removed the impurities from iron ore. The furnace did the job at such a low cost that steel replaced iron as a popular building material. At the cheaper prices other new industries used more steel.

Besides the discovery of rich ores, the improved transportation, and the new inventions, a tripling of the nation's population between 1860 and 1920 also worked in favor of the steel industry. More people meant not only more workers but also more customers. Nearly everyone bought products made from steel: pots and pans, stoves, bicycle parts, and all sorts of hardware. As the factories made more products, the cost of making them and of buying them went down. Low prices in turn attracted even more customers. Thus, the market for steel products boomed.

Carnegie and the Steel Industry

A number of talented and imaginative persons entered the steel industry and became successful. None was more exciting than Andrew

Carnegie. He came to the United States with his parents, poor immigrants from Scotland, in 1848. Carnegie first worked as a bobbin boy in a cotton factory at a wage of $1.20 a week. As fast as the bobbins on the spinning machines filled with thread, the child workers replaced them with empty spools. Later Carnegie became a telegraph operator and then assistant to a railroad executive. Although he had spent little time in school, Carnegie managed to educate himself through reading.

In 1865 Carnegie entered the iron and steel business. He gave it all his attention. When others cut back, Carnegie added to his plants. When a business slowdown left other steelmakers short of money in 1873, Carnegie bought them out and made more steel. He bought mining firms to control the flow of iron ore and coal to his plants. He added a steamship company and a railroad company to carry materials to and from the plants.

By the 1890s Carnegie himself had an income of $20 million a year. In 1901 he sold his business to the newly formed United States Steel Corporation for $500 million. He gave away hundreds of millions of dollars for education, libraries, scientific study, and the cause of world peace.

As early as 1901, the national press recognized Andrew Carnegie for his generous public gifts. *Harper's Weekly* printed the cartoon to the left, entitled "Building a Very Solid Temple of Fame." Carnegie gave more than $56 million to build libraries around the world—1,700 of them in the United States. Communities receiving library buildings still had to buy books and hire librarians.

The Oil Industry

When oil was first found in the United States, no one quite knew what to do with it. Some people sold it as a medicine. They said it would cure everything from colds to blindness.

It was not until the mid-1800s that a way was discovered to refine crude oil into something useful. That something was kerosene, which soon replaced whale oil as fuel for lamps. A heavier oil was made to keep machine parts moving smoothly and to cut down on wear. Oil for this purpose became more and more important with the greater use of machines.

Edwin L. Drake dug the first well in search of oil in 1859 near Titusville, Pennsylvania. Two years later the first oil gusher came in through his well. A man dashed into the Titusville Hotel shouting: "Oil! Millions of gallons! . . . Shootin' up in the air like a fountain." The rush for oil soon matched the gold rushes of the West in energy and excitement. By the early 1900s the United States was pumping 60 percent of the world's oil.

Rockefeller and the Oil Industry

The person who became known as the oil king was John D. Rockefeller. He was born on a farm in New York state, and one of his first jobs was as a clerk in a grocery store. He and a partner opened a store in Cleveland, Ohio, in 1859. Four years later Rockefeller entered the oil refining business in Cleveland. He founded the Standard Oil Company in 1870.

Rockefeller let little stand in his way as he took over the oil industry. At one time, key railroads gave him special low rates to carry his oil. In return for all his business these railroads also gave Rockefeller part of the fares they collected from his competitors. Rockefeller's company offered gifts to state legislators for yes votes on laws that favored the firm. Rockefeller bought out some competitors and forced out others. By the 1890s Standard Oil controlled about 90 percent of the nation's oil refineries. By 1914 Rockefeller was a billionaire.

Like Carnegie, Rockefeller gave away a great part of his fortune. Some money went to medicine, some to education, and some to the Baptist Church, of which he was a lifelong member.

John D. Rockefeller, shown here in 1922 at the age of eighty-three, had retired from the oil business by 1897 to devote his time and money to public causes.

Edison and the Electrical Industry

Like the oil industry, the electrical industry was new. Its rise began in the 1880s. Its leading figure was Thomas Alva Edison.

Edison began experimenting with science as a young boy, and he continued to do so until he died in 1931 at the age of eighty-five. In 1876 he set up a testing laboratory at Menlo Park, New Jersey. He wanted to turn out "a minor invention every ten days and a big thing

The oil industry, first shaped by Rockefeller in the 1800s, has become the key to worldwide industrial development in the 1980s.

every six months or so." People began to call him "the wizard of Menlo Park." Edison invented the phonograph in 1877. Two years later he made the first useful light bulb. He built the first electric power station. He improved the telegraph and the telephone, and he was among the first to work on motion picture machines.

By 1890 Edison's company was producing nearly a million light bulbs a year. Cities and towns began to light their streets with electricity. In 1887 Richmond, Virginia, installed the first electric streetcars. By 1890 over fifty cities had electric streetcar systems.

In the 1890s electricity began to take the place of steam power in many factories. Then came newfound electrical gadgets of all sorts. In 1906 Dr. Lee De Forest made a vacuum tube that allowed the sound of voices and of music to be carried over radio waves. Radio stations began operating in many major cities. By the mid-1920s, except for some rural areas, electricity and the radio were found everywhere.

Though not the first to do so, Henry Ford built a gas-powered tractor in 1906.

Henry Ford and the Assembly Line

Henry Ford, like Edison, was an inventor who helped develop an industry. Although born on a farm, Ford wanted no part of farming. He was interested in machines. He liked to take them apart to see what made them work. Later he said, "Every clock in the house shuddered when it saw me coming."

As a young man, Ford moved to Detroit. He later took a job in an electrical plant, but he spent all of his extra time working on a horseless carriage—an automobile powered by an engine. Other inventors were also working on the automobile. Ford called his first car a quadricycle because of its four wheels. It could go forward, but it could not back up. The important part of the car was its gasoline engine. Ford had built the engine himself.

Ford drove his new car out to the farm to show his father. Later a friend wrote of his father's reaction. "I could see that old Mr. Ford was ashamed of a grown-up man like his son Henry fussing over a little thing like a quadricycle."

Most people, however, were eager to know how Ford's car ran. Ford wrote: "If I left it [the car] alone for a minute, some curious person always tried to run it. Finally, I had to carry a chain and fasten it to a lamp post whenever I left it anywhere."

In the early 1900s Ford borrowed enough money to go into business with some partners. The company was small to start with, but it grew quickly. The Ford Motor Company was not the first company to make cars. In 1910 there were more than sixty such companies, but their total output was less than 200,000 cars a year. In those early years only the rich could afford motor cars.

Ford introduced a new way of building cars, a way that became widely used in other industries as well. The process was based on an idea that began with Eli Whitney—the idea of using interchangeable parts. In Ford's factory cars were put together as they traveled along on a moving belt. Workers along this assembly line added the same part to each car as it passed. Cars reached the end of the line finished and ready to be driven away.

By 1916 Ford's assembly line method allowed him to sell his Model T for as little as $360. This low price put the automobile within reach of most factory workers and farmers. Ford's business soared. In the same year, Ford's factories produced about 2,000 cars per day, or almost one car every 43 seconds. Ford and others were soon making 2 million cars each year.

The automobile brought about as great a revolution in transportation as the railroad had earlier. People could live farther from their places of business and drive to work each day. Suburbs around large cities mushroomed. People were able to travel for pleasure. Hundreds of thousands of miles of new roads were built for automobiles. Other industries profited, too. There was a demand for more steel for building car bodies and frames, more rubber for tires, and more oil for gasoline. This burst of industry meant even more jobs for workers.

3   Big Business

With such rapid industrial growth, business leaders turned to new ways of running factories and managing offices. In the smaller businesses of the early nineteenth century the owners were usually the managers. They watched over production. They often knew most or all of their workers by name. But as companies grew, business owners hired other people to manage their firms.

Corporations

One structure used to manage large industries is the corporation. A corporation is a business that is owned by many people called shareholders. A business becomes a corporation by getting a charter from a state. It can sell stock, or shares in the business, to other people. Hundreds of thousands of people may hold shares in a large corporation. Each shareholder owns part of the business and receives part

Section 2 Review

1. How did the Bessemer furnace aid the growth of the steel industry?
2. How did Andrew Carnegie increase his control of the steel business?
3. How did John D. Rockefeller use railroads and legislators to his company's advantage?
4. Name three devices that Edison invented or improved.

Critical Thinking

5. **Identifying Central Issues.** How did Henry Ford's assembly line method help automakers put many cars on the road in a short time?

LOOKING AHEAD: What new ways of managing and organizing businesses arose as industries grew larger?

Corporations, Trusts, and Holding Companies

Corporation X in a Trust

Trust

Trustees		
All shares X	All shares Y	All shares Z

1. X is bought by a trust that owns other corporations.
2. X no longer exists as a separate corporation. Its business affairs, and those of other companies in the trust, are directed by a single board of trustees.
3. In 1890 trusts were outlawed by the Sherman Antitrust Act.

Corporation X in a Holding Company

Holding Company

CORPORATION M   CORPORATION X

Board of Directors		Board of Directors
All shares	Controlling	Shares held by M
	shares	All other shares
M	Y Z	

of its profits. Many early corporations were owned by small groups of shareholders.

The advantages of the corporation are many. It can pool large sums of money—often borrowed from banks—to buy new machines and to expand factories. It can buy raw materials in large amounts, often at low prices. It can bring together the brain power and talent of many persons and put them to work where they are most needed. Its life is longer than that of a single manager or stockholder. Industrial leaders such as Carnegie and Rockefeller recognized these advantages and chose to manage their businesses as corporations.

Banking and Finance

With people buying and selling shares in corporations, a need arose for a central place where stock could be exchanged. New York City's Wall Street became that center. Banking companies specializing in buying and selling railroad stocks first appeared on Wall Street in the mid-1800s. These banking companies then grew by selling other industrial stocks.

A major organizer of corporations and of banks was John Pierpont Morgan. In 1895 he formed J.P. Morgan and Company. Most people called it the House of Morgan. It became the most important investment banking firm in the nation.

Morgan, a sharp business leader, began to take control of other banks, insurance companies, and railroads. He managed to work his way onto the board of directors of dozens of businesses. As a board member, he had important decision-making power.

In 1901 J. P. Morgan put together United States Steel, the nation's first billion-dollar corporation. When several banks failed in 1907, Morgan raised enough money to save the remaining ones. Even the federal government asked Morgan for advice or help in financial matters.

Trusts and Monopolies

From the 1870s through the early 1900s the trend in business was toward bigness. Corporations came together to form even larger businesses. One such business giant was the trust. When a trust was formed, the stock of several corporations would be handed over to a group of trustees, who acted as a board of directors for the new company. The trustees would manage all the different corporations as though they were a single firm. Rockefeller finally used this method to gain control of the oil industry. The trust multiplied the advantages of a corporation. But it gave great power to only a few people.

Although trusts were outlawed in 1890, holding companies were not. Holding companies would buy enough stock in different corporations to direct those corporations' business choices. The U.S. Steel Corporation was a holding company that also controlled some railroads. By 1904 six major business firms guided the operation of over a thousand railroad lines. And two men—Morgan and Rockefeller—had a hand in all six firms.

Many people worried about the trend toward bigness in business. If one person or a small group could control a whole industry, that industry would be a monopoly. A monopoly can set prices to its own advantage. Those who use its products or services have no choice—they either pay the price or do without. The American Telephone and Telegraph Company once held the telephone industry as a monopoly. Organized in 1885, AT&T owned or ran most telephone companies by 1900. These companies made the telephones, installed and repaired them, and handled almost all the calls made around the nation.

People were worried about how much power the Morgans, Rockefellers, and others had over the nation's economy. In the 1890s and early 1900s big business and monopolies became important issues in the nation's politics.

4 Labor

Growing industry needed more workers. Before the Civil War three out of every five persons in the United States worked on a farm. By 1880 more people worked in jobs off the farm than on the farm.

Immigrants as Workers

After 1880 great numbers of immigrants came to the United States from eastern and southern Europe—from Poland, Russia, Austria, Yugoslavia, Italy, Greece, and Spain. Between 1900 and 1915 more than 9 million immigrants arrived. Some settled on farms, but many more became factory workers. Employers were eager to hire the newcomers who so needed work that they accepted low wages. In 1907, in the Carnegie Steel Works alone, 15,000 out of 23,000 persons on the job were foreign born.

Workers' Problems

Workers—immigrant as well as native born—had many of the same problems. Personal exchanges between owners and workers disappeared as factories became larger. Workers had no protection against accidents on the job. And assembly line duties were often routine and dull. Only the drop in prices for many goods between 1865 and 1898 helped working people improve their standard of living. Prices began to rise rapidly after 1898, but workers' pay did not keep pace. Henry Ford shocked the business world when he

Section 3 Review

1. How does a business become a corporation?
2. What are three advantages of a corporation?
3. How did J. Pierpont Morgan gain power on Wall Street?
4. How does a trust differ from a holding company?
5. What is a monopoly?

Critical Thinking
6. **Expressing Problems Clearly.** What are the possible dangers of a monopoly?

LOOKING AHEAD: What problems did labor leaders try to solve for workers in growing industries?

Organized workers began to make their demands heard by 1914.

doubled his workers' salaries in 1914. He said that better paid workers would then have the money to become consumers. But few companies followed Ford's example.

Workers also faced the problem of unemployment. Even while industry grew, factories often slowed down or closed completely for long periods. Many workers were without jobs for months—even years—at a time.

Wage earners began to look to labor unions to solve their problems. By joining unions, workers could bargain together with business owners for higher pay and better working conditions. They could also threaten to strike—walk off the job—if they could not come to terms with the owners. Big business was against unions and tried to stamp them out. Some companies fired workers just for joining unions. Owners shut down plants to get rid of workers who asked for better conditions. The owners then reopened the plants and hired new workers. Some business owners hired police to report on union leaders and to upset union plans.

Unions grew—but slowly. By 1898 fewer than a half million out of 17 million non-farm workers belonged to a union. Not until the early twentieth century did unions gather enough strength to make themselves heard by big business.

Organized Labor Unions

Two unions best show how organized labor fared on a national level between 1865 and 1914. The Knights of Labor succeeded briefly; the American Federation of Labor lives on today.

Uriah Stephens, a man of faith whose goal was to improve all of society, founded the Knights of Labor in 1869. The group grew slowly. By the mid-1880s Terence V. Powderly, a good speaker and organizer, had gotten more than 700,000 workers to join. But in 1886 the Knights of Labor were blamed, without evidence, for the Haymarket riot in Chicago. In that clash between workers and police seven law officers were killed and seventy others injured by a bomb. No one knows who threw it.

Being blamed for the Haymarket riot hurt the Knights of Labor. The union had other problems as well. Its leaders were fighting over union goals. And among the Knights were many unskilled workers—those whose jobs almost anyone could do. The union found it hard to strike, since a business owner could easily fill the strikers' jobs with other unskilled workers. By 1893 membership in the Knights of Labor had dropped to 75,000. By the end of the century the union was all but dead.

The American Federation of Labor (AFL) was organized in 1886. Samuel Gompers was chosen president, an office he held in every year but one until 1924. The AFL was not a single union but a collection of many different craft unions. Among its members were groups of skilled workers such as brewers, carpenters, furniture makers, and cigar makers. Each group was composed of people who did similar work in a single industry. Its members shared the same kinds of problems and goals. At the same time, the federation, acting for the many separate groups, could seek ends that all the workers valued, such as safety on the job, shorter hours, and more pay. By 1901 the AFL had nearly 1 million members, and by 1920 it had grown to 4 million. As its numbers grew, the AFL became a political influence. The AFL urged members to vote for political candidates who favored better working conditions. Many candidates tried to win its support.

Labor vs. Business

The strike was labor's major weapon against business. From the late 1870s to the beginning of the First World War in 1914 there were numerous strikes. Many walkouts led to fighting, property damage, and death. Sometimes the unions won, but more often they were defeated.

The Pullman strike was the hardest fought. In 1894 the American Railway Union, headed by Eugene V. Debs, backed the striking workers at the Pullman Company, a firm that made railroad cars. The railway walkout tied up almost all train traffic. At first there was no violence. But Attorney General Richard Olney, cooperating with the railroads, was determined to crush the union. Federal troops were called in to make the union obey a court order to end the strike. A fight followed. Many people were jailed. Later Debs was also jailed. The strike was broken, and the union was crippled.

Less violent was a strike among New York garment workers in 1909. Women sewed most of the factory-made clothes at that time. They often worked in old, dirty buildings with little light and no fresh air. To improve their lot, the International Ladies' Garment Workers Union and the Women's Trade Union League called for a strike. Thousands of women walked off the job and stayed off the job for thirteen weeks. The court ordered them back to work, but the women held firm. Many were carried off to jail. The strike was finally called off in February 1910, with only a few small gains for the workers. But during the strike the union had added thousands of new members.

During its rise no one could foresee how much industry would influence every aspect of people's lives. Today huge businesses and unions are accepted as part of everyday life. So is the unending stream of goods turned out by factories all over the nation. New machines, new products, and new ways of working come into use every single day. You are an heir of the machine age.

Section 4 Review

1. What three problems did factory workers share?
2. What did business owners do to keep unions from gaining power?
3. Why did the American Federation of Labor succeed while the Knights of Labor failed?
4. Why was the 1894 strike by the American Railway Union so violent?

Critical Thinking

5. **Demonstrating Reasoned Judgement.** Did the 1909-1910 strike by New York's garment workers succeed? Explain.

511

Heritage   Of Enterprise

Daring, far-looking people have been part of American life since the country was first settled.

Enterprise is what moves people to try new ways and to dare to reach for certain goals. Founding a colony in a foreign land calls for enterprise. Forming a nation calls for enterprise. Moving west calls for enterprise. An enterprising spirit has been part of business in the United States from the nation's earliest days. In the industrial age many enterprising persons succeeded beyond their wildest dreams.

Individual Efforts

The enterprise of certain business owners often led to the growth of new factories or even whole industries. Gustavus Swift made his fortune in meat packing. Cyrus McCormick led the way in farm machinery. Marshall Field became famous in retail sales. Julius Rosenwald fathered a national mail order company, and John D. Rockefeller pioneered in refining and marketing oil. In each case a single person started a firm that often grew large enough to control an entire industry.

These business leaders succeeded mainly because they were bright, hard-working, and daring. But their efforts were favored by an abundance of natural resources and skilled workers, a growing body of customers, and generally good times for business.

These same leaders often bent the law and profited from the hard work of people less enterprising than they were. They also destroyed or used up many gifts of the land that belonged to all citizens, rich and poor. But it is a matter for debate where the nation would be today if they had acted otherwise.

Scientific Management

As firms grew, enterprising people thought up new devices and ideas

President Warren G. Harding (second from right) relaxes with (left to right) Henry Ford, Thomas Edison, and Harvey Firestone.

for increasing production. They used what is often called scientific management.

The parent of scientific management was Frederick W. Taylor. Taylor believed there was one best way to do any task. For example, he tried to find a way to walk that used the least amount of energy. And he designed a special tennis racket that helped him win a national championship.

The Bethlehem Steel Company hired Taylor to cut down on wasted work in its factory. In those days paying people to shovel coal and iron ore was a large part of the cost of making steel. Taylor studied what the workers did. He found that they used the same shovel to move coal that they used to move iron ore. A shovelful of coal weighed about three and a half pounds (1.6 kg), while one shovelful of iron ore weighed about thirty-eight pounds (17 kg).

Taylor reasoned that using the same shovel for coal and for iron ore wasted energy and time. He began to try different shovels that would serve each use better. He found that workers using a smaller shovel moved more ore in the same time and were less weary than workers had been before.

After Taylor had devised different shovels, only 140 persons were needed to do the job that 600 had done before. Although some people had to look for work elsewhere, those who were kept on received 50 percent higher pay.

Benefits of Enterprise

Taylor's approach was widely imitated. Chemists found better ways to make steel and other materials. Engineers learned how to

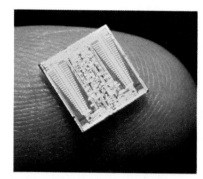

The invention of tiny computer chips started a new industry.

build long bridges. Today experimenters in electronics and computers have found a way to store great amounts of information on a piece of matter much smaller than your fingernail. All of these breakthroughs spring from the minds of enterprising and scientific people.

New methods or machines often cut down on the number of workers needed to produce goods. The loss of a job is a great hardship. But some inventions lead to whole new industries and thousands of new jobs.

The Productive Cycle

The goal of enterprise in business is to make more goods at a lower cost. In other words the goal is higher productivity. Lower costs bring more goods within reach of more people. At the same time, higher productivity leads to bigger profits, since less money is spent on making goods. Higher profits make it possible for companies to pay better wages. Workers are then spurred on to produce more goods. Business leaders enjoy the fruits of higher productivity, and everyone lives a little better for it.

Business enterprise is part of a lasting heritage in the United States. To keep up the nation's standard of living—the highest in the world—leaders of tomorrow must bring to their task the quick thinking and the boldness of their enterprising forebears.

Mass production of such goods as bathroom basins lowers the price of each individual item.

Chapter 26 Review

Chapter Summary

The completion of the first cross-country railroad in 1869, faster communication with the telegraph and the telephone, and other inventions led to a great spurt in industrial growth after the Civil War. Giant industries such as steelmaking and oil refining began to develop in this period.

Industrial workers, many of whom were immigrants, started joining unions. Using the strike, the unions' chief weapon, workers hoped to gain better working conditions.

Two unions in particular rose to power in the late 1800s. The Knights of Labor, founded in 1869, consisted mainly of unskilled workers. It lost its power in the 1890s after it was blamed for the Haymarket riot in 1886. The American Federation of Labor (AFL)—a collection of craft unions led by Samuel Gompers—won some important gains for workers and continues to bargain for its members today.

Reviewing Vocabulary

Match each of the following words with its correct definition. Write your answers on a separate sheet of paper.

energy	stock
communication	trust
charter	holding company
invention	monopoly
corporation	labor
competitor	union
assembly line	strike
shareholder	enterprise

1. a business owning enough stock in different companies to control the management of those companies
2. a line of workers each of whom attaches a piece to a product as it passes before them on a moving belt
3. an industry completely controlled by one person or small group
4. a written agreement or grant of rights and privileges
5. a willingness to start something new or take a daring step
6. workers, as a group
7. the process of sharing information
8. one or more shares in a business
9. to walk off the job until one's demands are met
10. a large business made up of several corporations and operated as a single firm by a board of trustees
11. an organization formed by workers to bargain for higher pay and better working conditions
12. a business chartered by the state and owned by shareholders
13. one who owns a share in a business
14. the ability or capacity to do work
15. a new device or way of doing something
16. a rival buyer or seller of goods and services in the marketplace

Understanding Main Ideas

1. Describe the important changes in transportation and communication that helped industry grow between 1870 and 1914.
2. How did Carnegie, Rockefeller, Edison, and Ford change the operation of business and industry in the United States?
3. How was the "Big Business" of the industrial age different from the small, independently owned businesses of earlier times?
4. Why did workers feel it was inportant to join labor unions?

Critical Thinking Skills

1. **Identifying Assumptions.** Why did the United States encourage railroad building

Social Studies Skills: Interpreting a Cartoon

The editorial cartoon on this page, like all political cartoons, expresses an opinion. The topic of this cartoon is the Standard Oil Company, which is depicted as an octopus.

Skill Review: Study the cartoon and then choose the correct ending for each statement below.

1. The cartoonist chose to show Standard Oil with octopus-like arms because
   (a) an octopus stands for hard work and a fighting spirit
   (b) an octopus has many arms that it uses to strangle its victims.
2. The cartoonist is trying to say that
   (a) trusts have control over too many elements of the nation's economy
   (b) trusts are good for America because they link many parts of the economy.
3. A good caption for this cartoon would be
   (a) "And I have more arms yet!"
   (b) "The good work continues."

with grants of money and land to the railroad companies?
2. **Recognizing Ideologies.** What beliefs about American society led the government to side with industry against striking unions in the early 1900s?
3. **Expressing Problems Clearly.** What is the contradiction between the way John D. Rockefeller made his fortune and the way he used it?

Writing About History

1. **Writing an Advertisement.** Write a "help wanted" ad that might have appeared in an American newspaper anytime between 1870 and 1914. Describe a typical job in this period and the experience, training, and work hours that the job requires.
2. **Writing an Opinion.** Select the one invention or development described in this chapter that you think is the most interesting. In a short essay, explain why you find it to be interesting and summarize the effect it had on the nation.

Your Region in History

Economics. What industries or businesses were important in your area in the late 1800s? Were labor unions active in your region's economy? How does the economic climate of your region in the 1800s compare with your area's economy today?

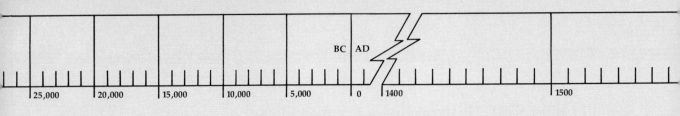

City
Lights

❧ **Chapter 27**

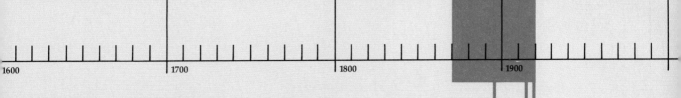

1600   1700   1800   1900

Vocabulary

rural	trolley
urban	suburb
slum	subway
ethnic	leisure
skyscraper	entertainment
terminal	vaudeville
apartment	jazz
tenement	motion picture

THE GROWTH OF INDUSTRY in the age of machines gave rise to city life. New cities came into being and older cities gained in size and numbers. In 1850 the United States was a rural nation. A few large trading and manufacturing cities were sprinkled among the farms, villages, and small towns. By 1890 most of today's cities had been founded. By 1910 parts of the nation were becoming urban, made up of cities that were growing centers for factories and businesses linked together by rail lines.

More and more people came to cities to work and live. In 1875 only one fourth of the nation's people lived in cities. By 1920 half of them had moved there. In some parts of the country—the Atlantic seaboard, for example—two out of three people lived in urban communities, places with populations of 2,500 or more. The astonishing growth of cities changed the face of the nation.

Prereading

1. What were some reasons for urban growth between 1850 and 1910?
2. How did the city change the lives of those who lived there?
3. In what free-time activities did city dwellers take part?

1   Urban Growth

Between 1880 and 1920 towns and cities grew quickly. A British visitor observed that "towns and villages have been raised by magic." Railroad agents, land companies, individual business owners, and others all helped found urban communities. An agent for a railroad wrote: "I shall have two or three more towns to name very soon. . . . [One] is now . . . a cornfield, so I cannot have it surveyed. But yesterday a man came to arrange to put a hotel there. This is a great country for hotels." One land promoter had a grand idea. "One of my plans was the creation of a chain of great towns across the continent, connecting Boston with San Francisco by a magnificent highway of cities."

Other promoters promised investors they would get rich quick. "Would you make money easy?" one advertisement asked. It quickly answered its own question. "Find then the site of a city and the farm it is to be built on! How many regret the non-purchase of that lot in New York; that block in Buffalo; that acre in Chicago; that quarter section in Omaha. Once these city properties could be bought for a song."

People from the countryside and from foreign lands were drawn to cities in the United States in greater numbers than ever before. The unending stream of people brought both prosperity and problems. The new urban centers struggled to provide housing, public transportation, schools, parks, public water and sewers, and police and fire protection for their ever-growing populations.

Migration from Farms to Cities

After 1900, farmers who earlier might have migrated west moved instead to the city. Between 1880 and 1910 at least 11 million people born in rural homes became urban dwellers. At the end of this period about one in four city dwellers was newly arrived from a farm or small town. A visitor to Vermont in the 1880s found a village nearly abandoned except for a few outlying farms. When he asked where all the villagers had gone, he was told they had left for the factory towns and the large cities. One American declared that the city had become the heart of the nation, "sending its streams of life . . . to the very fingertips of the whole land."

The city served as a magnet for farmers who had lost their farms and who were seeking other jobs. The city also offered music, art, and theater. In many ways the city was another frontier. It offered all comers a chance to improve themselves.

With all its charms, the city had its darker side. New York City reminded one visitor of "a lady in a ball costume, with diamonds in her ears, and her toes out at her boots." Alongside the beautiful

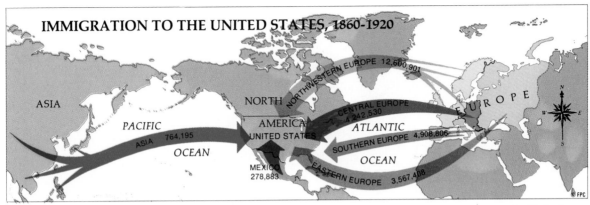

IMMIGRATION TO THE UNITED STATES, 1860-1920

ASIA

PACIFIC OCEAN

ASIA 764,195

NORTH AMERICA
UNITED STATES

MEXICO 278,883

NORTHWESTERN EUROPE 12,600,901

CENTRAL EUROPE 4,242,530

ATLANTIC OCEAN

SOUTHERN EUROPE 4,908,806

EASTERN EUROPE 3,567,408

EUROPE

© FPC

Immigrants came to the United States by the thousands, but all together they were still only a minority in the population.

homes, the stately churches, and the city's places of business and industry lay the slums. There many hopeless people lived out their lives in poverty.

Migration of Immigrants to Cities

Newly arrived immigrants came to the cities for the same reasons that farmers did—jobs and a better way of life. Between 1880 and 1910 the number of immigrants settling in the cities almost equaled the number of people moving to the cities from the farms. Between 1900 and 1910, however, more immigrants than farmers poured into urban centers.

As in the past, many newcomers arrived from the countries of western and northern Europe—from Britain, Ireland, Scotland, Norway, Sweden, Denmark, Germany, and France. But after 1880 an even greater number came from eastern and southern Europe—from Poland, Russia, Czechoslovakia, Austria-Hungary, Yugoslavia, Italy, Greece, Spain, and Portugal. Historians often call this influx from eastern and southern Europe the "new" immigration.

Most of the new immigrants had few of the skills needed for living in big cities or working at high-paying jobs. Only a few spoke English. While most earlier immigrants had been Protestants, many new arrivals were Catholics or Jews. They often faced prejudice. They were also distrusted, even hated, by workers who feared they would lose their jobs to the newcomers.

Most immigrants settled in the large cities where there were more jobs. Immigrants speaking the same language and following the same customs often kept together. Ethnic neighborhoods began taking shape in almost every large city—a Polish neighborhood next to an Italian neighborhood next to a Jewish neighborhood. Many ethnic groups published their own newspapers. In 1890 there were 800 German-language newspapers issued in the United States. The *Daily Journal of New York*, printed in Yiddish, was one of the best-selling papers in the city. The different ethnic groups also built their

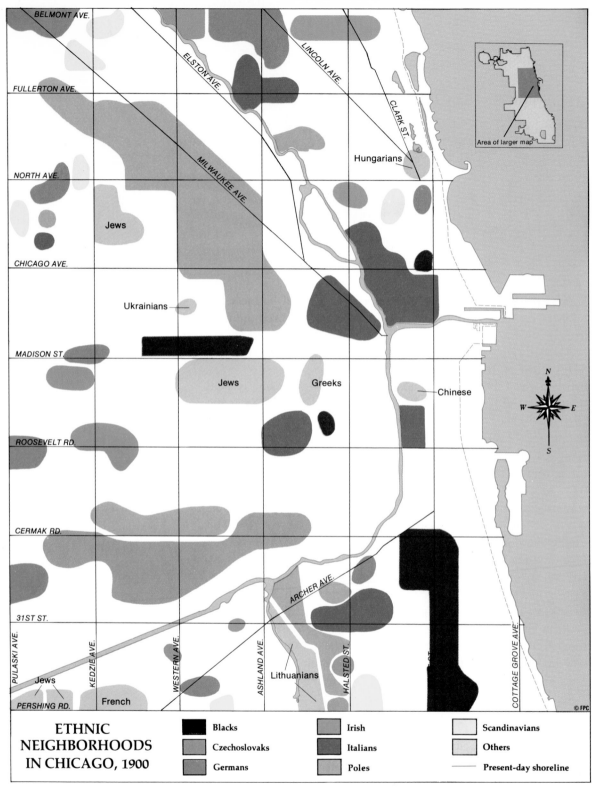

ETHNIC NEIGHBORHOODS IN CHICAGO, 1900

Map labels:
BELMONT AVE.
FULLERTON AVE.
NORTH AVE.
CHICAGO AVE.
MADISON ST.
ROOSEVELT RD.
CERMAK RD.
31ST ST.
PERSHING RD.

ELSTON AVE.
LINCOLN AVE.
CLARK ST.
MILWAUKEE AVE.
ARCHER AVE.
PULASKI AVE.
KEDZIE AVE.
WESTERN AVE.
ASHLAND AVE.
HALSTED ST.
COTTAGE GROVE AVE.

Hungarians
Jews
Ukrainians
Jews
Greeks
Chinese
Lithuanians
Jews
French

Area of larger map

N
W   E
S

© FPC

Legend:
Blacks
Czechoslovaks
Germans
Irish
Italians
Poles
Scandinavians
Others
Present-day shoreline

Factories and homes went up side by side in central Chicago as the city pushed out in all directions away from the lake.

own houses of worship. They spoke the language of their birthplace in their homes and shops. Their dress and food habits were also brought from the "old country."

In 1890 New York City had more foreign-born residents than any other city in the world. Four out of five people living there were either born in another country or had foreign-born parents. New York City had as many Italians as Naples, Italy, and as many Germans as Hamburg, Germany. There were twice as many Irish in New York City as in the city of Dublin. The number of Jews in New York City was more than twice the number of Jews in Warsaw, Poland.

In other large cities around the country—Cincinnati, Cleveland, St. Louis, and San Francisco—immigrant population was also high. Even today, more Poles live in Chicago than in any city in Poland except Warsaw.

Immigrants from Asia, especially China, swelled the ethnic populations of many western cities. Most of the Chinese who had come to work on the railroads in the West stayed on when the railroads were finished. Many settled along the West Coast in such cities as San Francisco and Los Angeles. Others moved elsewhere in the United States. Usually they lived together in one part of a city or small town, giving rise to the so-called Chinatowns found in many urban centers today. Japanese people came to the United States after 1890, but in smaller numbers than the Chinese. They too settled mainly on the West Coast.

Asian immigrants were saddled with strict rules. For a time the state of California would not allow Asians to own property or hold certain jobs. In 1882 Congress passed a law forbidding further immigration from China. Later the United States government asked the Japanese government to discourage Japanese people from coming. These bans lasted until 1952. Until then, immigrants from Asia were not allowed to become citizens of the United States.

A Building Boom

New building materials—steel, aluminum, and concrete—changed city skylines forever. The first modern skyscraper—the ten-story Home Insurance Building made with an iron frame—was built in Chicago in 1885. From that time on, developments in steelmaking and machinery made taller and taller buildings possible. High quality, low-priced steel was quickly put to use in big city skyscrapers. When the electric motor came along, together with safety devices, modern elevators became possible.

Most cities built huge train stations or terminals for the heavy passenger and freight traffic. South Station in Boston was completed in 1898. Union Station was built in Washington, D.C., in 1907. The Chicago and North Western Railway Station went up in Chicago in 1911. And Grand Central Station began to serve New York City in 1913. Some people saw these train terminals as monuments to the

Three separate rail companies shared New York's Grand Central Station when it was completed in 1871.

cities of the United States much as the giant cathedrals were monuments to European cities in earlier times. Many city dwellers and almost every visitor to the city passed through these great structures.

The high price of city land called for saving space in housing. Stacking housing units one on top of the other instead of building them side by side was one idea. Apartment buildings went up in great numbers between 1880 and 1910.

Tenement Housing

Some apartments became so crowded and ill-kept that they threatened the health, and even the life, of the residents. New York had the largest slum of any city in the United States. By 1901 two thirds of its 3.5 million people lived in tenements. Many of these tenements were dumbbell-shaped apartments—long, narrow buildings with six or seven rooms at each end. Only four rooms out of every fourteen on a floor had direct air and light. A room might measure three steps by five steps, or three steps by two steps. Often five people lived in a two-room apartment. The only light came from an air shaft between buildings into which people also tossed their garbage. Of this practice one man said, "It is better than breaking your legs running up and down the stairs in the dark." Toilets were placed in sheds in the alley. In 1900 the city of Baltimore still had 90,000 such outdoor toilets.

Few of these crowded tenements had water piped into the building. Instead, everyone went to a public pump in the street to get water for cooking and bathing. People living in tenements were said to receive only two good baths in their lives—one at birth and the other at death.

A reporter from a New York newspaper described tenement conditions in detail.

> The hall is dark, and you might stumble over the children. . . . Not that it would hurt them; kicks and cuffs are their daily diet. . . . Here where the hall turns and dives into utter darkness is a step. . . . You can feel your way, if you cannot see it. . . . All the fresh air that ever enters these stairs comes from the hall door that is forever slamming, and from the windows of dark bedrooms. . . . The sinks are in the hallway, that all tenants may have access—and all be poisoned alike by their summer stenches.

In 1901 the New York legislature passed a law that forbade further building of dumbbell-shaped apartments. Other states later copied this law.

Streets and Transportation

Roads made of concrete did not come into use until after 1900. In 1890 two thirds of Chicago's streets were dirt. The other streets were paved with wood blocks, gravel, cinders, or cobblestones. A person had to be alert to pass safely through the horses, buggies, wagons, people—and later, bicycles and cars—packed in the streets. Crossing busy streets was less dangerous after traffic signals came into use.

After 1900, steam trolleys carried passengers from place to place in many large cities. Overhead, or elevated, steam railways began to reach beyond the city into the suburbs. Tracks were laid for subway trains in underground tunnels in Boston in 1897 and in New York City in 1900. Ten years later New York had more than 100 miles of subways.

In the early 1900s many cities put electricity to work in trolleys and trains. Electric-powered engines were cheaper, faster, and cleaner for enclosed city stations than were noisy, smoky steam engines that burned wood or coal for fuel.

During this same period America took to bicycles as it later took to cars. Bicycles were mass-produced, and many people owned one. Tires filled with air replaced solid rubber tires and made riding safer and more comfortable.

Seattle: A Case Study

Between 1880 and 1914 cities began to be known for certain products or economic activities: Pittsburgh for steel; Cleveland, oil; New York, banking; Minneapolis and St. Paul, wheat and flour; Milwaukee, beer; Memphis, cottonseed oil; Chicago, meat packing; Detroit, automobiles; and Hershey, Pennsylvania, candy. Los Angeles and San Francisco on the Pacific Coast, though growing, had not yet made names for themselves in a single field.

In the South cities took shape slowly. Birmingham, Alabama, later grew into a steel- and iron-making city. Atlanta, Georgia, and Nashville, Tennessee, became important railroad centers. Cloth-making and tobacco towns thrived in North Carolina. Smaller towns of a few thousand people, such as Houston and Dallas, Texas, in time exploded into crowded, busy cities, with no end to their growth in sight.

Seattle, Washington, is a good case study of the swift changes that came to cities after 1870. Seattle already enjoyed profitable trade with other towns along the West Coast and a fine natural harbor that invited shipping. But as soon as the railroad linked Seattle with the East, one change quickly followed another. In 1883 a horse-drawn street railway began operating there. In 1888 Seattle was using an electric trolley—before New York City, Philadelphia, or Chicago. By this time Seattle's public buildings and a few private ones were lighted by electricity. A fire destroyed most of Seattle in 1889. But the city was rebuilt almost immediately with brick and iron. At that early date Seattle also was piping pure water from nearby mountain streams into city buildings. In 1890 Seattle had a population of 43,000—about 39,400 more people than it had ten years before.

Seattle's growth was only beginning. The city's vital fur and fish trade continued in full swing. But when gold was discovered in Alaska, Seattle's growth surged beyond belief.

In 1897 the ship *Portland* docked in Seattle's harbor carrying $800,000 worth of Yukon gold. Seattle became the jumping-off point for people joining the great Alaska gold rush. In 1898, hotels and houses were so crowded with people heading for "the mines" that stables were turned into dormitories. Seattle businesses grew rich selling miner's boots, "Yukon" stoves, blankets, canned goods, and other equipment. Soon Seattle began calling itself the "Queen City of the Pacific."

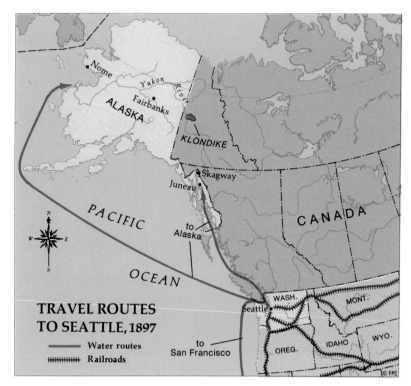

TRAVEL ROUTES TO SEATTLE, 1897

——— Water routes

++++++++ Railroads

Nome

Yukon River

Fairbanks

ALASKA

KLONDIKE

Skagway

Juneau

to Alaska

CANADA

PACIFIC

OCEAN

WASH.

Seattle

MONT.

OREG.

IDAHO

WYO.

to San Francisco

© FPC

As the first large seaport for ships moving along the northwest coast of the United States, Seattle found itself at the center of the Alaskan gold rush.

Seattle's population reached 250,000 by 1910. The city built more shipyards and improved its harbor. The completed harbor had enough space to hold *all* the naval fleets of the world *at one time*. By 1912 Seattle had become the fifth largest port in the nation, larger even than New Orleans. Workers could also find jobs in lumber mills that used wood from nearby forests and in newly built plants that canned the fruits and vegetables grown in the state.

Seattle also was a pleasant city. Open country lay only a long walk or a short trolley ride away. By 1912 Seattle could boast a symphony orchestra, several theaters, a public library, public schools, evening classes for adults, and a university that was gaining national attention.

To improve the city for business and shopping, hundred-foot hills standing in the center of town were slowly washed away with powerful streams of water. Buildings then went up on this flattened site. The whole project, begun in 1900, took about thirty years to complete.

In 1900 a reporter wrote that Seattle was like a small boy that had outgrown his clothes. By 1914 the city had begun to offer its large population more comfort and services. Seattle's high spirit and strength, like those of many urban centers blossoming during those years, live on in the present.

Section 1 Review

1. What were two reasons why rural people moved to the city?
2. What was the "new" immigration?
3. What were two reasons that native-born workers distrusted the newcomers?
4. What new inventions improved public transportation in cities?

Critical Thinking

5. **Recognizing Cause and Effect.** What were two reasons that native-born workers distrusted the newcomers?

LOOKING AHEAD: How did the city change the lives of those who lived there?

525

2   City Dwellers

Family life in the city differed from family life on the farm. On farms everyone worked together to do the chores and harvest the crops. The family usually went to town, to church, or to social events together. But in the city family members usually worked at different jobs in different locations. A father spent his day working in a factory, office, or store. Most children attended school, and a mother worked inside or outside the home. Each family member made friends individually, and each enjoyed different kinds of play. Families in cities usually ate their evening meal together. But home sometimes became mainly a place to sleep.

Women in the Cities

Magazines such as *The Ladies' Home Journal* (1883) and *Good Housekeeping* (1885) were aimed at women living in cities. Some city women took on full-time jobs outside the home to increase the family income. They worked as typists, nurses, salesclerks, librarians, and teachers. Immigrant wives and daughters or newcomers from the farms took jobs in factories or as house servants. In 1900 almost one half of the women working outside the home earned less than $6 a week. Few studied medicine or law. Yet one woman declared, "The crowning glory of the present age is that every woman is free to develop her own personality."

Women's independence showed up in dress fashions. Sometime after 1900, women's dress became simpler. Women wore skirts above the ankles or cut their hair short without being criticized. Women of all ages and of every economic class began to use cosmetics. However, the rewards of city living came mainly to women whose families had large incomes. As the use of electricity became commonplace in the city, home life was made easier. Electric appliances such as irons, toasters, stoves, and vacuum cleaners lightened family work loads.

Camp Fire Girls and Breaker Boys

Death rates were high among city children living in slums because of unsanitary and crowded conditions. In 1897, Rochester, New York, took the lead in passing public health laws. All milk sold in the city had to be pasteurized to free it from disease-causing bacteria. Rochester also ruled that milk had to be stored in clean bottles and kept cool enough to stay fresh.

Many cities began to pass special child care laws. Some cities established baby clinics and day nurseries. Some hired nurses to visit children in their homes. Public playgrounds were built. City buildings, crowded together, took up all the play space. So almost every

Poor city children, making artificial flowers at home in the evening, learned at an early age that they had to work to eat.

major city, beginning with Boston in 1898, began buying land for playgrounds. The Playground and Recreation Association of America was organized in 1906 to encourage such public works.

Some people feared that city children would lose all touch with the outdoors and the land. To offset this danger the Boy Scouts of America was formed in 1910. Its aim was to teach outdoor living and handicraft skills. In the same year, Dr. and Mrs. Luther Gulick organized the Camp Fire Girls. And in 1912 Juliette Low started the Girl Scouts of America.

The use of child labor continued to be a problem. In 1900 at least 1.7 million children under the age of sixteen worked for wages. Children working at night were kept awake by having cold water splashed in their faces. Some girls under sixteen worked sixteen hours a day in canning factories, capping forty cans per minute. Ten-year-old breaker boys crouched over dusty coal chutes for ten hours a day to pick slate out of the coal sliding past. In city tenements many children seven years and younger made artificial flowers at night to be sold the next day at street stands.

After 1905, states began passing useful child labor laws. By 1914 every state but one had a minimum working age limit for children. This age limit ranged from twelve to sixteen. In 1938 the federal government passed a law that prevented employers in most industries from hiring children under the age of sixteen.

Students and Schools

Primary schools changed in about 1900 when learning by doing was introduced. Instead of learning by memorizing, students learned arithmetic by organizing and running a store in the classroom. In upper-grade schools other skills besides the three so-called Rs— reading, writing, and arithmetic—were taught. After 1917, school-boys began to learn how to use carpenter's tools and to run and repair machines. Girls were trained in homemaking and office skills.

The greatest increase in the number of students after 1880 came in high schools, especially in cities. In 1878 there were only 500 high schools in the entire country. Most were private rather than public. Twenty years later there were 5,500 high schools, most of

The Boy Scouts of America and similar youth groups were formed to help children in towns and cities.

527

them paid for out of taxes. Between 1890 and 1918 one new public high school was opened in the United States for each day of the year. Total student enrollment doubled during that period.

High schools grew rapidly for several reasons. Business and industry needed trained young workers, men and women. The nation was becoming wealthy enough to pay more taxes for schooling. In earlier times families needed every penny that every member could earn just to feed, dress, and house themselves. After 1880, and especially after 1900, the father's income or the income of both parents allowed the family to meet its basic needs without help from the children. More children could therefore attend high school. Many people saw education as a way to better jobs and improved living conditions.

Public schools developed more slowly in the South. But after 1900, North Carolina, Virginia, Tennessee, and Georgia led a general move toward better schools for more students. More money was spent for equipment. Teachers were better trained. Enrollments jumped sharply. Blacks attended separate schools that often were not as well equipped as those for whites.

Many new colleges and universities in the United States were founded between 1870 and 1920. By the early 1900s, for the first time in history, the training for doctors and lawyers in the United States was as good or better than it was in Europe.

Reformers in the Cities

With the rise of cities and city problems many church leaders began to preach what has been called the social gospel. Church groups became interested in improving schools, hospitals, and orphanages. Many formed play centers and young people's groups. Church groups also tried to help newly arrived immigrants or farm families make new lives in the city. In 1892, on the first floor of a Greenwich Village store in New York City, the Missionaries of St. Charles opened a church called Our Lady of Pompeii. Their mission was to help the thousands of Italian immigrants who came to the United States.

Some church groups built places of worship in industrial centers to help workers as well as job-seekers. Such church groups pushed for laws to end child labor and to protect workers who handled dangerous machines. In 1908 the Federal Council of Churches was organized. Its main purpose was to discuss workers' needs and to speak for those who did not share in the general prosperity.

Other reformers also took on the task of improving the lives of city dwellers. Jane Addams is one of the most famous. She opened Hull House in 1889 in a part of Chicago where she could work closely with immigrants. Hull House was a combination social club,

Mary McDowell (holding the flag, above) once lived at Hull House (left). She started her own settlement house in Chicago, following the example of her friend Jane Addams (right, above).

children's center, and aid station for immigrants. It had a kindergarten, a recreation center, a gathering place for the elderly, a training ground for the theater, and a music school.

Addams had been sickly as a child because of a deformed spine. After finishing college in 1881, she entered medical school but became too ill to go on. In 1883 she was sent to Europe by her parents. She took a second trip several years later, feeling uncertain about what to do with her life. One evening in Madrid, Spain, after watching a bloody bullfight, she suddenly knew she should work on problems that affected human lives.

In 1888 Addams visited a center in London where she saw college students helping people in a working neighborhood. She decided to follow their example. She came to Chicago to set up a settlement house called Hull House. She sought out well-trained helpers.

Hull House stood in a neighborhood made up largely of people from eastern and southern Europe—Italians, Greeks, Poles, Russians, Jews, Bohemians—as well as Germans and French Canadians. Each day Addams wrestled with the problems of crowded tenements. She also grappled with other problems that immigrants faced on coming to America. She saw, for example, a German musician scrubbing floors in an office building and an Italian goldsmith shoveling coal in a factory. She grieved when a Russian peddler was pelted with rocks and the fruit cart of an Italian was overturned by a band of youngsters. She worked to bring pleasure and relaxation to children and adults whose lives would otherwise be gray and empty.

Addams later recalled that an Italian woman, impressed by the beauty of red roses at a party at Hull House, thought they had come directly from Italy. The Italian woman did not know that these roses came from a flower shop ten blocks from where she lived. She had never even taken a five-cent trolley car ride to a public park because she was afraid of the unknown.

Section 2 Review

1. What were two signs of women's growing independence?
2. What measures were taken to improve the lives of city children?
3. About what time were state legislatures passing useful child labor laws?
4. What were two reasons for the rapid increase in the number of public high schools?
5. Name two ways in which church groups and settlement workers tried to help city dwellers.

Critical Thinking
6. **Making Comparisons.** Why did city families spend less time together than farm families?

LOOKING AHEAD: In what free-time activities did city dwellers take part?

3 Leisure Time

With shorter workdays and higher pay—important social reforms in the period after 1880—people had more time and money for leisure. By 1920, leisure-time activities had become a big business in the United States.

Sports

The large and eager audiences in the cities showed great interest in professional sports. The first baseball world series was held in the 1880s. And both the National and the American baseball leagues had been formed by 1901. The names of John J. McGraw, manager of the New York Giants, and Ty Cobb, the ace hitter for the Detroit Tigers, became household words. The Brooklyn team, often called the Trolley Dodgers, later became known simply as the Dodgers. The name caught on because trolley traffic in Brooklyn was so heavy people had to dodge between the cars when crossing streets. Baseball appealed to rich and poor alike and became a favorite national sport.

The first All-American college football team was chosen in 1889. Basketball was started in the early 1890s. Professional boxing first came to wide public attention when James J. "Gentleman Jim" Corbett defeated John L. Sullivan, "The Strong Boy of Boston," in twenty-one rounds.

Golf and tennis were less popular sports at first because these games could be played only at private clubs. The first U.S. Open golf championship was played in 1895. A United States tennis team won the first two international Davis Cup matches in 1900 and 1902.

Two newspaper items of September 8, 1892, show how important sports were to Americans. One was a single column report on the death of John Greenleaf Whittier, one of the nation's leading poets. The other was a report of the Corbett-Sullivan fight—a full dozen columns long.

Popular Entertainment

Thomas Edison's phonograph, invented in 1877, brought music of all kinds to ever-larger audiences. Live band concerts served as popular summer fare in small towns and cities.

But around 1900 the most popular entertainment anywhere was vaudeville. Comedians, singers, jugglers, and dancers brought hours of fun and laughter to people in crowded theaters all around the country. The players used the same act in every city they visited. Their fame spread wherever they went.

Musical entertainment also included best-selling records. The singers who made these records generally remained in public favor

Jazz cornetist Louis Armstrong began his career in Chicago in 1922 with King Oliver's Creole Jazz Band. Lillian, his wife-to-be, was the band's pianist.

for only a few months or a few years. They sang such sad songs as "The Picture That Is Turned to the Wall" and "She May Have Seen Better Days." The songs often told the stories of the city:

I've come to this great city
To find a brother dear,
And you wouldn't dare insult me, Sir,
If Jack were only here.

Jazz originated with black musicians in New Orleans. After 1900 it spread to Chicago and later to New York, mainly through records. Years later jazz was to gain national and world attention as a truly American art form. King Oliver's Creole Jazz Band and a host of others were early stars in the field. Paul Whiteman, a well-known band leader, compared the rhythms of jazz to "the rhythm of machinery." He wrote, "Jazz is the folk music of the machine age."

The motion picture was a whole new idea in entertainment. In 1903 *The Great Train Robbery* told a complete story in film—a first in movie making. Although early films were scratchy and had no sound, audiences loved them. By 1925, movies, with their stars—Charlie Chaplin, Mary Pickford, Douglas Fairbanks—had become one of the largest industries in the country.

Newspapers and magazines increased in public favor. They appealed to readers in all walks of life—the new fortune makers as well as the factory workers and farmers. Photographers captured on film the best and worst of city life. Their pictures appeared in newspapers and magazines.

Since their rise in the 1880s, modern cities have continued to attract new residents from home and abroad. Urban dwellers have long enjoyed the opportunities and excitement of living and working in a busy city. They have faced its many problems. Although lately many people have left the cities for the suburbs, urban living seems to be a lasting trend in the nation's history. Even today, urban life is closely tied to the nation's great industrial strength.

Section 3 Review

1. Why were baseball and football more popular than golf and tennis in the late 1800s?
2. What kinds of acts made up a vaudeville show?

Critical Thinking

3. **Determining Relevance.** What was important about the 1903 film *The Great Train Robbery?*

Though indebted to cultures from all over the world, the United States has developed its own national culture.

For many years American authors, artists, musicians, and architects searched for a look and a sound that were distinctly American. Many tried to throw off the rule of European art. Between 1880 and 1914 these dreams of a distinct national culture began to come true.

The City as Inspiration

The city offered its artists inspiration. Architects discovered new ways to shape homes, apartments, stores, and factories. Engineers built bridges to link one section of a city with another. Writers covered subjects that were special to the United States and its growing cities. And painters recorded in color the experience and energy of city life.

Skyscrapers

The most exciting showpiece of the city was the towering skyscraper. And the city best known for building skyscrapers was Chicago. Among its most creative builders was Louis Sullivan, described as a scientist with "the soul of a dreamer and artist." Sullivan once said that freedom of design in building was as important as freedom of ideas in government.

Sullivan believed that the urban setting called for a new look. He believed in building with clean, strong lines, using the new materials of the machine age. His work was framed in straight, strong steel beams, and he used many windows to bring the outside world inside.

New York and other cities quickly followed Chicago's lead. The skyscraper was distinctly American. One person wrote, "I admire the daring, wisdom, and genius of the men who designed and erected them [skyscrapers] without reference . . . to any other nation on earth."

Long steel bridges such as the bay bridge between San Francisco and Oakland, California, (below) and tall steel buildings such as this Sullivan skyscraper in Chicago (right) changed the profile of American cities.

Frank Lloyd Wright preferred to build homes, not skyscrapers.

Wright's Prairie Style

Some architects in the United States did not like the skyscraper. Frank Lloyd Wright, a student of Sullivan, admired clean, modern lines. But he thought the skyscraper packed people together too tightly. His buildings set a different style.

Wright tried to match buildings with the land around them. He believed that in prairie towns and cities a house should hug the ground and be made from such natural materials as wood and stone. He also believed that the furniture inside the home was part of the building's whole effect.

Painters

While Wright focused on natural settings, many city painters focused on social settings. One group of artists chose such common city subjects as boxing matches, tenement dwellers, and crowded city streets. A painter from this group wrote, "A child of the slums will make a better painting than a drawing room lady gone over by a beauty shop."

Another group of painters, although following the lead of European artists, also focused on American city scenes. These were the abstract artists—those who used shapes and colors to express meaning without painting a scene as a camera might see it. They valued the energy of the city. One of them explained the keen desire for painting the new, urban society in symbols and shapes. "There was life in all these new things. There was excitement, there was a healthy revolt . . . , and an utterly new world. . . ."

Writers, Moviemakers, and Musicians

Writers also used the city as a subject. William Dean Howells, a best-selling author of the nineteenth century, wrote of the problems people faced when they left the country for the city. Poet Carl Sandburg wrote of Chicago as if it were a rugged person.

Hog Butcher for the World,
Tool Maker, Stacker of Wheat,
Player with Railroads, and the
   Nation's Freight Handler;
Stormy, husky, brawling,
City of the Big Shoulders.

Not all writers of the time described city life. One of the nation's greatest, Mark Twain, wrote about life along the Mississippi River and about youngsters growing up there. *The Adventures of Huckleberry Finn* and *Tom Sawyer* became best-sellers. Twain's writing came to be seen as uniquely American. No other nation could have produced Mark Twain.

Movies and jazz also came to be identified with the culture of the United States. Moviegoers all over the country shared an interest in the off-screen lives of their favorite stars. Hollywood, California—a symbol for the movies as well as the place where many were made—shaped the hopes and dreams of many Americans. And the words and music of many jazz songs touched hearts all around the country. Jazz became another distinct feature of American culture.

Each year new builders, artists, poets, and entertainers appear who enrich the national culture that is our heritage.

Lillian Gish starred in *The Birth of a Nation* in 1915.

Chapter 27 Review

Chapter Summary

Between 1850 and 1910, the United States shifted from being a mainly rural nation to a mainly urban one. Among the factors contributing to this urban growth were the arrival of many unskilled immigrants from Europe and Asia and the migration of many people from farms to cities within the United States.

The increase in the number of cities and the growth of city population brought on a building boom that changed the face of the cities. Skyscrapers, transportation terminals, and apartment buildings went up.

The lives of urban families became quite different from the lives of rural families. City families usually spent less time together than rural families. Many city women worked outside their homes.

Reviewing Vocabulary

Choose the word that best completes each sentence.

1. In 1850 the United States was a(n) (*rural/ urban*) nation, with only a few large cities.
2. As more people moved to the cities, the nation became increasingly (*urban/ agricultural*).
3. A (*suburb/slum*) is a crowded, poor area of a city.
4. An (*ethical/ethnic*) neighborhood is home to immigrants from the same foreign country.
5. (*Skyscrapers/Subways*) saved space by building high into the air.
6. Grand Central Station is one of the great railroad (*terminals/tenements*).
7. Many families can have homes in one (*apartment/terminal*) building.
8. Workers often chose to move from the cities to outlying towns called (*suburbs/ slums*).

9. An early form of public transportation was the (*bicycle/trolley*).
10. (*Leisure/Leeway*) is time for relaxation and recreation.
11. A form of public transportation that uses underground tunnels is the (*trolley/ subway*).
12. A crowded, run-down apartment building occupied by poor people is called a (*terminal/tenement*).
13. Popular (*entertainment/inventions*) in the early 1930s included vaudeville, phonographs, and motion pictures.
14. Live entertainment in the 1900s included (*vaudeville/phonograph records*).
15. The form of music that is truly an American art form is (*country/jazz*).
16. The first (*motion picture/subway*) made no sound.

Understanding Main Ideas

1. What were three factors that contributed to the growth of cities between 1850 and 1910?
2. In what ways did the city affect newcomers, poor people, and families?
3. Describe the leisure-time activities of city people around the turn of the century.

Critical Thinking Skills

1. **Identifying Central Issues.** What are the three primary reasons that people moved to the cities in the late 1800s?
2. **Testing Conclusions.** Provide evidence from this chapter to support the conclusion that the city was "another frontier."
3. **Recognizing Cause and Effect.** In the early 1900s Americans began to spend more time with people of their own age than with their families. What developments led to this change?

Social Studies Skills: Using a Line Graph

U.S. Population Density*
(number of persons per square mile of land area)

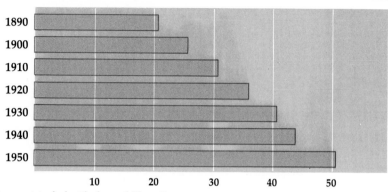

*Does not include Alaska and Hawaii.

Study the line graph above. It gives you information about the density of population within the continental United States. Density means the average number of persons living on a square mile of land.

Skill Review: Use the information on the graph to tell whether each of the conclusions that follow is true (T), false (F), or doubtful (D). A conclusion is doubtful if the graph lacks the information needed to prove the statement true or false.

1. On the average, twice as many people lived on a square mile of land in 1940 than in 1890.

2. Population density for the nation decreased between 1850 and 1950.

3. The number of square miles within the borders of the United States remained approximately the same between 1890 and 1950.

4. In 1930, every square mile of land in the United States had at least 51 people living on it.

5. Between 1910 and 1920, the total population of the United States increased 15 percent.

6. In 1950 there were about 51 people for each square mile of land.

Writing About History

Weighing Advantages and Disadvantages.
Write one paragraph about the advantages of city life at the turn of the century. Write a second paragraph about the disadvantages of life in a large city at that time. Were there more advantages or disadvantages? Would you have chosen to live in a city in that period? Explain.

Your Region in History

Geography. Write a case study for the city you live in or the city nearest you. Use the Seattle case study found on pages 524 and 525 as an example. In your study, include information about the population of the city around 1900, the major forms of transportation at that time, and the major attractions built in the late 1800s and early 1900s.

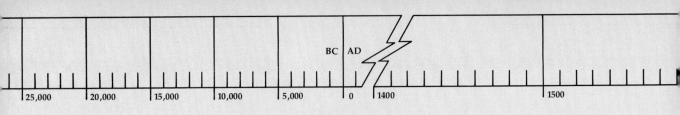

Politics
of Protest

❧ **Chapter 28**

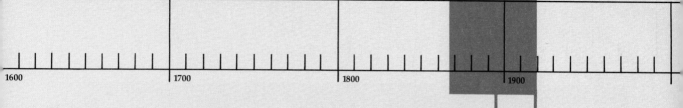

1600   1700   1800   1900

Vocabulary

regulate
alliance
commerce
competition
consumer
greenback
inflation
spoils system
civil service
corruption
primary
prejudice

AS MANUFACTURING AND BUSINESS GREW, owners of factories and big businesses became ever more powerful. Many people feared that the interests of small businesses, workers, and farmers would be overridden by the wishes of the industrial giants. In a message to Congress President Grover Cleveland warned that big businesses, which should be "the servants of the people, are fast becoming the people's master." Those who saw big business as a threat to democracy felt that only the federal government had enough power to regulate the huge industries.

Big business leaders disagreed. Abraham S. Hewitt, a pioneer in the steel industry, declared that "the invasion of the government into . . . industry must be met with [strong] opposition." In the view of business leaders a firm succeeded because it wasted neither time nor money and was well managed. If a firm was run so well that it took over a whole industry, then it was worthy of the power.

Prereading

1. What were the effects of the political protests begun by farmers in the last decades of the nineteenth century?
2. What reforms did the Populist party hope to make?
3. In what ways did the Progressive movement change state and local politics?
4. How did Progressive ideas influence national politics under Presidents Theodore Roosevelt and Woodrow Wilson?

1 The Beginnings of Protest

The view that big business should be regulated finally won out, but only after a long struggle. Leading the fight were the farmers. While

Local Grange groups often built halls where they held meetings, lectures on farming, and parties.

people were buying up goods as fast as factories could turn them out, farmers were falling deeper and deeper into debt.

Granges and Farmers' Alliances

In the last decades of the nineteenth century farmers were faced with rising costs for transportation and machinery. To cover their costs, farmers borrowed money from banks, often at high interest rates. Even the borrowed money did not always cover the rising costs, especially for shipping goods to market. Farmers had to pay about one third the price of a bushel of wheat just to ship it by train from Omaha, Nebraska, to Chicago, Illinois. They also had to pay for storing crops in warehouses owned by railroads.

Farmers in the Mississippi Valley and in the South, including Texas, began to band together to solve their problems. In 1867 they formed the Patrons of Husbandry. The Patrons in turn formed smaller groups called Granges in farm communities. Granges offered farmers a place where they could meet and exchange ideas.

As the problems of farmers piled up, Grange members began to talk more about political action. Many felt that the government and big businesses—mainly the railroads—were ignoring the needs of farmers. They wanted laws passed that would regulate railroad shipping costs and raise the price of farm products. To put more pressure on politicians, local Granges banded together in larger northern and southern groups called Farmers' Alliances. A black farmers' organization in the South joined in common cause with these alliance movements.

Partly because of the farmers' protests, Congress passed the Interstate Commerce Act of 1887 to regulate the railroads. The act set up a commission within the federal government to study and govern railroads. Members of the commission were named by the President and approved by the Senate. If commission members believed that a railroad line was charging unfair rates to haul goods or passengers, they took the case to a federal court. If the commission could prove its case, the court would order the railroad to lower its rates. The Interstate Commerce Act spelled out the role of the federal government in regulating trade or commerce among states.

Congress responded to another problem that had bothered farmers, workers, and owners of small businesses—the growth of monopolies. Farmers, battling on the market against cheaper goods from other countries, resented the freedom from competition that monopolies enjoyed. Workers and other consumers resented the higher prices that monopolies charged. And small business owners resented being forced out of business by monopolies.

In 1890 Congress passed the Sherman Antitrust Act. Its purpose was to break up large groups or combinations of big businesses that had become trusts. Supporters of the act hoped it would bring back competition and stop monopolistic trusts from charging almost any price they wished for the goods they made.

The act, however, did not work as planned. First, the wording of the act was not clear, so the act became hard to enforce. Second, the officials whose duty it was to carry out the act were not in favor of it. Attorney General Richard Olney spoke out against the act even after it had become law. Third, in a case brought before the Supreme Court in 1895, the Court decided that only firms engaged in trade and commerce fell under the terms of the act. The Court said that the act did not apply to manufacturing firms. The Court's narrow view of the antitrust act slowed government efforts to bring the giant industries into line.

2 The Populist Party

Farmers continued to suffer. Many felt that the government had not done enough and that neither political party would help them.

In 1892 the Farmers' Alliances helped start the Populist (People's) party. The Populists invited unhappy Republicans and Democrats to join them. They hoped to gain control of the national government.

Feeling ran high. One Populist leader, Ignatius Donnelly of Minnesota, claimed that unfair government practices were dividing

Section 1 Review

1. Give two reasons why many farmers fell into debt in the late 1800s.
2. Why did the Patrons of Husbandry form Granges?
3. What was the purpose of the Interstate Commerce Act of 1887?

Critical Thinking
4. **Identifying Central Ideas.** How did its wording, the attitude of federal officials, and the Supreme Court's decision take the teeth out of the Sherman Antitrust Act?

LOOKING AHEAD: What reforms did the Populist party hope to make?

the country into two camps—tramps and millionaires. Another, Senator "Pitchfork" Ben Tillman of South Carolina, warned senators that he would use his pitchfork to prod them into actions favoring the farmer. Mary Lease, a Kansas lawyer, spoke for farmers when she said, ". . . let the bloodhounds of money who have dogged us thus far beware!"

The Populists gathered for their first national convention in Omaha, Nebraska, in 1892. Every plank in their platform favored giving benefits and power to the many, not to the few. The platform called for:

1. Making government the owner of the railroad, telegraph, and telephone services.
2. Voting in secret rather than in the open where anyone could watch. Voting in the open was the practice at the time.
3. Allowing the people to elect their own senators directly. Under the Constitution senators were elected by state legislatures.
4. Limiting the President's and Vice-President's time in office to one term. The Populists believed that short terms would prevent powerful and wealthy groups from influencing the executive branch.
5. Shortening the workday.
6. Setting up an income tax that would tax large incomes more than small incomes.
7. Increasing the government's supply of paper money (greenbacks). The Populists believed that having more money in use would raise farm prices by bringing on inflation—a period of rising prices.
8. Minting coins from the silver newly found in Colorado and Nevada. In 1873 the government had stopped making silver coins. The Populists and mine owners wanted the government to buy the silver and use it as money once again. The "free silver," like the greenbacks, would bring on inflation, putting more money in the hands of buyers and helping raise prices.

Many ideas in the Populist platform were new in 1892. They seemed extreme to those who were against them. But over the years many Populist proposals became the law of the land.

The Populists ran James B. Weaver of Iowa for President in 1892. He received only 1 million votes. A number of Populist candidates for Congress, however, were winners. The Populists hoped to sweep the next elections in 1896. Instead, their ideas were taken over by the Democratic party.

Bryan and the Democrats

Between the election of President Rutherford B. Hayes in 1876 and the election of 1892, not one President caught the public's attention or made any bold political moves. Of this period, historian Henry

Election of 1880

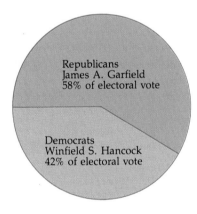

Republicans
James A. Garfield
58% of electoral vote

Democrats
Winfield S. Hancock
42% of electoral vote

Election of 1884

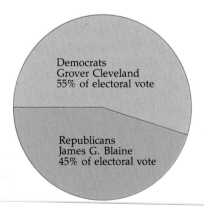

Democrats
Grover Cleveland
55% of electoral vote

Republicans
James G. Blaine
45% of electoral vote

Adams wrote, "No period so thoroughly ordinary had been known in American politics. . . ."

Rutherford B. Hayes, a Republican, had been followed as President by James A. Garfield, also a Republican. Garfield was shot in 1881 after only five months in office and died three months later. Vice-President Chester A. Arthur moved into the Presidency. Arthur failed to win favor with Congress or his own party. But during his term an important law, the Pendleton Act of 1883, was adopted. Usually called the Civil Service Act, this law stated that certain jobs in the federal government had to be filled on the basis of a worker's ability. People were to be rewarded for their good work, not for their political ties. Many people had objected to the earlier "spoils system" of giving good government jobs to loyal party workers. Today most jobs in the federal government are under the civil service.

Democrat Grover Cleveland, governor of New York, won the election for President in 1884 by one of the smallest margins in United States history. Troubled about the rise of big business, Cleveland tried to win votes in Congress for a lower tariff that would allow more foreign competition. His efforts failed. Cleveland was succeeded in 1889 by Republican Benjamin Harrison of Indiana, who favored the goals of big business.

Cleveland was again elected President in 1892. He lost much of his following, however, during his second term. Some people blamed him for the hard economic times. Farmers blamed him for fighting against measures that would have helped them. Workers blamed him for taking steps to break up labor unions and for failing to carry out the Sherman Antitrust Act of 1890.

When the Democratic party met in Chicago in 1896 to choose a candidate for President, its members turned to William Jennings Bryan. Bryan was a thirty-six-year-old delegate from Nebraska and a former congressman.

Bryan delivered a speech that stirred his audience, many of whom were farmers. "Burn down your cities and leave our farms, and your cities will spring up again as if by magic," he said. "But destroy our farms, and the grass will grow in the streets of every city in this country."

The Democrats named Bryan as their candidate for the Presidency. The Populists, not knowing what to do because the Democrats had taken over their causes, also came out for Bryan. But some businessmen warned that they would close their factories if Bryan were elected.

Bryan was defeated by William McKinley, the Republican candidate. McKinley was opposed to the free silver plan and favored big business. Bryan's defeat killed the Populist party, which by then had neither issues nor leaders around which to rally.

Election of 1888

Election of 1892

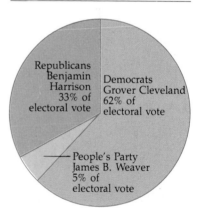

Election of 1896

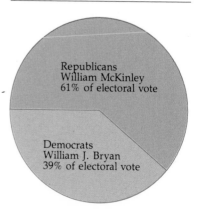

On the farm, as in the city, families depended on their children to work at least part of the year.

Section 2 Review

1. When did the Populist or the People's party begin?
2. List three planks in the 1892 platform of the Populist party.
3. Why did Populists want to print more paper money?
4. Why was the Pendleton Act of 1883 important?

Critical Thinking

5. **Recognizing Cause and Effect.** What finally caused the Populist party to die out?

LOOKING AHEAD: In what ways did the Progressive movement change state and local politics?

Improved Farm Conditions

Farmers' protests died down between 1900 and 1920 when farm conditions improved. More and better farm machinery and scientific farming methods increased crop yields. Farmers made use of improved strains of grain and corn, better ways of plowing, and fertilizer. And farm prices tripled because of greater demand in Europe for farm goods from the United States. As the nation's cities grew, so did the market for farm goods. Using trucks later freed the farmer from dependence on the railroad and cut transportation costs.

Farmers were to face lean years between 1920 and 1940. But the scientific farming practiced in the early 1900s paved the way for the United States to become the world's leading food producer.

3 The Progressive Movement

When the Populist movement ended, a new political movement emerged—the Progressive movement. It gained strength from 1900 to 1917 and influenced both major parties.

There were many differences between the Populists and Progressives. The Populists formed a political party. For many years the Progressives tried instead to gain supporters within both the Republican and the Democratic parties. The Populists were backed largely by farmers. The Progressives came mainly from small towns and cities. They were small business owners, doctors and teachers, and some workers. Blacks had been a part of the farmers' movements, but they were not part of the Progressive movement.

Goals of the Progressives

The Progressives wanted to correct injustices that kept people from enjoying the rewards of industrialization. They wanted to improve city life, keep child workers out of the factories, and offer a second chance to people in need.

Local Reforms

Congress tried to pass a bill in 1907 to end the use of child labor in mines and factories, but those against it put up a strong fight. Some members of Congress believed that it was against the Constitution to adopt such a law. Senator Albert Beveridge of Indiana answered those who opposed a child labor law. "They are the children of somebody else that are working twelve hours at night. If they were our children, we would forget lunch and not sit up at night [seeking ways] to show that the Constitution won't let us rescue them."

When the child labor law failed at the national level, Progressives began to work for change at local and state levels. Local reforms often centered on corruption in city politics.

A nationally known magazine reporter, Lincoln Steffens, looked into the politics of a number of major cities. In each city he found corruption. His articles on the subject appeared together in a book, *The Shame of the Cities*, printed in 1904.

People worked together to rid cities of corruption. Cleveland's Mayor Tom Johnson discovered in 1901 that people with friends in public office paid lower taxes than other citizens. The city's political

Farm specialties strongly influenced regional industrial development.

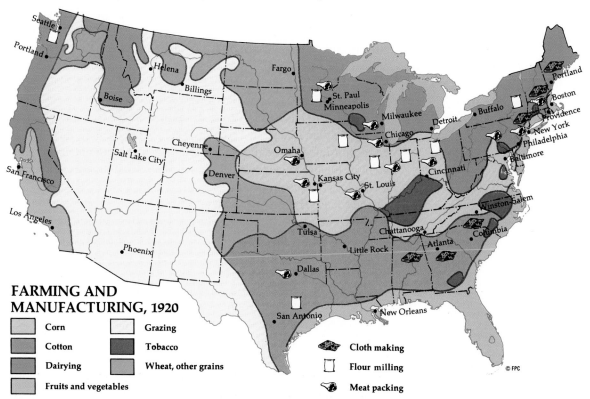

FARMING AND
MANUFACTURING, 1920

- Corn
- Cotton
- Dairying
- Fruits and vegetables
- Grazing
- Tobacco
- Wheat, other grains
- Cloth making
- Flour milling
- Meat packing

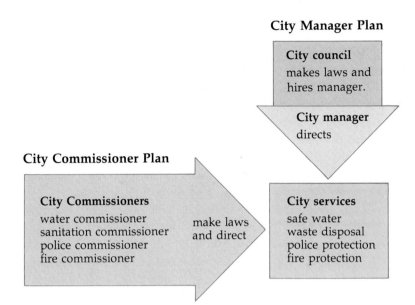

City Manager Plan

City council
makes laws and
hires manager.

City manager
directs

City Commissioner Plan

City Commissioners
water commissioner
sanitation commissioner
police commissioner
fire commissioner

make laws
and direct

City services
safe water
waste disposal
police protection
fire protection

By clearly defining what city officials were to do, voters hoped to improve their governments.

leaders often took payoffs for giving certain people big construction jobs. And big businesses often bribed city political bosses for special favors.

To halt corruption in government several cities turned to city managers. A city manager is specially trained to run a city. He or she sees that everyone shares in the city's services. Among these services are safe water, proper waste disposal, and honest, well-trained police officers and fire fighters. With a city manager in charge, the running of the city was separated from politics, and the spoils system no longer worked. If the city manager did not do the job, he or she would be fired and a new one hired.

In 1900 Galveston, Texas, developed a city commission plan. Under the plan four or five commissioners were elected. Each was to be responsible for one unit of government such as the police department or the fire department. Together the commissioners made laws for the city. Houston, Texas, and Des Moines, Iowa, followed Galveston's lead. By 1917 more than 500 cities were using the commission system of government. But in time the city manager plan became more popular.

State Reforms

States as well as cities were sometimes ruled by corrupt politicians. Robert La Follette, a Progressive from Wisconsin, said that entire states were often "ruled by a handful of men who destroyed . . . democracy . . . They [decided] practically all nominations for important offices, controlled conventions, dictated legislation, and had even sought to lay corrupt hands on the courts of justice." Beginning in 1900 Oregon and Wisconsin both tried to wipe out corruption in state government.

In states where Progressives gained control, senators were elected by the voters instead of by state legislators—a practice that had once been a Populist platform plank. Progressives also stood for the secret ballot, another Populist plank.

Many states also set up primary elections. In the past most candidates for office had been chosen by delegates to local or state party conventions. Many voters felt that no one spoke for them at these meetings. In primary elections the people could take part in choosing their party's candidates.

Reformers sought to win back from corrupt politicians the people's right to vote and to be heard. Through law, reformers hoped to curb the powerful forces that appeared to have too much control over people's daily lives. "To restore the government to the people" became a favorite theme of Progressives.

Women and Reform

Women led a number of reform movements. They worked to end child labor, to improve working conditions for women and other

Robert La Follette, as governor of Wisconsin, led in the successful reform of his state's laws.

laborers, and to outlaw alcoholic drinks. This last movement, called Prohibition, led to the organization of the Woman's Christian Temperance Union in 1874. Prohibition of alcohol became law in the 1920s with ratification of the Eighteenth Amendment. But it was repealed in 1933 by the Twenty-First Amendment.

By 1900, women had the right to vote in four western states—Wyoming, Colorado, Idaho, and Utah. Women's fight for the vote continued in other states. In August 1920 the Nineteenth Amendment, which gave women in all states the right to vote, became law.

Women also gained greater freedom in holding and managing property and in acting as guardians for children. Some were active in education, and more and more of them attended colleges and universities. By 1903 women had formed the American Association of University Women, the National Council of Jewish Women, the Women's Trade Union League, and other groups. The largest group, the General Federation of Women's Clubs, was founded in 1890 as a step toward continuing education for women. These organizations appealed to the middle classes rather than to the poor.

More women began to work outside the home. In 1880 there were 2.5 million female wage earners. By 1900 there were 5 million, about 20 percent of all women in the United States over the age of fifteen. By 1910 about 25 percent of women older than fifteen were working outside the home. Many women became teachers. Others worked in offices and factories. Those trying to enter such professions as medicine and law often faced prejudice from men. Almost every woman worker had fewer chances than a man to be hired for or promoted to a well-paying job. And almost every woman in the labor force received less pay than a man for doing the same work.

Before 1919, women had some voting rights in fifteen states.

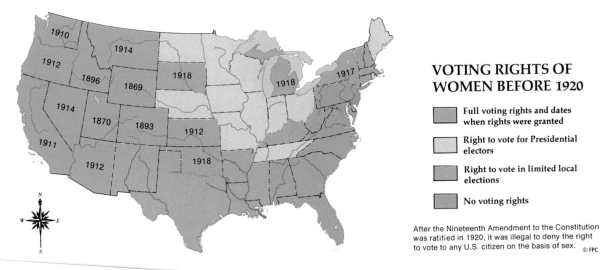

VOTING RIGHTS OF WOMEN BEFORE 1920

- Full voting rights and dates when rights were granted
- Right to vote for Presidential electors
- Right to vote in limited local elections
- No voting rights

After the Nineteenth Amendment to the Constitution was ratified in 1920, it was illegal to deny the right to vote to any U.S. citizen on the basis of sex. © FPC

Some black students went to private religious schools in the early twentieth century.

Problems for Blacks

While the Populists and Progressives were trying to correct some wrongs, many black Americans were losing their rights as citizens. In 1876 the Supreme Court ruled that a state could legally bar blacks from serving on juries or from giving evidence in court. In 1883 the Supreme Court overturned the Civil Rights Act of 1875. The Court ruled that the federal government could not guard the rights of blacks as citizens if states passed laws that took away those rights.

Especially in the South, states began to pass laws and draw up plans to limit the rights of blacks. Mississippi had worked out the first such plan in 1890. South Carolina and other southern states quickly followed. These states ruled that blacks and whites could not use the same parks, hospitals, schools, or waiting rooms in railway stations. The 1896 Supreme Court case of *Plessy* v. *Ferguson* upheld these "separate but equal" laws.

The state plans also included laws that kept blacks from qualifying to vote. Throughout the South, blacks were slowly turned away from the polls. In the election of 1896, for example, 130,000 blacks voted in Louisiana. Eight years later 1,342 blacks voted there.

Blacks set up separate churches, banks, and theaters in answer to the prejudice against them. They attended separate schools. But they knew their rights as citizens had been taken away. The National Association for the Advancement of Colored People (NAACP) was formed by both blacks and whites in 1910 to win back some of these rights. The struggle was long and hard. Not until the late 1950s and 1960s did blacks win major gains.

Section 3 Review

1. What were two differences between the Populist and the Progressive movements?
2. What did Progressive reformers such as Lincoln Steffens mean by "corruption" in city politics?
3. Name two reforms that Progressives achieved at the state level.
4. What was the purpose of the Woman's Christian Temperance Union?

Critical Thinking

5. **Identifying Central Issues.** Give three examples of how civil rights were taken away from black Americans between 1875 and 1910.

LOOKING AHEAD: How did Progressive ideas influence national politics under Presidents Theodore Roosevelt and Woodrow Wilson?

547

4 Progressives in National Politics

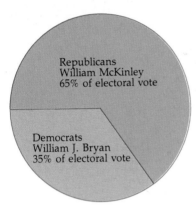

Republicans
William McKinley
65% of electoral vote

Democrats
William J. Bryan
35% of electoral vote

William McKinley was reelected to the Presidency in 1900. In 1901, shortly after beginning his second term, McKinley was shot by an assassin and died a week later. Vice-President Theodore Roosevelt became President. Bold and energetic, he soon was well liked.

Before 1900, Progressives had made their greatest mark at the state and local levels. When Theodore Roosevelt became President, however, Progressive politics rose to the national level.

Roosevelt's Background

Republican party leaders were uncertain about the stands Roosevelt would take on the issues. They feared he would act too boldly. When the party chose him to run on the Republican ticket as Vice-President, one Republican leader asked, "Don't any of you realize that there's only one life between this madman and the White House?" The same leader also spoke scornfully of that "cowboy in the White House."

But Roosevelt was well trained for the Presidency. He had served in the state legislature of New York. He had been a police commissioner in New York City. He also had held the office of assistant secretary of the navy, and in 1898 he was elected governor of New York.

Roosevelt seemed as much at ease in talking with cowhands as with kings. He wrote many books, some of them on the history of the American West. As a boy, Roosevelt had been sickly. So he spent part of his life on western ranches to improve his health. He became enthusiastic about the outdoors. He tried to preserve those parts of the western wilderness still owned by the national government, and he spoke in favor of the "strenuous life."

Being humble was not part of Roosevelt's character. When he completed his term as governor of New York, he said. "I think I have been the best governor within my time." Yet his frankness, his optimism, his energy, and his good faith won him the affection of most voters.

Roosevelt's Domestic Policies

President Roosevelt addressed the problem of big business. He felt that big business in itself was not wrong. Bigness, he said, should not be outlawed, but guided by government in the interest of all citizens. We are not attacking big businesses, he said. We only plan "to do away with the evil in them."

One of Roosevelt's goals was to enforce the Sherman Antitrust Act of 1890. A huge combination of railroads controlled in part by J. P. Morgan had been formed in 1901 as the Northern Securities

Before passage of the Meat Inspection Act of 1906, there was no guarantee of sanitary conditions at this cold storage plant.

Company. It ran the cross-country railroad lines in the Northwest. This company could charge any price it wished for freight or passenger fares. Roosevelt knew that every shipper and traveler would suffer as long as this company had such a grip on the railroads.

Roosevelt's attorney general brought suit against the Northern Securities Company under the Sherman Antitrust Act. In 1904 the Supreme Court ruled against the company and forced it to break up. One person wrote, "Even Morgan no longer rules the earth. . . ." The government brought other suits against the big business combinations. And Roosevelt pushed Congress to pass the Hepburn Act of 1906. This act gave the Interstate Commerce Commission the power to enforce its own rules about shipping across state lines.

President Roosevelt also won support in Congress for the Meat Inspection Act and the Pure Food and Drug Act in 1906. Before the Meat Inspection Act, meat-packing and other food-handling plants were not checked for healthy and sanitary conditions. Stories began to appear in the newspapers. They told of sick workers packing meat; of dirt, insects, and rats in the plants; and of spoiled food being canned and shipped out. Under the Meat Inspection Act government agents checked to see that meat and other foods were safe to eat. Without the government's stamp of approval the foods could not be sold. Under the Pure Food and Drug Act the government also ruled on the safety of certain medicines for human use.

Theodore Roosevelt was the first President to take into account labor's point of view in labor-management disputes. He believed workers and owners alike should get a "square deal." In 1902 the United Mine Workers went on strike against the coal companies. The mine operators refused to talk terms with the workers. The

The Dalles Dam on the Columbia River in Oregon produces electric power, stores water, and reduces the chances of flood.

strike dragged on. Because coal was then the major fuel used for heating, the whole East Coast began to suffer. Children in New York City stayed home from school. There was not enough coal to heat their classrooms.

Roosevelt stepped in. He called the mine operators and the leader of the striking workers to the White House. One mine operator still refused to talk to the union leader. Roosevelt became angry. He later wrote, "If it wasn't for the high office I hold, I would have taken him by the seat of the breeches and the nape of the neck and chucked him out the window." Roosevelt finally forced the two sides to settle the strike.

Roosevelt was elected to four more years in office in 1904. Roosevelt worked hard in his Presidency to save the nation's soil, its public lands, and its natural wilderness. Through his efforts the Newlands Act was passed in 1902. It laid the groundwork for the later building of such dams as the Grand Coulee Dam on the Columbia River and the Hoover Dam on the Colorado River. Besides harnessing these rivers for electric power, the dams stored water for dry times and stopped soil erosion. The President also called for a National Conservation Conference in 1908. He told Americans that they must care for the beautiful wilderness, the rich resources, the plentiful water, and all the good gifts of nature.

The Election of Taft

Republican William Howard Taft followed Theodore Roosevelt into the Presidency in 1909. Roosevelt favored Taft's candidacy and thought Taft would become a great President. But Taft failed to support the Progressives in Congress. So Taft and Roosevelt became political enemies, and both entered the race for the Republican nomination in 1912.

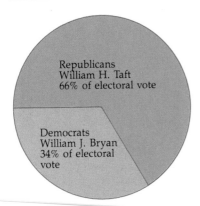

Election of 1904

Republicans
Theodore Roosevelt
71% of electoral vote

Democrats
Alton B. Parker
29% of electoral vote

Election of 1908

Republicans
William H. Taft
66% of electoral vote

Democrats
William J. Bryan
34% of electoral vote

Taft won the renomination. Roosevelt, unwilling to give up, organized a new third party—the Progressive party. Because Roosevelt had once said he felt "as strong as a bull moose," the party took the bull moose as its symbol. Roosevelt became the Progressives' candidate for President.

Roosevelt called both the Democratic and Republican parties "boss-ridden" and said they were controlled by big businesses asking for favors. Like the Populists, he favored an income tax that put the heaviest burden on the wealthy. He also believed that rich heirs should pay higher taxes than less well-to-do heirs. He called for pay for workers injured on their jobs, an end to night work in factories for women and children, and a decent living wage for workers. He said the national tariff should be lowered and big business should be regulated. With the Republican vote split between Roosevelt and Taft, the Democratic candidate, Woodrow Wilson, won the election of 1912.

Domestic Policies of Woodrow Wilson

Wilson believed in many of the Progressive plans. In battling big business, Wilson said, "I am fighting for the liberty of every man in America, and I am fighting for the liberty of American industry."

As he took office, Wilson spoke out for his beliefs. He praised the nation for what it had done and for its great government. But he said: "Evil has come with the good. . . . Our duty is to . . . correct the evil without impairing the good."

Wilson acted. Following his lead, Congress cut the tariff—for the first time since before the Civil War. Wilson also set up the Federal Reserve System, a stable chain of banks that is still vital today. He persuaded Congress to pass the Clayton Antitrust Act in 1914. This act, founded on the Sherman Antitrust Act, helped the government root out certain practices of big business that were unfair to consumers. He also came out for laws to help farmers and laborers. And during Wilson's term of office the Sixteenth Amendment was added to the Constitution to allow for a tax on income. Since then the income tax has been the chief source of revenue for the federal government. The Seventeenth Amendment was also added, calling for the election of senators by the people in the state, not by the state legislature.

During Wilson's first term in office (1913–1917) Congress passed more laws affecting industry than it had in the previous fifty years. In some ways Wilson's Presidency marked the end of the Progressive movement because so many of its reform ideas became laws. These laws did not always work the way their backers had planned. But their passage showed that many voters believed that better government was possible and well worth working to achieve.

Election of 1912

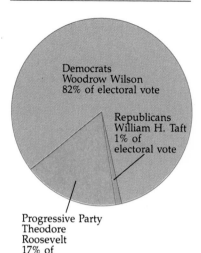

Democrats
Woodrow Wilson
82% of electoral vote

Republicans
William H. Taft
1% of
electoral vote

Progressive Party
Theodore
Roosevelt
17% of
electoral
vote

Section 4 Review

1. Name three steps President Roosevelt took to correct the abuses of big business.
2. Name two steps President Roosevelt took to preserve natural resources.
3. How did the formation of the Progressive party help Woodrow Wilson win the election of 1912?
4. Name three Progressive reforms that were enacted into law during Wilson's Presidency.

Critical Thinking

5. **Recognizing Ideologies.** What were Theodore Roosevelt's views on big business?

551

Ida Tarbell and Robert La Follette were Progressives who left their mark on the history of reform in the United States.

Before any reforms can take place, people first need to know there is a problem. In the Progressive era Ida Tarbell helped spread the word about injustices and corruption. And Robert La Follette acted through government to help bring about reform.

All in the Day's Work

Ida Tarbell was a writer and editor who favored Progressive ideas. She was born in 1857 on a farm in Erie County, Pennsylvania. She moved with her parents to Titusville. There Tarbell's father started an oil refining company that was later forced out of business by the Standard Oil Company.

Tarbell was the only girl in her class at school. As she grew up, she worked as an editor and writer, professions that in the past had been filled mainly by men. Tarbell believed that her successes in male-dominated fields would set an example for other women to follow.

Tarbell became best known as an editor and author for *McClure's Magazine*. Writers for *McClure's* often focused on social problems, believing that seeing faults was the first step in correcting them. President Theodore Roosevelt called these writers "muckrakers" for stirring up sticky social and political problems.

The Muckrakers

One Progressive author, Ray Stannard Baker, studied the unfair treatment of blacks. Another,

Lincoln Steffens, held up to public view the corruption in the cities and in politics in general.

Tarbell wrote about crooked business deals. One of her main subjects was the Standard Oil Company. She was the first person to make public the secret agreements between Standard Oil and the railroads over special oil shipping rates. She also showed how Standard Oil received a share of the rates the railroads charged other oil companies. Tarbell also wrote about the money Standard Oil paid to lawmakers.

Many books have since been written about the oil business from 1860 to 1905. But the facts Tarbell gathered are still a key part of the story. Later Tarbell looked with

Lincoln Steffens (inset) and Ida Tarbell—"muckrakers" to some—kept reform issues alive through their careful reporting.

Bob La Follette served nineteen years as a United States senator.

more favor on business and even wrote a friendly biography of one leader in the steel industry.

Tarbell also wrote about women. She praised home and family as important, although she herself never married. She also spoke out for better jobs and working conditions for women. She felt that women could best show how good they were by entering fields dominated by men.

Tarbell lived her beliefs. For her, work was everything. Her autobiography, *All in the Day's Work,* tells the full story of her unusual life.

"Fighting Bob" La Follette

Robert La Follette, a Progressive Republican, was every bit as strong-minded as Tarbell. He worked for reform through law.

La Follette was born on a farm near the small town of Primrose, Wisconsin. He worked his way through school and college and earned a law degree. His wife, Belle Case, also won her law degree, an unusual achievement for a woman in the 1880s. She became her husband's closest adviser. She also became a champion of women's right to vote.

La Follette at first had wanted to take up acting. He enjoyed debating and speaking. But he finally chose law. He was elected to office as a district attorney. Later he served in the House of Representatives in Washington, D.C.

A Wisconsin Reformer

La Follette was chiefly known for his work as a reformer in Wisconsin. He won the race for governor there in 1900 on a platform of fairer taxes, regulation of railroad rates, and direct primaries. La Follette was strongly against all government corruption. His ideas and acts in office made Wisconsin a model for reform in other states.

Wisconsin sent La Follette to the Senate in 1905. He spoke out there for national reforms. These included voting rights for women, direct primaries for national offices, and curbs on big business.

In 1924 La Follette ran for President on the Progressive party ticket. He lost the race. But he went on fighting for better government. In his autobiography he wrote that the Progressive movement stood for government by the people. "It expresses the hopes and desires of millions of men and women who are willing to fight for their ideals, to take defeat, if necessary, and still go on fighting."

In the 1950s the United States Senate named a committee to honor the five outstanding senators during the whole of United States history. "Fighting Bob" La Follette easily made the list.

Chapter 28 Review

Chapter Summary

As manufacturing and big business grew, some Americans felt that the industrial giants needed regulation before they overrode the interests of the country's citizens. The nation's farmers led the struggle to regulate big business and formed the Farmers' Alliances.

Farmers also organized the Populist party. As a third party, it offered voters many new ideas. In the presidential election of 1896 their candidate, William Jennings Bryan, was defeated by William McKinley, a Republican. This defeat ended the Populist party.

The call for reform was then taken up by those Democrats and Republicans who called themselves Progressives. These reformers wanted to end child labor, adopt new forms of government, and win the right for women to vote.

Reviewing Vocabulary

Use the following words to complete the sentences below. Write your answers on a separate sheet of paper.

regulate   inflation
alliance   spoils system
commerce   civil service
competition   corruption
consumer   primary
greenback   prejudice

1. _____ is another word for business or trade.
2. _____ is a nickname for a bill of United States currency.
3. Farmers formed a successful _____ to work together against the railroads.
4. A period of rising prices is called _____.
5. Most employees in the federal government are chosen through the _____ system.
6. Monopolies destroyed their _____ so they could raise prices freely.
7. Some Americans believe that the federal government should _____ big business.
8. In _____ elections, voters choose their party's candidates.
9. Women working in the professional world often met with _____ from men and other women.
10. The Civil Service Act ended the _____ _____ in the federal government.
11. During the early 1900s, many cities tried to end _____ by appointing a city manager.
12. A(n) _____ is a person who uses goods.

Understanding Main Ideas

1. What victories did farmers achieve in the late 1800s?
2. List the major reforms demanded by the Populist party.
3. How did the Progressives change state and local politics?
4. What Progressive reforms were enacted under Roosevelt and Wilson?

Critical Thinking Skills

1. **Identifying Central Issues.** Why did some Americans want the federal government to regulate big business?
2. **Making Comparisons.** Compare the Populists and Progressives in terms of the people who supported each movement, their goals, and their successes.
3. **Testing Conclusions.** In the early 1900s, many black Americans felt that the federal government had abandoned them. Give three arguments to support their claim.

Social Studies Skills: Making Generalizations from a Graph

Issues Causing Work Stoppages, 1896–1905

Year

Year	Better wages or hours	Right to unionize	Owner lockouts
1896	51%	28%	21%
1897	61%	18%	21%
1898	59%	21%	20%
1899	55%	26%	19%
1900	51%	22%	27%
1901	47%	34%	19%
1902	50%	32%	18%
1903	49%	33%	18%
1904	39%	40%	21%
1905	43%	37%	20%

The line graph on this page illustrates the percentages of strikes caused by each of three reasons in the years between 1896 and 1905. Each line of the graph represents 100 percent of the strikes occurring in one year. The percentage of strikes caused by each of the three reasons—the fight for better wages or hours, the right to unionize, and owner lockouts—is shown by color.

Skill Review: Study the graph and then select from the following list of generalizations those that the graph shows to be true. Write your answers on a separate sheet of paper.

1. Each year between 1896 and 1905, most work stoppages took place because workers wanted better wages and hours.
2. Some work stoppages took place every year because workers wanted the right to form unions.
3. Each year except for the years 1897 and 1900, work stoppages caused by owner lockouts represented the smallest percentage of total stoppages.
4. Work stoppages occurred each year because factory owners locked workers out.
5. The smallest percentage of stoppages for better wages and hours was in 1898.

Writing About History

1. **Defending an Opinion.** Select the reform discussed in this chapter that you think had the greatest effect on American life. In a short essay, give reasons for your choice.
2. **Expressing a Historical Viewpoint.** Imagine you are one of the following persons in the early 1900s: a child or adult working in a factory, a person living in a large city, or a Nebraska wheat farmer. Write a paragraph that describes the reform most wanted or needed by the person from whose viewpoint you are writing.

Your Region in History

Citizenship. Look at the map on page 546. What voting rights were held by women in your state? What factors accounted for their status? What do you think was the reaction in your state to the Nineteenth Amendment?

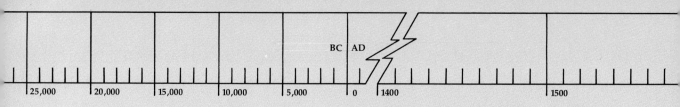

						BC	AD					
25,000	20,000	15,000	10,000	5,000		0	1400				1500	

The Nation as a World Power

Vocabulary

possession	imperialism
missionary	arbitration
annex	international
empire	isthmus

T HE UNITED STATES DEVELOPMENT as a major industrial nation led to its rise as a world power. On the strength of its drive in manufacturing and in trading the United States began to build influence beyond its borders and to gain new territories.

Some territory came under United States rule through trading ties in Asia and in the Pacific. Other territories were brought under the government's control through the Monroe Doctrine of 1823. That policy had warned that the United States would step in if European powers threatened any lands in the Western Hemisphere. Many people believed that the United States had a duty to govern and protect other lands. Among this group was Theodore Roosevelt, who said, "Our place must be great among the nations."

Prereading

1. Why was expansion of territory and trade in China, Japan, and the Pacific helpful to United States business interests?

2. What were the causes and the results of the Spanish-American War?

3. How did events in Mexico, Venezuela, and Panama give new life to the Monroe Doctrine?

1 China, Japan, and the Pacific

From their earliest days the colonies were linked to England and to its possessions by trade. After 1776 the independent United States developed overseas markets of its own. From 1815 to the 1880s,

Ships like the *John Bertram* were built to speed up the tea trade between New York and China.

however, most goods changed hands within the United States. But even during this period of domestic trade the search was on for possible trade ties abroad.

The China Trade

Trade with China had begun shortly after the revolutionary war. In 1784 the American ship *Empress of China* sailed from New York to Canton (Guangzhou), China. In its hold it carried ginseng—a plant the Chinese prized as medicine—brandy, wine, tar, turpentine, and $20,000 in cash. The *Empress* returned the following year with tea, silk, dishware, and other Chinese goods that were sold for a handsome profit. This venture was so well-paying that other traders tried their luck with China. In 1786 five American ships made the trip. By 1805 the value of cargo returning from China had passed the $5 million mark.

The War of 1812 slowed overseas trade. But the China trade was soon taken up again, reaching a peak in the 1850s. By then, sleek clipper ships built in the United States were breaking all speed records for oceangoing vessels. These many-sailed clippers outran even steamships. They ruled the seas until after the Civil War.

Most ships set sail for China from northeastern cities—New York, Philadelphia, and especially the New England ports. The early traders followed a southeastward course, sailing around the Cape of Good Hope at the southern tip of Africa, then on to Canton.

Later traders followed a southwestward route. They sailed around South America, then up the west coast of the Americas to the Pacific Northwest. There they traded cloth and iron products for seal furs. Well stocked, the ships then sailed west for China. Many stopped at the Hawaiian Islands to take on fresh food and water as well as sandlewood, another product the Chinese valued.

Diplomatic Relations with China

In 1843 the United States government sent a group to China to make a lasting trade agreement between the two nations. The group was led by Caleb Cushing. To impress the Chinese, the group arrived with four warships armed with more than 200 guns. The ships also carried gifts and goods made in the United States.

Cushing brought a letter from President John Tyler to the Emperor of China. In it the President expressed the hope of a treaty "so that nothing may happen to disturb the peace between China and America."

A treaty was signed in 1844 giving Americans full trading rights in the Chinese port cities. The treaty also made it possible for American missionaries to live in China. It did not, however, bring about full diplomatic ties between the two nations.

In 1861 Anson Burlingame was sent to serve as the American representative in Peking (Beijing), the Chinese capital. He resigned

Traders in the foreground buy tea as Chinese workers pack and weigh the dried leaves.

his position as United States minister to China in 1867. By then the Chinese were so taken with Burlingame's ability that they asked him to serve the Chinese government. In 1868, as a Chinese representative, Burlingame helped work out a new treaty between the two governments. One part of that treaty encouraged Chinese to come to the United States to work. They came in such numbers, however, that in 1882 Congress cut off further immigration from China.

By the end of the nineteenth century the United States looked to China, with its population of about 400 million, as a promising market for its factory-made goods. Other industrial nations—Great Britain, France, Germany, Russia, and Japan—were also trading with China. The United States feared that these other nations would gain the upper hand in China and that American trade would suffer. Business leaders began to pressure the government to act. They were backed by church groups that wanted to keep their missionary work alive in China.

In 1899 Secretary of State John Hay sent notes to each of the great trading powers asking them to follow an Open Door policy in China. By "open door" he meant that every nation should have equal rights to do business with the Chinese. No single country should receive special favors.

Some people in China were opposed to any foreign trade and influence in China. A secret group called the Boxers started a rebellion in 1900 to drive all "foreign devils" out of China. They killed hundreds of foreigners and Chinese Christians, and they surrounded the area where foreign citizens lived in Peking. Americans, British, Germans, Russians, French, and Japanese in China held out for nearly two months until troops from all of these nations came to their aid and ended the rebellion. The Chinese government was forced to pay $333 million in damages to the various countries. The United States used its share of the money to send Chinese students to school in America. This sign of good will helped improve relations between the two countries.

Relations with Japan

For centuries the Japanese had kept to themselves, not trusting foreigners. The Japanese government traded only with the Chinese and the Dutch, and only at the port of Nagasaki. In the late 1700s and early 1800s a number of American ships tried to land in Japan. All were driven off, some by gunfire. Ships just passing through Japanese waters in the 1840s were also driven out. Even shipwrecked sailors were captured and thrown into prisons.

In 1852 the United States sent Commodore Matthew C. Perry to Japan. Perry was told to make a treaty that would open trade with Japan and protect shipwrecked American sailors there. People in

A Japanese lady of 1874 rides in a ricksha as her servants follow on foot. Such scenes were common until much later in Japan's program of adopting western ways.

many nations were curious about Japan and followed every detail of Perry's voyage in the newspapers.

Perry arrived with four black warships in the bay outside Yedo, now Tokyo, in July 1853. Japanese officials tried to get Perry to leave, although they were impressed with his steam-driven warships that sailed against wind and current. Perry stubbornly refused. He said he would stay until he had talked with persons of high rank and delivered a letter from the President of the United States.

Perry was finally allowed to come ashore and meet with officials. He presented his letter and his requests and said that he would return the following year for an answer.

Perry returned to Yedo in February 1854, this time with seven ships. Meanwhile the Japanese had learned of a war between Britain and Russia. They feared that a war between great powers might spread to their island home. A treaty with the United States might offer Japan some protection, they thought.

Japanese officials attended a banquet aboard Perry's ships. They were delighted to see the model telegraph and steam locomotive that Perry had brought to show them. But the main business was the treaty. Each side gave in some to the other, but Perry gained his major goals. Two ports were to be opened to American ships, shipwrecked sailors would be protected, and a United States foreign office could be set up in Shimoda, one of the open ports. The treaty was signed on March 31, 1854.

An official United States reporter on one of Perry's vessels thought he heard one of the Japanese officials greet the occasion with the words "Nippon [Japan] and America, all the same heart." But despite these words the Japanese continued to distrust outsiders.

In 1868 a new Japanese emperor came to power and abruptly changed his country's attitude toward foreign ideas. The new ruler announced that "knowledge shall be sought from all over the world." Eager to learn new ways, the Japanese borrowed ideas from everywhere. They built a powerful new navy like that of the British and an army like that of the French. They borrowed political ideas from Germany. They fashioned their schools on the United States model. Japanese people visited the United States, and many Americans went to Japan to work. Within a few decades Japan became a modern, industrial nation. By the early 1900s Japan was a leading power in Asia.

The Alaska Purchase

The United States acquired lands as well as new trading partners beyond its borders. The largest land gain was the purchase of Alaska in 1867. The Russians, who owned Alaska, had offered to sell it to the United States in the 1850s. But the Civil War broke out, and the deal was not completed. After the war the Russians made another offer. Secretary of State William H. Seward, eager to obtain Alaska, was pleased with the low price of $7.2 million, less than two cents an acre. When the Russian minister told Seward late one night that the Russian government had agreed to the price, Seward wasted no time. The two men called their staffs together and worked all night. At 4 A.M. on March 30, 1867, the treaty of purchase was signed.

Many people thought Seward's buy was foolish. Although Alaska had more than half a million square miles of land, to many people it was an ice-covered wasteland. They called it "Seward's Icebox" and "Seward's Folly." The Senate voted for the treaty, however, and the House set aside money to pay for Alaska.

Over the years it became clear that Seward had made a splendid bargain. Alaska quickly became an important fishing center.

In the tradition of their ancestors, Eskimos in Alaska return from the hunt with walrus meat.

Gold was discovered there around 1900. In the twentieth century Alaska became the site of important military bases. And still later in the century great amounts of oil were found there. In 1959 Alaska became the forty-ninth state of the Union.

The Hawaiian Islands

In the same year that Congress approved the purchase of Alaska it also annexed—that is, claimed as its own—Midway Island in the Pacific Ocean. Seward wanted to annex Hawaii, too, but Congress refused. The Hawaiian Islands had been settled by peoples from other islands of the Pacific in the eighth century. The first European to reach Hawaii was Captain James Cook, a British naval officer on a voyage of discovery in 1778. The islands became an important stopping place for whaling ships and for trading vessels sailing between the United States and Asia. Missionaries soon arrived to convert the Hawaiians and to start schools. And families from the United States began to settle in the Hawaiian Islands.

European nations cast longing eyes toward Hawaii. To protect its interests, the United States in 1842 agreed to protect the islands. It also agreed to use force if necessary "to prevent its [Hawaii's] falling into the hands of one of the great powers of Europe."

In 1875 Hawaii and the United States signed a treaty that allowed Hawaii to send sugar, its main crop, to the United States without paying any tariffs. Hawaii, in turn, promised never to allow a power other than the United States to control any of its territory. In 1887 Hawaii gave the United States the great port of Pearl Harbor as a naval base.

By the 1890s people in the United States were divided in their views on Hawaii. Some people wanted closer ties with the islands. Others wanted Hawaii to remain independent. The first group, led by people in the sugar business, wanted the United States to annex Hawaii. The second group, led by Hawaiian Queen Liliuokalani (li·lē'ə·wō·kə·län'ē), believed in an independent Hawaii. United States business interests, with the help of American marines, started a revolution in Hawaii in 1893. They overthrew the queen, formed a new government, and asked the United States to annex the islands.

In his last day in office President Benjamin Harrison signed a treaty to annex Hawaii and sent the treaty to the Senate for approval. When Grover Cleveland took over the Presidency in 1893, however, he withdrew the treaty from Senate consideration. Hawaii remained an independent republic for a few more years. During the Spanish-American War in 1898 the United States finally annexed the islands. In 1900 Hawaii was made a territory and Hawaiians were made citizens of the United States. Not until 1959 did Hawaii become the fiftieth state of the Union.

Queen Liliuokalani held the throne of Hawaii for two years.

Section 1 Review

1. What was the meaning of the Open Door policy as it applied to trade with China?
2. Give three examples of how Japan changed after 1868.
3. Give three reasons why William H. Seward's purchase of Alaska was advantageous to the United States.

Critical Thinking

4. **Determining Relevance.** Why are these dates important in Hawaiian history: 1778, 1842, 1875, 1893, 1900, 1959?

LOOKING AHEAD: What were the causes and the results of the Spanish-American War?

2   The Spanish-American War

In the 1880s and 1890s European nations were in a race to claim lands all over the world. Some European nations had carved up and taken as colonies nearly all of Africa. The Europeans had trading ties in Asia and in islands of the Pacific. Their rule was more limited in the Western Hemisphere, but it did include some holdings in the Caribbean Sea. The practice of building an empire by taking over other parts of the world is called imperialism. The late nineteenth century was a time of European imperialism.

For a long time imperialism was not popular in the United States. The United States, after all, had fought a revolution to break free from the British empire. Moreover most Americans were far more interested in developing their own country. And control over other peoples, they said, ran counter to the ideals expressed in the Declaration of Independence.

Late in the nineteenth century, however, the United States changed its views. Starting in 1898, the United States extended its rule into far corners of the world. It had gained an empire of its own.

Background to Expansion

Although the move seemed sudden, the United States had earlier shown signs of joining the race for overseas possessions. Besides Seward, other important United States leaders had wanted to reach for land beyond the nation's borders. As early as 1858, Senator Stephen A. Douglas had stated, "It is our destiny to have Cuba, and it is folly to debate the question." In 1870 President Grant wanted to annex the Dominican Republic, but the Senate voted against it. Grant also toyed with the idea of obtaining the Danish Virgin Islands, but nothing came of it.

By the 1890s more and more people spoke of expansion. Some believed the nation needed raw materials from overseas for its growing industries. Business leaders and others began to look for wider markets. One person wrote, "The trade of the world must and shall be ours." Others believed that the blessings of republican government as practiced in the United States should be shared with other lands. Still others thought new territories were needed as ports for a strong navy worthy of the United States.

Troubles in Cuba

Although Spain had lost most of its colonies in the New World, it still held Cuba, the largest island in the Caribbean. For many years Cubans had been trying to free themselves from Spanish rule. Eight times between 1823 and 1853 Cubans took up arms against Spain. Each time the Spanish defeated the rebels. The Spanish put down other revolts from 1868 to 1878 and again in 1895. Stories about the cruel treatment of Cubans by Spanish soldiers circulated throughout the United States. More and more people grew angry over these reports. They sympathized with the Cubans.

American newspapers built the case against Spain. Their pages were filled with horror stories about "Spanish butchers" and the suffering of Cubans. Editorials in many newspapers wanted the United States to go to war with Spain to free the Cubans.

Finally, in 1898, two events brought matters to a head. On February 9 the New York *Journal* printed a letter written by the Spanish minister to the United States. The letter had been stolen by a Cuban rebel and turned over to the newspaper. In the letter the Spanish minister criticized President William McKinley, calling him weak and too eager to be admired. Americans were furious at this attack on their President.

On February 15 the second event took place: the United States battleship *Maine* exploded and sank in Havana harbor. The United States lost more then 250 sailors. Although no cause could be found for the explosion, most Americans, stirred by fiery newspaper reports, blamed the Spanish.

As the cry for war became louder, President William McKinley tried to keep peace. "I have been through one war [the Civil War]," he said, ". . . and I do not want to see another." But Theodore Roosevelt, who was then assistant secretary of the navy, ordered the United States fleet in Hong Kong to be ready for action in the Philippines, another Spanish possession.

McKinley finally gave in and laid the question of war before Congress. Congress debated for a week. On April 19, 1898, it acted. It recognized Cuba as independent, ordered the Spanish to leave the island, and authorized the President to use armed force if the Spanish refused. Congress also stated that Cuba would not be made a possession of the United States. Within a few days Spain and the United States were at war.

Victory for the United States

The United States Navy—trained and well equipped—was ready for action. Less than a week after the declaration of war the United States won a great naval victory—not in Cuba, but half a world away. On May 1 the United States Pacific fleet, led by Commodore George Dewey, steamed into Manila Bay in the Philippines. In a matter of hours United States warships smashed the rotting and outdated Spanish fleet. Army troops later landed and, with the help of Filipino forces, took Manila and other key cities.

Unlike the navy, the army was not prepared for war. There were plenty of volunteers—nearly 200,000 of them—but the troops

565

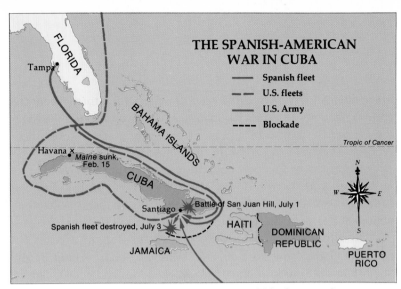

The Spanish-American War in Cuba was over within five months.

were untrained and ill-equipped. In the confusion soldiers were sent to Cuba without the proper uniforms or equipment. Many wore heavy winter uniforms as they fought under the hot Cuban sun. Trainloads of arms and equipment got lost on the way and sat on sidings in the United States for weeks. The port at Tampa, Florida, was crowded with troops, trains, and equipment. No one seemed to know how to match up the men with the right equipment and ships.

Fortunately for the United States the Spanish in Cuba were no better organized. Although the Spanish had nearly 200,000 trained and armed troops stationed in Cuba, they failed to use them to their advantage. An American army landed in Cuba without a fight. Among the American soldiers was Colonel Theodore Roosevelt. Roosevelt and his troops, called the Rough Riders, took the forts at San Juan Hill that guarded the city of Santiago in July 1898.

The United States Navy had blockaded the Spanish Caribbean fleet at Santiago Bay in May 1898. With United States ground forces now marching on the city, the Spanish fleet tried to escape. But it was destroyed by the United States Navy on July 3. On July 16 Santiago surrendered. Another United States army took the Spanish-held island of Puerto Rico on July 25 with little opposition.

The defeats in the Pacific and the Caribbean and the loss of their two fleets convinced the Spanish that they had nothing to gain from further fighting. They asked for peace. The war ended on August 12. A peace treaty was signed on December 10, 1898. Spain agreed to give Cuba and Puerto Rico in the Caribbean and Guam and the Philippines in the Pacific to the United States. The United States planned to use these islands as coaling stations where naval and trading ships could refuel.

The United States Empire

In a war that lasted less than four months the United States had freed Cuba from Spanish rule. But Cuba was not allowed to enjoy independence immediately. United States Army General Leonard Wood remained in Cuba as military governor until 1902. Even after that time, Congress acted as a "protector" of independent Cuba. Cuba's right to deal with other foreign powers was limited. Cuba also had to rent or sell naval stations to the United States.

Cubans did not like being treated this way. Finally, in 1934, the United States agreed to stay out of Cuba and honor that country's independence. The United States, however, has kept a naval base at Guantanamo Bay since the Spanish-American War.

Puerto Rico became a United States territory. In 1917 its people became United States citizens. Guam, also given up by the Spanish, and Wake Island, annexed by the United States in 1899, have remained United States possessions.

Some leaders wanted to see the Philippine Islands become independent. Others argued that the islands should become a United States possession. President McKinley hesitated. But finally he decided that the Filipinos were not ready to govern themselves. If the United States did not take over, he reasoned, some European power or Japan might do so. So McKinley chose to make the Philippines a possession of the United States.

By 1920 the United States had added islands in the Pacific and the Caribbean to the holdings it already had in Alaska and Panama.

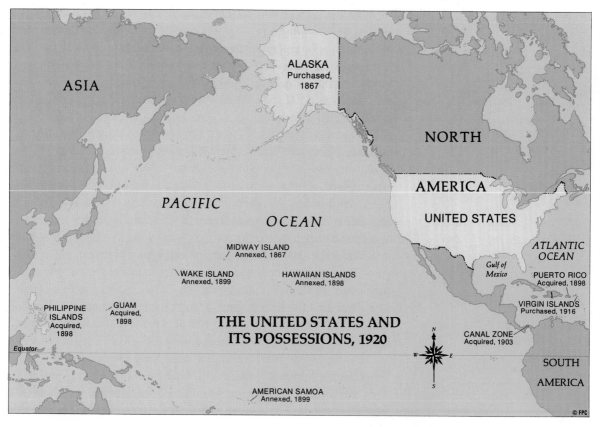

THE UNITED STATES AND ITS POSSESSIONS, 1920

Section 2 Review

1. Name three arguments given for expansion in the 1890s.
2. What role did the United States play in the affairs of Cuba and of the Philippines?

Critical Thinking

3. **Determining Relevance.** How did United States newspapers help bring about the Spanish-American War?

LOOKING AHEAD: How did events in Mexico, Venezuela, and Panama give new life to the Monroe Doctrine?

The Filipinos objected. Just as they had fought the Spanish for freedom, so they began to fight the United States troops moving into their country. Fighting lasted until 1902. More soldiers died in this conflict than in the war with Spain. But the Philippines remained a United States possession until 1946, when the islands became an independent nation.

With the signing of the peace treaty with Spain, the United States found itself to be a world power. On its list of overseas possessions were Alaska, the Hawaiian Islands, the Philippines, Midway Island, Puerto Rico, Guam, and later Wake Island. In 1899 the United States took over seven of the Samoan islands in the South Pacific. Holding lands all around the world changed the role of the United States in world affairs. Events taking place far from its shores could immediately affect the whole country. As Theodore Roosevelt said, "Even if we would, we cannot play a small part."

3 New Life for the Monroe Doctrine

The Monroe Doctrine of 1823 had warned the European powers against any further colonization in the Western Hemisphere. Before the Civil War, however, the United States lacked the might to follow through on its warning. Great Britain was ready to back up the United States only to protect its own interests. Spain, France, and other nations often paid little attention to the Monroe Doctrine. But as the United States became more powerful, the Monroe Doctrine began to take on new meaning.

France and Mexico

After Mexico freed itself from Spain in 1821, its government was unstable. Between 1857 and 1861 a new leader, Benito Juárez (hwär′əs), brought the people together under a republican form of government. At the same time, another European government had its eye on Mexico. Napoleon III of France sent troops into Mexico and defeated the forces of Juárez. He set up a puppet government—one whose strings he could control—under the Archduke Maximilian. Napoleon declared Maximilian emperor of Mexico.

The United States was against Napoleon's takeover, but there was little it could do. At that time the United States was fighting the Civil War and could not spare troops to fight against the French. Moreover the Union was afraid that if it went to the aid of Mexico, the French would help the Confederacy.

As the Civil War drew to a close, anti-French feeling grew. Shortly after Appomattox, General Grant was thinking of sending an army into Mexico to drive out the French. Meanwhile Napoleon III was beginning to have second thoughts about his bid for Mexico.

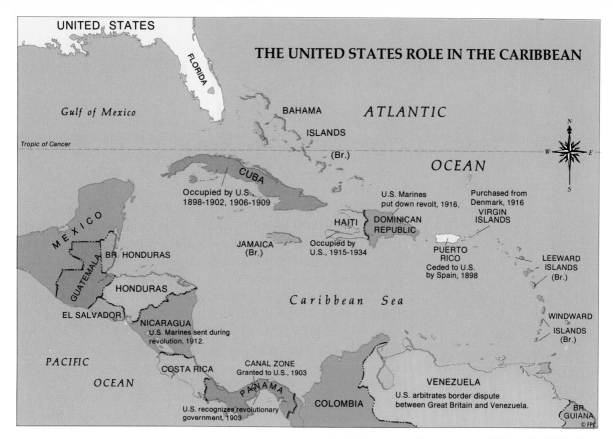

THE UNITED STATES ROLE IN THE CARIBBEAN

UNITED STATES

FLORIDA

Gulf of Mexico

BAHAMA

ISLANDS

ATLANTIC

OCEAN

(Br.)

Tropic of Cancer

CUBA

Occupied by U.S.,
1898-1902, 1906-1909

U.S. Marines
put down revolt, 1916.

Purchased from
Denmark, 1916
VIRGIN
ISLANDS

HAITI

DOMINICAN
REPUBLIC

JAMAICA
(Br.)

Occupied by
U.S., 1915-1934

PUERTO
RICO

Ceded to U.S.
by Spain, 1898

LEEWARD
ISLANDS
(Br.)

MEXICO

GUATEMALA

BR. HONDURAS

HONDURAS

EL SALVADOR

NICARAGUA

U.S. Marines sent during
revolution, 1912.

Caribbean Sea

WINDWARD

ISLANDS
(Br.)

PACIFIC

OCEAN

COSTA RICA

CANAL ZONE
Granted to U.S., 1903

PANAMA

U.S. recognizes revolutionary
government, 1903.

COLOMBIA

VENEZUELA

U.S. arbitrates border dispute
between Great Britain and Venezuela.

BR.
GUIANA

© FPC

Rebels there, once again united under Juárez, fought without rest against Maximilian. The cost of keeping an army in Mexico weighed heavily on the French treasury. And France had other troubles in Europe.

Under pressure from the United States Napoleon III finally withdrew his troops from Mexico. Maximilian was left without aid. On May 15, 1867, he was taken prisoner by Juárez's forces. He was tried, convicted, and executed.

Britain and Venezuela

In the 1890s a dispute arose over the boundary between Venezuela and British Guiana. A border line had been drawn years earlier by a British geographer, but the Venezuelans had never accepted it. When gold was discovered in the disputed territory, the argument became more heated.

To the United States, the matter seemed another case of a European imperialist power trying to force its way on a Latin American nation. Such action violated the Monroe Doctrine. So in 1895 the United States offered to act as arbitrator in the dispute between Britain and Venezuela—to listen to their claims, study the problem, and make a decision. Venezuela agreed to arbitration. Britain made no formal reply.

The British attitude angered Americans. One United States senator wrote: "If Great Britain is to be permitted to . . . take the territory of Venezuela, there is nothing to prevent her taking the

As a strong neighbor, the United States began to police conflicts in Central and South America.

whole of Venezuela or any other South American state. If Great Britain can do this . . . France and Germany will do it also. . . . The supremacy of the Monroe Doctrine should be established and at once—peaceably if we can, forcibly if we must."

The United States government stood fast in its offer of arbitration. The British did not answer for four months and then rejected the offer. This response made President Grover Cleveland "mad clear through." He asked Congress for the money to set up a commission to work on the boundary problem. Once the boundary was decided, he said, the United States should force the British to accept it—with troops, if necessary.

The British finally gave in and accepted arbitration by the United States. The new boundary gave only slightly more land to Venezuela than the old one. But the United States had forced a European power to honor the Monroe Doctrine.

Roosevelt and the Monroe Doctrine

Venezuela found itself in trouble again in 1902. It owed money to several European nations. So the Europeans set up a naval blockade of Venezuela. They intended to stay until they were paid. In time, the Europeans and Venezuelans settled the issue.

But Americans began to worry about the safety of the United States in situations that brought European troops into Latin America. So President Theodore Roosevelt read a new meaning into the Monroe Doctrine in a message to Congress in 1904. In cases of wrongdoing by Latin American nations, Roosevelt said, the United States might have to act as "an international police power." European fighting forces could remain at home. The United States would step in.

The United States soon began to carry out its self-assigned police duties. It stepped in when the Dominican Republic could not pay its debts to European countries. It sent marines there in 1916 to put down a revolution. Marines were also sent to Nicaragua in 1912 and to Haiti in 1915 to settle problems.

Theodore Roosevelt once told a friend that he was fond of a West African saying: "Speak softly and carry a big stick; you will go far." The United States, under Roosevelt and later Presidents, seldom spoke softly in dealing with Latin American countries and was often eager to use the big stick of military might. Only in the 1930s did the United States begin to change its approach to its southern neighbors.

The Panama Canal

Since the mid-1800s the United States had wanted to build a canal across the narrow isthmus that connects North and South America. People wanted a shorter and cheaper way to sail from one coast to

The Panama Canal shortened the trip between San Francisco and New York by about 7,800 miles (12,600 km).

the other without going around South America. But nothing came of the canal plans until early in the twentieth century.

In 1902 the United States asked Colombia, which then held Panama, for permission to build a canal in Panama. Talks between the two nations broke down when the Colombians seemed to be asking too much. On November 3, 1903, the Panamanians revolted against Colombia and declared their independence. The United States quickly began talks with the new government about the canal. In return for $10 million and $250,000 per year Panama gave the United States a zone ten miles (16 km) wide across Panama. The Canal Zone and the canal itself would belong to the United States.

Colombians complained that the United States had stirred up the Panamanian revolution to win the canal rights. The United States denied this charge. Later, in 1921, the United States paid Colombia $25 million for their loss of Panama.

President Theodore Roosevelt was eager to "make the dirt fly." Work on the canal began in 1904, directed by the United States Army Corps of Engineers. It went on for ten years. The builders had to come up with many new engineering ideas. They also had to fight such tropical diseases as malaria and yellow fever. The first ship passed through the completed canal in August 1914.

The canal proved to be of great value to the United States. But Panamanians began to demand control of it. In 1979 the United States agreed to give control of the canal to Panama by the year 2000 to keep good relations with all Latin American countries.

As a result of its economic and industrial strength, the United States could never again remain aloof from world problems. Before long, the United States would become a world leader.

Section 3 Review

1. Why did the United States not actively oppose the takeover of Mexico by France in 1861?
2. What were the results of the United States arbitration of the dispute between Britain and Venezuela in the 1890s?
3. Why did the United States want to build a canal across the Isthmus of Panama?

Critical Thinking

4. **Recognizing Bias.** Why did Theodore Roosevelt believe that the United States should act as a police power in Latin America?

People   And Empires

Henry Cabot Lodge supported an overseas empire for the United States, while Emilio Aguinaldo fought for Philippine independence.

When the United States gained lands overseas by defeating Spain in 1898, a heated debate broke out. Some people believed the United States should keep the territories, including the Philippine Islands. Others believed these countries should be self-ruled.

Lodge: Empire Supporter

Henry Cabot Lodge, senator from Massachusetts, spoke out for a United States empire. In 1895, three years before the war with Spain, Lodge wrote: "The great nations are rapidly absorbing for their future expansion and their present defence all the [developing] places of the earth. . . . As one of the great nations of the world, the United States must not fall out of the line of march."

Lodge and the Philippines

When Lodge heard that the United States Navy had crushed the Spanish navy in the Philippines, he wrote, "The American flag is up and it must stay!" The Philippines, said Lodge, opened more avenues for development than had anything since the purchase of Louisiana from France.

Lodge became excited about the possible "benefits to our trade, our industries, and our labor." With wider markets will come a great number of trading ships and a great navy, said Lodge. "Great colonies will grow about our ports of trade, and the American law, American order, American Civilization and the American flag will plant themselves on shores [once] bloody and [backward]."

The treaty with Spain that gave the Philippines to the United States was narrowly accepted by the Senate. Lodge took much of the credit when it did pass. In a letter to Theodore Roosevelt he compared his work on the treaty with that of a mechanic aboard ship. "We were down in the engine room and do not get flowers, but we did make the ship move."

The United States fleet won easily at Manila Bay (below). Henry Cabot Lodge (inset) helped work out the treaty with Spain.

Lodge's Opponents

Others in the United States were against holding the Philippines as a United States possession. Among them were Andrew Carnegie, former President Grover Cleveland, and labor leader Samuel Gompers. Senator William Jennings Bryan said that gaining an empire ran counter to the Declaration of Independence. The people of the United States, he said, had entered the war with Spain to free peoples under colonial rule. "Have the people so changed . . .," asked Bryan, that they are now willing to "force upon the Filipinos the same system of government against which the [American] colonists protested with fire and sword?"

Aguinaldo: Fighter for Independence

Emilio Aguinaldo (äg′ē·näl′dō) was a Filipino. He had attended a Catholic school in Manila. In 1896 a group led by twenty-six-year-old Aguinaldo tried to throw out Spanish representatives in the Philippines, mainly Catholic church leaders. The revolt failed. He and his followers agreed to leave the Philippines in 1897 in return for cash and promises of land and political changes. The promises were not kept.

After the United States defeated the Spanish fleet in Manila Bay, Admiral George Dewey sent a ship to Singapore to bring Aguinaldo and thirteen other leaders back to the Philippines. Aguinaldo and his Filipino friends fought side by side with United States soldiers to take control of Manila and other key cities in the Philippines away from the Spanish.

A government pulled together by Aguinaldo stood ready to take

Filipino rebel fighters, led by Aguinaldo (inset), battled United States troops for three years after the treaty with Spain was signed.

over when the fighting ended. This government declared self-rule for the Philippines on June 12, 1898. The United States commanders, however, received orders from Washington, D.C., that they were not to share the government of the Philippines with Aguinaldo. So Aguinaldo and his forces were told to withdraw from Manila.

Continued Rebel Fighting

Although Aguinaldo did leave Manila, fighting broke out between the United States Army and Aguinaldo's group. The Filipinos were willing to be protected but not ruled by the United States.

The United States brought in thousands more troops to fight Aguinaldo. In November 1899, short of weapons, Aguinaldo's army broke up into smaller bands of fighters. In small groups they hid in

the hills and forests and attacked when it was least expected.

Bitter fighting dragged on. The number killed, wounded, or dead from disease can only be estimated. The United States had about 245 soldiers killed and 490 wounded. The Filipinos lost about 3,850 killed and over 1,000 wounded. The cost to the United States was thought to be about $170 million.

Aguinaldo was finally caught in March 1901. He swore loyalty to the United States and accepted an uneasy peace. Those fighting with him, however, did not give up easily. In September 1901 almost a whole company of United States soldiers—three officers and 50 men—were killed in a surprise attack.

Aguinaldo's dream of an independent Philippine nation did not come true for almost fifty years.

Chapter 29 Review

Chapter Summary

The United States began trading heavily overseas in the late 1800s. At the end of the 1800s, the United States asked other industrial nations interested in trading with China to follow an Open Door policy. Trade with Japan began in 1854 when Commodore Perry persuaded Japanese officials to sign a trade treaty with the United States.

In 1860 the United States first acquired control of lands beyond its borders. The United States purchased Alaska from Russia in 1868. It annexed the Hawaiian Islands in 1898 to protect American shipping and sugar-growing interests. In the same year, the United States went to war with Spain. As a result of the war, the United States gained control over Cuba and Puerto Rico in the Caribbean, and Guam in the Pacific. The United States also acquired the Phillipines in the Pacific. The United States promised to stay out of Cuba in 1934, and the Philippines became independent in 1946. People living in Puerto Rico became United States citizens in 1917.

During this time, President Theodore Roosevelt strengthened the Monroe Doctrine. He warned all European nations that the United States intended to police the Western Hemisphere. The completion of the Panama Canal in 1914 provided a shorter route between the Atlantic and Pacific oceans. Its completion gave the United States an even more active role as a world leader.

Reviewing Vocabulary

Use the words below to complete the following sentences.

possession	imperialism	empire
missionary	arbitration	isthmus
annex	international	

1. Many Americans opposed the idea of building a(n) _____ overseas.
2. At one time, England held a(n) _____ on each continent.
3. A person with a(n) _____ reputation is known outside his or her own country.
4. The United States did not_____ the Hawaiian Islands at the time it claimed Midway Island.
5. In the late nineteenth century, European _____ led to a race to acquire new territories.
6. The United States acted as the neutral third party to settle a dispute between Venezuela and Britain by _____.
7. A(n) _____ hopes to teach religion and help others.
8. The Panama Canal is located on the _____ of Panama.

Understanding Main Ideas

1. In what ways was United States involvement in Asia and the Pacific helpful to United States business interests in the 1800s?
2. What caused the Spanish-American War? What were the results of that war according to the peace treaty?
3. How did United States actions in Mexico, Venezuela, and the Dominican Republic reflect a strong interpretation of the Monroe Doctrine?
4. What was the purpose of the Open Door policy in China? What events prompted the United States to pursue the passage of this policy?
5. How did the United States acquire each of the following territories: Midway Island, the Hawaiian Islands, the Philippines, and Alaska?

Social Studies Skills: Interpreting a Poster

Carefully study the poster to the right. The messages on the poster provide valuable clues to help you to answer the questions below.

Skill Review: Review the chapter, look up the words *sulphur* and *fumigation,* and answer the following questions.

1. Where and when was this poster probably used?
2. How was yellow fever passed to humans?
3. What is the difference between a theory and a fact?
4. What is does "sulphur for fumigation" mean?
5. How might the phrase "but we become EARNEST ONLY after it claims our own blood" have encouraged workers to follow the advice on the poster?

6. What group was directing the fumigation program?

---

6. Why did the United States want to build a canal in Panama?

Critical Thinking Skills

1. **Identifying Assumptions.** At the outbreak of the Spanish-American War, Theodore Roosevelt described it as a "splendid little war." How do you think Roosevelt felt about war in general and the position of the United States in the world?
2. **Recognizing Bias.** People living in the Hawaiian Islands strongly urged that the United States annex the islands. Why did they encourage annexation?
3. **Predicting Consequences.** Many people opposed the Spanish-American War. What might have happened to the United States if it had not entered that war?

Writing About History

Writing a Dialogue. Write a brief imaginary conversation between Theodore Roosevelt and President William McKinley in which McKinley tries to decide which option to choose regarding the future of the Philippines. Have the two discuss their views of the role that the United States should play in world affairs.

Your Region in History

Geography. What was the chief element of your region's economy when the United States began trading with China? Would any of the materials that your region produced then have been traded with China? What Chinese goods would have been valued by the people living in your area at that time?

Lifestyles: The Industrial Age

I N NO OTHER PERIOD of United States history did the everyday life of the average person change as much as it did between 1870 and 1914. More Americans lived among the noise, clutter, and activities of city life than among the peace and quiet of country life. Most children entering school in Boston at the end of the nineteenth century had never seen a sheep or a field of corn. But they knew electric lights, bicycles, and streetcars. Food to them was something they bought in a store rather than raised in a garden. Many people were not sure which was better—the security of the old ways or the excitement of the new.

Thomas Edison believed that his deafness began after a well-meaning friend pulled him aboard a moving train by grabbing his ears. Edison is shown here in his lab at West Orange, New Jersey.

Most men and women in the United States continued to marry and to live in families. But there were changes in family life in the late 1800s and early 1900s. Women who lived in cities tended to marry later and to have fewer children than women who lived in small towns and on farms.

Immigrant families made up a large part of the urban population. In most of these families both parents—and often the older children as well—had to work to earn enough to live. They also worked to learn the ways of their new country and to make better lives for themselves.

Romance by Morse Code

Thomas Edison, partly deaf from the age of twelve on, said that his deafness helped him in some ways. He believed that being deaf allowed him to concentrate on his inventions. And, he claimed, being deaf was an advantage in his romance with Mina Miller, whom he married in 1886.

In the first place it [deafness] excused me for getting quite a little nearer to her than I would have dared to if I hadn't had to be quite close in order to hear what she said. . . . My later courtship was carried on by telegraph. I taught her the Morse code, and when she could both send and receive we got along much better than we could have with spoken words by tapping our remarks to one another on our hands. Presently I asked her thus, in Morse code, if she would marry me. The word "Yes" is an easy one to send by telegraphic signals, and she sent it. . . . Nobody knew anything about many of our conversations. . . . If we had spoken words, others would have heard them. We could use pet names without the least embarrassment. . . . We still use the telegraphic code at times. When we go to hear a spoken play she keeps her hand upon my knee and telegraphs the words the actors use so that I know something about the drama though I hear nothing of the dialog.

A Family of "Greenhorns"

Mary Antin was born in Russia in 1881. When she was thirteen years old, she moved to the United States with her mother, two sisters, and brother. Her father had been in Boston for three years working to make a home for his family. In her autobiography, *The Promised Land*, Mary described her first day in the United States.

Our initiation into American ways began with the first step on the new soil. My father found occasion to instruct us or correct us even on the way from the pier to Wall Street, which journey we made crowded together in a rickety cab. He told us not to lean out of the windows, not to point, and explained the word "greenhorn" [an inexperienced newcomer]. We did not want to be "greenhorns" and

gave the strictest attention to my father's instructions. . . . My first meal was an object lesson of much variety. My father produced several kinds of food, ready to eat, without any cooking, from little tin cans that had printing all over them. He attempted to introduce us to a queer, slippery kind of fruit, which he called "banana," but had to give it up for the time being. After the meal, he had better luck with a curious piece of furniture on runners, which he called "rocking-chair. . . ." We laughed immoderately over our various experiments with the novelty, which was a wholesome way of letting off steam after the unusual excitement of the day.*

Free land under the Homestead Act, religious tolerance, and jobs created by the industrial revolution attracted immigrant families to the United States. In their homelands they had known terrible poverty, hunger, and religious persecution.

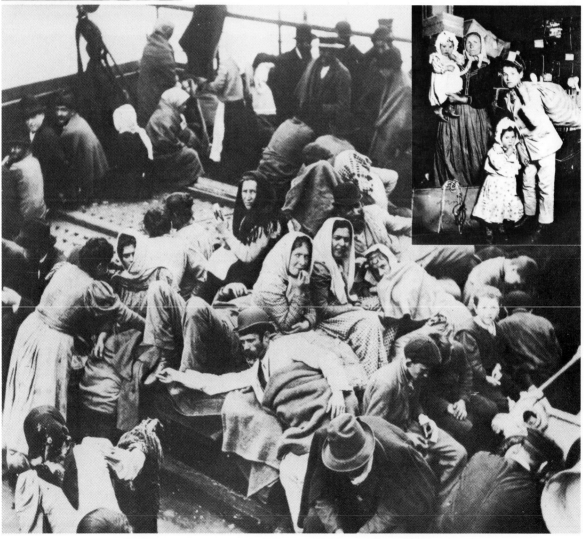

Stoves and fireplaces were the only sources of heat in homes at the turn of the century.

Many homes were built in the late 1800s and early 1900s. In the cities, high-priced apartments and row houses were built for middle-class families. The poor were crowded into larger, older houses that had been divided into many small apartments, or tenements. Many also lived in the newer dumbbell-shaped tenements. In tenements families shared what few bathroom and kitchen facilities there were.

As glass became cheaper and more plentiful, houses in all parts of the country were built with more windows. More and more houses had indoor bathrooms. Gas lighting—and later electric lighting—became more common.

Furnishings from the "Wish Book"

Furniture for the home changed rapidly in the early 1900s. Even in the country, families were buying labor-saving tools for their kitchens. They bought up-to-date chairs and tables as well as musical instruments for their sitting rooms. And they bought factory-made dishes for their dining rooms. All of these things and much, much more could be ordered from the Sears, Roebuck, and Company catalog. People called it the "wish book." Many read it cover to cover, dreaming about all the wonderful things they might someday order for themselves.

Sears, Roebuck, and Company was chartered in 1893. That year the catalog had 196 pages. Many of the ads were written by Richard Sears himself. In 1895 the catalog had 507 pages, including many special offers on items like kitchen tools, sewing machines, clothing, curtains, and potted plants. Almost everybody found something to order from the "wish book."

For only $15.50 Sears, Roebuck catalog customers could buy a large sofa, an armchair, a rocker, and two side chairs.

The reader in this well-furnished sitting room enjoys light from an electric lamp and heat from a steam radiator.

The drawings above show the bright and dark sides of tenement living.

Section 1 Review

1. How many people lived in the home workplace described by Jacob Riis?
2. Name three ways women today save time in keeping house.

Critical Thinking

3. **Making Comparisons.** Describe how city dwellings for the poor were different from those for the middle class.

At Home in a Tenement

In New York many newly arrived immigrants worked at home. In his book *How the Other Half Lives* reporter Jacob Riis, an immigrant from Denmark, described one such home workplace.

Five men and women, two young girls, not fifteen, and a boy who says . . . that he is fifteen . . . are at the machines sewing. . . . The floor is littered ankle-deep with half-sewn garments. In the alcove, on a couch of many dozens of "pants" ready for the finisher, a barelegged baby with pinched face is asleep. A fence of piled-up clothing keeps him from rolling off on the floor. The faces, hands and arms to the elbows of everyone in the room are black with the color of the cloth on which they are working.

Homes for Working Mothers

Charlotte Perkins Gilman believed that women should not have to depend on men for food, clothes, and housing. In her book *Women and Economics,* published in 1898, she argued that women, even women with children, should be free to choose jobs other than housework. She urged people to find time-saving ways of keeping house so that women would have more time for other work.

If there should be built and opened in any of our large cities to-day an . . . apartment house for professional women with families, it would be filled at once. . . . There would be a [common] kitchen . . . from which meals could be served to families in their rooms or in a common diningroom. . . . It would be a home where the cleaning was done by [hired] workers . . . ; and a roof-garden, day nursery, and kindergarten, under well-trained professional nurses and teachers, would insure proper care of the children. . . .

Many newcomers valued the customs of their former countries as much as the opportunities to make a good living in the United States.

Young women and men, converted during a religious meeting about 1910, line up to be baptized in a nearby creek.

Many people in the United States had great faith in the value of progress. They believed that life would be better for themselves, for their children, and for the country in the future. There would be more factory-made goods, more money to buy the goods, and better living conditions for all. They believed that success depended on a little luck and a lot of hard work.

Values for Success

Edward Bok's life was a true rags-to-riches story. He came to the United States from Holland when he was six years old, got his first job in a bakery at ten, became an office boy at thirteen. At nineteen he became a clerk in a publisher's office. Two years later he became an editor. And within five years he had both started his own publishing company and become editor-in-chief of a very popular magazine, *The Ladies' Home Journal.*

In his autobiography, *The Americanization of Edward Bok,* he praised America for the opportunity it offered the foreign-born. But he complained that American values fell short of the Dutch values he had learned from his parents.

Where the Dutchman saved, the American wasted. There was waste . . . on every hand. . . . The first time my mother saw [the wasted food in] the garbage pail of a family almost as poor as our own, . . . she could scarcely believe her eyes. . . . There was . . . nothing in American life to teach me thrift or economy; everything to teach me to spend and to waste.

Bok also complained that America taught that quantity counted for more than quality. How much a person did was more important than how well the work was done. Americans, he said, considered a job done when it was "good enough" or "would do."

Progress for Blacks—Two Programs

During the late nineteenth century, the leading spokesman for black Americans was one-time slave Booker T. Washington. He gave speeches and advised Presidents on how to improve the lives of black people. But during the early 1900s a young black leader, W.E.B. Du Bois, criticized Washington's leadership. He offered very different advice on how blacks could improve their lives.

Washington believed that blacks should remain in the South and work hard and well at the jobs that were open to them there. As productive citizens, he believed, they would be treated with justice and allowed to vote. In a speech made in 1903 he said:

I believe most earnestly that for years to come the education of the people of my race should be [concerned mostly with] the every-day practical things of life, upon something that is needed to be done, and something which they will be permitted to do in the community in which they [live].

In another speech he explained what he hoped would be the results of this program of practical education.

When a number of Negroes . . . own and operate the most successful farms, are among the largest tax-payers in their county, are moral and intelligent, I do not believe that in many portions of the South such [people] need long be denied the right to [vote]. . . .

Du Bois was twelve years younger than Washington and was the first black to earn Harvard's highest degree. He believed that more blacks should be enrolled in high schools, colleges, and universities. Blacks should not wait, he said, for equal rights and equal treatment under the law to be granted them by whites. They should demand those rights immediately. In his 1903 book *Souls of Black Folks* he said that Washington's leadership had

tended to make the whites, North and South, shift the burden of the Negro problem to the Negro's shoulders . . . when in fact the burden belongs to the nation, and the hands of none of us are clean if we bend not our energies to righting of these great wrongs.

Black and white auto makers worked side by side on the early Ford assembly lines.

Seventeen-year-old Virginia Fipps taught children of all ages in her Missouri school.

By the early twentieth century most children in the United States attended school. Some children attended only grade school. But more and more children went on to finish high school. For newcomers and for Native Americans, schools became a place to learn "American ways" and the English language.

Although experts in education and teachers in some city schools worked out learning-by-doing programs, many more teachers used the trusted way—drill, drill, and more drill—to teach the three Rs.

Manners in School

In her book *Lessons on Manners,* published in 1899, Julia M. Dewey outlined some rules for conduct in the schoolroom.

We should never slide down in our seat, . . . and when reciting we should stand erect and on both feet, without leaning on the desk. Neither should we swing the feet nor keep them in constant motion. . . .

Dewey stressed the need for quiet in the schoolroom.

It is absolutely necessary that the work of the school should be done quietly and in order. Whispering, loud studying, walking noisily, slamming books and scraping the feet on the floor, if [done] by all would make an unbearable [noise], and if [done] by a few would disturb the rest.

Even the raising of hands was considered bad manners.

Ghetto classrooms offered students little more than a place to sit and some warmth from a stove. In better schoolrooms in New York, students sat at desks and read from printed books (right).

Learning a New Lifestyle

In 1887 Batsinas, a young Apache, arrived at Carlisle Indian Industrial School in Carlisle, Pennsylvania. He was given a haircut, a blue uniform, and an English name, Jason Betzinez. He enjoyed wearing his new uniform. He had no trouble following the strict rules of the school. But learning English was a problem.

It was extremely difficult for me to learn to speak English. At first I was unable to make many of the sounds. I even had trouble pronouncing the letters of the alphabet. I couldn't tell the difference between the strange sounds as readily as the younger people in the class. . . . For the first three years it didn't seem that I would ever learn. . . . Finally I was pleased to have my teacher . . .[say] "Jason, you have made quite an advance. You are beginning to show improvement in your English." Thus encouraged I began to make better progress. . . .

Jason also learned blacksmithing and welding at Carlisle. After leaving school, Jason worked as a blacksmith.

The Purpose of Education

In 1897 Jane Addams, the founder of Hull House in Chicago, made a speech to the National Educational Association. She took American schools to task for failing to offer children of immigrant parents the means to lead more meaningful lives. She used as an example a young Italian boy who had come to America knowing no English and who had entered a public school.

[The teacher] has little idea of . . . Italian life. . . . No attempt is made to give a boy, who, we know, will certainly have to go into [a shop or factory] . . . any [idea] of his social value, and his activities [in school and at work] become perfectly mechanical. . . . Only occasionally . . . has he had a glimpse of the real joy of doing a thing for its own sake.

Section 2 Review

1. Name two ways that the behavior of Americans ran counter to Edward Bok's Dutch values.
2. List five rules that apply to student behavior in your classrooms.
3. What did Jane Addams expect the teacher to "give" the Italian student?

Critical Thinking

4. **Making Comparisons.** How did Du Bois's advice to blacks differ from Washington's advice?

Gasoline-powered machines made farm work easier. This man is harvesting potatoes in Florida.

By 1900 more Americans worked in factories than on farms. Both in the factory and on the farm the workday was long—ten to twelve hours or more. In the factory, however, there was more noise, stuffy air, and dull routine. Many workers began to join together to ask for better pay, shorter hours, and improved working conditions. And the celebration of a day for workers—Labor Day—was begun.

Anton's Job

Anton Kmet, an immigrant from eastern Europe, was thirty years old when he arrived in New York. He moved with other immigrants to Cleveland, Ohio. The day after he arrived he went to the American Steel and Wire Company to look for a job.

He was put to work moving large coils of wire from a loading platform into freight cars. When his boss discovered that he could lift the heavy loads without any problem, the other two men who had been working there were removed. Kmet now did the work of three men. Because he received twelve cents an hour and the other workers were paid only ten cents an hour, he was not unhappy.

Sweatshop Girl

Sadie Froune, an immigrant from Poland, told of what it was like to work in a sweatshop in the early 1900s.

At seven o'clock we all sit down to our machines and the boss brings to each one the pile of work that he or she is to finish during the day. . . . This pile is put down beside the machine, and as soon as a skirt is done it is laid on the other side of the machine. Sometimes the work is not all finished by six o'clock, and then the one who is behind must work overtime. Sometimes one is finished ahead of time and gets away at four or five o'clock. . . .

The machines go like mad all day, because the faster you work the more money you get. Sometimes in my haste I get my finger caught and the needle goes right through it. It goes so quick, though, that it does not hurt much. I bind the finger up with a piece of cotton and go on working. We all have accidents like that.

A Heartsick Ironworker

Some newcomers were not able to find work. A Russian immigrant sent the following letter to the *Jewish Daily Forward.*

I am an ironworker. I can work a milling machine and a drill press. I can also drive horses and train colts. I have been jobless for six months now, I have eaten the last shirt on my back and now there is nothing left for me. . . . One goes about with strong hands, one wants to sell them for a bit of bread, and no one wants to buy. They tell you coldbloodedly: We don't need you. Can you imagine how heartsick one gets? . . . Lately I have spent five cents a day on food, and the last two days I don't even have that. . . . If I had known it would be so bitter for me here, I wouldn't have come.

Labor Day

The custom of celebrating the first Monday in September as Labor Day started in 1882. Peter J. McGuire, the president of the United Brotherhood of Carpenters and Joiners of America, first suggested a parade in New York City to honor laborers. Workers were warned not to leave their jobs. But about ten thousand of them paraded around Union Square and up Fifth Avenue to Forty-Second Street. That afternoon the workers met for a big picnic. They ate, listened to speeches, and danced. A fireworks display ended the celebration.

In 1894 President Grover Cleveland signed a bill making Labor Day a national holiday.

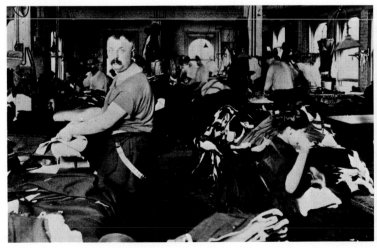

The clothing industry employed many workers—from ironers and tailors in New York garment shops (left) to bobbin boys in southern cotton mills.

Children enjoyed posing for
pictures in goat carts.

Electric lights turned Luna Park at
Coney Island into a glittering
nighttime playground for New
Yorkers (top). Out-of-town visitors
could send home picture postcards
of the entrance to the park.

On bicycles, streetcars, and other public transportation people left
home for entertainment and recreation. Spectator sports such as
baseball and football became far more popular. And amusement
parks and movie theaters drew large crowds.

A Coney Island Holiday

At Coney Island, near New York City, Americans learned to enjoy
the one-day holiday. Before the turn of the century Coney Island's
beaches, hotels, eating places, racetracks, and other amusements
had been mainly for the rich. But with new trolleys and trains
more people were able to enjoy Coney Island.

Men, women, and children flocked to the beaches. In
bathhouses they changed into rented bathing suits. Though most
people could not swim, they played in the water and the sand.

And the crowds loved the new amusement parks. The first
roller coaster was built on Coney Island in 1884. Amusement parks
also played up animal acts, oddities such as an Eskimo village and
a whale turned to stone, band music, and vaudeville theater. At
night, lights from the tall towers and castles housing the rides and
amusements made Coney Island seem like a dreamworld.

Holiday and weekend outings were often recorded on film at amusement parks (top). Louis Armstrong's Hot Five was one of many bands making records in the early 1900s.

Section 3 Review

1. Tell whether the following workers were skilled or unskilled: Anton Kmet, Sadie Froune, the Russian immigrant who wrote to the newspaper.
2. Name four new ideas used in movie making by David Griffith.

Critical Thinking

3. **Demonstrating Reasoned Judgement.** What sweatshop conditions described by Sadie Froune might a labor union try to change?

Wobbling Wheels

By 1896 more than 4 million Americans were riding bicycles, and more than 300 factories were manufacturing them.

Frances Willard, founder of the Woman's Christian Temperance Union, was fifty-three when she decided to learn to ride a bike. She bought a bicycle and named it Gladys. She set herself the task of learning Gladys's every bolt, spoke, and bearing. And every day she practiced riding for fifteen minutes. At first, Frances said, Gladys seemed "the embodiment of misfortune and dread." But she finally decided that "all failure was from a wobbling will rather than a wobbling wheel." She learned to ride, and she found the machine most "remarkable, ingenious, and inspiring. . . ."

Flickering Flicks

On April 24, 1896, the *New York Times* carried the story of the first public screening of a movie. "An unusually bright light fell upon the screen. Then came into view two precious persons of the variety stage, in pink and blue dresses, doing the umbrella dance. . . . Their motions were all clearly defined."

For a time anything on film excited audiences. Film companies such as Biograph, Vitagraph, and Kalem made about two short films a day. Each feature lasted ten minutes. The films all looked like scenes from a play. All the action was filmed from the same distance. Each scene started with the entrance of the actors and ended with their exit.

Director David Griffith was the first to use films to tell stories. He also used the movie camera in new ways. He moved the camera from place to place and mixed shots from far away with shots from close up. Griffith was also the first to make long films. In 1911 he made a two-reel film of about twenty minutes. In 1913 he made a four-reel film. In 1914 he made a two-hour movie, which is the standard length for films to this day.

The Ragtime Era

During the late 1800s a black composer named Scott Joplin changed the form and spirit of music in the United States. Joplin was born in 1868 in Texas. As a child, he learned to play the guitar, the bugle, and the piano. At fourteen he began playing the piano in dance halls and at sixteen, writing music. "The Maple-Leaf Rag" was his first big hit. With money from the sales of sheet music Joplin settled down in Missouri to write more songs.

In the 1970s Americans rediscovered Scott Joplin and ragtime. The 1902 rag "The Entertainer" became a hit all over again when it was used in a popular movie *The Sting*.

589

Focus on Unit 5

Lifestyles: Understanding Social History

To answer the following questions, review the lifestyles section from page 576 to page 589.

1. **Families and Homes.** The lives of families in the United States at the turn of the century differed widely depending upon the family's wealth and education, and the occupations of the family members. Reread Mary Antin's description of her first day in the United States on pages 578 and 579 and Charlotte Perkins Gilman's description of the professional family's ideal apartment house on page 581. What do you think Mary Antin would have thought of such an apartment?

2. **Values and Learning.** Booker T. Washington and W.E.B. DuBois disagreed on the method to achieve progress for black Americans in the early 1900s. Compare their positions as presented on page 583.

3. **Work and Play.** Immigrant workers often found themselves working long hours for very little money. Reread Anton Kmet and Sadie Froune's accounts of their work experiences on pages 586 and 587. How do they view their jobs? Do you think they were treated fairly?

Making Connections

Use the Unit 5 time line below to answer the following questions.

1. Which of the following events took place first: the Pullman strike, the founding of the Knights of Labor, or the United Mine Workers strike?

2. When was the Spanish-American War?

3. Reread the Unit Introduction on page 479 and give examples from the time line that show how political, economic, and social changes affected the United States.

4. **Drawing Conclusions.** Why were four Amendments to the Constitution adopted in a span of only four years?

Critical Thinking Skills

1. **Predicting Consequences.** If the United States had not become a great industrial nation, what major events discussed in this unit might not have occurred?

2. **Expressing Problems Clearly.** What problems arose because of the rapid growth of cities?

3. **Identifying Central Issues.** How did the Progressive movement promote democratic goals? What groups did not share the benefits of Progressive reforms?

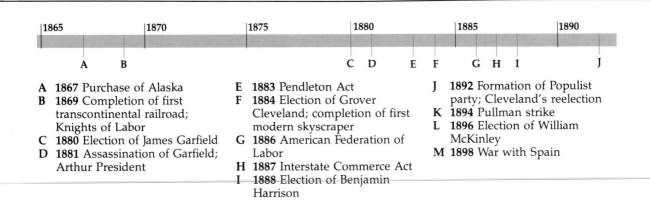

|1865 |1870 |1875 |1880 |1885 |1890 |
A   B   C   D   E   F   G   H I   J

A 1867 Purchase of Alaska
B 1869 Completion of first transcontinental railroad; Knights of Labor
C 1880 Election of James Garfield
D 1881 Assassination of Garfield; Arthur President
E 1883 Pendleton Act
F 1884 Election of Grover Cleveland; completion of first modern skyscraper
G 1886 American Federation of Labor
H 1887 Interstate Commerce Act
I 1888 Election of Benjamin Harrison
J 1892 Formation of Populist party; Cleveland's reelection
K 1894 Pullman strike
L 1896 Election of William McKinley
M 1898 War with Spain

4. **Formulating Questions.** What questions did the new role of the United States as a world power raise about American values and responsibilities?

Using Geography Skills

Refer to the map below to answer the following questions.

1. **Understanding Human Movement.** What industry does this map represent?
2. **Understanding Human and Environmental Interaction.** What city is at the hub, or center, of this map? What geographical reasons do you see that helped make this city the hub?
3. **Developing Locational Skills.** What cities shown on the map are located southwest of Indianapolis? What city shown on the map is located the furthest east of Chicago? The furthest west?

4. **Understanding World Regions.** If you were planning a map showing the major forms of transportation in the Midwest today, what transportation methods would you include? In what ways would your map differ from the map on this page?

Linking Past to Present

Determining Relevance. What reforms have strong support in the United States today? Which of today's reform movements have similarities to or actual roots in movements of the Progressive era?

Reviewing Social Studies Skills

1. **Historical Analysis.** What are the three major strands in the study of history presented on page 487? In a short essay, summarize the major events that took place in each of these areas in the United States between 1870 and 1914.
2. **Historical Synthesis.** Write a paragraph about the United States declaration of war on Spain in 1898. What events led to this action? In your paragraph, decide whether the United States had sound reasons for going to war. Use evidence from the text to support your stand.

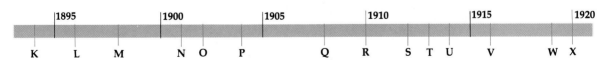

N 1901 Assassination of McKinley; T. Roosevelt President	**Q 1908** Election of William Taft	**T 1913** Sixteenth Amendment; Seventeenth Amendment
O 1902 United Mine Workers strike; Newlands Act	**R 1910** National Association for the Advancement of Colored People (NAACP)	**U 1914** Clayton Antitrust Act
P 1904 T. Roosevelt's reelection; 1904–1914 U.S. construction of Panama Canal	**S 1912** Progressive party; election of Woodrow Wilson	**V 1916** Wilson's reelection
		W 1919 Eighteenth Amendment
		X 1920 Nineteenth Amendment

GIVE HIM THE RIGHT
TO BARE ARMS!

HIRE THE

EMERGING AS A WORLD LEADER

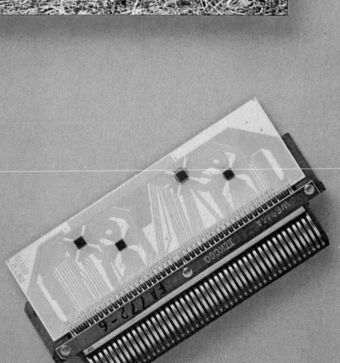

The empire building of the late 1800s led to fierce rivalries in Europe. A world war broke out in 1914. The United States was drawn into the war in 1917. Many people hoped that this would be "the war to end all wars." But the peace terms were disappointing.

The postwar prosperity came to a sudden halt in 1929. Millions were jobless during the depression. President Franklin Roosevelt's New Deal helped the nation recover.

The worldwide economic problems gave rise, however, to dictatorships in Europe and Asia. Again fighting broke out. The United States joined the war in 1941 and defeated its enemies. The two mightiest powers at the end of the war were the United States and the Soviet Union.

The United States became involved in two fierce fights in the 1950s and 1960s. But gains in civil rights were made at home.

As you read about modern times, try also to keep informed of current events. By following the news, you can link past and present and make informed choices about the future.

Unit 6

Understanding
Tomorrow's
History

Chapter 31

O N MAY 17, 1954, EVENING NEWSPAPERS around the country carried the story of the Supreme Court ruling on *Brown* v. *Board of Education of Topeka*. Americans reading the story wondered what would happen next. Those Americans were reading history in the making.

Tonight when you go home you may switch on the television. You may see and hear reports on the evening news about the President and Congress, or about peace talks, or about the rising price of oil. You will be learning about history in the making—tomorrow's history. Students in years to come will read about some of today's events in their history textbooks.

But which events will they read about? Which ones will have become the most important? And how can these events be seen as part of the flow of events that make up the nation's history? The skills you have learned in earlier chapters will help you answer these questions. And understanding the media that carry today's news will help you keep up to date about the present.

Before the days of television, press conferences were recorded on film to be shown in the newsreels at local movie houses.

1 Understanding the News Media

The news media include newspapers, newsmagazines, and radio and television news broadcasts. Many people do many different kinds of jobs in gathering and presenting the news. One important job is that of reporter—the person who finds out the news.

Gathering the News

Reporters get their stories in different ways. Sometimes they receive a printed handout which they must interpret. For example, reporters who write about the Supreme Court are given written copies of the Court's decisions. Other agencies or departments at all levels of governments often pass along written news reports. These are called press releases.

Often an official will also allow reporters to ask questions about a press release. A formal question-and-answer meeting is called a press conference. Presidential press conferences often appear on national television. Sometimes a President will begin with a short speech on a certain subject. Then reporters ask questions that dig deeper into that story.

Groups other than those in government also put out press releases and hold press conferences. An automobile maker, for example, might call in the press to tell about a new car model. Labor leaders might explain to reporters the union's reasons for striking against a factory owner. Scientists might hold a press conference to let the public know about a breakthrough in medicine that protects people against sickness.

People who use press releases to give news to the public are trying to control what the public will learn. Sometimes they do not tell the whole story. Reporters at a press conference will usually try to get more information than the official wants to give. Sometimes reporters learn more, sometimes not.

Some news items may concern facts that certain people may not want known. In such cases the reporter goes after a story in the same way that a police officer investigates a crime. Sometimes, in fact, what the reporter is looking into is a crime.

One of the biggest news stories of the 1970s was the Watergate scandal in Washington, D.C. It began in 1972 as the story of a burglary attempt. Five men were caught after breaking into a room in a Watergate office building. Two more men were later found to have taken part in the break-in. The room they broke into belonged to the Democratic National Committee.

The story of the break-in made headlines in all the media—television, radio, newspapers, and newsmagazines. But, as other big stories that seemed more important came in, the break-in at Watergate began to drift out of the headlines. It might have been forgotten altogether because the media were full of 1972 election year news.

The country's greatest and most recent political scandal began at Watergate, a group of apartment and office buildings in Washington, D.C.

Faced with possible impeachment, President Richard Nixon resigned from office on August 9, 1974 (top). John Dean (above) was chief witness in the hearings that uncovered the scandal.

Yet news reporters did not let the story die. They kept working on it. As good reporters, they began asking around, following leads from one person to another, getting more and more information. As you will read in Chapter 35, the story of the Watergate break-in and attempts to cover it up became more and more knotted. Watergate became one of the most important political stories in United States history. It led to the resignation of a President—the first in United States history.

Another story that drew everyone's attention developed much differently. On May 17, 1954, reporters covering the Supreme Court gathered for their usual Monday briefing. They were surprised to receive a decision in a case that had been in the Court for a long time. That decision—in a case called *Brown* v. *Board of Education of Topeka*—reversed the earlier Supreme Court decision on *Plessy* v. *Ferguson* and ruled that separate schools for blacks and whites were unconstitutional. The reporters had their big story for the day. But the story was by no means over with the announcement of the Court's decision.

What would the *Brown* v. *Board of Education* decision mean for the future? School segregation was the rule throughout the South and in much of the North as well. How soon would it end? What would school officers do? How did Americans—black and white—feel about the idea? How did other minority groups feel? What would politicians who were against integration do? In one sense the evening news reports on *Brown* v. *Board of Education* marked the end to the story of a court case. But they also marked the beginning of the even bigger story of bringing school segregation to an end. That story is still not finished. Now, decades later, you can still find stories about school desegregation in newspapers and newsmagazines, and on news broadcasts.

Most reporters in the Supreme Court press room that important day in 1954 had been there before and would be there again. The Supreme Court was their "beat"—a place they regularly came for news. Beat reporters cover stories on their assigned rounds every day. Some are assigned to places like the White House or Congress, where news is always breaking. Others may cover local news at a city hall. Still others may cover crime and spend a lot of time at police stations. Reporters often get to know their own fields very well. They come to know many people who are likely to play a part in news events. They develop "contacts"—people who are willing to help them get information.

Some reporters become specialists in certain areas of foreign news. Newspapers cannot send people flying all over the world every time something happens overseas. They want people on the spot at all times. So they station foreign correspondents in news centers all over the globe. American reporters and broadcast journalists live and work in London, in Moscow, in Cairo, in Tokyo—in almost every important place on earth. They come to know the people, the politics, and the facts about the place they cover. They send their stories back to the United States regularly. If you watch a television news program often enough, you will come to recognize some of the foreign correspondents. They appear every time there is a big story in their part of the world. If you read a newspaper every day, you will get to know the names of foreign correspondents who sign their stories.

Few newspapers, however, can afford to send reporters to every place news happens. Instead, they use wire services such as the Associated Press (AP) and United Press International (UPI). These services have more reporters in more countries than any one newspaper has. Wire services sell their stories to newspapers, magazines, or radio and television news departments. The initials AP or UPI at the beginning of stories in your local newspaper tell you that the story is from a wire service. Wire services also provide photos. You can see a few examples of these in *American Spirit*.

There is yet another way in which reporters gather news. They look into files, papers, and records in much the same way a historian

```
       a042
          d w czcuivbyl a0469
     PM-Washington Briefs,530
     WASHINGTON  AP  - The Reagan administration has been given an extra
     5 days to decide whether it will scrap the basic federal job test as
     art of the settlement of a job discrimination suit.
       U.S. District Judge Joyce Hens Green on Monday granted the Reagan
     administration's request for more time to decide whether to accept,
     withdraw or seek to modify a proposed consent decree filed days before
     the Carter administration left office.
       In the consent decree, proposed to settle a 1979 class action
     discrimination suit by blacks and Hispanics, the Carter administration
     agreed to phase out the Professional and Administrative Career
     Examination over the next three years.
     ap-ny-02-10 0526EST
```

Customers of the Associated Press and other news services receive reports daily from national and foreign correspondents.

digs out the facts about the past. Most newspapers have huge files of information that reporters can use to learn more on any subject. If, for example, a public figure becomes involved in a story, reporters can go to the files and find copies of past stories about that person. Facts from the past may shed light on the current story. Reporters may spend hours, even days, searching through old records for information. Papers important to a current story may be gathering dust in an old file cabinet somewhere. Reporters, like historians, must be good at shaking off the dust.

Practicing Your Skills

1. The top news stories of the day will start on the first page of a newspaper. Other big stories will appear in the first few pages. Get an edition of your local newspaper and pick out six stories highlighted for the day. Choose two stories in each of the following categories: foreign news, national news (news involving the whole country or the national government), and local news (news about your own town or city). Write out the headline of each story and then write a sentence or two of your own explaining the story. If any story is from Associated Press or United Press International, include that information.

Critical Thinking

2. **Demonstrating Reasoned Judgment.** Choose one story from each of the three kinds in Exercise 1. Tell how you think the reporter got the information for the story. Watch for clues such as "The mayor said" or "Records revealed that." List all the sources each reporter used. Later exercises will ask you to use all these stories again, so keep them in a folder.

As early as 1935, the Associated Press was offering telephoto service to the print media. Photos, such as this one taken after the attack on Pearl Harbor in 1941, could be sent great distances by wire.

Presenting the News

On a fateful day in the nation's history, newspapers around the country carried a story much like the following:

> Honolulu, Hawaii (December 7, 1941)—Early this morning the Japanese made a surprise attack on United States military installations in Hawaii. Japanese planes, taking off from aircraft carriers, destroyed most of the United States fleet at Pearl Harbor. They also destroyed planes of the United States Air Force on the ground at Hickam Field. The United States is certain to go to war against Japan and its allies.

Like all good news stories, whether on television or radio, or in newspapers or newsmagazines, this story tells the *who, what, where, why, when,* and *how* of the event—the six basic facts.

Who?	The Japanese
What?	Attacked Pearl Harbor
Where?	In Honolulu, Hawaii
Why?	To destroy the United States naval fleet
When?	December 7, 1941 (the date always appears on page 1 of a newspaper or on the cover of a newsmagazine.)
How?	By sending armed airplanes from nearby aircraft carriers

601

At the time of the Pearl Harbor attack most Americans got their news from newspapers and radio. Recent studies show that today about two thirds of all Americans get their news mainly from television. All the news media present the six main facts of a story. But they differ in how much they tell about the story and in the impact of their report.

Each of the four media has advantages and disadvantages. Radio and television can get the news out faster than printed media. In fact, you can often see news as it happens on television or hear it as it happens on radio. Newspapers and newsmagazines, on the other hand, can tell more about a news event. Radio and television are limited by time. Most television news broadcasts, for example, run for a half hour. Part of that half hour is taken up by commercials. Sports and weather take up more time. There may be only twenty minutes or less left for all other news.

Despite the time limits, television stories can have a great impact on the viewer. In Chapter 7 you learned how to understand pictures. You learned that pictures get across ideas and feelings. Many times seeing the faces or hearing the voices of people in the news leaves a deeper impression than reading about newsmakers. Think how thrilled people around the world must have felt when they actually saw, by means of satellite television, the first human being walk on the moon.

On the other hand, newspapers and magazines can print longer and more informative stories. In the case of the moon walk, print media presented more information than television about the wonderful technology that took men to the moon and brought them safely home. Some print stories are so long that they might take a half hour—the full length of a television newscast—to read out loud. Of course, you can read more news to yourself in less time.

Time is important in all the media. Television can cover a news event at the moment it happens. But if all events were covered instantly, people would be upset by repeated interruptions to their favorite shows. Newscasts generally appear at regular times, usually around noon, in the early evening, and late at night. Thus, much of the news you see on television was tape-recorded earlier. Still, when a big story breaks, television can interrupt its regular program and present an on-the-spot report.

Newspapers, unlike electronic media, always have some time lag, no matter how short. A story can never be printed in a newspaper as fast as it can be aired on radio or television. It takes time to write a story, set it in type, make up pages, print the newspaper, and distribute it to newsstands.

The time lag is even longer for newsmagazines. The three leading newsmagazines are *Time, Newsweek,* and *U.S. News & World*

Report. All three are printed once a week and take about a day to distribute. Anything you read in a newsmagazine is at least a day old and may be as much as a week old.

The print media can turn the time-lag disadvantage into an advantage. Newspaper writers can take more time to check into a story. They can present far more facts than a television news reporter can. A weekly newsmagazine can go even further. Few news stories begin and end in a single day. Hearing them on radio, seeing them on television, or reading them in a daily newspaper is like following a continued story from day to day. A newsmagazine can present more of the story—maybe even all of it—in a single issue. Sometimes it is easier to judge how important a story is from a report in a weekly newsmagazine.

Since television came into use, radio has become far less important as a source of news. A few radio stations present mainly news. But most radio stations today offer little more than short news reports several times a day. They do not have the money to hire their own reporters, so they depend on the wire services for news. Often these reports are little more than headlines, read quickly, one after the other, in about five minutes.

As the world watched, television cameras recorded astronaut Edwin Aldrin's walk on the moon.

Television and radio are best for on-the-spot news coverage. Newspapers lead in covering day-to-day news events fully. And newsmagazines present well-written summaries of a whole week's happenings. A person who wants to keep up with today's events will make use of all the news media. All can help you judge how important today's events may be for tomorrow's history.

Practicing Your Skills

1. Write out answers to the following questions.
   a. Watch an evening news program on television. Pick out one major event and take notes on what you have learned about it from television. Tell what pictures were shown. How did these pictures help you understand the news event? How did they make you feel about the story?
   b. Check that same story in a newspaper that evening or the next morning. What more, if anything, did you learn from the television newscast?
   c. Finally, check the story again in a newsmagazine the following week. If this report differs from the television report or the newspaper report, describe the differences.

Critical Thinking

2. **Identifying Central Issues.** Watch a TV newscast reporting local news and then watch one reporting national news. List the stories covered by each. Choose the one event from each broadcast that seems most important for the future. Explain why you think it is important.

2 Piecing Together Tomorrow's History

History, you will remember, is a record of change over time affecting people at a certain place. The changes that will become tomorrow's history are taking place today. Sometimes it is hard to know how today's news will be treated in tomorrow's history books. Time is needed to sort things out. Time is also needed to finish news stories that are ongoing. Still, you can make judgments about how important today's events are for tomorrow's history. Some of these judgments will prove to be better than others. Those that are based on a knowledge of the past and the present will probably come closest to the truth.

Using the News Media as Sources

News reports from electronic media—TV and radio—may be kept in a bank of tape recordings. Newspapers and magazines may be kept

on film. The pages are photographed, and the photographs are reduced to a tiny size. The small pictures are then stored on cards or rolls. The rolls are like a filmstrip. The picture may be enlarged on a machine so it can be read easily.

However it is kept, each news source must be carefully evaluated. The news story may not be accurate. Shown on these pages is a newspaper headline with a famous error. President Harry S. Truman, having just been reelected to office in 1948, is holding up a newspaper that says he lost the election. The newspaper printed its account before all the votes were counted. Thomas E. Dewey, Truman's opponent, seemed to be a sure winner. Election returns, coming in after the newspaper was printed, showed Truman had won.

A front-page mistake does not happen often. When it does, it is quickly corrected in the next edition of the newspaper. But the Truman headline does show that mistakes—even big mistakes—can be made in news media.

Newspapers are put out in a hurry. There is not always time to check every fact before going to press. And ideas that seem true today may turn out to be false tomorrow.

Care must also be taken in judging other news media. People make mistakes. You need not doubt everything presented in news media. Most of it will be true to fact. But there might be a mistake. And remember that there may be more to a story than appears in a single issue of a newspaper or newsmagazine, or on a single radio or television broadcast.

Another reason historians must be careful with news media is that sometimes an unexpected and spectacular event will get more play than an event that is of greater importance in the long run. The front page of the *New York Times* June 16, 1919, illustrates this case. Part of the major headline for the day read "ALCOCK AND BROWN FLY ACROSS ATLANTIC." The dramatic story described how two British fliers, John Alcock and Arthur W. Brown, had just become the first pilots to fly nonstop across the Atlantic Ocean. Much of the front page was taken up with this story.

Two other stories were given far less attention and space in the *Times* that day, though the stories turned out to be more important than that of Alcock and Brown. One story told of United States troops crossing the border into Mexico. Pancho Villa, a Mexican revolutionary leader who had turned outlaw, had been attacking towns in the United States and then riding back into Mexico. President Woodrow Wilson finally ordered American soldiers to go after Pancho Villa and his band in Mexico. Sending troops into another country is a serious act, in many ways an act of war. This action caused bad feelings between the two countries for years to come.

The other story in that June 16 issue of the *New York Times* told about Germany's objections to the peace talks being held in Europe. These were the talks about ending the First World War. The fighting had stopped the year before. The defeated Germans had no say in the treaties of 1919. They were just forced to accept the terms. Their ill will stirred up further problems in Europe for decades. The treaties became a major cause in bringing on World War II some twenty years later. This story was certainly far more important to readers of history than the one about Alcock and Brown.

To piece together tomorrow's history, you must use all the skills you have learned. You must understand the time and place of an event. You must make sense out of pictures, maps, and charts—including those shown on television—to gather the facts and recognize opinions. You must judge how true and fair the sources are. You must understand what led up to today's events and decide how important these events will be for the future. And you must separate political, social, and economic strands, and then weave them together to see the interplay of cause and effect in past history and today's events. Even after you have taken all these steps, you must finally wait for the passage of time to judge which events will be most important.

Practicing Your Skills

1. Return to the six stories you picked for Exercise 1 on page 600. Decide which of those stories is most likely to be of interest to tomorrow's historian. Write a paragraph explaining why you think so. Write another paragraph explaining why another of your six stories is least likely to have historical importance.

2. **Checking Consistency.** Save the stories and your answers to Exercise 1. Look at them again when you finish Unit 6. See if you would change your answers in any way.

Linking Past, Present, and Future

People like to predict the future. You look out your window on a cloudy day and decide that it probably will not rain later, because the wind is not coming from a direction that usually brings rain. So you leave home without an umbrella. If your predictions are right, you are pleased with yourself. If they are wrong, you get soaked.

The theories of Albert Einstein (above) have made it possible to harness nuclear power at plants such as the Trojan on the Columbia River in Oregon (top).

People try to predict the future by seeing trends in present happenings and past events. Knowing the past and present will not help the historian—or you—predict the future. But it may help you understand why events are happening when they happen.

One thing is sure. The future will bring changes. Some changes will come as complete surprises. But not all of them need surprise you, if you use what you know about the past and the present.

Energy is an issue that is constantly in the news today. The price of gasoline keeps rising because the oil from which gasoline is made is costly. Problems in the Middle East threaten to cut off the world's chief supply of oil. New ways of making energy come to light. An accident at sea spills oil into the ocean and pollutes a nation's coast. Some people speak against and others for building nuclear power plants. All these news stories are about energy.

Energy did not become an issue overnight. It has its roots in the past. The idea of using nuclear power, for example, can be traced back to the early part of this century. At that time Albert Einstein proved that atomic energy could produce huge amounts of power. The fear of nuclear power can be traced back to 1945 when the first atomic bombs were dropped on Japan, destroying two cities.

In the search for clean, renewable sources of energy some car makers have turned to electricity.

Oil is perhaps the subject of most energy stories today. The United States uses far more oil than it produces. Oil lubricates machine parts. It heats homes and runs electrical power plants. It is used to make many fabrics and most plastics. As gasoline, it powers automobiles. As with atomic power, the need for oil today has its roots in the past.

When inventors began working on cars, they tried a number of different kinds of engines. In the early days there were electric cars and steam-powered cars. But the engine that finally worked the best was the internal combustion engine—a motor that runs on gasoline. At that time gasoline was plentiful and cheap. Henry Ford turned out cars by the thousands. But no one guessed that there would be nearly 100 million cars on United States highways by 1980. Thus, decisions and events in the past are directly tied to one of today's most important issues—the need for oil as fuel.

In a like manner today's energy answers will affect the future. Scientists are working on many new forms of energy. One is solar power, which taps energy given off by the sun. Another new idea is really an old idea put to work again—wind power harnessed by huge windmills. Energy can also be drawn from the hot waters that lie beneath the earth. Some people believe energy can even be drawn from the tides, the daily in-and-out flow of large bodies of water.

People have also searched for fuels other than gasoline to run motors. Gasohol—gasoline and alcohol mixed—will make our oil go farther. It is already being produced and used on a small scale. People are also working on fuels made from plants and from wastes such as garbage. Car makers are already building cars that run more miles on each gallon of gas. Perhaps all of these ideas, and some we have not yet heard of, will solve the energy problem of the future.

The solution to the energy problem may be a painful one, or it may lead to new, unforeseen problems. Henry Ford's use of the assembly line was one promising solution to a production problem. But it has led in part to today's energy problem. There are no easy ways out of serious problems, but knowledge of the past may help us to find better answers for the future.

As you read the history of more recent times in the chapters to come, watch for the roots of the problems that you hear and read about in the daily news today. Knowledge of the past and the present will help you understand the direction of tomorrow's history. It may also guide your decisions—the choices you make that will shape tomorrow's history for you.

The energy needed to bake cookies in this solar oven is free—even if it is not always available.

Practicing Your Skills

Critical Thinking

Testing Conclusions. Below are sayings from famous people about the past, present, and future.

> "I know of no way of judging the future but by the past."— PATRICK HENRY
>
> "While we read history we make history."—G.W. CURTIS
>
> "Those who cannot remember the past are condemned to repeat it."—GEORGE SANTAYANA
>
> "The Present is the living sum-total of the whole Past."— THOMAS CARLYLE
>
> "The future is only the past again, entered through another gate."—SIR ARTHRUR WING PINERO

Choose one of these sayings as a theme for a five-paragraph essay. You may agree or disagree with the saying. In the first paragraph— the introduction—state your position. In the second, third, and fourth paragraphs—the body—provide examples that support your position. In the fifth paragraph—the conclusion—drive home the truth of your position and suggest ways that the study of history can be useful.

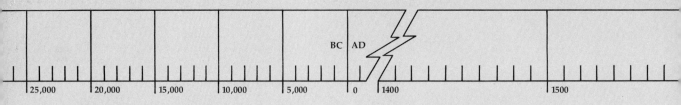

OVER THE TOP
FOR YOU

Buy U.S. Gov't Bonds
THIRD LIBERTY LOAN

World War I
and After

❧ **Chapter 32**

Vocabulary

alliance
nationalism
rivalry
neutrality
ration
draft
convoy
armistice
league
negotiate
idealism
prosperity
communism
installment
suffrage

B ETWEEN 1815 AND 1900 the United States paid far more attention to domestic affairs than to foreign affairs. After 1900, however, the United States held land in many parts of the world. Events abroad began to affect the United States directly, and foreign affairs demanded more and more attention.

In 1914 a major war broke out in Europe. Its influence spread to other continents. The conflict later became known as the First World War. For three years the United States refused to enter the contest. But gradually the country was drawn into the war. After the war the United States tried to pull out of world affairs. It soon found that it could not.

1   The War in Europe

You have read that the late nineteenth century was an age of imperialism. As European countries tried to add foreign lands to their empires, they fought among themselves. Power among nations began to shift. The older Ottoman and Russian empires began to decline. Newer empires, especially those of Germany and Italy, were on the rise. Some European nations banded together for protection,

Prereading

1. How did rivalries among European empires and the formation of alliances lead to World War I?

2. What series of events caused the United States to give up its neutrality and enter the First World War?

3. How did United States efforts on the home front, the fighting front, and the diplomatic front influence the outcome of the war and the peace that was made?

4. Describe the twenties in terms of its reforms, fears, heroes, and Presidents.

611

forming alliances that divided Europe into two main power groups. To add to these tensions, powerful feelings of nationalism began to sweep Europe. Nationalism is a belief that people with such common ties as language and customs should have their own nation.

Few people in the United States believed that these differences would lead to war. But war did break out, and the world witnessed bloodshed on a scale never before known.

Rivalries over Empires

European countries began dividing up foreign lands and building empires as early as the 1400s. At that time Spain, Portugal, England, France, and Holland founded colonies throughout the world. Long before 1900, however, many of these colonies, among them Mexico and the United States, had won their independence.

In the late 1800s the countries of Europe began a new round of empire building and rivalry. Some countries that had been left out of the first round—such as Germany—now began adding to their empires, especially overseas. Austria-Hungary, Turkey, and Russia built up giant empires by taking over neighboring lands.

Though imperialism touched nearly every part of the earth, most of the fighting was over rival claims in Africa and Asia. Britain fought with France over the Nile Valley in Africa and over Siam (Thailand) in Southeast Asia. Britain also clashed with Germany over East and West Africa and with Holland over South Africa. Britain and Russia disagreed about Persia (Iran) and Afghanistan in the Middle East. Germany disputed French and Belgian claims in Morocco and the Congo.

Colonies were important to European countries for many reasons. Europeans valued colonies for the raw materials they could provide. And workers in the colonies could be hired for little pay. Europeans put their colonists to work in the mines and fields, and in factories that the Europeans built. Europeans also saw the colonies as much-needed markets for goods made in the homeland. European missionaries looked to the colonies for possible converts. Business leaders saw the colonies as places to make good investments. And political leaders saw in them a chance to gain more power—and to outpace other European countries in empire building.

Rivalries and Alliances in Europe

Within Europe the countries fought among themselves. The Turkish Ottoman Empire had held parts of southeastern Europe and the Middle East for over 400 years. By the end of the 1800s it had become too weak to control its territory. Austria-Hungary, in the center of Europe, was also weakened by conflicts within. Other nations

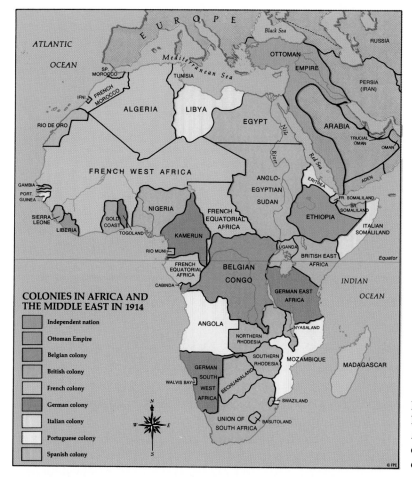

COLONIES IN AFRICA AND THE MIDDLE EAST IN 1914

- Independent nation
- Ottoman Empire
- Belgian colony
- British colony
- French colony
- German colony
- Italian colony
- Portuguese colony
- Spanish colony

Britain, France, Germany, and the Netherlands vied for land in Africa, while the Ottomans held on to what little was left of their once-great empire.

eyed the weaker countries of the Ottoman and Austro-Hungarian empires with a view to taking them over.

Germany, an empire that was rapidly growing stronger, had only become a nation in 1871. But by 1913 Germany was one of the world's leading industrial powers, producing more goods than either Britain or France. The older powers of Britain and Russia began to fear Germany. Britain feared that Germany might move into the Middle East and take over the Suez Canal. The canal was important to Britain's trade with its colonies in other parts of the world. Russia feared that Germany might take over Austria, which lay along Russia's western border. Austria, however, was afraid that Russia might take some of its land.

Germany, for its part, began to feel hemmed in by enemies—Russia to the east and France to the west. It also feared the British navy—the largest in the world. Though already protected by a mighty army, Germany began to build up its navy. This buildup further alarmed Germany's neighbors. To protect themselves, all the

EUROPE BEFORE WORLD WAR I

Triple Alliance   Triple Entente

© FPC

Even before the war, the Central Powers held a wide strip of land running straight through Europe.

major nations in Europe except Britain had formed standing armies numbering in the millions by 1913.

Besides building up their own armies, nations in Europe began looking for allies among the nations that were friendly to them. As early as 1879, Germany and Austria-Hungary had formed an alliance. In 1882, Italy joined them, forming the Triple Alliance, often called the Central Powers. The three countries promised to support each other if one of them was attacked by another country. By 1907, France, Russia, and Britain had also formed an alliance called the Triple Entente (än·tänt′). The two alliances were formed in part to prevent war. But, instead, they created a setting in which small differences could grow into major crises involving all the great powers in Europe.

At the same time that they were banding together, the nations were becoming ever prouder of their own heritage and people. Fired with nationalist spirit, each nation built up its own armies and wealth, the better to defend its independence. A series of crises in southeastern Europe, sparked by strong nationalist feeling, was to bring the whole world to war.

The Opening Guns

As early as 1890, the citizens of Serbia—today part of Yugoslavia— wanted to free the territory of Bosnia from Austria-Hungary because

The assassination of Archduke Ferdinand (left), heir to the throne of Austria-Hungary, brought on World War I.

many Serbs lived there. Members of a Serbian nationalist group called Union or Death swore to bring Serbia and Bosnia together into a larger nation or to die trying. A member of this terrorist group shot and killed Archduke Francis Ferdinand of Austria-Hungary on June 28, 1914. Ferdinand, heir to the throne of Austria-Hungary, was visiting the capital of Bosnia when he was shot.

To punish Serbia, Austria-Hungary demanded that its officers be allowed to search Serbia for members of Union or Death. When Serbia refused, Austria-Hungary declared war on Serbia on July 28, 1914. Germany, hoping to take over some lands in southeastern Europe, backed Austria-Hungary. When Russia threw its support to Serbia, Germany declared war on Russia and then on France, Russia's ally. Britain entered the war shortly afterward on the side of its ally France.

By the time fighting actually broke out almost all of Europe was divided into two camps. Germany, Austria-Hungary, the Ottoman Empire, and Bulgaria formed the Central Powers. Each nation in the group had declared war on Great Britain, France, Serbia, Russia, and Italy—a group that became known as the Allies. All Europe burst into flames.

Germany made the first move. In August 1914 seventy-eight German infantry divisions marched against France. To get there, they invaded the neutral country of Belgium. The invasion angered most neutral nations, including the United States. The Germans were stopped short of Paris, however, partly because they had sent many troops to fight the Russians on Germany's eastern border.

From their observation post French gunners in World War I looked out over no man's land between the trenches.

Section 1 Review

1. What part did nationalism play in bringing on war in Europe?
2. Give three reasons why European nations competed with one another for overseas colonies.
3. Why did Britain fear Germany and its rise to power?
4. Why did Germany fear Great Britain?

Critical Thinking

5. **Recognizing Cause and Effect.** Why did Austria-Hungary declare war on Serbia? For what reasons did Germany, Great Britain, Russia, and France enter the war?

LOOKING AHEAD: What series of events caused the United States to give up its neutrality and enter the First World War?

The war zone between France and Germany became known as the western front, in contrast to the eastern front that lay between Germany and Russia. Some of the most savage fighting and the heaviest loss of life in the history of the world took place on the western front. Each side dug trenches all the way from the borders of neutral Switzerland to the North Sea and fenced in the trenches with barbed wire. Huge guns fired across the battle line ceaselessly. Hundreds of thousands of soldiers were killed defending their positions. In one battle in 1916 the British lost 60,000 men in a single day. After an entire week they had moved forward only one mile. In one four-month period the Germans lost 500,000 men, the British 400,000, and the French 200,000.

Each year the two sides planned attacks that they believed would end the war on the western front. The two sides, however, were so evenly matched that after three years of fighting neither side had gained much ground.

Russia and Germany faced off in heavy fighting along Germany's eastern border for several years. Russian losses were high. Then revolution broke out in Russia in 1917. The ruling czar was overthrown, and the Communists came to power. Germany and the Soviet Union, as Russia was called after the revolution, signed a treaty in March 1918. With the Soviet Union out of the war Germany could now plan an all-out attack on the western front.

2 The United States and the War

For many people in the United States the outbreak of the war in Europe had come as a surprise. One southerner said, "This dreadful conflict of the nations came to most of us as lightning out of a clear sky." Other citizens had family and business ties in Europe. They found themselves taking sides.

Many people in the United States favored the Allies because they were so angered by Germany's attack on neutral Belgium. Stories were told about how cruelly the German army had treated the Belgian people. Later many of these stories were found to be false. But as one magazine stated, "For us the great, clear issue of this war is Belgium."

United States Neutrality

Though many citizens favored the Allies, President Wilson stood for complete neutrality from 1914 until 1917. United States neutrality was greatly tested when its shipping vessels came under attack, by Great Britain as well as Germany.

As part of their war plan, the Allies wanted to stop all goods from entering Germany. The British navy, the most powerful in the world, helped in this plan. British ships stopped all vessels, including those of the United States, from entering German ports. The British searched these vessels for "warlike goods." To the British, even food was considered warlike. The United States protested, believing that the Allies were taking away its right to trade.

These protests did not change the British plan. British officers continued to seize property—but never took the lives of United States citizens. Despite the loss of property the United States remained neutral.

Keeping goods away from the enemy was also part of Germany's war plan. Though Germany had the world's most powerful army, its navy could not match that of Britain. Germany did, however, have a large submarine fleet, with which it intended to sink all ships headed for enemy ports. Unlike the powerful surface vessels of the British that could overtake other ships, submarines could only sink surface-going vessels. When Germany decided to begin attacking ships without warning and endangering people's lives, the United States was drawn closer and closer to war.

Steps Toward War

On May 7, 1915, the British passenger liner *Lusitania* was sunk without warning by a German submarine. About 1,200 lives were lost, more than 120 of them citizens of the United States. Shocked United States newspaper editors and political leaders called the sinking "a crime." Many people believed it was time for war.

But President Wilson firmly defended neutrality. He demanded that Germany stop its attacks on unarmed ships. Germany finally agreed to stop sinking passenger ships without warning. No further attacks took place for a year. Then in March 1916 the French

Election of 1916

Democrats
Woodrow Wilson
52% of electoral vote

Republicans
Charles E. Hughes
48% of electoral vote

passenger ship *Sussex* was torpedoed by a German submarine. Several United States citizens were injured. Wilson warned that if Germany once again took up open submarine warfare, the United States would break all ties with Germany.

In the winter of 1916–1917 Germany planned to end the war in an all-out attack on the western front. To be certain of victory, Germany decided to renew submarine attacks on all shipping. Such a plan would cut off the flow of goods to the Allies. Germany announced its plan on January 31, 1917, knowing that announcement might bring the United States into the war. But Germany believed that the war would be over before the United States could arm itself.

Just a few weeks before, the Germans had hatched another plan that angered the United States. In January 1917, Germany sent a note to Mexico saying it would make an alliance with Mexico if the United States joined the Allies. Further, Germany promised to help Mexico win back Texas and other states from the United States. The note became public in late February. It only added to Americans' anger against Germany.

Declaration of War

When several United States vessels were sunk by German submarines in March 1917, President Wilson changed his stand and asked Congress for a declaration of war. In his message to Congress on April 2, 1917, Wilson spoke strongly against submarine warfare. He also said that the United States was fighting for democracy, for the liberty of small nations, and to "make the world itself . . . free." Congress did as Wilson asked. But some members still believed the United States "could and ought to have kept out of this war."

3 War and Peace

When the United States entered the war, it tipped the scales in favor of the Allies. The German belief that the United States could not arm itself fast enough to stop Germany's victory proved wrong.

The Home Front

President Wilson realized that the whole country had to go to war. "It is not our army that we must shape and train for the war," he said. "It is a nation." Men and women worked day and night in the factories to make enough war goods. Each person received only a small amount, or a ration, of certain foods such as sugar so that there would be more for Allied and United States soldiers. Materials used in making everyday items were used instead to make war goods.

Secretary of War Newton D. Baker called the war between the Allies and the Central Powers a "conflict of smokestacks." A War

Section 2 Review

1. What was the official stand of the United States toward the war in Europe from 1914 to 1917?
2. How was United States neutrality violated by Britain? By Germany?
3. Why did Germany's note to Mexico anger the United States?

Critical Thinking

4. **Recognizing Cause and Effect.** Why did President Wilson ask Congress to declare war against Germany in April 1917?

LOOKING AHEAD: How did United States efforts on the home front, the fighting front, and the diplomatic front influence the outcome of the war and the peace that was made?

Women machinists on the home front trimmed fuses for gun shells.

Industries Board was formed to plan production. Factories that were making cars were asked to make guns and tanks. Those making civilian clothes were asked to make uniforms. Factories making watches were asked to make gunsights. Transportation and agriculture were drawn into the war effort. Another government board decided what goods should be transported where, by what means, and in what amounts, and sold at what prices. Herbert Hoover, who was later to become President of the United States, was put in charge of food planning and rationing. To save food for the fighting forces, people at home were asked to have "wheatless Mondays" or "meatless Tuesdays."

The Fighting Front

The way the United States went about raising an army of 4 million men also was in keeping with the all-out war effort. This time the United States did not depend largely on volunteers. All males between the ages of twenty-one and thirty were called to sign up for the armed services by a Selective Service Act passed in 1917. Later the ages for the draft, as it was called, were changed to eighteen and forty-five. Almost 10 million young men answered the first draft call. Some 2 million were drafted into the army by the end of the war.

Every one of the 2 million United States soldiers sent to fight on the western front needed 50 pounds of supplies each day—food, uniforms, guns, and ammunition. The United States not only provided these but also outfitted British and French soldiers.

Shipping war goods to Europe was dangerous because of enemy submarines. To protect their ships, the United States and the Allies sailed in convoys. In a convoy, ships carrying soldiers and war goods were surrounded by battleships. By December 1917 the convoy system had kept the German submarine threat in check.

Fresh troops from the United States did much to swing the war toward victory for the Allies. The first soldiers to arrive in France were led by General John J. "Black Jack" Pershing. He and his men served as part of the French army under a French officer. But Pershing insisted that a separate United States command be put in charge of its own part of the western front. This separate United States army became caught up in the hard-fought Meuse-Argonne battle that began on September 20, 1918. The fighting went on for more than forty days and nights. More than 1 million United States soldiers, 840 airplanes, and 324 tanks took part. At times soldiers fought hand to hand. In the end the United States and the Allies won. It was the last major battle of the war.

Germany asked for peace terms. On November 11, 1918, an armistice brought the fighting to a halt so that peace terms could be worked out. Armistice Day—a name changed to Veterans Day in 1954—became a day to honor all soldiers who fought the nation's battles.

During the war 10 million persons were killed and another 20 million were wounded. Each major European country lost between 1 and 2 million persons. For these countries, a whole generation of young people was wiped out. The United States lost 116,000 soldiers in battles fought far from home.

Wilson's Fourteen Points

When Germany asked for peace, it expected the terms to be those outlined by President Wilson eleven months before. Of Wilson's fourteen points or goals, six were most important: (1) Secret agreements among countries should end. (2) Belgium, taken by Germany during the war, should be given its independence once again. (3) Poland should be formed as an independent country on the eastern border of Germany. (4) Freedom of the seas should be a right of all nations. (5) Where possible, borders in Europe should be changed to bring together people with the same cultural and language background. (6) All parties should make up a League of Nations to prevent wars.

The Allies did not agree with all of these points. Britain and France favored secret agreements. They also wanted a treaty with terms that would punish Germany. They wanted Germany to pay for Allied war debts. They called for Germany's land overseas to be divided among other nations. And they wanted to take away some of Germany's land in Europe as well. The Allies also believed that keeping Germany's armed forces small would do more to prevent war than would forming a League of Nations.

The Peace Conference

The peace talks began in Paris in January 1919. President Wilson decided to attend in person. He left for the meeting in high spirits.

Wilson had said that this war would end all wars. He believed that the world would finally work out a "lasting peace." His words had brought hope to many people.

When Wilson arrived in Europe, he was greeted as a hero. Many believed that he alone would and could end all wars. One woman wrote: "Wilson, you have given back the father to his home, the plowman to his field. . . . Wilson, you have saved our children. Through you, evil is punished. Wilson! Wilson! Glory to you. . . . Peace on Earth! . . ."

But Wilson soon learned that a lasting peace might not be possible. Missing at the peace table was defeated Germany. While Wilson had hoped Germany would be there, it soon became clear that the Allies were not willing to negotiate. They would spell out the peace terms, and Germany could take them or leave them.

Almost all parties were unhappy with the results. Germany got a forced rather than a negotiated peace. Peoples in Europe expecting lands of their own did not receive them. Other countries added to their empires by dividing up Germany's land overseas. France and Britain were not paid for their war losses. And Wilson faced a fight over the treaty at home.

The Treaty of Versailles was signed on June 28, 1919—exactly five years after the shooting of Archduke Ferdinand. President Wilson forwarded the treaty to the Senate for approval.

The Debate at Home

Exchanges in the Senate over the treaty stirred up anger on both sides. The treaty needed a two-thirds vote to pass. Senator Henry Cabot Lodge led the fight against it. He spent weeks reading every word of the treaty aloud to empty seats in a Senate hearing room just to gain time for others to line up votes against the agreement. He asked for changes that he knew Wilson would not accept. In the end the treaty failed to pass.

President Wilson did not believe that the Senate spoke for the people. So he toured the country looking for popular support. He believed that if the United States rejected the treaty and the League of Nations another war would surely come.

> You [the soldiers] have fought for something you did not get . . . and there will come . . . another struggle in which, not a few hundred thousand fine men from America will have to die, but as many as millions. . . .

During the tour Wilson's health failed. And he could not wring out enough votes for the treaty to get it past the Senate. The treaty's defeat at home was a blow from which Wilson never recovered.

Section 3 Review

1. What did the United States do on the home front that affected the outcome of the war?
2. How did the United States aid the fighting front?
3. On what day did the fighting in World War I end?
4. Name three ways that British and French ideas for peace differed from Woodrow Wilson's fourteen points.
5. Who led the fight in the Senate against passing the Versailles treaty by the United States?

Critical Thinking

6. **Identifying Assumptions.** Why did President Wilson try to win popular support for the treaty that the Senate rejected?

LOOKING AHEAD: Describe the twenties in terms of its reforms, fears, heroes, and Presidents.

The flapper came to stand for the new freedom in the lifestyles of the twenties.

4   The Twenties

The defeat of the Treaty of Versailles and the end of President Wilson's term of office in 1921 seemed to dash hopes for world peace and bring American idealism to an end. As the decade of the 1920s unfolded, the United States moved from the sacrifices of the war years to a time of rising prosperity. Historians have given many labels to the 1920s. Some call the 1920s the Jazz Age because jazz music was so popular then. The music gave performers and listeners alike great freedom of expression. Others have called the 1920s the Age of the Flapper because of the change in dress styles—a sign of a new social freedom. The Roaring Twenties also became a popular label. It described that burst of activity after the war when people followed their own wishes, living fairly free and open lives. Golden Twenties is also used to describe this seemingly rich decade. But despite the colorful names, the 1920s were a time when most families lived quiet, working lives. People were happy that the war was over. They could not know that much harder times were to come.

Reforms, Fears, and Heroes

Since the 1830s, reformers had worked for women's right to vote. Some states had even been won over, but the movement had stalled on the national level. In 1919 the Nineteenth Amendment was added to the Constitution. It gave all women twenty-one years of age and over the right to vote.

Reformers since the 1830s had also tried to get people to stop drinking alcoholic beverages. In 1919 the Eighteenth Amendment was added to the Constitution. It prohibited the making, selling, and transporting of liquor. Many people who still wanted liquor began breaking the law to get it. Selling illegal liquor became big business for criminals. The most famous of these public enemies was Al Capone. His gang and other gangs in Chicago carved out parts of the city for making and selling liquor. They fought "wars" over which part belonged to whom. In 1929 seven members of Bugs Moran's gang were killed by rivals thought to be part of Capone's gang. But law officers could not prove anything against Capone. He was finally jailed in 1931 for not paying his income taxes. In 1933 the Twenty-First Amendment to the Constitution repealed the Eighteenth Amendment and ended Prohibition.

While some reform groups worked for change through lawful means, other groups began taking the law into their own hands. The Ku Klux Klan, which was anti-Catholic, anti-Jewish, and anti-black, reorganized in 1915. It seemed at first to be within the law. A large number of state legislators around the country began listening to Klan members. The Klan grew particularly strong in the Midwest. Klan members terrorized blacks, Jews, and other minorities. But when scandals were reported about the private lives of some Klan leaders, the power of the Klan faded.

While the Klan was most feared by those it hated, the whole country was frightened by the Red Scare. Communists, or Reds as they were called, had come to power in Russia in 1917. Many people feared communism would also sweep the United States, even though only a few thousand persons in the country favored communism. The federal government acted on these fears. It tried to stop everyone from criticizing the government by calling these critics Communists even if they had no direct ties to communism.

To escape their fears and their faltering idealism, people in the 1920s turned to entertainment and sports. There they also found heroes. The music of Rudy Vallee and Guy Lombardo reached nearly every home by radio. The National Broadcasting Company, founded in 1926, was the first of the nationwide networks that turned radio into big business.

Perhaps the greatest sports hero was George Herman Ruth, better known as Babe Ruth. In 1927 he hit sixty home runs for the New York Yankees. This record remained unbroken for over thirty years. Jack Dempsey and Gene Tunney became boxing heroes. Twice they drew crowds of more than 100,000 people. In football the Four Horsemen of Notre Dame excited fans with their play.

Charles Lindbergh was photographed beside his single-engine plane before he flew nonstop across the Atlantic in 1927.

No hero was more loved than Charles A. Lindbergh, a young handsome, daring midwesterner. He was the first person to fly alone nonstop across the Atlantic, winning a prize of $25,000. In the *Spirit of St. Louis* Lindbergh took off in May 1927 from an airport on Long Island, New York, and landed thirty-three hours later at an airport near Paris. A joyful crowd rushed to welcome and praise him. Lindbergh won the hearts of many with his skill and daring.

Presidents in the 1920s

Republicans controlled the national government during the 1920s. Senator Warren G. Harding of Ohio was elected President in 1920 and took office in 1921. Harding was an easy-going, friendly person who often wondered whether he belonged in the Presidency. He depended too much on friends. Some of these friends, whom he had named to high office, let him down. Harding's attorney general, for example, took bribes to pardon and parole criminals. The head of the Veterans Bureau took bribes from people who wanted to do business with the government. And the secretary of the interior was

Election of 1920

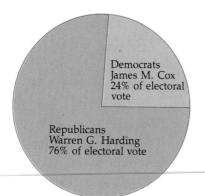

Democrats
James M. Cox
24% of electoral vote

Republicans
Warren G. Harding
76% of electoral vote

found guilty of taking money in exchange for leasing government property.

On a return trip from Alaska in 1923 Harding died suddenly from a heart attack. He was followed in office by Vice-President Calvin Coolidge of Massachusetts. Coolidge was a serious person of simple tastes. His father, a justice of peace, administered the Presidential oath of office. The room in the small New England farmhouse where they stood was lighted by a kerosene lamp. Coolidge was elected as President in his own right in 1924.

Unlike Theodore Roosevelt and Woodrow Wilson, President Coolidge believed that the federal government should act as little as possible. During his entire term of office he suggested no new laws and was against the few bills Congress did pass.

In 1928 Coolidge simply said that he did not wish to be President again. The Republicans then chose Herbert Hoover as their nominee. Hoover had served ably in the First World War as food administrator. As a youngster, Hoover had been poor, but later he made a fortune working as an engineer in South America and China.

Running against Hoover was Democrat Alfred E. Smith, governor of New York. Smith was a Catholic from New York City. Some voters feared that a Catholic President might blur the separation between church and state. Hoover finally defeated Smith in 1928, mainly because most people were happy with Republican policies in the 1920s.

Uneasy Prosperity

On the surface the 1920s seemed prosperous. The economy suffered a downturn in 1920. By 1922 it had recovered, and business boomed once again. More and more goods—especially such consumer items as radios, cars, bicycles, stoves, and sewing machines—appeared on the market and were eagerly snapped up.

This great flow of goods hid some serious economic weaknesses. One was the popularity of installment buying. Customers could pay a small part of the cost of an item. Then, while using the item, customers could pay the remaining charges in small, monthly installments. Problems arose when buyers lost their jobs. Then they could not meet the monthly payments. Another economic weakness was that workers' wages did not keep pace with the rising prices of many goods. At the same time, farm prices were dropping, keeping farmers from sharing in the good times. Some business leaders also encouraged people to put their money into risky deals.

Before the end of the 1920s the good times suddenly came to a halt. Though World War I was now history, a new war—a war against joblessness and hunger—took over at home as the United States entered the Great Depression.

Election of 1924

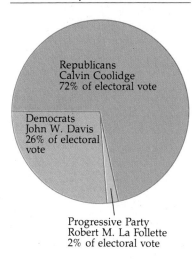

Republicans
Calvin Coolidge
72% of electoral vote

Democrats
John W. Davis
26% of electoral vote

Progressive Party
Robert M. La Follette
2% of electoral vote

Election of 1928

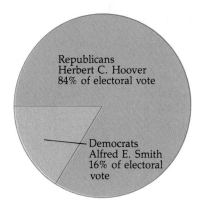

Republicans
Herbert C. Hoover
84% of electoral vote

Democrats
Alfred E. Smith
16% of electoral vote

Section 4 Review

1. Explain how life in the 1920s was influenced by the Eighteenth Amendment. The Nineteenth Amendment. The Ku Klux Klan.
2. In what ways was Lindbergh a symbol of the 1920s?

Critical Thinking
3. **Expressing Problems Clearly.** What two economic weaknesses brought an end to the seeming prosperity of the 1920s?

625

People   In War and Peace

Though opposites in many ways, Jeanette Rankin and George C. Marshall shared traits of character that won them lasting respect.

During the First World War two people of quite different backgrounds and views began careers that won them public attention. One stood for peace at all costs. The other stood for national security.

Go! Go! Go!

Jeanette Rankin was born in 1880 on a ranch in Montana. She attended public schools and then college. At first Jeanette was unable to channel her great energy. She wrote in her diary, "Go! Go! Go!"

But she did not yet have a clear direction. Only after searching for a few years did she find her goal— the crusade for women's rights.

In 1910 the Montana legislature, then made up entirely of men, invited Rankin to speak about voting rights for women. She was warmly applauded, and her speech was widely reported.

During the next six years Rankin spoke throughout the country for the National American Woman Suffrage Association. She led the Montana delegation in a suffrage

parade March 3, 1913. The following year women won the right to vote in Montana.

In 1916 Rankin became the first woman elected to Congress. Her victory made national headlines. She told a *New York Times* reporter: "I feel that it is my special duty to express . . . the point of view of women. . . ."

A Stand for Peace

Rankin's first vote as a member of Congress was on President Wilson's proposal that the United States

Peace advocate Jeanette Rankin (right) lived long enough to march for women's political rights in 1916 and for women's social rights in the 1960s (inset).

People

enter World War I. When the roll call vote was taken, Rankin stood up and said: "I want to stand by my country, but I cannot vote for war. I vote no." Although forty-nine male members of Congress also voted no, Rankin alone was bitterly criticized.

During the First World War Rankin fought for better working conditions for women. She helped get the Nineteenth Amendment to the Constitution accepted, which gave women the right to vote. She ran for a Senate seat in 1918, but she was defeated. In the following years Rankin gave all her energies to world peace.

Another Vote for Peace

In 1940 Rankin again ran for Congress and won. Once again she faced the question of whether the United States should go to war after the Japanese attack on Pearl Harbor in 1941. Once again she voted against war, saying, "As a woman I can't go to war, and I refuse to send anyone else." This time she stood alone.

After leaving Congress, Rankin spoke in favor of nonviolent protests to win human rights. She joined the movement for women's rights in the 1960s and 1970s. She joined the peace movement against the Vietnam War. She was celebrated by leaders of Congress and of the modern women's movement alike on her ninetieth birthday. She died on May 18, 1973.

Marshall: Soldier and Diplomat

Marshall was born in Uniontown, Pennsylvania, in 1880. As a teenager, George knew he wanted to be a soldier. He attended the Virginia Military Institute. He arrived as a tall, gawky boy, but he graduated a leader in his class.

Marshall first served in the Philippines shortly after the surrender of Aguinaldo's rebels in 1902. When he returned to the Philippines later, he showed himself to be a clever planner in battle games.

When the United States entered the First World War, Colonel Marshall was sent with troops to France. At first he trained new recruits to be soldiers. Then he was made chief of staff of his division. He began planning how best to attack the enemy and to move supplies from place to place. He did his job so well he was made General Pershing's chief of staff. Marshall served closely with Pershing during and after the war.

Ready for the Next War

Marshall believed that the United States had been poorly prepared for war. When Marshall was offered a higher-paying job outside the army, he replied: "I must stay on the job. I must see that the army is ready for the next war."

To prepare, Marshall made notes on the best young officers. In his plans for the next war he knew that troops and tanks would advance swiftly, not crawl slowly from trench to trench. He appreciated the lonely task of foot soldiers, seeing that in the end only they could win a war. He studied all the mistakes made before by the army.

Chief of Staff

Although he was bright and forward-looking, Marshall moved up slowly in rank in the peacetime army. Marshall did not become a

As secretary of state, George Marshall worked for peace.

general until he was fifty-six years old. Then suddenly he was called to Washington and named deputy chief of staff of the whole army. Soon President Franklin D. Roosevelt appointed him chief of staff during World War II.

Roosevelt knew that Marshall wished to lead the Allied armies onto the French coast of Normandy. But he did not want Marshall to leave his side. The President said that without Marshall near at hand to advise him he would not be able to sleep at night.

Marshall planned his country's part in the Second World War. He selected the commanders—including General Dwight Eisenhower—and decided how soldiers were to be trained, moved, and equipped on battlefields around the world. After the war, President Harry Truman named Marshall his secretary of state. The Marshall Plan to help the countries of Europe rebuild after the war was only one of his many achievements. Marshall devoted his life to making the nation safe in war and in peace.

Chapter 32 Review

Chapter Summary

World War I began in 1914 with the shooting of Austria-Hungary's Archduke by Serbian nationalists. The Allies—Britain, France, and Russia—joined the war on the side of Serbia. The Ottoman Empire and Germany came to the aid of Austria-Hungary. Hundreds of thousands died on the western front —the war zone between France and Germany. Fighting on Germany's eastern front ended in 1917 when a revolution in Russia overthrew the czar.

Although most people in the United States favored the Allies, President Wilson asked for neutrality between 1914 and 1917. German submarine warfare, however, led Congress to declare war against the Central Powers in 1917.

On November 11, 1918, an armistice brought an end to the fighting. The Treaty of Versailles punished Germany and Austria-Hungary. The treaty also set up the League of Nations which the Senate voted not to join.

Reviewing Vocabulary

Use the following words to complete the sentences below.

prosperity	ration	rivalries
negotiate	armistice	alliances
installment	suffrage	idealism
communism	nationalism	neutrality
league	convoy	draft

1. _____ that divided Europe into power groups and strong feelings of _____ added to the tensions that led to war.
2. The United States stayed out of European _____ but finally gave up its _____ and entered the war.

3. The war effort included the need to _____ goods and to _____ people into the army.
4. Soldiers and war supplies were shipped by _____.
5. A(n) _____ brought the fighting to a halt on November 11, 1918, and President Wilson proposed a _____ of Nations.
6. The failure of the Allies to _____ a lasting peace brought American _____ to an end.
7. Although the 1920s were a time of _____, fear of _____ swept the nation.
8. The practice of _____ buying caused a serious economic weakness in the nation.
9. Jeanette Rankin helped gain _____ for women.

Understanding Main Ideas

1. What part did rivalries and alliances in Europe play in bringing about war?
2. Why did the United States give up its neutrality and enter World War I?
3. What effect did United States efforts on the home front, the fighting front, and the diplomatic front have on the outcome of the war?
4. How did reforms, fears, heroes, and Presidents influence the 1920s?

Critical Thinking Skills

1. **Predicting Consequences.** Would the outcome of World War I have been different if the United States had remained neutral? Explain your answer.
2. **Identifying Alternatives.** How might the post-war treaties have helped to prevent future conflicts among nations?

Social Studies Skills: Comparing Information from Maps

EUROPE AFTER WORLD WAR I

Compare the map above showing Europe in 1919 after the signing of the Treaty of Versailles with the map on page 614 showing Europe at the start of World War I.

Skill Review: For each of the following countries, write a statement that describes a change shown on the map on this page.

Germany	Poland
Austria-Hungary	Latvia
Serbia	Bulgaria
Russia	Romania

Writing About History

Analyzing Heroes. Study the heroes of the 1920s. Make a list of qualities that people at that time seem to have admired. Make another list of the qualities that people admire today. How are your two lists different? How are they the same? Write two paragraphs comparing heroes of the 1920s with heroes that exist today.

Your Region in History

Government. What role did your community play in World War I? Check your local library or historic society for old newspapers, pictures, or mementos. See if any soldiers or nurses from your area were awarded medals for bravery. Also look for information on local factories providing supplies or munitions for the war.

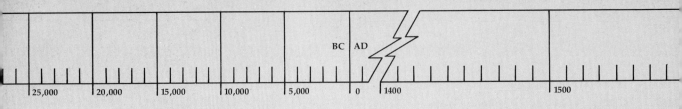

The New Deal

Chapter 33

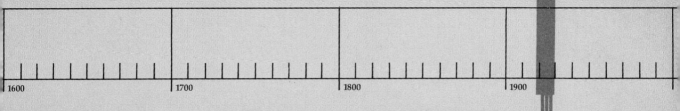

Vocabulary

downturn	handicap
cycle	investment
unemployment	emergency
relief	unconstitutional
recovery	bargain
bonus	retirement
veteran	sit-down strike

Hopes were high when Herbert Hoover accepted the Republican nomination for the Presidency in August 1928. "We in America today," he said, "are nearer to the final triumph over poverty than ever before in the history of any land. . . . We shall soon . . . be in sight of the day when poverty will be banished from this nation." In his inaugural address in March 1929 Hoover stated, "Our first objective must be to provide security from poverty and want. . . ." That summer the chairman of the Democratic party said, "I am firm in my belief that anyone not only can be rich, but ought to be rich."

Both party leaders were wrong. A few months later the price of stock in the biggest and best companies in the nation dropped to nearly nothing. The plunge became known as the Great Stock Market Crash of 1929. The hard times of the Great Depression set in and lasted for ten long years. Millions of people were not only without jobs, but also desperate for some way to feed, clothe, and house themselves each day.

1 The Deepening Depression

The United States had suffered business downturns before. Some experts believed that such downturns were a natural part of a business cycle. At one phase in the cycle, business slowed. Factories

Prereading

1. What did President Hoover do to help jobless workers, farmers and business owners when an economic downturn began in 1929?

2. What short-term measures did President Roosevelt use to ease the bank crisis and to create more jobs?

3. What long-range reforms were started during the New Deal to help business, agriculture, and labor recover from the depression?

4. Why did unions become more powerful during the 1930s?

Phases in the Business Cycle

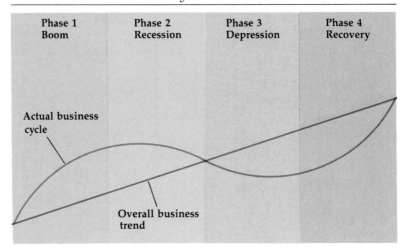

produced less or closed because they were making more goods than people were buying. More and more workers were laid off. They could not earn money to buy goods. But when the goods in stores or warehouses ran out, business began to pick up. Factories hired more workers to make more goods. Workers earned money, which they used to buy more goods. And business boomed once again. Since industrialization, business had gone through these cycles time and time again.

In the depression of the 1930s the downturn seemed endless. Each year conditions grew worse. Never before had so many people in the United States lived through such hard times.

Jobless Workers

People who had put their money in shares of stock often lost every penny when the companies closed. Risky and sometimes dishonest deals fell through, leaving investors penniless. People lost their savings when the banks closed. Families who could no longer make payments on their homes lost their homes as well.

Factories put out less as people stopped buying goods. Factory managers cut the hours and pay of most workers. They laid off many others. Some factories closed altogether, setting off a chain of closings in businesses that depended on the ones that failed. The closing of an automobile plant, for example, led to the closing of tire plants. Unemployment spread. With no money coming in, jobless workers were not able to buy goods. The shrinking number of customers forced more factories to close their doors, and even more workers lost their jobs.

By 1932 more than 13 million workers were unemployed, about one of every four. About 1 million workers in New York and

600,000 workers in Chicago were unable to find work. In Cleveland 50 percent of the workers were without jobs. In Akron, Ohio, the figure was 60 percent and in Toledo, 80 percent.

Young people—those with few or no skills and little experience—often could not find work of any kind. Thousands "rode the rails," sneaking onto freight trains and riding from city to city looking for work. The lucky ones might get a day or two of work now and then—just enough to keep them going. Others begged for money and food. Some stole.

On the outskirts of many towns and cities clusters of crude shacks sprang up. People used anything they could find to build with—scraps of metal, wood, or paper. These towns were sometimes called Hoovervilles by people who blamed President Herbert Hoover for the depression. Hundreds, even thousands, of these people lined up to apply for only a dozen or so jobs. Others stood for hours in long lines to get a free loaf of bread or a bowl of thin soup. Some people even rummaged through garbage dumps searching for scraps of food. One writer described this scene: "We saw a crowd of fifty men fighting over a barrel of garbage which had been set outside the back door of a restaurant. American citizens fighting for the scraps of food like animals!"

Despair on the Farms

Some people left the cities to try their luck on farms, slowing the flow of people to the cities. But farm life was no easier. Farmers were producing more food than people could buy, so prices kept falling.

Even a tar paper shack in a St. Louis Hooverville was worth protecting with a padlock during the depression.

Without rain, no amount of hard work could make the Great Plains produce enough food to keep a family alive.

Between 1929 and 1932 the price of a bushel of corn dropped lower than the cost of shipping it to market. Some farmers chose to burn their corn instead, using it as fuel to keep warm in the winter. Some farmers also joined in farm strikes, agreeing not to buy or sell anything until prices rose. But conditions got no better.

Thousands of farmers could not pay back loans they had taken out to buy land and machines. They lost everything and were forced to leave their land. Many took to the roads, strapping their few belongings to their cars or trucks. They drove from place to place looking for work, but there was little or no work to be found.

Farmers in the Great Plains also suffered from droughts in the early 1930s. Without rain, crops died. Precious topsoil was blown away by powerful winds. Great dust storms raged for days at a time. The hardest-hit parts in Colorado, Kansas, New Mexico, Oklahoma, and Texas formed the huge Dust Bowl. A Kansas newspaper editor wrote: "We can see nothing out our windows but dirt; every time our teeth . . . come together, you feel dirt and taste it; haven't heard a thing for hours, my ears are full; can't smell, my nose is full; can't walk, my shoes are full, but not of feet."

Great clouds of dust blown from the Plains darkened the skies as far away as Albany, New York. New England had red snow in the winter of 1935, colored by the topsoil from farms more than a thousand miles away. Farmers who had managed somehow to keep going through the early depression years now found themselves ruined by the weather. Even more of them packed up, left their useless land, and drove west looking for a place to start again.

Hoover and the Depression

President Hoover tried to end the depression, but most of his plans failed. In November 1929 he met with leaders from business, industry, and labor. He asked them to work together to keep people on the job at fair wages. But nothing seemed to stem the business downturn. Hoover told officers of the New York Stock Exchange to change their rules so that there would be less danger of another stock market crash. He also ordered the federal government to work with states and private charities to set up relief programs for those without jobs. But Hoover was dead set against a federal relief program. It was his belief that such a program would add to the national debt and take away powers that properly belonged to the states.

Hoover also favored the highest tariff in the nation's history. He hoped to stir up the sale of American goods at home by slowing down the sale of goods brought in from other countries. More than a thousand economic experts begged Hoover to kill the tariff. But Hoover signed it into law in 1930. As the economists had feared, other countries then raised their tariffs, making it harder for the United States to sell its goods abroad. The tariff turned out to hurt the nation's chances for recovery.

Hoover's most successful plan was the Reconstruction Finance Corporation (RFC). In 1932 the RFC was set up to spend as much as $2 billion helping businesses important to the national economy. Loans from the RFC kept a number of banks, insurance companies, and railroads from going broke. People against the RFC, however, called the plan a "breadline for business," believing that direct relief to the unemployed was a more important goal. Hoover would not try direct relief.

Even more unpopular than the RFC was Hoover's answer to the "bonus marchers." Veterans of World War I had been promised a bonus by the government, but the money was not to be paid until 1945. As more and more veterans lost their jobs, they began to demand that the government pay the bonus early. In 1931 Congress passed a bill that allowed veterans to borrow up to half of their bonus. The President vetoed the bill the first time. Veterans' groups then began asking for the whole amount. In June 1932 they camped in and around Washington, D.C., to bring attention to their cause.

On July 28, 1932, Hoover ordered the army to break up the rundown shelters in the camp. The army used tear gas and bayonets to drive out the families of veterans. The shelters were then burned. A Washington newspaper stated: "What a pitiful spectacle is that of

In the summer of 1937, veterans put up a tent city in Washington, D.C. They had come to the capital seeking their full war-service bonus.

Election of 1932

Democrats
Franklin D. Roosevelt
89% of electoral vote

Republicans
Herbert C. Hoover
11% of electoral vote

Section 1 Review

1. Explain how one factory closing often led to other plant closings.
2. What was the Dust Bowl?
3. List four actions that President Hoover took to deal with the depression.

Critical Thinking

4. **Checking Consistency.** Was Roosevelt's campaign pledge consistent with his record as governor of New York?

LOOKING AHEAD: What short-term measures did President Roosevelt use to ease the bank crisis and to create more jobs?

the great American Government, mightiest in the world, chasing unarmed men, women, and children with Army tanks. . . . If the Army must be called out to make war on unarmed citizens, this is no longer America."

The Election of 1932

In the election of 1932 the Republicans renominated Herbert Hoover. The Democrats nominated Governor Franklin D. Roosevelt of New York.

Franklin Roosevelt was a distant relative of President Theodore Roosevelt. Like the earlier Roosevelt, he had served as assistant secretary of the navy before entering national politics. In 1920 he had run for Vice-President of the United States.

An attack of polio, which crippled Roosevelt for life, seemed to end his chances for public office. But he was a cheerful man with a strong will. He would not let his handicap hold him back. He ran for governor of New York and won in 1928. He was praised for the steps his state took to fight the depression. Under Roosevelt, New York became the first state to offer money to citizens who had no jobs. Aid for the unemployed, he said, "must be extended by Government, not as a matter of charity, but as a matter of social duty."

The Democrats won by a landslide in 1932. Roosevelt received 23 million popular votes to Hoover's 16 million. Democrats won control of both the House and the Senate. Early in the campaign Roosevelt had said, "I pledge you, I pledge myself, to a new deal for the American people." A cartoonist picked up the phrase "new deal," and it became the motto for the Roosevelt administration.

2 Roosevelt and the New Deal

Roosevelt took office on March 4, 1933. The Twentieth Amendment to the Constitution called for a new President and a new Congress to begin work in January instead of March. But the amendment was not ratified in time to affect Roosevelt's swearing in. So the nation had to wait until March for Roosevelt's New Deal to begin. As it waited, still another crisis arose.

The Bank Crisis

All bankers lend out or invest the money that savers put into the bank. After the stock market crash in 1929 many banks suffered losses on their loans and investments. People who were worried about the safety of their money began to withdraw their savings. Many banks ran out of money entirely. Though the RFC managed to save some banks, others were forced to close. People who still had savings in the banks that closed lost their money.

Late in 1932 banks began to fail in greater numbers. Panic took over. People rushed to the banks to take out their savings before it was too late. As more and more people drew out their savings, more and more banks ran out of money and had to close. By the time Roosevelt took office the bank panic had spread throughout the country.

Roosevelt acted within hours after taking office. Using emergency powers that had been given to the President during World War I, he declared a "bank holiday." Banks all over the country were ordered to close. Roosevelt then called a special session of Congress. On March 9 Congress passed the Emergency Banking Act. The act set aside money to help troubled banks. It also included a plan to reopen as many banks as could be saved.

On Sunday evening, March 12, 1933, President Roosevelt spoke on the radio to the whole country about his plans. Talks such as this became known as "fireside chats." In his first chat Roosevelt told the people they need not be afraid to put their money in the reopened banks. "I can assure you,' he said, "that it is safer to keep your money in a reopened bank than under the mattress." Roosevelt's quick action and his comforting words over the radio helped end the bank panic. By April many banks were back in business and people were using them.

Under Roosevelt, new laws were passed to reform the nation's banks. The Federal Deposit Insurance Corporation (FDIC) was set up in June 1933. It protected people's savings, guaranteeing a certain return on money kept in the bank. Today most banks are members of the FDIC.

Congress also passed laws reforming the stock market to avoid another collapse. It set up a federal Securities and Exchange Commission (SEC) in 1934 to watch over the market's day-to-day sales.

These measures were characteristic of Roosevelt. He believed in trying new ideas. If one plan failed, he tried another. In 1933 Hoover said, "We are at the end of the string." But Roosevelt said, "This great nation will endure as it has endured, will revive and prosper." He assured the nation that "the only thing we have to fear is fear itself." Roosevelt said the nation wanted "action, and action now!"

Relief and Jobs

Roosevelt acted on many fronts as the New Deal took shape. Most New Deal plans are best described by at least one of three Rs: relief, recovery, or reform. The more than 12 million unemployed people and their families needed relief of some kind until they could find work. Business, industry, and agriculture needed help to recover from the depression. And reforms of many kinds were called for if the nation was to protect itself against another depression.

Under the New Deal, special agencies provided relief to the needy. Within two years $3 billion was divided among the states to

At a Public Works Administration site in Kentucky, workers used teams of oxen to clear land for a school.

help the poor. But most people wanted work, not handouts. So the New Deal Congress set up several work programs. In 1933 Congress created the Civilian Conservation Corps (CCC). Before it ended in 1940, the CCC provided jobs for more than 2 million young men between the ages of eighteen and twenty-five. In national parks and forests, CCC groups cleared out deadwood, built firebreaks, and planted new trees. Another organization set up in 1935, the National Youth Administration (NYA), offered training and aid to almost 2 million students in high school and college. By staying in school, these young people learned skills for future jobs. The plan also kept students out of the job market a little longer, making it somewhat easier for others to find work.

Over several years, beginning in 1933, the Public Works Administration (PWA) built bridges, dams, power plants, and government buildings. Many new jobs were created through these projects. The PWA was headed by Harold Ickes (ik'əs), who worked slowly and carefully, making sure that every cent of the government's money was well spent. But the President wanted people put to work faster. He also wanted to get large amounts of money flowing into the national economy quickly so that people could buy the goods they needed. When Roosevelt later set up the Works Progress Administration (WPA) in 1935, he asked his close adviser Harry Hopkins to help Ickes. "Ickes is a good administrator," Roosevelt said, "but often too slow. Harry gets things done. I am going to give this job to Harry."

Hopkins had worked as the director of the New York state relief agency while Roosevelt was governor of the state. Roosevelt brought him to Washington to oversee the federal program, and Hopkins soon became Roosevelt's favorite. When critics argued that relief might not be wise in the long run, Hopkins answered, "People don't eat in the long run—they eat every day."

Aided by Hopkins and Ickes, Roosevelt used the WPA to spend $11 billion in federal money between 1935 and 1941. At its peak the WPA provided jobs for over 3 million workers. The agency built more than half a million miles of roads and highways, 8,000 parks, and 850 airports. Thousands of schools and hospitals were built or repaired by the WPA. The agency also put writers, artists, actors, and musicians to work. It brought art, live theater, and concerts to millions of people all over the country. In almost every town and city in the nation, WPA parks, highways, and schools are still used today.

3 Recovery and Reform

The longer Roosevelt held office, the more he turned to long-range recovery and reform measures. Some of these recovery efforts failed.

Section 2 Review

1. What four steps did Roosevelt take to end the bank panic of 1933?
2. What purpose was served by the Federal Deposit Insurance Corporation? By the Securities and Exchange Commission?
3. What three agencies were set up to deal with unemployment? How did the National Youth Administration aid the jobless?

Critical Thinking

4. **Identifying Assumptions.** What attitude toward administrators did Roosevelt express when he appointed Harry Hopkins head of WPA?

LOOKING AHEAD: What long-range reforms were started during the New Deal to help business, agriculture, and labor recover from the depression?

Others are still a vital part of the nation's daily economic, political, and social life.

Business Recovery

Under Roosevelt, Congress set up the National Recovery Administration (NRA) to aid industry. Roosevelt called it "a shot in the arm" for industry. The NRA worked with many businesses to draw up sets of "fair practices." The act set aside earlier laws so that owners could fix prices and production goals. The country welcomed the NRA with parades, flags, signs, and speeches. But later workers charged that the NRA was too easy on business. And business groups often did not honor their promises to one another. In 1935 the NRA ended when the Supreme Court ruled that the law setting up the organization was unconstitutional.

Labor Reforms

The NRA did, however, bring about some important reforms for workers that were later restored by Congress. The Wagner Act of 1935 again gave workers the right to bargain as a group with their employers for better working conditions. The Wagner Act also said workers could form or join labor unions.

The Fair Labor Standards Act of 1938 set a minimum wage and a maximum work week for industries engaged in business and trade between states. At first the minimum wage was set at twenty-five cents an hour and the maximum work week at forty-four hours. The hourly rate seems low today, but five dollars in 1938 bought groceries for the average family for a week. The act also put an end to child labor by setting sixteen as the earliest legal working age.

Recovery and Reform for Farmers

The Agricultural Adjustment Administration (AAA) was set up in 1933 to help farmers. Their main problem was the low price of farm goods. Many people believed that prices could be raised by cutting production. The fewer the goods, the more valuable they would become and the higher the prices they would bring. But farmers were not willing to let some of their land lie idle. Under the AAA, farmers would be paid to leave parts of their fields unplanted. The AAA, however, was called unconstitutional by the Supreme Court in 1936. But in 1938 a new agricultural act with many of the same goals was passed.

Government agencies also loaned farmers money, helped them move from worn-out land to new farms, and taught them new ways of farming that made better use of the soil. One act of Congress allowed hundreds of thousands of sharecroppers and tenant farmers to get easy loans to buy their own farms. In 1935 another act brought

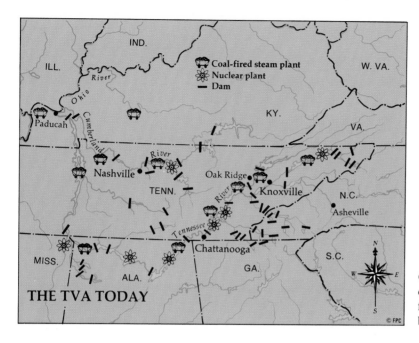

THE TVA TODAY

Coal-fired steam plant
Nuclear plant
— Dam

Coal and nuclear energy, instead of dammed-up water, now produce four fifths of the electricity used by customers of the TVA.

electricity to millions of farmers. By 1941 one out of every four farms was wired for electricity.

The TVA

High on the list of New Deal achievements was the Tennessee Valley Authority (TVA), created in 1933. People living in the Tennessee River Valley—40,000 square miles of land in parts of seven southern states—were some of the poorest in the nation. George Norris, a progressive Republican senator from Nebraska, had been trying since 1921 to get the federal government to bring electrical power to the Tennessee Valley. Twice he had guided bills through Congress, and twice the bills were vetoed by Republican Presidents—first by Coolidge, then by Hoover.

Roosevelt was for the TVA, and so it came into being. In twenty years the TVA repaired five dams and built twenty new ones along the Tennessee River and its smaller streams. On the new lakes formed by the dams people fished, swam, and sailed. Plants built along with the dams turned water power into cheap electricity for the whole valley. The TVA helped control floods and improved river transportation. It also made cheap fertilizer for local farmers. Its agents taught the people better farming methods. The TVA also planted millions of trees. The tree roots, spreading out in all directions, kept the soil from washing away during heavy rains.

Senator Norris wanted to start regional authorities like the TVA elsewhere in the country. Private power companies, which had to

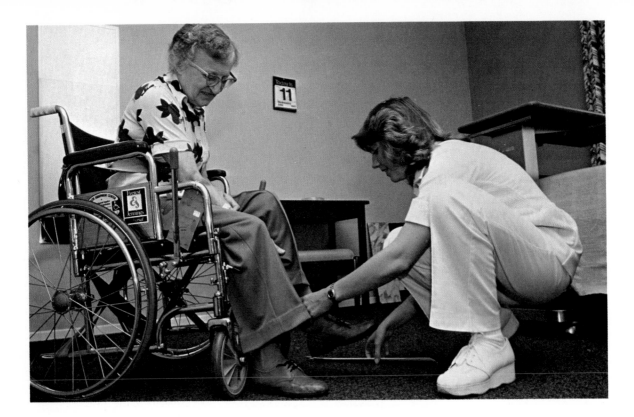

Under Social Security, workers suffering disabling illness or injury receive money in aid from the federal government.

Section 3 Review

1. Why was the National Recovery Administration criticized?
2. What three steps did the federal government take to help farmers?

Critical Thinking

3. **Demonstrating Reasoned Judgement.** Which of the long-range recovery and reform measures do you consider most important? Why?

LOOKING AHEAD: Why did unions become more powerful during the 1930s?

charge the same low rates for electricity as the TVA, spoke out loudly against the agency. Other people pointed out that tax money from the whole nation was being used to help just one part of the country. And still others thought it was wrong to pit an agency of the federal government against private power companies. Congress was slowed by criticism of the TVA and took no further action.

Social Security

Another lasting law was the Social Security Act of 1935. Most people believed that social security was long overdue. The Social Security Act was written under the direction of Secretary of Labor Frances Perkins, the first female cabinet member. It provided three types of aid: (1) payments to workers who lost their jobs, (2) payments to retired workers, and (3) payments to workers who became blind, crippled, or otherwise handicapped so they could not work. Money for Social Security came from a special tax paid by both workers and employers.

4   The Rise of Big Labor

Unions had lost members during the 1920s, partly because of growing prosperity. When the depression started, workers began returning to the unions. By the early 1940s organized labor carried much weight at the national level.

A new day for workers began with the Norris-La Guardia Act of 1932. Senator Norris and Representative Fiorello La Guardia of New York brought the bill before Congress. The act removed two weapons that business had used to keep workers on the job and out of unions. First, it made back-to-work orders from courts harder to obtain. Such court orders had been used to crush strikes by forcing striking workers to return to their jobs. Second, the act put an end to "yellow dog" contracts. Under such agreements job seekers swore not to join a union in exchange for being given a job.

Labor and the New Deal

On the whole, labor favored Roosevelt and the New Deal. The New Deal, in turn, did much for organized labor. The Wagner Act of 1935 gave workers the right to organize without fear of being fired. The Social Security Act of 1935 offered greater security for working people. And the Fair Labor Standards Act of 1938 improved working conditions.

Secretary of Labor Frances Perkins played a key part in these gains. At first, organized labor had been against her—in part because she had never been a union member and in part because she was a woman. William Green, president of the American Federation of Labor (AFL), said labor could never accept her. But twelve years later, just before her retirement from office, Perkins had shaped the department into an agency that made businesses deal fairly with working people.

A report prepared under the direction of Frances Perkins laid the groundwork for the Social Security Act of 1935.

The CIO

In the 1930s a split developed within organized labor. A number of union leaders, headed by John L. Lewis of the United Mine Workers, believed that the AFL did not speak for all workers. The AFL, Lewis said, spoke only for a special group of skilled workers in craft unions. Lewis and others wanted to organize the general workers—those on the assembly lines. In 1935 Lewis and the others formed a Committee for Industrial Organization (CIO) within the AFL. The CIO quickly began to sign up members. When AFL leaders, worried by CIO growth, ordered it to disband, Lewis said no. He and his followers left the AFL. In 1938 they changed the name of their group to the Congress of Industrial Organizations.

The AFL and the CIO, now separate organizations, were different in several important ways. The AFL was made up mainly of craft and other skilled workers. The CIO tried to sign up every worker in an industry, skilled or unskilled. The CIO did not group its members by the kind of work they did. Any worker in the automobile industry, for example, could become a member of the United Auto Workers.

Attempts to bring workers into the unions sometimes led to fighting. Strikers in South Chicago had to dodge police clubs in 1937.

Unlike the AFL, the CIO also brought black and white workers together in a single union. And the CIO was more active in politics than the AFL. In the 1936 election the United Mine Workers donated half a million dollars to Roosevelt's reelection campaign. Other CIO unions also put up large amounts of money for the candidates of their choice.

Union Growth

Throughout the 1930s union leaders worked hard to sign up members and start unions in different industries. Labor found a new weapon in the sit-down strike. Union members, seeking a hearing, simply stayed in the factory without working until employers began talks. Workers refused to be replaced by strikebreakers. The sit-down strike worked so well against General Motors that the company had to recognize the United Auto Workers union in 1937.

By late 1937 the CIO numbered 3,718,000. By 1939 total union membership in the country had reached 9 million. About 1 million of these were members of independent unions. The rest were almost equally divided between the AFL and the CIO. With so many members, most of voting age, unions became a strong force in politics.

Election of 1936

Democrats
Franklin D. Roosevelt
98% of electoral vote

Republicans
Alfred M. Landon
2% of electoral vote

Federal Income and Spending, 1928–1940

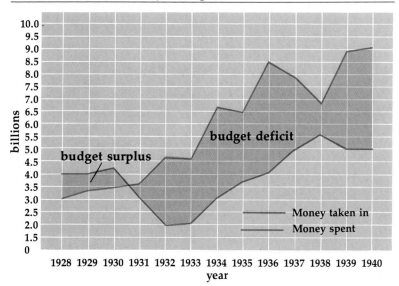

billions

budget surplus

budget deficit

—— Money taken in
—— Money spent

1928 1929 1930 1931 1932 1933 1934 1935 1936 1937 1938 1939 1940
year

The nation went into debt to pull itself out of the depression.

Candidates for office eagerly looked for contributions from organized labor. Organized labor could make or break a person politically. In many ways big labor became a counterforce to big business.

Reactions to the New Deal

During his first years in office President Roosevelt pleased almost everyone. Congress passed the acts Roosevelt wanted. Business and labor were also on the President's side. And the people believed in him. Will Rogers, the popular humorist, said: "Even if what (Roosevelt) does is wrong, (the people) are with him. Just so he does something. If he burned down the Capital, we would cheer and say, 'Well, we at least got a fire started anyhow.'"

This broad support did not last. The chief complaint was that the federal government was becoming too powerful. Government was telling business how to operate. It was spending large sums of money, piling up a big national debt. Many people thought that individuals were depending too heavily on the government. In 1936 Republican Senator Arthur H. Vandenberg of Michigan summed up some people's feelings, "I belong to but one bloc and it has but one slogan—stop Roosevelt." Yet Roosevelt was reelected in 1936, 1940, and 1944. He held office longer than any other President in United States history. Under the Twenty-Second Amendment to the Constitution, ratified in 1951, no future President would ever hold office for more than two complete terms.

By the time the New Deal ended in the 1930s there were still millions of people out of work. Business still had not fully recovered. But Roosevelt had raised the nation from despair. He said, "We have shown the world that democracy has within it the elements necessary to its own salvation."

Election of 1940

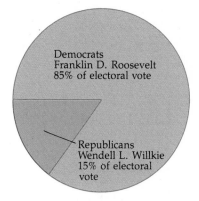

Democrats
Franklin D. Roosevelt
85% of electoral vote

Republicans
Wendell L. Willkie
15% of electoral vote

Election of 1944

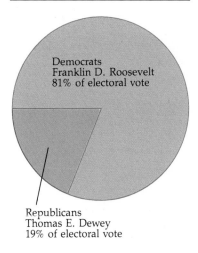

Democrats
Franklin D. Roosevelt
81% of electoral vote

Republicans
Thomas E. Dewey
19% of electoral vote

Section 4 Review

1. How did the New Deal strengthen organized labor?
2. What is a sit-down strike?

Critical Thinking

3. **Identifying Central Issues.** What were two criticisms of the New Deal in the late 1930s?

Heritage   Of the New Deal

The New Deal left a legacy of laws, federal responsibility for social welfare, and a strong and aggressive Presidency.

Critics and supporters of Franklin D. Roosevelt agree on at least one point: his Presidency gave the nation a lasting heritage. Roosevelt and the New Deal changed the federal government in three important ways.

A Long List of Laws

The New Deal introduced dozens of key laws that still guide the country today. Through Social Security most workers now save for retirement. The TVA sells power at a low price, manages lakes and rivers, and protects the soil in one region of the country. Land for national parks and forests has been set aside for coming generations.

Banking laws protect the savings of each citizen. The Wagner Act gives unions bargaining power, and another act states that factories and offices must be decent places in which to work. Laws governing the stock market keep investors from being tricked out of their money or stock. Farmers are sure to receive some help from the federal government when the price of their crops drops too low. The list of laws introduced in the 1930s and still working today goes on and on.

Government's Role in Social Welfare

The federal government played only a small part in the reform movements from 1830 to 1860. It played a much larger part during the Presidencies of Theodore Roosevelt and Woodrow Wilson. But in neither period was the federal government the main instrument of change.

During the New Deal, however, the federal government took the lead in almost all reforms. Unemployment and poverty gripped the country in the 1930s. These problems called for national rather than local or state solutions. Roosevelt once said that it is a "duty of the Federal government to keep its citizens from starving."

To feed the people and to put them back to work, Roosevelt spent huge sums of tax money. Some Presidents since Roosevelt have tried to cut government spending to lighten the tax load on citizens. But even today many people still look to the federal government for solutions to social problems.

The Modern Presidency

Roosevelt stretched the powers of the office of President and set an example for later Presidents. Most of the hundreds of laws adopted during the New Deal began in the executive branch. Members of the President's staff had the ideas, laid

Among the many benefits of the New Deal were Social Security payments to retired workers and better working conditions.

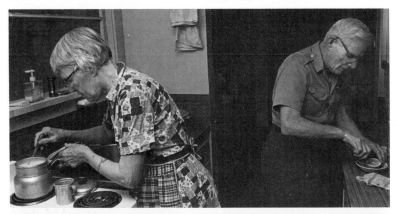

President Franklin Roosevelt appealed directly to the people in his fireside chats.

out plans of action, drew up bills, and worked with Congress to get the bills passed. Developing a legislative program has come to be expected of the President today.

The people were in favor of Roosevelt's programs, partly because he talked about them often with the people. His radio fireside chats reached every person willing to listen. A friend of Roosevelt wrote: "He was in a very special sense the people's President, because he made them feel that with him in the White House they shared the Presidency. The sense of sharing the Presidency gave even the most humble citizen a lively sense of belonging."

President Roosevelt's office was flooded with mail from all over the country. Before Roosevelt, a single person handled all the mail coming to the White House. Within months after Roosevelt took office fifty mail clerks were needed. Today hundreds of people handle the White House mail.

Roosevelt also spoke to the public through news or press conferences every two weeks. Reporters were invited into the President's office to ask questions, usually about New Deal plans or programs. The President became the number one newsmaker.

Roosevelt often used his public appeal to gain an edge over Congress. With the voters on his side Roosevelt could pressure senators and representatives into passing certain laws.

Stretching Too Far

Roosevelt also tried to stretch the power of the Presidency to influence the Supreme Court—the judicial branch. Roosevelt was annoyed when in 1936 the Supreme Court called certain laws of the New Deal unconstitutional. Many of the judges on the Supreme Court were over seventy years old. Roosevelt said that these "old men" were out of step with the times.

To stop the court from blocking New Deal laws, Roosevelt tried to increase the number of judges on the Supreme Court. His plan was to appoint one new judge for each judge over seventy years of age. Roosevelt planned to name new judges who favored the New Deal.

Though the plan was constitutional, the media called Roosevelt's bill "court packing." Even those who backed Roosevelt thought he was pushing his Presidential power too far. The plan failed. In the end the Supreme Court emerged with an even stronger sense of independence.

Roosevelt once said, "We Americans of today—all of us—we are characters in the living book of democracy." Though more chapters in American history are yet to be written, Roosevelt's New Deal and strong Presidency remain as important chapters in the "living book" of history.

The Supreme Court justices quashed some New Deal laws.

Chapter 33 Review

Chapter Summary

The economic depression that lasted for 10 years began in 1929. Many farmers lost their land. Drought turned much of the Great Plains into a Dust Bowl. By 1932 more than 13 million people were jobless. Yet President Hoover refused to set up federal relief programs for the unemployed.

In the presidential election of 1932, Democratic candidate Franklin D. Roosevelt promised a "new deal" for the American people. His New Deal programs provided federal relief payments for the needy and jobless. These programs included the CCC, PWA, WPA, AAA, the Wagner Act, and the Social Security Act.

During the 1930s a split developed between the AFL, which continued to represent workers mainly by craft or trade, and the CIO, which took in all workers in an industry. In many ways big labor became a counterforce to big business.

Reviewing Vocabulary

Match each of the following words with its correct definition. Write your answers on a separate sheet of paper.

relief	recovery
handicap	bargain
downturn	emergency
investment	sit-down strike
cycle	veteran
bonus	unemployment
retirement	unconstitutional

1. a decrease in business activity
2. a series of events that happen again from time to time, usually in the same order
3. a time when a worker is out of a job
4. money or goods given to help people without jobs, homes, or food
5. an upturn in business usually following a downturn
6. a payment for past military service
7. a person who has already served in a country's armed forces
8. a disability that makes doing certain tasks difficult or impossible
9. money loaned or spent to make a profit
10. an unexpected event calling for immediate action
11. not in agreement with the United States Constitution
12. the time in later life when a person stops working
13. a refusal to work by employees who continue to occupy their place of work

Understanding Main Ideas

1. How did President Hoover help jobless workers, farmers, and business owners in 1929 when an economic downturn began?
2. How did President Roosevelt's short-term measures ease the bank crisis and create more jobs?
3. How did long-range reforms and programs started during the New Deal help business, agriculture, and labor recover from the Depression?
4. How did unions in the United States gain power during the 1930s?
5. How did New Deal work programs differ from relief programs?

Critical Thinking Skills

1. **Making Comparisons.** How did Franklin Roosevelt's approach to dealing with the Great Depression differ from that of Herbert Hoover?
2. **Testing Conclusions.** Evaluate the following opinion: "Even if what Roosevelt

Social Studies Skills: Interpreting a Graph

Unemployment, 1929–1940 (in millions)

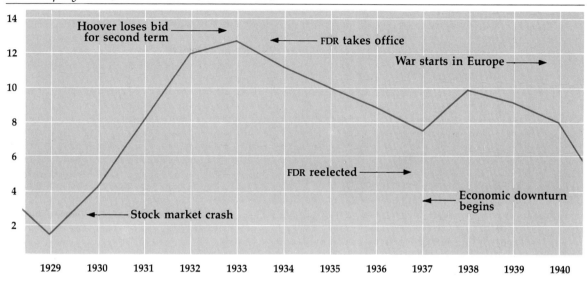

Study the line graph above which shows unemployment in the United States between 1929 and 1940.

Skill Review: Decide whether each of the following statements is true or false. Rewrite the false statements to make them true.

1. Unemployment grew steadily between 1929 and 1933.
2. Between 1933 and 1937, unemployed workers increased by about 6 million.
3. By 1940 the number of unemployed was 4 million lower than it had been in 1930.

---

does is wrong, the people are with him.'' What information in the chapter supports or contradicts this viewpoint?

3. **Formulating Questions.** What questions did New Deal policies raise about the role of the federal government in the lives of Americans?

Writing About History

Writing an Essay. Some people praise Franklin Roosevelt for pulling the American people out of the Great Depression. Others criticize Roosevelt for greatly expanding the role of the federal government. Choose one of these viewpoints and write a brief essay defending your position.

Your Region in History

Citizenship. Use the library and other community resources to find out how New Deal programs affected your community. Does your community have murals, buildings, parks, bridges, roads, or other projects completed by PWA or WPA workers? Prepare a bulletin-board display of pictures of such projects in your area.

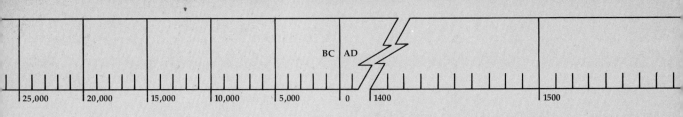

Leader
of the
Free World

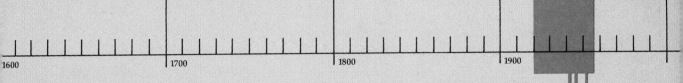

Vocabulary

policy
dictator
security
civilian
lend-lease
surrender
concentration camp
international
bloc
desegregation
loyalty
interdependence
pact
permanent
temporary

With the disappointing peace terms ending World War I and the trials of the Great Depression, the United States turned inward during the 1920s and 1930s. It followed a policy of isolationism—of keeping itself out of conflicts elsewhere, as much as possible.

The hardships of an economic depression had also weakened nations in Europe, Asia, and elsewhere. Despairing people in some of these nations turned to new leaders for direction. In return for promises of prosperity and worldwide glory for the homeland, these people gave their leaders almost limitless power. Some leaders became dictators, crushing democratic freedoms in their countries and assuming the powers of absolute rulers. These dictators then began to think about taking over neighboring lands.

Once again the world was torn by strife. Once again, despite its wish for neutrality, the United States was drawn into a world war. This time the United States became the leader of the free nations of the world.

Prereading

1. What efforts did the United States make to keep the peace after World War I and to avoid war once it had broken out again in Europe?
2. What strategies and tactics did the United States use in fighting World War II in Europe? In Asia?
3. What issues in foreign affairs kept United States leaders busy between 1945 and 1960?
4. What domestic issues kept United States leaders busy between 1945 and 1960?

1   Failure of a Lasting Peace

After World War I some critics said that European nations would not have been so willing to go to war if they had not had such

651

powerful armies. In the 1920s and 1930s many nations signed agreements to limit arms, respect one another's lands, and work together for peace.

Efforts to Avoid War

In the 1920s the United States took steps to cut back on its own military strength. It invited other nations to do the same. To this end, eight nations and the United States met in Washington in 1921. The United States, Britain, France, Japan, and Italy agreed to a Five-Power Treaty in 1922. Each nation would keep only a certain small number of battleships.

Two more security arrangements were signed about the same time. In the Four-Power Treaty of 1921 Japan, Britain, France, and the United States agreed to protect each other's possessions in the Pacific. In 1922 a Nine-Power Treaty guaranteed the boundaries of China and an Open Door policy there. Each of these treaties held out hope that the nations of the world wished to remain at peace. But each treaty had a serious flaw. None outlined the steps to be followed if the treaty were broken.

Though heading different types of governments, Germany's Adolf Hitler (top) and the Soviet Union's Joseph Stalin were both dictators.

The United States also hoped to work out a peaceful alliance with its neighbors to the south. In the 1920s the government had sent marines to Central and South American countries to settle disputes. These countries were angered by the interference of their giant northern neighbor.

President Herbert Hoover had started a so-called Good Neighbor policy toward Latin America. After taking office, President Franklin D. Roosevelt gave the idea a vigorous boost. Delegates to the International Conference of American States in 1933 agreed that "no State [nation] has a right to intervene in the internal or external affairs of another." Three years later President Roosevelt spoke out for mutual aid among all nations of the Western Hemisphere.

Outbreak of Fighting Abroad

The policy of good neighbors among nations of the Western Hemisphere contrasted with the keen rivalry among nations elsewhere. In country after country a single leader with a small group of close advisers came to power. In 1925 Benito Mussolini became the dictator in Italy. He wanted Italy to know again the glory it enjoyed in the old Roman Empire. Adolf Hitler, leading the Nazi party, gained control of Germany in early 1933. Hitler wished to win back the land lost by Germany after World War I. He also wanted to rule all of Europe—and one day the world. He believed that Germans were members of a super race and that Jews and dark-skinned peoples threatened the "purity" of that race. Millions of Jews were killed at the hands of the Nazis.

With the military help of Mussolini and Hitler, General Francisco Franco triumphed in a civil war in Spain and became dictator there in 1939. As early as 1929, Joseph Stalin headed the Communists, the ruling group in the Soviet Union. The Communists took over all factories and farms and provided food and goods for all citizens. But it also took from the people their freedom to choose where they would work and live.

At the same time, military leaders in Japan rose to power by murdering political leaders who opposed them. They planned to gain control in Asia and the islands of the Pacific—by conquest, if need be.

By 1930 the stage was set for violence as Hitler, Mussolini, and the Japanese leaders began their deadly march on other countries.

1931: Japan, without warning, took over Manchuria, an important Chinese manufacturing center on the Asian mainland.

1932: Japan set up its own puppet government in Manchuria.

1933: Hitler began to rebuild Germany's armed forces.

1935: Mussolini attacked defenseless Ethiopia in Africa and conquered it for Italy in 1936.

1936: Hitler sent German soldiers into the Rhineland, a neutral stretch of land between France and Germany.

1937: Japan swiftly moved into and took the Chinese capital city of Peking (Beijing).

1938: Hitler took Austria.

1939: Hitler marched into Czechoslovakia.

Problems of Strict Neutrality

After the Japanese entered Manchuria in 1931, Secretary of State Henry L. Stimson wanted the United States and other nations to stop the Japanese. But no one listened. The worldwide depression had turned each country's attention to its own troubles.

In 1935 the United States passed a Neutrality Act. The act forbade the United States to aid the defense of other neutral nations if they were attacked. It also outlawed the sale of United States war goods to any country. Later the United States refused to lend money to warring nations.

By late 1939 events in Europe caused the United States to take a second look at its stand on strict neutrality. In August, Germany and the Soviet Union agreed not to fight each other. On September 1, 1939, Hitler attacked Poland. Within weeks Poland was defeated, and its land was divided between Germany and the Soviet Union. France and Great Britain had warned Hitler that they would enter the war if Poland were attacked. Two days after the attack they kept their word, and World War II began.

Francisco Franco of Spain (top) and Benito Mussolini of Italy (center) came to power in the 1930s. Hirohito, emperor of Japan, was only a figurehead leader.

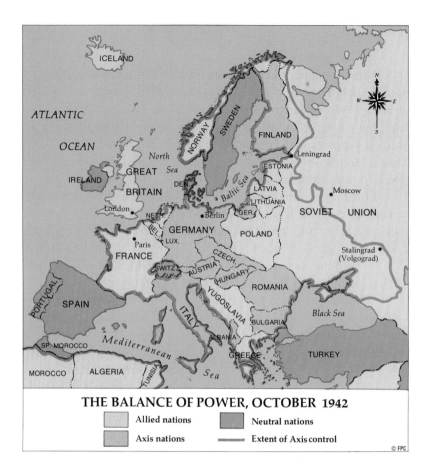

THE BALANCE OF POWER, OCTOBER 1942

Allied nations   Neutral nations

Axis nations   Extent of Axis control

© FPC

The Axis powers struck swiftly and occupied most of Europe and North Africa by September 1942.

Because of its treaty with the Soviet Union, Germany was able to direct all its military might against western Europe. In the spring of 1940 Hitler swept through the four neutral nations of Denmark, Norway, Belgium, and Holland. By June, Hitler had brought France to its knees and marched in victory into Paris. And in 1939–1941 Hitler helped Mussolini take over the Balkans, including Yugoslavia and Greece. Only Britain still stood free in western Europe.

The Brink of War

These events, especially the fall of France, stunned the United States. For the first time the people believed the United States was in grave danger. Strict neutrality was no longer possible. The United States and its American neighbors met and agreed to protect all lands in the Western Hemisphere. Congress voted to arm the nation, spending as much for military defense in 1940 as was spent during most of World War I. In 1940 Congress also passed the Selective Service Act to call men into the armed services.

In September 1940 President Roosevelt gave Britain fifty destroyers in exchange for bases in British Bermuda, Newfoundland, and the West Indies. Britain's leader, Winston Churchill, urged Roosevelt to go still further, but Roosevelt held back.

In the Atlantic Charter signed by President Franklin Roosevelt (seated left) and Prime Minister Winston Churchill (seated right) the United States and Britain declared themselves against tyranny and for peace and freedom.

In November 1940 Roosevelt was reelected for a third term, breaking the two-term precedent set by Washington. Many people expected Roosevelt to lead the nation through these war-troubled times as well as he had led them through the depression.

The storm of war began to darken the skies of Europe. Britain and Germany were locked in a battle of air power. Despite heavy losses the British still controlled the skies. Their pilots were guided by a new British invention called radar. Radar could detect German planes in flight long before they reached their target.

Unable to win the air war with Britain, Hitler decided not to invade the British mainland. Instead, he turned on the Soviet Union in June 1941, despite their treaty of friendship. At first the Soviets put up little or no fight. But in the winter of 1941–1942 they mounted a desperate defense of their major cities, especially Moscow and Stalingrad. The Soviets stopped the Germans after bitter fighting. The effort cost the Soviet Union the lives of millions of soldiers and civilians.

Meanwhile the United States stepped up its aid to Britain. Roosevelt asked Congress to accept a lend-lease plan under which countries fighting Germany, Italy, and Japan could borrow United States goods. After three months of debate the Lend-Lease Act passed.

Section 1 Review

1. Why did the United States sign treaties limiting military strength after World War I?
2. Which treaty limited the number of battleships built by Britain, the United States, France, Japan, and Italy?
3. What was the Good Neighbor policy?
4. What were the main goals of Germany's Adolf Hitler?
5. What were the terms of the Neutrality Act of 1935?

Critical Thinking

6. **Recognizing Cause and Effect.** Why did Japan attack the United States in 1941?

LOOKING AHEAD: What strategies and tactics did the United States use in fighting World War II in Europe? In Asia?

In 1944 metal tokens replaced paper stamps as the currency of wartime rationing.

United States vessels, protected by convoys of armed ships, carried the war goods to Britain. And in August 1941 Roosevelt and Churchill met on a United States cruiser to sign the Atlantic Charter. They pledged their two countries to stand for four freedoms: freedom from fear and want, and freedom of speech and worship. Little by little the United States drew closer to war.

Attack on Pearl Harbor

The final step toward war came out of events in the Pacific rather than in Europe. In September 1940 Japan had made an alliance with Germany and Italy. The group was known as the Axis powers. In 1941 the United States stopped shipping certain goods to Japan, especially oil. The embargo hurt Japan badly. Tensions between Japan and the United States mounted.

Early Sunday morning, December 7, 1941, the Japanese caught the United States off guard with an all-out attack on Pearl Harbor. Within hours Japanese planes had damaged most of the United States Pacific Fleet. Almost all the airplanes based in Hawaii were destroyed. Within a few months the Japanese had also taken most of Southeast Asia, including the great British ports of Hong Kong and Singapore. They captured the Philippine Islands and the Dutch East Indies, and were eyeing Australia. Their victories made them seem invincible.

2 The United States and World War II

On the day following the Japanese attack on Pearl Harbor, the United States declared war on Japan. Three days later the other Axis powers—Germany and Italy—declared war on the United States. In a message to Congress President Roosevelt said of the allied nations of Britain, the United States, and the Soviet Union, "We are going to win the war and we are going to win the peace that follows."

As in World War I, the whole nation joined the war effort. Factories open day and night turned out tanks, armed trucks, airplanes, and other supplies instead of goods for civilian use. The country produced twice as much steel and five times as much aluminum as it had before. Overall factory output tripled. Shipyards built freighters at top speed. More and more women joined the work force. All transportation was put to wartime use. Some foods were rationed. Wages, prices, and rents were controlled. The war touched everyone's life.

Strategy and Tactics

In the years before Pearl Harbor the top military leaders of the United States decided that if war broke out the United States must first defeat Germany. Even after the Japanese attack, the leaders held to their plan.

To defeat Germany, the United States first had to stop Germany's submarine attacks. In the early months of 1942 some eighty-two United States cargo ships were sunk along the northeastern coast of the United States. In June some 142 United States ships were sunk in the Caribbean. The United States fought back with powerful convoys and airplanes. And with remarkable speed the United States built new ships to replace those destroyed by the Germans. By 1943 the United States held the upper hand in the Atlantic.

Women welders, working on the third or swing shift, helped keep the nation's shipyards open twenty-four hours a day, seven days a week.

The War in North Africa and Europe

In October 1942 British and United States land forces stopped a march of German and Italian troops through Africa. German General Erwin Rommel and his soldiers were on their way to take over the Suez Canal. Soldiers under United States General Dwight D. Eisenhower and British General Bernard Montgomery surrounded Rommel's army, forcing surrender in May 1943. From then on Hitler gave up the idea of taking any new land and turned to defense.

In July 1943 the Allies captured Sicily—an Italian island in the Mediterranean Sea. Almost two months later they invaded Italy itself, using Sicily as a jumping-off place. Italy surrendered in September, two months after the overthrow of Mussolini, and supported the Allies. But the Germans fought on in Italy for two more years.

While the fighting went on in Italy, United States and British bombers ceaselessly pounded German cities and military bases from the air. These attacks gave the Allies control of the skies over western Europe. As Germany became weaker, the Allies grew stronger. For years the Allies had been planning the biggest military move yet—an invasion of Europe. After a great build-up of supplies, troops, and ships in England, D-Day arrived June 6, 1944. By this time the Soviets had won at home and were marching on Germany.

General Eisenhower, leader of the Allied forces, described what it was like before the attack:

> All southern England was one vast military camp, crowded with soldiers awaiting final word to go, and piled high with supplies and equipment awaiting transport to the far shore of the (English) Channel. . . . The mighty host [army] was tense as a coiled spring. . . .

The attack was launched. After a few weeks of heavy fighting the Allies broke through the German defenses to free France. The Allies took Paris in August 1944. More battles raged in the cruel winter months of 1944–1945. Finally, in March 1945, the Allies crossed the Rhine River into Germany.

657

Aircraft carriers (top) played a major role in the war in the Pacific. Soldiers of the Seventh Army, marching into Dachau, Germany, in April 1945, were greeted by 32,000 jubilant prisoners.

As the Allies approached from the west, the Soviets closed in from the east. By fall 1944 Soviet troops had reached the outskirts of Warsaw, Poland. After March 1945 the Soviets drew near Berlin, the capital of Germany, while the Allies took Germany's industrial heartland. On May 7, 1945, the Germans surrendered to the Allies. A few weeks before, Hitler had killed himself. But his deadly work was discovered by the Allied troops when they came upon concentration camps in Poland, Austria, and Germany. Among the 12 million killed in Nazi death camps were 6 million Jews who had been starved, tortured, and gassed to death. And millions of other Europeans had been forced to work as slaves for the Nazis. Though warned earlier about what Hitler was doing, the world was horrified.

Fighting in the Pacific

In the Pacific the Allied forces were made up mainly of Americans, with some Australians. Naval forces—especially aircraft carriers, the new weapon in World War II—proved to be the key in the Pacific theater of war.

The Allies won a major victory over the Japanese at the naval Battle of Midway in June 1942. This victory gave the Allies control of the Central Pacific.

About six months later Allied soldiers checked the Japanese advance in the Southwest Pacific islands of New Guinea and Guadalcanal. General Robert Eichelberger, who led the army in New Guinea, later described the war there as "a nightmare." Uniforms rotted in the wet climate. Food soon spoiled. Sick soldiers had to fight on because there were no replacements for them.

General Douglas MacArthur led United States and Australian forces across the Southwest Pacific to the Philippines in October 1944. Admiral Chester Nimitz led a second fighting force in the Central Pacific toward the home islands of Japan. The United States captured the Mariana Islands in the Central Pacific in June 1944. By fall, these islands had become a land base from which B-29 airplanes could bomb southern Japan. Meanwhile, many miles away, Allied troops were fighting the Japanese in Southeast Asia and China.

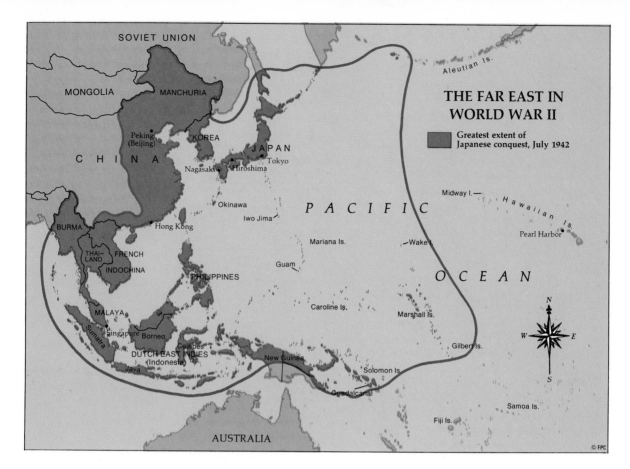

THE FAR EAST IN
WORLD WAR II

▮ Greatest extent of
Japanese conquest, July 1942

Island by island, Allied forces fought their way to the Marianas, where they built bases for bombers that could reach Japan.

After a strong warning to which the Japanese paid no attention, on August 6, 1945, the United States dropped the world's first atomic bomb on Hiroshima, Japan. Three days later the United States dropped a second bomb on Nagasaki, Japan. The two bombs laid waste the cities, killing thousands upon thousands of civilians. The course of war, as well as foreign policy, was now changed forever.

On August 15, 1945, the fighting ended. On September 2 General MacArthur accepted Japan's surrender in a meeting on the deck of the battleship *Missouri*.

The war that seemed to have no end was finally over. It had cost the lives of 250,000 American soldiers, 7 million European soldiers, and 1.5 million Japanese soldiers. Civilian losses were also great. The Soviet Union may have lost 12 million people. And those who died in concentration camps raise the numbers even higher.

President Roosevelt did not live to see the end of the war. He died suddenly on April 12, 1945, during his fourth term in office. Vice-President Harry S. Truman became President.

3 Postwar Foreign Issues

Two powerful nations came out of the Second World War—the United States and the Soviet Union. Germany, Japan, and Italy were

Section 2 Review

1. How did United States civilians take part in the war effort?
2. How did the United States deal with Germany's submarines?
3. Why was it important for the Allies to fight in Africa? In Italy?
4. What was D-Day?
5. Why were airplanes important to the war in the Pacific?

Critical Thinking

6. **Predicting Consequences.** Would the outcome of the war have been different if the United States had not used the atomic bomb? Why?

LOOKING AHEAD: What issues in foreign affairs kept United States leaders busy between 1945 and 1960?

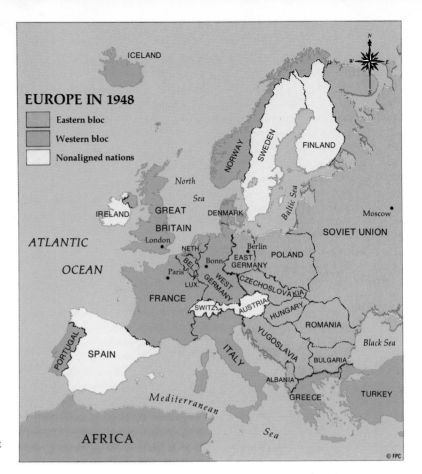

EUROPE IN 1948

Eastern bloc
Western bloc
Nonaligned nations

As the war ended, new lines were drawn in Europe between the Soviet satellite countries to the east and the allies of NATO to the west.

in ruins. Other major powers such as Britain were exhausted from six years of grinding conflict. In contrast, the Soviet Union, though worn out, had one of the mightiest armies in the world. And it now held many countries of Europe and Asia. The United States had the world's most powerful navy, one of the world's strongest armies, and an unequalled capacity for producing goods. Between 1948 and the early 1960s tensions between the United States and the Soviet Union surfaced in what became known as the Cold War.

The Yalta Agreement

Even before the war ended leaders from the Big Three—the United States, Britain, and the Soviet Union—met in Soviet Yalta to work out peace terms. The three nations decided to divide Germany, when defeated, into four separate zones. Each Big Three power would control one zone. France would control the fourth. They also agreed that the people of Poland, Hungary, and Romania—countries overrun by Germany and taken back by the Soviet Union—should vote on the kind of government they wanted. Finally, the Big Three agreed to form the United Nations, a new world organization to settle international disputes.

As it turned out, the Soviet Union refused to allow free elections in Eastern Europe. The Soviet Union said it needed to control these countries to protect its borders. The Soviets set up Communist

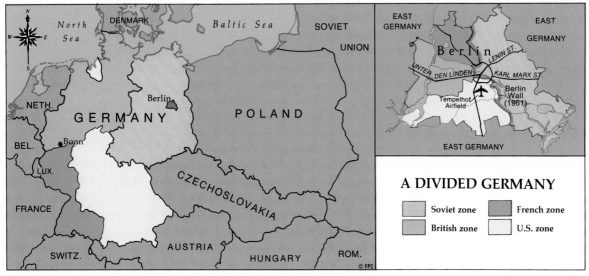

A DIVIDED GERMANY

Soviet zone   French zone

British zone   U.S. zone

Germany and its capital city Berlin were divided between the victors—the United States, the Soviet Union, Britain, and France.

governments in Poland, Hungary, Yugoslavia, and Romania over the protests of the United States and Great Britain. These Communist governments are still in power today, and together they make up the so-called eastern bloc.

The United Nations, however, was later formed as planned. At the conference held in San Francisco in April 1945 to set up the United Nations President Truman stated, "If we do not want to die together in war, we must learn to live together in peace."

Relations with Defeated Nations

The United States set the peace terms for Japan. General Douglas MacArthur carried them out. Japan's armed forces and secret police were disbanded. A new constitution was written that made Emperor Hirohito—a man once worshipped as a divine being—a mere figurehead in the government. The new constitution set up a democratic government and gave women the right to vote. The constitution also outlawed war.

With hard work the Japanese rebuilt their country. Today Japan is one of the most productive nations in the world, along with the United States and the Soviet Union.

All the Allies took part in setting the policy for defeated Germany. They formed an international court at Nuremberg, Germany. There they heard the frightening truth of how the Nazis treated the Jews and other people.

Together the Allies also carried out the four-part division of Germany agreed to at Yalta. Berlin, the capital of Germany before World War II, was also divided into four parts, even though it was located in the Soviet zone. The Soviets controlled only East Berlin.

In June 1948 the Soviet Union blocked the roads leading through eastern Germany to West Berlin to keep the western powers out of the capital. But the United States moved people and supplies into West Berlin by air to protect against a Soviet takeover. The Soviets finally lifted the blockade of Berlin in May 1949.

In April 1949 the United States, British, and French zones formed the nation of West Germany. The West Germans elected their own democratic government and called it the Federal Republic of Germany. Its constitution provides for active political parties.

The Soviets saw West Germany as a threat to the Soviet zone. So in 1949 the Soviets formed the nation of East Germany. It is called the German Democratic Republic.

The Marshall Plan

In 1947 President Truman offered full support to all free peoples who would resist Communist takeover. The Truman Doctrine was part of a larger United States plan to keep the Soviet Union within the boundaries agreed to in 1947. The United States feared that hard times in France, Italy, and other war-torn European countries might turn the people toward communism.

To help the free nations, the United States backed the Marshall Plan of 1947. George C. Marshall, former chief of staff of the army, had become secretary of state. Under his plan the United States offered money to help the countries of Europe get started again.

The nations of the Soviet bloc turned down the plan, but many other countries submitted lists of their recovery needs. Congress voted the money, and United States taxpayers bore the whole cost. In return the United States expected its friendly allies to help it keep the peace. The Marshall Plan became a keystone in Western Europe's struggle back to economic health.

Hostilities in Asia

The same idea that led to the Marshall Plan also led President Truman to send United States troops to Asia in 1950. He wanted to stop the spread of communism. It began in 1949 when Communists in China overthrew the Nationalist Chinese government and set up the People's Republic of China. The Nationalist government retreated to the tiny island of Formosa, now called Taiwan.

In 1950 the Communist government of North Korea, backed by both the Soviet Union and the People's Republic, sent troops into South Korea. The United Nations called for the defense of South Korea. Leaders of the UN feared that another world war might break out. They also feared the spread of communism. The United States answered the call.

Led by General Douglas MacArthur, combined United States and United Nations forces finally stopped the North Koreans in South Korea and pushed them back within their own borders. MacArthur then pushed on into North Korea. The Chinese Communists rushed to the defense of their ally. The two sides fought on for two years. In July 1953 everyone finally agreed to a truce.

President Harry Truman(left) recalled General Douglas MacArthur from Korea in 1951.

Section 3 Review

1. What was the Cold War?
2. What three decisions reached at Yalta affected postwar Europe?
3. Name three policies the United States set for postwar Japan.
4. What was the Truman Doctrine?

Critical Thinking

5. **Identifying Central Issues.** How did the Marshall Plan contain communism in Europe?

LOOKING AHEAD: What domestic issues kept United States leaders busy between 1945 and 1960?

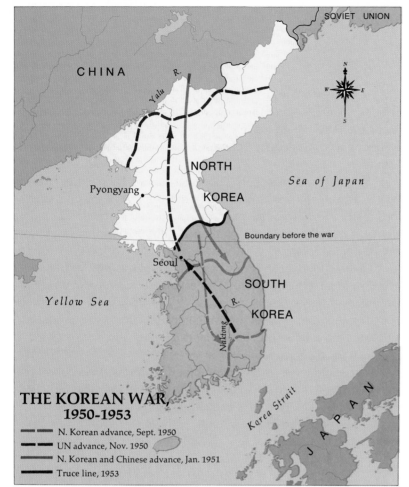

THE KOREAN WAR, 1950-1953

---- N. Korean advance, Sept. 1950
▬ ▬ UN advance, Nov. 1950
—— N. Korean and Chinese advance, Jan. 1951
▬▬ Truce line, 1953

The United States acted not as a country at war but as a fighting arm of the United Nations in Korea.

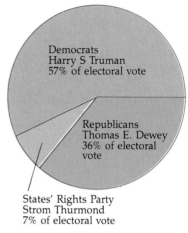

Election of 1948

Democrats
Harry S Truman
57% of electoral vote

Republicans
Thomas E. Dewey
36% of electoral vote

States' Rights Party
Strom Thurmond
7% of electoral vote

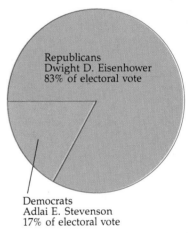

Election of 1952

Republicans
Dwight D. Eisenhower
83% of electoral vote

Democrats
Adlai E. Stevenson
17% of electoral vote

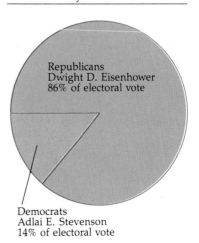

Election of 1956

Republicans
Dwight D. Eisenhower
86% of electoral vote

Democrats
Adlai E. Stevenson
14% of electoral vote

4 Postwar Issues at Home

Truman shouldered a heavy burden when he took over the Presidency after the death of Roosevelt. But he was scrappy and tough. He let people know he didn't duck the hard decisions by being a buck passer. A sign on his desk read "The buck stops here." Truman was elected President in his own right in 1948 in a close contest with Republican Thomas E. Dewey, governor of New York.

In 1952 Republican Dwight D. Eisenhower, the much-admired general of World War II, was elected President, defeating Democrat Adlai Stevenson of Illinois. Eisenhower served two terms. Truman and Eisenhower faced many of the same problems in office.

From War to Peace

When World War II ended, business boomed as Americans started buying the goods they had done without for so long. Many of the 15 million veterans of the armed services and even wartime workers found peacetime jobs, thanks to help from Congress.

Veterans of World War II and later conflicts were given many benefits. While looking for jobs, veterans could receive aid if they needed it. They could borrow money at low interest rates to build homes or buy businesses. Veterans could also get money to attend school.

Workers and managers had much to work out after World War II. During the war, wages had been frozen. At war's end, prices rose faster than workers' pay. Union members struck for more money. They also wanted long-term health and hospital insurance and retirement plans.

In 1947 the Republican Congress passed the Taft-Hartley Act over President Truman's veto. This act greatly limited the power of the unions. Many workers called it a "slave labor bill."

Farmers also had reasons to complain. They were producing far more than ever before. But farmers felt they were not receiving a fair price for their crops.

The nation was troubled by other problems. President Truman's answer to all these issues was a program in 1949 that he called the Fair Deal. The Fair Deal called for:

1. Repeal of the Taft-Hartley Act.
2. A higher minimum wage.
3. Government support for farm prices.
4. A housing program.
5. A civil rights program.

Republicans in Congress fought against much of the Fair Deal. But parts of the plan were carried out. The minimum wage was raised. The National Housing Act helped cities clear slums and build low-income housing. And more people received Social Security.

Farmers received some help from the government in the form of a price support plan. If a farmer could not sell crops to a buyer at a certain price, the government would buy the crops at a high percentage of that price. In exchange, farmers agreed to leave some land unplanted. Having fewer goods on the market would drive prices up. Farmers wanted even higher price supports, but neither Truman nor Eisenhower favored such a law.

When Eisenhower took office in 1953, he slowed down government spending on Fair Deal programs. The housing program was limited to one year. Cuts were made in taxes as well as government spending at home and abroad.

Minority Rights

During the Second World War the government sent about 110,000 persons of Japanese descent to ten guarded relocation camps. About two thirds of these people who lived on the West Coast were citizens, having been born in the United States. But the government feared that they might help the enemy. Not one single case of disloyalty, however, was ever discovered among them.

Those held in camps returned to their homes after the war. They needed to find jobs, rebuild their businesses, relearn old skills, or learn new skills. Those who owned property often found it run down after years of neglect. The government offered to pay part of their losses. But most people collected only about ten cents for each dollar lost.

After the war, many blacks were still denied their civil rights under the Constitution. In 1948 President Truman ordered all the armed services to end segregation and to offer blacks equal opportunity for higher rank and pay.

During Eisenhower's term the 1954 Supreme Court decided in *Brown* v. *Board of Education of Topeka* that communities could no longer have separate schools for blacks and whites. All nine justices on the Court agreed. This landmark decision overturned the "separate but equal" ruling of 1896 in *Plessy* v. *Ferguson*. School systems began planning for integration.

The Court ordered that desegregation be undertaken "with all deliberate speed." A storm of protest arose in the South. In a few cases federal troops or marshals were used to protect black students entering white schools. Desegregation was begun.

Though innocent of any wrongdoing, Japanese-Americans were confined to relocation camps during World War II.

Loyalty Oaths

During the Cold War many people began to fear that Communists held important positions in the federal government. Some even wanted every federal jobholder to take a "loyalty oath." Truman finally set up a loyalty board in 1947. Out of 3 million federal employees, only about 200 were fired for disloyalty.

During Eisenhower's term some politicians, especially Senator Joseph McCarthy of Wisconsin, used the loyalty issue to make wild, false charges. McCarthy cried that there were "200 card-carrying Communists" in the state department. Such claims were later found not true. But many scared people believed him—at least for a time.

McCarthy even attacked President Eisenhower. In a televised public hearing his charges were proved false. In 1954 the Senate censured—that is, condemned—the way McCarthy had behaved.

The charges McCarthy made were a sign that many United States citizens feared the power of the Soviet Union. After World War II the United States and the Soviet Union stood out as the two strongest nations in the world. The United States gathered its allies from among the western bloc nations. The Soviet Union had its allies in Eastern Europe. The postwar struggle to keep a balance of power between the United States and the Soviet Union, and their allies, continued into the sixties.

Section 4 Review

1. Name three points that were part of Truman's Fair Deal.
2. How did Japanese-Americans suffer from the way they were treated during and after World War II?
3. How did government try to right the wrongs suffered by blacks?
4. Why were charges of disloyalty made against government employees in the 1950s?

Critical Thinking

5. **Expressing Problems Clearly.** What have been the central problems in foreign policy in the postwar years?

Heritage   Of International Leadership

More than ever before, the United States and other nations are working together for mutual defense and economic well-being.

Goods from the United States are found everywhere in the world. And goods in the United States, like the people themselves, come from almost every other country on earth. Moreover, each year millions of United States citizens travel to other countries, and millions of citizens from other countries come to the United States.

The people of the world have become aware of the need for interdependence. The United States, as a large and powerful nation, is a leader in this movement toward interdependence.

Defense Pacts

The threat of nuclear war became real when the Soviet Union in 1949 became the second nation after the United States to build an atomic bomb. Under the threat of nuclear war friendly nations began to band together.

In 1949 the countries of Western Europe formed the North Atlantic Treaty Organization (NATO). The United States not only joined NATO but also put up more soldiers and weapons than any other country. Under NATO all members agreed to defend each other.

In 1955 the Soviet Union answered NATO with the Warsaw Pact. The Soviet Union and countries in Eastern Europe such as East Germany and Poland agreed to fight together in the event of an attack.

Both the Soviet Union and the United States have signed other defense pacts with countries elsewhere in the world.

The United Nations

While mutual defense pacts promise aid after an attack, the United Nations (UN) works to head off outbreaks of war. It also encourages fair dealing among nations.

To carry out its goals, the United Nations has six main bodies. The two bodies most often involved in international disputes are the General Assembly and the Security Council. All member nations are seated in the General Assembly. The Assembly hears each country's grievances and arguments.

The Security Council decides what course of action to follow

Delegates from fifteen nations sit on the Security Council and decide issues of world peace.

American and Soviet guards face each other daily at various checkpoints along the border in Berlin.

when peace is threatened. The Council is made up of permanent and temporary members. The five permanent members are the United States, the Soviet Union, Britain, France, and the People's Republic of China. Ten additional members are chosen for two-year terms. The veto of any permanent member can block action by the Security Council.

The remaining bodies of the UN promote human rights and higher standards of living. They also settle legal disputes among nations and watch over new countries as they develop self-rule. One UN agency fights hunger by helping developing nations grow more food.

The United States plays a leading role in the United Nations. It was first in the fight to stop North Korea from taking South Korea. It puts up much of the money to further self-help in developing nations. Its representatives speak out for human freedom.

Economic Ties

The United States also plays a big part in the World Bank, which lends money to developing countries. The United States sends food to hungry peoples around the world. It trades with countries that have their own marketing groups. Among these are the ten nations of Western Europe that form the Common Market. These ten countries exchange certain goods freely without tariff charges. Other countries have formed trading groups similar to the Common Market. The United States trades with each of them.

Energy Ties

One part of the world, the Middle East, has become more and more important in trade around the globe. Before World War II much of the Middle East was governed by European empires. After the war, newly independent countries began to take shape there.

The new nation of Israel, founded in the Middle East in 1948, became a homeland for many Jews who had been driven out of Europe by the Nazis.

Many Arab nations in the Middle East, however, were against the creation of Israel. They believed the land belonged to the Arabs who were living there. Bitter fights broke out, and relations are still tense today. The United States has tried to help settle these differences and promote lasting peace.

OPEC

The United States has its own reasons for wanting peace in the Middle East. The Middle East produces more oil than any other region. Industrial nations, including the United States, depend on oil to run most of their factories.

In 1960 five Arab nations formed the Organization of Petroleum Exporting Countries (OPEC). In the 1970s OPEC took complete control of producing and pricing Middle Eastern oil.

The United States and other nations need oil from the Middle East as fuel for their homes and factories. If Middle Eastern oil wells are shut down, all nations will suffer. Dependence on the Middle East for oil tests international cooperation time and time again.

Since World War II the United States has made many efforts to keep peace in the world community. In these efforts the United States has recognized that peace for one means peace for all.

Members of the Organization of Petroleum Exporting Countries meet regularly to decide how much oil to sell for how much money.

Chapter 34 Review

Chapter Summary

After World War I, aggressive dictators rose to power in Germany, Italy, and the Soviet Union. In 1935, Italy attacked and conquered Ethiopia, and Germany marched into the Rhineland in 1936. War in Europe finally broke out in 1939 when Germany attacked Poland.

The United States had declared its neutrality in 1935. By 1940, however, the United States was sending needed materials to the Allies through the Lend-Lease Act. On December 7, 1941, Japan made a surprise attack on Pearl Harbor. The attack left President Roosevelt no choice but to ask Congress to declare war and join the Allies in the fight against the Axis nations. Four years later, in May 1945, Germany surrendered. Japan surrendered in August 1945, shortly after President Truman gave the order to drop two atomic bombs—one on Hiroshima and one on Nagasaki.

Following the war, the United States aided the war-torn nations in Europe through the Marshall Plan. At home, General Eisenhower was elected President. Post-war issues included the Supreme Court decision in the case of *Brown* v. *Board of Education* which ended segregation. The fifties also saw the McCarthy hearings and the development of the Cold War.

Reviewing Vocabulary

Choose the word that best completes each sentence. Write your answers on a separate sheet of paper.

1. A (*policy/pact*) is a course of action based on the goals of a group or government.
2. The Soviet Union set up a (*concentration camp/bloc*) of nations with Communist governments in Eastern Europe.
3. After months of debate, Congress accepted a (*lend-lease/surrender*) plan which allowed the Allies to borrow United States goods.
4. Even before the war ended, the Big Three powers agreed to form a world organization for the purpose of settling (*national/international*) disputes.
5. A person not serving in a country's armed forces is a (*dictator/civilian*).
6. A landmark Supreme Court decision in 1954 ordered (*desegregation/interdependence*) in the nation's schools.
7. During the Cold War some people wanted all federal jobholders to take a (*loyalty/security*) oath stating they were true to their country.
8. A veto by any (*permanent/temporary*) member of the United Nations can block action by the Security Council.

Understanding Main Ideas

1. How did the United States try to keep the peace after World War I and avoid war once it had broken out again in Europe?
2. What strategies and tactics did the United States use to defeat Germany? To defeat Japan?
3. How did United States leaders deal with foreign affairs between 1945 and 1960?
4. How did United States leaders deal with domestic issues between 1945 and 1960?

Critical Thinking Skills

1. **Recognizing Cause and Effect.** Would the United States have entered World War II if Japan had not attacked the Pacific Fleet at Pearl Harbor? What other events caused the United States to reconsider its neutrality?

Social Studies Skills: Interpreting a Political Cartoon

The cartoon at the right appeared in 1947 when George C. Marshall proposed a plan to aid free nations in Europe.

Skill Review: Interpret the cartoon by selecting the answer that best completes each of the following statements.

1. The cartoonist compares the situation in Western Europe to a race between
   (a) the President and Congress
   (b) Congress and communism
   (c) communism and chaos.
2. The cartoonist thinks that communism
   (a) will throw a monkey wrench into Western Europe's recovery
   (b) will make Western Europe happy
   (c) will increase Europe's population.
3. The cartoonist is in favor of
   (a) communism
   (b) isolationism
   (c) quick approval of the Marshall Plan by the United States Congress.

Roy Justus. *The Minneapolis Star*, 1947.

4. Congress is called a doctor because
   (a) many members are doctors
   (b) communism is considered a sickness
   (c) Congress can save Europe with foreign aid just as doctors can save sick people with medicine.

---

2. **Identifying Alternatives.** What course of action did Truman follow to end the war against Japan? What alternatives might he have chosen? What advantages did Truman's decision have over other choices?
3. **Recognizing Bias.** How did treatment of Japanese-Americans and blacks in the 1940s represent violations of minority rights?

Writing About History

1. **Writing a Slogan.** World War II represented an all-out effort on the home front as well as on the battle front. Write a slogan or design a poster encouraging citizens to help the war effort.

2. **Writing Newspaper Headlines.** Choose ten events from this chapter and write a newspaper headline for each one. Be sure to include a date for each headline. Then arrange the headlines in chronological order to present an overview of the time period. Choose one headline and write a brief newspaper article.

Your Region in History

Citizenship. Invite World War II veterans from your community to speak to your class. Prepare questions about where the veterans served, conditions at home and on the battle front during the war, and how patriotism affected the war effort.

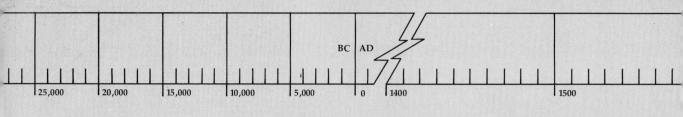

Only Yesterday

☙ Chapter 35

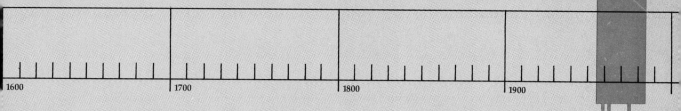

1600	1700	1800	1900	

T HE DECADES OF THE 1960s, the 1970s, and into the 1980s may seem a long time ago to you. But to a historian they are only yesterday. The events of those decades are almost too near in time for historians to judge without bias.

Yet the patterns and trends that emerged after World War II continued into the 1960s, the 1970s, and in the 1980s. In foreign affairs Communists and non-Communists competed for influence, sometimes with arms. One by one nations in Africa and Asia broke free from colonial rule and set up their own governments. The superpowers—the United States and the Soviet Union—competed with each other to win the new nations as allies. In domestic affairs the struggle for equal rights for all citizens continued—with some lasting victories. And the struggle to create a government that is honest and responsive to all citizens still makes front-page headlines today.

1 Kennedy in Office

With World War II soldiers returning to peacetime life back home, there was an increased number of births in the mid-1940s—a baby boom. Growing families began to move outside the city. Nine million people moved to the suburbs between 1947 and 1954. Cities

Vocabulary

missile	demonstrator
pollution	busing
minority	scandal
volunteer	pardon
integration	bicentennial
equality	energy
protest	inflation
perestroika	*glasnost*
supply-side economics	
Strategic Defense Initiative	

Prereading

1. What responses did President Kennedy make to Cold War moves by Communist nations? What gains were part of his New Frontier program at home?

2. What gains of Johnson's Great Society were overshadowed by ever-greater United States involvement in Vietnam?

3. What events of the Nixon years left the nation confused and divided?

4. What problems at home and abroad have United States Presidents faced since 1976?

once surrounded by prairies or farmlands soon were surrounded by suburbs. Throughout the nation suburbs of one city began to reach as far as suburbs of another city. These unbroken urban areas were called megalopolises (meg′ə·läp′ə·ləs·əz).

The generally good economic times of the 1960s allowed many people plenty of free time. Watching television became a favorite pastime. By 1960, 50 million homes had television sets. Besides entertainment, television brought news from home and around the world into everyone's living room. Television, in fact, played an important part in who won the 1960 election.

The Election of 1960

The Presidential election of 1960 was between two young men. Democrat John F. Kennedy was forty-three years old. Republican Richard M. Nixon was forty-seven. Not since President Theodore Roosevelt had the nation elected anyone to that office who was still in his forties. Kennedy, however, was not well known. Nixon, who had been Eisenhower's Vice-President for eight years, was better known. But Nixon was not wholly accepted by all members of his party. Both candidates had served in the House of Representatives. Both had gone on to win seats in the Senate.

The early political polls put Nixon well ahead of Kennedy, who was a Catholic. Those who favored Kennedy feared that he would lose votes because of his religion. As the campaign wore on, however, Kennedy attracted a broad range of support, mainly because of television.

The two candidates met in a series of four televised debates. For the first time in history Americans had a chance to see both Presidential candidates together on television. Surveys showed that many voters switched to Kennedy after seeing the debates. On election day Kennedy won—but by only 118,000 votes out of the more than 68 million votes cast.

The Cold War Near Home

In 1959 Fidel Castro had led a Communist overthrow of the dictator-controlled government in Cuba. Many anti-Castro Cubans fled to the United States. Cuba—only 90 miles (144 km) from Florida—became the first Communist government in the Americas. The United States, hoping to weaken Cuba, cut off all trade. The Soviet Union, however, stepped up its trade with the new Communist country.

The United States secretly began to help Cubans living in the Americas to take their country back from the Communists. Under Eisenhower the Central Intelligence Agency (CIA) trained these Cubans, hoping they would set off a general revolt in Cuba against Castro. When Kennedy took office, he continued the plan. About

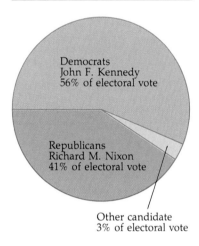

Election of 1960

Democrats
John F. Kennedy
56% of electoral vote

Republicans
Richard M. Nixon
41% of electoral vote

Other candidate
3% of electoral vote

Presidential candidates Richard M. Nixon (left) and John F. Kennedy faced off in a series of television debates before the American public in 1960.

1,400 trained anti-Castro Cubans invaded Cuba at the Bay of Pigs on April 17, 1961. Three days later the world and the citizens of the United States knew the effort to overthrow Castro had failed.

A second Cuban crisis arose in 1962. Photographs taken by American spy planes showed that the Soviet Union was building missile sites on the island. Nuclear missiles launched from those bases could easily reach any target in the United States.

Kennedy sent an urgent message to Soviet leaders telling them to remove the missiles. He also had United States diplomats take their evidence of Soviet bases in Cuba to the United Nations. And, most important, he ordered a naval blockade of Cuba to stop Soviet ships from delivering more missile parts to the island.

For a few days the nation—and the world—held its breath. What would the Soviet ships do when they reached the blockade? The ships got closer and closer. At the last minute they turned back and avoided a showdown. The Soviet Union agreed to remove the missile sites if the United States would lift the naval blockade and promise not to invade Cuba again. But Castro's government has kept its Communist ties to this day.

The Cold War Abroad

Only four months after the Bay of Pigs invasion another crisis arose in Berlin. For years many East Germans had been fleeing—against their government's wishes—to West Germany where they believed life was better. Most escaped by way of the divided city of Berlin. In August 1961 East Germans built the Berlin Wall. This mass of concrete and barbed wire totally separated East and West Berlin. Armed

When the Soviet Union built the Berlin Wall, President Kennedy sent armed troops to the city.

Section 1 Review

1. What factors helped John F. Kennedy win the election of 1960?
2. Why did President Kennedy order a naval blockade of Cuba?
3. Why did East Germany build the Berlin Wall?
4. Name four achievements of President Kennedy's New Frontier program.

Critical Thinking

5. **Demonstrating Reasoned Judgement.** Which of Kennedy's achievements do you consider most significant? Why?

LOOKING AHEAD: What gains of Johnson's Great Society were overshadowed by ever-greater United States involvement in Vietnam?

guards with shoot-to-kill orders kept watch day and night to stop East Germans from escaping.

The United States sent American troops to West Berlin. Kennedy's move showed his support for the non-Communist part of the city. President Kennedy told the people of West Germany that he would not allow the Communists to take over West Berlin. Two years later he was warmly welcomed when he visited West Berlin.

The New Frontier

Kennedy called for changes at home as part of his so-called New Frontier program, but Congress refused to pass many of them. Congress turned down medical aid for the aged, federal aid to education, and a new cabinet department for urban affairs and housing. Kennedy did win a higher minimum wage and better Social Security benefits. Kennedy also gained funds for mental health and for control of water pollution.

President Kennedy also brought about changes in civil rights, though Congress rejected a new, sweeping civil rights bill. Under Attorney General Robert Kennedy—the President's brother—the Justice Department enforced the *Brown v. Board of Education of Topeka* decision to integrate public schools. It also ruled against states that tried to keep blacks from voting. President Kennedy himself named a number of blacks to high offices. He also set up an agency to help employers hire more minority workers. And when some southern universities refused to admit blacks, President Kennedy called out federal police officers and the National Guard to guarantee their rights under the law.

The New Frontier reached beyond the country's borders. The Peace Corps, begun in 1961, still sends volunteers around the world to help people with programs in education, medicine, and farming.

After the Soviets took the lead in exploring space in the late 1950s, Kennedy started Project Apollo. Its goal was to put an American on the moon "before the decade is out." On July 20, 1969, while Richard Nixon was President, U.S. astronaut Neil A. Armstrong became the first person to walk on the moon.

2 Johnson and the Politics of Protest

On November 22, 1963, President Kennedy was shot and killed while riding in an open car through Dallas, Texas. Vice-President Lyndon B. Johnson became President. Johnson had served in the House and Senate for more than twenty years. He had been the majority leader in the Senate before becoming Vice-President. Now he entered the Presidency as the result of an assassin's bullets.

The Great Society

Johnson was as skilled a politician as ever entered the White House. He knew how to get people to vote his way. He persuaded Congress to pass many of the New Frontier bills that it had turned down earlier. Not since Franklin Roosevelt had a President moved laws through Congress so easily.

In 1964 Johnson swept to victory as President by a large vote over Republican Senator Barry M. Goldwater of Arizona. With Americans clearly behind him Johnson went to work on his Great Society, as it was called. His plans went much further than those of Kennedy's New Frontier. Johnson's war on poverty promised a better life for the poor.

Under Johnson, the laws poured out of Congress. Medicare offered older people help in paying their medical bills. The Manpower Development and Training Act gave workers a chance to prepare for better jobs. The food stamp program helped needy families pay for food. The Economic Opportunity Act of 1964 set up programs such as Head Start for preschool children, Upward Bound for college students, and Volunteers in Service to America (VISTA), a kind of Peace Corps for the United States. Federal aid to education went up sharply. The cabinet-level Department of Housing and Urban Development (HUD) was formed. Federal money flowed into the cities to help improve run-down neighborhoods.

Gains in Civil Rights

In 1964 President Johnson succeeded where Kennedy had failed by getting Congress to pass the Civil Rights Act. This act protected the voting rights of blacks. It outlawed segregation in such public places as restaurants and hotels. It gave the federal government the power to act in the integration of public schools. It denied federal money to public institutions that refused to serve anyone because of race. And it required private companies to open their job offers to members of minority groups.

A year later Johnson pushed through the Voting Rights Act of 1965. This gave the federal government the power to watch over voter registration in places where blacks and other minorities were being denied their voting rights. Soon more blacks began voting in the South.

Johnson also appointed blacks to high government posts. Robert C. Weaver, who headed HUD, became the first black cabinet member. Thurgood Marshall was the first black to serve on the Supreme Court.

Johnson was not alone in the fight for equality. Hundreds of thousands of people, both black and white, had been working hard

Vice-President Lyndon Johnson took over as President when Kennedy was assassinated in 1963. He guided the nation through a series of sweeping social reforms.

Election of 1964

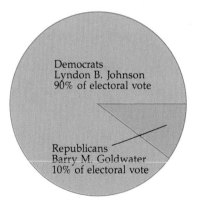

Democrats
Lyndon B. Johnson
90% of electoral vote

Republicans
Barry M. Goldwater
10% of electoral vote

Martin Luther King, Jr., (second from left) and his wife Coretta marched side by side from Selma to Montgomery, Alabama, in 1965 to support black voting rights.

for many years to bring about reform. Black leaders, especially Martin Luther King, Jr., led demonstrations, marches, and "freedom rides" through the South to bring the issues to national attention. The peaceful black marchers, however, were often jeered by white crowds and sometimes turned back by police with clubs, snarling dogs, and fire hoses. Attacks against blacks were common. And prejudice was as strong in many parts of the North as it was in Alabama or Mississippi.

Despite the new laws, change came slowly. In the mid-1960s some blacks, angered by the delays, rioted in cities all over the country. The shooting, burning, and looting began in Harlem—New York City's black ghetto—in the summer of 1964. In 1965 riots broke out in Watts, a section of Los Angeles, California. By 1967 a dozen cities had been torn by violence. When Martin Luther King, Jr., was shot and killed in 1968, the shock and horror set off a new wave of riots. Hundreds of people were killed, thousands were hurt, and millions of dollars worth of property was destroyed.

President Johnson's civil rights programs and his war on poverty offered some help to all disadvantaged Americans. But the promise of the Great Society seemed to fade away as the United States slipped deeper and deeper into the war between North and South Vietnam.

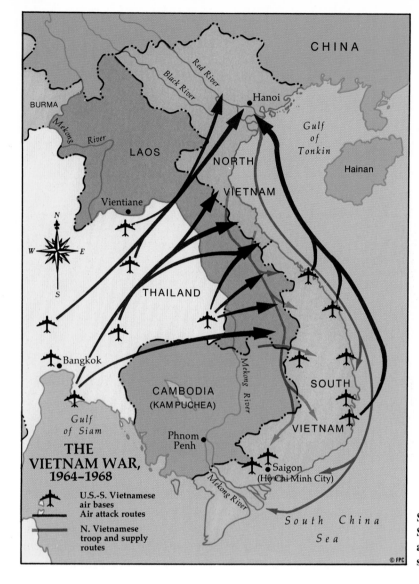

THE
VIETNAM WAR,
1964–1968

✈ U.S.-S. Vietnamese
air bases
━━ Air attack routes

━━ N. Vietnamese
troop and supply
routes

**South Vietnam and the United
States fought a jet-age air war
against North Vietnam's guerrilla-
style ground war.**

The Vietnam War

Vietnam, along with Laos and Cambodia, was once a French colony.
When Vietnam overthrew the French, the country was torn by civil
war between Communists in the north and non-Communists in the
south. The conflict stirred up some of the same fears that the Korean
conflict had. During the Eisenhower years the United States sent
some 650 military "advisers" and large amounts of money to South
Vietnam. Kennedy increased the number of military persons there to
more than 4,000.

Under Johnson the United States became far more involved in
Vietnam, though war was never officially declared. In 1964 Congress
said Johnson could use military force to defend Americans in Vietnam. Johnson used this power to order bombing raids on North
Vietnam and to send more soldiers to South Vietnam. By 1968 Johnson had sent more than 536,000 troops to Vietnam and had begun
drafting many more.

The nation's deep military involvement in Vietnam provoked strong antiwar feelings in the people back home.

As casualties mounted on both sides, many people began to criticize Johnson's handling of Vietnam. Before long the nation was divided into "doves," those who were against the war, and "hawks," those who were for it. Thousands of people joined peace marches and rallies protesting the war.

Election of 1968

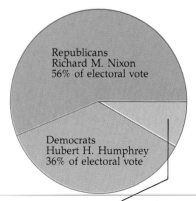

Republicans
Richard M. Nixon
56% of electoral vote

Democrats
Hubert H. Humphrey
36% of electoral vote

American Independent Party
George C. Wallace
8% of electoral vote

The Election of 1968

Differences between the hawks and doves greatly affected the 1968 election. In March 1968 Senator Eugene McCarthy, a dove, announced that he would run against Johnson for the Democratic Presidential nomination. A few days later Robert Kennedy announced that he, too, would run for the nomination. Kennedy had bowed out as attorney general a year after his brother's death and was serving as senator from New York. On March 31 President Johnson surprised the nation when he announced in a television speech that he would not run again.

In the following month Vice-President Hubert H. Humphrey became a third major Democratic candidate. Humphrey began to pick up votes from loyal party members.

In a mass outpouring of feelings and frustrations, 300,000 young Americans gathered at Bethel, New York, for the Woodstock Music and Art Fair in August 1969.

Then, on June 6, Robert Kennedy—like his brother before him and like Martin Luther King, Jr.—was assassinated. The fight for the nomination was now between McCarthy, an opponent of the war, and Vice-President Humphrey.

Chicago, where the Democratic national convention was held that summer, became a battleground. Fearing trouble from antiwar demonstrators, Chicago's Mayor Richard J. Daley refused to allow them to hold a public meeting. He also filled the streets with police dressed in riot gear. The National Guard was called out, and the convention hall was ringed by armed guards and barbed wire. While delegates inside the hall chose a Presidential nominee, police and demonstrators fought in the streets. Demonstrators threw stones and bottles at the police. The police used tear gas against the crowds and clubbed anyone who got in their way. Each side blamed the other for the fighting.

The Democrats selected Humphrey as their nominee. The Republicans, in a less stormy meeting, chose Richard M. Nixon. A third-party candidate—George Wallace, former governor of Alabama—entered the race. Nixon won in a close election.

3 The Resignation of a President

The events of the late 1960s and early 1970s left citizens confused and divided. Many people hoped that the country could be brought together again with Johnson out of office. But the gulfs between leaders and between citizens became even wider.

Social Divisions at Home

In the face of riots, war, and assassinations many young people began "dropping out" of what older citizens looked on as accepted, normal society. Thousands of draft-age men left the country, refusing to serve in what they thought was an unjust war in Vietnam. Many more burned their draft cards, and some went to prison rather than serve in the armed forces. Many eighteen-year-olds noted with anger that they were old enough to serve in the army but not old enough to vote. In 1971 the Twenty-Sixth Amendment to the Constitution lowered the voting age from twenty-one to eighteen.

Section 2 Review

1. Name five achievements of President Johnson's Great Society.
2. What gains for blacks were brought about by the Civil Rights Act of 1964? The Voting Rights Act of 1965?
3. How did President Johnson lead the United States ever deeper into war in Vietnam?

Critical Thinking

4. **Determining Relevance.** How did the conflict between hawks and doves influence the outcome of the 1968 presidential election?

LOOKING AHEAD: What events of the Nixon years left the nation confused and divided?

Unions sought to organize Mexican-American farm workers (above), while Native Americans in New York petitioned for the return of thirty sacred wampum belts held by the state government.

The nation was also divided over equal rights. Blacks kept up their fight for fair treatment under the law. Spanish-speaking Americans whose roots lay in such countries as Mexico and Puerto Rico also began to work together for greater freedom and better jobs. Many Native Americans began to tell of the wrongs suffered by their people. And growing numbers of women brought their call for equal rights before the public. Parades and speeches on equal rights became everyday events all over the United States.

Nixon did not favor far-reaching social plans aimed at the country as a whole. He closed the Office of Economic Opportunity—the office in charge of Johnson's war on poverty. He also refused to spend some money that Congress had set aside for social programs, believing that such programs should be handled mainly by state governments. He threw his weight behind a revenue-sharing program that would turn over billions of federal tax dollars to state and local governments. Congress voted in favor of this program in 1972. Nixon also worked for laws to prevent the courts from ordering busing to achieve school integration. But Congress did not pass these laws. Like the government itself, people throughout the country were divided on the busing question.

Vietnamization

In the campaign of 1968 Nixon had promised to bring peace in Vietnam. But, he said, it must be a "peace with honor." Nixon planned to turn command of the war over to the South Vietnamese and slowly withdraw U.S. troops. He called this plan Vietnamization.

Nixon gradually called home 75,000 troops. But he also stepped up other phases of the war. Peace talks, begun under President Johnson, dragged on without change. Nixon felt that another attack might force North Vietnam to accept United States terms. So, in a surprise move, he ordered United States and South Vietnamese soldiers into neighboring Cambodia (now Kampuchea) in April 1970. The Communist Vietcong fighters had been raiding South Vietnam through Cambodia.

The attack in Cambodia set off great protests at home, especially at colleges and universities. At Kent State University in Ohio,

National Guard troops fired into a crowd of shouting, flag-waving students on May 4, 1970, killing four and injuring several others. More protests and school closings followed.

Congress, which had not been asked about the Cambodian move, was also angry. Later that year Congress refused to spend any more money for operations in Cambodia. In early 1971 South Vietnamese troops invaded Laos, another of Vietnam's neighbors. No United States soldiers took part, and the attack failed. Americans began to doubt that Vietnamization was working.

Nixon continued to bring United States soldiers home, but he also stepped up the bombing of North Vietnam. The United States dropped three times more explosives during the Vietnam War than it had during World War II and the Korean conflict together.

Finally, in January 1973, the United States, South Vietnam, and North Vietnam signed a peace agreement. The remaining United States troops were pulled out within two months. The Vietnam War cost a total of 57,000 American lives and more than 300,000 wounded. It had also torn the United States apart. Within two years after the peace was signed, the South Vietnam government fell to the Communist government of North Vietnam.

New Directions in Foreign Policy

Outside of Southeast Asia, Nixon worked for peace with other countries. Relations with the Soviet Union improved. In 1972 the United States and the Soviet Union agreed to cut down on their nuclear weapons.

Nixon's greatest success was in opening talks with the People's Republic of China. Since 1949, the United States had treated the Nationalist government on Taiwan as the only Chinese government.

In July 1971 Nixon said that he would visit the People's Republic of China, home of nearly 1 billion people. Nixon made the trip early in 1972 and met with leaders of the People's Republic. In the following years there were further meetings and exchanges between the two countries.

Watergate

Nixon ran for reelection in 1972 against Democratic Senator George S. McGovern of South Dakota. Though his stand on the war was not popular, Nixon won an overwhelming victory. Then scandals uncovered during Nixon's second term turned victory to shame.

In June 1972, just months before Nixon swept to his second-term victory, five men were caught breaking into the national offices of the Democratic party. These Washington offices were located in a group of buildings called the Watergate. The burglars were known to those working for Nixon's reelection.

Election of 1972

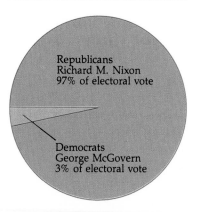

Republicans
Richard M. Nixon
97% of electoral vote

Democrats
George McGovern
3% of electoral vote

President Gerald Ford listens as Secretary of State Henry Kissinger tells of Israel's decision to withdraw from the Sinai peninsula in 1975.

Section 3 Review

1. What social differences became sharper during the Nixon years?
2. What did Vietnamization and opposition to it accomplish?
3. How did Nixon improve relations with the Soviet Union and the People's Republic of China?
4. What was the Watergate scandal?

Critical Thinking

5. **Recognizing Cause and Effect.** How did the Watergate scandal affect President Nixon?

LOOKING AHEAD: What problems at home and abroad have United States Presidents faced since 1976?

Newspaper reporters began to ask questions about the break-in. John J. Sirica, the judge in the burglars' trial, also studied the case. As more facts came to light, more people in high places were thought to have broken the law.

By 1973 Judge Sirica, members of the Senate, and a special lawyer were all looking into the Watergate break-in. Many Nixon aides, it seems, had been willing to go to almost any lengths to see him reelected. Charges of lying, blackmail, spying, and other such acts proved to be true. Fifty-six people eventually were fined or sent to jail, or both, for their part in the case. Among those found guilty was former Attorney General John Mitchell.

The President himself, it was learned, had secretly recorded talks with his advisers about these events. The Supreme Court ordered Nixon to turn over some of these tapes as evidence. The tapes showed that the President knew about the burglary and other scandals. He had even tried to help cover them up.

In July 1974 the Judiciary Committee of the House of Representatives voted to impeach President Nixon. As called for in the Constitution, the full House would have to vote on the impeachment. Then the Senate would hold a trial. Early counts showed that the House would certainly vote for impeachment. But before the House acted, Nixon resigned from office on August 9, 1974. Never before had a President removed himself from office.

Earlier, in 1973, Spiro T. Agnew had stepped down as Nixon's Vice-President because of a scandal. Following the steps given in the Twenty-Fifth Amendment for replacing an officer, Nixon had appointed Gerald R. Ford, Republican representative from Michigan, to the Vice-Presidency. Congress agreed. When Nixon himself left office, Vice-President Ford became President. He then named Nelson A. Rockefeller to the Vice-Presidency with the approval of Congress. For the first time in history the nation had both a President and a Vice-President who had been appointed, not elected, to office.

The Ford Presidency

Gerald Ford worked hard to wash away the stain of Watergate and rid the country of corruption in high places. Ford believed the good of the nation demanded an end to any further uncovering of Nixon's conduct. So a month after taking office, Ford issued a pardon to Nixon for any crimes he might have committed as President. Many persons were disappointed and angered by the pardon.

Ford made few changes in Nixon's domestic plans. Inflation and high unemployment, however, weakened the economy. Ford tried to curb rising prices by cutting federal spending for public housing, health care, and education. Congress, however, passed many bills over his veto.

4 Into the Third Century

In the bicentennial year 1976 the United States marked the two-hundredth anniversary of its independence. The year 1987 marks another anniversary—200 years since the writing of the Constitution. As it entered its third century, the United States faced challenges and opportunities at home and abroad.

The bicentennial year was also an election year. Ford ran against Democrat Jimmy Carter, former governor of Georgia. Carter promised a return to honest government. He said that he was not part of the Washington "establishment." Carter won the race. But he soon learned that he had to work closely with the lawmakers in Washington to get laws passed.

The Carter Years

Despite some opposition from Washington lawmakers, by 1979 Carter had succeeded in opening the way for a full exchange of ideas and goods with the Peoples Republic of China. He also continued talks with the Soviet Union to develop a treaty limiting arms, but the two nations failed to reach an agreement. Relations with the Soviet Union worsened when the Soviets marched into Afghanistan in 1979. Against very stout Senate opposition, Carter also won approval for treaties which gave control of the Panama Canal to Panama.

Jimmy Carter campaigned for many months among the voters to win the Presidency in 1976.

Election of 1976

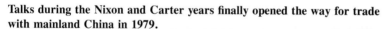

Democrats
Jimmy Carter
55% of electoral vote

Republicans
Gerald R. Ford
45% of electoral vote

Talks during the Nixon and Carter years finally opened the way for trade with mainland China in 1979.

Iranians enthusiastically welcomed the Ayatollah Khomeini back to Iran after the Shah fled in 1979.

Even Carter's critics, however, praised his success in bringing the leaders of Israel and Egypt together for peace talks. Since 1948 Israel had fought four wars with neighboring Arab nations in the Middle East, with Egypt as its chief enemy. Although the peace terms were upheld by all parties, conflict in the area did not end. Other Arab nations and Israel continued to fight.

Conflicts in the oil-rich Middle East gave rise to a worldwide concern over energy in the 1970s. Many nations feared that their oil supply might be cut off in a Middle Eastern war. President Carter established a new Department of Energy to help develop and conserve domestic energy sources. He also worked with Congress to write an energy act to encourage American firms to find and produce more oil. These measures eased the energy problem somewhat, but the cost of energy remained high.

Rapidly rising prices had troubled the administrations of Johnson, Nixon, and Ford. During the Carter years, the inflation rate continued to climb, exceeding 15% in early 1980. Inflation and the slowdown of the economy became critical issues in the election of 1980.

The Iran Hostage Crisis

In the late 1970s, the United States became involved with the Middle Eastern country of Iran. Iran had been an ally of the United States for more than 25 years. However, in 1979 the ailing leader of Iran, Shah Mohammad Reza Pahlavi, was overthrown in a revolution. The Shah had improved education and public health and created new opportunities for women in Iran. He had, however, achieved these and other goals through brutal methods.

A religious figure, the Ayatollah Khomeini, took over as Iran's leader. He detested the United States. Khomeini felt that the United States had supported the Shah's rule at the expense of the Iranian people. When the United States allowed the Shah to come to New York City for medical treatment in November 1979, Iranian terrorists protested. They stormed the United States embassy in

Election of 1980

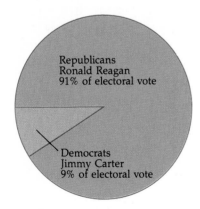

Republicans
Ronald Reagan
91% of electoral vote

Democrats
Jimmy Carter
9% of electoral vote

Democratic candidates Walter Mondale and Geraldine Ferraro (left) greet the crowds during the 1984 presidential campaign.

Iran and took 52 Americans hostage. The terrorists wanted the Shah returned to Iran to be tried for his crimes. They believed that the United States would exchange the Shah for the hostages.

President Carter would not give in to the terrorists' demands. He tried without success to negotiate the release of the hostages. His inability to free the hostages was yet another critical issue in the 1980 election.

The Reagan Revolution

In the 1980 election, Carter's Republican challenger was former California governor Ronald Reagan. Reagan and his running mate, George Bush of Texas, campaigned for lower taxes and less federal spending. They won by a landslide. Republicans also gained control of the Senate for the first time in 26 years and increased their seats in the House of Representatives.

On that sunny Inauguration Day, President Reagan called for a "new beginning." Reagan asked for a drastic reduction of the federal government's role in what he believed were state and local matters. "Government is not the solution to our problem," he said. "It is our problem."

Reagan's message had a wide appeal. The President's confidence in his programs inspired the nation. Three years into his presidency he declared with pride, "America is back—standing tall." By 1984 Reagan enjoyed widespread support. He easily defeated former Vice President Walter Mondale and his running mate, Representative Geraldine Ferraro of New York. Reagan was victorious in every state except Minnesota.

Domestic Affairs Under Reagan

From the outset, Reagan called for less federal spending—except for defense—and lower taxes. Lower taxes, he argued, would give people more money to spend. With more spending, Reagan believed the economy would grow. Thriving businesses would create more jobs for Americans, so more Americans could pay taxes. The revenue from a wider base of taxpayers would help pay off the national debt. This policy is known as "supply-side" economics.

Election of 1984

Republicans
Ronald Reagan
98% of electoral vote

Democrats
Walter Mondale
2% of electoral vote

Nancy Reagan campaigned alongside her husband, Republican candidate Ronald Reagan, during the presidential campaigns in 1980 and 1984.

The Supreme Court Justices pictured here are: (from left, front row) Thurgood Marshall, William Brennan, Jr., Chief Justice William H. Rehnquist, Byron R. White, and Harry A. Blackmun; (from left, back row) Antonin Scalia, John Paul Stevens, Sandra Day O'Connor, and Anthony M. Kennedy. Scalia, O'Connor, and Kennedy were appointed to the court by President Reagan.

Reagan moved swiftly to transform his views into law. He immediately proposed a 30% cut in income taxes over three years. He also proposed cutting back on such social programs as food stamps for the poor, job training for the unemployed, medicare for senior citizens, and loans for college students. At the same time, Reagan proposed a 10% increase in military spending each year for five years. He believed that a strong defense would reduce the threat of attack. Reagan also believed a strong military would allow a tough stand on terrorism. He made plans for a Strategic Defense Initiative (SDI), often called "Star Wars." It involved orbiting space platforms from which, he said, nuclear attacks on the United States could be halted.

Reagan's proposals met with a storm of protest from congressional leaders who did not want to see social programs seriously cut. Reagan's critics also feared that increased military spending, combined with lower taxes, would worsen the national debt. But Reagan stood by his views and promised that the federal government would be able to "balance the budget" by 1984. In slightly changed form, Reagan's proposals were eventually passed and signed into law.

When the economy slowed down in 1981, Reagan's domestic policies did not seem to be working. But by 1983, the economy had begun growing faster than at any time in a decade. Inflation went down from a high of 13% in 1980 to 4% in 1983. Unemployment went down as more than three million people found jobs. The good times continued into 1989. Not since after World War II had so many Americans enjoyed such a long period of prosperity.

Economic Woes

Nonetheless, some serious economic problems plagued the Reagan administration. The number of poor and homeless people increased during the Reagan years. Some industries, such as steelmaking and automobile manufacturing met with bad times and had to lay off

President Reagan called for a build-up of MX missiles capable of carrying nuclear warheads anywhere in the world.

In the late 1980s, many farmers had to auction off their farms. They were unable to pay their loans despite Reagan's farm credit bill.

thousands of workers. Farmers were also troubled. Their incomes fell sharply. To help those in danger of losing their farms, Congress and the President developed and passed a farm credit bill to make low-cost loans available. Nevertheless farm foreclosures were commonplace in the late 1980s.

Another economic problem facing Reagan was the balance of trade with other nations. The United States was buying foreign products at a faster rate than it was selling American goods overseas. In 1985, the difference between exports and imports was $140 billion. To narrow this gap, Reagan approved policies to encourage the sale of United States products to other countries.

Perhaps Reagan's most troubling economic problem was the ever-rising national debt. It grew from $1 trillion to more than $2.5 trillion during his presidency. The government's overspending during the Reagan years was greater than the combined overspending in all the years since George Washington took office in 1789. As a result, each year the government had to borrow more and more money to pay the interest on this huge debt.

Reactions to the Economic Problems

In an effort to bring down the national debt, Congress passed the Gramm-Rudman Act in December 1985. This act allowed for "across-the-board" cuts in most federal programs. The goal of the act was to have a balanced budget by the early 1990s. Then Congress passed the Tax Reform Act of 1986. It was an effort to promote the start-up of new enterprises which would invigorate the economy. To do this the act simplified the tax structure, reduced the tax rate on individuals, and increased corporate taxes.

Despite Reagan's efforts, trade problems and the growing national debt worried many investors on Wall Street. On October 19, 1987, the stock market dropped by more than 500 points—the largest decline ever. The "Crash of 1987," however, did not result in an immediate economic slowdown.

Many people on Wall Street worried that the "Crash of 1987" signaled an economic slowdown.

(From left to right) President Reagan, Raisa Gorbachev, Soviet Premier Gorbachev, and Nancy Reagan leave the Kremlin during the 1988 Moscow Summit.

The Soviet Union and the United States

When Reagan first came to office, he called the Soviet Union an "evil empire." But, like every President since World War II, he entered into talks with the Soviets to reduce the threat of nuclear war. Reagan's earliest arms proposals developed into the Strategic Arms Reductions Talks (START).

In 1985, talks between the Soviet Union and the United States grew more intense. During a meeting in Iceland, Soviet leader Mikhail Gorbachev made the bold proposal that all nuclear weapons be done away with and that the United States give up SDI. The United States was not prepared for such a bold move, and talks broke off.

However, the two superpowers continued discussing ways to reduce missiles in Europe. In December 1987, the United States and the Soviet Union signed the Intermediate Nuclear Force (INF) Treaty. This treaty called for the removal of all intermediate-range missiles in Europe. It was the first treaty in the history of the superpowers designed to reduce the size of nuclear forces. Plans went forward for another Reagan-Gorbachev meeting in Moscow in May 1988. At this meeting, the superpowers discussed a 50% reduction of all nuclear weapons.

The Moscow talks took place at a time of great change in the Soviet Union. Gorbachev demonstrated a new style of Soviet leadership which promoted new attitudes and new ways of thinking about old problems. Two Russian words represented Gorbachev's reforms: *glasnost* and *perestroika*. *Glasnost* meant the more open society that Gorbachev wanted for his country. *Perestroika* meant

Soviet citizens watch United States President Ronald Reagan on television during his Moscow visit.

Marines and Red Cross workers search through the wreckage after the bombing of the marine barracks in Lebanon in October 1983.

the reshaping of the economy, the communist party, and the government. This reshaping had to take place to create a freer society. These winds of change in the Soviet Union were well received in the United States and throughout the world.

The Middle East and Terrorism

Other pressing problems of foreign policy also challenged the Reagan administration. Renewed violence broke out in the Middle East. In 1982, Israel annexed the neighboring territory of the Golan Heights, where many Arabs lived.

During the 1980s, acts of terrorism increased worldwide. The United States believed that Libya, a North African country, was a major source of terrorist attacks. To punish Libya, in April 1986 the United States bombed targets in that country. The terrorism continued. At various times, at least nine Americans were held hostage in the Middle East. Reagan learned firsthand how hard it was to free political hostages.

Troubles in Latin America

Reagan also took a tough stand against communism, especially in Latin America. In 1984, a revolutionary group called the Sandinistas had legally won election to national office in Nicaragua. But Nicaraguans who opposed the Sandinistas, called the "contras," fought openly with government forces. Reagan backed the contras because the Sandinista government received aid from the Soviet Union. For a time the United States had secretly mined Nicaraguan harbors to prevent Soviet weapons from reaching the Sandinistas. Despite protests from many Americans, Reagan and his supporters sent military aid to the contras to help them overthrow the Sandinista government.

Sandinista soldiers prepare to fight the contras in Santos Lopez, Nicaragua.

689

Senator Daniel Inuoye of Hawaii chaired the congressional commission that investigated the Iran-contra affair.

The Iran-Contra Affair

In November 1986, the problems of the Middle East, terrorism, and Nicaragua came together in a scandal that outraged the nation. A newspaper in the Middle East printed a story claiming that the United States had secretly sold weapons to Iran in return for freeing three American hostages. This news directly contradicted Reagan's policy of avoiding all dealings with Iran. It also contradicted his policy of not doing business with terrorists holding hostages. In addition, the money obtained from the sale of weapons to Iran was secretly—and illegally—used to support the Nicaraguan contras.

Reagan responded to the storm of criticism by explaining that the sale of arms to Iran was intended to improve the relations between the two countries, not to serve as a bargaining tool to free the hostages. He fired two of his staff members who had played leading roles in the scandal. He also appointed a three-person commission to investigate the so-called "Iran-contra affair." The commission found that several presidential staff members carried out secret activities that did not follow official policies. But the commission found no evidence that the President himself had violated the law.

Congress was not satisfied with the commission's report and began its own investigation. After hearing much testimony, it concluded that staff members had indeed acted without the President's knowledge. These staff members had also knowingly lied to Congress in order to keep their deal a secret. In doing so, they had violated a number of laws. In the final report of August 1987, the congressional investigation condemned the President for lax management of his staff, but found no evidence that he had broken any laws. A special prosecutor later brought charges of unlawful conduct against former members of Reagan's staff.

The Election of 1988

Ronald Reagan was not eligible to run for reelection because he was completing his second term as President. As a result, the 1988 race was wide open. The battle for the nomination in each party was fought in the state primary elections.

Six Republicans entered the contest for the nomination, but the race soon narrowed down to two: Vice-President George Bush and Senator Robert Dole of Kansas. Bush overwhelmed Dole in the primaries and became the nominee at the Republican convention in August. He chose the little-known 41-year-old Senator J. Danforth Quayle of Indiana as his vice-presidential running mate.

Of the seven Democrats seeking the nomination, two soon emerged as front-runners. Governor Michael Dukakis of Massachusetts and Jesse Jackson, a civil rights leader from Chicago, became

The two leading Democratic candidates after the 1988 primaries were Jesse Jackson of Illinois and Governor Michael Dukakis of Massachusetts.

Republican George Bush defeated Democrat Michael Dukakis in the November 1988 presidential election to become the 41st president of the United States.

Election of 1988

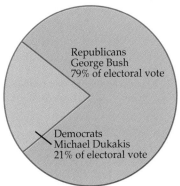

Republicans
George Bush
79% of electoral vote

Democrats
Michael Dukakis
21% of electoral vote

the leading candidates. With primary victories in New York, Pennsylvania, and California, Dukakis clinched the Democratic nomination. He chose Senator Lloyd Bentsen of Texas, a conservative, as his running mate.

Each candidate stressed his special qualifications and concerns for the nation's future. Bush, strongly supported by President Reagan, claimed responsibility for having made important national decisions that gave him greater experience than his opponent in handling the problems that face a President. Dukakis stressed his successful role as governor of Massachusetts and challenged voters to consider the future problems that would affect the economy, changing defense needs, and our environment.

After a hotly contested campaign, George Bush won the election and became the 41st President of the United States. With his victory, the new President had to address the vital questions that were to affect Americans well into the twenty-first century. What kind of defense should the United States maintain? What kind of relationship would be best with the Soviet Union? Could prosperous times be maintained? Could the environment be protected, providing Americans with clean air and water?

As the nation looked to its future, it also honored its past. The election of 1988 coincided with the celebration of the 200th anniversary of the first national election in the country's history. This birthday reminded Americans that the system of government, created more than 200 years ago, lives and thrives today. This precious heritage continues to affect every person living in the United States.

Section 4 Review

1. Explain why relations between the United States and the Soviet Union worsened in 1979.
2. What two steps did President Carter take to meet the energy problem?
3. What economic policies did President Reagan follow during his two terms in office?
4. What changes were taking place in the Soviet Union in the late 1980s?

Critical Thinking

5. **Making Comparisons.** Who were the presidential candidates in 1988? Which special qualifications did each candidate stress?

People   As Equals

"No, no, we are not satisfied, and we will not be satisfied until justice rolls down like waters and righteousness like a mighty stream."

Dr. Martin Luther King, Jr., spoke those words before a crowd of 250,000 blacks and whites who gathered in August 1963 at the Lincoln Memorial in Washington, D.C. People had come from all over the country to show peacefully that they were against injustice and inequality. Dr. King warned the crowd: "In . . . gaining our rightful place we must not be guilty of wrongful deeds. . . ."

The people you will read about on these pages are just a few who have worked peacefully for justice in our times.

Henry Gonzalez

After a revolution in Mexico in 1910, hundreds of thousands of Mexicans moved to the United States. Since then, the United States has received well over a million and a half Mexicans who have had immigration papers. Many other Mexicans have come into the country without these papers.

Spanish-speaking immigrants have also come from Cuba and other parts of Latin America. Like citizens from Puerto Rico who have come to live in the United States, these immigrants often have been treated unfairly and had trouble finding work.

Henry Gonzalez, the first Mexican-American elected to the Texas senate since 1846, became a champion of equal rights and of Spanish-speaking Americans. His parents had come to San Antonio, Texas, after the Mexican revolution. His father worked on a Spanish-language newspaper.

Born in 1916, Henry attended school in San Antonio and earned a law degree from St. Mary's University. Before entering politics, he taught English to Mexican-Americans. He began his political career in the San Antonio city government in the early 1950s. He worked to clear the slums, improve education, and end segregation. Gonzalez went on to the United States Congress in 1961 where he worked for voting rights, help for migrant workers, better housing, and a minimum wage.

Maggie Kuhn

In 1970, at the age of sixty-four, Maggie Kuhn and five of her

U.S. Representative Henry Gonzalez (inset) and civil rights leader Martin Luther King, Jr., both spoke for human equality.

People

Through the efforts of Maggie Kuhn (inset above), Shirley Chisholm, and John Stevens (below), elderly people, blacks, women, and Native Americans play more active roles in society today.

friends founded the Gray Panthers. This self-help organization, which now has over 7,000 members, speaks for people over sixty.

The Gray Panthers hope to end forced retirement at age sixty-five. They believe that many people older than sixty-five still carry out their jobs very well. Gray Panthers also keep an eye on poor government services and sky-high costs. Kuhn and other Gray Panthers teach people how to bring about reforms in their own community. They also work to protect the rights of others who one day will be over sixty.

John Stevens

In 1953 John Stevens was elected governor of the small Passamaquoddy (pa′sə·mə·kwä′dē) reservation in Maine. Stevens knew that at one time his ancestors and the neighboring Penobscot had owned over half the land in Maine. He set about finding out how the land was lost.

One day he came across a yellowed paper found by an old woman on the reservation. The paper was the Treaty of 1794 in which the Passamaquoddy had turned over all their land to the government.

Stevens found a lawyer, Tom Tureen, to help the Passamaquoddy try to win back some of their land. Tureen found a 1790 law that said land sales by Native Americans had to be approved by Congress. Since Congress had never approved the 1794 treaty, Tureen convinced judges in Maine to rule in favor of the Passamaquoddy.

Like claims have come to courts all across the country. In most cases the Native Americans do not expect the land to be returned to them. They just want fair payment for their losses. By 1975 the courts had awarded $561 million in claims to Native Americans.

Shirley Chisholm

Shirley Chisholm was born in 1924 in Brooklyn, New York. After earning a master's degree, Chisholm taught preschoolers. Later she served in the New York assembly.

In 1969 Chisholm became the first black woman to be elected to the United States Congress. She is also a member of the National Women's Political Caucus, an organization that favors the Equal Rights Amendment (ERA). The ERA calls for an end to unfair treatment of women on the basis of sex.

The facts show that women in many jobs earn less money than men who do the same work. They also show that women hold only a few of the well-paying jobs as managers. Chisholm and others are working within the law in hopes of improving pay and job opportunities for young women in future years.

Gonzalez, Kuhn, Stevens, and Chisholm, as well as millions more throughout the nation, owe a great debt to Martin Luther King, Jr. He led the way in peaceful protest against racial injustice, setting the stage for further reform. The last words of his speech at the Lincoln Memorial are part of his gift to all Americans. He called for ". . . the day when all God's children, black men and white men, Jews and Gentiles, Protestants and Catholics, will be able to join hands and sing in the words of the old Negro spiritual, 'Free at last, Free at last, Great God almighty, We are free at last'."

Chapter 35 Review

Chapter Summary

The Presidents of the 1960s faced challenges at home and overseas. John F. Kennedy's programs included the Peace Corps and the space program that put an American astronaut on the moon in 1969. Kennedy successfully stood up to the Soviets during the Cuban missile crisis.

After Kennedy's assassination in 1963, President Johnson persuaded Congress to pass New Frontier programs and launched a war on poverty at home. He also stepped up United States involvement in the Vietnam War. President Nixon withdrew all United States troops from Vietnam in 1973.

In the 1970s the Watergate scandal and the resignation of Richard Nixon brought Gerald Ford to the Presidency. The inflation and high unemployment that troubled Ford continued during the Carter years.

During the 1980s inflation declined under Reagan, but government overspending resulted in the greatest national debt in history. Reagan also faced problems of violence in the Middle East, terrorism, and the Iran-contra scandal. President Bush continued many of Reagan's policies, including the arms limitations talks.

Reviewing Vocabulary

Use the following words to complete the sentences below.

minority	pardon	inflation
protest	demonstrators	missile
integration	pollution	bicentennial
busing	equality	volunteer
glasnost	scandal	energy
Strategic Defense Initiative		*perestroika*
supply-side economics		

1. The Peace Corps sends _____ workers to aid other nations.

2. Kennedy's naval blockade stopped Soviet ships from delivering _____ parts to Cuba.

3. New Frontier programs included control of water _____ and help for _____ workers.

4. Civil rights legislation in the 1960s promoted school _____ and _____ in voting rights.

5. _____ against the Vietnam War led _____ to clash with police outside the Democratic national convention in Chicago.

6. Many people disagreed with court-ordered _____ to achieve school integration.

7. President Nixon, who had resigned because of the Watergate _____, received a(n) _____ from Ford.

8. In 1976 the United States celebrated its _____.

9. President Carter took measures to solve the _____ problem, but rising _____ and failure to secure the release of the hostages defeated him in 1980.

10. The terms _____ and _____ have come to represent the new directions taken in the Soviet Union.

11. Reagan vigorously pursued his economic policy, _____, and his defense plan, _____.

Understanding Main Ideas

1. How did Kennedy react to Cold War moves by Communist nations? What New Frontier programs succeeded at home?

2. In what way were the gains of Johnson's Great Society overshadowed by United States involvement in Vietnam?

3. Why did events of the Nixon years confuse and divide the nation?

Social Studies Skills: Interpreting a Table

Election year	Percent voting of voting-age population	Percent of population voting for winner
1968	61%	43.4%
1972	56%	60.7%
1976	54%	50%
1980	53%	50.7%
1984	54%	58.8%
1988	50%	53.9%

Examine the table above and complete the following exercise.

Skill Review: Indicate whether each of the following generalizations is true, false, or unknown based on the table.

1. Every President elected between 1968 and 1988 won a majority of the popular vote.

2. In every election between 1968 and 1988 more than half the voting-age population cast ballots.

3. No President has ever won 100% of the electoral vote.

4. Third-party candidates influenced the outcomes of elections in 1968 and 1980.

---

4. What foreign and domestic problems have Presidents faced since 1976?

Critical Thinking Skills

1. **Expressing Problems Clearly.** Why did civil rights legislation aimed at achieving the American ideal of equality lead to social conflict?

2. **Formulating Questions.** What questions did the Watergate scandal and the Iran-contra affair raise concerning the role of the President?

3. **Checking Consistency.** Did relations between the United States and the Soviet Union show consistent improvement in the 1970s and 1980s? What evidence from the text supports your answer?

Writing About History

1. **Writing a Nominating Speech.** Choose one presidential candidate between 1960 and 1988. Write a speech nominating that person at the party's national convention.

2. **Describing the American Spirit.** Write a paragraph describing examples of the American spirit in the years since 1960.

Your Region in History

Citizenship. Find out which presidential candidates your state supported in each election since 1960. What percent of the voting-age population of your state voted in each of these elections? Write three generalizations based on your findings.

❦ **Chapter 36**

BETWEEN 1914 AND TODAY lifestyles in the United States changed
faster than they ever had before. Such new inventions as cars,
televisions, and computers made great changes in the ways people
lived, learned, worked, played, and thought. Some of these changes
are illustrated on these pages. But you will be able to think of many,
many more changes that have come about in the years since your
grandparents were young.

697

The automobile lightened the family's workload and offered each member hours of pleasure as well.

From 1914 to the present American families changed along with the times. Except for the baby boom that followed World War II, families had fewer children. More couples decided not to have any children. More people divorced. By 1980 it was found that one third of American children would spend some time before they were eighteen in single-parent families. And after the children grew up, they usually lived apart from their parents and grandparents.

The Family Car

In 1925 two researchers studied changes in the life of a small Indiana city since 1900. Some of the biggest changes, they found, had come about because of the automobile.

Many families felt that the automobile helped hold them together as a group. "I never feel as close to my family as when we are all together in the car," one mother said. But others complained that their older children spent less time at home. Certainly the automobile brought about a change in family values. "We'd rather do without clothes than give up the car," said one mother of nine children.

Advice to Parents

In 1935 the Children's Bureau of the Department of Labor stated in a pamphlet, *Infant Care,* that the baby must be trained from

Lifestyles

birth to behave properly. "Good habits . . . may be built up if perfect regularity is observed in the performance of each act, [and] if the parents are consistent and logical in their demands. . . ." Ten years later, Benjamin Spock, M.D., published *The Common Sense Book of Baby and Child Care*. It has remained the most popular manual of advice to parents ever since. Dr. Spock held very different views about raising children.

You may hear people say that you have to get your baby strictly regulated in his feeding, sleeping, . . . and other habits—but don't believe this. . . . In all these habits he will fit into the family's way of doing things sooner or later without much effort on your part.

The same thing goes, later on, for discipline, good behavior, and pleasant manners. You can't drill these into a child. . . . The desire to get along with other people happily and considerately develops within him as part of the unfolding of his nature, provided he grows up with loving, self-respecting parents.

The Feminine Mystique

All through the 1940s, 1950s, and early 1960s most people believed that a woman's true reward lay in being a wife and mother. In 1963 Betty Friedan challenged this idea in the book *The Feminine Mystique*.

The suburban housewife—she was the dream image of the young American women and the envy, it was said, of women all over the world. . . . She was healthy, beautiful, educated, concerned only about her husband, her children, her home. . . .

If a woman had a problem in the 1950's and 1960's, she knew that something must be wrong with her marriage, or with herself. Other women were satisfied with their lives, she thought. . . . She was so ashamed to admit her dissatisfaction that she never knew how many other women shared it.

Sitting Up Here, Free

Vernon Jarrett, a columnist for the *Chicago Tribune*, recalls his mother's mother and his father's father.

My grandmother used to sit around and tell us these stories. . . . She was a little girl when slavery was ended. Dad's father was a runaway slave. He couldn't read and write. He heard that the Union army was freein' people and he cut out. . . .

Some Sundays in church when they started singin' those old hymns, these people would start laughing and answering each other from across the room. . . . They were really laughing about the fact that they had survived: Here we are sitting up here, free. These are our kids here with us. I've got a home, and my daughter is a schoolteacher.

As twentieth-century medicine improved, many more children were born in hospitals and many more children survived.

Family life was much the same for all Americans throughout the depression and the war years.

699

New housing went up all over the United States during the 1920s and after World War II. The first building boom took place mostly in the cities; the second, mostly in the suburbs. After 1900, people moved from home to home more often than before. Between 1948 and 1968 one family in five moved each year. Inside the home new kinds of appliances and furniture made housework easier than ever before. By 1980 most women with school-age children worked outside the home for pay. In many homes both parents shared in the housework.

From furnishings to labor-saving devices to solar-heated houses (inset), Americans have worked to improve the comfort and convenience of their homes.

Hooverville in California

Between 1932 and 1936, drought and dust storms drove 300,000 people from their farms on the Great Plains to California. Most of the refugees came by automobile from Oklahoma, Arkansas, Missouri, and Texas. But California was not the promised land they had been looking for. Many of them lived in camps like the one described in John Steinbeck's novel *The Grapes of Wrath.*

There was no order in the camp; little gray tents, shacks, cars were scattered about at random. . . . The south wall [of the first house]

After World War II, businesses joined their workers in the flight to the suburbs. High-rise housing projects went up in cities where slums once stood.

Section 1 Review

1. Name three conveniences besides the car that your family could not do without.
2. What was it about being free that made Vernon Jarrett's grandmother laugh?
3. List the different materials used to build shacks in Steinbeck's Hooverville.

Critical Thinking
4. **Making Comparisons.** What did suburbs like Park Forest offer families that cities like Chicago did not?

was made of three sheets of rusty corrugated iron, the east wall a square of moldy carpet tacked between two boards, the north wall a strip of roofing paper and a strip of tattered canvas, and the west wall six pieces of [coarse cloth]. Over the square frame, on untrimmed willow limbs, grass had been . . . heaped up. . . . A five-gallon kerosene can served for a stove . . . a collection of boxes lay about, boxes to sit on, to eat on. . . . There were forty tents and shacks, and beside each . . . some kind of automobile.

Flight to the Suburbs

Since the late 1800s there had been suburbs around cities. But after World War II many more people moved from cities to suburbs. Between 1960 and 1970 the twenty-five largest cities in the United States gained 710,000 people while the suburbs around these cities gained 8.9 million. A 1952 advertisement for Park Forest, a town about forty miles from Chicago, promises that those who move there will find friendships as well as grass and trees and bedrooms.

. . . a cup of coffee—symbol of PARK FOREST! Coffeepots bubble all day long in Park Forest. This sign of friendliness tells you how much neighbors enjoy each other's company—feel glad that they can share their daily joys—yes, and troubles, too.

Come out to Park Forest where smalltown friendships grow— and you still live so close to a big city.

Urban Renewal

Many young people are now moving from the suburbs to the city. Stephen Birmingham tells about one such urban newcomer and about one of his neighbors.

Not long ago the New York Times reported the cases of two Washington, D.C., neighbors who had never met and yet whose fates were closely linked. One was a twenty-eight-year-old white architect named Robert Corcoran, and the other was a poor black woman named Beatrice Poindexter, who lived just down the street. Mr. Corcoran . . . had bought a run-down house on a mostly black street in Washington's Adams-Morgan section. . . . He had paid very little for his house, but [had the money to fix it up]. All at once, the street became "hot" real estate property, and Miss Poindexter was being [told to leave] her . . . apartment. . . .

On the one hand, the well-to-do young newcomers are a blessing to the old cities. By [fixing up] once-fine houses, they are [breathing new life into old] neighborhoods. . . . [But] thousands of the poor are pushed elsewhere, often deeper into the poorer black or Puerto Rican ghettos. . . . Though Beatrice Poindexter does not know Robert Corcoran, she bitterly resents what is happening to her old neighborhood.

Through all the changes recorded in American history some values have remained unchanged. These are the principles of government by the people spelled out in the Declaration of Independence and the Constitution. "We the people" have struggled at home and abroad to protect these values for our children and our children's children.

Growing vegetables during World War I was looked on by some as an act of true patriotism.

An Indian America

Frank James, a Wampanoag, was invited to speak at a celebration marking 350 years since the Pilgrims' landing at Plymouth. Here is part of the speech he wrote for the 1970 celebration.

High on a hill, overlooking the famed Plymouth Rock stands the statue of our great Sachem, Massasoit. Massasoit has stood there many years in silence. We the descendants of this great sachem have been a silent People. . . . Today, I and many of my People are choosing to face the truth. We ARE Indians. . . . We stand tall and proud and before too many moons pass we'll right the wrongs we have allowed to happen to us. . . . today we work towards a more humane America, a more Indian America where men and nature once again are important; where the Indian values of honor, truth and brotherhood prevail.

With All My Heart, A Peaceful World

Eleanor Roosevelt, wife of President Franklin Roosevelt and delegate to the United Nations, records in her autobiography the goals of her later years in life.

I wanted, with all my heart, a peaceful world. And I knew it could never be achieved on a lasting basis without greater understanding between peoples. It is to these ends that I have, in the main, devoted the past years. . . . I think that one of the reasons it is so difficult for us, as a people, to understand other areas of the world is that we cannot put ourselves imaginatively in their place. We have no famine. But if we were actually to see people dying of starvation we would care quite a bit. We would be able to think, "These could be my people."

Two Cultures

Many Mexican-Americans feel the pull of both their Latin culture and the culture of the United States. One young Texas student said, "I don't know whether I am a Mexican or an American. I guess I'm neither." John Salazar, however, takes a different view.

My first name is English and my second name is Spanish. My ancestry is Mexican but if you ask me what I am, I'll tell you I'm an American and I'm a good American. I've worked for this country and fought for it. I would also die for it. But I want the right to be my

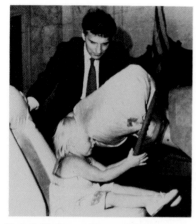

Ralph Nader, self-appointed spokesman for the American buyer, looks on as a three-year-old shows how an air bag promotes car safety.

own kind of American. I would no more renounce my Mexican heritage then the Anglos would renounce the English language. . . . I'm a Mexican-American and I'm proud of it. We Mexican-Americans can contribute to the greatness of our country. All we need to do is organize, state our wishes, and vote.

A Little Spaceship

John Muir once said, "When we try to pick out anything by itself, we find it hitched to everything else in the universe." The study of how things are "hitched" in nature is called ecology. Author Rachel Carson (*The Sea Around Us,* 1951, and *Silent Spring,* 1962) sounded the public alarm for ecology. And Adlai Stevenson, in his last address to the United Nations as U.S. ambassador in 1965, summed up the world's position in the matter.

We travel together, passengers on a little spaceship, dependent on its . . . resources of air and soil; all committed for our safety to its security and peace; preserved from [destruction] only by the care, the work, and, I will say, the love we give our fragile craft.

Citizens became alarmed and involved as oil spills at sea and other accidents threatened the environment. Ecologists took up the search for safer, saner ways of living.

Students in the 1980s may choose to attend vocational high schools and study such subjects as computer technology.

In the years after 1914 more people went to school than ever before. High school enrollment rose steadily. More students also went on to universities or colleges. Older people returned to school for more training. And young children attended preschools or watched "Sesame Street" at home. New machines and ways of teaching in the schools changed the way students learned.

High School Study Choices

With more high school students came many changes in curriculum. Students could ready themselves for work or college after graduation. In 1925 high school students in Muncie, Indiana, could choose from twelve courses of study.

1. General Course
2. College Preparatory Course
3. Music Course
4. Art Course
5. Shorthand Course
6. Bookkeeping Course
7. Applied Electricity Course
8. Mechanical Drafting Course
9. Printing Course
10. Machine Shop Course
11. Manual Arts Course
12. Home Economics Course

The Sputnik Crisis

On February 11, 1957, the Soviet Union sent the first spacecraft into orbit around the earth. Americans immediately began

Some modern-day youngsters prepare for classroom learning by watching educational programs on televison.

Section 2 Review

1. What does John Salazar say Mexican-Americans can do to contribute to their country's greatness?
2. What is the "little spaceship" and the "fragile craft" that Stevenson refers to in his speech?
3. Name three machines used in education today that probably were not used in 1925.

Critical Thinking

4. **Identifying Central Issues.** What event moved the United States to improve science education in the 1960s?

improving science training in their schools. *Life* magazine outlined what had to be done to bring about lasting change.

We must raise the low standards of our secondary schools and eliminate their trivial courses.

We must shore up the sagging quality of our science teaching, cut down on the teacher's extra jobs, give him time to become a professional scholar again.

We must provide both opportunity and incentive for our gifted children. There must be an unremitting search for talent and intellectual giftedness.

Reverse Discrimination?

In the 1960s many people began to feel that just being against discrimination was not enough. They wanted affirmative action— planned attempts to bring more minority group members and women into schools, businesses, and government.

In 1968 blacks made up about 12 percent of the nation's population. Yet only about 2 percent of the nation's medical students were blacks. In 1969 the University of California Medical School at Davis started an affirmative action program.

In 1974 a white student named Allan Bakke was turned down for the second time as a student at the Davis medical school. School officials admitted that Bakke was better qualified than some minority students they accepted. Bakke sued. His case reached the Supreme Court.

The Wall Street Journal reported on June 29, 1978, that the Court ordered the University of California to admit Bakke. But the Court also ruled that schools could take race into account in making admissions decisions. "The ruling means that universities may continue affirmative-action programs, so long as they consider candidates on an individual basis and don't set aside a rigid number of places for which whites can't compete."

Sesame Street

In November 1969 a new educational program for children was shown on American television. Soon everybody was talking about "Sesame Street." The program had been developed by Joan Ganz Cooney and the Children's Television Workshop. Cooney had studied young children watching television. "I'd found that kids were fascinated by commercials with fast action, catchy music, and cartoons. . . . We decided that our show would have to clip along at a fast pace. We wanted it to jump, move, and sound."

A study done in 1970 showed that children between three and five who watched "Sesame Street" regularly made some real gains. But some people still prefer a more traditional approach.

Lifestyles   Work and Play

Dolores Huerta worked with Cesar Chavez in the 1970s to bring underpaid Mexican-Americans into the United Farm Workers union.

The work force has changed greatly since the early 1900s. Women are on the job to stay. More women today work outside the home than in the home. Labor unions, too, have become a lasting part of work life, though they have not grown as fast as the work force.

Working part-time has become a common practice among teenagers, even those still in school. Many workers over the retirement age of sixty-five have also taken on part-time work.

Partly through affirmative action programs, more blacks, Spanish-speaking Americans, Asian-Americans, other minorities, and women are holding higher-paying jobs. White males, however, still hold most high-paying positions.

Up from the Sweatshop

A young Russian immigrant named Bessie Abramowitz worked as a button-sewer at Hart, Schaffner & Marx in Chicago. For each pair of pants she finished she earned 4 cents. To earn more money, fifteen-year-old Bessie took bundles of pants home to work on at night.

In the fall of 1910 Bessie's boss told her that her rate would be cut to 3.75 cents for a pair of pants. Bessie put down her needle and walked out. Seven other women joined her. Bessie was fired immediately. No other shop in the city would hire her.

Bessie called a secret meeting at Hull House to urge a strike. The next day 8,000 tailors walked off the job. The strike spread. Thirty thousand workers fought for five months for more money and better working conditions. Most of them had to go back to work with no change in workplace or pay.

But the workers at Bessie's shop, with the help of the famous lawyer Clarence Darrow, won some changes. A three-person committee was set up to settle the dispute between workers and employers. That committee was the first to bargain with American industry for a union of workers.

In 1914 Bessie and her husband Sidney Hillman founded the Amalgamated Clothing Workers of America. This union has continued to fight for social reforms from 1914 until today.

The Power of Ads

In the prosperous 1920s, businesses fought for the buyer's dollar. Advertising became more important as a sales tool. Historian Frederick Lewis Allen described the change in the advertising business.

The copy-writer was learning to pay less attention to the special qualities and advantages of his product, and more to the study of what the mass of . . . mankind wanted—to be young and desirable, to

be rich, to keep up with the Joneses, to be envied. The winning method was to associate his product with one or more of these ends . . . to draw a lesson from the dramatic case of some imaginary man or woman whose fate was altered by the use of X's soap. . . .

Something to Point To

In the 1970s interviewer Studs Terkel talked to people around the country about their jobs. He recorded what they said in the book *Working*. One person he talked to was Mike Lefevre, a worker in a midwestern steel mill.

You can't take pride any more. You remember when a guy could point to a house he built, how many logs he stacked. He built it and he was proud of it. . . . It's hard to take pride in a bridge you're never gonna cross, in a door you're never gonna open. You're mass-producing things and you never see the end result. . . . I would like to see a building, say, the Empire State, I would like to see on one side of it a foot-wide strip from top to bottom with the name of every bricklayer, the name of every electrician, with all the names. So when a guy walked by, he could take his son and say, "See, that's me over there on the forty-fifth floor. I put the steel beam in." . . . Everybody should have something to point to.

Officers in the Amalgamated Clothing Workers Union, started in 1914 by Bessie and Sidney Hillman, pose here with Eleanor Roosevelt (center).

Unemployed Americans stood hours each day in breadlines during the Great Depression waiting for free food.

Radio in the 1930s (top left) and television in the 1950s brought entertainment into the family living room. More Americans today are pursuing such solitary pastimes as jogging (left).

The biggest change in how Americans spent their free time came about because of television. By 1960, televisions were turned on in American homes an average of six hours a day, seven days a week. Television changed the way Americans thought about sports, entertainment, and even news. Other changes came about because of the new "youth culture" that emerged after World War II. A new word came into the language about this time—teenager. Teenagers had their own fashions, their own heroes, and their own music.

At forty-eight Satchel Paige pitched in the 1952 All-Star game.

Twenty-Two Years As a Rookie

. . . Leroy ("Satchelfoots") Paige . . . is regarded by many sportswriters as the greatest Negro pitcher of all time, as one of the greatest pitchers of any [color] in baseball history. Satchel has blinding speed, marvelous, control, and . . . is a [wonderful] hitter. . . . In 1933 he stretched a winning streak to 21 games, pitched 62 consecutive scoreless innings.

So said *Time* magazine in 1940. But in 1940 neither Satchel Paige nor any other black baseball player had any chance of playing on a major league baseball team.

The first black player to be hired by a major league team was Jackie Robinson. Robinson won the pennant for the Brooklyn

Dodgers and was named Rookie of the Year in his first season, 1947. In 1948 Satchel Paige, who by then was over forty years old, signed a contract with the Cleveland Indians and helped them win a pennant. When told that he might be named Rookie of the Year, Paige said, "Twenty-two years is a long time to be a rookie."

Reality or Drama?

In 1951 television news reporting was new in the United States. Social scientists Kurt and Gladys Lang wanted to find out how watching an event on television changed that event for viewers. The event they studied was "MacArthur Day" in Chicago. General Douglas MacArthur had recently been dismissed by President Truman as commander of the United Nations forces in Korea. MacArthur's fans in Chicago planned several events to honor him, including a parade through the city. The Langs asked thirty-one people who were on the spot to tell what they thought of the actual events. Then they compared those accounts with the television coverage.

Their findings were interesting. The television coverage was more exciting than the events themselves. For example, here is how the television announcer described the parade. "This is the most enthusiastic crowd *ever* in our city. . . . The whole city appears to be marching down State Street behind General MacArthur."

Here is how a person on the scene described the same parade: "A few seconds after he had passed most people merely turned around to shrug and to [say something like] 'That was it,' . . . 'What'll we do now?' Mostly teenagers . . . flocked into the street after MacArthur, but very soon got tired of following as there was no place to go and nothing to do. . . ."

Television tended to show the event as "a universal, enthusiastic, overwhelming ovation for the General"—"drama . . . at the expense of reality."

Beatlemania

In the 1960s the most popular music in America was that of the Beatles—four young rock singers from Liverpool, England. Rock 'n' roll had begun in America in the 1950s. But once the Beatles hit America in 1963, American rock groups tried to copy the Liverpool sound. Young people copied the Beatles' long hair and their "mod" clothing as well.

In many of their earlier songs the Beatles sang about the happiness that love and freedom could bring. A line in one of their hits sang out "All you need is love."

The Beatles spoke and sang for the cartoon versions of themselves in the animated movie *The Yellow Submarine.*

The popularity of VCRs increased sharply during the late 1980s. People liked being able to choose a film from a large selection. They also liked being able to watch films at their convenience.

Movies at Home

The viewing of movies on videocassette recorders (VCRs) has become very popular. Movie-rental stores have sprung up almost everywhere. Roger Ebert, film critic for the *Chicago Sun-Times*, compares watching movies at home with going to the theater.

[In my] last book, I wrote "Television is just not a first-class way to watch movies . . ."Have I changed my mind? Not at all. I still believe that the best way to see a movie is in a large, darkened room, with a giant screen at one end of it, and strangers all around. The strangers are especially important, because they set up a democracy in the dark . . . And yet I own a VCR, and I use it . . . The obvious reason to own and use videocassette players is, of course, that they exist, and that unless we happen to be Hollywood moguls or American Presidents with our private screening rooms, there is no other way to see the movie of our choice, at the time of our choice . . . Someday, I know, they will perfect TV screens the size of walls. You will be able to order the film of your choice, and it will arrive in your home via cable. The sound will be in perfect stereo . . . But when that day comes, I know I will still want to see new movies in real movie theaters, with real audiences, whenever I can. Who says you can't have it both ways?

The computer revolution made many jobs easier and led to the development of many new products for businesses and for the home.

Section 3 Review

1. What groups have been most helped by affirmative action programs?
2. According to Frederick Allen, what did advertisers find most people wanted?
3. What did Mike Lefevre see as the drawback for the worker in mass-producing goods?
4. What did Roger Ebert see as the final step in the viewing of movies at home?

Critical Thinking

5. **Identifying Central Issues.** How do workers and the company benefit from an on-site day-care center at Stride Rite Shoes?

The High-Tech Frontier

"We'll see a minimum of ten times as much progress in the next 12 years as we've seen in the past 12," claims John Peers, president of Novix Inc., a Silicon Valley company. Peers is describing the status of high-tech developments in the United States. Some of the high-tech breakthroughs that he and his colleagues predict are:

- book-sized computers that will fit in your shirt pocket or book bag and will answer to handwritten and spoken commands, possibly even gestures
- tiny cordless picture telephones
- electronic chefs that cook on command
- an electronic book that displays as many as 200 novels—all one will have to do is write the name of the desired novel and it will pop up on the screen
- a diagnostic machine through which one will walk and receive a complete physical examination.

On-The-Job Day Care

More than half the mothers with small children in the United States hold jobs outside the home. The need for the care and supervision of the children of working parents is a growing national concern. One company, Boston's Stride Rite Shoes, was one of the first companies to recognize this need. Back in 1971, the company started an on-site day-care center to provide care for the children of parents employed at Stride Rite. Author Fredelle Maynard describes the project.

Costs are shared by the company, the Massachusetts Department of Public Welfare, and the parents, who pay ten percent of their gross weekly salary for each child enrolled. The center cares for about fifty children, maintains a permanent staff of ten mostly college educated men and women, and gets a good deal of assistance from student volunteers . . . The center has access to all company facilities—the cafeteria, repair shops, accounting department, computers—and a bonanza of scrap material useful for crafts and building projects (cloth, leather, buckles, buttons, wood scraps, braid) . . . Stride Rite's president says . . . "There's a need for corporate management to begin to appreciate the economics of something like quality day care. Fifteen percent of American households are below the poverty line, and if business can get them to contribute to the gross national product, business will benefit."

Focus On Unit 6

Lifestyles: Understanding Social History

To answer the following questions, review the lifestyles section from page 696 to page 711.

1. **Families and Homes.** The move from the suburbs to the city and the resulting restoration of the inner city has a number of obvious and hidden costs. Reread Stephen Birmingham's account of such a move on page 701. What cost does he describe?
2. **Values and Learning.** By the end of World War II, the world had never seemed smaller or more interconnected than at any previous time in history. Review the passage from Eleanor Roosevelt's diary on page 702. Why does Eleanor Roosevelt believe it is important to imagine yourself in someone else's situation? How would doing this change your point of view?
3. **Work and Play.** Not only can we do things faster today due to advances in technology, but our lives have been made considerably easier. Reread Roger Ebert's account of movie-watching on page 710. What new development has affected the way we see movies? Does Ebert welcome this change? Make a chart showing the advantages and disadvantages of watching a movie at home.

Making Connections

Use the Unit 6 time line below to answer the following questions.

1. In what decade did each of the following events take place: Korean War, New Deal, Pearl Harbor, Panama Canal treaties, Kennedy assassination?
2. Which events show gains in civil rights?
3. Reread the Unit Introduction on page 593 and cite examples from the time line that prove that World War I was not "the war to end all wars."
4. **Predicting Consequences.** Imagine that you were 12 years old at the beginning of one of the decades on the time line. How would events of that decade have affected you?

Critical Thinking Skills

1. **Determining Relevance.** How did World War I influence American attitudes and lifestyles in the 1920s?
2. **Recognizing Cause and Effect.** How did the business downturn in 1929 cause widespread unemployment by 1932?
3. **Identifying Central Issues.** How was the issue of loyalty oaths part of the larger issue of the postwar struggle between the superpowers?

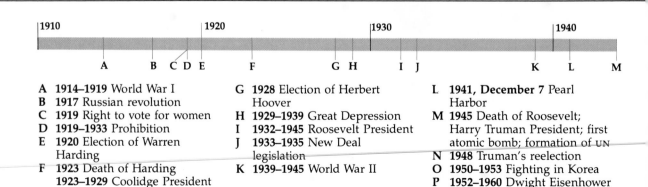

A 1914–1919 World War I	**G** 1928 Election of Herbert Hoover	**L** 1941, **December 7** Pearl Harbor
B 1917 Russian revolution	**H** 1929–1939 Great Depression	**M** 1945 Death of Roosevelt; Harry Truman President; first atomic bomb; formation of UN
C 1919 Right to vote for women	**I** 1932–1945 Roosevelt President	
D 1919–1933 Prohibition	**J** 1933–1935 New Deal legislation	**N** 1948 Truman's reelection
E 1920 Election of Warren Harding	**K** 1939–1945 World War II	**O** 1950–1953 Fighting in Korea
F 1923 Death of Harding 1923–1929 Coolidge President		**P** 1952–1960 Dwight Eisenhower President

Using Geography Skills

Use the map below to answer the following questions.

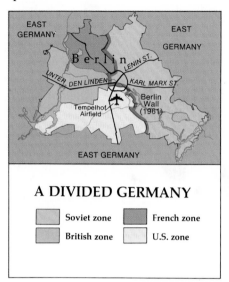

A DIVIDED GERMANY

Soviet zone French zone
British zone U.S. zone

1. **Developing Locational Skills.** In what country is Berlin located?
2. **Understanding Human and Environmental Interaction.** Name three Berlin landmarks made by people.
3. **Understanding World Regions.** How does the division of Berlin reflect the political reality of Europe after World War II?
4. **Understanding Human Movement.** What features on the map show that Berlin was once a united city? What feature shows that people can no longer move freely in the city?

Linking Past to Present

Drawing Conclusions. How did the United States move from its policy of isolationism in the early 1900s to its present position as leader of the free world? List events from this unit that drew the United States into involvement in world affairs. What role have Presidents since 1960 played in the struggle between the superpowers?

Reviewing Social Studies Skills

1. **Understanding the News Media.** List the four major news media. Then write one advantage and one disadvantage for each of the media. Which media are best for on-the-spot coverage? Which are best for full coverage or summaries?
2. **Tomorrow's History.** Choose one newspaper headline or one story from a television newscast. Write a summary of the event that tells *who, what, where, how,* or *why.* Then indicate whether you think the story is likely to have historical importance. Explain your answer.

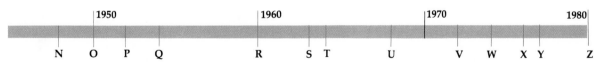

Q 1954 *Brown* v. *Board of Education of Topeka*
R 1960 Election of John F. Kennedy
S 1963 Assassination of Kennedy; Lyndon B. Johnson President

T 1964 Johnson's reelection; Civil Rights Act
U 1968 Assassinations of Martin Luther King, Jr., and Robert Kennedy; election of Richard Nixon

V 1972 Arms limitation treaty with U.S.S.R.; Watergate break-in; Nixon's reelection
W 1974 Nixon's resignation
X 1976 Election of Jimmy Carter
Y 1977 Panama Canal treaties
Z 1980 Election of Ronald Reagan

The Reference Shelf

Like a reference shelf in a library, this section of your book contains much information. The Atlas includes a world map as well as many maps of North America and the United States. The Declaration of Independence and the Constitution of the United States include both the full text and, in the margin, easier-to-read phrasing.

The charts in this section can tell you much about the territory of the United States. The Chronology provides a good review of the nation's history, and the Glossary defines many of the terms used in the text and shows how to pronounce them. The Index will help you find your way around the book by showing on what pages certain topics appear.

The Acknowledgments show the sources from which some quotes and all the pictures in this book have been taken. As you use this section, take a moment to think about all the people who have come before you. They have shaped your country's history, as you are doing now.

Atlas

ARCTIC OCEAN

ARctic circle

GREENLAND
(Denmark)

U.S.S.R.

Wrangel I.
Point Barrow
Barrow

UNITED STATES
ALASKA

Nome
Fairbanks
Yukon River
Dawson
Whitehorse
Anchorage
Juneau

Beaufort Sea

Banks Island

Victoria Island

Great Bear Lake
Port Radium
Great Slave Lake

Mackenzie River

Baffin Island

Ellesmere Island

Thule

Baffin Bay

Davis Strait

Godthaab

Julianehaab
Cape Farewell

Norwegia

Jan Mayen (Nor.)

ICELAND
Reykjavik

Bering Strait

St. Lawrence I.

Bering Sea

Pribilof Islands

Dutch Harbor

Kodiak I.

Gulf of Alaska

Queen Charlotte Islands

Vancouver Island

Seattle
Portland

NORTH

PACIFIC

OCEAN

Aleutian Islands

CANADA

Edmonton
Calgary
Regina
Winnipeg

Vancouver

Lake Winnipeg

Great Lakes

Minneapolis

Churchill

Hudson Bay

Goose Bay

Newfoundland I.
Gander
St. John's

Quebec
Ottawa
Montreal
Toronto
Boston
Halifax

NORTH

AMERICA

Chicago
Detroit
Cleveland
St. Louis
Washington, D.C.

New York
Philadelphia
Norfolk

NORTH

ATLANTIC

OCEAN

Faeroes (Den.)

Shetland Is.
Orkney Is.
UNITED
NO. IRELAND
IRELAND
Dublin

SCOTLA
SI
KINGDOM
ENGLAN
Lond

English Channel
Bay of Biscay
FRAN

Salt Lake City
Denver

San Francisco

Los Angeles

UNITED STATES

Dallas

Atlanta

Houston
New Orleans
Jacksonville

Bermuda (Br.)

Azores (Port.)

PORTUGAL
Lisbon
SPAIN
Madrid

Strait of Tangier Gibraltar
Rabat
Casablanca
MOROCCO

Madeira Is. (Port.)

Alg

PACIFIC

Honolulu
HAWAII
UNITED STATES

Hawaiian Islands

Johnston I. (U.S.)

Tropic of Cancer

Monterrey
MEXICO
Guadalajara
Mexico City
Veracruz

Gulf of Mexico

Miami

Havana
Key West
CUBA

BAHAMAS

West Indies

DOMINICAN REPUBLIC

Canary Is. (Sp.)

WESTERN SAHARA (Mor.)

MAURITANIA

A

OCEAN

TOKELAU

KIRIBATI

Line Is.

Marquesas Islands

AM. SAMOA

COOK ISLANDS

TONGA

Society Islands
Tahiti

Tuamotu Arch.

NIUE

FRENCH POLYNESIA

PITCAIRN ISLANDS GROUP

Equator

Galápagos Is. (Ecuador)

BELIZE
GUATEMALA
EL SALVADOR
HONDURAS
NICARAGUA
COSTA RICA
Central America
PANAMA
Panama Canal

JAMAICA
HAITI
Puerto Rico (U.S.)
Lesser Antilles

Caribbean Sea

Caracas
VENEZUELA
Medellín
Bogotá
COLOMBIA
Cali
Quito
Guayaquil
ECUADOR

TRINIDAD AND TOBAGO
GUYANA
SURINAME
FRENCH GUIANA (Fr.)

Manaus
Amazon R.
Belém

CAPE VERDE

SENEGAL
Dakar
GAMBIA
GUINEA-BISSAU
SIERRA LEONE
Monrovia
LIBERIA

MALI

BUR.
FASO
GUINEA
IVORY
COAST
Accra
TOGO
GHA

Niger R.

SOUTH

BRAZIL

Fortaleza
Recife

Ascension I. (Br.)

PERU
Callao
Lima
Cuzco

AMERICA

La Paz
BOLIVIA
Sucre

Brasília

Salvador

Belo Horizonte

SOUTH

St. Helena (Br.)

Tropic of Capricorn

Easter I. (Chile)

Antofagasta

Tucumán
Asunción
PARAGUAY

Paraná R.

Rio de Janeiro
São Paulo
Pôrto Alegre

Juan Fernández Is. (Chile)

Valparaíso
Santiago
Concepción

CHILE

ARGENTINA
Rosario
Buenos Aires

URUGUAY
Montevideo
Río de la Plata

ATLANTIC

SOUTH

PACIFIC

Punta Arenas

Strait of Magellan
Tierra del Fuego

Cape Horn

Falkland Islands (Br.)

South Georgia (Br.)

OCEAN

OCEAN

Drake Passage

Antarctic Circle

ANTAR

THE WORLD
Political Map

⊛ National Capitals
★ Other Capitals ● Other Cities

SCALE
One inch–about 1660 Miles

Miles
0   500 1000   2000   3000   4000   5000

Kilometers
0   2000   4000   6000   8000

Projection: Modified Van Der Grinten

NORTH AMERICA

Graphic-Relief Map

HEIGHT OF LAND

- OVER 13,000 FEET
- 6,600 TO 13,000
- 3,300 TO 6,600
- 1,650 TO 3,300
- 650 TO 1,650
- 0 TO 650 FEET
- BELOW SEA LEVEL

DEPTH OF WATER

- 0 TO 600 FEET
- BELOW 600 FEET

⊛ **National Capitals**

● **Other Cities**

SCALE
One inch–about 600 Miles

Miles
0   200   400   600   800   1000

Kilometers
0   400   800   1200   1600

Projection: Lambert's Azimuthal

719

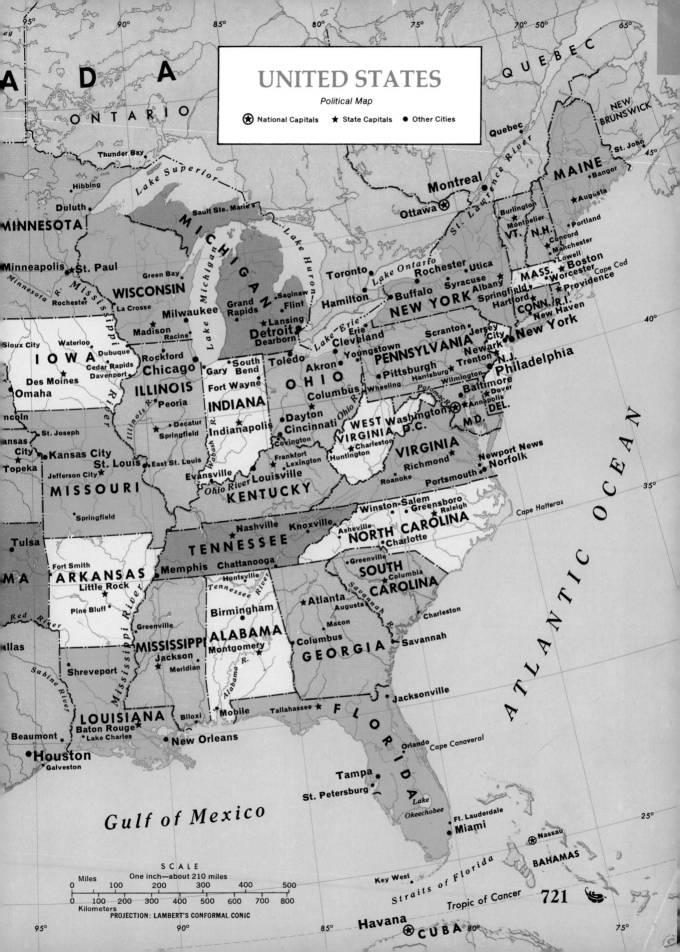

UNITED STATES
Political Map

⭐ National Capitals　　★ State Capitals　　● Other Cities

QUEBEC

NEW BRUNSWICK

ADA

ONTARIO

Quebec

MAINE

Bangor

Augusta

Thunder Bay

Hibbing

Duluth

Lake Superior

Sault Ste. Marie

Montreal

Ottawa ⭐

St. Lawrence River

Portland

MINNESOTA

Burlington

Montpelier

VT.

N.H.

Concord

Manchester

Lowell

Minneapolis　St. Paul

Green Bay

MICHIGAN

Lake Huron

Toronto

Lake Ontario

Rochester

Utica

MASS.

Boston

Worcester

Cape Cod

Minnesota R.

Rochester

WISCONSIN

La Crosse

Grand Rapids

Saginaw

Flint

Hamilton

Buffalo

Syracuse

Albany

Springfield

Providence

CONN.　R.I.

Hartford

Sioux City

Waterloo

Madison

Milwaukee

Lansing

Detroit

Lake Erie

Erie

Cleveland

NEW YORK

Scranton

Jersey City

New Haven

New York

Dubuque

Racine

Dearborn

Youngstown

PENNSYLVANIA

Newark

N.J.

IOWA

Cedar Rapids

Rockford

Chicago

Gary

South Bend

Toledo

Akron

Pittsburgh

Trenton

Philadelphia

Des Moines

Davenport

ILLINOIS

Fort Wayne

OHIO

Columbus

Wheeling

Harrisburg

Wilmington

DEL.

Omaha

Peoria

INDIANA

Dayton

Cincinnati

WEST VIRGINIA

Washington D.C. ⭐

Baltimore

Dover

Annapolis

MD.

ncoln

St. Joseph

Decatur

Springfield

Indianapolis

Covington

Frankfort

Lexington

Charleston

Huntington

VIRGINIA

Potomac R.

ansas City

Kansas City

St. Louis

East St. Louis

Evansville

Louisville

Richmond

Newport News

Norfolk

Topeka

Jefferson City

MISSOURI

Ohio River

KENTUCKY

Roanoke

Portsmouth

Springfield

Nashville

Knoxville

Asheville

Winston-Salem

Greensboro

Raleigh

Cape Hatteras

Tulsa

MA

Fort Smith

ARKANSAS

Little Rock

Memphis

TENNESSEE

Chattanooga

Huntsville

Tennessee River

NORTH CAROLINA

Charlotte

Greenville

SOUTH CAROLINA

Columbia

Charleston

Red River

Pine Bluff

Greenville

Birmingham

Atlanta

Augusta

Savannah R.

MISSISSIPPI

ALABAMA

Montgomery

Macon

Charleston

allas

Shreveport

Jackson

Meridian

Alabama R.

Columbus

GEORGIA

Savannah

Sabine River

LOUISIANA

Baton Rouge

Biloxi

Mobile

Tallahassee

Jacksonville

Beaumont

Lake Charles

New Orleans

FLORIDA

Houston

Galveston

Orlando

Cape Canaveral

Gulf of Mexico

Tampa

St. Petersburg

Lake Okeechobee

Ft. Lauderdale

Miami

ATLANTIC OCEAN

Nassau

BAHAMAS

Key West

Straits of Florida

Havana

Tropic of Cancer

CUBA

721

SCALE
One inch—about 210 miles

Miles
0　100　200　300　400　500

0　100　200　300　400　500　600　700　800
Kilometers

PROJECTION: LAMBERT'S CONFORMAL CONIC

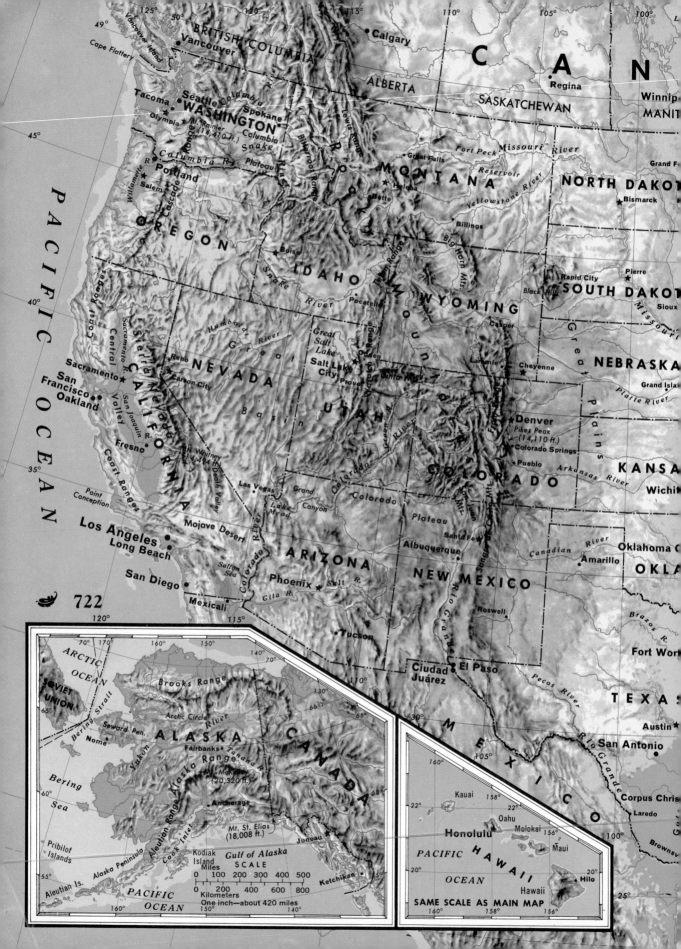

PACIFIC OCEAN

CANADA

BRITISH COLUMBIA

125°
120°
115°
110°
105°
100°

49°
Cape Flattery
Vancouver Island
Vancouver
Calgary
50°

ALBERTA
SASKATCHEWAN
Regina
Winnipeg
MANIT

Tacoma
Seattle
Spokane
Columbia
WASHINGTON
Olympia
Mt. Rainier
(14,410 ft.)
Columbia
Snake
45°
Columbia R.
Plateau
Great Falls
Fort Peck
Reservoir
Missouri
River
Grand F

Portland
Willamette
R.
Cascade
Range
Bitterroot Range
MONTANA
Helena
Yellowstone River
NORTH DAKOTA
Bismarck

Salem
OREGON
Butte
Billings

Boise
IDAHO
Snake
River
Rapid City
Black Hills
SOUTH DAKOTA
Pierre
Sioux

40°
Humboldt
River
WYOMING
Casper
Big Horn Mts.

Reno
NEVADA
Great
Salt
Lake
Salt Lake
City
Ogden
Provo
Laramie
Cheyenne
NEBRASKA
Grand Island

Carson City
Salt Lake
City
Uinta Mts.
Denver
Pikes Peak
(14,110 ft.)
Colorado Springs
Great Plains
Platte River

San
Francisco
Oakland
Sacramento
CALIFORNIA
Central
Valley
Sierra Nevada
UTAH
Colorado River
COLORADO
Pueblo
Arkansas River
KANSAS
Wichit

Fresno
San Joaquin
R.
35°
Mt. Whitney
(14,494 ft.)
Death Valley
Las Vegas
Grand
Canyon
Colorado
Plateau
Santa Fe
Sangre de Cristo Mts.

Point
Conception
Coast Ranges
Lake
Mead
Grand
Canyon
Colorado
Albuquerque
Canadian
River
Oklahoma C
Amarillo
OKLA

Los Angeles
Long Beach
Mojave Desert
Colorado River
ARIZONA
NEW MEXICO
Rio Grande

San Diego
Salton
Sea
Phoenix
Salt
R.
Roswell
Pecos River
TEXAS

Mexicali
Gila R.
Tucson
Fort Wort

722

120°
115°
110°
105°
100°

MEXICO
Ciudad
Juárez
El Paso
30°
Austin
San Antonio
Laredo
Corpus Chris
25°
Brownsv

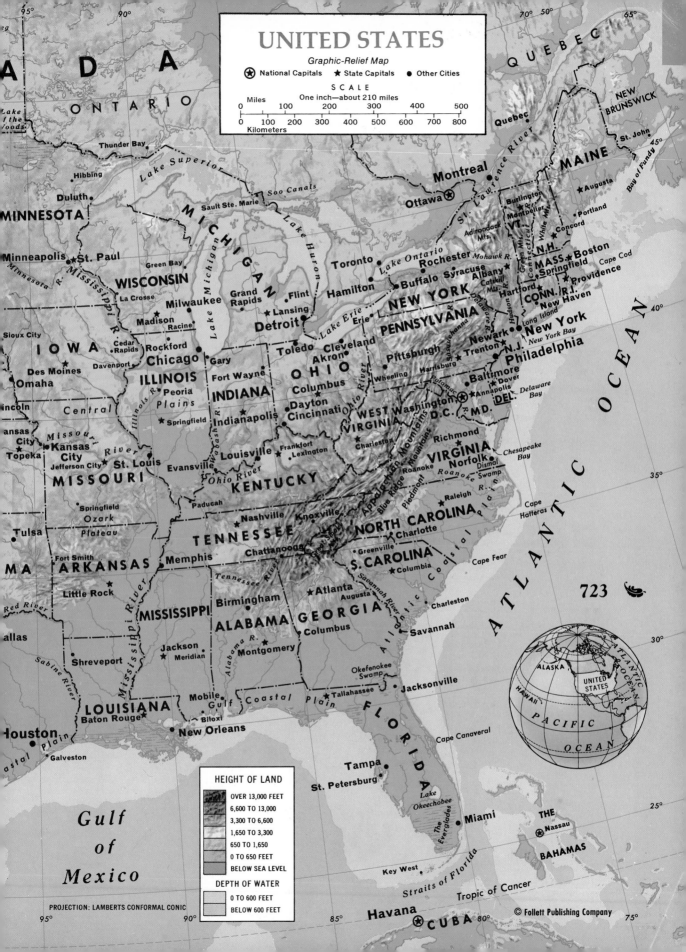

UNITED STATES

Graphic-Relief Map

⊛ National Capitals   ★ State Capitals   ● Other Cities

SCALE
One inch—about 210 miles

Miles
0   100   200   300   400   500

Kilometers
0 100 200 300 400 500 600 700 800

CANADA

QUEBEC

NEW BRUNSWICK

ONTARIO

Lake of the Woods

Thunder Bay

Hibbing
Duluth

MINNESOTA

Lake Superior

Soo Canals
Sault Ste. Marie

MICHIGAN

Lake Huron

Montreal
Ottawa ⊛

St. Lawrence River

MAINE

Bay of Fundy
St. John

Augusta

Portland
Concord

Burlington
Montpelier
VT.
Adirondack Mts.
White Mts.
N.H.

Minneapolis
St. Paul

Minnesota R.

Mississippi R.

Green Bay

WISCONSIN

La Crosse

Milwaukee

Madison
Racine

Lake Michigan

Grand Rapids
Flint
Lansing

Detroit

Toronto
Hamilton

Lake Ontario
Rochester
Buffalo Syracuse
Mohawk R.
Albany
Catskill Mts.
Hartford

MASS. Boston
Springfield
Providence
CONN. R.I.
New Haven

Long Island

Sioux City

IOWA

Cedar Rapids
Rockford
Davenport

Chicago
Gary

Lake Erie
Erie

NEW YORK

PENNSYLVANIA

Hudson R.

Newark
New York
New York Bay

Des Moines
Omaha

ILLINOIS

Peoria
Illinois R.
Central Plains

Fort Wayne

INDIANA

Toledo

Cleveland
Akron

OHIO

Columbus

Pittsburgh
Wheeling

Harrisburg
Susquehanna R.

Trenton
N.J.
Philadelphia

Baltimore
Dover
DEL.
Delaware Bay

Lincoln

Springfield

Indianapolis

Dayton
Cincinnati

Ohio River

WEST VIRGINIA
Washington
D.C. ⊛

Annapolis
MD.

kansas City

Missouri River

Kansas City

St. Louis

Evansville

Wabash R.

Louisville

Frankfort
Lexington

Charleston

VIRGINIA

Richmond

Norfolk
Chesapeake Bay

Topeka
Jefferson City

MISSOURI

Paducah

Ohio River

KENTUCKY

Roanoke
Blue Ridge Mountains
Piedmont
Dismal Swamp

Appalachian Mountains

Raleigh

Cape Hatteras

Springfield
Ozark Plateau

Nashville
Knoxville

Chattanooga
Great Smoky Mts.

NORTH CAROLINA
Charlotte

Greenville
S. CAROLINA
Columbia

Atlantic Coastal Plain

Cape Fear

Tulsa

TENNESSEE

Memphis

Tennessee River

ATLANTIC OCEAN

MA
Fort Smith

ARKANSAS

Little Rock

Mississippi River

Birmingham

ALABAMA

Atlanta
Augusta
GEORGIA
Columbus

Savannah River

Charleston

Savannah

723

Red River

Dallas

MISSISSIPPI

Jackson
Meridian

Alabama R.

Montgomery

Okefenokee Swamp

Jacksonville

Sabine River

Shreveport

Mississippi River

Mobile
Biloxi

LOUISIANA
Baton Rouge

Gulf Coastal Plain

Tallahassee

FLORIDA

Cape Canaveral

Houston

Coastal Plain

New Orleans

Galveston

Gulf of Mexico

Tampa
St. Petersburg

Lake Okeechobee

The Everglades

Miami

THE
Nassau ⊛

BAHAMAS

Key West

Straits of Florida

Tropic of Cancer

Havana
CUBA ⊛

ALASKA
HAWAII
UNITED STATES
ATLANTIC OCEAN
PACIFIC OCEAN

HEIGHT OF LAND

OVER 13,000 FEET
6,600 TO 13,000
3,300 TO 6,600
1,650 TO 3,300
650 TO 1,650
0 TO 650 FEET
BELOW SEA LEVEL

DEPTH OF WATER

0 TO 600 FEET
BELOW 600 FEET

PROJECTION: LAMBERTS CONFORMAL CONIC

© Follett Publishing Company

95° 90° 85° 80° 75° 70° 65°

45° 40° 35° 30° 25°

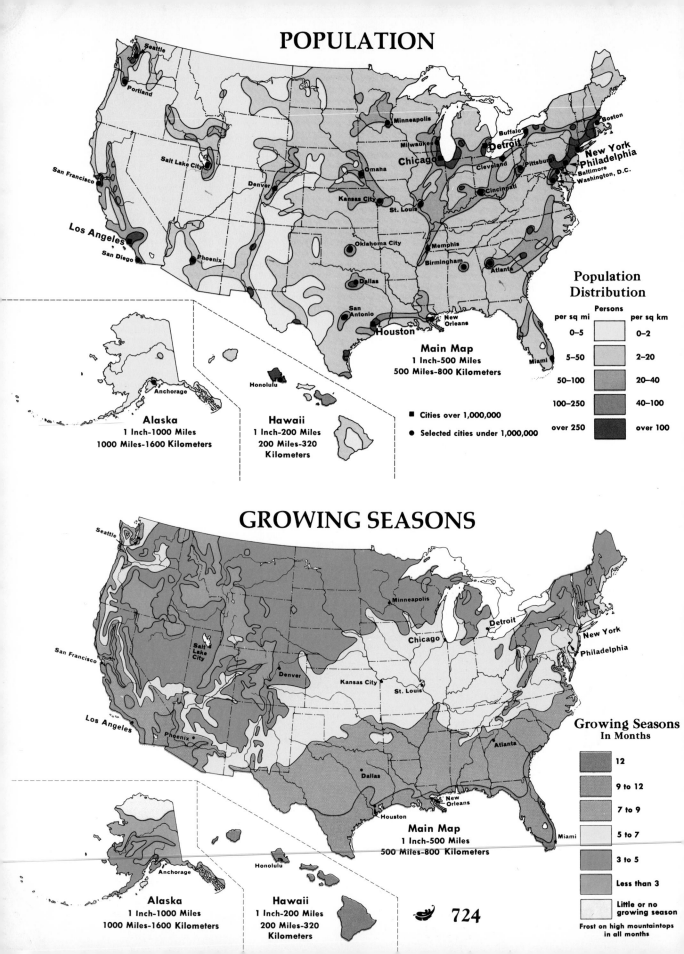

POPULATION

Population Distribution

Persons per sq mi	Persons per sq km
0–5	0–2
5–50	2–20
50–100	20–40
100–250	40–100
over 250	over 100

Main Map
1 Inch–500 Miles
500 Miles–800 Kilometers

Alaska
1 Inch–1000 Miles
1000 Miles–1600 Kilometers

Hawaii
1 Inch–200 Miles
200 Miles–320 Kilometers

■ Cities over 1,000,000

● Selected cities under 1,000,000

GROWING SEASONS

Growing Seasons
In Months

- 12
- 9 to 12
- 7 to 9
- 5 to 7
- 3 to 5
- Less than 3
- Little or no growing season

Frost on high mountaintops in all months

Main Map
1 Inch–500 Miles
500 Miles–800 Kilometers

Alaska
1 Inch–1000 Miles
1000 Miles–1600 Kilometers

Hawaii
1 Inch–200 Miles
200 Miles–320 Kilometers

724

LAND USE

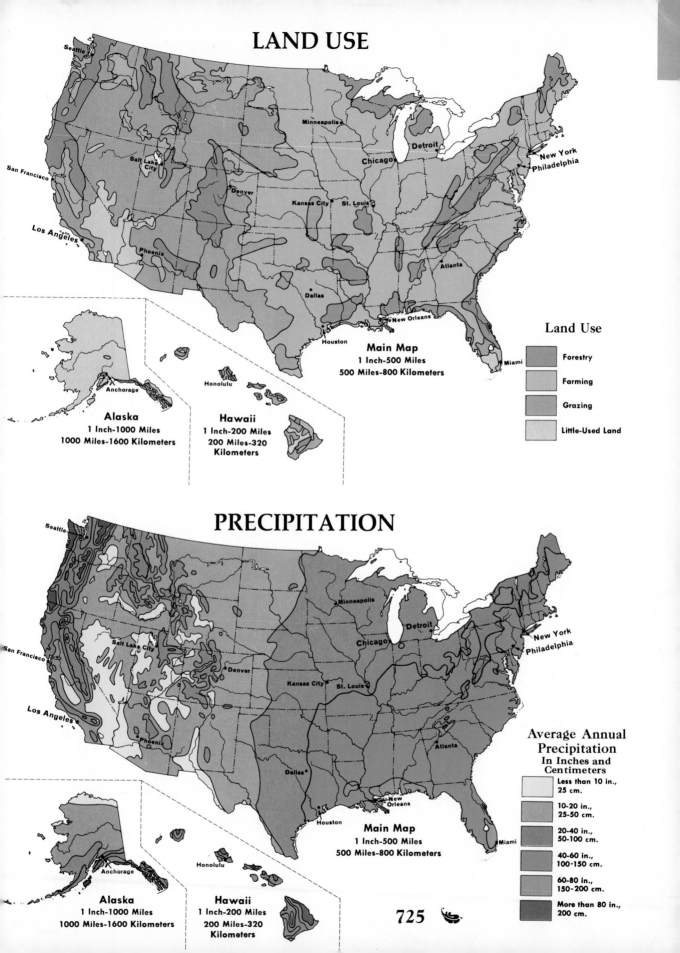

Seattle
San Francisco
Los Angeles
Phoenix
Salt Lake City
Denver
Minneapolis
Chicago
Detroit
Kansas City
St. Louis
Dallas
Houston
New Orleans
Atlanta
New York
Philadelphia
Miami

Main Map
1 Inch-500 Miles
500 Miles-800 Kilometers

Anchorage

Alaska
1 Inch-1000 Miles
1000 Miles-1600 Kilometers

Honolulu

Hawaii
1 Inch-200 Miles
200 Miles-320
Kilometers

Land Use

- Forestry
- Farming
- Grazing
- Little-Used Land

PRECIPITATION

Seattle
San Francisco
Los Angeles
Salt Lake City
Phoenix
Denver
Minneapolis
Chicago
Detroit
Kansas City
St. Louis
Dallas
Houston
New Orleans
Atlanta
New York
Philadelphia
Miami

Main Map
1 Inch-500 Miles
500 Miles-800 Kilometers

Anchorage

Alaska
1 Inch-1000 Miles
1000 Miles-1600 Kilometers

Honolulu

Hawaii
1 Inch-200 Miles
200 Miles-320
Kilometers

Average Annual
Precipitation
In Inches and
Centimeters

- Less than 10 in., 25 cm.
- 10-20 in., 25-50 cm.
- 20-40 in., 50-100 cm.
- 40-60 in., 100-150 cm.
- 60-80 in., 150-200 cm.
- More than 80 in., 200 cm.

725

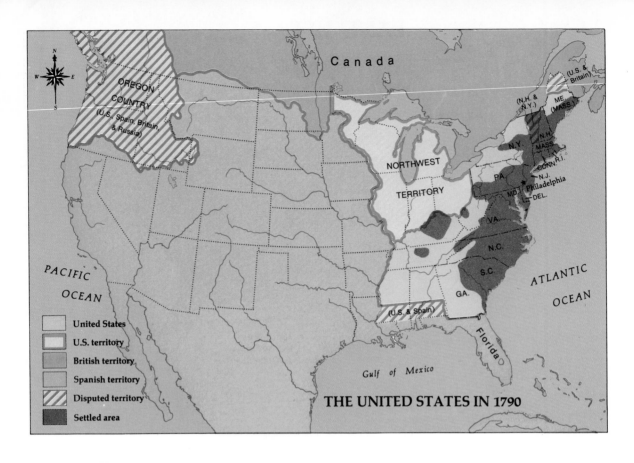

THE UNITED STATES IN 1790

Legend:
- United States
- U.S. territory
- British territory
- Spanish territory
- Disputed territory
- Settled area

OREGON COUNTRY (U.S., Spain, Britain, & Russia)

Canada

(U.S. & Britain)

(N.H. & N.Y.)

ME (MASS.)

NORTHWEST TERRITORY

N.Y.

N.H.

MASS.

CONN. R.I.

N.J.

PA.

MD. Philadelphia

DEL.

VA.

N.C.

S.C.

GA.

(U.S. & Spain)

Florida

PACIFIC OCEAN

ATLANTIC OCEAN

Gulf of Mexico

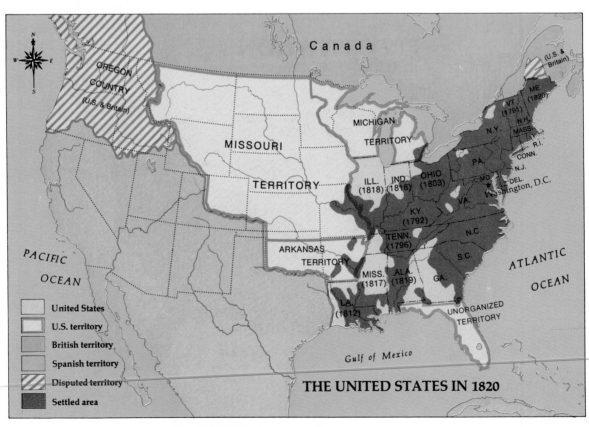

THE UNITED STATES IN 1820

Legend:
- United States
- U.S. territory
- British territory
- Spanish territory
- Disputed territory
- Settled area

OREGON COUNTRY (U.S. & Britain)

Canada

(U.S. & Britain)

MISSOURI TERRITORY

MICHIGAN TERRITORY

ILL. (1818)

IND. (1816)

OHIO (1803)

VT. (1791)

N.Y.

N.H.

MASS.

R.I.

CONN.

PA.

N.J.

MD.

DEL.

Washington, D.C.

ME (1820)

KY. (1792)

VA.

N.C.

ARKANSAS TERRITORY

TENN. (1796)

MISS. (1817)

ALA. (1819)

GA.

S.C.

LA. (1812)

UNORGANIZED TERRITORY

Florida

PACIFIC OCEAN

ATLANTIC OCEAN

Gulf of Mexico

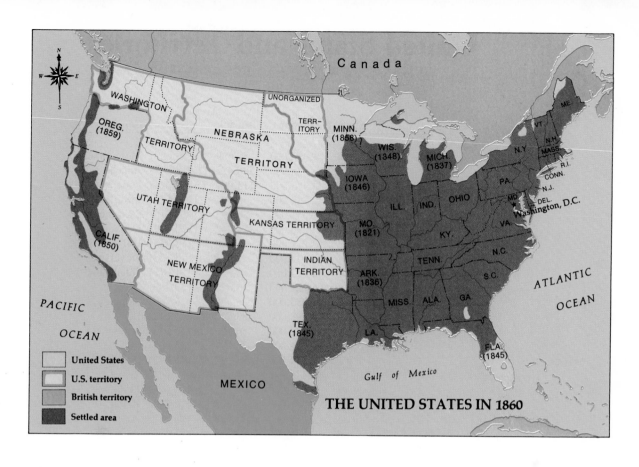

THE UNITED STATES IN 1860

Legend:
- United States
- U.S. territory
- British territory
- Settled area

Map labels (1860):
Canada, WASHINGTON TERRITORY, UNORGANIZED TERRITORY, OREG. (1859), NEBRASKA TERRITORY, MINN. (1858), WIS. (1848), MICH. (1837), N.Y., ME., VT, N.H., MASS., R.I., CONN., N.J., PA., UTAH TERRITORY, IOWA (1846), ILL., IND., OHIO, MD., DEL., Washington, D.C., CALIF. (1850), KANSAS TERRITORY, MO. (1821), KY., VA., NEW MEXICO TERRITORY, INDIAN TERRITORY, ARK. (1836), TENN., N.C., S.C., MISS., ALA., GA., TEX. (1845), LA., FLA. (1845), PACIFIC OCEAN, MEXICO, Gulf of Mexico, ATLANTIC OCEAN

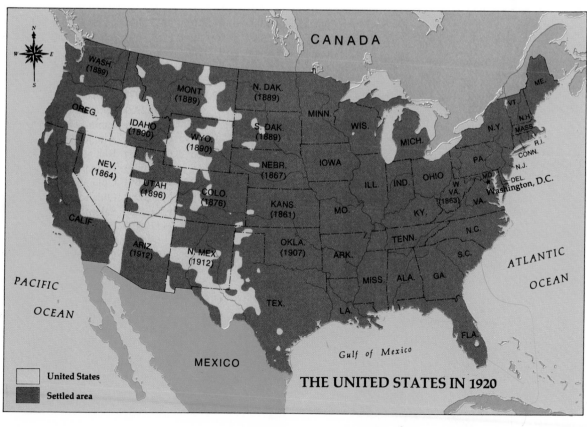

THE UNITED STATES IN 1920

Legend:
- United States
- Settled area

Map labels (1920):
CANADA, WASH. (1889), OREG., MONT. (1889), N. DAK. (1889), MINN., IDAHO (1890), WYO. (1890), S. DAK. (1889), WIS., MICH., NEV. (1864), UTAH (1896), COLO. (1876), NEBR. (1867), IOWA, ILL., IND., OHIO, W. VA. (1863), PA., N.Y., ME., VT, N.H., MASS., R.I., CONN., N.J., MD., DEL., Washington, D.C., CALIF., ARIZ. (1912), N. MEX. (1912), KANS. (1861), MO., KY., VA., OKLA. (1907), ARK., TENN., N.C., S.C., MISS., ALA., GA., TEX., LA., FLA., PACIFIC OCEAN, MEXICO, Gulf of Mexico, ATLANTIC OCEAN

United States and Territories by

State	Population	Area sq. mi.	(sq km)	Capital
Alabama	4,083,000	51,609	(133,667)	Montgomery
Alaska	525,000	586,412	(1,718,807)	Juneau
Arizona	3,386,000	113,909	(295,024)	Phoenix
Arkansas	2,388,000	53,104	(136,539)	Little Rock
California	27,663,000	158,693	(411,015)	Sacramento
Colorado	3,296,000	104,247	(270,000)	Denver
Connecticut	3,211,000	5,009	(12,973)	Hartford
Delaware	644,000	2,057	(5,328)	Dover
Florida	12,023,000	58,560	(151,671)	Tallahassee
Georgia	6,222,000	58,876	(152,489)	Atlanta
Hawaii	1,083,000	6,450	(16,706)	Honolulu
Idaho	998,000	83,557	(216,413)	Boise
Illinois	11,582,000	56,400	(146,076)	Springfield
Indiana	5,531,000	36,291	(93,995)	Indianapolis
Iowa	2,834,000	56,290	(145,791)	Des Moines
Kansas	2,476,000	82,264	(213,064)	Topeka
Kentucky	3,727,000	40,395	(104,623)	Frankfort
Louisiana	4,461,000	48,523	(125,875)	Baton Rouge
Maine	1,187,000	33,215	(86,017)	Augusta
Maryland	4,535,000	10,577	(27,394)	Annapolis
Massachusetts	5,855,000	8,257	(21,386)	Boston
Michigan	9,200,000	58,216	(150,779)	Lansing
Minnesota	4,246,000	84,068	(229,736)	St. Paul
Mississippi	2,625,000	47,716	(123,584)	Jackson
Missouri	5,103,000	69,686	(180,487)	Jefferson City
Montana	809,000	147,138	(381,087)	Helena
Nebraska	1,594,000	77,227	(200,018)	Lincoln
Nevada	1,007,000	110,540	(286,299)	Carson City
New Hampshire	1,057,000	9,304	(24,097)	Concord
New Jersey	7,672,000	7,836	(20,295)	Trenton
New Mexico	1,500,000	121,666	(315,115)	Santa Fe
New York	17,825,000	49,576	(128,405)	Albany
North Carolina	6,413,000	52,586	(136,198)	Raleigh
North Dakota	672,000	70,665	(183,022)	Bismarck
Ohio	10,784,000	41,222	(106,765)	Columbus
Oklahoma	3,272,000	69,919	(181,090)	Oklahoma City
Oregon	2,724,000	96,981	(251,181)	Salem
Pennsylvania	11,936,000	45,333	(117,412)	Harrisburg
Rhode Island	986,000	1,214	(3,144)	Providence
South Carolina	3,425,000	31,055	(80,432)	Columbia
South Dakota	709,000	77,047	(199,552)	Pierre
Tennessee	4,855,000	42,244	(109,412)	Nashville
Texas	16,789,000	267,339	(692,408)	Austin
Utah	1,680,000	84,916	(219,932)	Salt Lake City
Vermont	548,000	9,609	(24,887)	Montpelier

Population, Area, and Capital

State	Population	Area sq. mi.	(sq km)	Capital
Virginia	5,904,000	40,817	(105,716)	Richmond
Washington	4,538,000	68,192	(176,617)	Olympia
West Virginia	1,897,000	24,181	(62,629)	Charleston
Wisconsin	4,807,000	56,154	(145,439)	Madison
Wyoming	490,000	97,914	(253,687)	Cheyenne
District of Columbia	622,000	67	(174)	– – – – – –
U.S. total	**243,399,000**	**3,615,102**	**(9,363,114)**	**Washington, D.C.**

Territory	Population	Area sq. mi.	(sq km)	Capital
American Samoa	37,000*	76	(197)	Pago Pago
Guam	120,000*	209	(541)	Agaña
Puerto Rico	3,187,566*	3,421	(8,860)	San Juan
Republic of Palau	14,000	192	(499)	Koror
Virgin Islands	95,591*	132	(342)	Charlotte Amalie

*Estimated 1988 figure

The two-letter abbreviations shown on this map are called postal abbreviations. They are used by the United States Post Office to speed the sorting of mail.

© FPC

The Declaration of Independence

The words that follow in the wide column are the original words of the Declaration of Independence. Spelling and punctuation have been updated. The words in the margin help explain the original words.

Issued on July 4, 1776, the Declaration of Independence changed the course of history by asserting that the United States of America was a free and independent nation.

The opening paragraph explains that when people decide to free themselves from political ties with another country, they ought to explain their actions to the rest of the world.

WHEN, IN THE COURSE OF HUMAN EVENTS, it becomes necessary for one people to dissolve the political bands which have connected them with another, and to assume, among the powers of the earth, the separate and equal station to which the laws of nature and of nature's God entitle them, a decent respect to the opinions of mankind requires that they should declare the causes which impel them to the separation.

This paragraph contains ideas at the heart of American democracy. All people have certain natural, God-given rights. Governments are set up to protect these natural rights. If a government fails at this task, the people have the right to change or abolish their government. However, the reasons for such drastic action must be very serious.

We hold these truths to be self-evident: that all men are created equal; that they are endowed by their Creator with certain inalienable rights; that among these are life, liberty, and the pursuit of happiness. That, to secure these rights, governments are instituted among men, deriving their just powers from the consent of the governed; that, whenever any form of government becomes destructive of these ends, it is the right of the people to alter or to abolish it, and to institute new government, laying its foundation on such principles, and organizing its powers in such form, as to them shall seem most likely to effect their safety and happiness. Prudence, indeed, will dictate that governments long established should not be changed for light and transient causes; and accordingly, all experience hath shown, that mankind are more disposed to suffer, while evils are sufferable, than to right themselves by abolishing the forms to which they are accustomed. But, when a long train of abuses and usurpations, pursuing invariably the same object, evinces a design to reduce them under absolute despotism, it is their right, it is their duty, to throw off such government, and to provide new guards for their future security. Such has been the patient sufferance of these colonies, and such is now the necessity which constrains them to alter their former systems of government. The history of the present King of Great Britain is a history of repeated injuries and usurpations, all having, in direct object, the establishment of an absolute tyranny over these States. To prove this, let facts be submitted to a candid world.

> The colonists want the world to know what the king and his government have done to cause them to break away from British rule.

HE HAS refused his assent to laws the most wholesome and necessary for the public good.

> THE KING HAS: opposed needed laws.

HE HAS forbidden his governors to pass laws of immediate and pressing importance, unless suspended in their operation till his assent should be obtained; and, when so suspended, he has utterly neglected to attend to them.

> neglected pressing problems.

HE HAS refused to pass other laws for the accommodation of large districts of people, unless those people would relinquish the right of representation in the legislature—a right inestimable to them and formidable to tyrants only.

> demanded that people give up their self-government before he would approve needed laws.

HE HAS called together legislative bodies at places unusual, uncomfortable, and distant from the depository of their public records, for the sole purpose of fatiguing them into compliance with his measures.

> made self-government inconvenient.

HE HAS dissolved representative houses repeatedly, for opposing, with manly firmness, his invasions on the rights of the people.

> ordered lawmaking bodies to stop meeting.

HE HAS refused, for a long time after such dissolutions, to cause others to be elected; whereby the legislative powers, incapable of annihilation, have returned to the people at large for their exercise; the State remaining, in the meantime, exposed to all the dangers of invasions from without and convulsions within.

> left colonies unprotected after dissolving their legislatures.

HE HAS endeavored to prevent the population of these States; for that purpose obstructing the laws for naturalization of foreigners, refusing to pass others to encourage their migrations hither, and raising the conditions of new appropriations of lands.

> tried to limit the growth and expansion of the colonies.

HE HAS obstructed the administration of justice, by refusing his assent to laws for establishing judiciary powers.

> interfered with justice in the colonies.

HE HAS made judges dependent on his will alone for the tenure of their offices and the amount and payment of their salaries.

> kept colonial judges under British control.

HE HAS erected a multitude of new offices, and sent hither swarms of officers to harass our people, and eat out their substance.

> sent officers to harass the public.

HE HAS kept among us, in times of peace, standing armies, without the consent of our legislatures.

> quartered British soldiers in colonial homes without consent.

HE HAS affected to render the military independent of, and superior to, the civil power.

> replaced civilian rule and law with harsh military rule.

THE KING HAS: forced laws upon the colonists that

demand housing of troops;
protect criminals;

limit trade;
tax without consent;
deny trial by jury;
force trials overseas;
extend British rule into lands claimed by colonies;

change colonial governments;

deny lawmaking power.

THE KING HAS: waged war against the colonies.

destroyed lands and people.

used paid foreign soldiers, or mercenaries, on American soil.

captured colonists and forced them to fight on the British side.

used Native Americans as allies against the colonists.

After listing their complaints, the colonists mention their many attempts to settle these issues peacefully.

HE HAS combined with others to subject us to a jurisdiction foreign to our constitution, and unacknowledged by our laws, giving his assent to their acts of pretended legislation:
• For quartering large bodies of armed troops among us;
• For protecting them by a mock trial, from punishment for any murders which they should commit on the inhabitants of these States;
• For cutting off our trade with all parts of the world;
• For imposing taxes on us without our consent;
• For depriving us, in many cases, of the benefits of trial by jury;
• For transporting us beyond seas to be tried for pretended offences;
• For abolishing the free system of English laws in a neighboring province, establishing therein an arbitrary government, and enlarging its boundaries, so as to render it at once an example and fit instrument for introducing the same absolute rule into these colonies;
• For taking away our charters, abolishing our most valuable laws, and altering fundamentally the forms of our governments;
• For suspending our own legislatures, and declaring themselves invested with power to legislate for us in all cases whatsoever.

HE HAS abdicated government here, by declaring us out of his protection and waging war against us.

HE HAS plundered our seas, ravaged our coasts, burnt our towns, and destroyed the lives of our people.

HE IS, at this time, transporting large armies of foreign mercenaries to complete the works of death, desolation, and tyranny already begun, with circumstances of cruelty and perfidy scarcely paralleled in the most barbarous ages, and totally unworthy the head of a civilized nation.

HE HAS constrained our fellow-citizens, taken captive on the high seas, to bear arms against their country, to become the executioners of their friends and brethren, or to fall themselves by their hands.

HE HAS excited domestic insurrections amongst us and has endeavored to bring on the inhabitants of our frontiers, the merciless Indian savages, whose known rule of warfare is an undistinguished destruction of all ages, sexes, and conditions.

IN EVERY STAGE OF THESE OPPRESSIONS, we have petitioned for redress, in the most humble terms; our repeated petitions have been answered only by repeated injury. A prince, whose character is thus marked by every act which may define a tyrant, is unfit to be the ruler of a free people.

Nor have we been wanting in attentions to our British brethren. We have warned them, from time to time, of attempts by their legislature to extend an unwarrantable jurisdiction over us. We have reminded them of the circumstances of our emigration and settlement here. We have appealed to their native justice and magnanimity, and we have conjured them, by the ties of our common kindred, to disavow these usurpations, which would inevitably interrupt our connections and correspondence. They, too, have been deaf to the voice of justice and of consanguinity. We must, therefore, acquiesce in the necessity, which denounces our separation, and hold them, as we hold the rest of mankind, enemies in war; in peace, friends.

The colonists argue that all appeals to the king and to the people of Britain have failed.

WE, THEREFORE, THE REPRESENTATIVES of the United States of America, in General Congress assembled, appealing to the Supreme Judge of the world for the rectitude of our intentions, do, in the name, and by authority of the good people of these colonies, solemnly publish and declare: That these United Colonies are, and of right ought to be, free and independent States; that they are absolved from all allegiance to the British Crown, and that all political connection between them and the state of Great Britain is, and ought to be, totally dissolved; and that, as free and independent States, they have full power to levy war, conclude peace, contract alliances, establish commerce, and to do all other acts and things which independent States may of right do. And, for the support of this declaration, with a firm reliance on the protection of Divine Providence, we mutually pledge to each other our lives, our fortunes, and our sacred honor.

In the last paragraph the colonists declare that the colonies are now free and independent. They owe no loyalty to the king or to Britain. In taking this action, the colonists feel that they have the protection of God. In conclusion the colonists pledge their lives, property, and honor to their cause.

New Hampshire
Josiah Bartlett
Wm. Whipple
Matthew Thornton

Massachusetts-Bay
John Hancock
Saml. Adams
John Adams
Robt. Treat Paine
Elbridge Gerry

Rhode Island
Step. Hopkins
William Ellery

Connecticut
Roger Sherman
Sam'el Huntington
Wm. Williams
Oliver Wolcott

New York
Wm. Floyd
Phil. Livingston
Frans. Lewis
Lewis Morris

Pennsylvania
Robt. Morris
Benjamin Rush
Benja. Franklin
John Morton
Geo. Clymer
Jas. Smith
Geo. Taylor
James Wilson
Geo. Ross

Delaware
Caesar Rodney
Geo. Read
Tho. M'Kean

Georgia
Button Gwinnett
Lyman Hall
Geo. Walton

Maryland
Samuel Chase
Wm. Paca
Thos. Stone
Charles Carroll of
  Carrollton

Virginia
George Wythe
Richard Henry Lee
Th. Jefferson
Benja. Harrison
Ths. Nelson, Jr.
Francis Lightfoot Lee
Carter Braxton

North Carolina
Wm. Hooper
Joseph Hewes
John Penn

South Carolina
Edward Rutledge
Thos. Heyward, Junr.
Thomas Lynch, Junr.
Arthur Middleton

New Jersey
Richd. Stockton
Jno. Witherspoon
Fras. Hopkinson
John Hart
Abra. Clark

To help you understand the Constitution, the original words are in the wider column and an easier-to-read paraphrase is in the margin. Also in the margin is extra information. It is printed in *italics*. Parts of the Constitution that have been changed by amendments or that are no longer in effect have been crossed out. Spelling and punctuation have been updated, and a short introduction comes before each main part of the Constitution.

The Preamble

The Preamble sets the tone of the Constitution and states its goals. It begins with the famous words. "We the people . . ." These words show a major difference between the Constitution and the Articles of Confederation which it replaced. The Articles, with their stress on states' rights, begin "We the states . . ." Under the Articles, ruling power came from the states. Under the Constitution, all power comes from the people.

Preamble

The Preamble explains that the Constitution was written to guarantee peace and liberty for all United States citizens and their descendants.

We the people of the United States, in order to form a more perfect union, establish justice, insure domestic tranquility, provide for the common defense, promote the general welfare, and secure the blessings of liberty to ourselves and our posterity, do ordain and establish this Constitution for the United States of America.

The Preamble was written last, after all other parts of the Constitution were decided.

Introduction to Article I

Article I outlines the legislative or lawmaking branch of the government, made up of the House of Representatives and the Senate. The ten sections of this Article describe the day-by-day operations of Congress—such as qualifications for membership, the electing process, and the process by which a bill becomes a law—as well as the powers Congress has as one of the three branches in the federal government.

United States

Article I *Legislative Branch*

Section 1 *Congress in general*

All legislative powers herein granted shall be vested in a Congress of the United States, which shall consist of a Senate and House of Representatives.

The power to make laws is given to the Senate and the House of Representatives.

Section 2 *The House of Representatives*

1. The House of Representatives shall be composed of members chosen every second year by the people of the several states, and the electors in each state shall have the qualifications requisite for electors of the most numerous branch of the state legislature.

House members are elected every two years by people qualified to vote for members of the largest house of their state legislature.

2. No person shall be a representative who shall not have attained to the age of twenty-five years, and been seven years a citizen of the United States, and who shall not, when elected, be an inhabitant of that state in which he shall be chosen.

House members must be at least twenty-five years old, U.S. citizens for seven years, and residents of the states that elect them.

3. Representatives and direct taxes shall be apportioned among the several states which may be included within this Union, according to their respective numbers, [which shall be determined by adding to the whole number of free persons, including those bound to service for a term of years, and excluding Indians not taxed, three fifths of all other persons]. The actual enumeration shall be made within three years after the first meeting of the Congress of the United States, and within every subsequent term of ten years, in such manner as they shall by law direct. The number of representatives shall not exceed one for every thirty thousand, but each state shall have at least one representative; [and until such enumeration shall be made, the state of New Hampshire shall be entitled to choose 3, Massachusetts 8, Rhode Island and Providence Plantations 1, Connecticut 5, New York 6, New Jersey 4, Pennsylvania 8, Delaware 1, Maryland 6, Virginia 10, North Carolina 5, South Carolina 5, and Georgia 3].

The number of representatives allowed each state depends on the state's population.

This is known as the "three-fifths compromise," which settled the problem of how slaves were to be counted.

The population of the states shall be determined by a federal census taken every ten years.

The first census was taken in 1790.

4. When vacancies happen in the representation from any state, the executive authority thereof shall issue writs of election to fill such vacancies.

The governor of the state calls special elections to fill vacancies in that state's representation.

5. The House of Representatives shall choose their speaker and other officers; and shall have the sole power of impeachment.

The House chooses its own officers. It alone has the power to accuse a government official of a crime.

Section 3 *The Senate*

1. The Senate of the United States shall be composed of two senators from each state, chosen [by the legislature thereof,] for six years; and each senator shall have one vote.

Each state is allowed two senators.

Senators are now elected directly.

2. Immediately after they shall be assembled in consequence of the first election, they shall be divided as equally as may be into three

Senate elections are arranged so that one third of the senators are elected every two years for six-year terms.

Originally vacancies in the Senate were filled by the state legislature. This process was changed by Amendment 17.

Senators must be at least thirty years old, United States citizens for at least nine years, and residents of the states that elect them.

The Vice-President is president of the Senate but only votes in ties.

The Senate elects its own officers, including a temporary president if needed.

The Senate tries all impeachment cases. A two-thirds vote is necessary for conviction.

The Senate can remove from office those officials it convicts on impeachment charges, but any further punishment must come by way of trial in regular courts of law.

classes. [The seats of the senators of the first class shall be vacated at the expiration of the second year, of the second class at the expiration of the fourth year, and of the third class at the expiration of the sixth year,] so that one third may be chosen every second year; [and if vacancies happen by resignation, or otherwise, during the recess of the legislature of any state, the executive thereof may make temporary appointments until the next meeting of the legislature, which shall then fill such vacancies.]

3. No person shall be a senator who shall not have attained to the age of thirty years, and been nine years a citizen of the United States, and who shall not, when elected, be an inhabitant of that state for which he shall be chosen.

4. The Vice-President of the United States shall be president of the Senate, but shall have no vote, unless they be equally divided.

5. The Senate shall choose their other officers, and also a president pro tempore, in the absence of the Vice-President, or when he shall exercise the office of President of the United States.

6. The Senate shall have the sole power to try all impeachments. When sitting for that purpose, they shall be on oath or affirmation. When the President of the United States is tried, the chief justice shall preside; and no person shall be convicted without the concurrence of two thirds of the members present.

7. Judgment in cases of impeachment shall not extend further than to removal from office, and disqualification to hold and enjoy any office of honor, trust, or profit under the United States; but the party convicted shall, nevertheless, be liable and subject to indictment, trial, judgment, and punishment, according to law.

Section 4 *The electoral process*

1. The times, places, and manner of holding elections for senators and representatives shall be prescribed in each state by the legislature thereof; but the Congress may at any time by law make or alter such regulations, except as to the places of choosing senators.

Election regulations are left to the states, though Congress may pass certain laws concerning elections.

2. The Congress shall assemble at least once in every year, [and such meeting shall be on the first Monday in December,] unless they shall by law appoint a different day.

Congress must meet at least once a year.

Amendment 20 sets January 3 as the date for a session to begin.

Section 5 *Rules of procedure*

1. Each House shall be the judge of the elections, returns, and qualifications of its own members, and a majority of each shall constitute a quorum to do business; but a smaller number may adjourn from day to day, and may be authorized to compel the attendance of absent members, in such manner, and under such penalties, as each House may provide.

Each house of Congress has the right to judge the elections and qualifications of its members. To conduct official business, each house must have a majority of its members present.

2. Each House may determine the rules of its proceedings, punish its members for disorderly behavior, and, with the concurrence of two thirds, expel a member.

Each house may make rules for its members. Members may be expelled by a two-thirds vote.

3. Each House shall keep a journal of its proceedings, and from time to time publish the same, excepting such parts as may in their judgment require secrecy; and the yeas and nays of the members of either House on any question shall, at the desire of one fifth of those present, be entered on the journal.

Each house of Congress must keep a journal and publish a record of its activities.

4. Neither House, during the session of Congress, shall, without the consent of the other, adjourn for more than three days, nor to any other place than that in which the two Houses shall be sitting.

Neither house may adjourn for more than three days without the permission of the other house.

Section 6 *Compensation, privileges, and restrictions*

1. The senators and representatives shall receive a compensation for their services, to be ascertained by law, and paid out of the Treasury of the United States. They shall in all cases, except treason, felony, and breach of the peace, be privileged from arrest during their attendance at the session of their respective houses, and in going to and returning from the same; and for any speech or debate in either house, they shall not be questioned in any other place.

Members of Congress are paid a salary. With certain exceptions, members cannot be sued or arrested for anything they say in Congress.

2. No senator or representative shall, during the time for which he was elected, be appointed to any civil office under the authority of the United States, which shall have been created, or the emoluments whereof shall have been increased during such time; and no person holding any office under the United States shall be a member of either house during his continuance in office.

Members of Congress may not hold any other federal office while serving in Congress.

Section 7 *Method of passing laws*

1. All bills for raising revenue shall originate in the House of Representatives; but the Senate may propose or concur with amendments as on other bills.

All money bills must begin in the House. The Senate may amend such bills.

2. Every bill which shall have passed the House of Representatives and the Senate shall, before it become a law, be presented to the President of the United States; if he approve he shall sign it, but if not he shall return it with his objections to that house in which it shall have originated, who shall enter the objections at large on their journal, and proceed to reconsider it. If after such reconsideration two thirds of that house shall agree to pass the bill, it shall be sent, together with the objections, to the other house, by which it shall likewise be reconsidered, and if approved by two thirds of that house, it shall become a law. But in all such cases the votes of both houses shall be determined by yeas and nays, and the names of the persons voting for and against the bill shall be entered on the journal of each house respectively. If any bill shall not be returned by the

A bill passed by both houses of Congress goes to the President. If the President approves the bill, it becomes a law. If the President vetoes a bill, it goes back to Congress. Congress may pass a bill into law over the President's veto by a two-thirds vote.

The veto and the override are examples of the checks and balances built into the federal government. In 1947 the Taft-Hartley Act was passed over President Truman's veto.

A bill becomes a law if the President holds it unsigned for ten days, unless Congress adjourns.

Every order or resolution of Congress should be presented to the President.

Actually, many congressional resolutions do not go to the President. But any bill that is to become a law must be sent to the President.

Congress has the power to: collect taxes and pay debts; provide for the defense and welfare of the United States;

borrow money;
regulate trade;

establish uniform laws concerning citizenship and bankruptcy;

coin money and fix standards of weights and measures;

fix punishment for counterfeiting money;

establish post offices and roads;
issue patents and copyrights;

set up federal courts;
punish piracies;

declare war; raise and support armies;

maintain a navy;
make regulations for the armed forces;

provide, in case of emergency, for calling out the national guard;

maintain and train the national guard;

President within ten days (Sundays excepted) after it shall have been presented to him, the same shall be a law, in like manner as if he had signed it, unless the Congress by their adjournment prevent its return, in which case it shall not be a law.

3. Every order, resolution, or vote to which the concurrence of the Senate and House of Representatives may be necessary (except on a question of adjournment) shall be presented to the President of the United States; and before the same shall take effect, shall be approved by him, or being disapproved by him, shall be repassed by two thirds of the Senate and House of Representatives, according to the rules and limitations prescribed in the case of a bill.

Section 8 *Powers granted to Congress*
The Congress shall have power:

1. To lay and collect taxes, duties, imposts, and excises, to pay the debts and provide for the common defense and general welfare of the United States; but all duties, imposts, and excises shall be uniform throughout the United States;

2. To borrow money on the credit of the United States;

3. To regulate commerce with foreign nations, and among the several states, and with the Indian tribes;

4. To establish a uniform rule of naturalization, and uniform laws on the subject of bankruptcies throughout the United States;

5. To coin money, regulate the value thereof, and of foreign coin, and fix the standard of weights and measures;

6. To provide for the punishment of counterfeiting the securities and current coin of the United States;

7. To establish post offices and post roads;

8. To promote the progress of science and useful arts by securing for limited times to authors and inventors the exclusive right to their respective writings and discoveries;

9. To constitute tribunals inferior to the Supreme Court;

10. To define and punish piracies and felonies committed on the high seas, and offenses against the law of nations;

11. To declare war, [grant letters of marque and reprisal,] and make rules concerning captures on land and water;

12. To raise and support armies; but no appropriation of money to that use shall be for a longer term than two years;

13. To provide and maintain a navy;

14. To make rules for the government and regulation of the land and naval forces;

15. To provide for calling forth the militia to execute the laws of the union, suppress insurrections, and repel invasions;

16. To provide for organizing, arming, and disciplining the militia, and for governing such part of them as may be employed in the service of the United States, reserving to the states respectively the appointment of the officers and the authority of training the militia according to the discipline prescribed by Congress;

17. To exercise exclusive legislation in all cases whatsoever over such district—not exceeding ten miles square—as may, by cession of particular states, and the acceptance of Congress, become the seat of the government of the United States, and to exercise like authority over all places purchased by the consent of the legislature of the state in which the same shall be for the erection of forts, magazines, arsenals, dockyards, and other needful buildings; and

make laws for the District of Columbia and other federal properties;

To win southern support for his economic plan in 1790, Hamilton supported a southern city, Washington, D.C., as the capital.

18. To make all laws which shall be necessary and proper for carrying into execution the foregoing powers and all other powers vested by this Constitution in the government of the United States, or in any department or officer thereof.

make all laws "necessary and proper."

This is the "elastic clause," which allows Congress to make laws not specifically mentioned in the Constitution.

Section 9 *Powers denied to the federal government*

CONGRESS MAY NOT:

1. [The migration or importation of such persons as any of the states now existing shall think proper to admit shall not be prohibited by the Congress prior to the year one thousand eight hundred and eight, but a tax or duty may be imposed on such importation, not exceeding ten dollars for each person.]

This clause, referring to the slave trade until 1808, has no effect today.

2. The privilege of the writ of *habeas corpus* shall not be suspended, unless when in cases of rebellion or invasion the public safety may require it.

illegally imprison people;

3. No bill of attainder or *ex post facto* law shall be passed.

pass laws of unfair punishment;

4. No capitation or other direct tax shall be laid, unless in proportion to the census or enumeration herein before directed to be taken.

pass any direct tax unless it is in proportion to population (except the income tax, which is allowed by Amendment 16); tax exports;

5. No tax or duty shall be laid on articles exported from any state.

6. No preference shall be given by any regulation of commerce or revenue to the ports of one state over those of another; nor shall vessels bound to or from one state be obliged to enter, clear, or pay duties in another.

pass any law that would favor the trade of a particular state;

7. No money shall be drawn from the Treasury, but in consequence of appropriations made by law; and a regular statement and account of the receipts and expenditures of all public money shall be published from time to time.

spend money that has not been authorized by law;

8. No title of nobility shall be granted by the United States; and no person holding any office of profit or trust under them shall, without the consent of the Congress, accept of any present, emolument, office, or title of any kind whatever from any king, prince, or foreign state.

grant any title of nobility. No government officials may accept gifts or titles from other nations unless Congress approves.

Section 10 *Powers denied to the states*

STATE GOVERNMENTS MAY NOT:

1. No state shall enter into any treaty, alliance, or confederation; grant letters of marque and reprisal; coin money; emit bills of credit; make anything but gold and silver coin a tender in payment of debts;

make treaties or alliances; coin money; give bills of credit; grant titles of nobility;

pass any bill of attainder, *ex post facto* law, or law impairing the obligation of contracts, or grant any title of nobility.

tax imports or exports without the consent of Congress;

This section spells out the powers denied to the states in an attempt to avoid disputes like those that arose under the Articles of Confederation.

tax ships without the consent of Congress; keep a regular army; make agreements with other states or with foreign countries; or engage in war, unless invaded or in grave danger.

2. No state shall, without the consent of Congress, lay any imposts or duties on imports or exports, except what may be absolutely necessary for executing its inspection laws; and the net produce of all duties and imposts laid by any state on imports or exports shall be for the use of the Treasury of the United States; and all such laws shall be subject to the revision and control of the Congress.

3. No state shall, without the consent of Congress, lay any duty of tonnage, keep troops, or ships or war in time of peace, enter into any agreement or compact with another state, or with a foreign power, or engage in war, unless actually invaded, or in such imminent danger as will not admit of delay.

Introduction to Article II

Article II, which describes the executive branch, was the most hotly debated part of the Constitution. Experience during colonial times had shown many executives—the king and his governors in the colonies—to be tyrants. So the writers of the Constitution were careful to provide many checks on the President's power. Article II outlines the President's term of office, method of election, qualifications, powers, and duties. It also provides a way for removing a President from office if that President commits a high crime.

Article II *Executive Branch*

Section 1 *President and Vice-President*

The executive power is given to the President who holds office for a four-year term.

1. The executive power shall be vested in a President of the United States of America. He shall hold his office during the term of four years, and together with the Vice-President, chosen for the same term, be elected as follows:

The President is elected by an electoral college made up of electors appointed by the states. The number of electors given to each state equals the number of its senators and representatives.

2. Each state shall appoint, in such manner as the legislature thereof may direct, a number of electors equal to the whole number of senators and representatives to which the state may be entitled in the Congress; but no senator or representative, or person holding an office of trust or profit under the United States, shall be appointed an elector.

3. [The electors shall meet in their respective states, and vote by ballot for two persons, of whom one at least shall not be an inhabitant of the same state with themselves. And they shall make a list of all persons voted for, and of the number of votes for each; which list they shall sign and certify, and transmit sealed to the seat of the government of the United States, directed to the president of the Senate. The president of the Senate shall, in the presence of the Senate and House of Representatives, open all the certificates, and the votes shall then be counted. The person having the greatest number of votes shall be the President, if such number be a majority of the whole number of electors appointed; and if there be more than one who have such a majority, and have an equal number of votes, then the House of Representatives shall immediately choose by ballot one of them for President; and if no person have a majority, then from the five highest on the list the said house shall in like manner choose the President. But in choosing the President, the votes shall be taken by states, the representation from each state having one vote; a quorum for this purpose shall consist of a member or members from two thirds of the states, and a majority of all the states shall be necessary to a choice. In every case, after the choice of the President, the person having the greatest number of votes of the electors shall be the Vice-President. But if there should remain two or more who have equal votes, the Senate shall choose from them by ballot the Vice-President.]

This method of electing a President and Vice-President has been changed by Amendment 12.

4. The Congress may determine the time of choosing the electors, and the day on which they shall give their votes; which day shall be the same throughout the United States.

Congress determines when electors are chosen and when they will vote.

5. No person except a natural-born citizen [or a citizen of the United States at the time of the adoption of this Constitution,] shall be eligible to the office of President; neither shall any person be eligible to that office who shall not have attained to the age of thirty-five years and been fourteen years a resident within the United States.

The President must be a natural-born citizen of the United States, at least thirty-five years old, and a resident of the United States for at least fourteen years.

6. In case of the removal of the President from office, or of his death, resignation, or inability to discharge the powers and duties of the said office, the same shall devolve on the Vice-President, and the Congress may by law provide for the case of removal, death, resignation, or inability, both of the President and Vice-President, declaring what officer shall then act as President, and such officer shall act accordingly, until the disability be removed, or a President shall be elected.

This section has been modified by Amendment 25.

7. The President shall at stated times receive for his services a compensation, which shall neither be increased nor diminished during the period for which he shall have been elected, and he shall not

The President receives a salary, which cannot be lowered or raised during the term in office.

receive within that period any other emolument from the United States, or any of them.

8. Before he enter on the execution of his office, he shall take the following oath or affirmation:—"I do solemnly swear (or affirm) that I will faithfully execute the office of President of the United States, and will to the best of my ability, preserve, protect, and defend the Constitution of the United States."

Before taking office, the President takes this oath, which is usually administered by the chief justice of the Supreme Court.

Section 2 *Powers of the President*

1. The President shall be commander in chief of the army and navy of the United States, and of the militia of the several states, when called into the actual service of the United States; he may require the opinion in writing of the principal officer in each of the executive departments upon any subject relating to the duties of their respective offices, and he shall have power to grant reprieves and pardons for offenses against the United States, except in cases of impeachment.

The President is commander in chief of the armed forces.

The President can grant delays of punishment and pardons for offenses against the United States, except in impeachment cases.

2. He shall have power, by and with the advice and consent of the Senate, to make treaties, provided two thirds of the senators present concur; and he shall nominate and, by and with the advice and consent of the Senate, shall appoint ambassadors, other public ministers and consuls, judges of the Supreme Court, and all other officers of the United States whose appointments are not herein otherwise provided for, and which shall be established by law; but the Congress may by law vest the appointment of such inferior officers as they think proper in the President alone, in the courts of law, or in the heads of departments.

The President has the power to make treaties and to appoint ambassadors and other officers. The Senate must approve such appointments. Minor appointments may be made without Senate approval.

The right of the Senate to approve appointments was new with the Constitution.

When the Senate is not in session, the President may make temporary appointments to office.

3. The President shall have power to fill up all vacancies that may happen during the recess of the Senate, by granting commissions which shall expire at the end of their next session.

Section 3 *Duties of the President*

He shall from time to time give to the Congress information of the state of the Union, and recommend to their consideration such measures as he shall judge necessary and expedient; he may, on extraordinary occasions, convene both houses, or either of them, and in case of disagreement between them with respect to the time of adjournment, he may adjourn them to such time as he shall think proper; he shall receive ambassadors and other public ministers; he shall take care that the laws be faithfully executed, and shall commission all the officers of the United States.

The President is required to report to Congress on the state of the Union, to receive ambassadors, to see that all laws are executed, and to commission all officers of the United States. He also has the power to call special sessions of Congress.

Section 4 *Impeachment*

The President, Vice-President, and all civil officers of the United

States shall be removed from office on impeachment for, and conviction of, treason, bribery, or other high crimes and misdemeanors.

The President and all other civil officers of the United States may be removed from office if convicted of treason, bribery, or other high crimes.

Introduction to Article III

Article III outlines the last of the three branches of government—the judicial branch. By creating a court system, the writers of the Constitution found a way for the government to enforce its laws and settle disputes peacefully. Besides describing the federal court system, Article III defines the crime and punishment of treason.

Article III *Judicial Branch*

Section 1 *The federal courts*

The judicial power of the United States shall be vested in one Supreme Court, and in such inferior courts as the Congress may from time to time ordain and establish. The judges, both of the Supreme and inferior courts, shall hold their offices during good behavior and shall at stated times receive for their services a compensation, which shall not be diminished during their continuance in office.

Judicial power is given to a Supreme Court and other lesser courts authorized by Congress. Federal judges can hold office for life if they are not impeached and convicted for committing crimes.

Section 2 *Jurisdiction of the federal courts*

1. The judicial power shall extend to all cases in law and equity arising under this Constitution, the laws of the United States, and treaties made, or which shall be made, under their authority; to all cases affecting ambassadors, other public ministers and consuls; to all cases of admiralty and maritime jurisdiction; to controversies to which the United States shall be a party; to controversies between two or more states; [between a state and citizens of another state;] between citizens of different states; between citizens of the same state claiming lands under grants of different states, and between a state, or the citizens thereof, and foreign states, citizens, or subjects. **2.** In all cases affecting ambassadors, other public ministers and consuls, and those in which a state shall be a party, the Supreme Court shall have original jurisdiction. In all the other cases before mentioned, the Supreme Court shall have appellate jurisdiction, both as to law and fact, with such exceptions, and under such regulations as the Congress shall make.

The federal courts try all cases involving the Constitution, federal laws, and treaties. Lawsuits involving the federal government, two states, or citizens of different states are tried in federal courts.

Amendment 11 changes this part. The case of Cherokee Nation v. Georgia *in 1831 rested on this part of the Constitution.*

Cases involving ambassadors or officials of foreign nations or those involving states are tried in the Supreme Court. Other cases begin in lesser courts but may be appealed to the Supreme Court.

All crimes, except in cases of impeachment, shall be tried by jury.

3. The trial of all crimes, except in cases of impeachment, shall be by jury; and such trial shall be held in the state where the said crimes shall have been committed; but when not committed within any state, the trial shall be at such place or places as the Congress may by law have directed.

Section 3 *Treason*

It is an act of treason to wage war against the United States or to give aid to its enemies.

1. Treason against the United States shall consist only in levying war against them, or in adhering to their enemies, giving them aid and comfort. No person shall be convicted of treason, unless on the testimony of two witnesses to the same overt act or on confession in open court.

Congress may fix the punishment for treason, but it may not punish the families of those found guilty of treason.

2. The Congress shall have power to declare the punishment of treason, but no attainder of treason shall work corruption of blood, or forfeiture except during the life of the person attained.

Introduction to Article IV

Article IV describes the relation of the states to one another, new states and territories, and the rights of states that the federal government guarantees.

Article IV *The States and the Federal Government*

Section 1 *State records*

The official acts of one state must be recognized as legal by all other states.

Full faith and credit shall be given in each state to the public acts, records, and judicial proceedings of every other state. And the Congress may by general laws prescribe the manner in which such acts, records, and proceedings shall be proved, and the effect thereof.

Section 2 *Privileges and immunities of citizens*

States must treat citizens of another state as fairly as their own citizens.

1. The citizens of each state shall be entitled to all privileges and immunities of citizens in the several states.

A state governor may demand the return of a criminal who has fled to another state.

2. A person charged in any state with treason, felony, or other crime, who shall flee from justice and be found in another state, shall, on demand of the executive authority of the state from which he fled, be delivered up to be removed to the state, having jurisdiction of the crime.

3. [No person held to service or labor in one state, under the laws thereof, escaping into another shall, in consequence of any law or regulation therein, be discharged from such service or labor, but shall be delivered up on claim of the party to whom such service or labor may be due.]

This provision for the return of runaway slaves has had no effect since Amendment 13 was adopted in 1865.

Section 3 *New states and territories*

1. New states may be admitted by the Congress into this Union; but no new state shall be formed or erected within the jurisdiction of any other state; nor any state be formed by the junction of two or more states, or parts of states, without the consent of the legislatures of the states concerned, as well as of the Congress.

New states may be admitted into the Union by Congress.

2. The Congress shall have power to dispose of and make all needful rules and regulations respecting the territory or other property belonging to the United States; and nothing in this Constitution shall be so construed as to prejudice any claims of the United States, or of any particular state.

Congress has power to make rules and regulations for territories and federal property.

Section 4 *Guarantees to the states*

The United States shall guarantee to every state in this union a republican form of government, and shall protect each of them against invasion; and on application of the legislature, or of the executive—when the legislature cannot be convened—against domestic violence.

The federal government guarantees to each state a republican form of government, protection against invasion, and protection against disturbances within the state.

Introduction to Article V

Article V describes the amending process, the means by which the Constitution can be changed to meet the needs of a changing and growing nation.

Article V *Method of Amendment*

The Congress, whenever two thirds of both houses shall deem it necessary, shall propose amendments to this Constitution or, on the

Amendments to the Constitution may be proposed by either two thirds of both houses of Congress or by two thirds of the states. Amendments may be ratified by either the legislatures of three fourths of the states or by conventions in three fourths of the states.

This clause has not been in effect since 1808.

application of the legislatures of two thirds of the several states, shall call a convention for proposing amendments, which in either case shall be valid to all intents and purposes as part of this Constitution when ratified by the legislatures of three fourths of the several states, or by conventions in three fourths thereof, as the one or the other mode of ratification may be proposed by the Congress; provided that [no amendment which may be made prior to the year one thousand eight hundred and eight shall in any manner affect the first and fourth clauses in the ninth section of the first article, and that]no state, without its consent, shall be deprived of its equal suffrage in the Senate.

Introduction to Article VI

Article VI includes a clause that allows all the other parts of the Constitution to work. It declares that the Constitution is "the supreme law of the land." As such, it overrides local or state laws that may be in conflict with it.

Article VI *General Provisions*

All money previously borrowed by the confederation government will be repaid under the Constitution.

The Constitution, federal laws, and the treaties of the United States are the supreme law of the land.

1. All debts contracted and engagements entered into before the adoption of this Constitution shall be as valid against the United States under this Constitution as under the Confederation.

2. This Constitution, and the laws of the United States which shall be made in pursuance thereof; and all treaties made, or which shall be made, under the authority of the United States, shall be the supreme law of the land; and the judges in every state shall be bound thereby, anything in the constitution or laws of any state to the contrary notwithstanding.

All federal and state officials must take an oath of office promising to support the Constitution. There can be no religious requirement for holding office.

3. The senators and representatives before mentioned, and the members of the several state legislatures, and all executive and judicial officers, both of the United States and of the several states, shall be bound by oath or affirmation, to support this Constitution; but no religious test shall ever be required as a qualification to any office or public trust under the United States.

This clause shows the separation between church and state in the United States.

Introduction to Article VII
This brief article explains the approval needed before the Constitution can take effect.

Article VII *Ratification of the Constitution*

The ratification of the conventions of nine states shall be sufficient for the establishment of this Constitution between the states so ratifying the same.

The Constitution will take effect when it is approved by nine states. *The Constitution went into effect on March 4, 1789.*

Amendments to the Constitution
The first ten amendments are known as the Bill of Rights. The dates on which these and the other amendments were declared ratified are shown in parentheses.

Amendment 1 *(1791)*

Congress shall make no law respecting an establishment of religion, or prohibiting the free exercise thereof; or abridging the freedom of speech, or of the press; or the right of the people peaceably to assemble, and to petition the government for a redress of grievances.

The Congress may not make laws interfering with the freedoms of religion, speech, the press, assembly, and petition.

Amendment 2 *(1791)*

A well-regulated militia being necessary to the security of a free state, the right of the people to keep and bear arms shall not be infringed.

The states have the right to maintain national guard units.

Amendment 3 *(1791)*

No soldier shall, in time of peace, be quartered in any house without the consent of the owner, nor in time of war, but in a manner to be prescribed by law.

Troops cannot be lodged in private homes during peacetime.

Amendment 4 *(1791)*

The right of the people to be secure in their persons, houses, papers, and effects against unreasonable searches and seizures shall not be

People are protected against unreasonable searches and arrests.

Amendments 3 and 4 grew out of colonial grievances against the acts of British Parliament.

violated, and no warrants shall issue but upon probable cause, supported by oath or affirmation, and particularly describing the place to be searched and the persons or things to be seized.

Amendment 5 *(1791)*

A person cannot be tried for a crime punishable by death unless charged by a grand jury, be tried twice for the same crime, nor be forced to testify against himself or herself. A person may not be deprived of life, liberty, or property except by lawful means. The government must pay a fair price for property taken for public use.

No person shall be held to answer for a capital or otherwise infamous crime, unless on a presentment or indictment of a grand jury, except in cases arising in the land or naval forces, or in the militia, when in actual service in time of war or public danger; nor shall any person be subject for the same offense to be twice put in jeopardy of life or limb; nor shall be compelled in any criminal case to be a witness against himself, nor be deprived of life, liberty, or property without due process of law; nor shall private property be taken for public use without just compensation.

Amendment 6 *(1791)*

A person accused of a crime has a right to a speedy public trial by jury, information about the accusation, help from the court in bringing favorable witnesses to the trial, and the aid of a lawyer.

Amendments 4, 5, 6, and 8 are sometimes called a "bill of rights" for people accused of a crime.

In all criminal prosecutions the accused shall enjoy the right to a speedy and public trial by an impartial jury of the state and district wherein the crime shall have been committed, which district shall have been previously ascertained by law, and to be informed of the nature and cause of the accusation; to be confronted with the witnesses against him; to have compulsory process for obtaining witnesses in his favor, and to have the assistance of counsel for his defense.

Amendment 7 *(1791)*

In civil lawsuits involving more than $20, the right to a jury trial is guaranteed.

In suits at common law, where the value in controversy shall exceed twenty dollars, the right of trial by jury shall be preserved, and no fact tried by a jury shall be otherwise reexamined in any court of the United States than according to the rules of the common law.

Amendment 8 *(1791)*

Bails, fines, and punishments cannot be unreasonable.

Excessive bail shall not be required, nor excessive fines imposed, nor cruel and unusual punishments inflicted.

Amendment 9 *(1791)*

The basic rights of the people cannot be denied, even those not named in the Constitution.

The enumeration in the Constitution of certain rights shall not be construed to deny or disparage others retained by the people.

Amendment 10 *(1791)*

The powers not delegated to the United States by the Constitution, nor prohibited by it to the states, are reserved to the states respectively, or to the people.

The powers not given to the federal government are to be held by the states or the people.

Amendment 11 *(1798)*

The judicial power of the United States shall not be construed to extend to any suit in law or equity, commenced or prosecuted against one of the United States by citizens of another state, or by citizens or subjects of any foreign state.

Federal courts do not have the power to hear suits brought against a state by the citizens of another state or by foreigners.

Amendment 12 *(1804)*

The electors shall meet in their respective states and vote by ballot for President and Vice-President, one of whom at least shall not be an inhabitant of the same state with themselves; they shall name in their ballots the person voted for as President, and in distinct ballots the person voted for as Vice-President, and they shall make distinct lists of all persons voted for as President, and of all persons voted for as Vice-President, and of the number of votes for each, which lists they shall sign and certify, and transmit sealed to the seat of the government of the United States, directed to the president of the Senate; the president of the Senate shall, in the presence of the Senate and House of Representatives, open all the certificates, and the votes shall then be counted; the person having the greatest number of votes for President shall be President, if such number be a majority of the whole number of electors appointed; and if no person have such majority, then from the persons having the highest numbers not exceeding three on the list of those voted for as President the House of Representatives shall choose immediately by ballot the President. But in choosing the President, the votes shall be taken by states, the representation from each state having one vote; a quorum for this purpose shall consist of a member or members from two thirds of the states, and a majority of all the states shall be necessary to a choice. And if the House of Representatives shall not choose a President whenever the right of choice shall devolve upon them, [before the fourth day of March next following,] then the Vice-President shall act as President, as in the case of the death or other constitutional disability of the President. The person having the greatest number of votes as Vice-President shall be the Vice-President, if such number be a majority of the whole number of electors appointed; and if no person have a majority, then from the two highest

The members of the electoral college vote for the President and Vice-President on separate ballots. If no person receives a majority of the electoral votes for President, the House of Representatives elects the President. In such an election the representatives from each state have one vote among them. A majority of these votes is necessary to elect the President.

This amendment was brought about as a result of the election of 1800, when Jefferson and Burr, candidates of the same party, received the same number of votes. Although it was understood that Burr was the candidate for Vice-President, he could have been named President by the House of Representatives.

The reference to March 4 does not apply today, since the President takes office in January. (See Amendment 20.)

If no person receives a majority of the votes for Vice-President, the Senate elects the Vice-President. A majority vote is necessary.

numbers on the list the Senate shall choose the Vice-President; a quorum for the purpose shall consist of two thirds of the whole number of senators, and a majority of the whole number shall be necessary to a choice. But no person constitutionally ineligible to the office of President shall be eligible to that of Vice-President of the United States.

Amendment 13 *(1865)*

Section 1 *Abolition of slavery*

Slavery is prohibited. Congress is given the power to enforce the abolition of slavery.

Neither slavery nor involuntary servitude, except as a punishment of crime whereof the party shall have been duly convicted, shall exist within the United States, or any place subject to their jurisdiction.

After the Civil War three amendments, numbers 13, 14, and 15, were quickly ratified. The last amendment had passed sixty-one years before.

Section 2 *Enforcement*

Congress shall have power to enforce this article by appropriate legislation.

Amendment 14 *(1868)*

Section 1 *Definition of citizenship*

All people born or naturalized in the United States are citizens. No state may infringe on the rights of citizens of the United States.

All persons born or naturalized in the United States and subject to the jurisdiction thereof are citizens of the United States and of the state wherein they reside. No state shall make or enforce any law which shall abridge the privileges or immunities of citizens of the United States; nor shall any state deprive any person of life, liberty, or property without due process of law; nor deny to any person within its jurisdiction the equal protection of the laws.

This extended the civil rights protection of Amendment 5 to the citizens of individual states.

Section 2 *Apportionment of representatives*

If a state prevents certain citizens from voting, that state's representation in Congress may be reduced.

Representatives shall be apportioned among the several states according to their respective numbers, counting the whole number of persons in each state, excluding Indians not taxed. But when the right to vote at any election for the choice of electors for President and Vice-President of the United States, representatives in Congress, the executive and judicial officers of a state, or the members of the legislature thereof, is denied to any of the male inhabitants of such state, being twenty-one years of age and citizens of the United States, or in any way abridged, except for participation in rebellion or other crime, the basis of representation therein shall be reduced in the proportion which the number of such male citizens shall bear to the whole number of male citizens twenty-one years of age in such state.

This amendment was passed to guarantee newly freed slaves the right to vote. Congress has never applied this penalty.

Section 3 *Disability resulting from insurrection*

No person shall be a senator or representative in Congress, or elector of President and Vice-President, or hold any office, civil or military, under the United States, or under any state, who having previously taken an oath as a member of Congress, or as an officer of the United States, or as a member of any state legislature, or as an executive or judicial officer of any state, to support the Constitution of the United States, shall have engaged in insurrection or rebellion against the same, or given aid or comfort to the enemies thereof. But Congress may by a vote of two thirds of each house, remove such disability.

If a federal officeholder goes against the oath of office and rebels against the country or helps its enemies, that person cannot ever hold a federal office again. Congress may, however, allow such a person to hold office if two thirds of both houses agree.

This section was aimed at keeping former Confederate officials from holding public office after the Civil War.

Section 4 *Confederate debt void*

The validity of the public debt of the United States, authorized by law, including debts incurred for payments of pensions and bounties for services in suppressing insurrection or rebellion, shall not be questioned. But neither the United States nor any state shall assume or pay any debt or obligation incurred in aid of insurrection or rebellion against the United States, [or any claim for the loss or emancipation of any slave]; but all such debts, obligations, and claims shall be held illegal and void.

All debts of the Confederate states are declared invalid and may not be paid.

Section 5 *Enforcement*

The Congress shall have power to enforce, by appropriate legislation, the provisions of this article.

Amendment 15 *(1870)*

Section 1 *The suffrage*

The right of citizens of the United States to vote shall not be denied or abridged by the United States or by any state on account of race, color, or previous condition of servitude.

No citizen can be denied the right to vote because of race or color, or because he or she was formerly a slave.

Section 2 *Enforcement*

The Congress shall have power to enforce this article by appropriate legislation.

Amendment 16 *(1913)*

The Congress shall have power to lay and collect taxes on incomes, from whatever source derived, without apportionment among the several states, and without regard to any census or enumeration.

Congress has the right to pass an income tax law.

See Article I, Section 9, Clause 4.

Amendment 17 *(1913)*

Senators are to be elected directly by the voters rather than by state legislatures. A vacancy in the Senate is to be filled by a special election called by the governor. The governor may be given power by the state legislature to appoint someone to fill the vacancy until a special election is held.

See Article I, Section 3, first paragraph.

1. The Senate of the United States shall be composed of two senators from each state, elected by the people thereof for six years; and each senator shall have one vote. The electors in each state shall have the qualifications requisite for electors of the most numerous branch of the state legislatures.

2. When vacancies happen in the representation of any state in the Senate, the executive authority of such state shall issue writs of election to fill such vacancies, provided that the legislature of any state may empower the executive thereof to make temporary appointments until the people fill the vacancies by election as the legislature may direct.

3. [This amendment shall not be so construed as to affect the election or term of any senator chosen before it becomes valid as part of the Constitution.]

Amendment 18 *(1919)*

This entire amendment (forbidding the manufacture, sale, or transporting of alcoholic beverages) was repealed by Amendment 21.

Section 1 *Prohibition of intoxicating liquors*
[After one year from the ratification of this article the manufacture, sale, or transportation of intoxicating liquors within, the importation thereof into, or the exportation thereof from the United States and all territory subject to the jurisdiction thereof for beverage purposes is hereby prohibited.]

Section 2 *Enforcement*
[The Congress and the several states shall have concurrent power to enforce this article by appropriate legislation.]

Amendments 16–19, all ratified within seven years, grew out of a major period of reform in the nation.

Section 3 *Limited time for ratification*
[This article shall be inoperative unless it shall have been ratified as an amendment to the Constitution by the legislatures of the several states, as provided in the Constitution, within seven years from the date of the submission hereof to the states by the Congress.]

Amendment 19 *(1920)*

Women have the right to vote.

This amendment was ratified in time for women to vote in the Presidential election of 1920.

The right of citizens of the United States to vote shall not be denied or abridged by the United States or by any state on account of sex.

The Congress shall have power to enforce this article by appropriate legislation.

Amendment 20 *(1933)*

Section 1 *Terms of President, Vice-President, and Congress*

The terms of the President and Vice-President shall end at noon on the 20th day of January, and the terms of senators and representatives at noon on the third day of January, of the years in which such terms would have ended if this article had not been ratified; and the terms of their successors shall then begin.

The terms of senators and representatives end on January 3 instead of March 4, and the terms of the President and Vice-President end on January 20 rather than March 4.

This is the "lame duck" amendment. By specifying earlier dates for starting new terms of office, this amendment assured that officials who were defeated in an election would not continue to serve (as "lame ducks") for a long time.

Section 2 *Sessions of Congress*

The Congress shall assemble at least once in every year, and such meeting shall begin at noon on the third day of January, unless they shall by law appoint a different day.

Section 3 *Presidential succession*

If, at the time fixed for the beginning of the term of the President, the President-elect shall have died, the Vice-President-elect shall become President. If a President shall not have been chosen before the time fixed for the beginning of his term, or if the President-elect shall have failed to qualify, then the Vice-President-elect shall act as President until a President shall have qualified; and the Congress may by law provide for the case wherein neither a President-elect nor a Vice-President-elect shall have qualified, declaring who shall then act as President, or the manner in which one who is to act shall be selected, and such person shall act accordingly until a President or Vice-President shall have qualified.

If a President-elect dies before taking office, the Vice-President-elect will become President.

If a President-elect is disqualified, the Vice-President-elect will serve as President until the President-elect qualifies. Congress may declare who will serve as President if neither the President-elect nor the Vice-President-elect qualifies.

Section 4 *Choice of President by House*

The Congress may by law provide for the case of the death of any of the persons from whom the House of Representatives may choose a President whenever the right of choice shall have devolved upon them, and for the case of the death of any of the persons from whom the Senate may choose a Vice-President whenever the right of choice shall have devolved upon them.

A law in effect today provides that the Speaker of the House will serve as President until a President or Vice-President qualifies.

Section 5 *Date effective*

[Sections 1 and 2 shall take effect on the 15th of October following the ratification of this article.]

Section 6 *Limited time for ratification*

[This article shall be inoperative unless it shall have been ratified as an amendment to the Constitution by the legislatures of three-fourths of the several states within seven years from the date of its submission.]

753

Amendment 21 *(1933)*

Section 1 *Repeal of Amendment 18*

Amendment 18 is repealed.

The eighteenth article of amendment to the Constitution of the United States is hereby repealed.

Section 2 *States protected*

The transportation or importation into any state, territory, or possession of the United States for delivery or use therein of intoxicating liquors in violation of the laws thereof is hereby prohibited.

Section 3 *Limited time for ratification*

[This article shall be inoperative unless it shall have been ratified as an amendment to the Constitution by convention in the several states, as provided in the Constitution, within seven years from date of the submission hereof to the states by the Congress.]

Amendment 22 *(1951)*

Section 1 *Presidential term limited*

The President is limited to two terms of office.

No person shall be elected to the office of the President more than twice, and no person who has held the office of President, or acted as President, for more than two years of a term to which some other person was elected President shall be elected to the office of the President more than once. [But this article shall not apply to any person holding the office of President when this article was proposed by the Congress, and shall not prevent any person who may be holding the office of President, or acting as President, during the term within which this article becomes operative from holding the office of President or acting as President during the remainder of such term.]

Until 1940 no President had served more than two terms in office. This amendment was proposed after Franklin D. Roosevelt won a fourth term as President. Roosevelt died early in his fourth term.

Section 2 *Limited time for ratification*

[This article shall be inoperative unless it shall have been ratified as an amendment to the Constitution by the legislatures of three fourths of the several states within seven years from the date of its submission to the states by the Congress.]

Amendment 23 *(1961)*

Section 1 *Voting rights of residents of the District of Columbia*

The District constituting the seat of government of the United States shall appoint in such manner as the Congress may direct: A number of electors of President and Vice-President equal to the whole number of senators and representatives in Congress to which the district would be entitled if it were a state, but in no event more than the least populous state; they shall be in addition to those appointed by the states, but they shall be considered, for the purposes of the election of President and Vice-President, to be electors appointed by a state; and they shall meet in the district and perform such duties as provided by the twelfth article of amendment.

The residents of the District of Columbia are given the right to vote for President and Vice-President.

Section 2 *Enforcement*
The Congress shall have power to enforce this article by appropriate legislation.

Amendment 24 *(1964)*

Section 1 *Abolition of poll taxes*
The right of citizens of the United States to vote in any primary or other election for President or Vice-President, for electors for President or Vice-President, or for senator or representative in Congress, shall not be denied or abridged by the United States or any state by reason of failure to pay any poll tax or other tax.

No citizen can be made to pay a tax for the right to vote in a federal election.

In 1966 a Supreme Court case found poll taxes on state elections unconstitutional.

Section 2 *Enforcement*
The Congress shall have the power to enforce this article by appropriate legislation.

Amendment 25 *(1967)*

Section 1 *Presidential succession*
In case of the removal of the President from office or his death or resignation, the Vice-President shall become President.

The Vice-President becomes President if the President dies or must leave office.

Section 2 *Appointment of new Vice-President*
Whenever there is a vacancy in the office of the Vice-President, the President shall nominate a Vice-President who shall take the office upon confirmation by a majority vote of both houses of Congress.

If the office of Vice-President is vacant, the President shall appoint and the Congress approve a new Vice-President.

Section 3 *Creation of acting President*
Whenever the President transmits to the president pro tempore of the Senate and the Speaker of the House of Representatives his written declaration that he is unable to discharge the powers and duties of his office, and until he transmits to them a written declaration to the contrary, such powers and duties shall be discharged by the Vice-President as acting President.

If the President declares himself unable to continue as President, the Vice-President becomes acting President.

Section 4 *Provisions for Presidential disability*

Whenever the Vice-President and a majority of other officers declare that the President is disabled, the Vice-President becomes acting President.

Whenever the Vice-President and a majority of either the principal officers of the executive departments, or of such other body as Congress may by law provide, transmit to the president pro tempore of the Senate and the Speaker of the House of Representatives their written declaration that the President is unable to discharge the powers and duties of his office, the Vice-President shall immediately assume the powers and duties of the office as acting President.

When the President declares that he is again able, he resumes his duties. But if the Vice-President and other officers disagree, Congress decides whether or not the President is able to resume the powers and duties of the office.

Amendment 25 sought a solution to problems that came up in the 1900s when two Presidents—Wilson and Eisenhower—were very sick during their terms. To avoid disputes over who should be in control at such times, this amendment spells out the line of responsibility.

Thereafter, when the President transmits to the president pro tempore of the Senate and the Speaker of the House of Representatives his written declaration that no inability exists, he shall resume the powers and duties of his office unless the Vice-President and a majority of either the principal officers of the executive department, or of such other body as Congress may by law provide, transmit within four days to the president pro tempore of the Senate and the Speaker of the House of Representatives their written declaration that the President is unable to discharge the powers and duties of his office. Thereupon Congress shall decide the issue, assembling within forty-eight hours for that purpose if not in session. If the Congress, within twenty-one days after receipt of the latter written declaration, or if Congress is not in session, within twenty-one days after Congress is required to assemble, determines by two-thirds vote of both houses that the President is unable to discharge the powers and duties of his office, the Vice-President shall continue to discharge the same as acting President; otherwise, the President shall resume the powers and duties of his office.

Amendment 26 *(1971)*

Section 1 *Voting age lowered*

Eighteen-year-olds are given the right to vote.

The right of citizens of the United States who are eighteen years of age or older to vote shall not be denied or abridged by the United States or by any state on account of age.

A Senate report of 1971 concluded that the nation would benefit from the "idealism and concern and energy" of eighteen-year-olds.

Section 2 *Enforcement*

The Congress shall have the power to enforce this article by appropriate legislation.

Presidents and Vice-Presidents

No.	President	Birth–Death	State*	Term	Party	Vice-President
1	George Washington	1732–1799	Va.	1789–1797	None	John Adams
2	John Adams	1735–1826	Md. (Mass.)	1797–1801	Federalist	Thomas Jefferson
3	Thomas Jefferson	1743–1826	Va.	1801–1805	Republican**	Aaron Burr
				1805–1809		George Clinton
4	James Madison	1751–1836	Va.	1809–1813	Republican	George Clinton
				1813–1817		Elbridge Gerry
5	James Monroe	1758–1831	Va.	1817–1825	Republican	Daniel D. Tompkins
6	John Quincy Adams	1767–1848	Md. (Mass.)	1825–1829	Republican	John C. Calhoun
7	Andrew Jackson	1767–1845	Tenn. (S.C.)	1829–1833	Democratic	John C. Calhoun
				1833–1837		Martin Van Buren
8	Martin Van Buren	1782–1862	N.Y.	1837–1841	Democratic	Richard M. Johnson
9	William H. Harrison	1773–1841	Ohio (Va.)	1841	Whig	John Tyler
10	John Tyler	1790–1862	Va.	1841–1845	Whig	
11	James K. Polk	1795–1849	Tenn. (N.C.)	1845–1849	Democratic	George M. Dallas
12	Zachary Taylor	1784–1850	Iowa (Va.)	1849–1850	Whig	Millard Fillmore
13	Millard Fillmore	1800–1874	N.Y.	1850–1853	Whig	
14	Franklin Pierce	1804–1869	N.H.	1853–1857	Democratic	William R. King
15	James Buchanan	1791–1868	Pa.	1857–1861	Democratic	John G. Breckinridge
16	Abraham Lincoln	1809–1865	Ill. (Ky.)	1861–1865	Republican**	Hannibal Hamlin
				1865		Andrew Johnson
17	Andrew Johnson	1808–1875	Tenn. (N.C.)	1865–1869	Republican	
18	Ulysses S. Grant	1822–1885	Ill. (Ohio)	1869–1873	Republican	Schuyler Colfax
				1873–1877		Henry Wilson
19	Rutherford B. Hayes	1822–1893	Ohio	1877–1881	Republican	William A. Wheeler
20	James A. Garfield	1831–1881	Ohio	1881	Republican	Chester A. Arthur
21	Chester A. Arthur	1830–1886	N.Y. (Vt.)	1881–1885	Republican	
22	Grover Cleveland	1837–1908	N.Y. (N.J.)	1885–1889	Democratic	Thomas A. Hendricks
23	Benjamin Harrison	1833–1901	Ind. (Ohio)	1889–1893	Republican	Levi P. Morton
24	Grover Cleveland	1837–1908	N.Y. (N.J.)	1893–1897	Democratic	Adlai E. Stevenson
25	William McKinley	1843–1901	Ohio	1897–1901	Republican	Garret A. Hobart
				1901		Theodore Roosevelt
26	Theodore Roosevelt	1858–1919	N.Y.	1901–1905	Republican	
				1905–1909		Charles W. Fairbanks
27	William H. Taft	1857–1930	Ohio	1909–1913	Republican	James S. Sherman
28	Woodrow Wilson	1856–1924	N.J. (Va.)	1913–1921	Democratic	Thomas R. Marshall
29	Warren G. Harding	1865–1923	Ohio	1921–1923	Republican	Calvin Coolidge
30	Calvin Coolidge	1872–1933	Md. (Vt.)	1923–1925	Republican	
				1925–1929		Charles G. Dawes
31	Herbert C. Hoover	1874–1964	Calif. (Iowa)	1929–1933	Republican	Charles Curtis
32	Franklin D. Roosevelt	1882–1945	N.Y.	1933–1937	Democratic	John N. Garner
				1937–1941		John N. Garner
				1941–1945		Henry A. Wallace
				1945		Harry S Truman
33	Harry S Truman	1884–1972	Mo.	1945–1949	Democratic	
				1949–1953		Alben W. Barkley
34	Dwight D. Eisenhower	1890–1969	N.Y. (Tex.)	1953–1957	Republican	Richard M. Nixon
				1957–1961		Richard M. Nixon
35	John F. Kennedy	1917–1963	Mass.	1961–1963	Democratic	Lyndon B. Johnson
36	Lyndon B. Johnson	1908–1973	Tex.	1963–1965	Democratic	
				1965–1969		Hubert H. Humphrey
37	Richard M. Nixon	1913–	N.Y. (Calif.)	1969–1973	Republican	Spiro T. Agnew
				1973–1974		Agnew; Gerald R. Ford
38	Gerald R. Ford	1913–	Mich.	1974–1977	Republican	Nelson R. Rockefeller
39	Jimmy Carter	1924–	Ga.	1977–1981	Democratic	Walter F. Mondale
40	Ronald Reagan	1911–	Calif. (Ill.)	1981–1989	Republican	George H.W. Bush
41	George H.W. Bush	1924–	Tex. (Mass.)	1989–	Republican	J. Danforth Quayle

*State of residence at time of election. ()State of birth, if different.
**The Republican party of the third through the sixth Presidents is not the same party that elected Lincoln in 1860. Lincoln's party was formed in 1854.

Chronology

25,000 B.C.	Asian hunters enter North America in pursuit of game.
21,000 B.C.	Early Americans push south into the Los Angeles area.
8000 B.C.	The Ice Age ends.
	Native Americans hunt bison near Folsom, New Mexico.
3500 B.C.	Early farmers in the Southwest grow corn, beans, and squash.
	The Adena build mounds as graves for the dead.
1000 B.C.	People in the Eastern Woodlands begin to farm.
700 B.C.–A.D. 500	The eastern Hopewell culture flourishes.
100 B.C.	Hohokam farmers in the Southwest irrigate their crops.
A.D. 700–1700	The Mississippian mound–building society flourishes, then declines.
900	The Anasazi build cliffside pueblos in the Southwest.
1001	Leif Ericsson, a Norse seafarer, explores lands in North America.
1096–1291	Christian Crusaders fight to win back Jerusalem from the Muslims.
1200–1531	Incas build an empire along the western coast of South America.
1271–1295	Marco Polo travels through central Asia and China.
1300	The Anasazi disappear from their homes in the Southwest.
1300–1519	The Aztecs build a great empire in Mexico.
1488	Diaz of Portugal sails around Africa as far as the Cape of Good Hope.
1492	Columbus lands on San Salvador.
1497–1498	Cabot pilots the first English ship to the shores of North America.
	Da Gama of Portugal sails to India.
1513	Ponce de León explores Florida.
	Balboa discovers what is later called the Pacific Ocean.
1519	Cortes defeats the Aztecs and claims Mexico for Spain.
1519–1522	Magellan's crew makes the first voyage around the world.
1523–1524	Verrazano probes the coastline of North America for France.
1531	Pizarro conquers the Incas, taking their land for Spain.
1534–1541	Cartier explores the St. Lawrence River as far west as Montreal.
1539–1542	De Soto of Spain leads an expedition through the Southeast.
1540	Coronado searches the Southwest for gold.
1565	The Spanish establish St. Augustine, Florida.
1570–1784	Six eastern tribal groups make up the League of the Iroquois.
1578–1580	Francis Drake of England sails around the world.
1588	England defeats the Spanish Armada.
1590	White searches for the lost colonists on Roanoke Island.
1607	The settlement of Jamestown, England's first lasting settlement in the New World, begins.
1608	Champlain founds Quebec, first lasting French colony in the Americas.
1619	The first shipload of slaves arrives in Virginia.
	The House of Burgesses, America's first legislature, meets.
1620	Pilgrims landing at Plymouth sign the Mayflower Compact.
1629	Puritans start a model religious community in Massachusetts.
1647–1671	Most New England colonies open public schools for children.
1651	Britain restricts colonial trade with the passage of several Navigation Acts.
1673	Marquette and Joliet explore the upper Mississippi River for France.
1682	La Salle claims for France all lands drained by the Mississippi River.
1707	England and Scotland form Great Britain.
1718	The French found the city of New Orleans.
1732	Britain forbids the export of beaver hats from the colonies.
1733	Britain passes the Molasses Act to halt colonial trade with France.
1741	Britain forbids the colonists to form banks.
1750	Britain's Iron Act stifles colonial trade in finished iron products.
1754	Britain and France begin the Great War for Empire in America.

1763	France cedes to Britain most of its lands in North America, ending the Great War for Empire.
	King George III issues the Proclamation of 1763.
1764	Britain halts the printing of paper money in the colonies.
1765	Britain passes the Quartering Act and the Stamp Act.
	The Stamp Act Congress urges colonists to boycott British goods.
1766	Britain repeals the Stamp Act.
1767	Britain taxes goods bought by colonists.
1770	Britain responds to a colonial boycott with tax repeals.
	A clash between colonists and British soldiers erupts into the so-called Boston Massacre.
1773	Colonists dump British tea into Boston harbor.
1774	Britain passes the Intolerable Acts and the Quebec Act.
	The First Continental Congress meets in Philadelphia.
1775	Colonists and British troops clash at Lexington and Concord.
	The Second Continental Congress meets.
1776	Thomas Paine publishes *Common Sense*, urging separation of the thirteen colonies from Great Britain.
	The Continental Congress issues the Declaration of Independence.
1781	The colonies win independence defeating the British at Yorktown.
	The colonies become the United States with the adoption of the Articles of Confederation.
1783	The Treaty of Paris ends the American Revolution.
1785	Congress passes the Land Ordinance.
1786	Shays's Rebellion tests the strength of the new federal government.
1787	Congress passes the Northwest Ordinance.
1787–1788	The United States Constitution is written and ratified.
1788	George Washington is named President in the first national elections.
1789	Samuel Slater introduces cloth making in New England.
	Congress passes its first tariff and defines the court system.
1789–1792	France declares itself a republic.
1791	Congress passes an excise tax on whiskey and charters a national bank.
1792	Washington wins a second term as President.
1793	Washington issues the Proclamation of Neutrality.
	Eli Whitney invents the cotton gin.
1794	The Whiskey Rebellion takes place.
1795	The Senate accepts the Jay Treaty with Great Britain.
1796	John Adams is made President by a close vote.
1797	The XYZ affair arouses anger against France.
1798	Federalists pass the Alien and Sedition Acts.
1800	The United States and France agree on a trade treaty.
1800	Thomas Jefferson wins the Presidency.
	Napoleon Bonaparte becomes ruler of France.
1801	Federalists create new judgeships under the Judiciary Act.
1803	The Supreme Court rules on the constitutionality of a law in *Marbury v. Madison*.
	The United States buys Louisiana from France for $15 million.
	Britain and France go to war.
1804	Jefferson wins a second term as President.
1804–1806	Lewis and Clark travel northwest to the Pacific Ocean, exploring parts of the Louisiana Territory.
1805–1816	Naval victories and treaties end piracies along the Barbary coast.
1806	Congress bans British imports with the Non-Importation Act.

1807	Congress passes the Embargo Act.
	The Supreme Court finds Burr not guilty of treason.
	Fulton's steamboat speeds river travel.
1808	James Madison wins election as President.
1809	The Non-Intercourse Act stops trade with Britain and France.
1810	Congress passes the Macon Act to fight blockades by Britain and France.
1812	President Madison wins reelection.
	The United States declares war with Britain.
1813	The invention of the power loom speeds up cloth making.
1814	The Peace of Ghent ends the War of 1812.
1815	Jackson defeats the British at the Battle of New Orleans.
1816	James Monroe succeeds Madison as President.
1817	Gallaudet founds the nation's first school for the deaf.
1817–1825	Work on the Erie Canal from Albany to Buffalo, New York, takes place.
1818	Britain agrees to an eastern border between the United States and Canada.
1819	Spain sells Florida to the United States for $5 million.
1820	Boston opens schools for blacks.
1820	James Monroe wins a second term as President.
	Congress passes the Missouri Compromise.
1820s–1840s	Mountain men trap and trade throughout the Rocky Mountains.
1820s–1850s	Reformers work to aid the handicapped and end the use of alcoholic drinks.
	The antislavery movement gains strength in the North.
1820s–1860s	Immigrants from northern and western Europe enter the United States.
1821	Mexico wins independence from Spain.
1821–1826	Boston opens the nation's first high schools.
1822	Austin establishes a colony in Mexican Texas.
1823	The United States adopts the Monroe Doctrine in foreign affairs.
1824	John Quincy Adams wins the Presidency by a vote in the House of Representatives.
1827	*Freedom's Journal*, the first black newspaper, begins publication.
	Frederick Douglass writes the story of his life in *My Bondage and My Freedom*.
1828	Andrew Jackson defeats Adams for the Presidency.
	Congress passes a high tariff—a Tariff of Abominations to its critics.
1830	Congress passes the Indian Removal Act.
1830–1860	Unions grow stronger among skilled workers.
1831	Cyrus McCormick perfects the reaper.
	William Lloyd Garrison starts the antislavery paper *The Liberator*.
	Nat Turner leads a slave revolt in Virginia.
1832	Jackson is reelected President.
	Jackson vetoes a new charter for the bank of the United States.
	Chief Black Hawk suffers defeat at the Battle of Bad Axe.
1833	Congress lowers the tariff of 1828.
	Oberlin College admits women.
	Mexico opens California mission lands to its nation's pioneers.
1833–1834	Settlers under Wyeth blaze the trail to Oregon.
1836	Texas declares its independence from Mexico.
	Santa Anna wins at the Alamo but loses war with Texas at San Jacinto.
1836	Martin Van Buren is elected President.
1837	Mount Holyoke becomes the first women's college.
1838	The Cherokee follow the Trail of Tears to Indian Territory.
1839	Charles Goodyear discovers how to make strong, flexible rubber.

1840	William Henry Harrison is elected President.
1841	President Harrison dies; Vice-President John Tyler becomes President.
1843	Whitman guides the Burnett party to settlement in Oregon.
1844	Samuel Morse invents the telegraph.
1844	James Polk defeats Henry Clay for the Presidency.
	China grants the United States full trading rights.
1846	Congress declares war against Mexico.
	Britain and the United States agree to a western boundary for Canada.
	A band of 15,000 Mormons migrates to present-day Utah.
1848	Zachary Taylor wins the Presidency.
	Peace with Mexico adds the Mexican Cession to United States territory.
	Gold is discovered at Sutter's Fort in California.
	Women declare their rights as citizens at Seneca Falls, New York.
1850	Vice-President Millard Fillmore becomes President on Taylor's death.
	Congress passes the package of bills known as Clay's Compromise.
	The Know-Nothings form the American party.
1852	*Uncle Tom's Cabin* feeds the fires of antislavery.
1852	Franklin Pierce wins election as President.
1853	The National Council of Colored People is formed.
1854	The United States signs a trade treaty with Japan.
	The Republican party is formed.
	Kansas-Nebraska Act establishes popular sovereignty in the formation of new states.
1855	Blacks and whites attend school together in Boston and New Bedford.
1856	James Buchanan narrowly wins election as President.
1857	The Supreme Court rules against freedom for slave Dred Scott.
1858	Gold is discovered near Pike's Peak.
	The Lincoln-Douglas debates in Illinois draw national attention.
1859	Edwin L. Drake digs the first well in search of oil in Pennsylvania.
	Miners discover the Comstock Lode in Nevada Territory.
	Abolitionist John Brown raids the arsenal at Harpers Ferry, Virginia.
1860	Abraham Lincoln is elected President.
1861	Southern states secede and form the Confederate States of America.
	The Civil War begins as Confederates fire on Fort Sumter.
	The first coast-to-coast telegraph line is completed.
1862	Congress encourages settlement of public lands through the Homestead Act.
	Congress authorizes the formation of transcontinental railroads.
	President Lincoln issues the Emancipation Proclamation.
1862–1863	Confederate and Union governments pass draft laws.
1863	President Lincoln announces his plan for readmitting southern states into the Union.
1864	Volunteer militia kill 450 Cheyenne in the Sand Creek Massacre.
1864	Lincoln wins a second term as President.
1865	Lee surrenders to Grant at Appomattox Court House, Virginia.
1865	John Wilkes Booth assassinates President Lincoln. Vice-President Andrew Johnson succeeds to the Presidency.
	The Ku Klux Klan is formed.
1865–1870	Congress passes the Thirteenth, Fourteenth, and Fifteenth amendments to assure the rights of black people.
1865–1874	The Freedmen's Bureau helps ex-slaves find homes, jobs, and education.
1865–1877	Congress directs Reconstruction in the South.
1866	Congress passes a civil rights act over President Johnson's veto.

1867	Christopher Sholes builds the first useful typewriter.
	Farmers form the Patrons of Husbandry.
	The United States buys Alaska from Russia for $7.2 million.
	Congress annexes Midway Island in the Pacific Ocean.
	The United States pressures France to withdraw from Mexico.
1868	Congress fails to remove President Johnson from office.
1868	Ulysses S. Grant is elected President.
1869	Uriah Stephens founds the Knights of Labor.
	Workers join tracks in Utah, forming the first coast-to-coast railroad.
	Wyoming Territory grants women the right to vote.
	George Westinghouse invents air brakes for trains.
1870	John D. Rockefeller founds Standard Oil Company.
1872	President Grant is reelected.
1873	The Big Bonanza strike produces $200 million in gold and silver.
1874	Joseph F. Glidden invents barbed wire.
	Gold is discovered in the Black Hills of the Dakotas.
1874	The Woman's Christian Temperance Union is formed.
1876	General George Custer and his soldiers die at Little Big Horn.
	Alexander Graham Bell invents the telephone.
1876	Rutherford B. Hayes is elected President.
1877–1879	Thomas A. Edison invents the phonograph and the first useful light bulb.
1880–1900	Interest in professional sports begins to develop.
1880	James A. Garfield wins the Presidency.
1881	President James A. Garfield's assassination after five months in office brings Vice-President Chester A. Arthur into the Presidency.
1882	Congress forbids further immigration from China.
	Italy joins Germany and Austria-Hungary in the Triple Alliance.
1883	The Pendleton Act establishes a federal civil service.
1884	Grover Cleveland wins the Presidency by a slim margin.
1885	The first modern skycraper is built in Chicago.
1886	Samuel Gompers heads the newly formed American Federation of Labor.
	Workers and police clash in the Haymarket riot in Chicago.
1887	The Dawes Act rules that Native Americans be treated as individuals.
	Congress regulates railroad rates through the Interstate Commerce Act.
1888	Benjamin Harrison succeeds Cleveland as President.
1889	Jane Addams starts Hull House in Chicago.
	Congress opens Indian Territory to white settlers.
1890	The General Federation of Women's Clubs is formed.
	Congress passes the Sherman Antitrust Act.
1892	Cleveland is reelected President after four years out of office.
	The Farmers' Alliances help start the Populist party.
1893	Queen Liliuokalani of Hawaii is overthrown in a revolution.
1894	The American Railway Union backs strikers at the Pullman Company.
1895	The United States arbitrates a dispute between Britain and Venezuela.
1896	In *Plessy v. Ferguson* the Court rules separate facilities for blacks legal.
1896	William McKinley defeats William Jennings Bryan for the Presidency.
1897	Gold is discovered in Alaska.
1898	Winning the Spanish-American War increases the nation's land holdings.
	The United States annexes Hawaii.
1898–1913	Huge train terminals go up in most of the nation's major cities.
1899	John Hay announces an Open Door policy in world trade with China.
1900	President McKinley is reelected.
	The Boxers try to drive foreigners out of China.

1901	President McKinley is shot. Vice-President Theodore Roosevelt succeeds him.
	New York state halts the building of slum-type apartments.
	J.P. Morgan puts together U.S. Steel Corporation.
1902–1916	The United States polices conflicts in Latin America.
1902	The Newlands Act lays the groundwork for later dam building in the West.
	President Roosevelt forces settlement of the United Mine Workers strike.
1903	*The Great Train Robbery* becomes the first film to tell a complete story.
	Henry Ford borrows money to begin building automobiles.
1904	Roosevelt uses the Sherman Antitrust Act to attack giant businesses.
	Lincoln Steffens describes corruption in government in *The Shame of Cities*.
1904	Roosevelt is elected President in his own right.
1904–1914	The United States constructs a canal across Panama.
1906	Congress passes the Meat Inspection Act, the Pure Food and Drug Act, and the Hepburn Act.
	Dr. Lee De Forest invents the vacuum tube used in radios.
1907	France, Russia, and Britain ally themselves in the Triple Entente.
1908	President Roosevelt sounds the call for national conservation.
1908	William H. Taft is elected to succeed President Roosevelt.
1909–1910	Women garment workers in New York strike for thirteen weeks.
1910	The National Association for the Advancement of Colored People is formed.
1910–1912	Concerned citizens form scouting and youth groups.
1912	Woodrow Wilson wins the Presidency over Roosevelt and Taft.
1913	The Constitution is amended to allow a federal tax on income.
1914	Congress strengthens earlier laws with the Clayton Antitrust Act.
	Wilson sets up the Federal Reserve System.
	With the assassination of Archduke Ferdinand, war breaks out in Europe.
1916	President Wilson wins reelection.
1917	Communist revolutionists overthrow the czar in Russia.
	Congress declares war against the Central Powers and begins the draft.
1918	An armistice ends World War I fighting in Europe.
1919	Women gain the right to vote.
1919–1933	The making and selling of liquor is prohibited.
1920	Warren G. Harding is elected President.
1920–1921	The United States signs a series of defense treaties with other nations.
1923	President Harding dies. Calvin Coolidge succeeds him in office.
1924	Congress grants all Native Americans full citizenship.
1924	Coolidge is elected President in his own right.
1925	Benito Mussolini comes to power in Italy.
1926	The National Broadcasting Company of radio is founded.
1927	Babe Ruth hits sixty home runs for the New York Yankees.
	Charles Lindbergh flies alone nonstop across the Atlantic.
1928	Herbert Hoover defeats Al Smith for President.
1929	Joseph Stalin heads the ruling Communist party in the Soviet Union.
	Stock prices drop suddenly in the Great Stock Market Crash.
	Congress limits immigration.
1931	Japan invades Manchuria.
1932	The Reconstruction Finance Corporation is founded.
	The Norris-La Guardia Act gives workers more freedom in union activities.
	Veterans march on Washington, demanding full service bonuses.
1932	Franklin D. Roosevelt is elected President by a landslide.

1933   Congress passes the Emergency Banking Act.

President Roosevelt holds the first of his many fireside chats.

Under the New Deal, Congress sets up the TVA, the AAA, the CCC, the FDIC, and the NRA.

Adolf Hitler and his Nazi party gain control of Germany.

1933–1935   The Public Works Administration and the Works Progress Administration are formed.

1934   Congress forms the Securities and Exchange Commission.

1935   Congress passes the Neutrality Act, sets up the Social Security System, establishes the National Labor Relations Board with the Wagner Act, and provides for a National Youth Administration.

The Supreme Court finds the National Recovery Administration unconstitutional.

1936   The AAA is declared unconstitutional.

Mussolini's troops conquer Ethiopia.

Hitler's German soldiers march into the Rhineland.

1936   President Roosevelt wins a second term, while war clouds gather in Europe.

1937   Japan seizes China's capital city.

1938   The Fair Labor Standards Act improves workers' wages and hours.

Congress sets 16 as the minimum working age in most industries.

John L. Lewis and others form the CIO.

Germany takes Austria.

1939   Franco takes over as dictator in Spain, following civil war.

Hitler's troops cross into Czechoslovakia.

1940   Congress drafts men for the armed forces.

Japan forms an alliance with the Axis powers of Germany and Italy.

1940   President Roosevelt is elected to a third term.

1941   The United States pledges aid to the Allies in the Lend-Lease Act.

President Roosevelt and Britain's Churchill sign the Atlantic Charter.

Japan attacks the U.S. Pacific fleet at Pearl Harbor.

The United States enters World War II.

1941–1945   The United States joins the Allies in fighting World War II.

Japanese citizens are relocated in guarded camps during World War II.

1944   Roosevelt is elected to a fourth term as President.

1945   Leaders of the Big Three work out peace terms at Yalta.

1945   President Roosevelt dies. Vice-President Harry S Truman succeeds him.

The United Nations is formed at a meeting in San Francisco.

Germany surrenders to the Allies.

The United States drops the first atomic bomb on Hiroshima, Japan.

General Douglas MacArthur accepts Japan's surrender.

1947   The United States offers postwar aid to Europe under the Marshall Plan.

Congress passes the Taft-Hartley Act over President Truman's veto.

1947–1954   Families in the United States start a new movement to the suburbs.

1948   Truman is elected President over Thomas Dewey.

President Truman orders desegregation of all armed forces.

1948–1949   The Berlin airlift takes place.

1949   A Communist revolution sets up the People's Republic of China.

1950–1953   United Nations forces stop the invasion of South Korea by North Korea.

1952   Dwight D. Eisenhower defeats Adlai Stevenson for President.

1954   The Supreme Court orders desegregation of all public schools.

1956   President Eisenhower wins a second term.

1960   John F. Kennedy defeats Richard M. Nixon in the race for President.

1961	Cuban exiles fail in their Bay of Pigs invasion attempt.
	East Germany builds a wall between East and West Berlin.
	The United States begins its Peace Corps volunteer program.
1962	The United States forces the Soviet Union to remove missiles from Cuba.
1963	An assassin kills President Kennedy in Texas. Vice-President Lyndon B. Johnson assumes office as President.
1964	President Johnson is elected to continue in office.
	Congress passes numerous programs to improve social services under Johnson's Great Society.
	Congress passes the Civil Rights Act to protect blacks and other minorities.
	The Department of Housing and Urban Development is formed.
	Congress gives the President power to send more troops into Vietnam.
1968	Martin Luther King, Jr., and Robert Kennedy are assassinated.
1968	Richard M. Nixon is elected President.
1969	Astronaut Neil A. Armstrong walks on the moon.
1970	President Nixon orders troops into Cambodia.
	Four students are killed during a protest at Kent State University in Ohio.
1971	Congress gives eighteen-year-olds the right to vote.
1972	The United States and the Soviet Union agree to limit stores of nuclear arms.
	President Nixon favors revenue-sharing with state and local governments.
	Burglars are caught breaking into Democratic headquarters at Watergate.
1972	President Nixon is reelected to office.
1973	The United States, North Vietnam, and South Vietnam sign a peace agreement.
1974	Vice-President Gerald Ford steps in as President after Nixon resigns.
1976	Jimmy Carter is elected President.
1977	President Carter establishes a Department of Energy.
1979	The United States and Communist China resume full trading relations.
	Soviet troops invade Afghanistan.
1980	Ronald Reagan wins the Presidency from Carter.
1981	President Reagan survives an attempted assassination.
	The space shuttle *Columbia,* piloted by astronauts Young and Crippen, lands safely after space orbit.
1981	The first woman, Sandra Day O'Connor, is appointed to the Supreme Court.
1982	Reagan's tax cut program becomes law.
1984	President Reagan is reelected to office.
1986	The space shuttle *Challenger* disaster halts the space shuttle program for two years.
	The national debt exceeds $2 trillion.
	Congress passes the Balanced Budget and Emergency Deficit Control Act, called the Gramm-Rudman Act.
1987	The United States and the Soviet Union sign a treaty eliminating all intermediate nuclear missiles in Europe.
1988	Fifth year without recession, the longest such period since World War II.
	President Reagan meets with General Secretary Gorbachev in Moscow to discuss further arms reductions.
	The launch of the space shuttle *Discovery* resumes America's space shuttle program.
	Republican George Bush defeats Democrat Michael Dukakis in the 1988 presidential election.
1989	George Bush is sworn in as the 41st President of the United States.

Glossary

In this Glossary you will find all the terms listed at the beginning of chapters. You may use the Glossary as you would a dictionary. But only the meanings most helpful to you in the study of history are given. All of the words have been spelled phonetically (using symbols within parentheses following the word) to help you pronounce them. The Pronunciation Key below shows what the symbols mean and gives examples of how to pronounce the sounds.

Pronunciation Key

a	at	e	met	ī	hike	ŏŏ	good
ā	fade	ē	me	ō	open	ōō	soon
ā	air	ə	about	ô	awful	ou	loud
ä	father	i	it	oi	oil	zh	vision

abolition (ab'ə·lish'ən) the work of ending slavery (p. 333)

accuracy (ak'yər·ə·sē) correctness; truthfulness; the lack of error or mistake (p. 263)

acquisition (ak'wə·zish'ən) the act of gaining something from another person; something gained from another person (p. 387)

agriculture (ag'ri·kəl'chər) the raising of animals and the growing of crops; farming (p. 114)

alliance (ə·lī'əns) an organization to foster common interests or defense among members (p. 614)

ally (al'ī) a person, nation, or group willing to help another person, nation, or group (p. 117)

amend (ə·mend') to change; to add to, delete from, or otherwise revise the wording of a document, such as the Constitution (p. 191)

analysis (ə·nal'ə·səs) a study that separates something into its simple parts to discover how the parts work together and relate to one another (p. 482)

ancestor (an'ses'tər) a person who came before another person in a family line, usually related more distantly than a grandparent (p. 43)

annex (an'eks') to claim a certain area as part of the nation (p. 564)

antislavery (an'tī·slāv'ə·rē) against the practice of buying or selling people as property (p. 323)

apartment (ə·pärt'mənt) a building with separate living units; one of many separate housing units in a building (p. 522)

appeal (ə·pēl') (*noun*) a request for the rehearing of a case in a higher court (p. 380)

appeal (ə·pēl') (*verb*) to request the hearing of a case in a higher court (p. 380)

apprentice (ə·prent'əs) a person who learns a trade or skill from another person (p. 112)

arbitration (ar'bə·trā'shən) the hearing and settlement by a third party of a dispute between two parties (p. 570)

archaeologist (är'kē·äl'ə·jəst) a person who studies such material remains as fossils, bones, and objects made by people to learn about human history (p. 45)

armistice (är'mə·stəs) an agreement between armies to stop fighting for a time (p. 620)

artifact (ärt'ə·fakt') an item from an earlier time made with human skill (p. 256)

assembly line (ə·sem'blē līn) a line of workers who each places a piece in a product as it passes before them, usually on a moving belt (p. 506)

autobiography (ôt'ə·bī'äg'rə·fē) self-written story of one's life (p. 253)

balance (bal'əns) an evenness of

treatment in presenting two or more views of an issue or event (p. 191)

bar graph (bär' graf') a drawing made up of bars of different lengths showing amounts or numbers of something and how they compare (p. 115)

bargain (bär'gən) to discuss working terms and conditions (p. 640)

bibliography (bib'lē·äg'rə·fē) a list of books (p. 259)

bicentennial (bī'sen·ten'ē·əl) having to do with the two-hundredth anniversary of an event (p. 683)

bison (bīs'ən) buffalo; a wild ox of the American Great Plains (p. 448)

black code (blak' kōd') a set of laws passed by the southern states after the Civil War, applying only to blacks (p. 427)

bloc (bläk) a group of nations sharing a common interest or united by a treaty (p. 662)

blockade (blä·kād') (*noun*) a barrier imposed by an enemy nation to another nation's foreign trade and communications (p. 223)

blockade (blä·kād') (*verb*) to stop or interrupt another nation's foreign trade and communications (p. 226)

bonus (bō'nəs) a payment of money or other gifts given for past military service or for reenlistment in a military service (p. 635)

border (bôrd′ər) an imaginary line that separates one area from another (p. 310)

boundary (boun′də·rē) a line separating two areas or defining the limits of a single area (p. 385)

boycott (boi′kät) (*noun*) the refusal to do further business with a company or nation until certain conditions or practices are changed (p. 163)

boycott (boi′kät) (*verb*) to refuse to do further business with a company or nation until certain conditions or practices are changed (p. 163)

bribe (brīb) (*noun*) an offer of money or gifts to a person for making choices favorable to the giver (p. 208)

bribe (brīb) (*verb*) to offer a person money or gifts for making choices favorable to the giver (p. 208)

bribery (brī′bə·rē) the act of offering or accepting money or gifts for making choices favorable to the giver (p. 436)

busing (bəs′ing) the transporting of students by bus from their neighborhood to a school in another neighborhood to achieve racial balance (p. 680)

cabinet (kab′ə·nət) a group of governmental department heads advising the President (p. 199)

campaign (kam′pān′) (*noun*) a series of actions to bring about a certain outcome, such as the election of a candidate (p. 211)

candidate (kan′də·dāt′) a person seeking a political office (p. 208)

caption (kap′shən) an explanation found near an illustration (p. 144)

caricature (kar′i·kə·chər′) a cartoon that exaggerates a person's physical features (p. 147)

cash crop (kash′ kräp′) a farm product raised to be sold for a profit (p. 330)

cause and effect (kôz′ ən i·fekt′) a relationship between events in which one event (cause) leads to another event (effect) (p. 490)

cede (sēd) to award or grant, usually by agreement (p. 387)

census (sen′səs) an official count of the number of people living in a given area (p. 338)

century (sench′ə·rē) a period of 100 years (p. 28)

cession (sesh′ən) a surrendering of something to another; that which is surrendered to another, usually by formal agreement (p. 387)

chart (chärt) a graphic arrangement of data for the purpose of showing relationships among the data (p. 114)

charter (chärt′ər) a written agreement or grant of rights and privileges (p. 90)

checks and balances (cheks′ ən bal′ən·səz) a system of the United States Constitution that provides for the consent and approval of decisions and acts among the executive, legislative, and judicial branches of government (p. 191)

civil service (siv′əl sər′vəs) a system of government employment under which workers for nonelective offices are hired (p. 541)

civilian (sə·vil′yən) a person not serving in a country's armed forces (p. 655)

claim (klām) (*noun*) land or other resource staked out as one's own (p. 446)

claim (klām) (*verb*) to declare one's right to an area or resource (p. 446)

climate (klī′mət) the usual weather of an area, including average temperature and precipitation (p. 33)

colony (käl′ə·nē) a group of people from the same country living in a new country but keeping ties with their old country; a settlement made by such a group of people (p. 69)

commerce (käm′ərs) the overall exchange of goods, including the transportation (p. 539)

commission (kə·mish′ən) a group assigned to carry out a particular task (p. 436)

communication (kə·myoo′nə·kā′shən) the process of exchanging information (p. 498)

communism (käm′yə niz′əm) the belief that all property belongs to the state rather than to individuals and that the state should control all the means of production and distribution of goods; the principles practiced by the Soviet Union and other nations in the eastern bloc (p. 623)

competition (käm′pə·tish′ən) the effort engaged in by two or more people or groups acting independently to achieve the same goal (p. 539)

competitor (käm·pet′ət·ər) a rival buyer or seller of goods or services in the marketplace (p. 504)

compromise (käm′prə·mīz′) (*noun*) an agreement among differing parties based on concessions granted by each (p. 188)

compromise (käm′prə·mīz′) (*verb*) to reach agreement by the mutual granting of concessions (p. 188)

concentration camp (kän′sən·trā′ shən kamp′) a wartime prison for captured soldiers or civilians regarded as potentially dangerous by their captors (p. 658)

conclusion (kən·kloo′zhən) an opinion or theory based on careful study and logical thought (p. 493)

confederation (kən·fed′ə·rā′shən) a union of several small groups for mutual aid or action; a large group formed by such a union; the form of government in the United States between 1781 and 1789 (p. 186)

consequence (käns′ə·kwens′) an outcome produced by previous actions or conditions (p. 371)

constitution (kän′stə·tyoo′shən) the basic laws of a government (p. 186)

consumer (kən·soo′mər) a user of goods (p. 539)

continent (kant′ə·nənt) one of the earth's great land masses (p. 43)

controversial (kän′trə·vər′shəl) having the characteristics of a dispute that arises from a difference in views (p. 384)

convoy (kän′voi′) a system used for ocean crossings in wartime by which battleships and other armed ships surround unarmed ships for their protection (p. 619)

corporation (kôr′pə·rā′shən) a business chartered by the state and owned by shareholders (p. 507)

corruption (kə·rəp′shən) a state of widespread wrongdoing, including bribery (p. 543)

council (koun′səl) a group that meets to discuss and decide issues (p. 53)

cultural (kəlch′ə·rəl) having to do with the life patterns of a group of people (p. 487)

culture (kəl′chər) art, language, the production of material goods, customs, and beliefs of a group of people (p. 48)

cycle (sī′kəl) a series of events that recur from time to time, usually in the same order (p. 631)

debtor (det′ər) a person who owes money or service (p. 98)

decade (dek′ād) a period of ten years (p. 28)

decision (di·sizh′ən) the choice of a position or course of action, often made after a thoughtful consideration of alternatives (p. 367)

declaration (dek′lə·rā′shən) a statement of one's belief or position on an issue (p. 170)

define (di·fīn′) to outline; to state the meaning of; to describe in complete detail (p. 368)

delegate (del′i·gət) (*noun*) a person chosen to act for others in a meeting or a government (p. 53)

delegate (del′i·gāt′) (*verb*) to choose a person as one's representative (p. 53)

demonstrator (dem′ən·strāt′ər) a person publicly expressing opinions or feelings about an issue (p. 679)

deposit (di·päz′ət) an accumulation of matter formed by natural forces (p. 444)

descendant (di·sen′dənt) a person born of another person or in a family line directly traceable from earlier ancestors (p. 43)

desegregation (dē′seg′ri·gā′shən) a movement to halt the division of people into separate groups on the basis of race, class, or ethnic background (p. 665)

dictator (dik′tāt′ər) a ruler with almost limitless power over the people in a nation (p. 651)

disaster (diz·as′tər) an event occurring suddenly and bringing great misfortune (p. 215)

discrimination (dis·krim′ə·nā′shən) an act that judges people on the basis of something other than individual merit or value (p. 340)

displace (dis·plās′) to remove from a usual place (p. 275)

dissent (dis·ent′) a difference of opinion; on the Supreme Court the act of a justice who disagrees with the majority opinion and publicly airs the difference in a written statement (p. 380)

doctrine (däk′trən) a statement of government policy, often about foreign relations (p. 311)

document (däk′yə·ment′) an official record or statement (p. 254)

domestic (də·mes′tik) having to do with one's own country (p. 302)

downturn (doun′tərn′) a decrease in business activity usually resulting in an increase in unemployment (p. 631)

draft (draft) (*noun*) the selection of persons for military service (p. 407)

draft (draft) (*verb*) to select for military service (p. 619)

drought (drout) a long period of dry weather, usually resulting in damage to crops (p. 48)

duty (dyo͞ot′ē) a tax on goods brought into a country, usually at their point of entry (p. 416)

economic (ek′ə·näm′ik) having to do with producing, trading, and using goods and services to meet the needs of people (p. 160)

economy (i·kän′ə·mē) a system through which people meet their needs and wants by producing, exchanging, and using goods and services (p. 105)

edition (i·dish′ən) an issue of a newspaper or magazine; also a newscast aired at a stated time on television or radio (p. 605)

elector (i·lek′tər) a person entitled to vote in an election; in the U.S., a member of the electoral college (p. 208)

elevation (el′ə·vā′shən) the height of land above sea level (p. 34)

embargo (im·bär′gō) a governmental order halting all trade with another nation (p. 225)

emergency (i·mər′jən·sē′) an unexpected event that usually calls for quick action (p. 637)

empire (em′pī′ər) a large territory or group of territories having a single government (p. 69)

energy (en′ər·jē) the ability or capacity to do work (p. 497)

enlist (in·list′) to sign up for military service (p. 407)

enterprise (ent′ər·prīz′) a willingness to start something new or to take a daring step (p. 513)

entertainment (ent′ər·tān′mənt) a pleasing, amusing, or stimulating activity (p. 530)

environment (in·vī′rən·mənt) the surroundings in which an individual or a group functions (p. 54)

equality (i·kwäl′ət·ē) a condition in which a person or a group has the same rights or standing as every other person or group (p. 675)

ethnic (eth′nik) having to do with a group of people of like origin and culture (p. 519)

evaluate (i·val′yə·wāt′) to decide the value of something through careful study (p. 260)

evidence (ev′əd·əns) a statement or fact that supports the truth of a matter (p. 378)

excise tax (ek′sīz′ taks′) a fee paid on the manufacture, sale, and use of goods made within a country (p. 201)

executive (ig·zek′yət·iv) of that branch of government responsible for carrying out programs or enforcing laws (p. 191)

expansion (ik·span′chən) a growth in area, in number, or in volume (p. 283)

expedition (ek′spə·dish′ən) a trip taken for a particular reason; the persons making the trip (p. 75)

export (ek′spôrt′) (*noun*) a product sent to another country for sale (p. 97)

export (ek·spôrt′) (*verb*) to send a product to another country for sale (p. 98)

federal (fed′ə·rəl) of a government formed by agreement among several political units in which strong and clearly defined powers belong to the central government while other powers are retained by the member units; of the United States government (p. 189)

federal aid (fed′ə·rəl ād′) money or supplies given to state and local governments and other institutions by the national government (p. 302)

fiction (fik′shən) an account that is made up or imagined, such as a story (p. 260)

focus (fō′kəs) (*noun*) a main subject of attention or discussion (p. 481)

focus (fō′kəs) (*verb*) to concentrate attention on (p. 481)

foreign affairs (fôr′ən ə·fārz′) the activities of one government in relation to the governments of other countries (p. 222)

foreign-born (fôr′ən·bôrn) (*adjective*) having a birthplace outside the United States (p. 291)

foreign-born (fôr′ən·bôrn) (*noun*) a person whose birth occurred in a country other than the United States (p. 291)

foreign correspondent (fôr′ən cor′ə·spän′dənt) a reporter who specializes in gathering news outside the boundaries of the United States (p. 599)

foreign policy (fôr′ən päl′ə·sē) the

position taken by one government in relation to governments of other countries (p. 222)

fraud (frôd) an act achieved through trickery (p. 437)

frontier (frən′tiər′) a boundary between settled and largely unsettled land (p. 443)

generation (jen′ə·rā′shən) the time span between the birth of parents and the births of their children; all the children born during such a time span (p. 28)

glasnost (gläs′nōst) a Russian word meaning a more open society (p. 688)

graft (graft) the dishonest or illegal gain of money and favors (p. 436)

graph (graf) a drawing that compares different sets of facts by using points, lines, bars, or symbols (p. 151)

graphic (graf′ik) any picture, map, or chart that presents facts and ideas (p. 143)

grassland (gras′land′) a large area of flat or rolling land covered with coarse grass (p. 448)

greenback (grēn′bak′) paper money in the United States; United States political party favoring an increase in the supply of paper money (p. 540)

handicap (hand′di·kap) a disability that makes doing certain tasks difficult or impossible (p. 642)

headline (hed′līn′) a short summary statement preceding a news story (p. 597)

heritage (her′ə·tij) knowledge, customs, and beliefs passed on to a person or group of a present generation by members of each past generation (p. 58)

hill (hil) a landform of 1,650 to 6,600 feet (495 to 1,980 m) having moderate relief (p. 35)

history (his′tə·rē) a record of change over a period of time that affects people living in a certain place (p. 23)

holding company (hōl′ding kəmp′

ə·nē) a business owning enough stock in different companies to control the management of those companies (p. 508)

idealism (ī·dē′ə·liz′əm) belief in perfectibility and excellence (p. 620)

identify (ī·dent′ə·fī) to name; to establish the like character of a group of things (p. 368)

immigrant (im′i·grənt) a person born in one country who has entered another country with the intention of taking up permanent residence (p. 106)

immigration (im′ə·grā′shən) the entrance of people into one country from another with the intention of permanent residence (p. 291)

impeach (im·pēch′) to bring charges against a public official for crime or misbehavior (p. 378)

imperialism (im·pir′ē·ə·liz′əm) the practice of building an empire by taking over other parts of the world (p. 75)

import (im′pôrt′) (*noun*) a good brought into one country from another country (p. 75)

import (im·pôrt′) (*verb*) to bring goods into one country from another country (p. 75)

impress (im·pres′) to force into service, especially naval service (p. 224)

inauguration (in·ô′gyə·rā′shən) a ceremony of taking office (p. 216)

indentured servant (in·den′chərd sər′vənt) a person committed to work for another for a certain length of time (p. 106)

independence (in′də·pen′dəns) the freedom to act on one's own (p. 170)

inflation (in·flā′shən) a period of rising prices (p. 540)

installment (in·stôl′mənt) (*adjective*) having to do with payments made at regular intervals (p. 625)

installment (in·stôl′mənt) (*noun*) one of several equal payments, usually part of a debt that is being repaid with interest (p. 625)

integration (int′ə·grā′shən) a bringing together of two or more separate groups (p. 675)

intellectual (int′əl·ek′chə·wəl) having to do with thought, ideas, or study (p. 487)

interdependence(int′ər-di·pen′dəns) a relationship in which individuals, groups, and nations trust and help one another (p. 666)

interest (in′trəst) the extra money paid by a borrower and received by a lender as a fee for the use of loaned money (p. 203)

international (int′ər·nash′nəl) having to do with two or more nations (p. 570)

invention (in·ven′chən) a new device or way of doing something (p. 501)

investment (in·vest′mənt) a sum of money loaned or spent to make a profit (p. 637)

irrigation (ir′ə·gā′shən) supplying water to a dry area for the purpose of growing crops (p. 46)

isthmus (is′məs) a narrow neck of land connecting two larger land masses (p. 570)

jazz (jaz) a style of music originated by black musicians (p. 531)

joint-stock company (joint′stäk′ kəmp′ə·nē) a trading group formed to do business for the profit of individual stockholders (p. 86)

judicial (ju·dish′shəl) of that branch of government responsible for hearing cases in a court system (p. 191)

justice (jəs′təs) a judge; as a term of address, usually used for state or federal supreme court judges (p. 201)

labor (lā′bər) workers, as a group; an organization or group of persons that represents workers (p. 509)

landform (land′fôrm) a natural feature of the earth's surface such as mountains, hills, plateaus, and plains (p. 34)

league (lēg) a group of persons or nations with a common cause (p. 620)

legislative (lej′ə·slāt′iv) of that branch of government responsible for making laws (p. 190)

legislature (lej′ə·slā′chər) a branch of government with the power to make laws (p. 86)

leisure (lēzh′ər) time free from work and other responsibilities (p. 530)

lend-lease (len′dlēs′) agreement under which one country borrows or rents goods or services from another country (p. 655)

lifestyle (līf′stīəl′) usual way of going about one's daily life (p. 18)

lifetime (līf′tīm′) average amount of time a person usually lives (p. 26)

line graph (līn′ graf′) a line joining points on a grid and showing changes in the quantity of something over a period of time (p. 153)

longhorn (lông′hôrn) a breed of cattle derived from Spanish stock that once roamed wild in the southwestern United States (p. 452)

loom (loom) a frame or machine on which to weave threads into cloth (p. 297)

loyalty (loi′əl·tē) being true to one's country, party, leader, or cause (p. 665)

manufacture (man′yə·fak′chər) (*noun*) the process of making goods from raw materials, by hand or by machine (p. 159)

manufacture (man′yə·fak′chər) (*verb*) to make goods from raw materials, by hand or by machine (p. 159)

market (mär′kət) a place where goods are bought and sold (p. 159)

massacre (mas′i·kər) a large-scale killing of defenseless people (p. 449)

media (mēd′ē·ə) the various forms of mass communication, such as television, radio, and newspapers (p. 595)

midwife (mid′wīf′) a person who helps women during childbirth (p. 126)

migrate (mī′grāt′) to move to a new country or place (p. 43)

migration (mī·grā′shən) the act of moving from one country or place to another (p. 43)

militia (mə·lish′ə) a group of armed citizens subject to call for military service (p. 114)

minority (mə·nôr′ət·ē) (*adjective*) having to do with a group that makes up less than half of the total population of a nation or other group (p. 675)

minority (mə·nôr′ət·ē) (*noun*) a group whose members total less than half of the population of a nation or other group (p. 675)

missile (mis′əl) a guided rocket used as a weapon (p. 673)

missionary (mish′ə·när′ē) a person who goes to another country to teach a religion or to help others (p. 79)

mission station (mish′ən stā′shən) a Spanish settlement built along the Pacific Coast and run by Spanish priests during the late 1700s (p. 279)

monopoly (mə·näp′ə·lē) an industry completely controlled by one person or a small group (p. 508)

motion picture (mō′shən pik′chər) a movie (p. 531)

mountain (mount′ən) a landform of 6,600 feet (1,980 m) or more with high relief (p. 34)

mountain man (mount′ən man) a white trapper and trader who explored the central Rocky Mountains in the 1820s (p. 277)

nationalism (nash′nəl·iz′əm) a belief that people with such common ties as language and customs should form their own nation; great loyalty to one's country (p. 612)

native-born (nāt′iv·bôrn) a person born in the United States (p. 289)

natural feature (nach′ə·rəl fē′chər) a physical characteristic of an area such as a landform, body of water, climate, or natural resource (p. 34)

natural resource (nach′ə·rəl rē′ sôrs′) a physical characteristic of the earth such as soil, a forest, a mineral, or a lake, that is useful to human beings (p. 37)

navigation (nav′ə·gā′shən) the act of guiding a ship (p. 66)

negotiate (ni·gō′shē·āt′) to bargain with another party to reach a settlement (p. 621)

neutral (nyoo′trəl) not taking sides in conflicts (p. 222)

neutrality (nyoo·tral′ət·ē) the policy of not taking sides in conflicts among groups or governments (p. 617)

nonfiction (nän′fik′shən) stories of actual events (p. 259)

nuclear power (nyoo′klē·ər pou′ər) a form of energy supplied by splitting the nucleus of an atom (p. 607)

nullification (nəl′ə·fə·kā′shən) a theory that a state may declare a federal law of no force within its boundaries if it thought the law to be unconstitutional (p. 316)

nullify (nəl′ə·fī′) to declare a law or an action of no force or value (p. 388)

opinion (ə·pin′yən) one's belief or judgment about a particular matter; in law, a written judicial decision that states the legal reasons for the decision (p. 253)

opposition (äp′ə·zish′ən) resistance; a group of people who offer the resistance (p. 404)

option (äp′shən) a choice; the right to choose (p. 368)

organization chart (ôr′gə·nə·zā′ shən′ chârt) an illustration showing the structure of a group, such as a business, school, political party, or government (p. 150)

outpost (out′pōst′) a military base or settlement located on a frontier (p. 279)

overseer (ō′vər·siər′) a supervisor of slaves on a plantation (p. 334)

pact (pakt) an agreement; a treaty (p. 666)

parallel (pãr′ə·lel) an imaginary east-west line on a globe or map that marks latitude (p. 385)

pardon (pärd′ən) (*noun*) the act of forgiving a person for wrongdoing (p. 682)

pardon (pärd′ən) (*verb*) to forgive a person for wrongdoing (p. 682)

patent (pat′ənt) an official document stating one's rights to an invention (p. 135)

patroon (pə·troon′) an owner of an estate in the Dutch colony of New Netherland (p. 96)

perestroika (pe′res·troi′kä) a Russian word meaning to restructure the economy, the party, and the government (p. 688)

periodical (pir′ē·äd′i·kəl) a publication printed at regular intervals, such as daily, weekly, or monthly (p. 255)

permanent (pərm′ə·nənt) lasting; continuing in existence, often without change (p. 67)

phase (fāz) an identifiable stage or period occurring within a series of events (p. 410)

pictograph (pik′tə·graf′) a drawing that uses symbols to compare different quantities of things (p. 156)

pie graph (pī′ graf′) a drawing that divides a circle into wedge-shaped parts to show the relationship of each part to the whole (p. 151)

pioneer (pī′ə·nir′) a person who blazes a trail to a new area or is among the first settlers in a new area (p. 276)

plains (plānz) an area of broad flat land (p. 36)

plantation (plan·tā′shən) a new settlement; a large farm, usually planted in a single crop and requiring a large resident work force (p. 330)

plateau (pla·tō′) an area of mostly high flat land (p. 35)

platform (plat′fôrm) a statement of the beliefs and proposed actions of a group, especially a political party (p. 210)

policy (päl′ə·sē) a course of action based on the goals of a group or government (p. 651)

political (pə·lit′i·kəl) having to do with government (p. 481)

political cartoon (pə·lit′i·kəl kär·toon′) a drawing that expresses an opinion about current government policies or events (p. 146)

pollution (pə·loo′shən) an unclean condition in the environment caused by the release of chemical or other wastes (p. 674)

popular sovereignty (päp′yə·lər säv′rən·tē) a United States policy of the 1850s that allowed people in the territories to decide for themselves whether or not they wanted slavery (p. 390)

possession (pə·zesh′ən) land outside of a government's boundaries that comes under its control (p. 557)

prairie (prãr′ē) a stretch of level land covered with grass (p. 272)

prediction (pri·dik′shən) the act of foretelling an event (p. 607)

prehistory (prē′his′tə·rē) time before written records (p. 27)

prejudice (prej′əd·əs) a disapproving attitude toward some group or thing in the absence of cause or adequate knowledge (p. 427)

preservation (prez′ər·vā′shən) maintaining or preventing the destruction of an object or idea (p. 389)

press conference (pres′ kän′fə·rəns) a formal question-and-answer meeting between public officials and reporters (p. 596)

press release (pres′ ri·lēs′) an official news announcement given to reporters and other members of the media (p. 596)

primary (prī′mãr′ē) an election in which each party selects candidates for various state and federal offices (p. 545)

primary source (prī′mãr′ē sôrs′) an account, drawing, photograph, or other record of an event made at the time an event took place, or an account made at a later time by someone who lived through the event (p. 253)

proclamation (präk'lə·mā'shən) a formal declaration of policy or intent by an official (p. 414)

profit (präf'ət) money gained over and above the original cost of goods or services (p. 86)

proprietary colony (prə·prī'ə·ter'ē käl'ə·nē) a settlement owned and governed by a single person or group (p. 98)

proposal (prə·pō'zəl) a suggested plan (p. 203)

prosperity (prä·sper'ət·ē) a condition of general well-being and economic plenty (p. 622)

protective tariff (prə·tek'tiv tār'əf) a tax on foreign-made goods that raises the cost of certain goods high enough to allow similar domestic goods to be lower priced and more attractive to a buyer (p. 301)

protest (prō'test') (*noun*) a statement or demonstration of disapproval (p. 165)

protest (prə·test') (*verb*) to voice objection to or to demonstrate disapproval for an action, plan, or idea (p. 165)

pueblo (poo·eb'lō) a flat-roofed house built of stone or of bricks made from mud, water, and straw (p. 279)

rancho (ran'chō') a land where a Mexican settler raised livestock, grain, and food crops during the early 1800s (p. 279)

range (rānj) an open country where cattle may roam and graze (p. 453)

ratify (rat'ə·fī') to approve in a formal way (p. 186)

ration (rash'ən) (*noun*) a set amount of certain goods granted to each person (p. 618)

ration (rash'ən) (*verb*) to limit the use of certain goods (p. 618)

recovery (ri·kəv'ə·rē) an upturn in business following a downturn (p. 639)

reform (ri·fôrm') a change that im-

proves or corrects an existing condition in society or politics (p. 318)

regulate (reg'yə·lāt') to govern or control through rules; to put under the control of government (p. 537)

relief (ri·lēf') the changes in elevation from one point to another in a given stretch of land; money or goods given to help people without jobs, homes, or food (p. 39)

removal (ri·moo'vəl) the transfer of people from one location to another sometimes by force (p. 274)

repeal (ri·pēl') (*noun*) a legislative action that nullifies a law (p. 164)

repeal (ri·pēl') (*verb*) to nullify by legislative action (p. 164)

reporter (ri·pōrt'ər) a person who gathers news for publication (p. 596)

representative (rep'ri·zent'ət·iv') (*adjective*) characteristic of a government in which some members of a group are chosen to speak and act for other members (p. 162)

representative (rep'ri·zent'ət·iv') (*noun*) a person who speaks for others, particularly in a lawmaking body (p. 162)

reservation (rez'ər·vā'shən) a piece of land set aside by the federal government for the use of Native Americans (p. 274)

retirement (ri·tīər'mənt) a period in later life when a person stops working (p. 642)

rivalry (rī'vəl·rē) a contest between two or more parties to outdo each other (p. 612)

roundup (roun'dəp) a herding together of scattered cattle (p. 452)

rural (rur'əl) having to do with the countryside or farming (p. 517)

sachem (sā'chem) a chief in some Native American groups (p. 31)

scandal (skan'dəl) a condition of outrage generated by a report of illegal or unethical behavior, particularly by a public official (p. 681)

seafarer (sē'fãr'ər) one who helps run a ship; a sailor (p. 63)

secession (si·sesh'ən) the act of a state withdrawing from the United States government (p. 229)

secondary source (sek'ən·där'ē sôrs') an account based on facts gathered from original sources (p. 254)

security (si·kyoor'ət·ē) (*adjective*) having to do with safety (p. 203)

security (si·kyoor'ət·ē) (*noun*) a promise in the form of a note to pay back a loan with interest (p. 204)

segregation (seg'ri·gā'shən) separation of one group from other groups on the basis of race, class, or ethnic background (p. 599)

sharecropper (shãr'kräp'ər) one who raises crops for another and receives a share of the crop's selling price minus the cost of seed, tools, and other expenses (p. 426)

shareholder (shãr'hōl'dər) one who owns a share in a business (p. 508)

shortage (shôrt'ij) a lack of something (p. 409)

sit-down strike (sit'doun' strīk') a refusal to work by employees who continue to occupy their place of work (p. 644)

skyscraper (skī'skrā'pər) a very tall building (p. 521)

slaveholder (slāv'hōl·dər) the owner of a person bought as property (p. 332)

slum (sləm) a crowded, run-down housing area, usually in a city (p. 519)

solar power (sō'lər pou'ər) a form of energy that comes from the sun (p. 608)

source (sôrs) a place from which something is obtained; the giver of information to a reporter (p. 660)

spoils system (spoilz' sis'təm) the practice of giving government jobs to loyal party workers, regardless of thier ability (p. 541)

stock (stäk) one or more shares in a business (p. 508)

 772

strand (strand) a cluster of ideas and events that form a specialized area of history and that intertwine with one or more other clusters to form a general history of a time or place (p. 481)

Strategic Defense Initiative (SDI) (stra·tē′jik di·fens′ in·ish′at′iv) a defensive shield of advanced weapons, some operating in outer space, to make the United States safe from nuclear attack, popularly known as Star Wars (p. 686)

strike (strīk) (*noun*) a walkout; a refusal to work until one's demands are met (p. 322)

strike (strīk) (*verb*) to walk off the job until one's demands are met (p. 322)

stronghold (strông′hōld′) a position that is well-defended (p. 119)

suburb (sab′arb′) an area or smaller town lying just outside a larger city and joined to it by one or more transportation systems (p. 523)

subway (sab′wā′) an underground rail system (p. 523)

suffrage (saf′rij) the right to vote (p. 626)

supply-side economics (sa·plī′sīd ek′a·näm′iks) the theory that the government can best help the economy by cutting taxes and encouraging businesses, thus increasing the supply of goods (p. 685)

surrender (sa·ren′dar) (*noun*) the act of giving up one's freedom of choice and action to another (p. 415)

surrender (sa·ren′dar) (*verb*) to give up one's freedom of choice and action to another (p. 657)

synagogue (sin′a·gäg′) a Jewish house of worship (p. 120)

synthesis (sin′tha·sas) an act that combines separate elements or strands of history in a way that shows how they are related (p. 490)

table (tā′bal) a graphic presentation of information in words and figures arranged in related groups (p. 149)

tariff (tär′af) a tax on foreign-made goods entering a country (p. 201)

temperance (tem′pa·rans) the practice of not using or of limiting the use of intoxicating drinks (p. 320)

temporary (tem′pa·rär′ē) continuing for a short time (p. 667)

tenant farmer (ten′ant far′mar) one who raises crops on the land of another and who pays rent or a share of the crops to the owner of the land (p. 426)

tenement (ten′a·mant) a crowded, run-down apartment house usually found in large cities and occupied by poor people (p. 521)

terminal (tarm′nal) a train station (p. 521)

territory (tär′a·tôr′ē) land belonging to or ruled by a government (p. 161)

time lag (tīm′ lag′) a delay between the occurrence of an event and the public report of it (p. 602)

trail (trāl) a path through unsettled country (p. 452)

transportation (trans′par·tā′shan) the means by which people and goods are moved or carried from one place to another (p. 289)

treason (trēz′an) an action by which a person betrays his or her own government (p. 222)

tributary (trib′ya·tär′ē) a river or stream that flows into a larger river or stream (p. 79)

trolley (träl′ē) a carriage running on tracks, at first pulled by horses and later powered by steam or electricity (p. 523)

trust (trast) a large business made up of several corporations and operated as a single firm by a board of trustees (p. 508)

turnpike (tarn′pīk′) a main road on which a traveler often pays a fee (p. 293)

unconstitutional (an′kän′sta·tyoosh′nal) not in agreement with the Constitution of the United States (p. 640)

unemployment (an′im·ploi′mant) a time when a worker is out of a job (p. 632)

union (yoo′nyan) an organization formed by a group of workers to bargain for higher pay and better working conditions (p. 321)

urban (ar′ban) having to do with the city (p. 517)

value (val′yoo′) a belief, attitude, or overall policy that shows what is important to a person (p. 130)

value judgment (val′yoo jaj′mant) an opinion that reflects the worth placed on a person, object, idea, action, or event of the past (p. 493)

vaudeville (vôd′a·val) a stage show offering a variety of acts (p. 530)

veteran (vet′a·ran) a person who has previously served in a country's armed forces (p. 635)

veto (vēt′ō) (*noun*) a refusal to pass or to approve the acts of another (p. 317)

veto (vēt′ō) (*verb*) to refuse to approve the acts of another (p. 317)

volunteer (väl′an·tiar′) (*noun*) a person who freely offers to be of service to others (p. 404)

volunteer (väl′an·tiar′) (*verb*) to offer one's services freely to others (p. 675)

warrior (wôr′yar) one who is experienced in warfare (p. 448)

waterpower (wôt′ar·pou′ar′) a form of energy produced by a flow or a fall of water (p. 297)

waterway (wôt′ar·wā′) a body of water on which people can travel (p. 289)

wire service (wīr′ sar′vas) a business that sells original news stories and photos to the media (p. 599)

An italic letter before a page number indicates a reference to information contained in an illustration. In this Index *c* stands for chart or table; *g* stands for graph; *m* stands for map; and *p* stands for picture.

Acknowledgements

Text

Grateful acknowledgment is made to the following sources for permission to reprint copyright material:

Page 33: Text excerpt from *Little House in the Big Woods* by Laura Ingalls Wilder. Copyright, 1932, as to text, by Laura Ingalls Wilder. Renewed 1959 by Roger L. MacBride. By permission of Harper & Row, Publishers, Inc.

Page 126: From *Colonial Virginia: Its People and Customs* by Mary Newton Stanard, published by J. B. Lippincott Co. Copyright 1917 by J.B. Lippincott Co.

Page 133: From *The Ursulines in New Orleans and Our Lady of Prompt Succor* edited by H. C. Semple (New York: P. J. Kenedy & Sons, 1925).

Page 134: From *Colonial Women of Affairs* by Elisabeth Dexter, published by Houghton Mifflin Company. Copyright 1924 and 1931 by Elisabeth Anthony Dexter. Reprinted by permission of the publisher.

Page 137: Text excerpts from *Everyday Life in Colonial America* by Louis B. Wright, published by G. P. Putnam's Sons. Copyright 1965 by Louis B. Wright.

Page 157: © 1980 by The New York Times Company. Reprinted by permission.

Page 173: From *The Poems of Phillis Wheatley*, edited by Julian D. Mason, Jr. Copyright 1966 The University of North Carolina Press.

Page 237: © 1969 American Heritage Publishing Company, Inc. Reprinted by permission from *American Manners & Morals* by Mary Cable.

Page 255: From *The Journals of Lewis and Clark* edited by Bernard DeVoto. Copyright, 1953, by Bernard DeVoto. Reprinted by permission of Houghton Mifflin Company.

Pages 262–263: From *Journals and Other Documents on the Life and Voyages of Christopher Columbus* edited by Samuel Eliot Morison. Reprinted by permission of Curtis Brown, Ltd. © 1963 by Samuel Eliot Morison.

Page 264: From *The Correspondence of General Thomas Gage* edited by Clarence E. Carter, published by Yale University Press. Copyright 1931 by Yale University Press.

Page 323: Reprinted by permission of Hawthorn Properties (Elsevier-Dutton Publishing Co., Inc.). From the book *Her Name Was Sojourner Truth* by Hertha Pauli. Copyright © 1962 by Hertha Pauli.

Pages 352–353: Abridged from pp. 4, 7, 8 in *The Autobiography of Mark Twain* edited by Charles Neider. Copyright © 1959 by Charles Neider. Reprinted by permission of Harper & Row, Publishers, Inc.

Page 356: Abridged from pp.50–52, 82 in *Life on the Mississippi* by Mark Twain. Reprinted by permission of Harper & Row, Publishers, Inc.

Page 465: Text excerpt from *Little House in the Big Woods* by Laura Ingalls Wilder. Copyright, 1932, as to text, by Laura Ingalls Wilder. Renewed 1959 by Roger L. MacBride. By permission of Harper & Row, Publishers, Inc.

Page 470: Reprinted by permission of Howard University from *Howard University: The First Hundred Years, 1867–1967* by Rayford W. Logan. © 1968 by Howard University.

Page 533: From "Chicago" in *The Complete Poems of Carl Sandburg*. Reprinted by permission of Harcourt Brace Jovanovich, Inc.

Page 578: From *The Diary and Sundry Observations of Thomas Alva Edison* edited by Dr. Dagobert D. Runes, published by Philosophical Library, Inc. Copyright 1948 by Philosophical Library, Inc.

Pages 578–579: From *The Promised Land* by Mary Antin. Copyright 1912 by Houghton Mifflin Company. Copyright 1940 by Mary Antin. Reprinted by permission of Houghton Mifflin Company.

Page 585: From *I Fought With Geronimo* by Jason Betzinez with Wilbur S. Nye. Reprinted by permission of Stackpole Books.

Page 600: From the Associated Press PM–Washington Briefs, February 10, 1981. Reprinted by permission of AP Newsfeatures.

Page 693: Reprinted by permission of Hawthorn Properties (Elsevier-Dutton Publishing Co., Inc.). From the book *The Common Sense Book of Baby and Child Care* by Benjamin Spock. Copyright ©1945, 1946 by Benjamin Spock.

Page 693: From *The Feminine Mystique* by Betty Friedan. Copyright 1974, 1963 by Betty Friedan. Reprinted by permission of W. W. Norton, Inc.

Page 693: From *American Dreams: Lost and Found* by Studs Terkel. © 1980 by Studs Terkel. Reprinted by permission of Pantheon Books, a division of Random House, Inc.

Pages 694–695: A selection from *The Grapes of Wrath* by John Steinbeck. Copyright 1939 by John Steinbeck. Copyright renewed © 1967 by John Steinbeck. Reprinted by permission of Viking Penguin Inc.

Page 695: Abridged and adapted from pp. 199-200 in *The Golden Dream* by Stephen Birmingham. Copyright © 1978 by Stephen Birmingham. Reprinted by permission of Harper & Row, Publishers, Inc.

Page 696: Abridged from pp. 412–413 in *The Autobiography of Eleanor Roosevelt*. Copyright © 1961 by Anna Eleanor Roosevelt. Reprinted by permission of Harper & Row, Publishers, Inc.

Page 696: From *The Mexican-Americans of South Texas* by William Madsen. Copyright ©1964 by Holt, Rinehart and Winston, Inc. Reprinted by permission of Holt, Rinehart and Winston.

Page 701: From *Working* by Studs Terkel. © 1972, 1974 by Studs Terkel. Reprinted by permission of Pantheon Books, a division of Random House, Inc.

Page 710: Excerpted from *Roger Ebert's Movie Home Companion*, by Roger Ebert. © 1985 by Andrews & McMeel. Reprinted by permission of the author.

Page 711: Abridged from *The Child Care Crisis*, by Fredelle Maynard. © 1985 by Viking Press. Reprinted by permission of the publisher.

Page 711: By Gene Bylinski from *Fortune*, © July 1988 Time Inc. All rights reserved.

Illustrations

1: HALF-TITLE PAGE: The Bettmann Archive

TITLE SPREAD: Styled by Barbara L. Bowman/ Photosynthesis

2: *left*, NASA; *right*, The Bettmann Archive; *top*, Black Star/Flip Schulke; *bottom*, Shelburne Museum Inc.

3: *left*, TSW/Click, Chicago/Rohan; *right*, Masterfile/Imtek Imagineering; *far left*, David Edward Dempster/Off-Shoot Special Stock Collections

TABLE OF CONTENTS

5: *top*, The New York Public Library; *bottom*, Peter Bloomer, Flagstaff, Ariz.

6: *top*, Roloc Color Slides, Washington, D.C.; *bottom*, courtesy, American Antiquarian Society

7: *top*, Historical Pictures Service, Inc., Chicago; *bottom*, The Bettmann Archive

8: *top* and *bottom*, Historical Pictures Service, Inc., Chicago

9: *top*, The Bettmann Archive; *center*, Historical Pictures Service, Inc., Chicago; *bottom*, Historical Pictures Service, Inc., Chicago

10: *top*, NASA; *bottom*, SYGMA Photo News/Ira Wyman

20: Milt and Joan Mann, Chicago

22: *top* and *bottom*, The Bettmann Archive

23: *top*, photo by Ray Hillstrom, Chicago; *left*, © Robert Frerck, Chicago; *right*, The Bettmann Archive

24: *top*, Milt and Joan Mann, Chicago; *bottom*, Historical Pictures Service, Inc., Chicago

25: Colonial Williamsburg

26: John Running, Flagstaff, Ariz.

28: Gary Truman, Nitro, W. Va.

31: Historical Pictures Service, Inc., Chicago

34: Milt and Joan Mann, Chicago

35: Milt and Joan Mann, Chicago

36: Milt and Joan Mann, Chicago

42: *top left* courtesy, Field Museum of Natural History, Chicago

43: *left* and *right*, courtesy Field Museum of Natural History, Chicago

45: Museum of Anthropology, University of Michigan

47: Arizona State Museum/Helga Teiwes

48: Allan Bruce Zee, Portland, Oreg.

49: Ohio Historical Society

50: courtesy, Field Museum of Natural History, Chicago

53: courtesy of American Museum of Natural History

54: courtesy, Field Museum of Natural History, Chicago/Ron Testa

56: courtesy, Field Museum of Natural History, Chicago

59: John Running, Flagstaff, Ariz..

62: *left*, Historical Pictures Service, Inc., Chicago; *right* and *bottom*, Roloc Color Slides, Washington, D.C.

63: Historical Pictures Service, Inc., Chicago

64: The Bettmann Archive

67: The Bettmann Archive

73: courtesy of American Museum of Natural History

74: © Danga Variakojis, 1977

81: *top*, Peter Bloomer, Flagstaff, Ariz.; *bottom*, Historical Pictures Service, Inc., Chicago

84: *top left*, The New York Public Library; *bottom*, Colour Library International

85: Historical Pictures Service, Inc., Chicago

87: Historical Pictures Service, Inc., Chicago

88: Historical Pictures Service, Inc., Chicago

89: Historical Pictures Service, Inc., Chicago

90: Historical Pictures Service, Inc., Chicago

92: reproduced from the collection of the Library of Congress

93: The Granger Collection, New York

94: Historical Pictures Service, Inc., Chicago

96: The Bettmann Archive

99: Historical Pictures Service, Inc., Chicago

100: © Michael Phillip Manheim, Marblehead, Ma.

101: *top left* and *right*, photos by Ray Hillstrom, Chicago; *bottom*, James R. Holland/Stock, Boston

104: *left*, New York Public Library; *right*, Roloc Color Slides, Washington, D.C.

105: Historical Pictures Service, Inc., Chicago

107: *left*, courtesy, American Antiquarian Society; *right*, Historical Pictures Service, Inc., Chicago

109: Historical Pictures Service, Inc., Chicago

110: *left*, Milt and Joan Mann, Chicago; *right*, Historical Pictures Service, Inc., Chicago

113: *top* and *center,* Colonial Williamsburg
117: Chicago Public Library
120: *top,* Historical Pictures Service, Inc., Chicago; *bottom,* courtesy of the American Jewish Historical Society
121: Newport Historical Society
124: *top,* Colour Library International; *bottom,* Historical Pictures Service, Inc., Chicago
125: *left,* courtesy, American Antiquarian Society; *top right,* Colour Library International; *bottom right,* courtesy, Field Museum of Natural History, Chicago
126: Historical Pictures Service, Inc., Chicago
127: Historical Pictures Service, Inc., Chicago
128: *top,* Milt and Joan Mann, Chicago; *center,* Historical Pictures Service, Inc., Chicago; *bottom,* Phil and Judy Sublett, Plymouth, Minn.
129: *top,* The Bettman Archive; *center,* courtesy of Fairbanks House; *bottom,* Colour Library International
130: Historical Pictures Service, Inc., Chicago
131: courtesy, Chicago Historical Society
132: The Bettmann Archive
133: Historical Pictures Service, Inc., Chicago
134: Colonial Williamsburg
135: *top, center,* and *bottom,* Colonial Williamsburg
136: *top,* Historical Pictures Service, Inc., Chicago; *center left, center,* and *center right,* Colonial Williamsburg
137: *left* and *right,* Historical Pictures Service, Inc., Chicago
140: *left* and *right,* Historical Pictures Service, Inc., Chicago; *bottom, left* and *right.* The Bettmann Archive
141: *top,* The Bettmann Archive; *bottom,* powderhorn, courtesy, Chicago Historical Society
143: by permission of Wil-Jo Associates and Bill Mauldin, Inc.
144: Historical Pictures Service, Inc., Chicago
145: *top,* by permission of the Folger Shakespeare Library; *bottom,* New York Public Library
146: Historical Pictures, Service, Inc., Chicago
147: *top,* by permission of Bill Mauldin and Wil-Jo Associates, Inc.; *bottom,* courtesy, American Antiquarian Society
148: *top,* Historical Pictures Services Inc., Chicago; *center left, center right,* and *center bottom,* United Press International; *bottom,* Culver Pictures
149: reprinted, courtesy of the Chicago Tribune
158: *top* and *bottom,* Roloc Color Slides, Washington, D.C.
159: Roloc Color Slides, Washington, D.C.
162: Chicago Public Library
163: Historical Pictures Service, Inc., Chicago
168: Roloc Color Slides, Washington, D.C.
169: Roloc Color Slides, Washington, D.C.
170: Historical Pictures Service, Inc., Chicago
172: Roloc Color Slides, Washington, D.C.
173: *top,* Roloc Color Slides, Washington, D.C.; *bottom,* Historical Pictures Service, Inc., Chicago
175: The Granger Collection, New York
176: *top,* courtesy, Chicago Historical Society; *bottom,* Roloc Color Slides, Washington, D.C.
177: Roloc Color Slides, Washington, D.C.
178: Historical Pictures Service, Inc., Chicago
179: *top* and *bottom,* Roloc Color Slides, Washington, D.C.
183: Historical Pictures Service, Inc., Chicago
184: *top left* and *right,* Roloc Color Slides, Washington, D.C.; *center left,* Historical Pictures Service, Inc., Chicago; *center right* and *bottom,* Roloc Color Slides, Washington, D.C.
185: *left* and *right,* Historical Pictures Service, Inc., Chicago
193: Historical Pictures Service, Inc., Chicago

196: *top,* Historical Pictures Service, Inc., Chicago; *bottom,* Roloc Color Slides, Washington, D.C.; *right,* Free Library of Philadelphia
197: *left* and *right,* Historical Pictures Service, Inc., Chicago
198: Historical Pictures Service, Inc., Chicago
199: Roloc Color Slides, Washington, D.C.
201: Historical Pictures Service, Inc., Chicago
203: Historical Pictures Service, Inc., Chicago
206: Historical Pictures Service, Inc., Chicago
211: *top,* Historical Pictures Service, Inc., Chicago; *bottom,* Jim Pickerell, Bethesda, Md.; *bottom right,* Everett McKinley Dirksen Congressional Leadership Research Center
214: *left,* Roloc Color Slides, Washington, D.C.; *right,* Robert L. Pollock/Uniphoto, Washington, D.C.
215: Roloc Color Slides, Washington, D.C.
217: Historical Pictures Service, Inc., Chicago
221: *top right* and *center right,* Historical Pictures Service, Inc., Chicago; *bottom left,* Richard Hodge/Uniphoto; *bottom,* courtesy of the Edward E. Ayer Collection, the Newberry Library, Chicago
223: Roloc Color Slides, Washington, D.C.
228: Roloc Color Slides, Washington, D.C.
230: Roloc Color Slides, Washington, D.C.
231: Historical Pictures Service, Inc., Chicago
234: *top* and *bottom,* Roloc Color Slides, Washington, D.C.; *right,* the Bettmann Archive
235: *top,* Historical Pictures Service, Inc., Chicago; *bottom,* The Bettmann Archive
236: Historical Pictures Service, Inc., Chicago
237: courtesy, American Antiquarian Society
238: *top,* Roloc Color Slides, Washington, D.C.; *bottom left,* Milton Feinberg/Stock, Boston; *bottom right,* Colonial Williamsburg
239: *top,* Museum of the City of New York; *center,* National Gallery of Art
240: Historical Pictures Service, Inc., Chicago
241: *top right,* Historical Pictures Service, Inc., Chicago; *top left,* The Bettmann Archive; *bottom left,* National Gallery of Art
242: courtesy, American Antiquarian Society
243: *top,* Historical Pictures Service, Inc., Chicago; *center,* Historical Pictures Service, Inc., Chicago
244: *top,* Yale University Art Gallery; *bottom,* The Mariners Museum
245: Historical Pictures Service, Inc., Chicago
246: *top,* courtesy, The Henry Francis Du Pont Winterthur Museum, Delaware; *bottom,* Historical Pictures Service, Inc., Chicago
247: Historical Pictures Service, Inc., Chicago
250: *top, center,* and *bottom,* The Bettmann Archive; *left,* David Phillips, Chicago Architectural Photographing Company; *right,* National Museum of American Art
252: *top,* Milt and Joan Mann, Chicago; *bottom,* courtesy, Field Museum of Natural History, Chicago
253: The Bettmann Archive
254: The Public Roads Administration, Washington, D.C.
255: *left,* reproduced from the collection of the Library of Congress; *right,* The Missouri Historical Society
256: reproduced from the collection of the Library of Congress
261: reproduced from the collection of the Library of Congress
262: Historical Pictures Service, Inc., Chicago
263: The Bettmann Archive
267: Roloc Color Slides, Washington, D.C.
268: *left* and *right,* Historical Pictures Service, Inc., Chicago; *bottom,* Yale University Art Gallery, The Mabel Brady Garvan Collection
269: *left,* The Bettmann Archive; *right,* The Missouri Historical Society
272: Historical Pictures Service, Inc., Chicago

274: Historical Pictures Service, Inc., Chicago
276: Woolaroc Museum, Bartlesville, Oklahoma
278: The Walters Art Gallery, Baltimore
279: Historical Pictures Service, Inc., Chicago
281: courtesy of the New York Historical Society, New York City
282: from the collection of Mr. and Mrs. Ernst Schuchard
283: The Bettmann Archive
284: *left,* courtesy of the Daughters of the Republic of Texas Museum, Austin; *right,* Historical Pictures Service, Inc., Chicago
285: *left,* Historical Pictures Service, Inc., Chicago; *right,* courtesy Warren Shetter, Oregon Chamber of Commerce, Illinois
288: *left,* Historical Pictures Service, Inc., Chicago; *right,* courtesy, Chicago Historical Society
289: Historical Pictures Service, Inc., Chicago
293: *left,* The Bettmann Archive; *right,* Historical Pictures Service, Inc., Chicago
295: *top,* Michigan Bell Telephone Company; *center* and *bottom,* Historical Pictures Service, Inc., Chicago
296: Culver Pictures
297: Historical Pictures Service, Inc.; Chicago
301: courtesy, Chicago Historical Society
304: *left,* courtesy, Chicago Historical Society; *right,* Historical Pictures Service, Inc., Chicago
305: *top,* Culver Pictures; *center* and *bottom,* Historical Pictures Service, Inc., Chicago
307: *left,* courtesy International Harvester; *right,* The Bettmann Archive
308: courtesy, The Henry Francis Du Pont Winterthur Museum, Delaware
309: *left* and *right,* Historical Pictures Service, Inc., Chicago
311: Culver Pictures
314: *left,* Historical Pictures Service, Inc., Chicago; *right,* The Old Print Shop, Inc.
317: The Bettmann Archive
319: The Bettmann Archive
320: *top,* The Bettmann Archive; *bottom,* Historical Pictures Service, Inc., Chicago
321: Historical Pictures Service, Inc., Chicago
322: courtesy, Chicago Historical Society
323: *left,* Historical Pictures Service, Inc., Chicago; *right,* Museum of the City of New York
324: *left,* © Karen Yops, Follett Publishing Company; *right,* The Bettmann Archive
325: *top,* The Bettmann Archive; *bottom,* Charles Harbutt/Magnum Photos
327: Historical Pictures Service, Inc., Chicago
328: *left, center,* and *right,* Historical Pictures Service, Inc., Chicago
332: Free Library of Philadelphia
335: Historical Pictures Service, Inc., Chicago
337: Roloc Color Slides, Washington, D.C.
339: The Brooklyn Museum, gift of the Brooklyn Institute of Arts and Sciences
341: Historical Pictures Service, Inc., Chicago
343: Historical Pictures Service, Inc., Chicago
344: *left,* Historical Pictures Service, Inc., Chicago; *right,* Sophia Smith Collection, Smith College
345: *left* and *right,* Historical Pictures Service, Inc., Chicago
348: *top left,* Historical Pictures Service, Inc., Chicago; *top right,* American Antiquarian Society; *bottom left,* Wisconsin Historical Society; *bottom right,* Culver Pictures
349: Bob Sitkowski, Follett Publishing Company
350: The Bettmann Archive
351: *left* and *right,* The Bettmann Archive
352: The Bettmann Archive

353: *left,* Wisconsin Historical Society; *right,* The Newberry Library, Chicago
354: California State Library
355: Historical Pictures Service, Inc., Chicago
356: Watertown Historical Society, Wisconsin
357: The Bettmann Archive
358: *top,* Bob Sitkowski, Follett Publishing Company; *bottom,* courtesy, Museum of Fine Arts, Boston
359: Vincennes University Files, Indiana
360: *top,* The Bettmann Archive; *bottom,* courtesy, Circus World Museum, Baraboo, Wisconsin
361: courtesy, Circus World Museum, Baraboo, Wisconsin
364: *left,* The Bettmann Archive; *right,* courtesy, Chicago Historical Society; *bottom left,* Roloc Color Slides, Washington D.C.; *bottom right,* The Bettmann Archive
365: *top,* The Bettmann Archive; *bottom,* Lincoln's glasses, courtesy, Chicago Historical Society
366: *top* and *bottom,* Everett McKinley Dirksen Congressional Leadership Research Center
367: Everett McKinley Dirksen Congressional Leadership Research Center
370: Sophia Smith Collection, Smith College
371: The Bettmann Archive
372: The Remington Art Museum, Ogdensburg, New York
374: The Bettmann Archive
377: Historical Pictures Service, Inc., Chicago
379: Brown Brothers
380: The Bettmann Archive
382: *left* and *right,* Historical Pictures Service, Inc., Chicago
383: Historical Pictures Service, Inc., Chicago
385: Historical Pictures Service, Inc., Chicago
388: Historical Pictures Service, Inc., Chicago
391: Brown Brothers
392: Historical Pictures Service, Inc., Chicago
394: courtesy, Chicago Historical Society
397: Historical Pictures Service, Inc., Chicago
398: *top* and *bottom,* Historical Pictures Service, Inc., Chicago
399: *top* and *bottom,* Historical Pictures Service, Inc., Chicago
402: *left,* reproduced from the collection of the Library of Congress; *right,* Historical Pictures Service, Inc., Chicago
403: reproduced from the collection of the Library of Congress
407: Historical Pictures Service, Inc., Chicago
408: Historical Pictures Service, Inc., Chicago
409: Historical Pictures Service, Inc., Chicago
410: courtesy, Chicago Historical Society
417: Historical Pictures Service, Inc., Chicago
418: *top* and *right,* Historical Pictures Service, Inc., Chicago; *left,* The Bettmann Archive
419: Historical Pictures Service, Inc., Chicago
421: Historical Pictures Service, Inc., Chicago
422: *left,* Colour Library International; *right,* Historical Pictures Service, Inc., Chicago
423: reproduced from the collection of the Library of Congress
424: Historical Pictures Service, Inc., Chicago
425: reproduced from the collection of the Library of Congress
427: Historical Pictures Service, Inc., Chicago
429: reproduced from the collection of the Library of Congress
430: reproduced from the collection of the Library of Congress
433: *top,* Historical Pictures Service, Inc., Chicago; *bottom,* reproduced from the collection of the Library of Congress
435: Historical Pictures Service, Inc., Chicago

437: *left* and *right,* Historical Pictures Service, Inc., Chicago
438: *left* and *right,* Historical Pictures Service, Inc., Chicago
439: *left* and *right,* Historical Pictures Service, Inc., Chicago
442: Historical Pictures Service, Inc., Chicago
443: *left,* The Bettman Archive; *right,* Historical Pictures Service, Inc., Chicago
446: Historical Pictures Service, Inc., Chicago
447: Culver Pictures
448: Historical Pictures Service, Inc., Chicago
449: Woolaroc Museum, Bartlesville, Oklahoma
452: The Bettmann Archive
454: The Bettmann Archive
457: Milt and Joan Mann, Chicago
458: *top,* Historical Pictures Service, Inc., Chicago; *bottom,* State Historical Society of Wisconsin
459: Historical Pictures Service, Inc., Chicago
461: Historical Pictures Service, Inc., Chicago
462: *top* and *bottom,* Historical Pictures Service, Inc., Chicago
463: The Bettmann Archive
464: Historical Pictures Service, Inc., Chicago
465: Nebraska State Historical Society
466: *left,* Bob Sitkowski, Follett Publishing Company; *right,* Brown Brothers
467: Bob Sitkowski, Follett Publishing Company
469: Historical Pictures Service, Inc., Chicago
470: courtesy, Field Museum of Natural History, Chicago
471: Historical Pictures Service, Inc., Chicago
472: *left* and *right,* Historical Pictures Service Inc., Chicago
473: Historical Pictures Service, Inc., Chicago
474: *top* and *bottom,* Historical Pictures Service, Inc., Chicago
475: Historical Pictures Service, Inc., Chicago
478: *top* and *center,* The Bettmann Archive; *left,* Roloc Color Slides, Washington, D.C.; *right,* David Phillips, Chicago Architectural Photographing Company
480: *top,* Historical Pictures Service, Inc., Chicago; The Bettmann Archive
481: reproduced from the collection of the Library of Congress
483: Historical Pictures Service, Inc., Chicago
485: The Bettmann Archive
486: reproduced from the Library of Congress
487: Historical Pictures Service, Inc., Chicago
488: The Bettmann Archive
489: *top* and *bottom,* The Bettmann Archive
490: Historical Pictures Service, Inc., Chicago
491: Historical Pictures Service, Inc., Chicago
494: Historical Pictures Service, Inc., Chicago
495: courtesy of the New York Historical Society, New York City
496: *left,* The Bettmann Archive; *right,* reproduced from the collection of the Library of Congress
497: The Bettmann Archive
498: Historical Pictures Service, Inc., Chicago
500: The Bettmann Archive
503: *left,* Historical Pictures Service, Inc., Chicago; *right,* The Bettmann Archive
504: The Bettmann Archive
505: Tom Stack and Associates
506: Historical Pictures Service, Inc., Chicago
510: The Bettmann Archive
512: Historical Pictures Service, Inc., Chicago
513: *top,* courtesy, International Business Machines; *bottom,* Horst Schafer/Peter Arnold, Inc.
515: Historical Pictures Service, Inc., Chicago
516: *left* and *right,* Historical Pictures Service, Inc., Chicago
517: Historical Pictures Service, Inc., Chicago

522: New York Central System
527: *top,* The Bettmann Archive; *bottom,* Historical Pictures Service, Inc., Chicago
529: *left* and *right,* Historical Pictures Service, Inc., Chicago
531: Historical Pictures Service, Inc., Chicago
532: *top,* photo by Ray Hillstrom, Chicago; *bottom,* Ed Cooper photo, El Verano, Calif.
533: *top,* photographed by Douglas Brooks/Brooks and Van Kirk Photography, Chicago; *bottom,* Historical Pictures Service, Inc., Chicago
536: *top,* United Press International; *bottom,* Historical Pictures Service, Inc., Chicago
537: Historical Pictures Service, Inc., Chicago
538: Historical Pictures Service, Inc., Chicago
542: Ann Granacki, Follett Publishing Company
545: Historical Pictures Service, Inc., Chicago
547: David Phillips/Chicago Architectural Photographing Company
549: The Bettmann Archive
550: Ed Cooper Photo, El Verano, Calif.
552: *left,* The Bettmann Archive; *right,* Historical Pictures Service, Inc., Chicago
553: Historical Pictures Service, Inc., Chicago
556: *left,* photo by Ray Hillstrom, Chicago; *right,* The Bettmann Archive
557: Historical Pictures Service, Inc., Chicago
558: Historical Pictures Service, Inc., Chicago
559: Peabody Museum of Salem, Photo by Mark Sexton
561: The Bettmann Archive
562: Steve McCutcheon, Alaska
563: The Bettmann Archive
571: The Bettmann Archive
572: *top* and *bottom,* The Bettmann Archive
573: *left* and *right,* Historical Pictures Service, Inc., Chicago
575: Historical Pictures Service, Inc., Chicago
576: *left,* Historical Pictures Service, Inc., Chicago; *right,* Brown Brothers; *bottom,* The Bettmann Archive
577: *left,* Historical Pictures Service, Inc., Chicago; *right,* from the collection of Lea Heir, Follett Publishing Company
578: The Bettmann Archive
579: *left,* from the collection of Michael Lipkin, Follett Publishing Company; *right* and *bottom,* Historical Pictures Service, Inc., Chicago
580: *top,* Historical Pictures Service, Inc., Chicago; *bottom,* courtesy, D.B.I., Inc.
581: *top* and *bottom,* Historical Pictures Service, Inc., Chicago; *right,* courtesy of Myrtle Allman, Chicago
582: *right* and *left,* from the collections of June Huitt and Karen Swan, Follett Publishing Company; *bottom,* courtesy, Edna Ebner, Chicago
583: Historical Pictures Service, Inc., Chicago
584: from the collection of June Huitt, Follett Publishing Company
585: *left* and *right,* The Bettmann Archive
586: Historical Pictures Service, Inc., Chicago
587: *left* and *right,* The Bettmann Archive
588: *top,* The Bettmann Archive; *left,* Historical Pictures Service, Inc., Chicago; *right,* Follett Publishing Company photo
589: from the collection of Michael Lipkin, Follett Publishing Company; *bottom,* Bettmann Film Archive
592: *left,* Roloc Color Slides, Washington, D.C.; *right,* © Bill Grimes/Black Star; *center,* © Jack Zehrt, St. Louis, Mo.; *bottom,* Roloc Color Slides, Washington, D.C.